Natural Computing for Simulation and Knowledge Discovery

Leandro Nunes de Castro
Mackenzie University, Brazil

Medical Information Science
REFERENCE
An Imprint of IGI Global

Managing Director: Lindsay Johnston
Production Manager: Jennifer Yoder
Publishing Systems Analyst: Adrienne Freeland
Development Editor: Joel Gamon
Acquisitions Editor: Kayla Wolfe
Typesetter: Travis Gundrum
Cover Design: Jason Mull

Published in the United States of America by
Medical Information Science Reference (an imprint of IGI Global)
701 E. Chocolate Avenue
Hershey PA 17033
Tel: 717-533-8845
Fax: 717-533-8661
E-mail: cust@igi-global.com
Web site: http://www.igi-global.com

Library of Congress Cataloging-in-Publication Data

Natural computing for simulation and knowledge discovery / Leandro Nunes de Castro, editor.
pages cm
Summary: "This book investigates the latest developments in nature-influenced technologies, offering an in-depth analysis of such advances as cryptographic solutions based on cell division, the creation and manipulation of biological computers, and particle swarm optimization techniques"-- Provided by publisher.
Includes bibliographical references and index.
ISBN 978-1-4666-4253-9 (hardcover) -- ISBN 978-1-4666-4254-6 (ebook) -- ISBN (invalid) 978-1-4666-4255-3 (print & perpetual access) 1. Natural computation. 2. Computational biology. 3. Swarm intelligence. I. De Castro, Leandro Nunes, 1974- editor of compilation.
QA76.9.N37N37 2014
006.3--dc23
2013011179

British Cataloguing in Publication Data
A Cataloguing in Publication record for this book is available from the British Library.

Table of Contents

Preface xvi

Chapter 1
PSO-CGO: A Particle Swarm Algorithm for Cluster Geometry Optimization 1
Nuno Lourenço, Centro de Informática e Sistemas da Universidade de Coimbra (CISUC), Portugal
Francisco Baptista Pereira, Centro de Informática e Sistemas da Universidade de Coimbra (CISUC) & Instituto Superior de Engenharia de Coimbra, Portugal

Chapter 2
Phylogenetic Differential Evolution 22
Vinícius Veloso de Melo, University of São Paulo, Brazil
Danilo Vasconcellos Vargas, University of São Paulo, Brazil
Marcio Kassouf Crocomo, University of São Paulo, Brazil

Chapter 3
Head Motion Stabilization During Quadruped Robot Locomotion: Combining CPGs and Stochastic Optimization Methods 41
Miguel Oliveira, University of Minho, Portugal
Cristina P. Santos, University of Minho, Portugal
Lino Costa, University of Minho, Portugal
Ana Maria A. C. Rocha, University of Minho, Portugal
Manuel Ferreira, University of Minho, Portugal

Chapter 4
Incorporation of Preferences in an Evolutionary Algorithm Using an Outranking Relation: The EvABOR Approach 66
Eunice Oliveira, Polytechnic Institute of Leiria, Portugal & R&D Unit INESC Coimbra, Portugal
Carlos Henggeler Antunes, University of Coimbra, Portugal & R&D Unit INESC Coimbra, Portugal
Álvaro Gomes, University of Coimbra, Portugal & R&D Unit INESC Coimbra, Portugal

Chapter 12
Implementation on CUDA of the Smoothing Problem with Tissue-Like P Systems 184
Francisco Peña-Cantillana, University of Sevilla, Spain
Daniel Díaz-Pernil, University of Sevilla, Spain
Hepzibah A. Christinal, University of Sevilla, Spain & Karunya University, India
Miguel A. Gutiérrez-Naranjo, University of Sevilla, Spain

Chapter 13
Elementary Active Membranes Have the Power of Counting 194
Antonio E. Porreca, Università degli Studi di Milano–Bicocca, Italy
Alberto Leporati, Università degli Studi di Milano–Bicocca, Italy
Giancarlo Mauri, Università degli Studi di Milano–Bicocca, Italy
Claudio Zandron, Università degli Studi di Milano–Bicocca, Italy

Chapter 14
Linear Time Solution to Prime Factorization by Tissue P Systems with Cell Division 207
Xingyi Zhang, Anhui University, China
Yunyun Niu, Huazhong University of Science and Technology, China
Linqiang Pan, Huazhong University of Science and Technology, China
Mario J. Pérez-Jiménez, University of Sevilla, Spain

Chapter 15
Unorganized Machines: From Turing's Ideas to Modern Connectionist Approaches 221
Levy Boccato, University of Campinas (UNICAMP), Brazil
Everton S. Soares, University of Campinas (UNICAMP), Brazil
Marcos M. L. P. Fernandes, Faculdade de Engenharia de Sorocaba (FACENS), Brazil
Diogo C. Soriano, Federal University of ABC (UFABC), Brazil
Romis Attux, University of Campinas (UNICAMP), Brazil

Chapter 16
The Grand Challenges in Natural Computing Research: The Quest for a New Science 237
Leandro Nunes de Castro, Natural Computing Laboratory (LCoN), Mackenzie University, Brazil
Rafael Silveira Xavier, Natural Computing Laboratory (LCoN), Mackenzie University, Brazil
Rodrigo Pasti, Laboratory of Bioinformatics and Bio-Inspired Computing (LBiC), State University of Campinas (UNICAMP), Brazil
Renato Dourado Maia, State University of Montes Claros, Brazil
Alexandre Szabo, Natural Computing Laboratory (LCoN), Mackenzie University, Brazil
Daniel Gomes Ferrari, Natural Computing Laboratory (LCoN), Mackenzie University, Brazil

Chapter 17
Trans-Canada Slimeways: Slime Mould Imitates the Canadian Transport Network 251
Andrew Adamatzky, University of the West of England, UK
Selim G. Akl, Queen's University, Canada

Chapter 18
Ecosystems Computing: Introduction to Biogeographic Computation 266
Rodrigo Pasti, Laboratory of Bioinformatics and Bio-Inspired Computing (LBiC), University of Campinas (UNICAMP), Brazil
Fernando José Von Zuben, Laboratory of Bioinformatics and Bio-Inspired Computing (LBiC), University of Campinas (UNICAMP), Brazil
Leandro Nunes de Castro, Natural Computing Laboratory (LCoN), Mackenzie University, Brazil

Compilation of References 288

About the Contributors 315

Index 323

Detailed Table of Contents

Preface xvi

Chapter 1
PSO-CGO: A Particle Swarm Algorithm for Cluster Geometry Optimization 1
Nuno Lourenço, Centro de Informática e Sistemas da Universidade de Coimbra (CISUC), Portugal
Francisco Baptista Pereira, Centro de Informática e Sistemas da Universidade de Coimbra (CISUC) & Instituto Superior de Engenharia de Coimbra, Portugal

In this chapter the authors present PSO-CGO, a novel particle swarm algorithm for cluster geometry optimization. The proposed approach combines a steady-state strategy to update solutions with a structural distance measure that helps to maintain population diversity. Also, it adopts a novel rule to update particles, which applies velocity only to a subset of the variables and is therefore able to promote limited modifications in the structure of atomic clusters. Results are promising, as PSO-CGO is able to discover all putative global optima for short-ranged Morse clusters between 30 and 50 atoms. A comprehensive analysis is presented and reveals that the proposed components are essential to enhance the search effectiveness of the PSO.

Chapter 2
Phylogenetic Differential Evolution 22
Vinícius Veloso de Melo, University of São Paulo, Brazil
Danilo Vasconcellos Vargas, University of São Paulo, Brazil
Marcio Kassouf Crocomo, University of São Paulo, Brazil

This chapter presents a new technique for optimizing binary problems with building blocks. The authors have developed a different approach to existing Estimation of Distribution Algorithms (EDAs). Our technique, called Phylogenetic Differential Evolution (PhyDE), combines the Phylogenetic Algorithm and the Differential Evolution Algorithm. The first one is employed to identify the building blocks and to generate metavariables. The second one is used to find the best instance of each metavariable. In contrast to existing EDAs that identify the related variables at each iteration, the presented technique finds the related variables only once at the beginning of the algorithm, and not through the generations. This paper shows that the proposed technique is more efficient than the well known EDA called Extended Compact Genetic Algorithm (ECGA), especially for large-scale systems which are commonly found in real world problems.

In this work, the authors propose a combined approach based on a controller architecture that is able to generate locomotion for a quadruped robot and a global optimization algorithm to generate head movement stabilization. The movement controllers are biologically inspired in the concept of Central Pattern Generators (CPGs) that are modelled based on nonlinear dynamical systems, coupled Hopf oscillators. This approach allows for explicitly specified parameters such as amplitude, offset and frequency of movement and to smoothly modulate the generated oscillations according to changes in these parameters. The overall idea is to generate head movement opposed to the one induced by locomotion, such that the head remains stabilized. Thus, in order to achieve this desired head movement, it is necessary to appropriately tune the CPG parameters. Three different global optimization algorithms search for this best set of parameters. In order to evaluate the resulting head movement, a fitness function based on the Euclidean norm is investigated. Moreover, a constraint-handling technique based on tournament selection was implemented.

The incorporation of preferences into Evolutionary Algorithms (EA) presents some relevant advantages, namely to deal with complex real-world problems. It enables focus on the search thus avoiding the computation of irrelevant solutions from the point of view of the practical exploitation of results (thus minimizing the computational effort), and it facilitates the integration of the DM's expertise into the solution search process (thus minimizing the cognitive effort). These issues are particularly important whenever the number of conflicting objective functions and/or the number of non-dominated solutions in the population is large. In EvABOR (Evolutionary Algorithm Based on an Outranking Relation) approaches preferences are elicited from a decision maker (DM) with the aim of guiding the evolutionary process to the regions of the space more in accordance with the DM's preferences. The preferences are captured and made operational by using the technical parameters of the ELECTRE TRI method. This approach is presented and analyzed using some illustrative results of a case study of electrical networks.

In this chapter, the authors propose a new approach to fully asynchronous P systems, and a matching complexity measure, both inspired from the field of distributed algorithms. The authors validate the proposed approach by implementing several well-known distributed depth-first search (DFS) and breadth-first search (BFS) algorithms. Empirical results show that the proposed P algorithms have shorter descriptions and achieve a performance comparable to the corresponding distributed algorithms.

In this chapter, the authors discuss the simulation of a P system variant known as Spiking Neural P systems (SNP systems), using Graphics Processing Units (GPUs). GPUs are well suited for highly parallel computations because of their intentional and massively parallel architecture. General purpose GPU computing has seen the use of GPUs for computationally intensive applications, not just in graphics and video processing. P systems, including SNP systems, are maximally parallel computing models taking inspiration from the functioning and dynamics of a living cell. In particular, SNP systems take inspiration from a type of cell known as a neuron. The nature of SNP systems allowed for their representation as matrices, which is an elegant step toward their simulation on GPUs. In this paper, the simulation algorithms, design considerations, and implementation are presented. Finally, simulation results, observations, and analyses using a simple but non-trivial SNP system as an example are discussed, including recommendations for future work.

In this chapter, the authors continue the investigation of P colonies introduced in Kelemen, Kelemenová, and Păun (2004). This paper examines a class of abstract computing devices composed of independent agents, acting and evolving in a shared environment. The first part is devoted to the P colonies of the capacity one. The authors present improved results concerning the computational power of the P colonies with capacity one and without using checking programs. The second part of the paper examines the modularity of the P colonies. The authors then divide the agents into modules.

Local search is currently one of the most used methods for finding solutions in real-life problems. It is usually considered when the research is interested in the final solution of the problem instead of the how the solution is reached. In this paper, the authors present an implementation of local search with Membrane Computing techniques applied to the N-queens problem as a case study. A CLIPS program inspired in the Membrane Computing design has been implemented and several experiments have been performed. The obtained results show better average times than those obtained with other Membrane Computing implementations that solve the N-queens problem.

One of the concepts that lie at the basis of membrane computing is the multiset rewriting rule. On the other hand, the paradigm of rules is profusely used in computer science for representing and dealing with knowledge. Therefore, establishing a "bridge" between these domains is important, for instance, by designing P systems reproducing the modus ponens-based forward and backward chaining that can be used as tools for reasoning in propositional logic. In this paper, the authors show how powerful and intuitive the formalism of membrane computing is and how it can be used to represent concepts and notions from unrelated areas.

This chapter presents an approach to P systems verification using the Spin model checker. The authors have developed a tool which implements the proposed approach and can automatically transform P system specifications from P-Lingua into Promela, the language accepted by the well known model checker Spin. The properties expected for the P system are specified using some patterns, representing high level descriptions of frequently asked questions, formulated in natural language. These properties are automatically translated into LTL specifications for the Promela model and the Spin model checker is run against them. In case a counterexample is received, the Spin trace is decoded and expressed as a P system computation. The tool has been tested on a number of examples and the results obtained are presented in the paper.

The Intravenous Glucose Tolerance Test is an experimental procedure used to study the glucose-insulin endocrine regulatory system. An open problem is to construct a model representing simultaneously the entire regulative mechanism. In the past three decades, several models have appeared, but they have not escaped criticisms and drawbacks. In this paper, the authors apply the Metabolic P systems theory for developing new physiologically based models of the glucose-insulin system, which can be applied to the IVGTT. Ten data-sets obtained from literature were considered and an MP model was found for each, which fits the data and explains the regulations of the dynamics. Finally, each model is analysed to define a common pattern which explains, in general, the action of the glucose-insulin control system.

Smoothing is often used in Digital Imagery for improving the quality of an image by reducing its level of noise. This paper presents a parallel implementation of an algorithm for smoothing 2D images in the framework of Membrane Computing. The chosen formal framework has been tissue-like P systems. The algorithm has been implemented by using a novel device architecture called CUDA (Compute Unified Device Architecture) which allows the parallel NVIDIA Graphics Processors Units (GPUs) to solve many complex computational problems. Some examples are presented and compared; research lines for the future are also discussed.

P systems with active membranes have the ability of solving computationally hard problems. In this paper, the authors prove that uniform families of P systems with active membranes operating in polynomial time can solve the whole class of PP decision problems, without using nonelementary membrane division or dissolution rules. This result also holds for families having a stricter uniformity condition than the usual one.

Prime factorization is useful and crucial for public-key cryptography, and its application in public-key cryptography is possible only because prime factorization has been presumed to be difficult. A polynomial-time algorithm for prime factorization on a quantum computer was given by P. W. Shor in 1997. In this work, it is considered as a function problem, and in the framework of tissue P systems with cell division, a linear-time solution to prime factorization problem is given on biochemical computational devices – tissue P systems with cell division, instead of computational devices based on the laws of quantum physical.

This work presents a discussion about the relationship between the contributions of Alan Turing – the centenary of whose birth is celebrated in 2012 – to the field of artificial neural networks and modern unorganized machines: reservoir computing (RC) approaches and extreme learning machines (ELMs). Firstly, the authors review Turing's connectionist proposals and also expose the fundamentals of the main RC paradigms – echo state networks and liquid state machines, - as well as of the design and training of ELMs. Throughout this exposition, the main points of contact between Turing's ideas and these modern perspectives are outlined, being, then, duly summarized in the second and final part of the work. This paper is useful in offering a distinct appreciation of Turing's pioneering contributions to the field of neural networks and also in indicating some perspectives for the future development of the field that may arise from the synergy between these views.

An important premise of Natural Computing is that some form of computation goes on in Nature, and that computing capability has to be understood, modeled, abstracted, and used for different objectives and in different contexts. Therefore, it is necessary to propose a new language capable of describing and allowing the comprehension of natural systems as a union of computing phenomena, bringing

Preface

Natural Computing for Simulation and Knowledge Discovery is a compilation of the second volume of the *International Journal of Natural Computing Research* (IJNCR), published in 2011. The field continues maturing and some interesting initiatives have arisen. In this second volume, four issues were published, three of them special issues, and the last one a spontaneous submission issue.

Issue 1 contains the papers titled "PSO-CGO: A Particle Swarm Algorithm for Cluster Geometry Optimization," "Phylogenetic Differential Evolution," "Head Motion Stabilization During Quadruped Robot Locomotion: Combining CPGs and Stochastic Optimization Methods," "Incorporation of Preferences in an Evolutionary Algorithm Using an Outranking Relation: The EvABOR Approach" selected from the Second Luso-Brazilian Evolutionary Computational School that occurred in June 2010 at the University of Minho in Guimaraes, Portugal.

Issues 2 and 3 contain a selection of papers from the 9th Brainstorming Week on Membrane Computing, held in Seville, Spain, from late January 2011 to early February 2011. The papers published were "Asynchronous P Systems," "Simulating Spiking Neural P Systems Without Delays Using GPUs," "P Colonies of Capacity One and Modularity," "Local Search with P Systems: A Case Study," "Forward and Backward Chaining with P Systems," "Towards Automated Verification of P Systems Using Spin," "MP Modelling of Glucose-Insulin Interactions in the Intravenous Glucose Tolerance Test," "Implementation on CUDA of the Smoothing Problem with Tissue-Like P Systems," "Elementary Active Membranes Have the Power of Counting," and "Linear Time Solution to Prime Factorization by Tissue P Systems with Cell Division."

The last issue was the only spontaneous issue of the year and contained four papers emphasizing more conceptual aspects of Natural Computing. The first paper titled "Unorganized Machines: From Turing's Ideas to Modern Connectionist Approaches" presents a discussion relating A. Turing's contributions with Neural Networks. The paper titled "The Grand Challenges in Natural Computing Research: The Quest for a New Science" brings the Natural Computing field to the context of the Grand Challenges in science, with the proposition of three grand challenges for the field. In the third paper, titled "Trans-Canada Slimeways: Slime Mould Imitates the Canadian Transport Network," the authors make a parallel between the protoplasmic network and the Canadian national highway network, analyze the networks, and evaluate slime mould's network response. Finally, paper four titled "Ecosystems Computing: Introduction to Biogeographic Computation" proposes a new bioinspired approach with roots in Biogeography.

In "PSO-CGO: A Particle Swarm Algorithm for Cluster Geometry Optimization," the authors present PSO-CGO, a novel particle swarm algorithm for cluster geometry optimization. The proposed approach combines a steady-state strategy to update solutions with a structural distance measure that helps to maintain population diversity. In addition, it adopts a novel rule to update particles, which applies velocity only to a subset of the variables and is therefore able to promote limited modifications in the structure of atomic clusters. Results are promising, as PSO-CGO is able to discover all putative global optima for short-ranged Morse clusters between 30 and 50 atoms. A comprehensive analysis is presented and reveals that the proposed components are essential to enhance the search effectiveness of the PSO.

"Phylogenetic Differential Evolution" presents a new technique for optimizing binary problems with building blocks. The authors have developed a different approach to existing Estimation of Distribution Algorithms (EDAs). Our technique, called Phylogenetic Differential Evolution (PhyDE), combines the Phylogenetic Algorithm and the Differential Evolution Algorithm. The first one is employed to identify the building blocks and to generate metavariables. The second one is used to find the best instance of each metavariable. In contrast to existing EDAs that identify the related variables at each iteration, the presented technique finds the related variables only once at the beginning of the algorithm, and not through the generations. This chapter shows that the proposed technique is more efficient than the well known EDA called Extended Compact Genetic Algorithm (ECGA), especially for large-scale systems which are commonly found in real world problems.

In "Head Motion Stabilization during Quadruped Robot Locomotion: Combining CPGs and Stochastic Optimization Methods," the authors propose a combined approach based on a controller architecture that is able to generate locomotion for a quadruped robot and a global optimization algorithm to generate head movement stabilization. The movement controllers are biologically inspired in the concept of Central Pattern Generators (CPGs) that are modelled based on nonlinear dynamical systems, coupled Hopf oscillators. This approach allows for explicitly specified parameters such as amplitude, offset, and frequency of movement, and to smoothly modulate the generated oscillations according to changes in these parameters. The overall idea is to generate head movement opposed to the one induced by locomotion, such that the head remains stabilized. Thus, in order to achieve this desired head movement, it is necessary to appropriately tune the CPG parameters. Three different global optimization algorithms search for this best set of parameters. In order to evaluate the resulting head movement, a fitness function based on the Euclidean norm is investigated. Moreover, a constraint-handling technique based on tournament selection is implemented.

The incorporation of preferences into Evolutionary Algorithms (EA) presents some relevant advantages, namely to deal with complex real-world problems. It enables focus on the search, thus avoiding the computation of irrelevant solutions from the point of view of the practical exploitation of results (thus minimizing the computational effort), and it facilitates the integration of the DM's expertise into the solution search process (thus minimizing the cognitive effort). These issues are particularly important whenever the number of conflicting objective functions and/or the number of non-dominated solutions in the population is large. In EvABOR (Evolutionary Algorithm Based on an Outranking Relation) approaches, preferences are elicited from a Decision Maker (DM) with the aim of guiding the evolutionary process to the regions of the space more in accordance with the DM's preferences. The preferences are captured and made operational by using the technical parameters of the ELECTRE TRI method. This approach is presented and analyzed in "Incorporation of Preferences in an Evolutionary Algorithm Using an Outranking Relation: The EvABOR Approach" using some illustrative results of a case study of electrical networks.

In "Asynchronous P Systems," the authors propose a new approach to fully asynchronous P systems and a matching complexity measure, both inspired from the field of distributed algorithms. The authors validate the proposed approach by implementing several well-known distributed Depth-First Search (DFS) and Breadth-First Search (BFS) algorithms. Empirical results show that the proposed P algorithms have shorter descriptions and achieve a performance comparable to the corresponding distributed algorithms.

In "Simulating Spiking Neural P Systems without Delays Using GPUs," the authors discuss the simulation of a P system variant known as Spiking Neural P systems (SNP systems), using Graphics Processing Units (GPUs). GPUs are well suited for highly parallel computations because of their intentional and massively parallel architecture. General purpose GPU computing has seen the use of GPUs for computationally intensive applications, not just in graphics and video processing. P systems, including SNP systems, are maximally parallel computing models taking inspiration from the functioning and dynamics of a living cell. In particular, SNP systems take inspiration from a type of cell known as a neuron. The nature of SNP systems allowed for their representation as matrices, which is an elegant step toward their simulation on GPUs. In this chapter, the simulation algorithms, design considerations, and implementation are presented. Finally, simulation results, observations, and analyses using a simple but non-trivial SNP system as an example are discussed, including recommendations for future work.

In "P Colonies of Capacity One and Modularity," the authors continue the investigation of P colonies introduced in Kelemen, Kelemenová, and Păun (2004). This chapter examines a class of abstract computing devices composed of independent agents, acting and evolving in a shared environment. The first part is devoted to the P colonies of the capacity one. The authors present improved results concerning the computational power of the P colonies with capacity one and without using checking programs. The second part of the chapter examines the modularity of the P colonies. The authors then divide the agents into modules.

Local search is currently one of the most used methods for finding solutions in real-life problems. It is usually considered when the research is interested in the final solution of the problem instead of the how the solution is reached. In this chapter, the authors present an implementation of local search with Membrane Computing techniques applied to the *N*-queens problem as a case study. A CLIPS program inspired in the Membrane Computing design has been implemented and several experiments have been performed. The obtained results in "Local Search with P Systems: A Case Study" show better average times than those obtained with other Membrane Computing implementations that solve the N-queens problem.

One of the concepts that lie at the basis of membrane computing is the multiset rewriting rule. On the other hand, the paradigm of rules is profusely used in computer science for representing and dealing with knowledge. Therefore, establishing a "bridge" between these domains is important, for instance, by designing P systems reproducing the modus ponens-based forward and backward chaining that can be used as tools for reasoning in propositional logic. In "Forward and Backward Chaining with P Systems," the authors show how powerful and intuitive the formalism of membrane computing is and how it can be used to represent concepts and notions from unrelated areas.

"Towards Automated Verification of P Systems using Spin" presents an approach to P systems verification using the Spin model checker. The authors have developed a tool, which implements the proposed approach and can automatically transform P system specifications from P-Lingua into Promela, the language accepted by the well-known model checker Spin. The properties expected for the P system are specified using some patterns, representing high-level descriptions of frequently asked questions, formulated in natural language. These properties are automatically translated into LTL specifications for the Promela model and the Spin model checker is run against them. In case a counterexample is received, the Spin trace is decoded and expressed as a P system computation. The tool has been tested on a number of examples and the results obtained are presented in the chapter.

The Intra Venous Glucose Tolerance Test (IVGTT) is an experimental procedure used to study the glucose-insulin endocrine regulatory system. An open problem is to construct a model representing simultaneously the entire regulative mechanism. In the past three decades, several models have appeared, but they have not escaped criticisms and drawbacks. In "MP Modelling of Glucose-Insulin Interactions in the Intravenous Glucose Tolerance Test," the authors apply the Metabolic P systems theory for developing new physiologically based models of the glucose-insulin system, which can be applied to the IVGTT. Ten data sets obtained from literature were considered and an MP model was found for each, which fits the data and explains the regulations of the dynamics. Finally, each model is analysed to define a common pattern, which explains, in general, the action of the glucose-insulin control system.

Smoothing is often used in Digital Imagery for improving the quality of an image by reducing its level of noise. " Implementation on CUDA of the Smoothing Problem with Tissue-Like P Systems" presents a parallel implementation of an algorithm for smoothing 2D images in the framework of Membrane Computing. The chosen formal framework has been tissue-like P systems. The algorithm has been implemented by using a novel device architecture called CUDA™ (Compute Unified Device Architecture), which allows the parallel NVIDIA Graphics Processors Units (GPUs) to solve many complex computational problems. Some examples are presented and compared; research lines for the future are also discussed.

P systems with active membranes have the ability of solving computationally hard problems. In "Elementary Active Membranes Have the Power of Counting," the authors prove that uniform families of P systems with active membranes operating in polynomial time can solve the whole class of PP decision problems, without using nonelementary membrane division or dissolution rules. This result also holds for families having a stricter uniformity condition than the usual one.

Prime factorization is useful and crucial for public-key cryptography, and its application in public-key cryptography is possible only because prime factorization has been presumed to be difficult. A polynomial-time algorithm for prime factorization on a quantum computer was given by P. W. Shor in 1997. In "Linear Time Solution to Prime Factorization by Tissue P Systems with Cell Division," it is considered as a function problem, and in the framework of tissue P systems with cell division, a linear-time solution to prime factorization problem is given on biochemical computational devices – tissue P systems with cell division, instead of computational devices based on the laws of quantum physical.

"Unorganized Machines: From Turing's Ideas to Modern Connectionist Approaches" presents a discussion about the relationship between the contributions of Alan Turing—the centenary of whose birth is celebrated in 2012—to the field of artificial neural networks and modern unorganized machines: Reservoir Computing (RC) approaches and Extreme Learning Machines (ELMs). Firstly, the authors review Turing's connectionist proposals and also expose the fundamentals of the main RC paradigms—echo state networks and liquid state machines—as well as of the design and training of ELMs. Throughout this exposition, the main points of contact between Turing's ideas and these modern perspectives are outlined, being, then, duly summarized in the second and final part of the work. This chapter is useful in offering a distinct appreciation of Turing's pioneering contributions to the field of neural networks and also in indicating some perspectives for the future development of the field that may arise from the synergy between these views.

An important premise of Natural Computing is that some form of computation goes on in Nature, and that computing capability has to be understood, modeled, abstracted, and used for different objectives and in different contexts. Therefore, it is necessary to propose a new language capable of describing and allowing the comprehension of natural systems as a union of computing phenomena, bringing an information processing perspective to Nature. To develop this new language and convert Natural Computing into a new science, it is imperative to overcome three specific Grand Challenges in Natural Computing Research: Transforming Natural Computing into a Transdisciplinary Discipline, Unveiling and Harnessing Information Processing in Natural Systems, Engineering Natural Computing Systems. This is explored in "The Grand Challenges in Natural Computing Research: The Quest for a New Science."

Slime mould *Physarum polycephalum* builds up sophisticated networks to transport nutrients between distant parts of its extended body. The slime mould's protoplasmic network is optimised for maximum coverage of nutrients yet minimum energy spent on transportation of the intra-cellular material. In laboratory experiments with *P. polycephalum,* the authors represent Canadian major urban areas with rolled oats and inoculated slime mould in the Toronto area. The plasmodium spans the urban areas with its network of protoplasmic tubes. The authors uncover similarities and differences between the protoplasmic network and the Canadian national highway network, analyse the networks in terms of proximity graphs, and evaluate slime mould's network response to contamination in "Trans-Canada Slimeways: Slime Mould Imitates the Canadian Transport Network."

The main issue presented in "Ecosystems Computing: Introduction to Biogeographic Computation" is based on the premise that Nature computes, that is, processes information. This is the fundamental of Natural Computing. Biogeographic Computation is presented as a Natural Computing approach aimed at investigating ecosystems computing. The first step towards formalizing Biogeographic Computation is given by defining a metamodel, a framework capable of generating models that compute through the elements of an ecosystem. It is also discussed how this computing can be realized in current computers.

Leandro Nunes de Castro
Mackenzie University, Brazil
July 2013

Chapter 1
PSO-CGO:
A Particle Swarm Algorithm for Cluster Geometry Optimization

Nuno Lourenço
Centro de Informática e Sistemas da Universidade de Coimbra (CISUC), Portugal

Francisco Baptista Pereira
Centro de Informática e Sistemas da Universidade de Coimbra (CISUC) & Instituto Superior de Engenharia de Coimbra, Portugal

ABSTRACT

In this paper the authors present PSO-CGO, a novel particle swarm algorithm for cluster geometry optimization. The proposed approach combines a steady-state strategy to update solutions with a structural distance measure that helps to maintain population diversity. Also, it adopts a novel rule to update particles, which applies velocity only to a subset of the variables and is therefore able to promote limited modifications in the structure of atomic clusters. Results are promising, as PSO-CGO is able to discover all putative global optima for short-ranged Morse clusters between 30 and 50 atoms. A comprehensive analysis is presented and reveals that the proposed components are essential to enhance the search effectiveness of the PSO.

1. INTRODUCTION

A chemical cluster is an aggregate of between a few and millions of atoms or molecules. A better understanding of the properties of clusters is relevant for many areas, from protein structure prediction to the field of nanotechnology. The overall organization of a cluster leads to distinct physical traits from those of a single particle or bulk matter and a multidimensional function is used to describe the interactions occurring in the aggregate. This mathematical function, known as the Potential Energy Surface (PES), contains all the relevant information about the chemical system and models all reciprocal actions between particles (Doye, 2006).

DOI: 10.4018/978-1-4666-4253-9.ch001

The goal of cluster geometry optimization is to determine the optimal structural organization for the set of particles that compose a given aggregate, i.e., to position all atoms/molecules in the 3D space in such a way that the structure corresponds to the lowest potential energy. Due to efficiency reasons, model PES are usually adopted when studying large clusters. Pair-wise PES are simplified potentials that only consider the distance between every pair of particles composing the cluster to calculate the energy of the aggregate. The most common model potentials are Lennard-Jones (1931) and Morse (1929) functions. The latter is particularly relevant, since it provides accurate approximations of real materials (e.g., C_{60} molecules or alkali metal clusters) (Braier et al., 1990; Smirnov et al., 1999).

A PES usually generates a highly roughed energy landscape, with multiple funnel topography (Stillinger, 1999). Moreover, it has been proved that the global minimization of most PES is NP-hard, since the number of local minima increases exponentially as the clusters grow in size (Wille & Vennik, 1985). It follows that stochastic global optimization methods are the most effective approaches for identifying low energy configurations for different cluster compositions. In particular, Morse clusters define challenging benchmarks and are regularly adopted to access the effectiveness of new optimization methods (Doye & Wales, 1997). Examples of current state-of-the-art approaches for Morse cluster optimization are hybrid evolutionary algorithms (Johnston 2003; Pereira & Marques, 2009), dynamic lattice searching (Cheng & Yang, 2007) or population basin-hopping (Grosso et al., 2007).

In this paper we propose a Particle Swarm Optimization (PSO) algorithm for cluster geometry optimization. PSO algorithms were proposed by Kennedy and Eberhart (1995) and are inspired by the dynamics of social interactions. They maintain a set of particles (potential solutions) that travel across the search landscape defined by the problem being solved. The movement of each particle takes into consideration its own previous history and also relevant information gathered from neighbor solutions. PSO are particularly well suited to continuous optimization scenarios and they have been successfully applied to a large number of problems (Poli, 2008). Nevertheless, there are just a few simple proposals described in the literature reporting the application of PSO algorithms to cluster geometry optimization problems (Call et al., 2007; Hodgson, 2002).

Here we present PSO-CGO, a novel PSO approach for this problem and perform a comprehensive study of the methods' strengths and weaknesses. We concentrate our analysis on two relevant issues: how to update the positions of the particles that belong to the swarm and how to maintain an appropriate level of diversity inside the swarm. PSO-CGO adopts a steady state model to manage the population of particles. This vital component helps to maintain a stable and diverse set of promising solutions and is combined with a balanced approach to modify the current position of particles. In concrete, velocity is applied only to a subset of the atoms that compose the cluster, thereby ensuring a limited modification in the structure of the aggregate. Short-ranged Morse instances are adopted as a benchmark to the aforementioned study. Results presented confirm that algorithmic components specifically designed for PSO-CGO enhance the likelihood of discovering good quality solution. Therefore, the framework proposed in paper is a relevant contribution towards the development of effective swarm intelligence algorithms for cluster geometry optimization.

The structure of the paper is the following: in Section 2 we describe the Morse potential and provide a brief overview of existing optimization algorithms for this problem. Then, in Section 3 we introduce the most relevant properties of existing PSO algorithms. Section 4 comprises a detailed explanation of the proposed PSO for cluster geometry optimization. A complete analysis of the PSO optimization performance is accomplished in Section 5 and, finally, Section 6 gathers the main conclusions and suggests directions for future work.

2. MORSE CLUSTERS

Model potentials are widely adopted both to understand chemical properties of real materials and as benchmarks to access the efficacy of new optimization algorithms. The Lennard-Jones (1931) and the Morse (1929) potentials are the most common pair-wise models described in the literature. The optimization of Morse clusters is the problem addressed in our study. The total potential energy of a N-cluster Morse aggregate is obtained by summing all pair-wise contributions that occur between atoms and is given by the following equation:

$$V_{Morse} = \epsilon \sum_{i=1}^{N-1} \sum_{j=i+1}^{N} \left(e^{-2\beta\left(r_{ij}-r_0\right)} - 2e^{-\beta\left(r_{ij}-r_0\right)} \right) \quad (1)$$

where r_{ij} is the distance between particles i and j in the cluster structure, ε is the bond dissociation energy, r_0 is the equilibrium bond length and β is the range exponent of the potential. Following Doye and Wales (1997), both ε and r_0 are set to 1.0, thus leading to a scaled version of the Morse function with non-atom specific interactions. Then, the potential has single parameter β that determines the shape of the energy contribution of every pair of atoms (Doye et al., 2004). Figure 1 contains a chart illustrating how this pair-wise contribution is modeled as a function of the distance between atoms (distance is displayed in the *xx* axis). Two different β values are exemplified: in both cases, the optimal potential energy is achieved when atoms are placed at a distance corresponding to the equilibrium bond length. However, moving from a long-ranged potential (β =6.0) to a short-ranged version (β =14.0) leads to a narrower potential curvature, promoting the appearance of very roughed search landscapes, with the number of local minima increasing exponentially as the number of atoms increases (Doye et al., 2004). Furthermore, the global minima for instances with a different number of atoms have distinct 3D geometries, therefore preventing the application of optimization methods that are biased to search for a specific structural organization (Chen & Yang, 2007; Doye & Wales, 1997; Grosso et al., 2007). The value of parameter β is set to 14.0 for all experiments described in this paper.

The application of gradient-driven local search, as described in Section 4, requires the specification of the first derivative of the PES function given in Equation 1. In Cartesian coordinates, the generic element *n* of the Morse potential gradient is given by:

$$g_n = -2\beta\epsilon \sum_{i \neq n}^{N} \left(\frac{x_{ni}}{r_{ni}}\right)\left(e^{-2\beta(r_{ni}-r_0)} - e^{-\beta(r_{ni}-r_0)}\right) \quad (2)$$

where $x_{ni} = x_n - x_i$. Similar expressions apply for the *y* and *z* directions.

2.1. Related Work: Optimization of Morse Clusters

The first report describing the application of a bio-inspired algorithm to cluster geometry optimization dates back from 1993 (Hartke, 1993). The reader is referred to Hartke (2004) for an historical overview on this topic. Here we focus our attention on key achievements related to the minimization of the Morse potential. Doye and Wales (1997) pioneered the application of global methods to this function. They used a basin-hopping algorithm, which is a combination of a Monte Carlo method with local search, and were able to discover most of the putative global minima for clusters up to 80 atoms.

In 2000, Roberts et al. (2000) were the first to apply evolutionary algorithms (EAs) to Morse clusters. The EA contained several specific com-

Figure 1. The Morse potential for different values of β

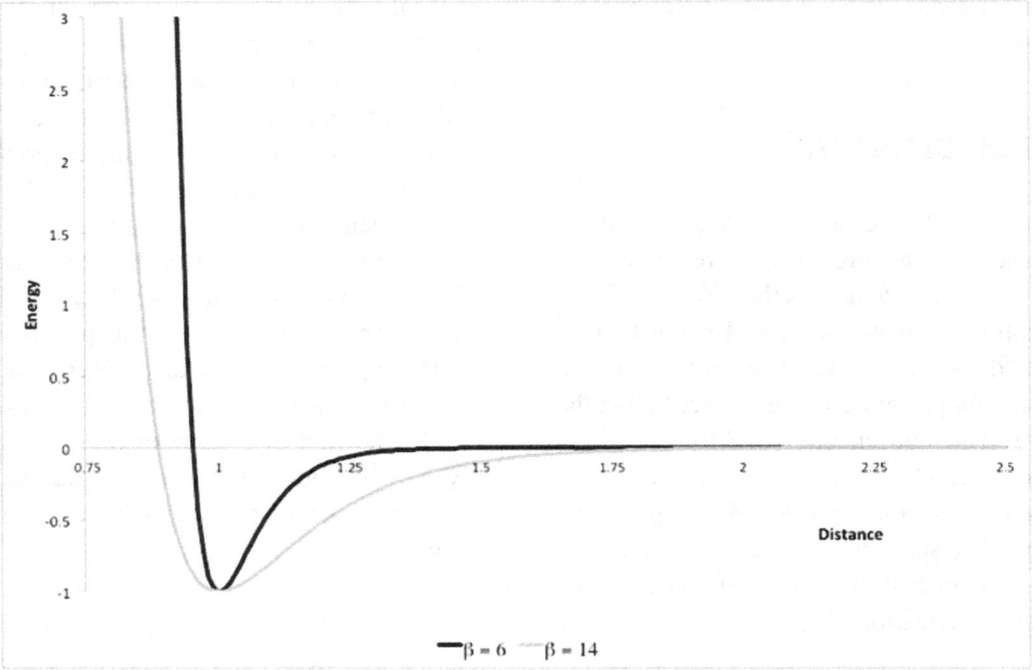

ponents previously proposed for other cluster optimization tasks, such as a real valued representation encoding the Cartesian coordinates of the atoms (Zeiri, 1995) and structural genetic operators (Deaven & Ho, 1995) sensitive to the solutions being manipulated (3D clusters). Moreover, the optimization framework incorporated a local search procedure that was applied to every solution generated by the EA. This hybrid approach was applied to medium and short-ranged Morse instances between 19 and 50 atoms and discovered nearly all putative global optima. The same research group presented a revised version of their algorithm in 2003 and reported success in finding all known best solutions for the aforementioned instances (Johnston, 2003).

Grosso et al. (2007) recently proposed a hybrid population-based algorithm that was able to discover all putative global optima for Morse clusters between 41 and 80 atoms. The key idea of this approach is the application of a two-phase local optimization to increase the efficiency of the search (Locatelli & Schoen, 2002). In this framework, local optimization is first applied on a modified potential, followed by a search performed on the real PES. The goal of the initial local step is to bias search towards promising areas of the search space. Despite the high rate of success achieved, this approach has an important drawback, since the design of the modified potential requires the specification of a set of parameters that are related to specific properties of the optimal solution being searched (e.g., some parameters create a bias towards the appearance of clusters with a given geometrical shape). Optimization frameworks incorporating two-phase local search are then unsuitable to situations where the structure of the optimal solutions is not known in advance. To overcome this limitation, Pereira and Marques (2008) proposed a hybrid EA that is able to self adapt on-the-fly the set of parameters used by the first step of local search. The same authors recently proposed a hybrid EA that is able to discover all putative global optima for Morse clusters until 80 atoms (Pereira & Marques, 2009). This method combines a steady-state EA and a single step local gradient driven optimization procedure that operates just on the true PES. The key to its success lies at the definition and application of a distance measure that helps to maintain diversity in the population.

Dynamic lattice searching (DLS) is another effective approach for cluster geometry optimization (Chen & Yang, 2007). It starts with a randomly generated local minimum and iteratively applies a greedy strategy to seek for better solutions in the neighborhood. The method is restarted several times to ensure a proper exploration of the search space. DLS was applied to Morse clusters and was able to establish several new upper bounds for instances ranging between 81 and 160 atoms.

To the best of our knowledge, there are just two reports describing the application of PSO algorithms to cluster geometry optimization. In Hodgson (2002), a straightforward PSO is applied in the optimization of Lennard-Jones clusters between 4 and 15 atoms. Even though the aggregates are small, the failure rate of the method, i.e., the number of runs that failed to discover the putative global optimum, is high (above 90% for clusters with more than 9 atoms). This result confirms that, for cluster geometry optimization tasks, unbiased global methods must be complemented with a local search procedure.

Call et al. (2007) recently proposed a modified PSO for cluster geometry optimization. Several specific issues were proposed with the aim to increase its efficiency and reliability. Relevant features described in the aforementioned publication include the adoption of a distance metric to estimate similarity between structures, therefore preventing the inclusion of similar solutions in the population and the enforcement of minimum distance constraint between particles. A noteworthy feature of the proposed method is that it does not incorporate local optimization of the generated solutions. The PSO was applied to small and medium size atomic and molecular clusters, namely the Lennard-Jones cluster with 26 atoms, the anionic silicon hydride ($Si_2H_5^-$) and the triply hydrated hydroxide ion ($OH^-(H_2O)_3$).

3. PARTICLE SWARM OPTIMIZATION

The key idea of Particle Swarm Optimization (PSO) is to develop optimization algorithms that mimic the behavior of a group of animals engaged in social interactions (Eberhart & Kennedy, 1995; Kennedy & Eberhart, 1995). Prominent examples are synchronous bird flocking or fish shoals escaping from a predator. For a detailed introduction on PSO algorithms, including the main variants and specializations that were proposed in recent years, consult (Banks et al., 2007, 2008; Poli et al., 2007) and references therein. In the next subsections we provide a brief overview of its main components, emphasizing issues that are relevant to the optimization approach proposed in this paper.

3.1. Canonical PSO

When solving a problem, PSO algorithms maintain a set of simple entities, called particles, which travel across the search space and try to identify promising solutions. At each moment, the fitness of a particle is the quality of its current location. Particles iteratively move around the search landscape, guided by knowledge previously acquired and by information inherited from promising particles in the neighborhood. In concrete, a given particle calculates its own movement by combining its previous search history and the best locations of the closest neighbors. A PSO individual encoding is composed by three D-dimensional vectors (y_1, y_2, …, y_D), $y_i \in \mathfrak{R}$, where D is the dimensionality of the search space. The first vector x encodes the set of coordinates that define the current position of the particle in the search space. The second vector p keeps the coordinates of the best position ever seen by that particle (i.e., it is a memory of a good location visited in the past that will bias future explorations). As for the third vector v, it stores the velocity of the particle and helps to establish the direction and strength of movement.

Swarm entities interact to enhance search effectiveness. Then, when a particle is calculating its new location, it also takes into account the best position found by any of its neighbors.

To establish a neighborhood, populations are organized into some kind of undirected topological structure connecting sets of particles. In this paper we concentrate on static topologies, which may consider either Euclidian neighborhoods (proximity in the search space) or social arrangements (Poli et al., 2007). We do not consider the first class of topologies, due to the high computational requirements involved and to its tendency to lead to premature convergence (Poli et al., 2007). In social neighborhoods, the swarm is represented as an undirected graph. Each particle is represented as a vertex, whereas edges link neighbors. Many different graph topologies were proposed in the literature, with differences in how the specific neighborhood is defined (Mendes, 2004; Kennedy & Mendes, 2002). One well-known example is the *lbest-k* topology, where the graph adopts a ring lattice arrangement and every particle is connected to k×2 neighbors (the k closest particles in each side of the ring) (Eberhart & Kennedy, 1995). Figure 2 illustrates two examples of *lbest-k* topologies. Another example of a topology is obtained with a fully connected graph. This social structure is known as the global best topology (*gbest*), since the whole swarm composes the neighborhood of the every particle.

In the original PSO proposed by Kennedy and Eberhart (1995), the velocity and position of a particle i are updated according to the following equation:

$$\begin{cases} v_i = v_i + U(0,\phi_1) \otimes \left(p_i - x_i\right) + U(0,\phi_2) \otimes (p_g - x_i) \\ x_i = x_i + v_i + \end{cases} \tag{3}$$

where p_g represents the best p vector in the neighborhood of particle i (i.e., the best solution ever found by a neighbor of particle i) and U(0, ϕ_1) (respectively U(0, ϕ_2)) represents a vector of random numbers uniformly distributed in [0, ϕ_1] (respectively [0, ϕ_2]). Acceleration coefficients ϕ_1 and ϕ_2 determine the relative contribution of the

Figure 2. The lbest topology with two different neighborhood sizes: the graph on the left illustrates lbest-1, whereas the one on the right exemplifies lbest-2. Figure reprinted with permission from (Mendes, 2004).

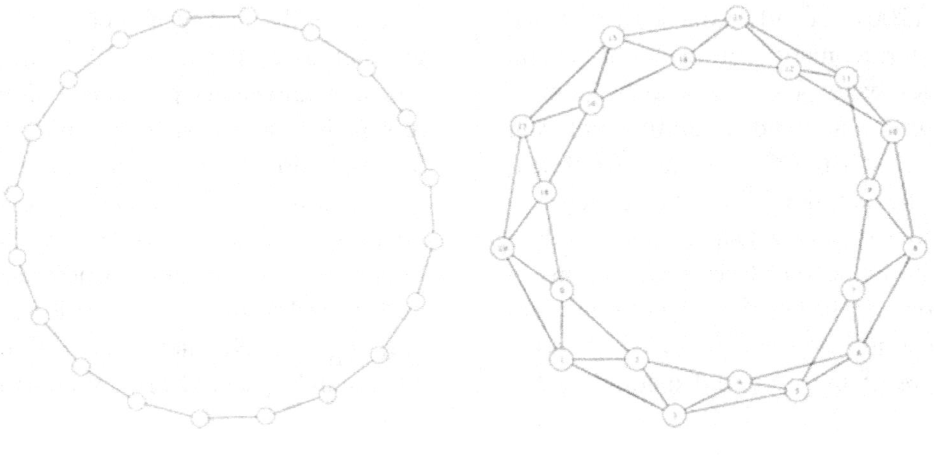

personal best and neighborhood best in calculating v (see, e.g., Poli et al., 2007) for details on how to set these parameters). The original PSO proposal enforces that the velocity must be kept within the range $[-V_{max}, +V_{max}]$. The hard bounds on velocity are a parameter of the algorithm and usually are problem-specific.

With the aim to achieve a better control of particle movement, a few modifications to the PSO update rule have been introduced. One of them proposed the adoption of an inertia weight (Shi & Eberhart, 1998), whilst another relies on constriction coefficients (Clerc & Kennedy, 2002). We adopt this last update rule, widely considered as the canonical version of the PSO algorithm (Poli et al., 2007). According to the constriction coefficient strategy, the position of a particle is updated according to the following rule:

$$\begin{cases} v_i = \chi(v_i + U(0,\phi_1) \otimes \left(p_i - x_i\right) + \\ U(0,\phi_2) \otimes (p_g - x_i) \ ) \\ x_i = x_i + v_i \end{cases} \tag{4}$$

The introduction of the constriction coefficient χ allows for a controlled convergence of the algorithm and removes the need to specify hard bounds for the velocity. This coefficient is obtained in the following way:

$$\chi = \frac{2}{\phi - 2 + \sqrt{\phi^2 - 4\phi}} \tag{5}$$

where $\phi = \phi_1 + \phi_2$. In this variant, ϕ is commonly set to 4.1 and $\phi_1 = \phi_2$.

Algorithm 1 presents an overview of the general organization of the canonical PSO algorithm. Following random initialization, the iterative process goes on, either until all particles converge to an optimum, or a maximum number of iterations is reached.

3.2. Extensions to the Canonical PSO

In the past few years, a large number of extensions to the canonical PSO have been proposed. New proposals either address specific situations or aim to describe a more generic variant that might be successfully applied in a wide range of situations. Here we briefly review some key achievements mainly related to hybridization and diversity control, as these components are essential to the development of an effective PSO for cluster geometry optimization.

From all variants proposed in the last decade, Kennedy's (2003) bare-bones is probably the most relevant to our work, as some of its components inspired the development of PSO-CGO.

Algorithm 1. Canonical PSO algorithm

```
Initialize population of particles with random positions and velocities
While termination condition not met do
For each particle do
        Evaluate current position
    If the current position x_i is better than the previous best position p_i then
            Update best position p_i
    Identify the best particle in the neighborhood, and assign it to p_g
    Apply selected update rule to change the velocity v_i and the current position x_i
    end do
end while
Return optimization result
```

It was presented in 2003 and its most distinctive feature is the absence of velocity. Instead, for all particles, every component from the *x* vector is updated with a random value sampled from a Gaussian distribution with mean $(p_i(k)+p_g(k))/2$ and standard deviation $|p_i(k)-p_g(k)|$, where $p_i(k)$ (respectively, $p_g(k)$) stands for the *k-th* component of the p_i (respectively p_g) vector. A later work replaced the original distribution by a Lévy distribution, further enhancing the performance of the optimization method (Richer & Blackwell, 2006). The bare-bones PSO adopts a static local topology with 4 neighbors. However, when calculating the new position of a given particle, the neighbor p_g is randomly selected (instead of the canonical best neighbor selection). Moreover, this variant includes an interaction probability (IP) parameter that specifies the likelihood of updating the components of vector *x* with the values drawn from the probability distribution. Results presented in Kennedy (2003) reveal that setting IP to 0.5 coupled with random neighbor selection helps to enhance performance of the PSO when seeking for the global optimum of a set of mathematical functions.

Hybrid proposals can by classified in two, possibly overlapping categories: they either combine a PSO algorithm with another optimization method or incorporate specific components from other algorithms into the regular PSO framework. Relevant examples of hybrid combinations of methods are the LifeCycle model that simultaneously applies a PSO, a genetic algorithm and stochastic hill-climbing (Krink & Loøvbjerg, 2002), the DEPSO that relies on a PSO and a differential evolution algorithm in alternate iterations (Zhang & Xie, 2003), or the approach by Holden and Freitas (2005) joining PSO and ant colony optimization for designing effective data mining classification rules.

A popular approach to modify the usual PSO modus operandi is to incorporate specific components borrowed from evolutionary algorithms (EA). Angeline (1998) pioneered this line of research by proposing a tournament selection mechanism that identifies and removes the worst particles from the swarm. The two standard genetic operators have also been incorporated in the PSO framework: mutation can be applied with a given probability to every component of a recently updated particle, thereby helping to speed up convergence and avoiding local optima traps (Higashi & Iba, 2003; Stacey et al., 2003); Loøvbjerg et al. (2001) presented an arithmetic crossover operator that creates two descendant particles by combining the velocities and positions of two randomly chosen parents. A recent work from Deb and Padhye (2010) goes one step further by incorporating a large number of EA components, e.g., selection, mutation, crossover or elitism, into a PSO framework. The resulting hybrid approach obtained results that are comparable to those achieved by state-of the-art EAs on the optimization of 100-variable unimodal mathematical functions.

PSO algorithms are prone to premature convergence to local optima (Banks et al., 2007; Poli et al., 2007) and many approaches have been proposed to postpone stagnation. A few well-known examples include the collision avoidance system by Krink et al. (2002), the predator/prey model by Silva et al. (2002), or the dissipative PSO by Xie et al. (2002) that relies on negative entropy to maintain the swarm far from an equilibrium state. Also, a careful definition of the topology might help to postpone convergence (Mendes, 2004).

4. PSO-CGO: A PSO FOR CLUSTER GEOMETRY OPTIMIZATION

In this section we present the specific issues that must be considered when designing a PSO for the optimization of the geometry of Morse clusters. There are two key topics regularly addressed in the literature that reports the application of effective population-based methods for cluster geometry optimization: the advantage of adopting a steady-state model and the need to maintain an appropriate level of diversity (Grosso et al., 2007; Pereira & Marques, 2009). Additionally, state-of-the-art approaches are hybrid frameworks combining a global optimization method with local search procedures that rely on gradient information to guide solutions into the nearest local optima (Deaven & Ho, 1995; Roberts et al., 2000; Grosso et al., 2007; Pereira & Marques, 2009). In the next sections we describe how the canonical PSO algorithm is modified to incorporate these topics. Special attention is given to population and particle update strategies, as they differ from those adopted by standard PSO frameworks. The population update rule implements a novel steady-state PSO that resembles other population-based approaches for cluster geometry optimization. The update of the current particle solution combines contributions from the velocity vector with random modifications introduced by a mutation operator. The joint application of these two forces aims to maintain a balance between keeping relevant information already discovered and promoting further exploration. Hopefully, the modified PSO, which we identify as PSO-CGO, will have increased effectiveness when seeking for low energy Morse clusters.

4.1. Solution Encoding and Evaluation

A solution for a cluster geometry optimization problem must specify the 3D location of all atoms that compose the aggregate. For an instance with N atoms, solutions encode 3N real values specifying the corresponding Cartesian coordinates. The coordinate values belong to the interval $[0, N^{1/3}]$, as this enables the cluster to scale correctly with N (Johnston, 2003). An important constraint is that inter-atomic distances cannot fall below a pre-specified parameter δ. If this constraint is not satisfied the potential becomes too repulsive and the energy tends to infinity, leading to arithmetic overflow. Following previous works (Pereira & Marques, 2009), the value of δ is set to 0.5. A PSO particle (i.e., a complete solution) contains 3 vectors with 3N real values. Vectors x and p encode the coordinates of the current solution and of the best solution ever seen by this particle, respectively. Vector v encodes the current velocity.

The evaluation of a new position discovered by a PSO-CGO particle proceeds in two steps. First, the Broyden-Fletcher-Goldfarb-Shannon (L-BFGS) quasi-Newton method (Liu & Nocedal, 1989) relaxes the solution into the nearest local optimum. Then Equation 1 is used to determine the potential energy of the resulting cluster. In this framework, all solutions kept by the PSO are local optima.

L-BFGS is an efficient local optimization technique that combines the modest storage and computational requirements of conjugate gradient methods with the superlinear convergence exhibited by full memory quasi-Newton strategies. This is the local optimization algorithm regularly adopted by hybrid approaches for cluster geometry optimization problems (Grosso et al., 2007; Johnston, 2003; Pereira & Marques, 2009).

4.2. Population Update

The model adopted for the update of the particles that compose the swarm requires the definition of a distance measure to estimate the similarity between two solutions. Many different descriptors were proposed in the literature to evaluate how similar two atomic clusters are (Marques et al., 2010) and references therein for a comprehensive description and analysis). In this work we adopt the center of mass distance (CMD), an accurate estimator for cluster similarity. CMD was proposed by Grosso et al. (2007) and it is based on the distance of atoms to the corresponding center of mass (see the aforementioned references for a detailed description).

The update and replacement strategy of the λ solutions composing the swarm proceeds in three main periods, detailed in Algorithm 2. First, a replica of the actual population is created. In the replicated population, the current position of every particle is reset to the corresponding best location, i.e., $x_i = p_i$, $i=1, \ldots, \lambda$. This operation moves all particles from Rep to the best location they ever seen, thereby ensuring that particles from Pop and Rep explore the search space departing from different locations. In the second period, the velocity and current position of all particles from both populations are updated. The last period is required to reduce the existing particles to half. Particles are merged into a single sorted set, ordered by increasing potential energy of current solutions. Starting with the first solution (the best one), particles are then selected to appear in the next PSO-CGO population. A solution at a given position *P* is discarded if it is similar to another solution previously selected. CMD is used to estimate the similarity between two solutions. If the calculated value is lower than a pre-specified minimum distance threshold, then solutions are considered as similar.

The PSO-CGO swarm update resembles the ($\lambda+\lambda$) selection scheme adopted by evolutionary strategies. First, the existing λ particles generate λ offspring and, then, the whole set of solutions is reduced to half. There are nevertheless two noteworthy differences in the framework described in this paper: parents are also updated and the selection of survivors considers both quality and diversity. The second criterion is essential to maintain diversity in the population, therefore preventing premature convergence.

To estimate the minimum distance threshold we follow the rule proposed in Pereira and Marques (2009). First, we generate a large set of random solutions and use them to make an educated guess on the average distance between two arbitrary structures (d_{rnd}). Then, the minimum distance threshold is set to $0.25 \times d_{rnd}$. We did some preliminary experiments with a different tightness for the threshold and verified that PSO-CGO was fairly insensitive to variations in this parameter.

4.3. Particle Update

Each particle performs the steps presented in Algorithm 3 to update its current position. The PSO-CGO adopts a *lbest-2* topology, meaning that each solution has four neighbors. The most similar neighbor, as determined by the CMD measure, is selected to influence the velocity update, which is accomplished by the application of Equation 4. The update of the current position has some differences from standard PSO applications. Preliminary experiments revealed that a complete update of all atoms that compose the cluster tends to disrupt its geometrical structure, compromising the effectiveness of the optimization. On the other hand, we observed that moving just a subset of atoms regularly led to premature convergence. As a consequence, we propose a novel approach that aims to find a balance between these unwanted extremes. First, velocity is applied with probability p_{vel} to atoms that compose the cluster. It is important to notice that updates are applied to

Algorithm 2. PSO-CGO swarm update

```
Given t he current PSO population Pop: ((x₁, p₁, v₁), (x₂, p₂, v₂), ..., (x_λ, p_λ, v_λ)) Do:
1. Create a copy Rep: ((p₁, p₁, v₁), (p₂, p₂, v₂), ..., (p_λ, p_λ, v_λ))
2. Update the velocity and current position of solutions from Pop
3. Update the velocity and current position of solutions from Rep
4. Merge Pop and Rep
5. Sort merged population by increasing potential energy of current solutions
6. Select the best λ solutions to appear in the next PSO-CGO population
```

Algorithm 3. PSO-CGO particle update

```
1. Select most similar neighbor
2. Update velocity
3. Update atoms with probability p_vel
4. Apply mutation to all atoms not updated by velocity
```

atoms, i.e., changes are made to groups of three coordinates that specify a given 3D location. Precautions are taken to ensure that two atoms do not approach too much. If any inter-atomic distance falls below the minimum distance threshold, then the movement that leads to the violation is reverted. In the last step of the update, mutation is applied to particles that were not moved by the velocity. Sigma mutation, an operator widely adopted in cluster geometry optimization is used in this step (Pereira & Marques, 2009). When mutating an atom, it slightly perturbs each of its three coordinates with a random value sampled from a Gaussian distribution with mean 0 and standard deviation σ.

5. EXPERIMENTS

The experimental analysis will focus on the application of PSO-CGO to several instances of short-ranged Morse clusters. More specifically, we selected instances with a number of atoms that ranges between 30 and 50. With these experiments we pursue two goals: 1) to access the performance effectiveness of PSO-CGO and 2) to gain insight into the role played by the main components of the algorithm. In concrete, we aim to determine if the novel steady-state swarm update strategy and the combined particle update rule indeed help to enhance the effectiveness of the PSO.

Two criteria are used to evaluate the performance of the optimization methods. The ability of an algorithm to discover the putative optima (within a pre-specified computational effort) is a widely adopted performance measure in cluster geometry optimization. Therefore, for all selected instances, we show if PSO-CGO was able to discover the best-known solution and what was its success rate (number of runs that found the putative optimum). For completeness, we provide the mean best fitness (MBF) as a second performance criterion, as it will help to understand if the PSO is reliably converging to promising areas of the search space.

The absolute performance of PSO-CGO will be accessed by comparing its results with those achieved by an EA recently described in Pereira and Marques (2009). This is a hybrid approach, combining a steady-state EA with a quasi-Newton local search procedure and is one of the most effective unbiased methods for Morse clusters optimization.

The settings of the algorithm are the following: Number of runs: 30; Number of particles: 50; Number of evaluations: 5,000,000; p_{vel}: 0.35; σ: $0.05 \times N^{1/3}$. Each iteration performed by L-BFGS counts as 1 evaluation and the accuracy of local search is set to 1.0E-8. Initial populations are randomly generated. Even though parameter values were set heuristically, we did some additional tests and verified that moderate variations have no significant impact on the performance of PSO-CGO.

5.1. Optimization Results

In Table 1 we provide an overview of the optimization results. The first column identifies the number of atoms of each instance and the second column (labeled *optimum*) displays the potential energy of the best-known solution. The next two columns present the success rate (column SR) and the MBF of PSO-CGO. The fourth column

Table 1. Optimization results of Morse clusters between 30 and 50 atoms obtained by PSO-CGO and the hybrid EA (with CMD) from (Pereira & Marques, 2009)

		PSO-CGO			Hybrid EA	
	Optimum	**SR**	**MBF**	**Deviation**	**SR**	**MBF**
30	-106.8357	4	-106.7182	0.11	22	-106.7947
31	-111.7606	19	-111.6309	0.12	30	-111.7606
32	-115.7675	20	-115.6863	0.07	29	-115.7666
33	-120.7413	19	-120.6902	0.04	28	-120.6976
34	-124.7482	15	-124.6052	0.11	28	-124.7154
35	-129.7373	6	-129.0789	0.51	27	-129.6232
36	-133.7446	14	-133.4948	0.19	28	-133.7151
37	-138.7085	12	-138.1474	0.40	25	-138.6105
38	-144.3210	8	-142.5455	1.23	8	-143.1304
39	-148.3274	7	-147.3619	0.65	14	-147.9580
40	-152.3337	7	-151.5165	0.54	9	-151.8860
41	-156.6334	2	-155.8986	0.47	15	-156.5479
42	-160.6410	4	-160.0271	0.38	12	-160.5181
43	-165.6349	4	-164.6498	0.59	14	-165.2548
44	-169.6424	3	-168.9085	0.43	7	-169.3036
45	-174.5116	3	-173.1605	0.77	5	-174.1021
46	-178.5193	1	-177.5135	0.56	9	-178.3897
47	-183.5082	1	-182.0811	0.78	2	-183.1536
48	-188.8889	2	-186.7820	1.12	14	-188.1606
49	-192.8984	4	-191.4960	0.73	18	-192.6278
50	-198.4556	1	-195.8160	1.33	5	-197.6889

measures of how the MBF deviates from the putative optimum. Results from Table 1 confirm the effectiveness of the proposed approach, as it was able to discover all putative optima for sort-ranged Morse clusters between 30 and 50 atoms. This is an important outcome, as it is the first PSO algorithm that succeeds in this difficult optimization task. As expected, the variation in the success rate is somehow irregular. Some specific instances (the so called magic numbers – e.g., 30, 38, 47, Doye & Wales, 1997)) define particularly rugged landscapes and it expectable that unbiased approximate algorithms might frequently converge to local optima (Doye & Wales, 1997; Roberts et al., 2000; Grosso et al., 2007). In any case, there is a general trend for the success rate of the PSO to decrease as the number of atoms increases. This might be partially explained by the fact that we keep the number of evaluations fixed for all cluster sizes. More atoms lead to larger search spaces and it is likely that the performance of the optimization algorithm gradually declines. Nevertheless, the success rate for instances with more than 40 atoms is always below 15%, suggesting that there is still room for additional modifications in the PSO framework, which might further improve its performance.

An overview of the MBF values achieved reveals that they are always close to the optimum (deviation ranges between 0.04% and 1.33%). This result shows that, even when the PSO converges to local optima, it can reliably identify low potential energy structures.

Recalling algorithm 2, the swarm update strategy obtains the solutions for a new iteration by selecting some particles from two sets identified as Pop and Rep. Individuals from Pop explore the search space taking the current location as a starting point, whereas individuals from Rep start exploring from the best solution ever seen by that particle. In the chart from Figure 3 we show how many of the solutions that appear in the next iteration were selected from each one of these sets. Results are averages of 30 runs and were obtained with the Morse instance with 50 atoms, although the same trend is visible for other instances. The lines displayed in Figure 3 reveal that, throughout the optimization, both Pop and Rep contribute with solutions to the new swarm, i.e., both search strategies are helpful in discovering promising and diverse solutions.

5.2. Comparison with Other Approaches

It is important to compare the absolute performance of PSO-CGO against other optimization methods. A direct comparison with other PSO approaches is not possible, as there are no reports describing the application of swarm algorithms to the optimization of Morse clusters. We then selected an EA recently described in Pereira and Marques (2009), which is one of the most effective unbiased methods for Morse clusters optimization. This is a hybrid approach, combining a steady-state EA with a quasi-Newton local search procedure. The EA relies on the CMD measure to maintain population diversity. On the last two columns of Table 1, we show the success rate and MBF achieved by the hybrid EA on the instances considered in this study. Results were taken from Pereira and Marques (2009) and were obtained with the same number of evaluations that

Figure 3. Evolution of the number of particles from Pop and Rep that are selected for the next PSO population (see algorithm 2). Results are averages of 30 runs and were obtained with the Morse instance with 50 atoms.

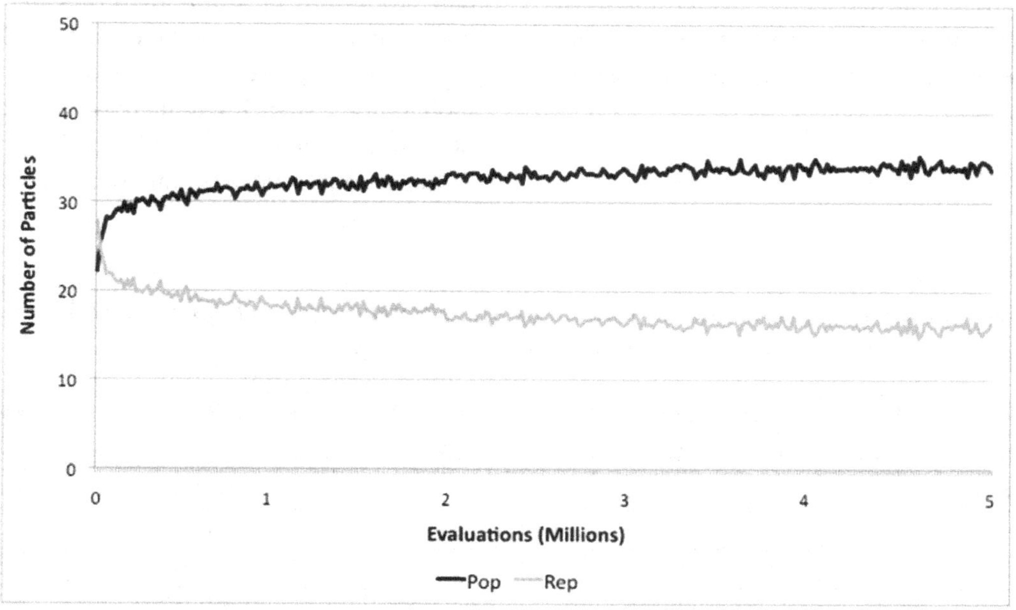

were granted to the PSO. A brief perusal of the outcomes reveals that PSO-CGO is not as effective as the EA, both in the success rate and the MBF values. This result is not unexpected. The selected hybrid EA is the final result of the development of evolutionary approaches for cluster geometry optimization. As for the PSO proposed in this paper, it should be considered as a relevant step of ongoing research toward the development of effective swarm intelligence algorithms for this problem. Additional results presented in the next sections support this claim, by showing that the novel components are important to enhance the effectiveness of PSO-CGO.

5.3. Detailed Analysis of the PSO-CGO Framework

PSO-CGO contains some novel components, particularly designed to enhance its effectiveness in cluster geometry optimization problems. In this section we present an additional set of results obtained in a subset of instances by several slightly modified PSO-CGO variants. We selected clusters with size N={30, 38, 45, 50} and changes range from a simple parameter setting variation to structural modifications in the PSO-CGO framework. A comparison of results will help to clarify the relevance of the different components proposed in Section 4.

5.4. Particle Update

Vector x components are updated either by velocity or by mutation. This compromise aims to promote a controlled modification of the current solution, thereby preventing both excessive disturbance and premature convergence. Parameter p_{vel} establishes the balance between the two contributions and its value was set to 0.35 in the experiments previously described. In Table 2 we present results obtained with additional settings, p_{vel} = *{0.2, 0.35, 0.5, 0.65, 0.8}*, in the selected subset of instances. An inspection of this table immediately reveals that the value of p_{vel} does not have to be set with excessive care, as different proportions of velocity vs. mutation in particle update lead to similar outcomes. This is partially a consequence of the strategy adopted for particle update. Step 3 of algorithm 3 states that atoms are updated with probability p_{vel}. However, changes are not accepted if they lead to a situation where two atoms approach too much. As the optimization progresses, PSO-CGO gradually starts to discover good quality solutions. They typically correspond to packed clusters, where the displacement of a few atoms often leads to a violation of the minimum distance constraint. Therefore, the real proportion of atoms modified by velocity is usually lower than the value specified by p_{vel}. This is particularly true in situations with high p_{vel} probabilities, since it will increase the likelihood of unwanted interactions between atoms. The displacement induced by mutation is smaller (due

Table 2. Optimization results obtained by PSO-CGO with different values of p_{vel} in selected Morse clusters instances. The symbol '-' indicates that the optimum was never found.

	P_{vel} = 0.2		P_{vel} = 0.35		P_{vel} = 0.5		P_{vel} = 0.65		P_{vel} = 0.8	
	SR	**MFB**	**SR**	**MFB**	**SR**	**MFB**	**SR**	**MFB**	**SR**	**MFB**
30	8	-106.7107	4	-106.7182	11	-106.7415	5	-106.7458	5	-106.7127
38	8	-143.0960	8	-142.5455	3	-143.3354	11	-143.1128	11	-142.8916
45	1	-173.0446	3	-173.1605	1	-173.1218	-	-173.2293	-	-172.9061
50	1	-195.7586	1	-195.8160	-	-195.4535	-	-195.5851	1	-195.5610

to the low standard deviation adopted) and, for that reason, this operator only infrequently will cause a minimum distance constraint violation.

5.5. Swarm Topological Structure

PSO-CGO adopts a social *lbest-2* topology. Each particle has 4 neighbors and the most similar one (as estimated by CMD measure) is selected to influence velocity update. Here we study the impact of two possible modifications in the definition of the neighborhood. The first change addresses two alternative rules to select the neighbor: by fitness (the best neighbor is selected) or randomly (a random particle in the neighborhood is selected). The other modification deals with the definition of a global best topology *gbest*. The results obtained by the six possible configurations on the subset of instances are presented in Tables 3 and 4, respectively for the *lbest-2* and *gbest* topologies.

The outcomes obtained by the six social topologies are similar. There is a slight trend for the fitness-based neighborhoods to obtain results of inferior quality (e.g., it fails to discover the optimal solution for the instances with 45 and 50 atoms in every run), but differences in performance are very small. On the contrary, a random neighbor selection proves to be a viable option, both for the *lbest* and *gbest* topologies. This result is in accordance with the findings obtained by the bare bones PSO (Kennedy, 2003). The existence of a steady-state model for the population of particles helps to understand the comparable results obtained by the different topologies. The diversity enforcement mechanism prevents the existence of similar solutions in the swarm. Then, the neighborhood of a given particle tends to be composed by good quality clusters with distinct properties, and the selection strategy adopted is somehow irrelevant.

5.6. Population Update

The population update strategy is the most distinctive feature of PSO-CGO. There are some noteworthy differences between the rules followed by the canonical PSO algorithm and those proposed for PSO-CGO. This design was specifically formulated for cluster geometry optimization problems and we will now analyze how it impacts performance. The additional set of results presented in this section clearly shows that these features are essential to enhance performance. To succeed in the analysis we created a set of variants, which were obtained from PSO-CGO by removing some of its components. All alternatives maintain the representation encoding described in Section 4 and apply L-BFGS to all solutions generated by the algorithm. We consider three different variants:

Table 3. Optimization results obtained by PSO-CGO with lbest-2 topology in selected Morse clusters instances. Results obtained with three different rules for neighbor selection are presented. The symbol '-' indicates that the optimum was never found.

	Structural		Fitness		Random	
	SR	MFB	SR	MFB	SR	MFB
30	4	-106.7182	5	-106.6916	9	-106.7563
38	8	-142.5455	7	-142.4964	9	-142.8840
45	3	-173.1605	-	-172.6205	-	-173.0912
50	1	-195.8160	-	-194.8282	1	-195.7150

Table 4. Optimization results obtained by PSO-CGO with gbest topology in selected Morse clusters instances. Results obtained with three different rules for neighbor selection are presented. The symbol '-' indicates that the optimum was never found.

	Structural		Fitness		Random	
	SR	MFB	SR	MFB	SR	MFB
30	6	-106.7316	2	-106.7102	7	-106.7521
38	9	-143.0000	9	-142.8973	7	-142.7664
45	-	-172.9415	-	-172.5513	-	-172.4953
50	-	-195.4261	-	-195.1080	2	-195.6925

- **PSO-V1:** Canonical PSO with the constriction coefficient update rule. It does not consider the population update strategy described in algorithm 2 and applies velocity to change the location of all atoms (i.e., p_{vel} is set to 1.0).
- **PSO-V2:** Canonical PSO with mutation. The only difference from PSO-V1 is that p_{vel} is set to 0.35 and the remaining atoms are updated by sigma mutation. This is the same particle update strategy adopted by PSO-CGO.
- **PSO-V3:** This variant is almost identical to PSO-CGO. It follows algorithm 2 to update the population and algorithm 3 to perform particle update. The only difference is that it does not consider structural similarity to select individuals that appear in the next PSO population (step 6 of algorithm 2). Hence, potential energy is the single criterion considered by selection to choose the 50 particles that survive.

Optimization results are presented in Table 5 for the selected subset of instances. To simplify the comparison, we report again the results achieved by PSO-CGO. The outcomes clearly show that the framework specifically proposed for cluster geometry optimization helps to enhance search effectiveness. Both PSO-V1 and PSO-V2 follow the canonical population update and, for every instance of the selected subset, converge to local optima in all runs. This confirms the advantage in following a strategy that simultaneously searches for promising cluster structures in the neighborhood of current solutions and in the neighborhood of best ever seen solutions. Moreover, the steady-state nature of PSO-CGO helps to maintain a stable and diverse set of solutions that guide future explorations and amplifies the ability to discover the putative global optima. Also, results obtained by PSO-V1 and PSO-V2 are similar, revealing that the particle update strategy proposed in algorithm 2 does not provide a noticeable advantage if it is not combined with the modified population strategy update.

The results obtained by PSO-V3 are disappointing. It always fails to discover the best-known solutions and the final MBFs are even worse than those of both PSO-V1 and PSO-V2. The evident advantage of PSO-CGO over PSO-V3 confirms the vital importance of promoting diversity when seeking for good solutions in cluster geometry optimization problems. The chart from Figure 4 displays the evolution of the MBF for all PSO variants considered in this section. Results are from the Morse instance with 50 atoms, but the same trend is visible for other instances. The information in this chart clearly illustrates the premature convergence of PSO-V3, whereas PSO-CGO maintains the ability to improve solutions through all the course of optimization. Additionally, towards the end of the run PSO-V1 and PSO-V2 outperform PSO-V3, confirming that it is mandatory to combine a steady-state approach with a method that helps to maintain diversity.

Table 5. Optimization results obtained by several PSO variants in selected Morse clusters instances. The symbol '-' indicates that the optimum was never found.

	PSO-CGO		PSO-V1		PSO-V2		PSO-V3	
	SR	**MFB**	**SR**	**MFB**	**SR**	**MFB**	**SR**	**MFB**
30	4	-106.7182	-	-105.8146	-	-106.1442	-	-104.0080
38	8	-142.5455	-	-138.9613	-	-140.1084	-	-137.3954
45	3	-173.1605	-	-168.5571	-	-169.1759	-	-167.0014
50	1	-195.8160	-	-190.1797	-	-191.2081	-	-189.5750

6. CONCLUSION AND FUTURE WORK

In this paper we presented PSO-CGO, a PSO algorithm for cluster geometry optimization. The proposed framework contains several features that were specifically designed to enhance search effectiveness when seeking for low energy structures of atomic clusters. The most noteworthy distinctions between PSO-CGO and the canonical PSO algorithm are: 1) the adoption of specific rules to update the current positions of particles, where velocity is applied only to a fraction of the variables that encode a solution; and 2) the embracing of a steady-state strategy to update the population of particles. This strategy allows for a simultaneous exploration of the neighborhoods of the current locations and of the best ever seen solutions and is coupled with a mechanism to maintain diversity, therefore postponing convergence.

Optimization results described in Section 5 are promising. We applied PSO-CGO to short-ranged Morse instances between 30 and 50 atoms and verified that it is able to discover all putative global optima. To the best of our knowledge, this is the first PSO algorithm to succeed in this difficult cluster geometry optimization benchmark. Moreover, PSO-CGO always achieves MBF values close to the optimum, showing that it can reliably identify low potential energy structures. A comprehensive analysis of the optimization behavior revealed that the steady-state strategy specifically designed for this problem is the vital component to enhance the search effectiveness of PSO-CGO.

The research described in this paper is a relevant step towards the development of state-of-the-art PSO algorithms for cluster geometry optimization. It is important, nevertheless, to recognize that the success rate of PSO-CGO is somehow irregular and tends to decrease as the number of atoms increases. Also, its absolute performance is still not comparable with state-of-the-art approaches for cluster geometry optimization. In accordance, our future research efforts will be directed towards modifications that can further enhance the robustness and scalability of PSO-CGO. In concrete, we will study alternatives for the particle update strategy that might replace the current approach. One possibility is the adaptation of the bare-bones PSO update strategy (Kennedy, 2003). This is an elegant approach that combines, in a single rule, information from

Figure 4. Evolution of the MBF of PSO-CGO and of three additional PSO variants. Results were obtained with the Morse instance with 50 atoms.

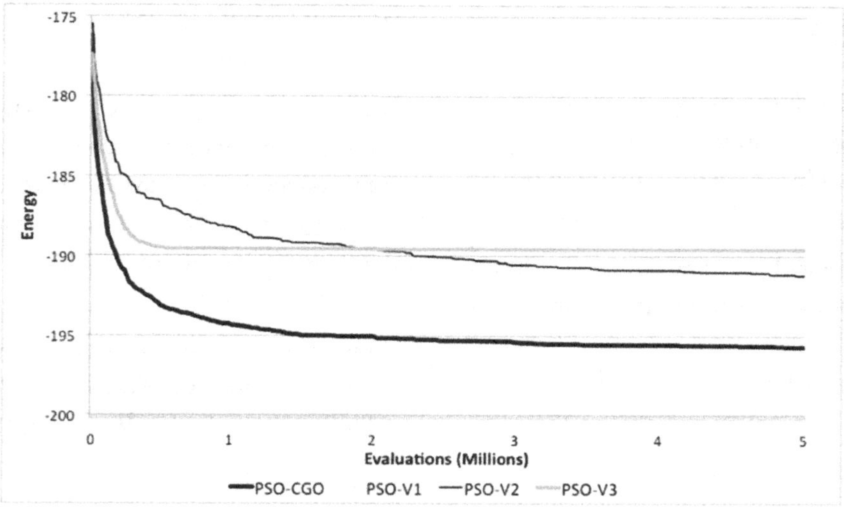

neighbor particles and a stochastic perturbation. Accordingly, the current two-step particle update strategy could be replaced by a simplified framework, while maintaining the balance between exploitation of previously acquired knowledge and exploration of new areas of the search space. Another option is the development of a crossover operator for obtaining new solutions through the combination of several particles from the swarm. There are reports in the literature describing the advantages of adding crossover-like operators to PSO algorithms (Løvbjerg et al., 2001; Deb et al., 2010). In the optimization problem addressed in this paper, it could be relevant to consider the application of a recombination operator working on the 3D space (Froltsov & Reuter, 2009). This would allow it to consider the spatial distribution of atoms, therefore maximizing the probability of performing a meaningful combination of relevant features from different parents.

ACKNOWLEDGMENT

This work was supported by Fundação para a Ciência e Tecnologia (FCT), Portugal, under project PTDC/QUI/69422/2006, which is financed by Programa Operacional Factores de Competitividade (COMPETE) of QREN and FEDER programs.

REFERENCES

Angeline, P. (1998). Using selection to improve particle swarm optimization. In *Proceedings of the IEEE Congress on Evolutionary Computation* (pp. 84-89). Washington, DC: IEEE Computer Society.

Banks, A., Vincent, J., & Anyakoha, C. (2007). A review of particle swarm optimization. Part I: Background and development. *Natural Computing*, *6*, 467–484. doi:10.1007/s11047-007-9049-5.

Banks, A., Vincent, J., & Anyakoha, C. (2008). A review of particle swarm optimization. Part II: Hybridisation, combinatorial, multicriteria and constrained optimization, and indicative applications. *Natural Computing*, *7*, 109–124. doi:10.1007/s11047-007-9050-z.

Braier, P., Berry, R., & Wales, D. (1990). How the range of pair interactions govern features of multidimensional potentials. *The Journal of Chemical Physics*, *93*(12), 8745–8756. doi:10.1063/1.459263.

Call, S., Zubarev, D., & Boldyrev, A. (2007). Global minimum structure searches via particle swarm optimization. *Journal of Computational Chemistry*, *28*(7), 1177–1186. doi:10.1002/jcc.20621.

Cheng, L., & Yang, J. (2007). Global minimum structures of morse clusters as a function of the range of the potential: 81 ≤ n ≤160. *The Journal of Physical Chemistry A*, *111*, 5287–5293. doi:10.1021/jp072238g.

Clerc, M., & Kennedy, J. (2002). The particle swarm explosion, stability, and convergence in a multidimensional complex space. *IEEE Transactions on Evolutionary Computation*, *6*(1), 58–73. doi:10.1109/4235.985692.

Deaven, D., & Ho, K. (1995). Molecular geometry optimization with a genetic algorithm. *Physical Review Letters*, *75*, 288–291. doi:10.1103/PhysRevLett.75.288.

Deb, K., & Padhye, N. (2010). Development of efficient particle swarm optimizers by using concepts from evolutionary algorithms. In *Proceedings of the Genetic and Evolutionary Computation Conference* (pp. 55-62). New York, NY: ACM Press.

Doye, J. P. K. (2006). Physical perspectives on the global optimization of atomic clusters. *Nonconvex Optimization and its Applications*, *85*, 103-139.

Doye, J. P. K., Leary, R., Locatelli, M., & Schoen, F. (2004). Global optimization of morse clusters by potential energy transformations. *INFORMS Journal on Computing*, *16*, 371–379. doi:10.1287/ijoc.1040.0084.

Doye, J. P. K., & Wales, D. (1997). Structural consequences of the range of the interatomic potential. A menagerie of clusters. *Journal of the Chemical Society, Faraday Transactions*, *93*, 4233–4243. doi:10.1039/a706221d.

Eberhart, R. C., & Kennedy, J. (1995). A new optimizer using particle swarm theory. In *Proceedings of the Sixth International Symposium on Micro Machine and Human Science* (pp. 39-43). Washington, DC: IEEE Computer Society.

Froltsov, V., & Reuter, K. (2009). Robustness of 'cut and splice' genetic algorithms in the structural optimization of atomic clsuters. *Chemical Physics Letters*, *473*, 363–366. doi:10.1016/j.cplett.2009.04.015.

Grosso, A., Locatelli, M., & Schoen, F. (2007). A population-based approach for hard global optimization problems based on dissimilarity measures. *Mathematical Programming Services A*, *110*, 373–404. doi:10.1007/s10107-006-0006-3.

Hartke, B. (1993). Global geometry optimization of clusters using genetic algorithms. *Journal of Physical Chemistry*, *97*, 9973–9976. doi:10.1021/j100141a013.

Hartke, B. (2004). Application of evolutionary algorithms to global cluster geometry optimization. In Johnston, R. L. (Ed.), *Applications of evolutionary computation in chemistry: Structure and bonding* (pp. 33–53). Berlin, Germany: Springer-Verlag.

Higashi, N., & Iba, H. (2003). Particle swarm optimization with gaussian mutation. In *Proceedings of the IEEE Swarm Intelligence Symposium* (pp. 72-79). Washington, DC: IEEE Computer Society.

Hodgson, R. (2002). Particle swarm optimization applied to the atomic cluster optimization problem. In *Proceedings of the Genetic and Evolutionary Computation Conference* (pp. 68-73). New York, NY: ACM Press.

Holden, N., & Freitas, A. (2005). A hybrid particle swarm/ant colony algorithm for the classification of hierarchical biological data. In *Proceedings of the IEEE Swarm Intelligence Symposium* (pp. 100-107). Washington, DC: IEEE Computer Society.

Johnston, R. (2003). Evolving better nanoparticles: Genetic algorithms for optimising cluster geometries. *Dalton Transactions (Cambridge, England)*, *22*, 4193–4207. doi:10.1039/b305686d.

Kennedy, J. (2003). Bare bones particle swarms. In *Proceedings of the IEEE Swarm Intelligence Symposium* (pp. 80-87). Washington, DC: IEEE Computer Society.

Kennedy, J., & Eberhart, R. C. (1995). Particle swarm optimization. In [Washington, DC: IEEE Computer Society.]. *Proceedings of the IEEE International Conference on Neural Networks*, *IV*, 1942–1948. doi:10.1109/ICNN.1995.488968.

Kennedy, J., & Mendes, R. (2002). Population structure and particle swarm performance. In *Proceedings of the IEEE Congress on Evolutionary Computation* (pp. 1671-1676). Washington, DC: IEEE Computer Society.

Krink, T., & Loøvbjerg, M. (2002). The lifecycle model: Combining particle swarm optimization, genetic algorithms and hillclimbers. In J. Julián-Merelo Guervós, P. Adamidis, H.-G. Beyer, H.-P. Schwefel, & J.-L. Fernández-Villacañas (Eds.), *Proceedings of the 7th International Conference on Parallel Problem Solving from Nature* (LNCS 2439, pp. 621-630).

Krink, T., Vesterstroøm, J. S., & Riget, J. (2002). Particle swarm optimization with spatial particle extension. In *Proceedings of the IEEE Congress on Evolutionary Computation* (pp. 1474-1479). Washington, DC: IEEE Computer Society.

Lennard-Jones, J. E. (1931). Cohesion. *Proceedings of the Physical Society*, *43*, 461–482. doi:10.1088/0959-5309/43/5/301.

Liu, D., & Nocedal, J. (1989). On the limited memory method for large scale optimization. *Mathematical Programming B*, *45*, 503–528. doi:10.1007/BF01589116.

Locatelli, M., & Schoen, F. (2002). Fast global optimization of difficult Lennard-Jones clusters. *Computational Optimization and Applications*, *21*, 55–70. doi:10.1023/A:1013596313166.

Loøvbjerg, M., Rasmussen, T. K., & Krink, T. (2001). Hybrid particle swarm optimiser with breeding and subpopulations. In *Proceedings of the Third Genetic and Evolutionary Computation Conference* (pp. 469-476).

Marques, J. M. C., Llanio-Trujillo, J. L., Abreu, P. E., & Pereira, F. B. (2010). How different are two chemical structures? *Journal of Chemical Information and Modeling*, *50*(12), 2129–2140. doi:10.1021/ci100219f.

Mendes, R. (2004). *Population topologies and their influence in particle swarm performance*. Unpublished doctoral dissertation, Universidade do Minho, Braga, Portugal.

Morse, P. (1929). Diatomic molecules according to the wave mechanics: Vibrational levels. *Physical Review*, *34*, 57–64. doi:10.1103/PhysRev.34.57.

Pereira, F. B., & Marques, J. M. C. (2008). A self-adaptive evolutionary algorithm for cluster geometry optimization. In *Proceedings of the Eight International Conference on Hybrid Intelligent Systems* (pp. 678-683). Washington, DC: IEEE Computer Society.

Pereira, F. B., & Marques, J. M. C. (2009). A study on diversity for cluster geometry optimization. *Evolutionary Intelligence*, *2*, 121–140. doi:10.1007/s12065-009-0020-5.

Poli, R. (2008). Analysis of the publications on the applications of particle swarm optimization. *Journal of Artificial Evolution and Applications*.

Poli, R., Kennedy, J., & Blackwell, T. (2007). Particle swarm optimization: An overview. *Swarm Intelligence*, *1*, 33–57. doi:10.1007/s11721-007-0002-0.

Richer, T., & Blackwell, T. M. (2006). The Lévy particle swarm. In *Proceedings of the IEEE Congress on Evolutionary Computation* (pp. 3150-3157). Washington, DC: IEEE Computer Society.

Roberts, C., Johnston, R., & Wilson, N. (2000). A genetic algorithm for the structural optimization of morse clusters. *Theoretical Chemistry Accounts*, *104*, 123–130. doi:10.1007/s002140000117.

Shi, Y., & Eberhart, R. C. (1998). A modified particle swarm optimizer. In *Proceedings of the IEEE International Conference on Evolutionary Computation* (pp. 69-73). Washington, DC: IEEE Computer Society.

Silva, A., Neves, A., & Costa, E. (2002). An empirical comparison of particle swarm and predator prey optimization. In M. O'Neill, R. F. E. Sutcliffe, C. Ryan, M. Eaton, & N. J. L. Griffith (Eds.), *Proceedings of 13th Irish International Conference on Artificial Intelligence and Cognitive Science* (LNCS 2464, pp. 103-110).

Smirnov, B., Strizhev, Y., & Berry, R. (1999). Structures of large morse clusters. *The Journal of Chemical Physics*, *110*(15), 7412–7420. doi:10.1063/1.478643.

Stacey, A., Jancic, M., & Grundy, I. (2003). Particle swarm optimization with mutation. In *Proceedings of the IEEE Congress on Evolutionary Computation* (pp. 1425-1430). Washington, DC: IEEE Computer Society.

Stillinger, F. (1999). Exponential multiplicity of inherent structures. *Physical Review E: Statistical Physics, Plasmas, Fluids, and Related Interdisciplinary Topics, 59*, 48–51. doi:10.1103/PhysRevE.59.48.

Wille, L., & Vennik, J. (1985). Computational complexity of the ground-state determination of atomic clusters. *Journal of Physics. A, Mathematical and General, 18*(8), 419–422. doi:10.1088/0305-4470/18/8/003.

Xie, X., Zhang, W., & Yang, Z. (2002). Dissipative particle swarm optimization. In *Proceedings of the IEEE Congress on Evolutionary Computation* (pp. 1456-1461). Washington, DC: IEEE Computer Society.

Zeiri, Y. (1995). Prediction of the lowest energy structure of clusters using a genetic algorithm. *Physical Review, 51*, 2769–2772.

Zhang, W.-J., & Xie, X.-F. (2003). DEPSO: Hybrid particle swarm with differential evolution operator. In *Proceedings of the IEEE International Conference on Systems, Man and Cybernetics* (pp. 3816-3821). Washington, DC: IEEE Computer Society.

This work was previously published in the International Journal of Natural Computing Research (IJNCR), Volume 2, Issue 1, edited by Leandro Nunes de Castro, pp. 1-20, copyright 2011 by IGI Publishing (an imprint of IGI Global).

Chapter 2
Phylogenetic Differential Evolution

Vinícius Veloso de Melo
University of São Paulo, Brazil

Danilo Vasconcellos Vargas
University of São Paulo, Brazil

Marcio Kassouf Crocomo
University of São Paulo, Brazil

ABSTRACT

This paper presents a new technique for optimizing binary problems with building blocks. The authors have developed a different approach to existing Estimation of Distribution Algorithms (EDAs). Our technique, called Phylogenetic Differential Evolution (PhyDE), combines the Phylogenetic Algorithm and the Differential Evolution Algorithm. The first one is employed to identify the building blocks and to generate metavariables. The second one is used to find the best instance of each metavariable. In contrast to existing EDAs that identify the related variables at each iteration, the presented technique finds the related variables only once at the beginning of the algorithm, and not through the generations. This paper shows that the proposed technique is more efficient than the well known EDA called Extended Compact Genetic Algorithm (ECGA), especially for large-scale systems which are commonly found in real world problems.

1. INTRODUCTION

The resolution of several black-box optimization problems has been possible due to the development of metaheuristics (Larrañaga & Lozano, 2001; Goldberg, 2002; Chakraborty, 2008). Also, engineering design problems have been solved by those same algorithms (Ruela, Cabral, & Aquino, 2010; Taroco, Carrano, & Neto, 2010). However, when the problem has strong correlated variables - as the deceptive problems (Goldberg, 2002) - classical metaheuristics may not have a high

DOI: 10.4018/978-1-4666-4253-9.ch002

probability of success. The Evolutionary Compact Genetic Algorithm (ECGA) (Harik, Lobo, & Sastry, 2006) - based on the Compact Genetic Algorithm (Harik, Lobo, & Goldberg, 1999) - is an Estimation of Distribution Algorithm (EDA) (Larrañaga & Lozano, 2001) that identifies the correlated variables, called Building Blocks (BBs), and uses a recombination operator to combine the best found partial solutions of each BB in order to generate a new full solution of the problem.

This paper proposes the use of the Phylogenetic Differential Evolution (PhyDE) to identify the BBs of a deceptive problem. This technique employs a clustering algorithm named Neighbor Joining (Saitou & Nei, 1987), commonly used in Biology to create Phylogenetic Trees (Felsenstein, 2003).

While most EDAs, including ECGA, aim to find the BBs in each generation, Phylogenetic Algorithms (Vargas, Delbem, & de Melo 2010) first applies a process to identify the BBs of a problem, and soon after the BBs have been known, a local search algorithm, usually an exhaustive search, is applied to each BB in order to find its optimum configuration.

However, an exhaustive search must be avoided when a BB is composed of several bits, due to the exponential complexity of the problem. Thus, a better alternative to locate the optimum configuration must be used. The idea is to replace the exhaustive search with metaheuristics, and more than that, to employ an efficient metaheuristic incapable of solving large deceptive problems. To achieve this goal, a type conversion from binary to integer is required. Since the Differential Evolution (DE) algorithm presents one of the best results in the resolution of several problems (García, Molina, Lozano, & Herrera, 2009), it was chosen as the optimization algorithm to be used in this project.

Hard problems solved by EDAs are usually characterized by the number of variables, number of BBs that compose the problem, and their size. While the problem size is appropriately treated by existing algorithms, the size of the BBs is not. This is the main contribution of the proposed PhyDE. EDAs solve these problems using large number of evaluations (Harik, Lobo, & Sastry, 2006; Pelikan, Goldberg, & Cantú-Paz, 1999). By contrast, the proposed method is capable of solving problems with larger BBs in as few as half the number of evaluations. In general, results of EDAs are presented for BBs of size four. The experiments presented in this paper show a comparison using BBs composed of eight variables.

This paper is organized as followed: the next section introduces the concept of BBs and deceptive functions which are commonly used to test the performance of different EDAs. After that, we briefly present the way other algorithms find BBs, and then, we present methods of phylogenetic reconstruction used to identify BBs. Following this, two sections introduce the Phylogenetic Algorithms and the proposed PhyDE algorithm, which is composed of three sections detailing its steps: the construction of the Distance Matrix, the Neighbor Joining method and the construction of metavariables, and the Differential Evolution algorithm, used by the PhyDE to locate the optimum configuration for the identified BBs. Finally, the last section contains the explanation of the conducted experiments, and the results that show its efficiency. The results have shown that the technique proposed in this paper is approximately twice more efficient than the known ECGA.

2. BUILDING BLOCKS AND DECEPTIVE FUNCTIONS

It is usual to evaluate the size of its search space to determine the difficulty of an optimization problem. However, two other factors (Goldberg, 2002) that are also important in determining difficulty are the number of Building Blocks (BBs) and the number of variables in each BB.

Consider the deceptive problem described by Equation 1. This problem accepts an 8-bit string as input and calculates the fitness based on the number of bits '1'. To illustrate a deceptive function, consider the input 00001111. This string has 4 bits marked as '1'. Applying $u = 4$ to the equation below, the returned fitness is 7-4=3. When we use a metaheuristic to find the value for the 8-bit string that maximizes the obtained fitness, this type of function usually converges to a local optimum (00000000 in this example). This result occurs because the fitness increases in conjunction with the number of bits '0', but the global optimum is a string of bits '1'.

$$trap8(u) = \begin{cases} 7-u & if\ u < 8 \\ 8 & otherwise \end{cases} \tag{1}$$

Due to their deceiving behavior, functions like this one are called deceptive or trap functions. There are also problems that are composed of a sum of trap functions. When the value of one bit is altered, the change in the respective fitness value is also related to the other correlated variables (in this example, the 7 remaining bits that are used as input for the trap function). Each set of correlated variables (input for the trap function) is called a BB. The number of variables belonging to a BB and the number of BBs that compose a problem are, respectively, represented by letters *k* and *m*.

Equation 2 below shows the estimated population size required to represent all the possible instances of each of the *m* building blocks, composed of *k* variables of cardinality χ (Goldberg, 2002). The equation shows that the complexity of the problem grows exponentially in relation to *k*. Therefore, it is important that researchers continue to develop more efficient algorithms to solve problems with higher values of *k* and *m* than the existing algorithms.

$$n = \chi^k(k * ln\chi + ln(m)) \tag{2}$$

The idea used by EDAs is to build probabilistic models (Pelikan, Goldberg, & Lobo, 2002) that identify the existing BBs of a problem. The created probabilistic model can then be used to sample new solutions for the next generation which tend to be closer to the global optimum, since this model was built based on a sample of promising solutions selected from the existing population.

3. HOW TO FIND BUILDING BLOCKS

To identify the relationship among variables, probabilistic methods are usually employed. When they consider the dependency of more than two variables they are called multivariate models, which is the most complex stage of the algorithm. More complex models are more powerful and accurate, but require large computational effort. The opposite occurs with simpler models. In general, there is a compromise between the accuracy of the constructed model and the efficiency of the estimation process (Pelikan, Goldberg, & Lobo, 2002). To generate models, EDAs use the concept of joint probability distribution (JPD), which is the probability distribution of all possible combinations of two or more variables of a sample. As that JPD is difficult to be obtained in large-scale problems, simplifications are applied to find an estimate for this distribution. In multivariate models, JPD is given by:

$$P(x) = \prod_{i=1}^{D} p(x_i \mid pa_i), \tag{3}$$

where x is one element of the sample, *D* is the number of variables, pa_i are instances of Pa_i (set of variables from which x_i depends). The construction of a network of probabilities that represents those dependencies can be considerably more complex. Therefore, the computational time to build it can grow exponentially. Thus, an exhaustive search for the best network, testing all possible connections, is impractical. Therefore, it is common to use greedy heuristics, given their efficiency in building such a model. There is no guarantee that the best network will be found, but the quality of the models generated by the heuristic is usually acceptable. Examples of algorithms with multivariable models are the Extended Compact Genetic Algorithm, the Factorized Distribution Algorithm, and the Bayesian Optimization Algorithm.

1. **Extended Compact Genetic Algorithm (ECGA) (Harik, 1999):** Is an extension of the compact Genetic Algorithm (Harik, Lobo, & Goldberg, 1999), which is a probabilistic version of the Genetic Algorithm. The probability model used in ECGA is called Marginal Product Model (MPM). This model accepts univariate, bivariate or multivariate marginal distribution. However, it does not accept conditional probability or overlapping dependencies. This means that variables within a group interact with each other but cannot interact with variables of other groups. To generate the MPM, at each iteration a greedy search algorithm merges all possible pairs of variables, or groups of variables, similarly to a hierarchical clustering algorithm. The merge which presents the best improvement on a specific metric is maintained. This process is repeated until no improvements can be made. The metric used by ECGA is the Minimum Description Length (MDL).
2. **Factorized Distribution Algorithm (FDA) (Mühlenbein, 1999):** Can be considered as an extension of the Bivariate Marginal Distribution Algorithm (BMDA) (Pelikan & Mühlenbein, 1999). According to the Factorization Theorem, it is possible to say which schemes (schemata theory, (Holland, 1975) are needed to generate the current population distribution by using the Boltzmann distribution. To achieve this, the distribution is factored into a product of marginal and conditional probabilities. The main disadvantage is that FDA requires that the factorization problem be informed by the user as a function of decomposition, which is not always available in real-world problems.
3. **Bayesian Optimization Algorithm (BOA) (Pelikan, 1999):** Encodes the joint probability distribution of the problem using a Bayesian Network. Unlike FDA, which requires the model to handmade and presented to the optimization algorithm, BOA builds the network using a greedy algorithm that adds edges to connect the variables of the problem. Once an edge is added, a particular metric is calculated to evaluate the new formation of the network. If the metric is improved, the edge is maintained. The process is repeated until no more improvement can be made. The data used to build the network are a subset of the promising solutions, extracted from the population (sample/solutions).

BOA and ECGA are very similar. The main differences are the model construction and the sampling from the model. Instead of using the MPM, BOA employs a simplification of the original metric BD (Bayesian Dirichlet) called K2, defined in Pelikan (1999). This metric combines the a-priori knowledge about a problem and statistical information in a given data set. The objective is to measure how close is a sample generated from a Bayesian network from the data set used to build the network.

4. METHODS OF PHYLOGENETIC RECONSTRUCTION

Phylogenetic reconstruction methods were first proposed by Charles R. Darwin to study the relationship among ancestors involved in an evolutionary process (Darwin, 2003). The relations among species or organisms are represented in a tree structure, called a phylogenetic tree. Since the information from ancestors is generally lost, the ancestors from a phylogenetic tree (its internal nodes) and their relation to other nodes are only hypotheses. The reliable information (leaf nodes) is the current species. Thus, finding the inference (a tree) that best fits the data is a difficult task.

For many years, EAs have been used with success in the construction of phylogenetic trees (Lewis, 1998; Lemmon & Milinkovitch, 2002; Zwickl, 2006). However, the proposed PhyDE algorithm works the other way around, using phylogenetic trees in the construction of an EA, more specifically, an EDA in which the construction of a phylogenetic tree is part of the process that creates the used probabilistic model.

The number of possible tree topologies from a non-trivial dataset is huge, making the phylogenetic tree reconstruction a computationally complex problem. Fortunately, there exist several methods of inference that have different characteristics and, naturally, advantages and disadvantages. The Neighbor Joining (NJ) (Saitou & Nei, 1987; Studier & Keppler, 1988) has been noted for its computational efficiency and high quality of the trees it produces (Gascuel & Steel, 2006).

NJ was developed a while ago (Saitou & Nei, 1987), but it is still one of the state of the art algorithms used to validate relevant phylogenetic researches (Gascuel & Steel, 2006). The fact that NJ has been resilient over the decades motivated its selection from a large set of phylogenetic reconstruction methods to compose this EDA.

NJ was used to develop EDAs in a recent new trend of Genetic Algorithms called Phylogenetic Algorithms (PhyGA) (Vargas, Delbem, & de Melo 2010; de Melo, Vargas, & Delbem, 2010). This type of EDAs will be described in the following section.

5. PHYLOGENETIC ALGORITHMS

Inspired by the idea that a phylogeny can describe how species (variables of a problem) interrelate with each other, the PhyGA employs the NJ to generate models. Those algorithms use a phylogenetic tree and a distance metric to discover correlated variables. This procedure is called linkage learning (Harik, Lobo, & Sastry, 2006). In other words, the PhyGAs are EDAs that use phylogenetic tree reconstruction methods to generate a model that represents a sample of promising solutions.

The motivation behind the use of phylogenetic tree reconstruction methods as model for EDAs lies between two different points. First, their success as relational clustering algorithms for the complex real world problem of phylogenetic reconstruction. And second, the ideological motivation that phylogeny can describe how species (variables of a problem) interrelate with each other.

There are two main differences between the PhyGAs employed in (Vargas, Delbem, & de Melo 2010; de Melo, Vargas, & Delbem, 2010; Martins, Soares, Vargas, & Delbem, 2011) and the proposed approach:

1. The framework employed before did not use BBs as metavariables (as shown in Figure 3). The BBs were instead seen as independent problems solved separately. Therefore, the proposed algorithm is an increment of the framework previously used. With this new framework, it is possible to solve problems where there is interrelation between BBs.
2. The optimization stage used before consisted simply of an exhaustive search. Now, it employs a Differential Evolution algorithm.

6. PHYLOGENETIC DIFFERENTIAL EVOLUTION

The proposed algorithm, the Phylogenetic Differential Evolution (PhyDE), is an EDA and, in particular, a PhyGA, which uses NJ associated with Mutual Information measure to correctly find the BBs of a problem in only one generation. This approach to accurately solve the linkage learning problem in the first generation was first explored by de Melo, Vargas, and Delbem (2010). PhyDE's pseudocode is described in Table 1.

Figure 1 shows a diagram of the PhyDE's steps, composed by two main procedures: (1) problem decomposition and (2) the DE algorithm, responsible for the problem optimization. The problem decomposition is formed by 4 steps. The first 4 steps of the Figure 1 correspond to the five first steps of the pseudocode. The first step is the creation of an initial random population, as it is done in most Evolutionary Algorithms. The second step applies a tournament selection method, resulting on a set of promising solutions.

The following two steps are responsible for solving the linkage learning problem. First, a Distance matrix is calculated using the set of promising solutions and a distance metric. This matrix represents the correlation between variables, and is the input for the next step of the algorithm, that uses a hierarchical clustering method - the NJ algorithm, to identify the BBs. Then, the algorithm joins the variables of each BB to form metavariables that are used as input for the DE algorithm, responsible for finding the optimal solution for the problem.

The following sections explain in more details: (1) the Distance Matrix and the metric used for its construction, (2) the NJ algorithm as well as the construction of the metavariables and (3) the DE algorithm. It is important to observe that the DE is not the focus of this research. The investigation is mainly the creation of the metavariables, performed by the Problem Decomposition procedure. The optimization process tends to fail if the decomposition is inadequate.

6.1. Distance Matrix

The NJ method, explained in the next section, uses a Distance Matrix D. In order to calculate D, a metric that could represent the correlation between variables is required. Mutual information (Kraskov, Andrzejak, & Grassberger, 2005) is a measure of similarity between two variables, expressed by Equation 4:

Table 1. Pseudocode for the phylogenetic differential evolution algorithm

1. Generate random initial population and evaluate.
2. Select population.
3. Use Mutual Information to calculate the distance matrix based on the selected population.
4. Apply Neighbor Joining to the distance matrix and cut the tree in partitions.
5. Create the metavariables based on the created partitions.
6. Apply DE in the set of metavariables.

Figure 1. Basic steps of the PhyDE algorithm

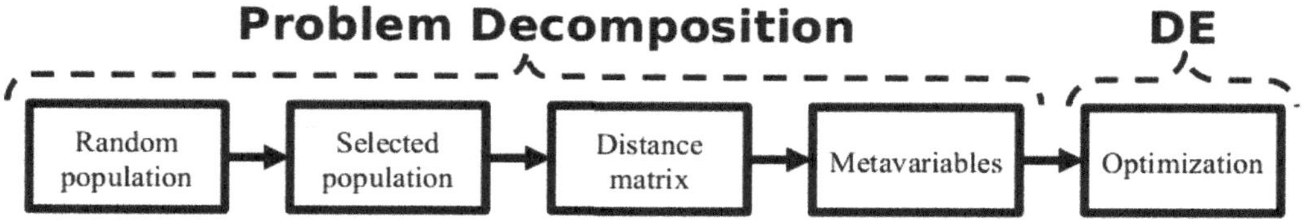

$$I(x,y) = H(x) + H(y) - H(x,y)$$
$$= \sum_{i,j} p_{ij} \log \frac{p_{ij}}{p_i(x)p_j(y)}, \quad (4)$$

where x and y are random uniform variables, and $H(x)$, $H(y)$, $H(x,y)$ are the entropies of x, y, and pair (x,y), respectively.

Mutual information is not a metric, as it does not satisfy the triangle inequality. Therefore, the following metric (Equation 5) is used based on the work from (Kraskov, Andrzejak, & Grassberger, 2005):

$$d(x,y) = H(x,y) - I(x,y) \quad (5)$$

This metric has been widely used in the literature (Aghagolzadeh, Soltanian-Zadeh, Araabi, & Aghagolzadeh, 2007; Kraskov, 2008), specially because it satisfies the triangle inequality, non-negativity, indiscernibility and symmetry. Metric d is also a universal metric; i.e., any non-trivial distance measure that places x and y close, will also be judged close according to d (Kraskov, Andrzejak, & Grassberger, 2005).

6.2. Neighbor Joining and the Construction of Metavariables

The NJ can be viewed as a hierarchical agglomerative clustering method (Jain, Murty, & Flynn, 1999) used in computational phylogeny to create a phylogenetic tree (Saitou & Nei, 1987). It can be briefly described by the pseudocode in Table 2 as any agglomerative hierarchical clustering algorithm.

This pseudocode can be used as a guide for the detailed description of the algorithm that follows. As shown in the pseudocode, it uses a distance matrix D as an input, and then, constructs a star tree with a leaf node for each variable (column) of the distance matrix (Figure 2 illustrates a star tree).

Subsequently, NJ calculates the net divergence (r_i) for each node, which is the sum of all distances that refer to a node. A new distance matrix M is calculated using Equation 6:

$$M_{i,j} = D_{i,j} - \frac{r_i + r_j}{n-2}, \quad (6)$$

where $D_{i,j}$ is the element at position (i,j) in D (which is the input of the NJ method), r_i is the net divergence of node i, and n is the number of *taxa* (one unit within any level of a taxonomy). The M matrix is very important for the NJ, since the joining nodes will derive from it.

The two nodes (a and b) corresponding to the smallest $M_{i,j}$ are removed from the star tree (exemplified in Figure 1). Then, a new node, called u, is inserted and connected to a and b, starting the formation of a binary tree.

Table 2. Pseudocode for the neighbor joining algorithm

```
Input: dissimilarity matrix
1. Initialize with each object in a cluster
2. Repeat until only two clusters remain in the matrix
a. Find closest cluster pair in the matrix
b. Join the closest cluster pair in a new single cluster
c. Update the matrix with the new cluster and remove joined clusters
3. Join remaining two clusters in a single cluster
4. Return solution
```

Figure 2. Star tree of a problem with 6 variables

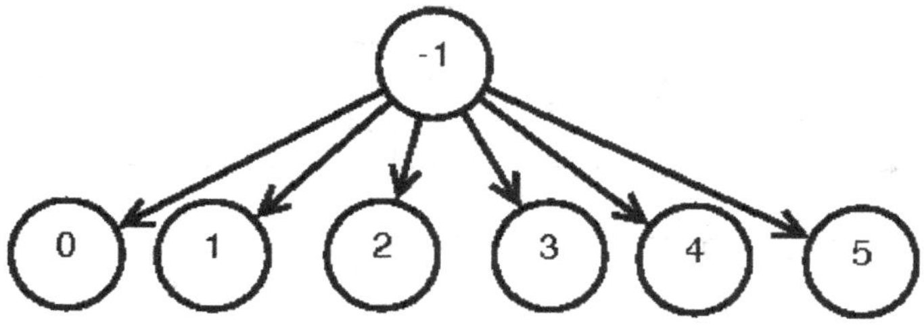

The calculation of the branch length can be found in Equation 7:

$$s_{a,u} = \frac{D_{a,b}}{2} + \frac{r_a - r_b}{2(n-2)}, \quad (7)$$

where $s_{a,u}$ is the branch length between *a* and *u*. The branch length from *u* to *b* uses the same equation as above, but exchanges the variable *a* with the variable *b*. In the next step, the distances from *u* to the other variables are calculated (see Equation 8) in order to fulfill a new *D* (without the columns related to *a* and *b* and with a new column for *u*).

$$D_{i,u} = \frac{D_{a,i} + D_{b,i} - D_{a,b}}{2}, \quad (8)$$

where *i* is necessarily a node different from *u* in *D*. *D* has its size decreased from *n* x *n* to $(n-1)\times(n-1)$. This new *D* is then used to calculate *M*, repeating the whole process described above until the size of *D* has reached 2. The two remaining nodes are joined and, finally, this created node is set as the root of the tree.

In order to find the BBs, first the information from matrix *M*, at the iteration *t*, is used to construct two variables. The first one is α_t, which is related to the accuracy of the NJ in choosing to join two variables. α_t is defined by the following equation:

$$\alpha_t = average(M,t) - minimum(M,t) \quad (9)$$

On the other hand, β_t is defined as a normalized α_t with the following equation:

$$\beta_t = \frac{\alpha_t - \alpha_{t-1}}{\alpha_t}, \quad (10)$$

By obtaining the maximum β_t, it is possible to infer a point at which the NJ should have stopped clustering. This value *t* is denoted *t** and used to cut the phylogenetic tree with values of nodes where $t > t*$. The leaf nodes of obtained subtrees are then joined in a single BB.

After finding the BBs, the algorithm joins the variables of each BB to form metavariables. Assume an integer array with the same size of the problem's input size, with each metavariable being a set of positions in this array (a similar modeling schema was used by Harik (1999). For instance, a deceptive problem of 2 traps of size 4 can be mapped (due to the variable's correlations intensity) to two metavariables (indexes 1 and 2) as an array $mv = \{1,1,1,1,2,2,2,2\}$. This array of metavariables is then passed to the DE to solve the problem efficiently. Figure 3 illustrates the described process.

Each metavariable is treated as an integer, ranging from 0 to $2_i^k - 1$, where k_i is the number of bits of BBi. A simple rounding procedure is applied to convert floating point variables (gener-

Figure 3. Conversion from a binary array to an integer array of metavariables

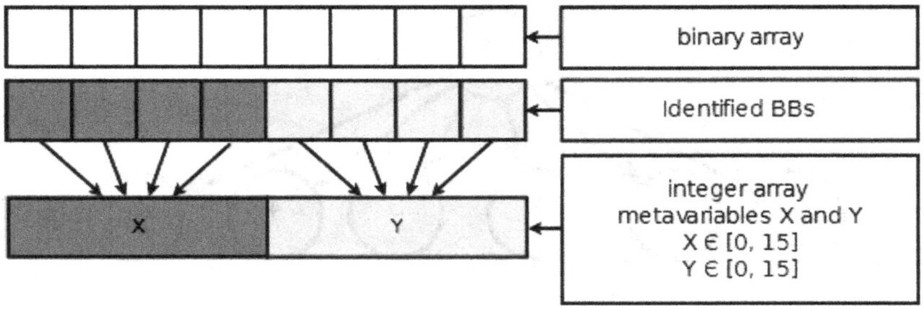

ated by DE) to the integer representation of the metavariables. When DE generates a solution composed of m integers, each integer is converted to binary format and each bit is positioned according to mv. Then, the resulting binary solution is evaluated. As DE is a populational metaheuristic, there is a population of integer solutions which will be converted and evaluated, until the optimization process stops.

6.3. Differential Evolution

The Differential Evolution algorithm (DE) is a simple yet effective metaheuristic that uses difference vectors to recreate the vector population. DE uses operators and strategies developed specifically to maintain the population's diversity for longer periods and delay premature convergence, while acting as a local optimizer in the previous generations. Besides, it may suffer from premature convergence if the parameter values are not well chosen or if the problem size increases to a very large number of variables. On the other hand, DE presents higher success rate in solving optimization problems when compared to other EAs, like genetic algorithms and particle swarm optimization, for instance.

The algorithm starts by creating a random initial population with uniform distribution (potential solutions) given the limits of each variable of the problem. At a given generation *g*, the mutation operator used to generate new vectors requires 3 randomly chosen and distinct vectors X from the population, named $X\alpha$, $X\beta$, and $X\gamma$. This operator calculates the difference of two of those selected vectors $\left(X\beta\ \text{-}\ X\gamma\right)$ and multiplies it by *f*, generating a vector called weighted difference $\left(w\right)$. Vector w is used to perturb a third vector $\left(X\alpha\right.$ or the best population's vector, $\left.Xbest\right)$, which results in the donor vector $V_{(g+1)}$. *f* is a constant $\in R$ in the interval [0,2] that controls the amplitude of the weighted difference.

The operator responsible for increasing diversity in the donor vector is the recombination operator, similar to the genetic operator known as crossover. The components (variables) of the mutated vector are mixed with the components of another predetermined vector, called target vector. The new vector, after the recombination, is called the trial vector.

The last operation, called selection, replaces the target vector by the trial vector if the objective function value of the trial vector is better than the value of the target vector. This means that there is neither elitism nor proportional selection. This process (mutation, recombination, selection) is repeated until a stopping criterion, e.g., number of generations, is achieved.

DE has presented excellent results in solving several optimization problems (Vesterstrom & Thomsen, 2004; García et al., 2009; Prado, Silva, Guimarães, & Neto, 2010), possibly due to the fact that it employs a mutation operator based on the difference between vectors. As the vectors become more similar, or closer to each other in the Euclidean space, the difference among them decreases. This can lead to a kind of local search.

In the next section, the proposed algorithm (PhyDE) is presented, co-relating the methods described up to this point.

7. EXPERIMENTS

To verify the efficiency of the proposed algorithm, experiments were conducted using the functions described in Equations 11 (onemax), 12 (f3 deceptive) and 13 (trap).

$$f_{one\max}(x) = \sum_{i=0}^{D} x_i \quad (11)$$

where x is the solution (binary string) and D is the dimension of the problem (number of bits).

$$f_{3deceptive}(u) = \begin{cases} 0.9 & if\ u = 0 \\ 0.8 & if\ u = 1 \\ 0 & if\ u = 2 \\ 1 & otherwise \end{cases}, \quad (12)$$

where u is the number of 1s in the string.

$$f_{trap}(u) = \begin{cases} 1, & if\ u = k \\ 1 - d - u * \dfrac{1-d}{k-1} & otherwise \end{cases}, \quad (13)$$

where u is the number of 1s in the string, k is the size of the trap function and d $\left(d = \frac{1}{k}\right)$ is the fitness signal. As the trap gets bigger, the complexity of the problem increases exponentially. For this reason, we chose to test our approach using a trap larger than 4 bits, usually tested in the literature (Harik, 1999; Sastry, Pelikan, & Goldberg, 2004). The corresponding population and problem sizes for each algorithm were obtained using the bisection method (Sastry, 2001). It is important to remember that $f_{3deceptive}$ solves blocks of 3 binary variables (k=3) and f_{trap} was applied to solve blocks of k (4, 6 or 8) variables. However, the whole problem is evaluated summing the values of m blocks.

After the problem decomposition, the DE is executed on the metavariables to find the best solution. The configuration for DE is CR=0.3 to maintain the diversity for longer periods; F=1.1 to allow bigger increments, because we use only the integer part of each vector; and DE/rand/1/bin (classical strategy). The population size for DE was also found using a bisection algorithm. We employed de DEoptim package for R (Mullen et al., 2011).

7.1. Results

This section presents the results on running PhyDE, implemented in this research, and ECGA (available in http://www.illigal.uiuc.edu/web/source-code), on Equations 11, 12 and 13 (Equation 13 with k=4, 6, and 8), with several sizes of m. All charts were created using the average results from 30 runs (onemax k=1, 3-deceptive k=3, and trap k=4 and 6) or 5 runs (trap k=8), for each problem size. All runs returned at least m-1 traps solved correctly. The population size was obtained by running the bisection method.

For the Onemax problem, the results are presented in Figure 4 (where $L = k*m$). As we do not have a mathematical theory for number of evaluations and running time, we did a regression to fit an order-3 curve.

By analyzing the regression coefficients and the curve, it is clear that for this problem PhyDE is not recommended for large values of L. PhyDE is able to recognize that all bits, or almost all of them, are independent using less than 200 evalu-

Figure 4. Onemax: (a) number of objective function evaluations and (b) running times

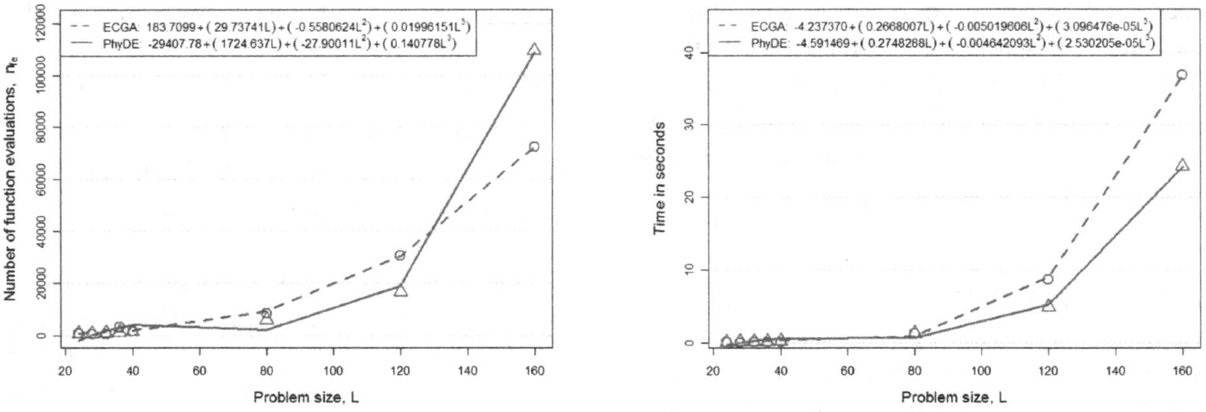

ations for any of the problem sizes. However, DE requires thousands of evaluations to reach the global optimum (Table 2). DE is an optimization tool for continuous problems, so we apply a round on the value to convert a real number to integer. We concluded that the high number of evaluations was caused by this behavior. As shown in Figure 4, ECGA uses much less evaluations. On the other hand, even using more evaluations, PhyDE can run in lower times, while the running time of ECGA seems to grow faster. Another important aspect of the running time (Figure 4(b)) is that, as one can see in Table 3, the computational time for this problem is largely spent by DE.

Table 3. Number of objective function evaluations used by DE in the PhyDE for Onemax

L	Pop Size	Evaluations	Time (s)
24	48	473.60	0.07
28	56	628.13	0.09
32	64	790.40	0.11
36	72	1,069.20	0.15
40	80	1,249.33	0.18
80	162	5,845.33	1.04
120	260	16,548.00	4.24
160	320	109,264	22.92

To compare the mean number of function evaluations of ECGA and PhyDE for each problem size, we did run Wilcoxon rank-sum test with $\alpha=5\%$. The results indicate that the means are statistically different.

The other problem studied in this paper is the 3-deceptive problem. The results are presented in Figure 5. We also applied regression of order-3 to estimate growing behavior.

In this problem, the result is considerably different from the Onemax problem. While in the previous problem PhyDE required a larger number of evaluations than ECGA using fewer seconds, in the 3-deceptive problem the growing in number of function evaluations is much lower. In the regression of the number of function evaluations, there is a clear difference among the coefficients of the two models, where the coefficients for ECGA are much higher. With respect to the running time, PhyDE is more time-consuming needing more than double of the time of ECGA.

Comparing Figure 5 with Table 4, it is also possible to see that now the larger computational cost is taken by PhyGA. In Onemax, for instance, when L=160 DE required 109,264 evaluations and 22.3 seconds. For the 3-deceptive problem when L=162, DE required only 10,076 evaluations in 9.3 seconds, totalizing 47,683 evaluations and 426 seconds for PhyDE. On the other hand,

Figure 5. 3-deceptive function: (a) number of objective function evaluations and (b) running times

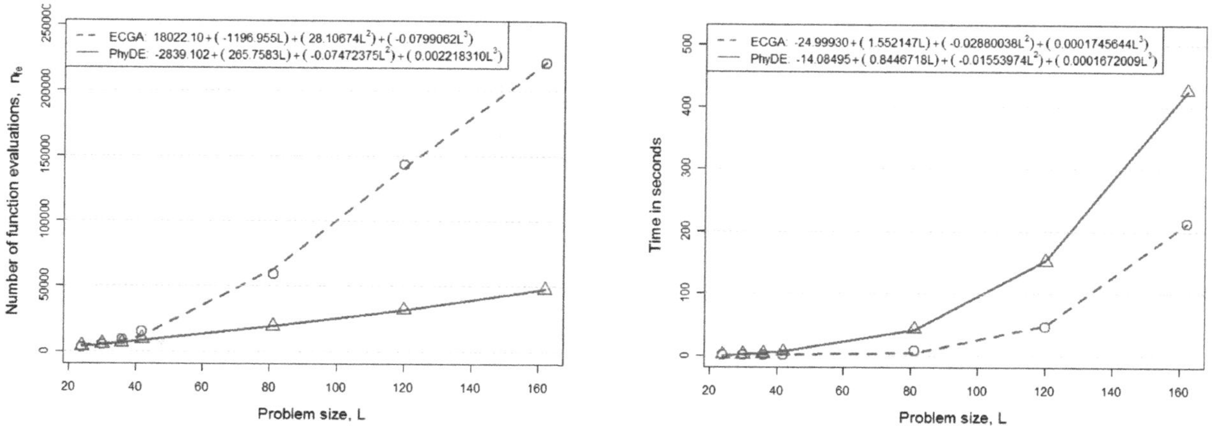

Table 4. Number of objective function evaluations used by DE in the PhyDE for the 3- deceptive problem

L	Pop Size	Evaluations	Time (s)
24	48	611.20	0.14
30	46	728.33	0.14
36	66	1,161.60	0.25
42	72	1,555.20	0.35
81	121	4,162.40	1.74
120	150	7,225.00	4.36
162	162	10,076.40	9.32

ECGA used more than 220,000 evaluations and approximately 220 seconds. In contrast with Onemax, we can conclude that PhyDE is highly recommended to solve the 3-deceptive problem in number of evaluations and that the algorithm to build the model must be improved to achieve better performance.

Again, Wilcoxon rank-sum test with α=5% indicated difference in the means of number of function evaluations.

The next problem is the *trap* in Equation 13. The results of the experiments when *k*=4 can be seen in Figure 6 and Table 5. In Figure 6a, it is possible to see that for smaller problems, ECGA can be superior in terms of number of evaluations. However, as the problem gets bigger, the advantage of PhyDE's approach is very clear. ECGA presents a more quadratic growing whereas PhyDE is smoother. Moreover, the output of the NJ algorithm allows identifying only the metavariables used as input for the DE algorithm. This means that DE must recalculate individuals previously generated. Treating this issue, the number of function evaluation should be much lower. This is one of the future works.

On the other hand, the running times (Figure 6b) of ECGA are lower. As one can see, we fitted an order-3 regression. And by analyzing the regression coefficients, it is possible to verify that ECGA's are higher than PhyDE's. This means that as the problem size increases, the ECGA's running time will surpass PhyDE's.

Other important point is that PhyDE's running time is directly related to a parameter named factor. If lowered, the running times decreases, but the number of function evaluations increases. In this paper we focus on the evaluations. So, the running times are more illustrative.

Table 5 presents the DE running times for *k*=4. It is possible to see that the time consumed in PhyDE is largely due to the Problem Decomposition procedure. After the metavariables are created, the optimization process can be very fast for smaller problems. However, DE presents

Figure 6. Trap size 4: (a) number of objective function evaluations and (b) running times

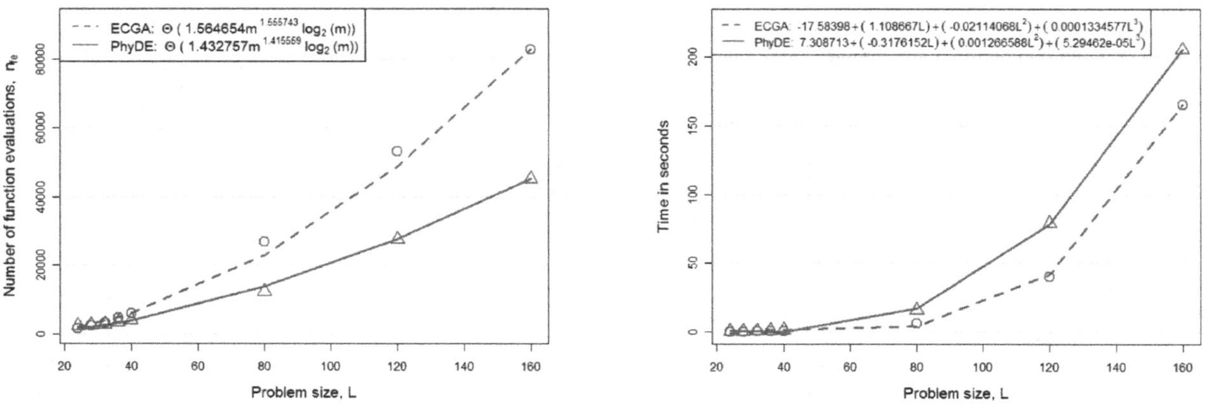

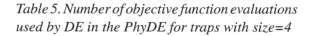

Table 5. Number of objective function evaluations used by DE in the PhyDE for traps with size=4

L	Pop Size	Evaluations	Time (s)
24	48	281.6	0.11
28	56	384.53	0.16
32	64	535.47	0.24
36	72	650.4	0.30
40	80	866.67	0.43
80	162	3,626.67	2.74
120	260	9,216	10.20
160	320	16,896	23.06

some difficult to solve larger problems, requiring almost the same number of function evaluations as the decomposition procedure. This slow decomposition is an important issue to be investigated using efficient enhancement techniques. Also, as mentioned before, the solutions evaluated by the decomposition procedure are not being used in DE.

The statistical analysis of means resulted that the means are different with $\alpha=5\%$.

The following experiment uses a trap of size 6. In this experiment, one can see that the growing behavior of the number of evaluations required by PhyDE and ECGA are quite different (Figure 7a). ECGA's number of evaluations increases very fast, while PhyDE's starts to grow later. This resulted is almost half the number of function evaluations required by ECGA. This difference tends to increase with problems size.

Figure 7b, which presents the running times, is a very different scenario when compared to Figure 6b. With k=6, ECGA's running time also possesses an almost quadratic form (as in Figure 6b, k=4) but now the time was multiplied by 10. On the other hand, the strategy adopted in the PhyDE algorithm allows it to achieve the same result with an increase in running time of less than 3 times.

The results regarding DE results are presented in Table 6. Both the number of evaluations and running time are about 4-13% and 1-7% of the required by the decomposition procedure, respectively. If it is possible to avoid reevaluation of solutions (caching), this percentage will be even lower, resulting in a faster PhyDE. The test with Wilcoxon presented difference in all comparisons of number of function evaluations.

In the experiments with $k = 8$, ECGA solved problems using approximately two times more function evaluations than the proposed algorithm (PhyDE). Moreover, this behavior was observed to hold true throughout the experiments and asymptotically. This can be observed by the asymptotic behavior of both algorithms, since the PhyDE required $3.635m^{1.76}\log_2(m)$ while the ECGA

Figure 7. Trap size 6: (a) number of objective function evaluations and (b) running times

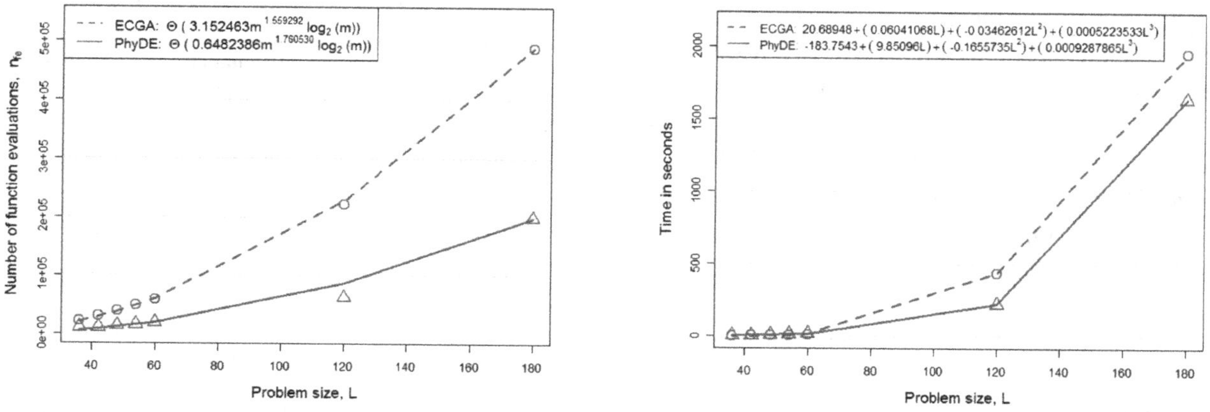

Table 6. Number of objective function evaluations used by DE in the PhyDE for traps with size=6

L	Pop Size	Evaluations	Time (s)
36	72	333.6	0.338
42	84	501.2	0.535
48	96	665.6	0.762
54	108	860.4	1.063
60	120	1064	1.386
120	240	4848	9.799
180	360	11484	21.581

required $7.018m^{1.77}\log_2(m)$ number of evaluations (Figure 8a). Both seem to grow at very similar rates (approximately $m^{1.77}$), with PhyDE requiring about 50% of the evaluations.

Figure 8b presents the running time needed by each algorithm. Even needing more time to solve the problems, the number of function evaluations is considerably lower, which means that PhyDE's approach to identify the relationship among variable seems more adequate than the used in ECGA.

Figure 8. Trap size 8: (a) number of objective function evaluations and (b) running times

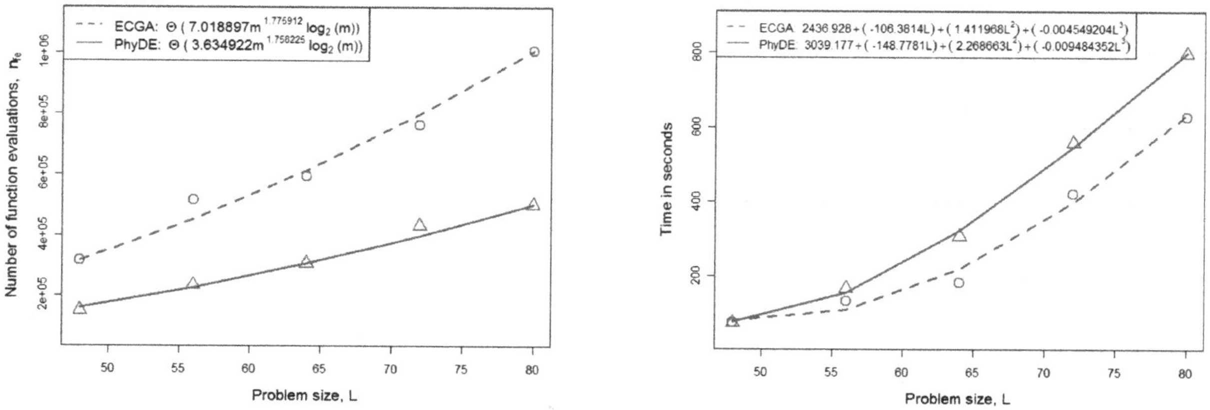

In Table 7, the evaluations and time consumed by DE can be considered insignificant when compared to the ones required by PhyGA. Moreover, they are equivalent to the results presented in Tables 3 and 4. This is a very important aspect of this approach. In all DE experiments, the trap size (*k*) presented a small impact in performance whereas the number of traps (*m*) is where DE suffers the most. In this paper, we didn't investigate other DE running strategies or parameters. Possibly, tuning DE can lead to better results for larger values of *L*.

The results presented for the trap function allows comparing both optimization algorithms with the increase of *m*. It was verified that the number of evaluations required by the PhyDE is always inferior to the required by the ECGA. This difference increases with *m*, indicating a better growing behavior for the PhyDE method.

Table 7. Number of objective function evaluations used by DE in the PhyDE for traps with size=8

L	Pop Size	Evaluations	Time (s)
36	96	409,60	0,41
42	112	578,67	0,61
48	128	776,53	0,88
54	144	1060,80	1,32
60	160	1290,67	1,70

As previously discussed, it is also important to compare both methods regarding the value of *k*, since it represents the most important factor in

Figure 9. Number of objective function evaluations for different values of k. Each graphic represents experiments done for different values of m.

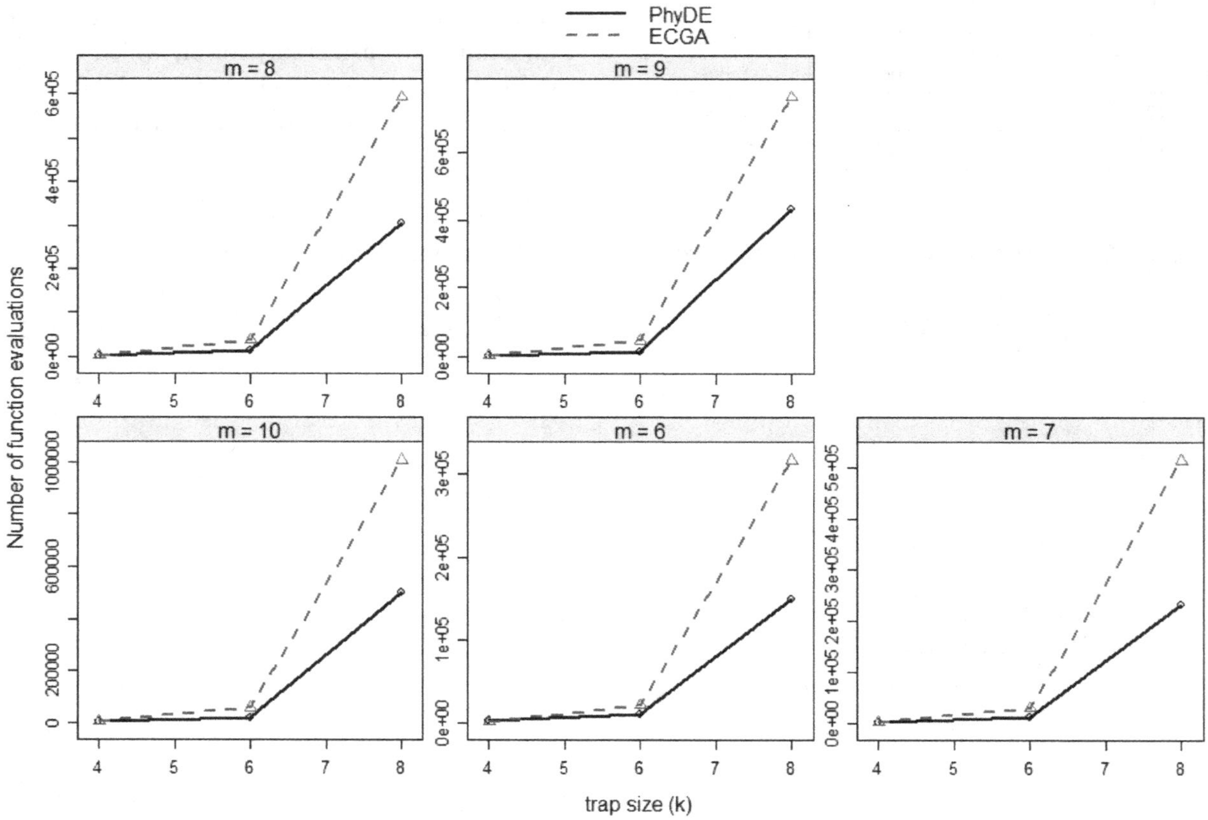

determining the problem difficulty, as illustrated by Equation 2. Figure 9 shows the results of tests comparing both algorithms in respect to parameter k. Each graphic presents, for a fixed m value, the number of evaluations needed regarding different values of k. The results show that the PhyDE always requires an inferior number of evaluations. The difference between the numbers of evaluations drastically increases as k increases, which highly favors the use of the PhyDE algorithm.

8. CONCLUSION

This paper validated a new approach for decomposing problems, involving only one stage to find metavariables, without the necessity of further iterating the algorithm, followed by one optimization stage to solve these metavariables.

Since the PhyDE presents a high precision for identifying the BBs, the binary problem could be treated as a problem with integer variables, in which the variables inside the same BB are treated as one integer value (metavariable). Therefore, it was possible to use DE, a real-valued optimization algorithm, for solving these metavariables.

From these results, it can be concluded that it is viable to use real-valued metaheuristics to solve certain binary problems efficiently, as the deceptive ones. Considering the number of evaluations, the results indicate that the PhyDE is more efficient than the ECGA. Additionally, this result showed to hold true asymptotically, that is, the ECGA showed to be unsuitable for solving problems with large BBs, due to its high number of function evaluations required. On the other hand, the PhyDE was verified to be capable of solving such problems efficiently since the results have shown a smaller constant multiplying the asymptotic behavior. One point that needs to be improved is the model building process. As shown in the charts, PhyGA is the bottleneck of PhyDE. This slow decomposition is an important issue to be investigated using efficient enhancement techniques or even other strategies.

To determine the efficiency of an EDA in solving difficult problems, it is important to verify the number of evaluations required for solving problems with big values of m and k. The PhyDE, has shown better results than ECGA for all tests, with different values of m, k, and consequently, L. Moreover, the difference regarding the number of evaluations between both algorithms increases as m and k increases, which highly favors the use of PhyDE, since it can solve a broader range of real-world problems.

ACKNOWLEDGMENT

D. V. Vargas would like to thank the support given by FAPESP (grant 2010/01634-5); M. K. Crocomo would like to thank the support given by CAPES (grant DS-4907210/D); V. V. de Melo would like to thank the support given by CNPq (grant 384122/2009-4).

REFERENCES

Aghagolzadeh, M., Soltanian-Zadeh, H., Araabi, B., & Aghagolzadeh, A. (2007). A hierarchical clustering based on mutual information maximization. In *Proceedings of the IEEE International Conference on Image Processing* (Vol. 1).

Chakraborty, U. K. (2008). *Advances in differential evolution*. New York, NY: Springer. doi:10.1007/978-3-540-68830-3.

Darwin, C. (2003). *The origin of species*. New York, NY: Signet Classic.

de Melo, V. V., Vargas, D. V., & Delbem, A. C. B. (2010). *Uso de otimização contínua na resolução de problemas binários: um estudo com evolução diferencial e algoritmo filo-genético em problemas deceptivos aditivos*. Paper presented at the 2ª Escola Luso-Brasileira De Computação Evolutiva (elbce), Guimarães, Portugal.

Felsenstein, J. (2003). *Inferring phylogenies*. Sunderland, MA: Sinauer Associates.

García, S., Molina, D., Lozano, M., & Herrera, F. (2009). A study on the use of non-parametric tests for analyzing the evolutionary algorithms' behavior: A case study on the CEC'2005 special session on real parameter optimization. *Journal of Heuristics*, *15*, 617–644. doi:10.1007/s10732-008-9080-4.

Gascuel, O., & Steel, M. (2006). Neighbor-joining revealed. *Molecular Biology and Evolution*, *23*(11), 1997. doi:10.1093/molbev/msl072.

Goldberg, D. E. (2002). *The design of innovation: Lessons from and for competent genetic algorithms*. Boston, MA: Kluwer Academic.

Harik, G. R. (1999). *Linkage learning via probabilistic modeling in the ecga* (Tech. Rep. No. 99010). Urbana, IL: University of Illinois at Urbana-Champaign.

Harik, G. R., Lobo, F. G., & Goldberg, D. E. (1999). The compact genetic algorithm. *IEEE Transactions on Evolutionary Computation*, *3*(4), 287–297. doi:10.1109/4235.797971.

Harik, G. R., Lobo, F. G., & Sastry, K. (2006). Linkage learning via probabilistic modeling in the extended compact genetic algorithm (ecga). In M. Pelikan, K. Sastry, & E. CantúPaz (Eds.), Scalable optimization via probabilistic modeling (p. 39-61). Berlin, Germany: Springer-Verlag.

Holland, J. H. (1975). *Adaptation in natural artificial systems*. Ann Arbor, MI: University of Michigan Press.

Jain, A., Murty, M., & Flynn, P. (1999). Data clustering: A review. *ACM Computing Surveys*, *31*(3), 264–323. doi:10.1145/331499.331504.

Kraskov, A. (2008). *Synchronization and interdependence measures and their application to the electroencephalogram of epilepsy patients and clustering of data*. Retrieved from http://eprints.ucl.ac.uk/69978/

Kraskov, A., Andrzejak, R., & Grassberger, P. (2005). Hierarchical clustering based on mutual information. *Europhysics Letters*, *70*(2), 278. doi:10.1209/epl/i2004-10483-y.

Larrañaga, P., & Lozano, J. A. (2001). *Estimation of distribution algorithms: A new tool for evolutionary computation (genetic algorithms and evolutionary computation)*. New York, NY: Springer.

Lemmon, A. R., & Milinkovitch, M. C. (2002). The metapopulation genetic algorithm: An efficient solution for the problem of large phylogeny estimation. *Proceedings of the National Academy of Sciences*, 10516-10521.

Lewis, P. O. (1998). A genetic algorithm for maximum-likelihood phylogeny inference using nucleotide sequence data. *Molecular Biology and Evolution*, *15*(3), 277–283.

Martins, J. P., Soares, A. H. M., Vargas, D. V., & Delbem, A. C. B. (2011). Multi-objective phylogenetic algorithm: Solving multi-objective decomposable deceptive problems. In R. H. C. Takahashi, K. Deb, E. F. Wanner, & S. Greco (Eds.), *Proceedings of the Sixth International Conference on Evolutionary Multi-criterion Optimization* (LNCS 6575, pp. 285-297).

Morzy, T., Wojciechowski, M., & Zakrzewicz, M. (2009). Pattern-oriented hierarchical clustering. In *Proceedings of the Third East European Conference on Advances in Databases and Information Systems* (pp. 179-190).

Mühlenbein, H., & Mahnig, T. (1999). Fda - a scalable evolutionary algorithm for the optimization of additively decomposed functions. *Evolutionary Computation*, *7*(4), 353–376. doi:10.1162/evco.1999.7.4.353.

Mullen, K., Ardia, D., Gil, D., Windover, D., & Cline, J. (2011). DEoptim: An R package for global optimization by differential evolution. *Journal of Statistical Software*, *40*(6), 1–26.

Pelikan, M., Goldberg, D. E., & Cantú-Paz, E. (1999). BOA: The Bayesian optimization algorithm. In *Proceedings of the Genetic and Evolutionary Computation Conference*, Orlando, FL (Vol. 1, pp. 525-532).

Pelikan, M., Goldberg, D. E., & Lobo, F. G. (2002). A survey of optimization by building and using probabilistic models. *Computational Optimization and Applications*, *21*(1), 5–20. doi:10.1023/A:1013500812258.

Pelikan, M., & Mühlenbein, H. (1999). Marginal distributions in evolutionary algorithms. In *Proceedings of the International Conference on Genetic Algorithms* (pp. 90-95).

Prado, R. S., Silva, R. C., Guimarães, F. G., & Neto, O. M. (2010). A new differential evolution based metaheuristic for discrete optimization. *International Journal of Natural Computing Research*, *1*(2), 15–32. doi:10.4018/jncr.2010040102.

Ruela, A. S., Cabral, R. D., Aquino, A. L., & Guimarães, F. G. (2010). Memetic and evolutionary design of wireless sensor networks based on complex network characteristics. *International Journal of Natural Computing Research*, *1*(2), 33–53. doi:10.4018/jncr.2010040103.

Saitou, N., & Nei, M. (1987). The neighbor-joining method: A new method for reconstructing phylogenetic trees. *Molecular Biology and Evolution*, *4*(4), 406–425.

Sastry, K. (2001). *Evaluation-relaxation schemes for genetic and evolutionary algorithms.* Unpublished master's thesis, University of Illinois at Urbana-Champaign, Urbana, IL.

Sastry, K., Pelikan, M., & Goldberg, D. (2004). Efficiency enhancement of genetic algorithms via building-block-wise fitness estimation. In *Proceedings of the IEEE Congress on Evolutionary Computing* (pp. 720-727).

Storn, R., & Price, K. (1997). Differential evolution - a simple and efficient heuristic for global optimization over continuous spaces. *Journal of Global Optimization*, *11*(4), 341–359. doi:10.1023/A:1008202821328.

Studier, J., & Keppler, K. (1988). A note on the neighbor-joining algorithm of Saitou and Nei. *Molecular Biology and Evolution*, *5*(6), 729.

Taroco, C. G., Carrano, E. G., & Neto, O. M. (2010). Robust design of power distribution systems using an enhanced multi-objective genetic algorithm. *International Journal of Natural Computing Research*, *1*(2), 92–112. doi:10.4018/jncr.2010040106.

Vargas, D. V., & Delbem, A. C. B. (2010). *Algoritmo filo-genético* (Tech. Rep. No. 350). San Paulo, Brazil: Universidade de Sao Paulo.

Vargas, D. V., Delbem, A. C. B., & de Melo, V. V. (2010). *Algoritmo filo-genético*. Paper presented at the 2ª Escola Luso-Brasileira De Computação Evolutiva (elbce), Guimarães, Portugal.

Vesterstrom, J., & Thomsen, R. (2004, June). A comparative study of differential evolution, particle swarm optimization, and evolutionary algorithms on numerical benchmark problems. In *Proceedings of the IEEE Congress on Evolutionary Computation*, Portland. *OR*, *3*, 1980–1987.

Zwickl, D. J. (2006). *Genetic algorithm approaches for the phylogenetic analysis of large biological sequence datasets under the maximum likelihood criterion.* Unpublished doctoral dissertation, University of Texas at Austin, Austin, TX.

This work was previously published in the International Journal of Natural Computing Research (IJNCR), Volume 2, Issue 1, edited by Leandro Nunes de Castro, pp. 21-38, copyright 2011 by IGI Publishing (an imprint of IGI Global).

Chapter 3
Head Motion Stabilization During Quadruped Robot Locomotion:
Combining CPGs and Stochastic Optimization Methods

Miguel Oliveira
University of Minho, Portugal

Cristina P. Santos
University of Minho, Portugal

Lino Costa
University of Minho, Portugal

Ana Maria A. C. Rocha
University of Minho, Portugal

Manuel Ferreira
University of Minho, Portugal

ABSTRACT

In this work, the authors propose a combined approach based on a controller architecture that is able to generate locomotion for a quadruped robot and a global optimization algorithm to generate head movement stabilization. The movement controllers are biologically inspired in the concept of Central Pattern Generators (CPGs) that are modelled based on nonlinear dynamical systems, coupled Hopf oscillators. This approach allows for explicitly specified parameters such as amplitude, offset and frequency of movement and to smoothly modulate the generated oscillations according to changes in these parameters. The overall idea is to generate head movement opposed to the one induced by locomotion, such that the head remains stabilized. Thus, in order to achieve this desired head movement, it is necessary to appropriately tune the CPG parameters. Three different global optimization algorithms search for this best set of parameters. In order to evaluate the resulting head movement, a fitness function based on the Euclidean norm is investigated. Moreover, a constraint-handling technique based on tournament selection was implemented.

DOI: 10.4018/978-1-4666-4253-9.ch003

1. INTRODUCTION

Visually-guided locomotion is important for autonomous robotics. However, there are several difficulties; for instance, the locomotion of quadruped, biped or snake-like robots induces head shaking that restricts stable image acquisition and the possibility to rely on that information to act accordingly.

This kind of disturbances, generated by locomotion itself, introduces image oscillations, increasing the difficulty in achieving image depending tasks like: search, visual navigation, distance measurement, etc. On the contrary, the robotics counterpart biological mechanisms are able to stabilize the head movement, even when they change the type of gait or adapt to the terrain.

In this work, we propose a combined approach to generate head movement stabilization on an ers-7 AIBO quadruped robot that walks with a walking gait, using Central Pattern Generators (CPGs) and an optimization algorithm. Our aim is to minimize the head movement induced by locomotion. We propose to generate head movement on a feedforward manner, such that the head moves in a manner opposed to the head movement induced by locomotion, in an open loop fashion. For this, we save the head movement induced by a certain walking gait, on a certain floor, during a certain amount of time. The generated head movement has to be opposed to this one.

We propose two movement controllers based on CPGs, one to generate locomotion and another to generate head movement. The first one generates movement for the joints of the robot limbs and the second one generates trajectories for tilt, pan and nod head joints. The CPG controller generates movement according to a set of parameters. A different tuning of these parameters results in a different movement. Moreover, this CPG approach enables to modulate the generated trajectories according to explicit changes in the controller parameters, such that movement is generated as required. This provides for a set of controller parameters that constitute the feedforward model, setting in an open loop manner.

In order to determine the best set of CPG control parameters that generates the head movement opposed to the one induced by the locomotion when no stabilization movement was performed, we apply optimization algorithms. We apply three stochastic optimization methods: evolution strategies (Schwefel, 1995; Goldberg, 1989) and the electromagnetism-like mechanism (Birbil & Fang, 2003). These approaches were adopted since, from the optimization point of view, this problem can be seen as a black-box type because the evaluation of the objective function implies running the model that is testing the solution by simulation. We want to remark that these optimization methods have been developed for problems with simple bounds. Hence, because several constraints are imposed in this optimization problem two constraint-handling approaches are implemented: a repairing method and the tournament based constraint method (Deb, 1998).

The usefulness of the proposed controller is verified in a physically realistic simulation environment, and the experimental results show the effectiveness of the proposed controller in reducing head motion during walking. These results enable to compare the performance of the three optimization algorithms and the distinct constraint-handling techniques, in terms of the simulation time, rate of convergence and robustness.

This represents a first step towards the achievement of head stabilization. The final solution should integrate both feedforward and feedback controllers, probably according to visual sensory information.

Considering real-world applications of visual sensors, such as visually-guided locomotion, errors in the head orientation rather than in head position should be considered and taken into consideration. However, the available degrees-of-freedom of the used ers-7 AIBO robot do not enable to directly control the camera or head orientation, and further, this issue could be tackled by an additional feedback controller.

The remainder of this paper is organized as follows. Firstly, the state-of-the-art is presented with a special focus on biological observations that may support the chosen approach. In Section 4, the system architecture and the locomotion generation and head movement are described. Also, the main ideas concerning the optimization process are presented. In Section 5 the problem formulation and the different optimization algorithms used to optimize the CPG parameters are described. Further, some numerical results are also discussed. Simulated results are showed in Section 5. Conclusions are discussed in Section 6.

2. STATE-OF-THE-ART

Research has shown that in humans head motion is important and necessary to permit that an individual can shift direction (Imai, 2008; Pozzo et al., 1990) achieve equilibrium (Nadeau et al., 2003) and to help the vestibular system to stabilize the retinal image. Further, the head movement induced by locomotion introduces image oscillations that increase the complexity of tasks such as image analysis, object localization and object tracking. This head stabilization problem is very relevant both from a robotics and biological points of view.

This difficulty may be minimized using gaze and image stabilization procedures (Kaushik et al., 2007; Gu & Kanade, 2006). The main goal of gaze stabilization is to maintain the image centered in a specific point, whereas in image stabilization the main purpose is to guarantee that a sequence of acquired frames results in a smooth video stream.

In animals, in order to the brain neuronal circuits be able to acquire important visual features, such as, distance perception, form and relative depth, it is required that the image obtained by the retina be relatively still. In vertebrates, like primates, image stabilization relies on compensatory eyes movement and is mainly based on the Vestibulo-Ocular Reflex (VOR). The vestibulo-ocular reflex is a reflex eye movement that stabilizes images on the retina during head movement by producing an eye movement in the direction opposite to head movement, thus preserving the image on the center of the visual field.

Techniques proposed in literature devoted to image stabilization are typically based on image registration algorithms. The rotation and translation of the image plane are firstly estimated, based on features extracted from images of the video sequence. The images are then registered using the estimated parameters (Cherubini et al., 2007; Wörz & Rohr, 2007). These types of approaches generally present high computational costs, meaning that it can be difficult to implement in some robots. Other concern is the drift on the scene viewed by the camera, since during the robot movement some objects can appear inside or outside the image. These difficult operations such as tracking objects and for that, gaze stabilization must be achieved.

Gaze stabilization is a mechanism that animals are not aware off and it is executed automatically. Basically, two most important reflexes are used in gaze stabilization: Optokinetic Reflex (OKR) and vestibulo-ocular reflex. The goal of OKR is to keep the image still on the fovea, the center of the retina, when the head remains stationary. This reflex allows the eye to follow objects in motion.

The overall of the gaze stabilization approaches can be divided into two types of techniques. One uses specific hardware, like accelerometers and gyroscope to estimate the 3D posture of the head, and complex control algorithms to compensate the oscillations. The use of inertial information was already proposed by several authors (Kaushik et al., 2007; Patane et al., 2004; Asuni et al., 2005; Gu & Kanade, 2006; Panerai et al., 2000). Typically this kind of techniques is used in binocular robot heads, where gaze is implemented through the coordination of the two eye movements. Most of the approaches are inspired in biological systems, specifically in the human VOR. In robots with fixed eyes, the fixation point procedure is achieved by compensatory head or body movements, based on multisensory information of the head. Additionally, nowadays there is an increasing number of studies and applications based on biological concepts (Panerai et al., 2000; Shibata & Schaal, 2001).

In Panerai et al. (2000), Shibata and Schaal (2001), and Panerai et al. (2002) approaches for binocular image stabilization are discussed. Both rely on inertial sensory measurements and learning algorithms to compensate for camera movements. In Panerai et al. (2000), they are interested in performing dynamical visual measurements during the robot movement and use fixation references for navigation or manipulation. They achieve low computational costs by using adaptive control to compensate the camera image information. A gaze stabilization methodology that depends on the geometric parameters of head and camera system, and the use of inertial information in dynamical contexts simplify the motor control of the head and eye systems.

In Shibata and Schaal (2001), it is presented a bio-inspired gaze stabilization method based on a feedback-error-learning (FEL) used to train a neural-network. The FEL maps the sensory errors onto the motor errors, and is used to train the network by supervised learning mechanism. A Newton method is used for fast stable learning. They show that FEL in association with nonparametric regression applied to the learn of the oculor-motor control leads to a fast learning convergence for a nonlinear oculor-motor plant and reduces the delays provoked by feedback systems similar to Panerai et al. (2000). This work is a first step towards applying biological concepts and reinforcing learning for gaze stabilization.

In Panerai et al. (2002), it is proposed a system based in a neural-network that combines two models: the growing neural gas (GNG) and SoftMax basis function networks, of the GNG-Soft architecture. The compensatory oculo-motor commands are calculated through a sensory map build by an unsupervised learning scheme.

The other type of techniques for gaze stabilization use visual servoing algorithms (Hosoda et al., 1995; Sandini et al., 2004; Panerai et al., 2002; Hutchinson et al., 1996). In these algorithms, a set of features extracted from the images are used to control the pose of the robot head. These features may be any measurable relationship in the image and must be located unambiguously in different views of the scene. Given knowledge of the geometric relationship between the features point, the pose can be evaluated. Sanderson and Weiss (1980) classify visual servoing in position-based and image-based. In the first, features are extracted from the image of a target, and through the knowledge about its geometry it is possible to determine the posture of the target with respect to the camera (Malis, 2004). In the second, image-base approaches, the servoing is done directly on the image domain without the need of the geometry model of the target (Kapur et al., 2005; Soria et al., 2006).This kind of approaches may reduce computational delays and minimize some errors due to camera calibration. Nevertheless, it is necessary to compute or estimate the feature Jacobian matrix, which represents a difficulty for the control architecture since the process is non-linear and high coupled. There are several works that combine these two types of approaches to achieve higher robust performance while maintaining a good efficiency (Panerai et al., 2000).

In Kurazume and Hirose (2000), it is described a system that moves a high speed camera mounted on the robot head. The movement of the head is calculated based on inertial-sensory information according to a neural-network. It compensates the image oscillation and the remaining error is processed by a template matching method. The head movement is not the result of sensory-feedback but results from a previous learned motion response of motor sensors.

In del Solar and Vallejos (2005), it is presented an approach based on Kalman filters to process the motion of the image and track objects.

Another bio-inspired solution for a quadruped robot is proposed in Kaushik et al. (2007) based on the VOR. This binocular solution has 9 DOF in the robot head that permits 3D rotations (pitch, roll, yaw). However, solutions based in binocular vision systems require additional hardware in the robot. Other works have successfully achieved gaze stabilization that consists on image stabilization during head movements in space.

In Yamada et al. (2007) it is presented a head stabilization of a snake like robot. This stabilization is achieved by controlling the neck joints that create a head motion that opposes to the undulation of the robot body. It is proposed a method for the head direction stabilization and another for position and direction stabilization of the head. The proposed motion and gaze stabilization is based on a new adaptive approach designed Model Reference Adaptative Control (MRAC). It is based on feedback and feed-forward controllers for a 2 DOF structure. They modeled the head motion schedule in other to minimize the actual head motion to achieve gaze stabilization. The gaze stabilization system performs head movement based on the sensory system and presents small error measurements and delay responses to the motion in the image plane.

However, biological systems seem to generally rely on both feedback and feedforward for the purpose of gaze stabilization. In Combes et al. (2008) they report and conclude that efference copies of rhythmic neural signals produced by locomotor pattern-generating circuitry within the spinal cord of several vertebrates are probably conveyed to the brainstem extraocular motor nuclei and potentially contribute to gaze stabilization during locomotion. Thus, they provide for an intrinsic feed-forward mechanism for vertebrate gaze stabilization. Further, several studies (Held & Hein, 1963; Imai, 2008) have led to the conclusion that in nature, perception depends both and equally on the sensory system available to the organism and on its motor activity.

Therefore, in this work we address as a first step to the head stabilization problem, a head motion stabilization system for an ers-7 AIBO quadruped robot, according to a feedforward controller. We generate robot movement, both for limbs and for the head, according to CPGs, modeled by coupled nonlinear oscillators and solved using numeric integration. CPGs are neural-networks located in the spine of vertebrates, able to generate coordinated rhythmic movements, namely locomotion (Grillner, 1985).

On the one hand, the use of control approaches based on CPGs and nonlinear dynamical systems are widely used in robotics to achieve tasks which involve rhythmic motions such as biped and quadruped autonomous adaptive locomotion over irregular terrain (Kimura et al., 2007; Taga, 1994), juggling (Buhler et al., 1994), drumming (Degallier et al., 2006), playing with a slinky toy, basis field approaches for limb movements (Bizzi et al., 2002) and postural control Matos and Santos (2010). Some of these works present a high degree of sensor-driven and/or learned autonomy. However, no feedforward model is generally proposed and it is not attempted the combination of CPGs with learning systems.

On the other hand, several similar works have been proposed in literature (Yamada et al., 2007; Kaushik et al., 2007) based on different approaches. However, despite proposing feedforward models, these methods consider that the robot moves according to a scheduled robot motion plan, which imply that space and time constraints on robot motion must be known before hand as well as robot and environment models. As such, control is based on this scheduled plan.

The proposed network of CPGs enables to explicitly specify parameters such as amplitude, offset and frequency, and to smoothly modulate the generated trajectories according to changes in these parameters, such that movement is generated as expected. A set of values of the CPG parameters corresponds to a determined movement. In order to minimize the head movement induced by locomotion, we generate movement for the head in a manner opposed to the head movement induced by locomotion when no stabilization procedure was performed. The required head CPG parameters are determined offline by optimization algorithms. The best set of head CPG parameters constitute the proposed feedforward head controller and are then sent to the robot when walking. The proposed solution models the robot behavior when walking with a certain gait over a flat type of terrain, for a certain time. This feedforward issue is an innovative aspect of our work. Further, the proposed approach seems to generalize to other different platforms.

The intrinsic properties of the dynamical systems are an advantage of the proposed approach. For instance, the intrinsic robustness of these oscillators to small perturbations allows the inclusion of feedback mechanisms to close the control-loop, as shown in Righetti and Ijspeert (2008), and ensure robust control of the movements in time-varying environments (Degallier et al., 2006; Matos & Santos, 2010). This applies well to adaptation of motion generation through the sensory information and the robot dynamics, once feedback is also included to gaze stabilization. This property would enable to make the controller more adaptive, able to deal both with gait changes, terrain uncertainties and adjustments to different platforms and physical changes due to time.

Furthermore, the rhythmic nature of locomotion applies well to build such a feedforward model that could a posteriori be adapted online according to the environment and robot dynamical changes.

A different approach would be to apply simple head kinematics to solve this problem or at least to optimize kinematics relations of interest. However, in order to later on deal with feedback, for consistency in the different controllers and also due to the periodic nature of locomotion, we believe that the oscillator based trajectory generators are well suited for the problematic herein addressed.

3. SYSTEM ARCHITECTURE

In this work, we want to minimize the head movement induced by the locomotion. We propose to generate head movement on a feedforward manner, such that the head moves in a manner opposed to the head movement induced by locomotion, in an open loop fashion. For this, we save the head movement induced by a certain walking gait, on a certain floor, during a certain amount of time.

We consider that we have two independent movement controllers. A locomotion controller generates hip and knee trajectories that result in a walking pattern. A head controller specifies the planned neck tilt, pan and nod joint values, such that the head moves as desired. These are CPG controllers model by coupled nonlinear oscillators. The generated trajectories are used as input for the PID controllers of these joints.

The head controller parameters have to be tuned such that the resultant movement is opposed to the one induced by locomotion. Our CPG approach allows us to assign explicit parameters for each of the nonlinear oscillators, independently controlling the amplitude, offset and frequency of the movement. We apply optimization algorithms, in order to determine the best set of CPG control parameters that results in, or close to the desired movement. This set of parameters constitutes the feedforward model. The overall system architecture is depicted in Figure 1.

In the following, we detail each of the modules of the proposed architecture.

Figure 1. Overall system architecture

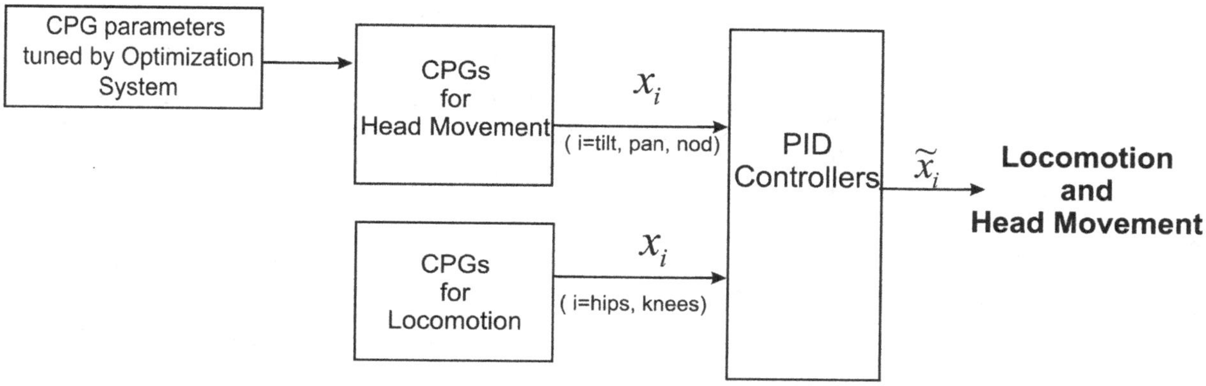

3.1. Locomotion Generation

3.1.1. Rhythmic Movement Generation

The rhythmic locomotor movements for a robot joint are generated by the x variable of the following Hopf oscillator

$$\begin{aligned} \dot{x} &= \alpha\left(\mu - r^2\right)\left(x - O\right) - \omega z, \\ \dot{z} &= \alpha\left(\mu - r^2\right) z + \omega\left(x - O\right), \end{aligned} \tag{1}$$

where $r = \sqrt{\left(x - O\right)^2 + z^2}$, peak-to-peak amplitude of the oscillations is given by $A = \sqrt{\mu}$ for $\mu > 0$, ω specifies the oscillations frequency (in rad s^{-1}) and relaxation to the limit cycle is given by $\dfrac{1}{2\alpha\mu}$.

This oscillator contains an Hopf bifurcation from a stable fixed point at $x = O$ (when $\mu < 0$) to a structurally stable, harmonic limit cycle, for $\mu > 0$. The fixed point x has an offset given by O.

It generates smooth trajectories due to the stable solutions of the dynamical solutions, despite small changes in the parameters. It exhibits limit cycle behaviour and describes a stable rhythmic motion where parameters μ, ω and O control the desired amplitude, frequency and offset of the resultant oscillations.

The generated x solution of this nonlinear oscillator is used as the control trajectory for the hip swing and knee joints of the robot limbs. These trajectories encode the values of the joint's angles and are sent online for the lower level PID controllers of each hip swing joint.

3.1.2. Locomotion Controller Architecture

We have to couple the oscillators in order to ensure phase-locked synchronization between the hip and knee DOFs of the robot, and generate locomotion with a desired gait. These couplings ensure that the limbs stay synchronized.

Figure 2 depicts the network structure used to generate locomotion for a quadruped robot. Interlimb coordination is achieved by bilaterally coupling the dynamics of the four hip swing oscillators (illustrated by right-left arrows in Figure 2). Intralimb coordination is achieved by unilaterally coupling each hip swing oscillator to the corresponding knee oscillator.

Figure 2. Structural view of the CPG network for generating locomotion

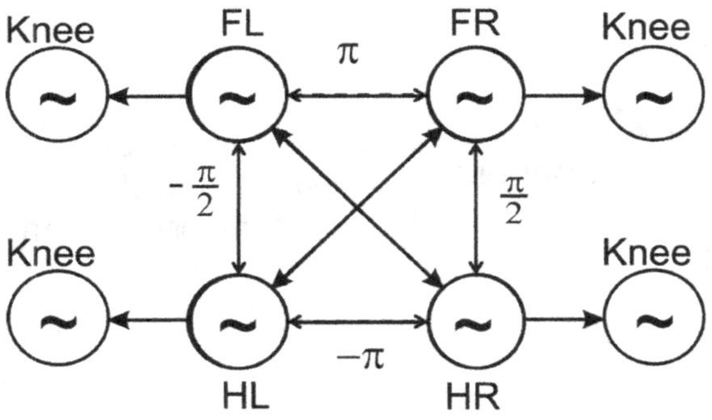

For the hip joints, identified by subscript [1], this is achieved by modifying (1) as follows:

$$\begin{bmatrix} \dot{x}_{i[1]} \\ \dot{z}_{i[1]} \end{bmatrix} = \begin{bmatrix} \alpha\left(\mu - r_{i[1]}^2\right) & \text{-}\omega \\ \omega & \alpha\left(\mu - r_{i[1]}^2\right) \end{bmatrix} \begin{bmatrix} x_{i[1]} - O_{i[1]} \\ z_{i[1]} \end{bmatrix} + \sum_{j \neq i} \mathbf{R}\left(\theta_{i[1]}^{j[1]}\right) \begin{bmatrix} x_{j[1]} - O_{j[1]} \\ z_{j[1]} \end{bmatrix} \tag{2}$$

For the knee joints, identified by subscript [3], we modify (1) as follows:

$$\begin{bmatrix} \dot{x}_{i[3]} \\ \dot{z}_{i[3]} \end{bmatrix} = \begin{bmatrix} \alpha\left(\mu - r_{i[3]}^2\right) & \text{-}\omega \\ \omega & \alpha\left(\mu - r_{i[3]}^2\right) \end{bmatrix} \begin{bmatrix} x_{i[3]} - O_{i[3]} \\ z_{i[3]} \end{bmatrix} + \frac{1}{2} \mathbf{R}\left(\psi_{i[3]}^{j[1]}\right) \begin{bmatrix} x_{j[1]} - O_{j[1]} \\ z_{j[1]} \end{bmatrix} \tag{3}$$

where *i,j* = Fore Left (FL), Fore Right (FR), Hind Left (HL) and Hind Right (HR) limbs. The linear terms are rotated onto each other by rotation matrices $\mathbf{R}(\theta_{i[1]}^{j[1]})$ and $\mathbf{R}(\psi_{i[3]}^{j[1]})$, where $\theta_{i[1]}^{j[1]}$ is the relative phase among the i[1]'s and j[1]'s hip oscillators and represents bidirectional couplings between these oscillators such that $\theta_{i[1]}^{j[1]} = -\theta_{j[1]}^{i[1]}$ and $\psi_{i[3]}^{j[1]}$ is the required relative phase among the i[3]'s and j[1]'s oscillators (Figure 2). We assure that closed-loop interoscillator couplings have phase biases that sum up to a multiple of 360 deg.

Each hip oscillator lags a quarter of a cycle from the previous. The relative phases between hips and knees, $\psi_{i[3]}^{j[1]}$, were all set to 180 deg.

Equation 2 provides a stable periodic solution (limit cycle attractor) for two oscillators *i*[1] and *j*[1] given by the closed form solutions

$$x_{i[1]}(t) = O_i + \frac{A_i[1]}{2}\cos\left(\omega t + \theta_{i[1]}^{j[1]} + \phi_0\right)$$

$$x_{j[1]}(t) = O_i + \frac{A_j[1]}{2}\cos\left(\omega t + \theta_{j[1]}^{i[1]} + \phi_0\right)$$

This system generates phase-locked oscillations for all connected oscillators with ϕ_0 depending on the system initial conditions. Further, these oscillations can be modulated according to the control parameters: A_i that controls individual amplitudes; O_i that controls the individual offsets and ω that controls the frequency of all the oscillators.

Due to the properties of this type of coupling among oscillators, the generated trajectories are stable and smooth and thus potentially useful for trajectory generation in a robot.

The final result is a network of oscillators with controlled phase relationships, able to generate more complex, synchronized behavior such as locomotion. It generates coordinated rhythmic movements in a stable and flexible way. The generated trajectories are smooth, stable and robust to perturbations. A complete description of the locomotion generation controller is described in Matos and Santos (2010).

3.1.3. Generating a Walking Gait

A gait event sequence is specified using the duty factor (β) and the relative phases, where the first event, and the start of the stride, is chosen as the event when the fore left leg (reference leg) is set down.

Parameters were chosen in order to respect feasibility of the experiment. We set the frequency to $\omega = 2.044$ rad s^{-1} in regards with the motor limitations. Speed of convergence of rhythmic systems was set to 0.08s ($\frac{1}{2\alpha\mu_i}$), in regard to stability during the integration process and to feasibility of the desired trajectories. The μ_i parameters of the front and hind limbs were set to 6.25 and 25, respectively.

This yield a non-singular, regular and symmetric gait with a FL-HR-FR-HL gait even sequence, a duty factor $\beta = 0.73$ and a velocity of $19\text{mm}s^{-1}$ (measured in the Z direction, see Figure 4).

We have implemented in webots (Michel, 2004) and in a real ers-7 AIBO robot this locomotion controller (simulation results and the experiment description is detailed explained in Section 5). The gait diagram is shown in Figure 3.

3.2. Head Movement Generation

Head movement is generated similarly to locomotion, but a CPG for a given DOF is modelled as a Hopf oscillator, not coupled to any other oscillator. Each CPG, therefore, generates a rhythmic movement according to

$$\begin{bmatrix} \dot{x}_i \\ \dot{z}_i \end{bmatrix} = \begin{bmatrix} \alpha\left(\mu - r_i^2\right) & -\omega_i \\ \omega & \alpha\left(\mu - r_i^2\right) \end{bmatrix} \begin{bmatrix} x_i - O_i \\ z_i \end{bmatrix}, \quad (4)$$

where *i*=tilt, pan, nod. The control policy is the x_i variable, obtained by integrating the CPGs dynamical systems, and represents tilt, pan and nod joint angles in our experiments.

Figure 3. Interlimb coordination during a simulated quadruped walk. Periods of foot contact are shown for both limbs. Relative phase i is plotted in the top.

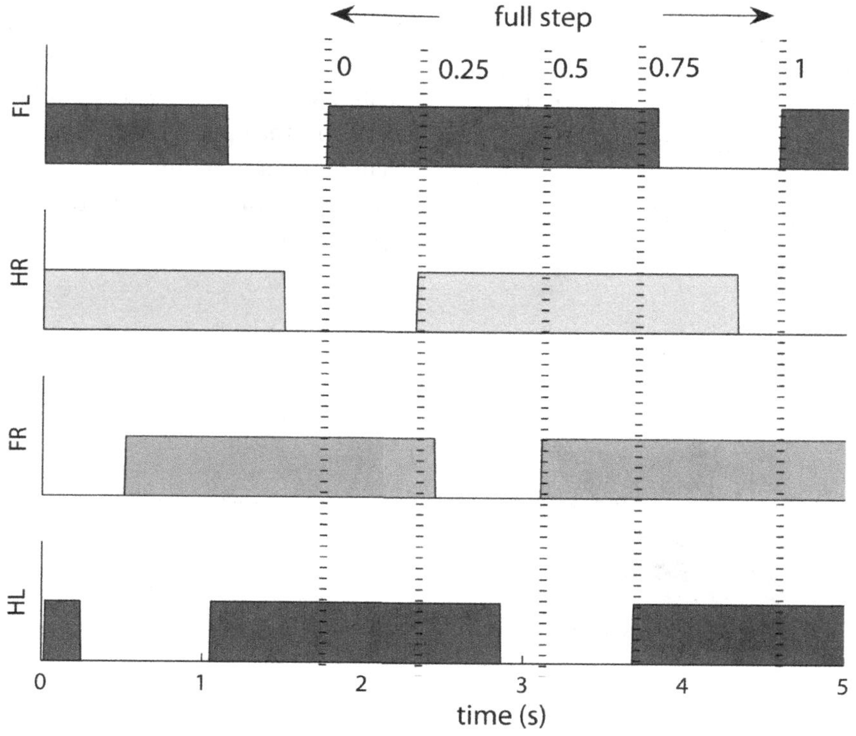

Note that the final movement for each of these joints is a rhythmic motion which amplitude of movement is specified by μ_i, offset by O_i and its frequency by ω_i.

The differential equations for locomotion and head movement are solved using Euler integration with a fixed time step of 1ms. The x_i trajectories represent angular positions and are directly sent to the PID controllers of the joint servomotors, and result in the actual $\tilde{x}_i$ trajectories (Figure 1).

3.3. Optimization System

The CPG approach allows assigning explicit parameters for each of the nonlinear oscillators, independently controlling the amplitude, offset and frequency of the resultant head movement. The multitude of parameter combinations is large, and it is difficult to derive an accurate model for the tested quadruped robot and for the environment. Besides, such a model based approach would also require some post-adaptation of results (because of backlash, friction, etc).

In this study, the search of suitable parameters for the implementation of the required head motion was carried out based on the data from a simulated quadruped robot. The *(X,Y,Z)* head coordinates, in a world coordinate system (Figure 4), are recorded when a simulated robot walks straightforward with a pre-specified given forward velocity (no angular movement) during 30s and no head stabilization is performed. We are interested in the opposite of this movement around the *(X,Y,Z)* coordinates. This data was mathematically treated such as to keep only the oscillations in the movement and remove the drift that the robot has in the *X* coordinate and also the forward movement in the *Z* coordinate. From now on, this data is referred to as $(X,Y,Z)_{\text{observed}}$. In the simulation, we have set a cycle time of 30ms, that is, the time needed to perform sensory acquisitions, calculate the planned trajectories (integrating the differential equations) and send this data to the servomotors. The $(X,Y,Z)_{\text{observed}}$ data is sampled with a sample time of 30ms, meaning we have a total of 1000 samples. A simulated time of 30s corresponds to 10 strides of locomotion. This time is arbitrary and could have been chosen differently but seems well suited to find a model representative of the head movement induced by the locomotion controller.

4. OPTIMIZATION PROCESS

In this section the optimization process associated to the robot head movement stabilization is explained. Therefore, we develop a model that performs the opposite movement of the observed data in order to minimize the head movement induced by locomotion. Three optimization methods are used and their numerical results are reported.

Figure 4. World coordinate system

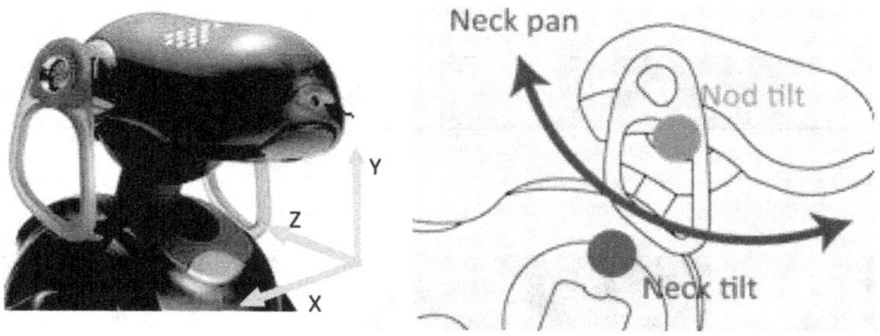

4.1. Problem Formulation

We formulate an optimization problem which objective is to find a set of head CPG control parameters that minimizes the distance between the generated head movement induced by locomotion and the one induced by locomotion without any stabilization mechanism. The basic idea is to combine the CPG model for head movement generation with the optimization algorithm. Figure 5 illustrates a schematic of the overall optimization system.

Three head CPGs (see (4)) generate during 30s rhythmic motions for the tilt, pan and nod joints. By applying forward kinematics, we calculate the resultant set of 1000 samples of $(X, Y, Z)_{\text{calculated}}$ head coordinates in the world coordinate system.

The Euclidean distance between the observed and calculated head coordinates is the evaluated criterion used to explore the parameter space of the CPG model to identify the head movement that minimizes the one induced by locomotion itself. Thus, the constrained optimization problem can be mathematically formulated as follows:

$$\begin{aligned}
&\min_{\text{s.t.}} f(x) = \| (X,Y,Z)_{\text{observed}} - (X,Y,Z)_{\text{calculated}} \|_2 \\
&-75 + \frac{\mu_{\text{tilt}}}{2} \le y_{\text{tilt}} \le -\frac{\mu_{\text{tilt}}}{2} \\
&-88 + \frac{\mu_{\text{pan}}}{2} \le y_{\text{pan}} \le 88 - \frac{\mu_{\text{pan}}}{2} \\
&-88 + \frac{\mu_{\text{nod}}}{2} \le y_{\text{nod}} \le 45 - \frac{\mu_{\text{nod}}}{2} \\
&0 \le \mu_{\text{tilt}} \le 75 \\
&-75 \le y_{\text{tilt}} \le 0 \\
&1 \le \omega_{\text{tilt}} \le 12 \\
&0 \le A_{\text{pan}} \le 176 \\
&-88 \le y_{\text{pan}} \le 88 \\
&1 \le \omega_{\text{pan}} \le 12 \\
&0 \le A_{\text{nod}} \le 60 \\
&-88 \le y_{\text{nod}} \le 45 \\
&1 \le \omega_{\text{nod}} \le 12
\end{aligned} \tag{5}$$

Therefore, we solve this optimization problem to obtain a set of head controller parameters that allows tuning the head movement of the robot. The objective function computation involves the input of the CPG parameters to the head move-

Figure 5. Schematics of the optimization system

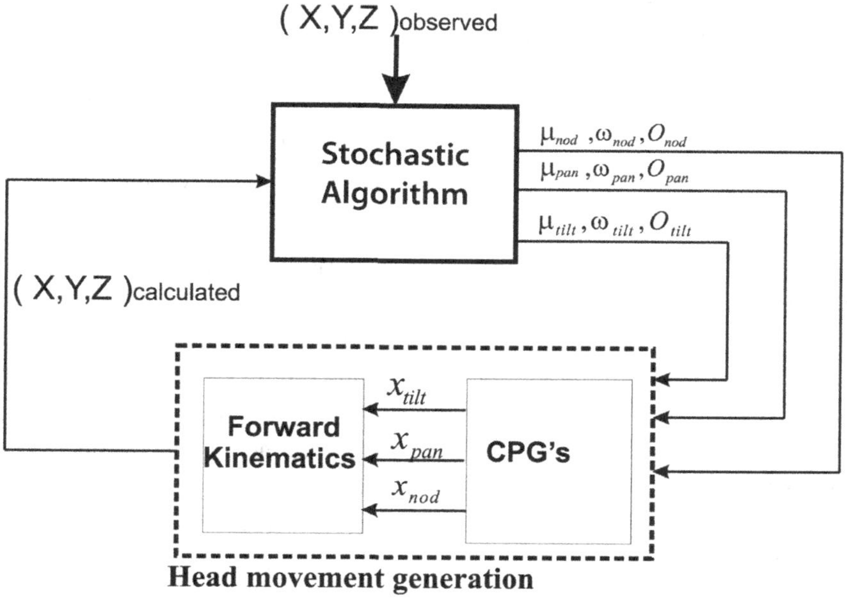

ment generation process (Figure 5) and the application of forward kinematics to obtain the resultant $(X,Y,Z)_{\text{calculated}}$ head coordinates.

In order to search for the optimal combinations of the head CPG control parameters, three stochastic optimization methods - evolution strategies, genetic algorithm and the electromagnetism-like algorithm are used. Then, their obtained best solutions are compared, since the global optimal solution of problem (5) is unknown.

4.2. Constraint-Handling Methods

In order to handle the simple boundary constraints, each new generated point is projected component by component in order to satisfy boundary constraints as follows:

$$x_k = \begin{cases} l_k & \text{if } x_k < l_k \\ x_k & \text{if } l_k \leq x_k \leq u_k \\ u_k & \text{if } x_k > u_k \end{cases} \qquad (6)$$

where l_k, u_k are the lower and upper limit of the kth component of the variables defined in problem (5), respectively.

In order to handle the inequality constraints, two approaches are implemented: a repairing method and the tournament based constraint method (Deb, 1998). In the approach based on a repairing mechanism, any infeasible solution is repaired exploring the relations among variables expressed by the inequality constraints, i.e., the values $y_{\text{tilt}}, y_{\text{pan}}$ and y_{nod} are repaired in order to satisfy the constraints of (5). The application of this repairing mechanism to all infeasible solutions in the population, guarantees that all solutions become feasible. Thus, the fitness function can be defined as $F(x) = f(x)$. We want to remark that the weakness of the repairing methods lies in their problem dependence. Different repairing procedures have to be designed for each particular problem. There are no standard heuristics for accomplishing this. Sometimes repairing infeasible solutions might become as a complex task as solving the original problem.

The second approach is based on the tournament based constraint method proposed by Deb (1998) that is based on a penalty function which does not require any penalty parameter. For comparison purposes, tournament selection is exploited to make sure that:

1. When two feasible solutions are compared, the one with better fitness function value is chosen;
2. When one feasible and one infeasible solutions are compared, the feasible solution is chosen;
3. When two infeasible solutions are compared the one with smaller constraint violation is chosen.

Therefore, the fitness function, in which infeasible solutions are compared based on their constraint violation, can be expressed by:

$$F(x) = \begin{cases} f(x) & \text{if } g_j(x) \leq 0, \forall_j \\ f_{\max} + \sum_{j=1}^{m} |\max(0, g_j(x))| & \text{otherwise} \end{cases} \qquad (7)$$

where $f_{\max}$ is the objective function value of the worst feasible solution in the population and $g_j(x)$ are the m inequality constraints to be satisfied ($g_j(x) \leq 0$, as presented in (5)). If no feasible solution exists $f_{\max}$ is set to 0. This approach can be only applicable to population-based search methods such as the adopted in this work. Thus, the fitness of an infeasible solution not only depends on the amount of constraint violation, but also on the population of solutions at hand. An important advantage of this approach is that it is not required to compute the objective function value for infeasible solutions.

4.3. Optimization Methods

Problem (5) is a nonlinear problem where continuity and convexity conditions are not guaranteed. Thus, searching for a global optimum is a difficult task that can be done by using stochastic-type algorithms. We apply three stochastic optimization methods - evolution strategies (Schwefel, 1995), the genetic algorithms (Goldberg, 1989) and the electromagnetism-like mechanism (Birbil & Fang, 2003), - in order to determine the best set of CPG control parameters that results in, or close to the desired movement. Evolutionary approaches like Genetic Algorithms Goldberg (1989) and Evolution Strategies (Schwefel, 1995) have been applied to global optimization problems in science, economy, and research and development with success.

Electromagnetism-like (EM) mechanism had been tested on available test problems in Birbil and Fang (2003), and it showed that EM can converge to the optimal solution. A theoretical study of EM analysis for convergence to the optimal solution was presented in Birbil et al. (2004). Recently, EM had been applied to solve various optimization problems successfully, such as scheduling optimization Yurtkuran and Emel (2010), multi-objective optimization Tsou and Kao (2006), NP optimizations problems Wu et al. (2006) and so on. According to conclusions in Birbil and Fang (2003), this problem appears to be easily solved by EM theoretically.

These methods are population-based techniques, that are easy to implement and require only data based on the objective function and constraints, and no derivatives or other auxiliary knowledge. Evolution Strategies (ESs) are a subclass of nature-inspired optimization methods belonging to the class of Evolutionary Algorithms (EAs) which use mutation, recombination, and selection applied to a population of individuals containing candidate solutions in order to evolve iteratively better and better solutions. Genetic Algorithms (GAs) are EAs that use techniques inspired by evolutionary biology such as inheritance, mutation, selection, and crossover Goldberg (1989). The electromagnetism-like algorithm simulates the electromagnetism theory of physics by considering each point in the population as an electrical charge. The method uses an attraction-repulsion mechanism to move a population of points towards optimality Birbil and Fang (2003).

4.3.1. Evolution Strategies

ESs work directly with the real representation of the parameter set, searching from an initial population of individuals that is uniformly generated at random within the feasible region. Each individual is evaluated through the fitness function value (5).

Traditionally, two distinct types of ESs differing basically on the selection procedure are considered: the $(\mu+\lambda)$-ES and the (μ,λ)-ES. In spite of, at first, the generation of new individuals being based on one single operator, the mutation operator, ESs benefit with the introduction of the recombination operator. Thus, the nomenclature for ESs is extended, and ESs with recombination is usually referred as $(\mu\,/\,\rho+\lambda)$-ES or $(\mu\,/\,\rho,\lambda)$-ES. In this nomenclature, μ and λ represent, respectively, the parent and offspring population sizes (for many problems, $\lambda\,/\,\mu\approx 7$ is suggested Schwefel (1995); ρ represents the number of parents that are selected for recombination.

Each population member consists on a tuple of two vectors: a vector of real values representing the decision variables and a vector of real standard deviations used to adapt step sizes during the search. It should be noted that one of the most promising features of ESs is that they use adaptive step sizes for mutation. So, these parameters of the algorithm are themselves optimized during the search. Thus, each decision variable k has an associated standard deviation σ_k, with $k=1,\ldots,n$, where n is the number of decision variables. The search starts from an initial population which individuals are, in general, randomly generated. The initial standard deviations σ_k were set according to (8)

$$\sigma_k = \frac{u_k - l_k}{\lambda\sqrt{n}} \tag{8}$$

Thus, in a $(\mu / \rho + \lambda)$-ES, at a given generation, there are μ parents, and λ offspring are generated by recombination and mutation. Basically, the recombination operator consists on, before mutation, to recombine a set of chosen parents to find a new solution. On other hand, mutation creates new individuals by adding random normal distributed quantities. Next, the $\mu + \lambda$ individuals are sorted according to their fitness function values. Finally, the best μ of all the $\mu + \lambda$ members become the parents of the next generation (i.e., the selection takes place between the $\mu + \lambda$ members). The $(\mu / \rho, \lambda)$-ES is similar differing, basically, on the selection procedure that is restricted to the offspring population, i.e., the selection takes place between the λ offspring.

Basically, the recombination operator consists on, before mutation, to recombine a set of chosen parents to find a new solution. A given number $\rho\left(1 \le \rho \le \mu\right)$ of parents are randomly chosen for recombination. When $\rho = 1$ then there is no recombination. Two types of recombination are, mainly, considered: intermediate and discrete recombination. Since, in this work, the recombination implemented was the discrete recombination, only this recombination will be described in detail. In the discrete recombination, each component of the offspring is chosen from one of the ρ parents at random.

Thus, for ρ chosen parents (randomly selected from population), the offspring x_p is given by

$$x_p = (x_{u_1,1}, \ldots, x_{u_n,n})$$

with $u_1 \in \{1, \ldots, \rho\}, \ldots, u_n \in \{1, \ldots, \rho\}$ and $p = 1, \ldots, \mu$. In discrete recombination, the integer uniform random values u_i, for $i = 1, \ldots, n$, allow the selection of which of the ρ parents will give the value of decision variable i. This procedure allows different combinations of the values of the decision variables from existing solutions in the population. Standard deviations are similarly recombined.

During the search, the step sizes for mutation are adapted. Several self-adaptation schemes are possible. One possibility is to actualize the standard deviations σ_i (for each decision variable) according to the equation Schwefel (1995):

$$\sigma_k \leftarrow \sigma_k e^{z_k} e^{z} \tag{9}$$

where $z_k \sim N(0, \Delta\sigma^2)$, $z \sim N(0, \Delta\sigma`^2)$ and $\Delta\sigma$ and $\Delta\sigma`$ are parameters of the algorithm. In the experiments conducted only this non-isotropic adaptation rule was considered.

Usually, the random numbers z are generated according to a Gaussian or Normal distribution. Besides, it is convenient that small changes occur frequently, but large ones only rarely. In this sense, the random numbers z_k can be generated according to a Normal distribution with mean zero and variance σ_k^2

$$z_k \sim N(0, \sigma_k^2) \tag{10}$$

So, mutation consists on adding random numbers with mean zero and variance σ_k^2 to the vector of decision variables, i.e., $x_d = x_u + z$. Each generated individual should be evaluated in terms of fitness function value, so they should go to the head movement generation process.

4.3.2. Genetic Algorithm

A Genetic Algorithm (GA) is a population based algorithm that uses techniques inspired by evolutionary biology such as inheritance, mutation, selection, and crossover Goldberg (1989). Thus, unlike conventional algorithms, GAs start from a population of points of size popsize. In spite of the traditional binary representation used by GAs, in our implementation, a real representation is used since we are leading with a continuous problem. Therefore, each point of the population z^i, for $i = 1, \ldots \text{popsize}$, is an n dimensional vector. The initial population is randomly generated. A fitness function is defined in order to compare the points of the population (in terms of objective function value and constraint violation). We implement a stochastic selection that guarantees that better points are more likely to be selected. New points in the search space are generated by the application of genetic operators (crossover and mutation) to the selected points from population.

Crossover combines two points in order to generate new ones. A Simulated Binary Crossover (SBX) Agrawal and Deb (1994) that simulates the working principle of single-point crossover operator for binary strings is implemented. Two points, z_1 and z_2, are randomly selected from the pool and, with probability p_c, two new points, w_1 and w_2 are generated according to

$$w_k^1 = 0.5\left((1+\beta_k)z_k^1 + (1-\beta_k)z_k^2\right)$$
$$w_k^2 = 0.5\left((1-\beta_k)z_k^1 + (1+\beta_k)z_k^2\right),$$
$$\beta_k = \begin{cases} (2r_k)^{\frac{1}{\eta_c+1}} & \text{if } r_k \le 0.5 \\ \left(\dfrac{1}{2(1-r_k)}\right)^{\frac{1}{\eta_c+1}} & \text{if } r_k > 0.5 \end{cases} \tag{11}$$

for $k = 1, \ldots, n$, where $r_k \sim U(0,1)$, (r_k is a random number uniformly distributed in [0, 1]) and $\eta_c > 0$ is an external parameter of the distribution. This procedure is repeated until the number of generated points equals the number of points in the pool.

A Polynomial Mutation is applied, with a probability p_m, to the points produced by the crossover operator. Mutation introduces diversity in the population since crossover, exclusively, could not assure the exploration of new regions of the search space. This operator guarantees that the probability of creating a new point t^i closer to the previous one w^i $\left(i = 1, \ldots, \text{popsize}\right)$ is more than the probability of creating one away from it. It can be expressed by:

$$t_k^i = w_k^i + (u_k - l_k)\iota_k,$$
$$\$\iota_k = \begin{cases} (2r_k)^{\frac{1}{\eta_m+1}} - 1 & \text{if } r_k < 0.5 \\ 1 - \left(2(1-r_k)\right)^{\frac{1}{\eta_m+1}} & \text{if } r_k \ge 0.5 \end{cases} \tag{12}$$

for $k = 1, \ldots, n$, where $r_k \sim U(0,1)$ and $\eta_m > 0$ is an external parameter of the distribution. The GA proceeds as the following algorithm.

Elitism is implemented by maintaining, during the search, a given number *e*, of best points in the population. This iterative procedure stops when a given stopping criterion is satisfied. The best point in the final population is returned and corresponds to the best approximation to the solution of the problem defined by (5), i.e., the point that minimizes the distance between the observed and computed head coordinates of the robot.

4.3.3. Electromagnetism-Like Algorithm

The electromagnetism-like algorithm (Birbil & Fang, 2003) is a population-based meta-heuristic which has been proposed to solve bounded problems effectively.

The EM algorithm starts with a population of randomly generated points from the feasible region. Analogous to electromagnetism, each point is a charged particle that is released to the space. The charge of each point is related to the fitness function value and determines the magnitude of attraction of the point over the population. The better the fitness function value, the higher the magnitude of attraction. The charges are used to find a direction for each point to move in subsequent iterations. The regions that have higher attraction will signal other points to move towards them. In addition, a repulsion mechanism is also introduced to explore new regions for even better solutions.

EM algorithm comprises three procedures: *Initialize*, *CalcF* and *Move*. A more detailed explanation of the EM algorithm follows. *Initialize* is a procedure that aims to randomly generate popsize points from the feasible region. After computing the fitness function value for all the points in the population, the procedure identifies the best point, x^{best}, which is the point with the best function value.

For the *CalcF* procedure, the Coulomb's law of the electromagnetism theory is used. It states that the force exerted on a point via other points is inversely proportional to the square of the distance between the points and directly proportional to the product of their charges. Then, we compute the charges of the points according to their fitness function values. As the charge q^i of point x^i determines the power of attraction or repulsion for that point, the charge is computed according to the fitness function value by

$$q^i = \exp\left(-n\frac{F(x^i) - F(x^{best})}{\sum_{j=1}^{\text{popsize}}(F(x^j) - F(x^{best}))}\right), \quad i = 1, \ldots, \text{popsize}. \tag{13}$$

where x^i is the ith point of the population, n is the number of decision variables and popsize is the population size. In this way the points that have better fitness function values possess higher charges. This is a scaled distance of the function value at x^i to the function value of the best point in the population.

The total force vector F^i_{orce} exerted on each point x^i is then calculated by adding the individual component forces between any pair of points x^i and x^j. As the charges (see (13)) are all positive, the direction of a force depends on the fitness function values at x^i and x^j. Thus, the total force exerted on point x^i of the population is evaluated as

$$F^i_{orce} = \sum_{j \neq i}^{popsize} \begin{cases} (x^j - x^i)\dfrac{q^i q^j}{\left\|x^j - x^i\right\|^3} & if \;\; F(x^j) < F(x^i)\,(attraction) \\ (x^i - x^j)\dfrac{q^i q^j}{\left\|x^j - x^i\right\|^3} & if \;\; F(x^j) \geq F(x^i)\,(repulsion) \end{cases},$$

for $i = 1, \ldots, \text{popsize}$.

The *Move* procedure uses the total force vector, F^i_{orce}, to move the point x^i in the direction of the scaled force by a random step length. The best point, x^{best}, is not moved and is carried out to the subsequent iteration. To ensure feasibility in this movement algorithm we define the projection of each coordinate of the point to the feasible region (see (7)).

In the original EM algorithm (Birbil & Fang, 2003), after the *Move* procedure, it performs a local search procedure only applied to the best point in the population. In this approach, we did not introduce it because it was too much expensive in terms of time and function evaluations.

4.4. Numerical Results

The optimization system was implemented in Matlab (Version 7.5) running in an Intel Pentium CPU 3.20 GHz (1024 MB of RAM) PC. The system of equations was integrated using the Euler method with 1ms fixed integration steps. The evaluation time for head movement generation is 30s.

In our implementation, for ES, the optimization system ends when the number of generations exceeds 150, or the population variability is inferior to a threshold set *a priori*. In this study, the number of parents was 10 and the number of offspring was 100, i.e., (10/10+100)-ES was used. For GA, the optimization system ends when the number of generations exceeds 300 and for this study, we use a population of 100 chromosomes. In EM the number of points in the population was set to \$20\$ and we depict results when the number of iterations exceeds 2000 iterations

Table 1 contains the Best, Mean and Standard Deviation (SD) values of the solutions found (in terms of fitness function and time) over the 10 runs, for the two constraint-handling techniques used. Note that, in all experiments, the evaluation time for locomotion generation is 30s. Comparing the performance of the two mechanisms, by analyzing Table 1, we conclude that the two mechanisms to handle constraints are competitive. In terms of best fitness found we see that for all algorithms, the approach using repairing solutions is the one who has least value. However the average fitness value found over the 10 runs is better for the tournament selection mechanism. We remark that the metric in terms of average values is indeed the most important when comparing stochastic algorithms, since it reports the central tendency of the results over the runs. A number of runs of the order herein used (a small sample) implies the use of non-parametric statistical tests. For this purpose we have adopted the Mann-Whitney test for independent samples. In Table 2, we present the results of the application of the statistical test to all pairwise combinations of the algorithms. The values below the diagonal of the table are the p-values of the statistical test. We consider that the performance of the algorithms is significantly different for a significance value of 0.05. In the table, the symbol $\approx$ indicates that there is no significant difference between the algorithms; $\lhd$ means that the algorithm in row has an inferior performance when compared with the algorithm in column; $\rhd$ means that the algorithm in row has a superior performance when compared with the algorithm in column. We

Table 1. Performance of the algorithms in the optimization system

Constraint-Handling Technique	Algorithm	Time (hours)			Fitness		
		Best	Mean	SD	Best	Mean	SD
Tournament	ES	0.860	1.634	0.445	3986.5	4130.7	173.4
	GA	4.926	5.482	0.290	3983.8	4877.0	839.4
	EM	5.432	5.993	0.342	4318.3	4559.9	538.2
Repairing	ES	1.984	2.421	0.333	3776.0	4183.1	572.7
	GA	9.206	9.961	0.717	3978.6	5232.3	762.7
	EM	6.502	7.033	0.263	4258.8	5053.3	863.0

Table 2. Results of pairwise statistical tests

		ES		GA		EM	
		Repairing	**Tournament**	**Repairing**	**Tournament**	**Repairing**	**Tournament**
ES	Repairing	-	≈	▷	≈	▷	▷
	Tournament	0.677	-	▷	≈	▷	▷
GA	Repairing	0.045	0.017	-	≈	≈	≈
	Tournament	0.212	0.212	0.570	-	≈	≈
EM	Repairing	0.009	0.009	0.677	0.241	-	≈
	Tournament	0.002	0.004	0.344	0.734		-

observe that the best average results were obtained by ES. There is no significant difference between ES with repairing mechanism and tournament technique. However, it should be noted that the computational effort required by the tournament technique is lesser than the repairing mechanism.

In Table 3, we present, in average terms, the number of generations, the computational time and the corresponding percentage of the total optimization time to achieve the best solution for tournament constraint-handling technique. Again, ES seems to present the best performance according to this criterion.

Clearly, the tournament selection method is the least time consuming algorithm. This is because, this algorithm deals not only with feasible but with infeasible points, and in this latter case the forward kinematics is not activated.

Table 3. Number of generations, computational time and percentage of the total optimization time (average values) for the tournament constraint-handling technique

	Number of Generation	Computational Time (hours)	Percentage of the Total Optimization Time (%)
ES	70	0.76	46.7
GA	75	1.37	24.5
EM	1980	5.93	99.0

Figure 6 shows the fitness evolution of the best and mean point for each of the three stochastic optimization methods when using the tournament method, for 10 runs.

Figure 7 depicts the time courses of the (X, Y, Z) calculated and observed head movement according to the CPG parameters of the best solutions found for each of the optimization algorithms, with the tournament mechanism. This data was mathematically treated such as to keep only the oscillations in the movement and remove the drift that the robot has in the X coordinate and also the forward movement in the Z coordinate.

We conclude that the generated movements are quite similar in the X coordinate. The calculated movement is quite different in the Z coordinate. This results from the fact that the pan joint controls movement in the X coordinate, while both the tilt and nod joints control the Y and Z coordinates. If we are able to mimic movement in the Y coordinate, in the Z coordinate this mimic is therefore difficult to achieve.

5. EXPERIMENTAL RESULTS

In this section, we describe the experiment done in a simulated ers-7 AIBO robot using Webots (Michel, 2004). Webots is a software for the

Figure 6. Best (solid line) and mean (dashed line) fitness evolution, with tournament mechanism, for each of the three stochastic optimization methods, for 10 runs: a) ES algorithm; b) GA algorithm and; c) EM algorithm.

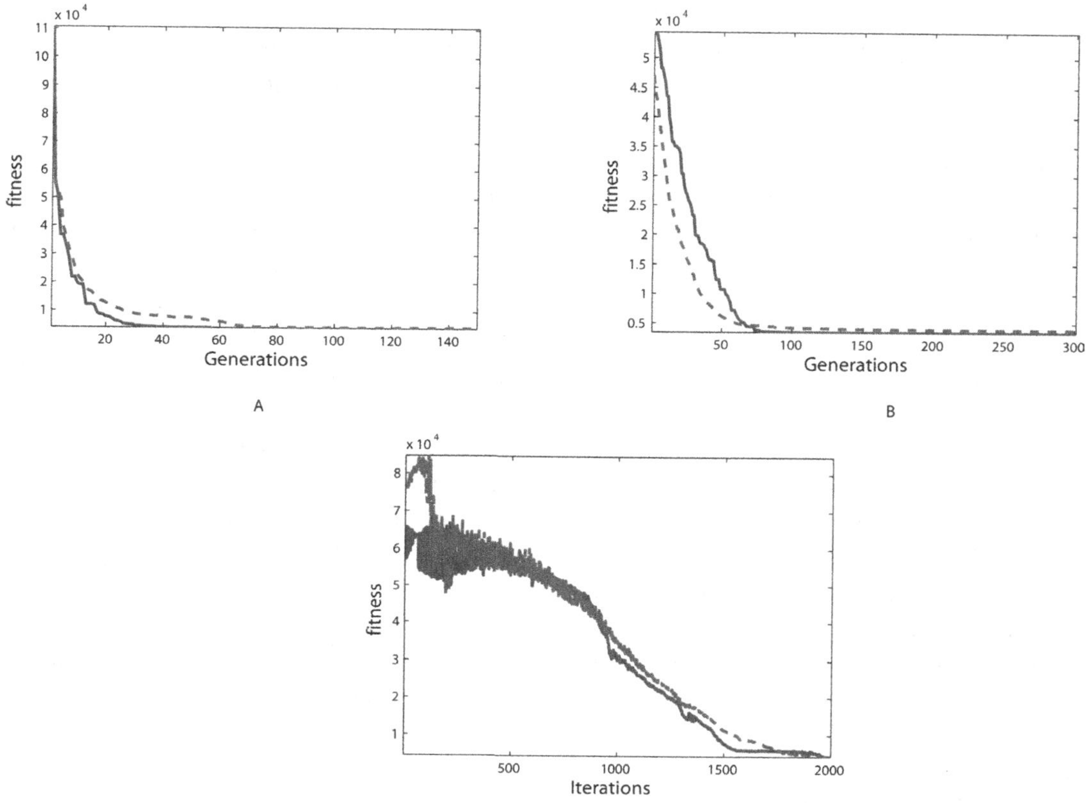

Figure 7. (X,Y,Z) observed (gray dashed line) and calculated (blue solid line, ES algorithm; green dotted line, GA algorithm and; black dashed line, EM algorithm), according to the CPG parameters of the best solutions found for each optimization algorithm with the tournament mechanism: a) the overall head movement during 30 s. b) detailed head movement between 5 to 10 seconds

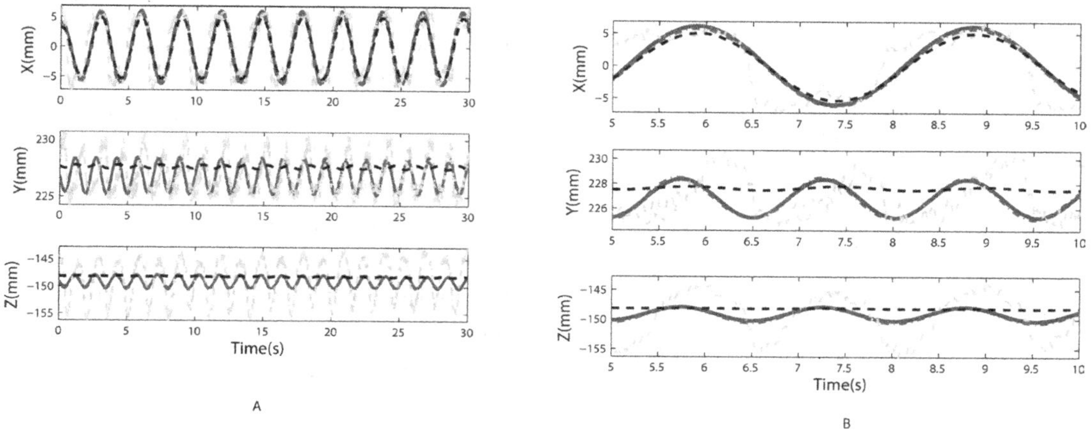

physic simulation of robots based on ODE, an open source physics engine for simulating 3D rigid body dynamics.

The ers-7 AIBO dog robot is a 18 DOFs quadruped robot made by Sony. The locomotion controller generates the joint angles of the hip and knee joints in the sagittal plane that is 8 DOFs of the robot, 2 DOFs in each leg. Only the previously described walk gait is generated and tested. Figure 8 depicts a schematics of the overall AIBO kinematics.

The head controller generates the joint angles of the 3 DOFs: tilt, pan and nod. The other DOFs are not used for the moment, and remain fixed to an appropriately chosen value during the experiments.

The AIBO has a camera built into its head. At each sensorial cycle (30ms), sensory information is acquired. The dynamics of the CPGs are numerically integrated using the Euler method with a fixed time step of 1ms thus specifying servo positions. Locomotion parameters were set as previously described.

Because we are working in a simulated environment, we are able to build a GPS into the AIBO camera that enable us to verify how the head effectively moves in an external coordinate system.

Figure 8. Schematics of the Aibo robot. The used joints are shown in red

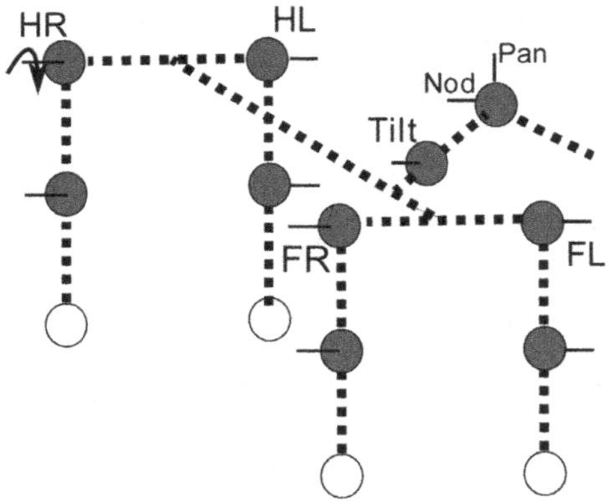

Ideally, during locomotion the head movement would have no oscillations in (*X,Y,Z*) oordinates and should only exhibit the navigational movement given by a straightforward movement.

Several simulations are performed: the robot walks during 30s without and with each of the best of the feedforward solutions found, and its GPS coordinates are recorded. Figure 9 shows the recorded GPS coordinates for the experiments with and without the found feedforward solutions. To analyze the oscillations in each (*X,Y,Z*) coordinate, we removed the natural drift of the robot in the *X* coordinate and the forward motion in the *Z* coordinate. We observe that the *X* coordinates of the marker position oscillate less. Note that there is some drift in the *X* coordinates, meaning the robot slightly deviates towards its side while walking. The observed peaks in the *Y* coordinate reflect the final stage of the swing phase and the beginning of the stance phases of the four legs, corresponding to an accentuated movement of the robot center of mass. This problem will be addressed in current work, by improving the locomotion controller and take into account balance control (Sousa et al., 2010).

Further, we calculate the standard deviation (sd) independently for each coordinate of the recorded oscillatory head movement, for each solution found and also for the observed movement. Table 4 depicts the obtained results. As previously verified offline, the resultant oscillation in *X* coordinate shows a greater decrease, of 39.3%, for the solution found by ES algorithm. In *Y* and *Z* coordinates the improvement is less significant

In order to further verify if the proposed head controller helps to stabilize the camera in this particular environment, we calculate the 3D distance between the resultant head movement and the ideal head movement (with no oscillations at all), for the same locomotion experiment (identical locomotion controllers), when head movement is generated by the best set of CPG parameters

Figure 9. (X, Y, Z) GPS coordinates of the AIBO head without drift in the X coordinate and without forward motion in the Z coordinate. Observed (gray dashed line) and calculated (blue solid line, ES algorithm; green dotted line, GA algorithm and; black dashed line, EM algorithm), according to the CPG parameters of the best solutions found for each optimization algorithm with the tournament mechanism: a) the overall head movement during 30 s. b) detailed head movement between 5 to 10 seconds

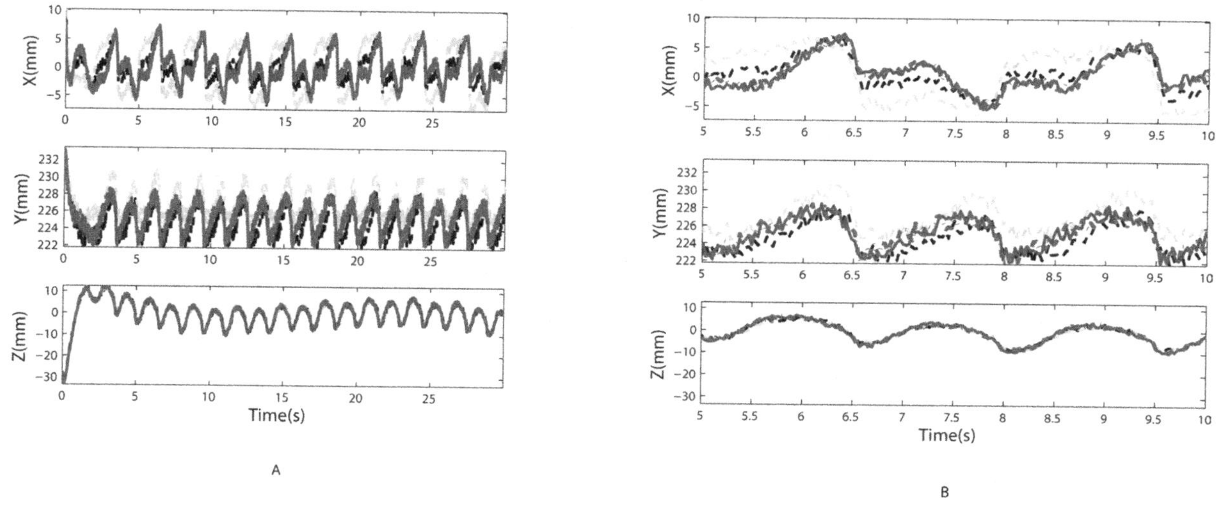

Table 4. Standard deviations of achieved (X,Y,Z) oscillations

	sd in X	sd in Y	sd in Z
obs movement	4.485	1.827	6.276
ES	2.722 (39.30%)	1.752 (4.1%)	6.158 (0.93%)
GA	2.742 (38.86%)	1.729 (5.4%)	6.190 (0.42%)
EM	2.953 (38.86%)	1.803 (1.31%)	5.878 (5.44%)

determined for each of the three optimization algorithms and also when no head movement is generated at all (the observed head movement). We expect that the proposed feedforward solution minimizes the variation of the head movement, meaning that the head remains near the same position during the experiment.

Table 5 presents the standard deviations of these 3D distances. If we compare these values to the one achieved by the observed movement, when no head movement was generated, we observe there is a decrease of this distance of: 13,1% when using the ES algorithm; 11.9% when using the GA algorithm and 9.3% when using the EM algorithm.

Table 5. Standard deviation of the 3D distance between resultant and ideal head movement

	ES	GA	EM	Observed
distance (mm)	3.06	3.10	3.19	3.52

An important result, is to verify whether the obtained control parameters generalize. Therefore, Figure 10 shows the GPS coordinates for another experiment without (dotted line) and with (solid line) the best ES feedforward solution for a sequence of time longer than the one used to off-line determine the control parameters.

Note that there is some drift in the *X* coordinate, meaning the robot slightly deviates towards its side while walking. Results seem to verify a tendency to generalize in the obtained control pa-

Figure 10. (X, Y, Z) Coordinates of the GPS positioned in the AIBO head when the robot walks during 60s. Solid and dotted lines indicate the experiment in which the feedforward solution is and is not implemented, respectively.

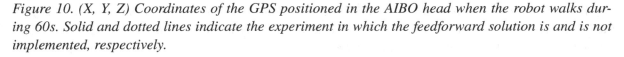

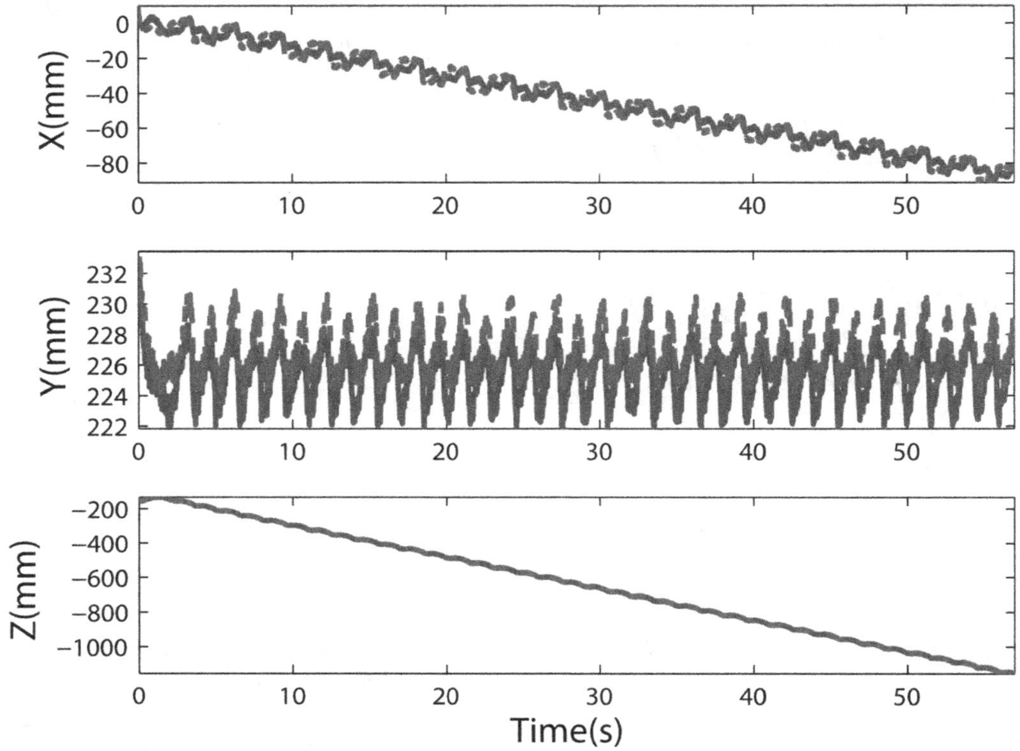

rameters. These results are as expected due to the periodic nature of locomotion and terrain homogeneity.

In conclusion, the proposed feedforward solution is able to minimize the head movement induced by the locomotion, but it is not able to eliminate it.

6. CONCLUSION AND FUTURE WORKS

In this article, we focus on the development of a head controller able to minimize the head motion induced by locomotion itself, on a quadruped robot. Our aim was to build a system able to eliminate or reduce the head motion of a robot that walks in the environment. For that, we set a dynamical controller generating trajectories for the head joints such that the final head movement is opposite to the one induced by locomotion. Specifically, we propose a combined approach to generate head movement stabilization, using CPG model for head movement generation and stochastic methods that search for the optimal combinations of the CPG parameters.

We implemented and compared the performance of three stochastic methods: the genetic algorithm, the electromagnetism-like algorithm and evolution strategies. Two constraint-handling techniques based on a repair mechanism or a tournament selection mechanism was embedded in the optimization algorithm to solve the constrained optimization problem.

Experimental results on a simulated AIBO robot demonstrate that the proposed approaches generate head movement that does not eliminate but reduce the one induced by locomotion. Furthermore, the comparing results show that both techniques are competitive in terms of fitness value found, despite the computational cost for the repairing method. Nevertheless, the repairing methods are problem dependent.

In this study, the search of parameters suitable for the implementation of the required head motion was carried out based on the data from a simulated quadruped robot. We further plan to extend our current work to online learning of the head movement similarly to Sproewitz et al. (2007) and to implement multiobjective strategies instead. Further, the inclusion of feedback mechanisms onto the overall system architecture is also currently being developed.

ACKNOWLEDGMENT

Work supported by the Portuguese Science Foundation (grant PTDC/EEA-CRO/100655/2008).

REFERENCES

Agrawal, R. B., & Deb, K. (1994). Simulated binary crossover for continuous search space. *Complex Systems*, *9*, 115–148.

Asuni, G., Teti, G., Laschi, C., Guglielmelli, E., & Dario, P. (2005). A robotic head neuro-controller based on biologically-inspired neural models. In *Proceedings of the IEEE International Conference on Robotics and Automation* (pp. 2362-2367).

Birbil, C. I., & Fang, S.-C. (2003). An electromagnetism-like mechanism for global optimization. *Journal of Global Optimization*, *25*, 263–282. doi:10.1023/A:1022452626305.

Birbil, C. I., Fang, S.-C., & Sheu, R.-L. (2004). On the convergence of a population-based global optimization algorithm. *Journal of Global Optimization*, *30*, 301–318. doi:10.1007/s10898-004-8270-3.

Bizzi, E., dAvella, A., Saltiel, P., & Trensch, M. (2002). Modular organization of spinal motor systems. *The Neuroscientist*, 8.

Buhler, M., Koditschek, D. E., & Kindlmann, P. J. (1994). Planning and control of a juggling robot. *The International Journal of Robotics Research*, *3*, 101–118. doi:10.1177/027836499401300201.

Cherubini, A., Oriolo, G., Macrì, F., Aloise, F., Cincotti, F., & Mattia, D. (2007). A vision-based path planner/follower for an assistive robotics project. In *Proceedings of the Workshop on Robot Vision* (pp. 77-86).

Combes, D., Le Ray, D., Lambert, F., Simmers, J., & Straka, H. (2008). An intrinsic feed-forward mechanism for vertebrate gaze stabilization. *Current Biology*, *18*(5), 241–243. doi:10.1016/j.cub.2008.02.018.

Deb, K. (1998). An efficient constraint handling method for genetic algorithms. *Computer Methods in Applied Mechanics and Engineering*, *186*, 311–338. doi:10.1016/S0045-7825(99)00389-8.

Degallier, S., Santos, C., Righetti, L., & Ijspeert, A. (2006). Movement generation using dynamical systems: A humanoid robot performing a drumming task. In *Proceedings of the IEEE-RAS International Conference on Humanoid Robots* (pp. 512-517).

del Solar, J. R., & Vallejos, P. A. (2005). Motion detection and tracking for an aibo robot using camera motion compensation and kalman filtering. In D. Nardi, M. Riedmiller, C. Sammut, & J. Santos-Victor (Eds.), *Proceedings of the 8th Robot Soccer World Cup* (LNCS 3276 pp. 619-627).

Goldberg, D. E. (1989). *Genetic algorithms in search, optimization and machine learning* (1st ed.). Reading, MA: Addison-Wesley.

Grillner, S. (1985). Neurobiological bases of rhythmic motor acts in vertebrates. *Science, 228*, 143–149. doi:10.1126/science.3975635.

Gu, L., & Kanade, T. (2006). 3d alignment of face in a single image. In. *Proceedings of the IEEE Conference on Computer Vision and Pattern Recognition, 1*, 1305–1312.

Held, R., & Hein, A. (1963). Movement-produced stimulation in the development of visually guided behavior. *Journal of Comparative and Physiological Psychology, 56*(5), 872–876. doi:10.1037/h0040546.

Hosoda, K., Sakamoto, K., & Asada, M. (1995). Trajectory generation for obstacle avoidance of uncalibrated stereo visual servoing without 3d reconstruction. In *Proceedings of the IEEE/RSJ International Conference on Intelligent Robots and Systems* (Vol. 1, p. 29).

Hutchinson, S., Hager, G., & Corke, P. (1996). A tutorial on visual servo control. *IEEE Transactions on Robotics and Automation, 12*(5), 651–670. doi:10.1109/70.538972.

Imai, T. (2008). Interaction of the body, head, and eyes during walking and turning. *Experimental Brain Research, 136*(1), 1–18. doi:10.1007/s002210000533.

Kapur, A., Virji-Babul, N., Tzanetakis, G., & Driessen, P. F. (2005). Gesture-based affective computing on motion capture data. In *Proceedings of the First International Conference on Affective Computing and Intelligent Interaction* (Vol. 1, pp. 1-7).

Kaushik, R., Marcinkiewicz, M., Xiao, J., Parsons, S., & Raphan, T. (2007). Implementation of bio-inspired vestibulo-ocular reflex in a quadrupedal robot. In *Proceedings of the IEEE International Conference on Robotics and Automation* (pp. 4861-4866).

Kimura, H., Fukuoka, Y., & Cohen, A. H. (2007). Adaptive dynamic walking of a quadruped robot on natural ground based on biological concepts. *The International Journal of Robotics Research, 26*(5), 475–490. doi:10.1177/0278364907078089.

Kurazume, R., & Hirose, S. (2000). Development of image stabilization system for remote operation of walking robots. In. *Proceedings of the IEEE International Conference on Robotics and Automation, 2*, 1856–1861.

Malis, E. (2004). Visual servoing invariant to changes in camera-intrinsic parameters. *IEEE Transactions on Robotics and Automation, 20*(1), 72–81. doi:10.1109/TRA.2003.820847.

Matos, V., & Santos, C. (2010). Omnidirectional locomotion in a quadruped robot: A CPG-based approach. In *Proceedings of the IEEE/RSJ International Conference on Intelligent Robots and Systems*, Taipei, Taiwan (pp. 3392-3397).

Michel, O. (2004). Webots: Professional mobile robot simulation. *Journal of Advanced Robotics Systems, 1*(1), 39–42.

Nadeau, S., Amblard, B., Mesure, S., & Bourbonnais, D. (2003). Head and trunk stabilization strategies during forward and backward walking in healthy adults. *Gait & Posture, 18*(3), 134–142. doi:10.1016/S0966-6362(02)00070-X.

Panerai, F., Metta, G., & Sandini, G. (2000). Visuo-inertial stabilization in space-variant binocular systems. *Robot and Autonomous Systems*, 195-214.

Panerai, F., Metta, G., & Sandini, G. (2002). Learning visual stabilization reflexes in robots with moving eyes. *Neurocomputing, 48*(1-4), 323–337. doi:10.1016/S0925-2312(01)00645-2.

Patane, F., Laschi, C., Miwa, H., Guglielmelli, E., Dario, P., & Takanishi, A. (2004). Design and development of a biologically-inspired artificial vestibular system for robot heads. In *Proceedings of the IEEE/RSJ International Conference on Intelligent Robots and Systems* (pp. 1317-1322).

Pozzo, T., Berthoz, A., & Lefort, L. (1990). Head stabilization during various locomotor tasks in humans. *Experimental Brain Research*, *82*, 97–106. doi:10.1007/BF00230842.

Righetti, L., & Ijspeert, A. J. (2008). Pattern generators with sensory feedback for the control of quadruped locomotion. In *Proceedings of the IEEE International Conference on Robotics and Automation* (pp. 819-824).

Sanderson, A., & Weiss, L. (1980). Image-based visual servo control using relational graph error signals. *Proc. IEEE*, pp. 1074-1077.

Sandini, G., Metta, G., & Vernon, D. (2004). Robotcub: An open framework for research in embodied cognition. In *Proceedings of the 4th IEEE/RAS International Conference on Humanoid Robots* (Vol. 1, pp. 13-32).

Schwefel, H.-P. P. (1995). *Evolution and optimum seeking*. New York, NY: John Wiley & Sons.

Shibata, T., & Schaal, S. (2001). Biomimetic gaze stabilization based on feedback-error-learning with nonparametric regression networks. *Neural Networks*, *14*, 201–216. doi:10.1016/S0893-6080(00)00084-8.

Soria, C. M., Carelli, R., Kelly, R., & Zannatha, J. M. I. (2006). Coordinated control of mobile robots based on artificial vision. *International Journal of Computers, Communications & Control*, *1*(2), 85–94.

Sousa, J., Matos, V., & Santos, C. (2010). A bio-inspired postural control for a quadruped robot: An attractor-based dynamics. In *Proceedings of the IEEE/RSJ International Conference on Intelligent Robots and Systems*, Taipei, Taiwan (pp. 5329-5334).

Sproewitz, A., Moeckel, R., Maye, J., Asadpour, M., & Ijspeert, A. J. (2007). Adaptive locomotion control in modular robotics. In *Proceedings of the Workshop on Self-Reconfigurable Robots/Systems and Applications* (pp. 81-84).

Taga, G. (1994). Emergence of bipedal locomotion through entrainment among the neuro-musculoskeletal system and the environment. In *Proceedings of the NATO Advanced Research Workshop and EGS Topical Workshop on Chaotic Advection, Tracer Dynamics and Turbulent Dispersion* (pp. 190-208).

Tsou, C.-S., & Kao, C.-H. (2006). An electromagnetism-like meta-heuristic for multi-objective optimization. In *Proceedings of the IEEE Congress on Evolutionary Computation* (pp. 1172-1178).

Wörz, S., & Rohr, K. (2007). Spline-based elastic image registration with matrix-valued basis functions using landmark and intensity information. In F. A. Hamprecht, C. Schnörr, & B. Jähne (Eds.), *Proceedings of the 29th DAGM Conference on Pattern Recognition* (LNCS 4713, pp. 537-546).

Wu, P., Yang, K.-J., & Fang, H.-C. (2006). A revised em-like algorithm + k-opt method for solving the traveling salesman problem. In *Proceedings of the First International Conference on Innovative Computing. Information and Control*, *1*, 546–549.

Yamada, H., Mori, M., & Hirose, S. (2007). Stabilization of the head of an undulating snake-like robot. In *Proceedings of the IEEE/RSJ International Conference on Intelligent Robots and Systems* (pp. 3566-3571).

Yurtkuran, A., & Emel, E. (2010). A new hybrid electromagnetism-like algorithm for capacitated vehicle routing problems. *Expert Systems with Applications*, *37*, 3427–3433. doi:10.1016/j.eswa.2009.10.005.

This work was previously published in the International Journal of Natural Computing Research (IJNCR), Volume 2, Issue 1, edited by Leandro Nunes de Castro, pp. 39-62, copyright 2011 by IGI Publishing (an imprint of IGI Global).

Chapter 4
Incorporation of Preferences in an Evolutionary Algorithm Using an Outranking Relation:
The EvABOR Approach

Eunice Oliveira
Polytechnic Institute of Leiria, Portugal & R&D Unit INESC Coimbra, Portugal

Carlos Henggeler Antunes
University of Coimbra, Portugal & R&D Unit INESC Coimbra, Portugal

Álvaro Gomes
University of Coimbra, Portugal & R&D Unit INESC Coimbra, Portugal

ABSTRACT

The incorporation of preferences into Evolutionary Algorithms (EA) presents some relevant advantages, namely to deal with complex real-world problems. It enables focus on the search thus avoiding the computation of irrelevant solutions from the point of view of the practical exploitation of results (thus minimizing the computational effort), and it facilitates the integration of the DM's expertise into the solution search process (thus minimizing the cognitive effort). These issues are particularly important whenever the number of conflicting objective functions and/or the number of non-dominated solutions in the population is large. In EvABOR (Evolutionary Algorithm Based on an Outranking Relation) approaches preferences are elicited from a decision maker (DM) with the aim of guiding the evolutionary process to the regions of the space more in accordance with the DM's preferences. The preferences are captured and made operational by using the technical parameters of the ELECTRE TRI method. This approach is presented and analyzed using some illustrative results of a case study of electrical networks.

DOI: 10.4018/978-1-4666-4253-9.ch004

1. INTRODUCTION

In real-world multi-objective optimization (MOO) problems, the dimension of the search space is usually very large and irregular due to the number of objective functions to be evaluated and the non-linear and/or combinatorial characteristics of the mathematical model. This leads to a prohibitive computational effort for the characterization of the non-dominated front or, at least, obtaining a well spread non-dominated solution set. Besides this, when the number of conflicting objectives to be dealt with increases, the number of non-dominated solutions also increases significantly. Despite the success of EAs in dealing with these issues (Coello et al., 2002; Deb, 2001), whenever a high number of non-dominated solutions exists the selection operator is usually less effective and the selection of solutions to the next generations becomes practically random thus making the evolutionary process slow (di Pierro et al., 2007; Garza-Fabre et al., 2009; Deb et al., 2010). This further complicates the practical exploitation of results in real-world problems when a solution (or a small set of solutions for further screening) must be chosen, due to the large number of solutions in the non-dominated front that generally occurs.

The difficult characteristics of most real-world MOO problems and the associated issues mentioned above require methodological tools to improve the efficiency and the efficacy of the solution search methods. The incorporation of preferences in EAs aimed at providing decision support in real-world problems presents two main advantages: it contributes to reducing the computational effort by focusing the search on regions of the search space that appear more interesting according to the preferences elicited from a DM, and it reduces the cognitive effort imposed on the DM by offering him/her solutions more in accordance with those expressed preferences and therefore displaying, in principle, more satisfactory trade-offs between the competing objectives (Branke & Deb, 2004; Coello, 2004). As a result, the overall efficiency of the algorithm is increased, as well as the effectiveness of the decision support process since the search process has been guided towards a final non-dominated solution (or a reduced set of the most preferred solutions) according to meaningful preference expression mechanisms having in mind a practical implementation.

An EA has been developed which incorporates and makes the preferences elicited from a DM by means of the technical parameters of the ELECTRE TRI method operational during the search process. The version of the algorithm presented in this work (EvABOR-III) is based on an outranking relation combining it with the non-dominance relation.

The motivation to this work has been presented is this section. In Section 2 some issues about the incorporation of preferences in EAs are presented and discussed. The ELECTRE TRI method is briefly described in Section 3 and the EvABOR-III approach is presented in Section 4. The main features of the algorithm are exploited in Section 5 using a case study of electrical networks. Finally, some conclusions are drawn in Section 6.

2. INCORPORATION OF PREFERENCE INFORMATION IN EAs

As in MOO mathematical programming algorithms, the incorporation of preferences into an EA can be done using one of the three main approaches classified in Horn (1997) as *a priori*, *a posteriori* and progressively (interactive).

In the *a priori* approach (Fonseca & Fleming, 1993; Deb, 1999) the preferences are elicited from the DM before the EA starts. A value (or utility) function is usually considered to transform the MOO problem into a scalar optimization problem, in which the single objective function embodies the preference expression parameters. A disadvantage usually pointed out to this approach lies in the fact that it is necessary to elicit all the preference information from the DM without knowledge of the possible alternatives, particularly in complex MOO mathematical models. Other drawbacks at stake in this "scalarization" process are the non-commensurability of objectives (which often cannot be adequately taken into account) and the existence of good compromise solutions in non-convex regions (which may not be effectively searched).

The *a posteriori* approach is the most used in evolutionary multi-objective problems. In this approach the non-dominated front is evaluated exhaustively with the aim of obtaining the whole Pareto-optimal front or at least the best approximation to this front. In *a posteriori* approaches a significant computational effort is generally devoted to the search of solutions that could be uninteresting from a practical point of view and convey no value-added for decision support purposes. The well-known algorithms NSGA-II (Deb et al., 2002), SPEA2 (Zitzler et al., 2002) and PAES (Knowles & Corne, 1999) are examples of *a posteriori* methods, which are aimed at characterizing thoroughly the Pareto-optimal front.

In the progressive (interactive) approach the preferences elicited from the DM are used to guide the search during the evolutionary process (Thiele et al., 2009; Chaudhuri & Deb, 2010; Branke et al., 2010; Deb et al., 2010). It is assumed that those preferences may change over time as more knowledge is gathered, not just about the solution space and the trade-offs at stake between the objective functions, but also about the shaping of a DM's preference structure. That is, the solutions provided by the EA contribute to a preference refinement process that in turn leads to focusing the search in the regions in which solutions more in accordance with the preferences expressed by the DM are located. This enables a learning process of the trade-offs at stake between the competing objectives in different regions of the search space. Interactive approaches may require *a priori* specification of a few preference information parameters, while other parameters may be provided during the evolutionary process. In some interactive algorithms the preferences are elicited based on a set of solutions which are presented to the DM during the evolutionary process. This is the approach used in Branke et al. (2010) and Deb et al. (2010) where, after a certain number of generations, a small set of alternatives is presented to the DM for choosing her/his preferred one or for assessing intensities of preference between pairs of alternatives. Using this information the algorithm determines one (Deb et al., 2010), or more (Branke et al., 2010), value functions and the EA searches for non-dominated solutions compatible with these functions.

The previous classification is done according to the point in the search process at which the incorporation of preferences occurs. Preference information may be incorporated into an EA using distinct sets of technical parameters, which may also be representative of different DM's attitudes. Different processes can be referred to, such as goal attainment (Fonseca & Fleming, 1993) (in which the main idea is to be as close as possible to goals the DM would like to attain in each objective function), the specification of acceptable trade-off between objectives (Branke et al., 2001) (thus using the notion of marginal rates of substitution) and the relative importance between objectives (Cvetkovic & Parmee, 2002; Jin & Sendhoff, 2002) (assigning importance weights to the objectives). In other cases the concept of non-dominance is modified and/or replaced by other constructs (Fernández et al., 2010; Said et al., 2010). Some recent works use an outranking relation (between a pair of alternatives) for preference incorporation into an EA. Rekiek et al. (2000) combines the PROMETHEE II method (Brans & Mareschal, 1986) with an EA to rank each population during the evolutionary process based on preferences elicited *a priori*. Also, Coelho et al. (2003) use PROMETHEE II during the EA, in a new method called PAMUC, to deal with preferences and constraints in an *a priori* approach. An *a posteriori* approach based on concepts of ELECTRE III and PROMETHEE methods is presented in Fonteix et al. (2004). In Parreiras et al., (2006) and Parreiras and Vasconcelos (2007) the PROMETHEE II method, or a modified PROMETHEE II, is also applied in an *a posteriori* manner for further analyzing the solutions in the Pareto optimal front.

In the algorithm proposed herein, an outranking relation is used to enrich the non-dominance relation. The preferences are captured and made operational by using the parameters of the ELECTRE TRI method. The choice of this method relies on the fact that it is devoted to the sorting problem, allowing a comparison of each solution with predefined standards rather than using comparisons between solutions as in methods devoted to the choice and ranking problems as, for example, ELECTRE I and ELECTRE II/III. Another important advantage of ELECTRE TRI is the possibility of using a veto threshold to account for non-compensatory aspects. Although the non-dominance relation is the essential one, it is not sufficient to include further non-controversial elements of the DM's preferences in order to discriminate between non-dominated solutions. As happens with other methods, ELECTRE TRI also allows us to consider the relative importance of each objective function using a set of weights. However, in ELECTRE TRI, these values are scale independent and are truly coefficients of importance assigned to the objective functions and they are not used to build a value function. Also, ELECTRE TRI enables the preference relation to be established in a gradual manner using indifference and preference thresholds and it is possible to express the exigency of the sorting defining a cutting-level. In EvABOR-III all the genetic operators are influenced by the preference expression parameters to guide the evolutionary search to regions of the solution space more in accordance with the preferences elicited from the DM, in order to improve the EA convergence to relevant solutions.

A review of incorporation of preferences in multi-objective evolutionary algorithms as well as some other representative works in this area is presented in Branke (2008), Coello (2004), and Rachmawati and Srinivasan (2006).

3. THE ELECTRE TRI METHOD

The ELECTRE TRI method (Mousseau et al., 2000) belongs to the ELECTRE (Elimination and Choice Translating Reality) family of multi-criteria methods developed by Roy et al. (1996). ELECTRE methods involve two main steps: the construction of an outranking relation and the exploitation of this relation in face of the problem to be dealt with (choice, ranking or sorting). ELECTRE TRI deals with the sorting problem, which consists in assigning each alternative solution to one of a set of pre-defined ordered categories (classes of merit) taking into account multiple evaluation criteria (objective functions, in the EA context). Reference profiles, which may be seen as playing the role of fictitious actions, define the boundaries of each category solutions should be assigned to. Each category C^i is bounded by two reference profiles b_{i-1} and b_i, $i=1,\ldots,n$ for all objective functions g_j, $j=1,\ldots,k$. A solution is assigned to a predefined class based on the magnitude of the difference between its objective function values and the reference profiles, the importance (weight) of each objective function and the level of exigency of the classification.

Other parameters required by the ELECTRE TRI method are a set of indifference, preference and veto thresholds for each criterion and for each reference profile. The aim of indifference (q_j) and preference (p_j) thresholds is to introduce the acceptance of some imprecision when comparing two alternatives by considering them as indifferent if their individual performances in each criterion j differ less than q_j. The transition from indifference to preference changes gradually in a linear manner from q_j to p_j (Figure 1). This acceptance is trans-

Figure 1. Computation of criterion concordance index c_j

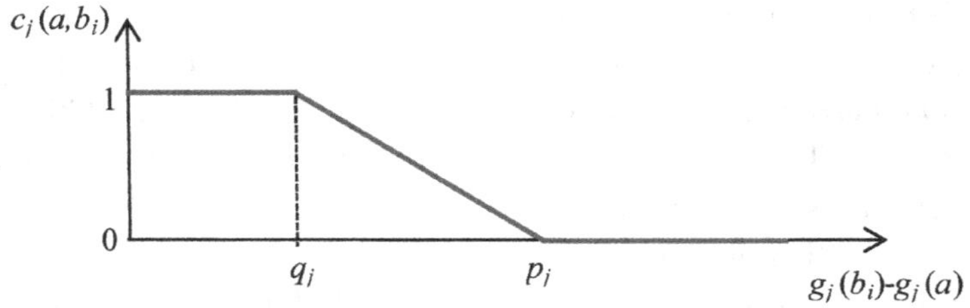

lated by the criterion concordance indexes c_j and is evaluated for each criterion (Equation 1). The veto thresholds (v_j) may prevent an alternative with very bad performance in this criterion from being classified in the best category, or may force it to be classified in the worst category independently of having very good scores in all other criteria. In this way, non-compensatory aspects are included into the evaluation process. The transition from p_j to v_j changes also in a linear manner.

Stating that "alternative a_1 outranks alternative a_2" may be interpreted as "a_1 is at least as good as a_2", in the sense that there are sufficiently strong reasons to confirm this assertion (concordance principle) and there are no impeditive reasons to contradict it (non-discordance principle). The assignment of a given alternative a to a category results from the comparison of its performances in each criterion with the corresponding performances of the reference profiles that bound the categories. The concordance and the non-discordance principles are translated using the concordance c_j and the discordance d_j indexes for each criterion (Equations 1 and 2).

$$c_j\left(a,b_i\right) = min\left\{1, max\left[0, \frac{g_j\left(a\right) - g_j\left(b_i\right) + p_j}{p_j - q_j}\right]\right\} \quad (1)$$

$$d_j\left(a,b_i\right) = min\left\{1, max\left[0, \frac{g_j\left(b_i\right) - g_j\left(a\right) - p_j}{v_j - p_j}\right]\right\} \quad (2)$$

In the pessimistic version of ELECTRE TRI an alternative is assigned to the highest category such that the alternative outranks the category's lower bound. The outranking relation is verified through the comparison of a credibility index (Equation 3), which is computed using the differences in performances and the criterion weights w_j, with a cutting-level λ defining the exigency of the classification (the "majority requirement" for the concordant criteria). In the framework of ELECTRE methods, weights take in the meaning of genuine coefficients of importance assigned to the criteria, expressing the "voting power" of each criterion for the "coalition" of criteria deciding the validity of the outranking relation. That is, they are not used as technical parameters for aggregating the criteria in a scalar function and computing a common value measure as in weighted-sum approaches. Therefore, weights in ELECTRE TRI are scale-independent, which facilitates their elicitation from DMs.

The credibility index is given by

$$\left(a,b_i\right) = C\left(a,b_i\right)\prod_{j\in S}\frac{1 - d_j\left(a,b_i\right)}{1 - C\left(a,b_i\right)} \quad (3)$$

where $C\left(a,b_i\right)$ is the global concordance index defined as $C\left(a,b_i\right) = \frac{\sum_{j=1}^{k} w_j . c_j\left(a,b_i\right)}{\sum_{j=1}^{k} w_j}$ and S is the subset of the criteria for which the discordance index (Equation 2) is larger than the global concordance index.

The use of the ELECTRE TRI method requires the setting of a non-negligible number of those technical parameters that convey the preference information elicited from the DM: criterion weights, reference profiles establishing the bounds between the categories, cutting-level, as well as indifference, preference and veto thresholds for each criterion. These parameters embody the preference information into the sorting process, and they should be elicited from the DM (with the help of an analyst with technical expertise who is able to mediate this communication). The elicitation of these parameters may require an important (cognitive) effort from the DM. Nevertheless, some of those values can be predetermined thus easing the DM effort for their specification; for instance, indifference and preference thresholds can be fixed as percentages (e.g., 2% and 10%, respectively) of the value ranges in each category.

For further operational details about the ELECTRE TRI method see Mousseau et al. (2000).

4. THE EvABOR-III APPROACH

In the EvABOR-III approach the non-dominance relation is enriched by an outranking relation, in order to capture and include the DM's preferences into the EA. One of the main goals is not losing solutions more in accordance with the preferences elicited, as could happen with an algorithm based on the non-dominance relation only (Oliveira & Antunes, 2010a). The preferences are captured by using the parameters of the ELECTRE TRI method and are then included in the operational framework of the EA.

The evolutionary process of EvABOR-III is performed using modified genetic operators (crossover, mutation and selection) in order to include the preference information. The selection operator has an important role in EvABOR-III guaranteeing that non-dominated solutions belonging to the best class of merit in the population remain in the next generation. The crossover and the mutation operators are also modified to improve the convergence of the algorithm to the regions of the search space in agreement with the preference expression.

Figure 2 displays the pseudo-code of the main function of EvABOR-III. The initial population is generated randomly and the evolutionary process is applied until a non-dominated set belonging to the best class of merit is obtained or a maximum number of iterations is reached. The non-dominated solutions in the final population are sorted into classes of merit. This classification results directly from the selection operator and no post-evaluation is necessary.

The idea underlying the crossover operator is that parents that better fulfill the DM's preferences have more probability of producing offspring with the same characteristics. Consequently, in EvABOR-III, solutions that belong to the best class of merit have a higher probability of being selected as a parent. A binary tournament process is used to choose each one of the parents (Figure 3). An advantage of the binary tournament process is that all individuals compete to be one of the parents. The crossover operator is applied according to the crossover probability and a 2-point crossover has been implemented to obtain the offspring.

In EvABOR-III several mutation operators are implemented being this mutation operator portfolio strongly dependent on the physical characteristics of the problem to be tackled. The choice of one of these operators is based on the criterion discordance indexes (evaluated in ELECTRE TRI). These values provide information about which objective function has the worst performance according to the DM's preferences. So, the mutation operators that could improve the objective function with worst performance have more probability of being chosen. The mutation operator is then applied according to the mutation probability as usual.

Figure 2. Pseudo-code of the main function of EvABOR-III

```
Generate randomly the initial population
Sort the initial population using the ELECTRE TRI method
while not Stop condition
        prob_cross = random number ∈ [0,1]
        if prob_cross <= crossover probability
                Apply the modified crossover
        end
        prob_mut = random number ∈ [0,1]
        if prob_mut <= mutation probability
                Evaluate the criterion discordance indexes of the offspring set
                Apply the modified mutation
        end
Select the next generation
end
Select non-dominated solutions from population, if necessary
```

Figure 3. Pseudo-code to choose one of the parents for the crossover operator in EvABOR-III

```
p_1 = permutation of the population
p_2 = other permutation of the population
dim_pop = dimension of the population
for i =1 to dim_pop
        if class of (p_1(i)) > class of (p_2(i))
                parent_1 = p_1(i)
        elseif class of (p_1(i)) < class of (p_2(i))
                parent_1 = p_2(i)
        else choose the solution that has better values for more objective functions
        end
end
```

The selection operator implemented is similar to the one used in NSGA-II (Deb et al., 2002) but in EvABOR-III it combines the non-dominance relation with the outranking relation. First, the set of non-dominated solutions is selected from the population (parents and offspring). The procedure depends on the number of non-dominated solutions in the population. If the number of non-dominated solutions is larger than the dimension of the population, then the non-dominated solutions are filtered using the outranking relation and solutions belonging to the best class of merit are chosen to pass to the next generation (Figure 4). If these solutions are not enough to complete the population, the solutions that belong to the next class of merit are chosen and this process is repeated until the population reaches the dimension defined. When a class of merit has more solutions than necessary, they are selected according to the setting of the EvABOR-III parameter α. If $\alpha=0$ then a random process is used to select the solutions from that class. If α=1 then an elitist process is used: a set of solutions that provide the best values for each objective function are chosen, its number being directly proportional to the weight of each objective function. Therefore, functions that the DM considers more important have more solutions favouring that objective in the next generation. A value of $\alpha \in]0,1[$ means that $(1-\alpha).NS$ solutions are randomly chosen and $\alpha.NS$ are chosen from the ones that have the best values for each objective function (always proportionally to the weight of each objective function). *NS* denotes the necessary number of solutions to complete the next generation.

If the number of non-dominated solutions is lower than the dimension of the population then all these solutions pass to the next generation and the population is completed with dominated solutions. The dominated solutions are sorted into classes of merit and the solutions belonging to the best classes of merit pass to the next generation. The procedure applied is similar to the one described before for the non-dominated solutions (Figure 4).

Figure 4. Scheme of selection of the next generation from non-dominated solutions in EvABOR-III

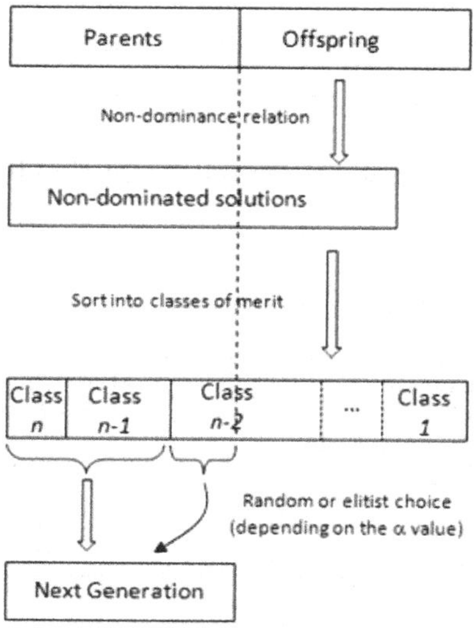

If the number of non-dominated solutions is equal to the dimension of the population then the next generation consists of these solutions.

The structure of EvABOR-III is modular, which means that the algorithm is prepared to use other type of multi-criteria approaches to replace (or to complement) the method used in this work. In these circumstances, the modules that use ELECTRE TRI may be replaced, for instance, the function that selects the parents to the crossover, the function that identifies the mutation operator within the portfolio and/or the one that determines the individuals that pass to the next generation.

In each generation the outranking relation is assessed using the performances of each individual according to each objective function and the corresponding values of each reference profile. Consequently, for a population of m individuals, r reference profiles and k objective functions the computational effort of the outranking relation involves $m.r.k$ comparison operators. It is important to note that r and k values are, in general, low. One advantage of ELECTRE TRI over other methods is the lower number of pairwise comparisons, since these are made between each individual and the reference profiles rather than other methods where the pairwise comparisons are made between all the individuals.

5. ILLUSTRATIVE RESULTS FROM A REACTIVE POWER COMPENSATION PROBLEM

In this section some illustrative results are presented to show the influence of the preference information parameters elicited from the DM on the results generated by the EA. The EvABOR-III approach is applied to an MOO problem of reactive power compensation in an electrical distribution network. The network does not respect some quality of service requirements related to the voltage in peak conditions. Therefore, shunt capacitors (local sources of reactive power) must be installed in the network. The MOO problem consists in determining the network nodes at which the capacitors should be installed and the corresponding types to minimize the costs of installation, resistive power losses and the maximum voltage deviation with respect to nominal values in the network. Eight types of capacitors are considered with capacities in the range 50 kVAr to 400 kVAr and cost in the range 2035€ to 9395€. Model constraints include power flow equations and technical restrictions limiting the maximum number of capacitors that may be installed. A similar mathematical model considering only two objective functions (cost and resistive power losses) has been developed in Antunes et al. (2009) in which the voltage deviation has been considered as a constraint.

The solution encoding is an array with 94 positions, each one corresponding to a network node. A zero value means that no capacitor is installed at this node and a non-zero value (an integer belonging to the interval [1,8]) provides the information about the type of capacitor to be installed in the corresponding position. Five mutation operators have been developed for this specific problem (Oliveira & Antunes, 2010a, 2010b), each one with a well-defined physical meaning in the context of the problem.

Several preference expression scenarios have been considered for evaluating the performance of EvABOR-III. These scenarios represent different DM's stances, which are captured by the ELECTRE TRI parameters. In Table 1 and Table 2 the reference profiles and the threshold values that make operational the DM's preferences are presented. In this scenario, the importance of each objective function, and consequently the corresponding weights, is considered the same. The level of exigency of the classification, captured by the cutting-level λ, is 0.5 (the minimum level of exigency, that is a simple majority of criteria). According to the reference profiles defined the solutions shall be sorted into 5 classes of merit (the best class is class 5). The probabilities of the crossover and the mutation operators are 1 and 0.2, respectively. Populations with different sizes are considered for this scenario.

The desirable situation would be obtaining solutions with performances lower than the inferior reference profiles (or, at least, near these values) in all objective functions, as happens with the solution marked with a red asterisk in Figure 5. In this case the solution will be clearly classified in class 5. However, due to the conflicting nature of the objective functions the previous situation is in general very difficult to obtain. Despite this, it is possible to achieve solutions belonging to the best class of merit with different but yet satisfactory (according to the preferences elicited) trade-offs between the objective functions. For example, the solution marked with a green rectangle in Figure 5 belongs also to class 5. However, the value of the maximum voltage deviation is high (0.07147) when compared with the inferior reference profile. As, in this scenario, the cutting-level is 0.5 and the veto threshold is high (0.08), it does not preclude the solution from being classified in the best class of merit.

Based on the weight of each objective function, the reference profiles, the thresholds and the cutting-level, the ELECTRE-TRI method has the capability to classify solutions with different trade-offs between the objective functions. For example, the solution marked with a blue circle in Figure 5 has different performances in the three objective functions. Based on the technical parameters elicited from the DM the solution is classified in class 3. A similar situation is repre-

Table 1. Reference profiles

Resistive Losses (kW)	Cost (€)	Maximum Voltage Deviation (p.u.)
240	38000	0.01
260	60000	0.03
290	85000	0.065
320	100000	0.09

Table 2. Threshold values

	Resistive Losses (kW)	Cost (€)	Maximum Voltage Deviation (p.u.)
Indifference	5	8000	0.005
Preference	10	15000	0.01
Veto	30	40000	0.08

sented with a pink triangle, but in this case the solution is classified in class 4. In fact, in the first case the discordance criteria index is greater than in the second one, which forces the solution to be classified in the class 3 instead of class 4.

The α parameter controls the level of elitism when solutions are chosen within the same class of merit. The results for 100 and 200 iterations, with a population size of 50 and 100 individuals and different values for the α parameter are summarized in Tables 3-5. The main conclusions are similar for both situations regarding the number of iterations. EvABOR-III provides better results obtaining a higher number of solutions in the best classes of merit with fewer iterations when α=0, which means that the solutions are picked from the different classes randomly. The increase of the α parameter leads to a sort of speciation process in which niches of solutions are created, located near the areas of the search space where the objective functions attain their optimal values (Figure 6 (a)), slowing the evolutionary process. In this case the algorithm needs some more time to achieve the region more in accordance with the preferences elicited from the DM. This niche effect tends to disappear with the increase of the number of iterations (Figure 6 (b)). The optimal values obtained for each objective functions are achieved considering α=1 (Table 5). This result is expected due to the fact that solutions that pass to the next generation are chosen from the classes of merit in an elitist manner.

Figures 7 and 8 present the evolution of the population concerning the number of non-dominated solutions and the number of solutions that

Figure 5. Examples of classification of solutions using ELECTRE TRI

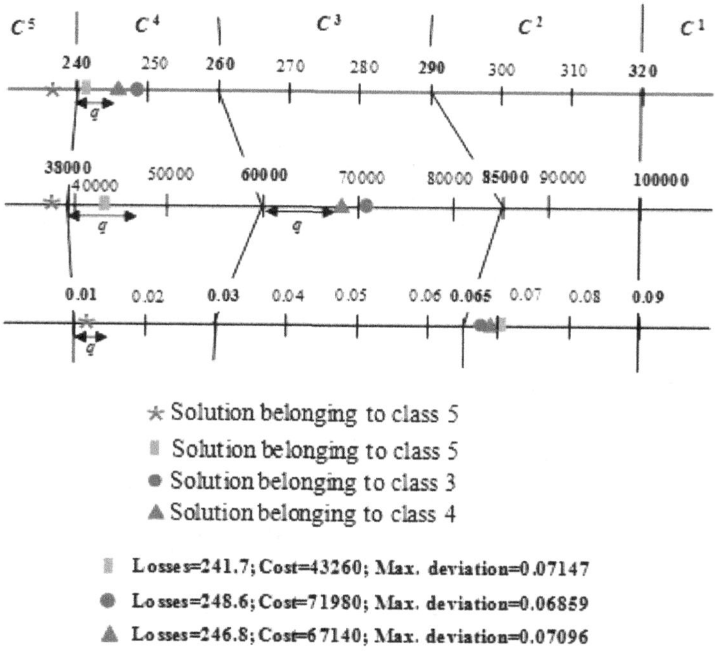

Table 3. Average results from 30 runs with a maximum of 100 iterations

Dimension of the Population	50			100		
α	0	0.5	1	0	0.5	1
Dimension of the non-dominated front	50	50	50	100	100	100
No. of executed iterations	99.47	100	100	95.63	99.07	99.47
No. of solutions in class 5	11.33	2.40	1.23	85.43	18.60	44.53
No. of solutions in class 4	38.67	47.60	48.77	14.57	81.40	55.47

Table 4. Average results from 30 runs with a maximum of 200 iterations

Dimension of the Population	50			100		
α	0	0.5	1	0	0.5	1
Dimension of the non-dominated front	50	50	50	100	100	100
No. of executed iterations	136.56	192.06	196.23	112.53	147.86	174.36
No. of solutions in class 5	44.6	22.03	11.9	98.67	98.63	83.7
No. of solutions in class 4	5.4	27.97	38.1	1.33	1.37	16.3

Table 5. Average values of the objective functions from 30 runs with a maximum of 200 iterations

Dimension of the Population		50			100		
α		0	0.5	1	0	0.5	1
Losses	Minimum	240.85	237.03	236.48	240.29	240.31	238.77
	Maximum	246.41	262.72	264.78	246.29	246.48	253.97
	Average	243.26	247.39	251.23	243.12	243.27	245.02
	Standard deviation	1.41	7.47	10.91	1.46	1.57	4.29
Cost	Minimum	42253	27265	24738	41662	41193	33854
	Maximum	49688	66893	68705	47510	48004	56652
	Average	46244	49810	51883	45151	45353	46643
	Standard deviation	1746.2	11464.9	17565.4	1391.1	1611.9	5976.0
Maximum Voltage Deviation	Minimum	0.0654	0.0488	0.0472	0.0655	0.0650	0.0580
	Maximum	0.0737	0.0886	0.0902	0.0728	0.0731	0.0803
	Average	0.0698	0.0696	0.0700	0.0695	0.0693	0.0694
	Standard deviation	0.0020	0.0101	0.0151	0.0018	0.0020	0.0054

remain in the population from one generation to the next ("equal solutions") during the evolutionary process. When $\alpha = 1$ (Figure 7) the number of solutions that remain in the population from one generation to the next is high and the algorithm has more difficulty in producing new solutions to improve the convergence to obtain solutions belonging to the best class of merit. For α=0 that number is lower when compared with the situation α=1, which indicates the algorithm's capability to generate more new solutions increasing the convergence to the region of the search space more in accordance with the DM's preferences (Figure 8). Another interesting aspect unveiled in Figure 8 is the increase of the number of solutions that remain in the population with the increase of the number of solutions belonging to the best class of merit. This aspect is clear when comparing Figures 8 and 9, which display the evolution of the population as far as classes of merit are concerned. As presented in Tables 3 and 4, in all runs the number of solutions in the non-dominated front is equal to the dimension of the population. This is due to the large number of non-dominated solutions in the population from early iterations (Figures 7 to 9) which is a common situation in problems with several contradictory objectives.

Although in this scenario $\alpha = 0$ is the value that leads to the best results, it must be noted that with other parameters a value of α near 0.5 (that is, just 50% of the solutions are randomly obtained within the same class of merit) gave the best results (Oliveira & Antunes, 2010a). Therefore, α in the interval [0, 0.5] provides the best results according to our experiments. A general situation that arises in all scenarios is the fact that values of α near 1 lead to an excessive elitism and never provide the best results. In the remaining examples the α parameter is considered equal to 0 since the best results in previous runs have been obtained using this value.

As described in Section 4, the parents for the crossover operator are selected using a tournament technique. In this procedure the parents that are more in accordance with the preferences elicited are chosen to generate the next generation. Figure 10 presents the percentages of parents chosen according to the condition: belong to the best class or present better performance in more objective functions. These values are the average from 30 runs with 100 individuals and a maximum of 100 iterations. The other parameters are the ones considered in the initial scenario (Tables 1 and 2) and the crossover and mutation probabilities are 1 and 0.2, respectively.

Figure 6. α=1 and different maximum number of iterations: (a) 100 (b) 200

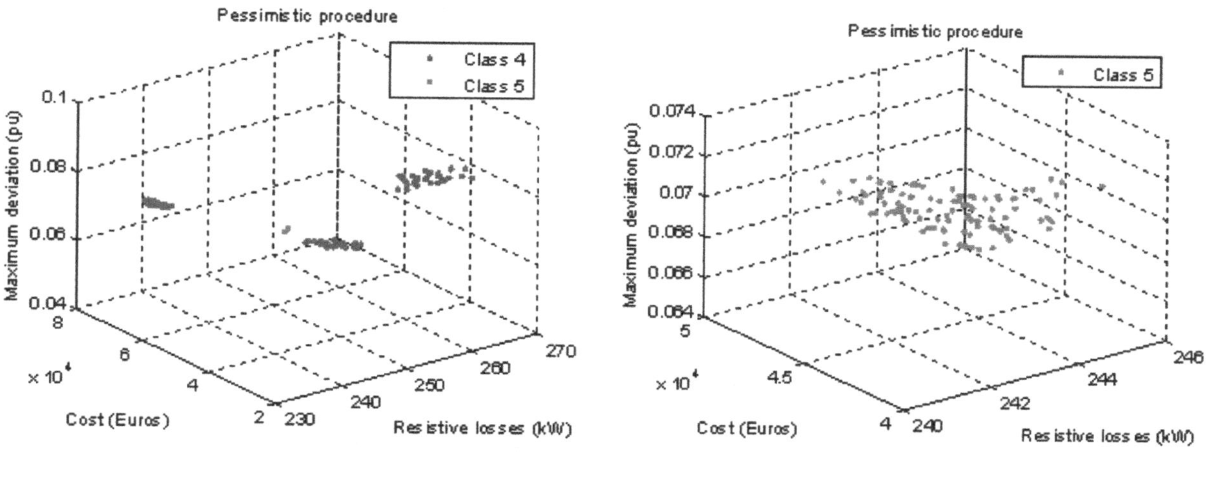

Figure 7. Evolution of the population during the evolutionary process (α=1)

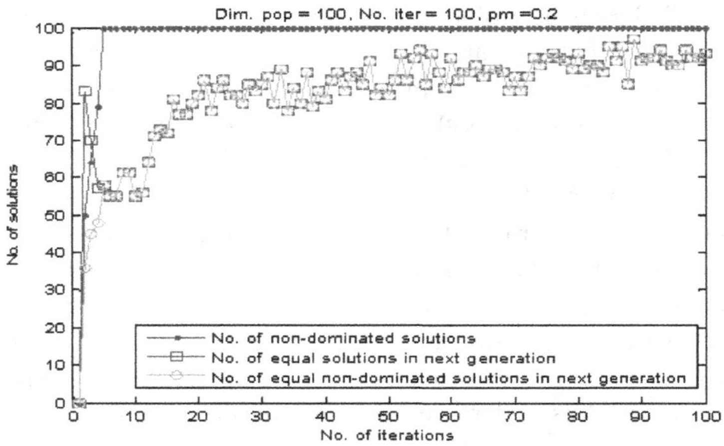

The analysis of these percentages during the evolutionary process enables to conclude that when the number of classes decreases the parents tend to be chosen according to their performance in the objective functions (Figures 9 and 11).

However, the previous percentages strongly depend on several factors, such as the maximum number of classes (a higher number of classes increases the probability to have more than one class in a particular generation), the number of classes in each generation and the maximum number of iterations.

To analyse the influence of weights in EvA-BOR-III, three different situations have been considered: - all the objective functions have the same weight (weighting vector=[100/3, 100/3, 100/3]); - the loss function has the largest weight (weighting vector=[60, 20, 20]); - the cost function has the largest weight (weighting vector=[20, 60, 20]). Figure 12 shows 3D and 2D plots of the non-dominated front obtained from runs with the three situations described before. Comparing the regions highlighted with a green dashed rectangle in Figure 12 ((b), (d) and (f)), it can be seen that

Figure 8. Evolution of the population during the evolutionary process (α=0)

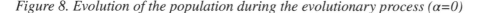

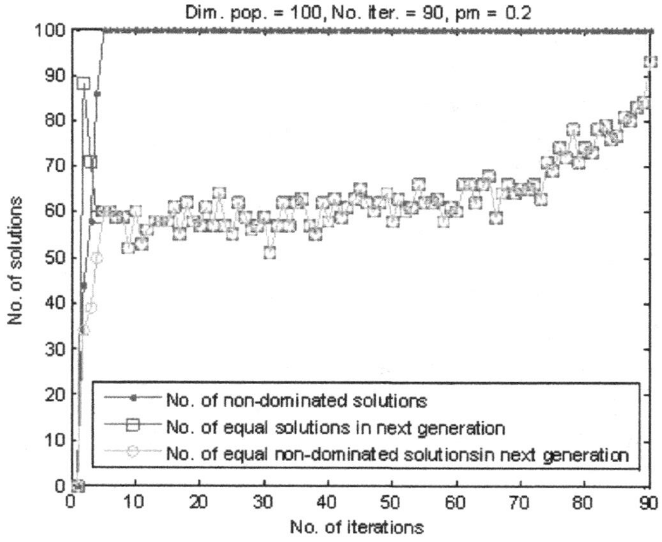

Figure 9. Evolution of the population by classes of merit (α=0)

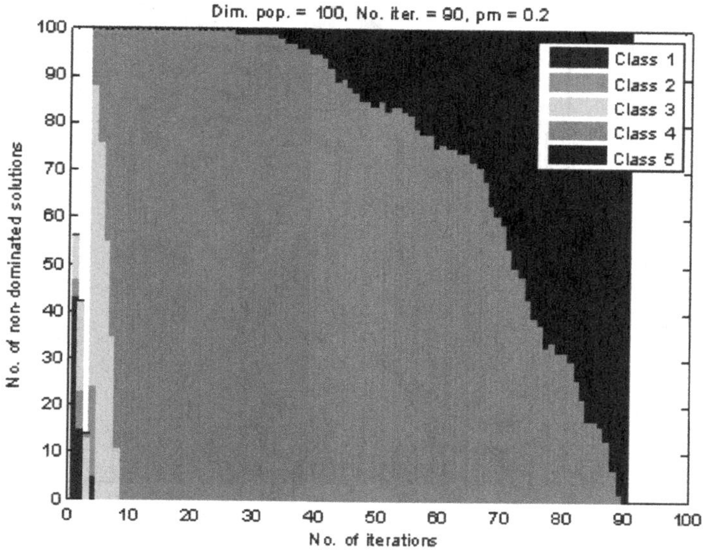

the solutions computed are predominantly located in regions of the search space in agreement with the preference information conveyed by these weights. For instance, when resistive losses is the objective function with higher weight there is a predominance of solutions with lower losses (Figure 12 (d)) with respect to the other cases and there are no solutions in the region with higher loss values (marked by a blue rectangle). However, if the cost is considered as the most important objective function, EvABOR-III obtains more

Figure 10. Selection of the parents for tournament

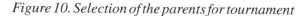

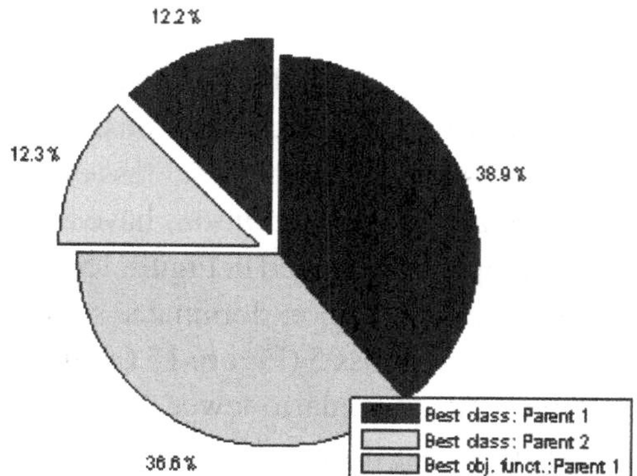

solutions in the region of the search space with minimum cost (see the zone within the ellipse). A similar conclusion can be reached by analyzing the representation of the statistical data in Figure 13. More information from 30 runs (average values) is provided in Table 6. The components of the weighting vector refer to the resistive losses, cost, and voltage deviation objective functions, respectively. The EvABOR-III approach has more facility to obtain solutions in the best class of merit when the objective function with a large weight is the resistive losses (Table 6). In this situation the number of iterations to obtain all the solutions in the non-dominated front belonging to the best class of merit is lower than in the other situations. It is also possible to verify that the minimum values for each objective function are obtained when the corresponding weight is the highest.

The veto threshold is an important parameter in ELECTRE TRI. This parameter precludes a solution having a bad performance in a given objective function from being classified in the best class of merit even if its performance is very good in the other objective functions. EvABOR-

Figure 11. Selection of the parents for tournament during the evolutionary process

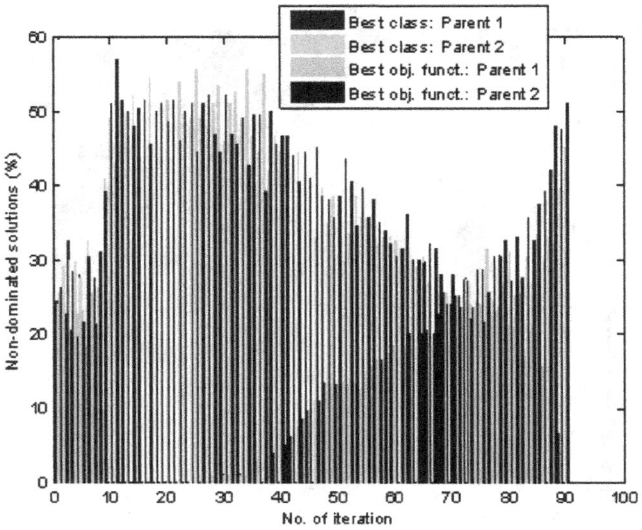

III has been tested with distinct veto thresholds for each objective function. Different values for the veto threshold (0.08, 0.075 and 0.04) for the maximum voltage deviation objective are presented below for illustrative purposes. All other parameters are the same in all runs (Tables 1 and 2). The three values of the veto threshold have distinct impacts on the results. While the less demanding value practically does not influence the sorting of solutions into categories, a slightly more demanding value (0.075) already prevents most solutions from being classified in the best class of merit. A strongly more demanding value (0.04) shows a situation where no solution obtained is classified in the best class of merit. Figure 14 shows two similar solutions classified in different classes of merit (class 5 in (a) and class 4 in (b)) due to the different values of the veto threshold. When the veto threshold is 0.08 the solution is classified in class 5. However, when this threshold is a little more demanding (0.075) a similar solution is classified in class 4. For a more demanding value for this threshold (0.04) all solutions in the non-dominated front belong to the class 4. Table 7 summarises some results from 30 runs with different veto thresholds for the maximum voltage deviation objective function. Note that when the veto threshold is 0.08 EvABOR-III obtains a non-dominated set with almost all solutions belonging to class 5.

The role of the indifference and the preference thresholds is translated in a larger or a lower acceptance of the difference between the performances of a solution with the respective reference profiles. To illustrate this situation, new values for the indifference and the preference thresholds are considered for the cost objective function (6000€ and 10000€, respectively). All the other parameters are the same as in Tables 1 and 2.

In this scenario, for a solution to be classified in the best class of merit it is necessary that the value of the cost objective function is nearer to the inferior reference profile for this objective function (38000€) than in the initial scenario. Consequently, the number of solutions in the best class of merit tends to decrease but these solutions have a lower cost. An example is presented in Figure 15, where in the initial scenario all non-dominated solutions obtained belong to class 5 (Figure 15 (a) and (b)) and in the modified scenario fewer solutions are obtained in this class (Figure 15 (c) and (d)). Table 8 presents the average values from 30 runs. In the

Figure 12. Impacts of different weights in the EvaBOR-III results

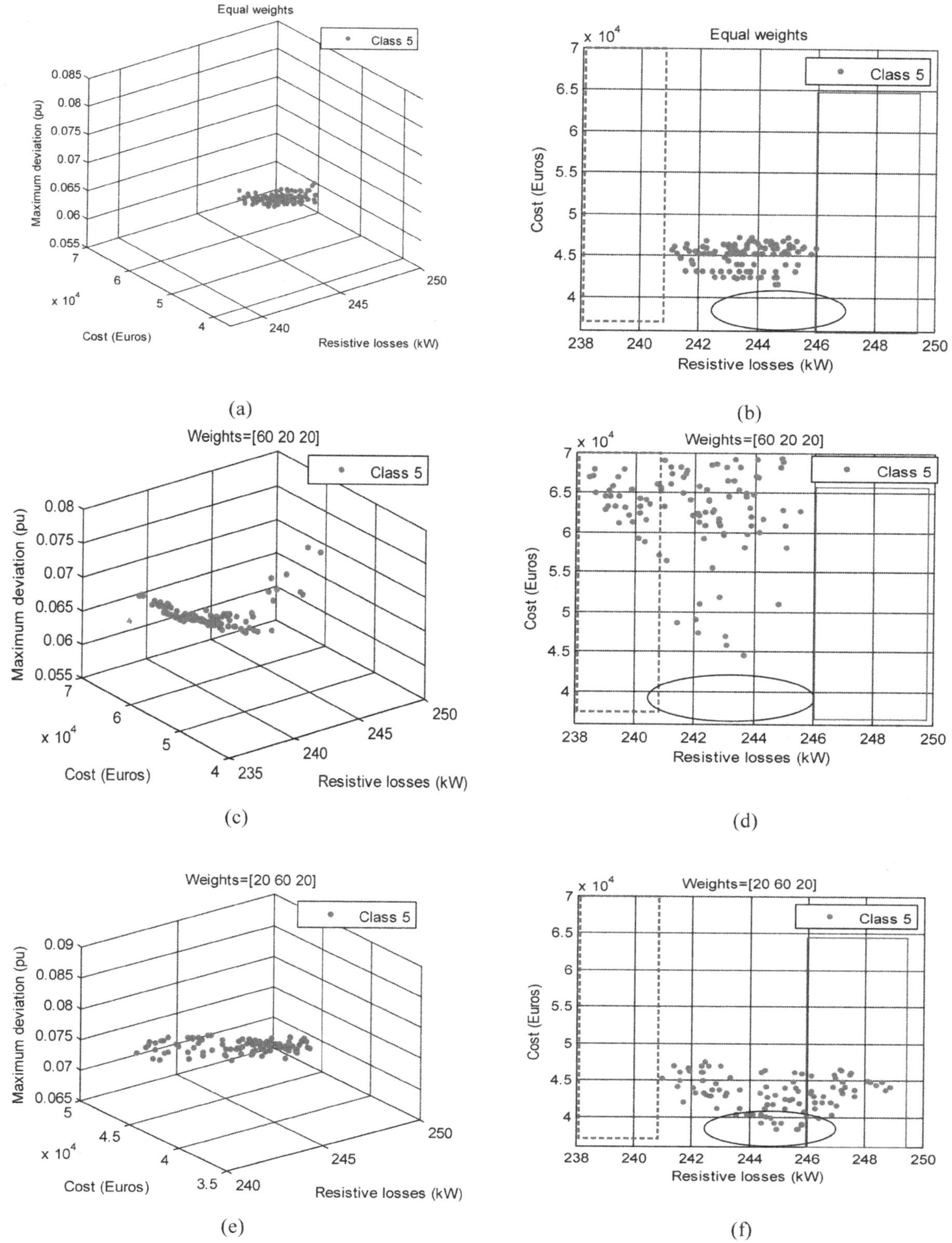

Figure 13. Statistical data representation for resistive losses (a) and cost (b)

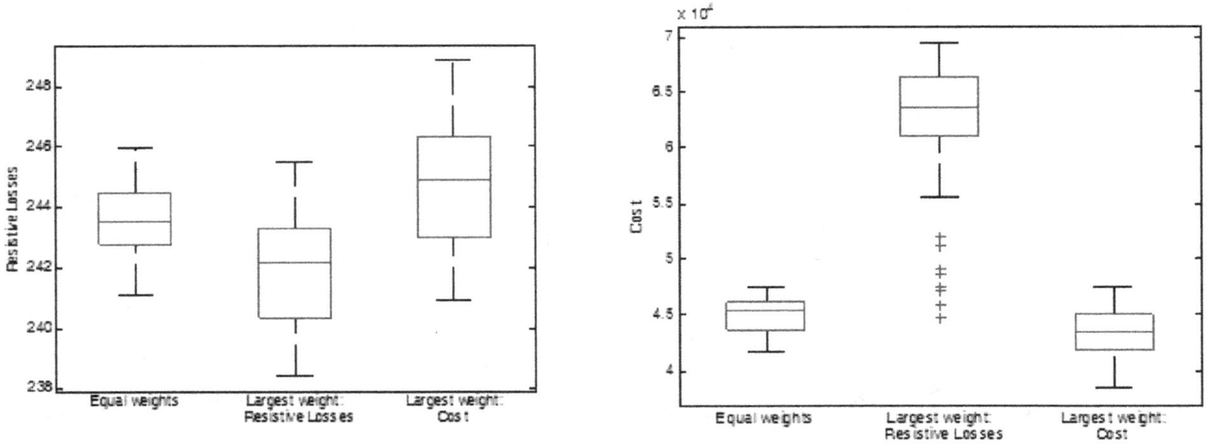

a b

Table 6. Average values from 30 runs and different weight values

Weight Vector		[100/3 100/3 100/3]	[60 20 20]	[20 60 20]
Maximum no. of iterations		200	200	200
No. of executed iterations		112.53	21	30.86
Dimension of the population		100	100	100
Dimension of the non-dominated front		100	100	100
No. of solutions in class 5		98.67	100	100
No. of solutions in class 4		1.33	0	0
No. of solutions in class 3		0	0	0
No. of solutions in class 2		0	0	0
No. of solutions in class 1		0	0	0
Losses	Minimum	240.29	239.31	239.89
	Maximum	246.29	245.50	253.90
	Average	243.12	242.60	243.87
	Standard deviation	1.46	1.56	2.57
Cost	Minimum	41662.37	41611.5	37316.5
	Maximum	47509.63	69232.03	47829.6
	Average	45151.14	58896.6	43322.5
	Standard deviation	1391.1	7297.6	2654.1
Maximum Voltage Deviation	Minimum	0.06547	0.05848	0.06566
	Maximum	0.07281	0.08027	0.08097
	Average	0.06953	0.06586	0.07436
	Standard deviation	0.0018	0.0054	0.0036

Figure 14. Comparative examples for different veto thresholds

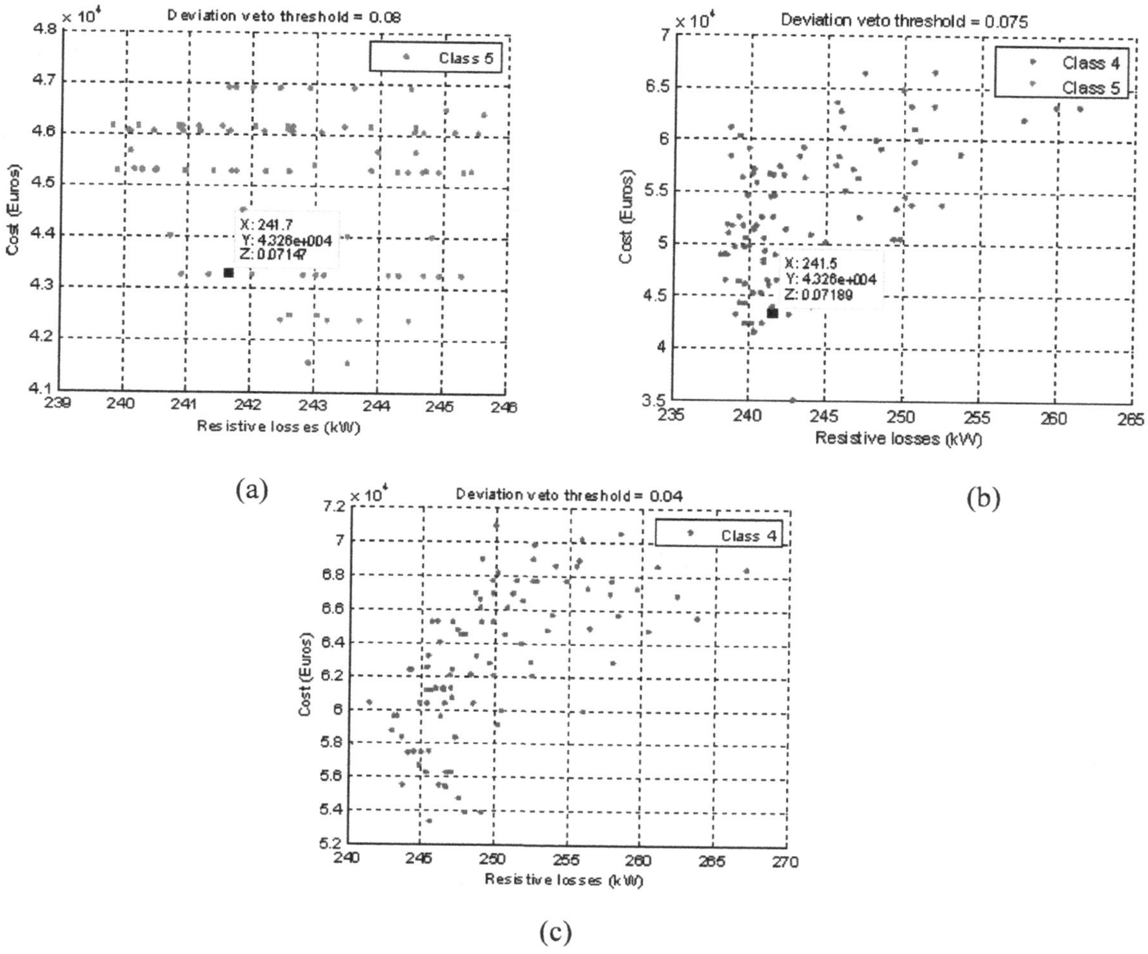

Table 7. Average values from 30 runs with different deviation veto thresholds

Deviation Veto Threshold	0.08	0.075	0.04
Maximum no. of iterations	200	200	200
No. of executed iterations	112.53	200	200
Dimension of the population	100	100	100
Dimension of the non-dominated front	100	100	100
No. of solutions in class 5	98.67	14.3	0
No. of solutions in class 4	1.33	85.7	100

Figure 15. Illustrative example of the indifference and the preference thresholds influence in EvABOR-III

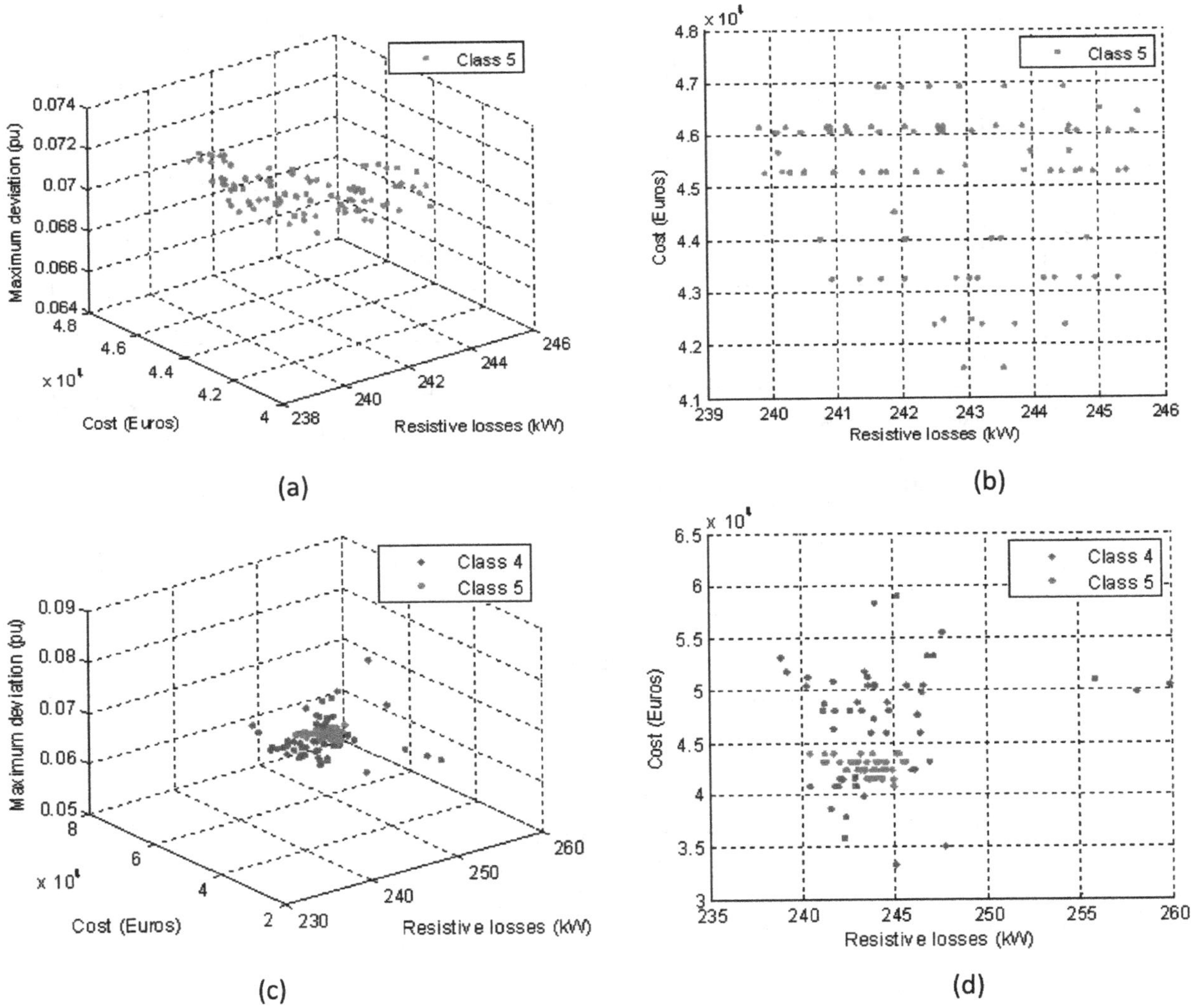

Table 8. Average values from 30 runs with different indifference and preference thresholds

Indifference and Preference Thresholds	**Initial Scenario** q_{cost} **=8000€** p_{cost} **=15000€**	**New Scenario** q_{cost} **=6000€** p_{cost} **=10000€**
Maximum no. of iterations	200	200
Average no. of executed iterations	112.53	200
Dimension of the population	100	100
Dimension of the non-dominated front	100	100
Average no. of solutions in class 5	98.67	47.27
Average no. of solutions in class 4	1.33	52.73

Figure 16. Illustrative example of the cutting-level influence in EvABOR-III

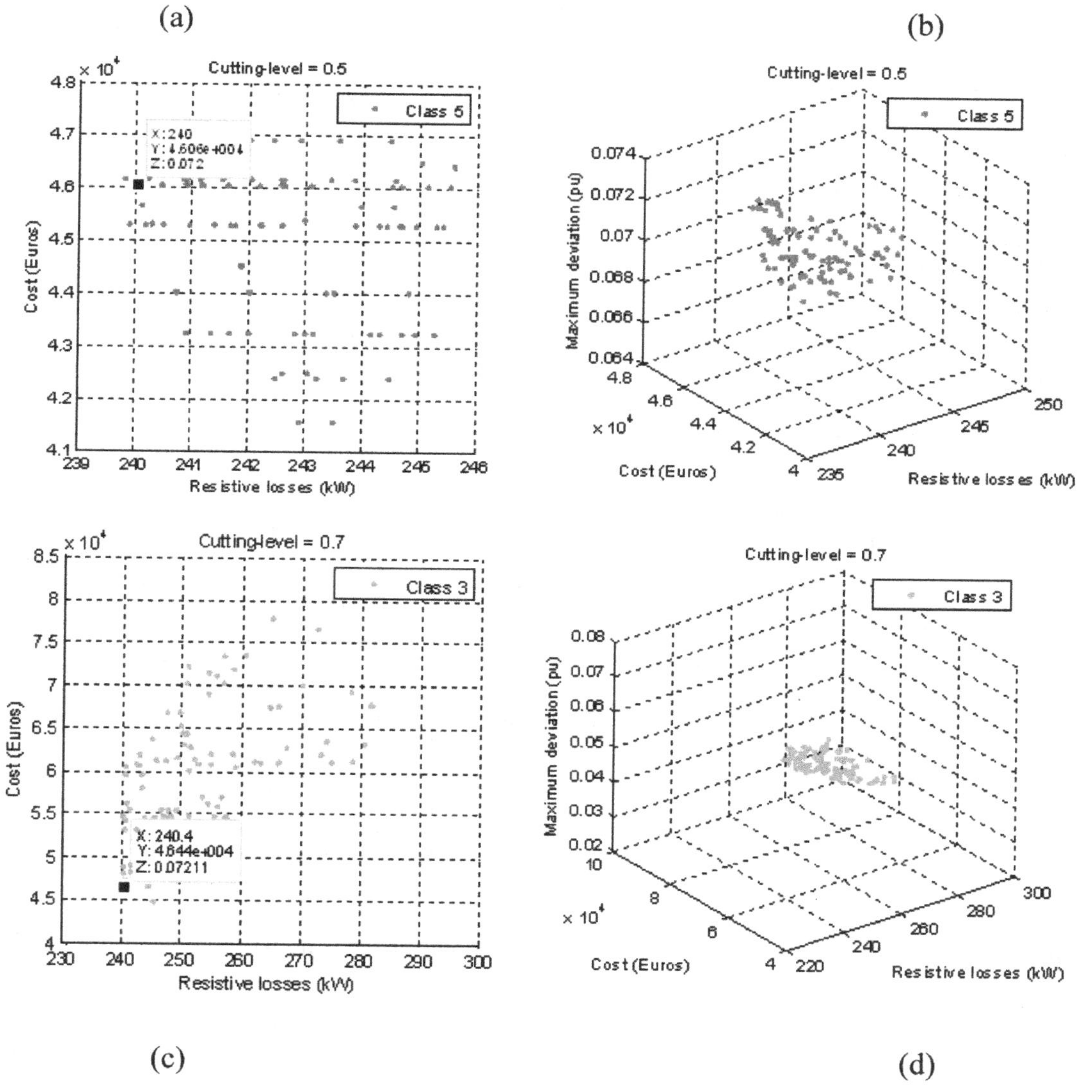

new scenario just about 47% of the solutions are classified in the best class of merit while in the initial scenario about 98% of the solutions are in this class and are obtained without achieving the maximum number of iterations.

The level of exigency of the classification (majority requirement) is defined by the cutting-level λ. The minimum value of λ has been considered in the first scenario presented (see results in Tables 3 through 5). When the cutting-level λ is increased to 0.7, solutions found by EvABOR-III are classified in different classes of merit (Figure 16). In this case a majority requiring two objective functions is necessary. For this reason, for instance, solution (240.4; 46440; 0.07211) is not classified in class 5 (Figure 16 (c)) but a similar solution (240; 46060; 0.072) is classified in class 5 when λ is equal to 0.5 (Figure 16 (a)).

Table 9 shows the average results for 30 runs with population sizes of 50 and 100 and a maxi-

Table 9. Average values from 30 runs and different cutting-level values

Cutting-Level Value		0.5	0.7	0.5	0.7
Dimension of the population		50		100	
Maximum no. of iterations		200	200	200	200
No. of executed iterations		136.57	200	112.53	200
Dimension of the non-dominated front		50	50	100	100
No. of solutions in class 5		44.6	0	98.67	0
No. of solutions in class 4		5.4	0	1.33	0
No. of solutions in class 3		0	50	0	100
No. of solutions in class 2		0	0	0	0
No. of solutions in class 1		0	0	0	0
Losses	Minimum	240.85	238.13	240.29	237.87
	Maximum	246.41	264.27	246.29	270.50
	Average	243.26	244.30	243.12	244.97
	Standard deviation	1.41	5.90	1.46	6.40
Cost	Minimum	42253.5	47798.7	41662.4	44610.7
	Maximum	49688.4	75556.7	47509.6	76674.2
	Average	46243.6	59923.4	45151.1	58437.3
	Standard deviation	1746.2	6365.6	1391.1	6702.2
Maximum Voltage Deviation	Minimum	0.06538	0.04563	0.06548	0.04148
	Maximum	0.07369	0.07289	0.07281	0.07381
	Average	0.06985	0.06207	0.06953	0.06113
	Standard deviation	0.00202	0.00647	0.00180	0.00700

mum number of iterations equal to 200. It is possible to see that when the cutting-level λ=0.7 the algorithm was not able to compute solutions belonging to the best class of merit even using all the maximum number of iterations allowed, while when λ=0.5 it was able to identify a significant number of solutions belonging to the best class even without using up all the iterations.

The computational effort associated with the main operations within EvABOR-III is analyzed from a set of 30 runs performed considering the parameters presented in Tables 1 and 2. The average percentage of the CPU time devoted to each task in each generation is evaluated. As it was expected the larger percentage of time (56.51%) is expended in the power flow algorithm which computes the (active and reactive) power and the voltage at each network node resulting from a given compensation scheme (that is, a solution representing a given location and sizing of the capacitors). The average percentage of time devoted to the outranking relation is 8.24% of the total time, considering all the steps in which preferences are used (crossover, mutation and selection operators). As the non-dominance relation is only performed in the selection operator it consumes 0.91% of the total time. The crossover, mutation and the selection operators spend 3.95%, 1.29% and 0.27%, respectively. The remaining time is consumed in other auxiliary tasks.

The average time expended in a run is 25.8 seconds. The experiments are done in a Core 2 Duo, 2.80 GHz with 4GB of RAM and the algorithm has been developed using Matlab® R2008b software.

6. CONCLUSION

EvABOR-III is an evolutionary algorithm that incorporates the preferences elicited from a DM using the parameters of the ELECTRE TRI method devoted to multi-criteria sorting problems. The aim is to use meaningful preference information to guide the evolutionary process to the regions of the search space more in accordance with the preferences elicited from the DM, thus minimizing both the computational effort in computing non-dominated solutions and the cognitive effort required to process an exhaustive characterization of the Pareto optimal frontier for practical decision support purposes.

The parameters of the ELECTRE TRI method make the preferences operational in the evolutionary process. Experiments carried out with real-world problems, namely in electrical networks, reveal that this EA based on an outranking relation has the capability of providing solutions in agreement with different preference expressions that capture distinct attitudes from the DM.

REFERENCES

Antunes, C. H., Barrico, C., Gomes, A., Pires, D. F., & Martins, A. G. (2009). An evolutionary algorithm for reactive power compensation in radial distribution networks. *Applied Energy*, *86*, 977–984. doi:10.1016/j.apenergy.2008.09.008.

Branke, J. (2008). Consideration of a partial user preferences in evolutionary multi-objective optimization. In J. Branke, K. Deb, K. Miettinen, & R. Slowinski (Eds.), *Proceedings of the Conference on Multiobjective Optimization - Interactive and Evolutionary Approaches* (LNCS 5252, pp. 157-178).

Branke, J., & Deb, K. (2004). Integrating user preferences into evolutionary multi-objective optimization. In Jin, Y. (Ed.), *Knowledge incorporation in evolutionary computation* (pp. 461–477). New York, NY: Springer.

Branke, J., Greco, S., Slowinski, R., & Zielniewicz, P. (2010). Interactive evolutionary multiobjective optimization driven by robust ordinal regression. *Bulletin of the Polish Academy of Sciences. Technical Sciences*, *58*(3), 347–358.

Branke, J., Kaußlera, T., & Schmeck, H. (2001). Guidance in evolutionary multi-objective optimization. *Advances in Engineering Software*, *32*, 499–507. doi:10.1016/S0965-9978(00)00110-1.

Brans, J.-P., & Mareschal, B. (1986). How to select and how to rank projects: The PROMETHEE method for MCDM. *European Journal on Operation Research*, *24*, 228–238. doi:10.1016/0377-2217(86)90044-5.

Chaudhuri, S., & Deb, K. (2010). An interactive multiobjective optimization and decision-making using evolutionary methods. *Applied Soft Computing*, *10*, 496–511. doi:10.1016/j.asoc.2009.08.019.

Coelho, R. F., Bersini, H., & Bouillard, Ph. (2003). Parametrical mechanical design with constraints and preferences: Application to a purge valve. *Computer Methods in Applied Mechanics and Engineering*, *192*, 4355–4378. doi:10.1016/S0045-7825(03)00418-3.

Coello, C. A. C. (2004). Handling preferences in evolutionary multi-objective optimization: A survey. In *Proceedings of the Congress on Evolutionary Computation* (pp. 30-37).

Coello, C. A. C., Veldhuizen, D. V., & Lamont, G. B. (2002). *Evolutionary algorithms for solving multiobjective problems*. Boston, MA: Kluwer Academic.

Cvetkovic, D., & Parmee, I. C. (2002). Preferences and their application in evolutionary multiobjective optimization. *IEEE Transactions on Evolutionary Computation*, *6*(1), 42–57. doi:10.1109/4235.985691.

Deb, K. (1999). Solving goal programming problems using multi-objective genetic algorithms. In *Proceedings of the IEEE Congress on Evolutionary Computation* (pp. 77-84).

Deb, K. (2001). *Multi-objective optimization using evolutionary algorithms*. Chichester, UK: John Wiley & Sons.

Deb, K., Pratap, A., Agrawal, S., & Meyarivan, T. (2002). A fast and elitist multi-objective genetic algorithm: NSGA-II. *IEEE Transactions on Evolutionary Computation*, *6*(2), 182–197. doi:10.1109/4235.996017.

Deb, K., Sinha, A., Korhonen, P. J., & Wallenius, J. (2010). An interactive evolutionary multiobjective optimization method based on progressively approximated value functions. *IEEE Transactions on Evolutionary Computation*, *14*(5), 723–739. doi:10.1109/TEVC.2010.2064323.

di Pierro, F., Khu, S.-T., & Savic, D. A. (2007). An investigation on preference order ranking scheme for multiobjective evolutionary optimization. *IEEE Transactions on Evolutionary Computation*, *11*(1), 17–45. doi:10.1109/TEVC.2006.876362.

Fernández, E., López, E., Bernal, S., Coello, C. A. C., & Navarro, J. (2010). Evolutionary multiobjective optimization using an outranking-based dominance generalization. *Computers & Operations Research*, *37*(2), 390–395. doi:10.1016/j.cor.2009.06.004.

Fonseca, C. M., & Fleming, P. J. (1993). Genetic algorithms for multiobjective optimization: Formulation, discussion and generalization. In *Proceedings of the Fifth International Conference on Genetic Algorithms*, San Mateo, CA (pp. 416-423).

Fonteix, C., Massebeuf, S., Pla, F., & Kiss, L. N. (2004). Multicriteria optimization of an emulsion polymerization process. *European Journal of Operational Research*, *153*, 350–359. doi:10.1016/S0377-2217(03)00157-7.

Garza-Fabre, M., Pulido, G. T., & Coello, C. A. C. (2009). Ranking methods for many-objective optimization. In *Proceedings of the 8th Mexican International Conference on Artificial Intelligence* (pp. 633-645).

Horn, J. (1997). Multicriterion decision making. In Bäck, T., Fogel, D., & Michalewicz, Z. (Eds.), *Handbook of evolutionary computation* (*Vol. 1*, pp. 1–15). New York, NY: Oxford University Press. doi:10.1887/0750308958/b386c85.

Jin, Y., & Sendhoff, B. (2002). Incorporation of fuzzy preferences into evolutionary multiobjective optimization. In *Proceedings of the 4th Asia Pacific Conference on Simulated Evolution and Learning* (Vol. 1, pp. 26-30).

Knowles, J., & Corne, D. (1999). The Pareto archived evolution strategy: A new baseline algorithm for multiobjective optimization. In *Proceedings of the Congress on Evolutionary Computation* (pp. 98-105).

Mousseau, V., Slowinski, R., & Zielniewicz, P. (2000). A user-oriented implementation of the ELECTRE-TRI method integrating preference elicitation support. *Computers & Operations Research*, *27*, 757–777. doi:10.1016/S0305-0548(99)00117-3.

Oliveira, E., & Antunes, C. H. (2010a). An evolutionary algorithm based on an outranking relation for sorting problems. In *Proceedings of the IEEE International Conference on Systems Man and Cybernetics*, Istanbul, Turkey (pp. 2732-2739).

Oliveira, E., & Antunes, C. H. (2010b). An evolutionary algorithm guided by preferences elicited according to the ELECTRE TRI method principles. In P. Cowling & P. Merz (Eds.), *Proceedings of the 10th European Conference on Evolutionary Computation in Combinatorial Optimization* (LNCS 6022, pp. 214-225).

Parreiras, R. O., Maciel, J. H. R. D., & Vasconcelos, J. A. (2006). The a posteriori decision in multiobjective optimization problems with smarts, Promethee II and a fuzzy algorithm. *IEEE Transactions on Magnetics*, *42*(4), 1139–1142. doi:10.1109/TMAG.2006.871986.

Parreiras, R. O., & Vasconcelos, J. A. (2007). A multiplicative version of Promethee II applied to multiobjective optimization problems. *European Journal of Operational Research, 183*(2), 729–740. doi:10.1016/j.ejor.2006.10.002.

Rachmawati, L., & Srinivasan, D. (2006, July). Preference incorporation in multi-objective evolutionary algorithms: A survey. *IEEE Congress on Evolutionary Computation*, Vancouver, BC, Canada (pp. 3385-3391).

Rekiek, B., De Lit, P., Pellichero, F., L'Eglise, T., Falkenauer, E., & Delchambre, A. (2000). Dealing with user's preferences in hybrid assembly lines design. In *Proceedings of the Management and Control of Production and Logistics Conference*.

Roy, B. (1996). *Multicriteria methodology for decision aiding*. Dordrecht, The Netherlands: Springer-Verlag.

Said, L. B., Bechikh, S., & Ghedira, K. (2010). The r-dominance: A new dominance relation for interactive evolutionary multicriteria decision making. *IEEE Transactions on Evolutionary Computation, 14*(5), 801–818. doi:10.1109/TEVC.2010.2041060.

Thiele, L., Miettinen, K., Korhonen, P. J., & Molina, J. (2009). A preference-based interactive evolutionary algorithm for multiobjective optimization. *Evolutionary Computation Journal, 17*(3), 411–436. doi:10.1162/evco.2009.17.3.411.

Zitzler, E., Laumanns, M., & Thiele, L. (2002). SPEA2: Improving the strength pareto evolutionary algorithm for multiobjective optimization. In *Proceedings of the Evolutionary Methods for Design, Optimisation and Control with Application to Industrial Problems* (pp. 95-100).

This work was previously published in the International Journal of Natural Computing Research (IJNCR), Volume 2, Issue 1, edited by Leandro Nunes de Castro, pp. 63-85, copyright 2011 by IGI Publishing (an imprint of IGI Global).

Chapter 5
Asynchronous P Systems

Tudor Bălănescu
University of Piteşti, Romania

Radu Nicolescu
University of Auckland, New Zealand

Huiling Wu
University of Auckland, New Zealand

ABSTRACT

In this paper, the authors propose a new approach to fully asynchronous P systems, and a matching complexity measure, both inspired from the field of distributed algorithms. The authors validate the proposed approach by implementing several well-known distributed depth-first search (DFS) and breadth-first search (BFS) algorithms. Empirical results show that the proposed P algorithms have shorter descriptions and achieve a performance comparable to the corresponding distributed algorithms.

1. INTRODUCTION

A P system is a computational model inspired by the structure and interactions of cell membranes, introduced by Păun (1998) and Păun, Rozenberg, and Salomaa (2010). The essential specification of a P system includes a membrane structure, objects and rules. Cells evolve by applying rules in a non-deterministic and (potentially maximally) parallel manner. These characteristics make P systems a promising candidate as a model for distributed and parallel computing.

The traditional P system model is *synchronous*, i.e., all cells evolution is controlled by a single global clock. P systems with various *asynchronous* features have been investigated by recent research (Frisco, 2004; Casiraghi, Ferretti, Gallini, & Mauri, 2005; Cavaliere & Sburlan, 2004; Cavaliere et al., 2008; Cavaliere & Mura, 2008; Cavaliere et al., 2009; Freund, 2005; Gutiérrez-Naranjo & Pérez-Jiménez, 2010; Kleijn & Koutny, 2006; Pan, Zeng, & Zhang, 2011; Yuan & Zhang, 2007). Here we are looking for similar but simpler definitions, closer to the definitions used in

DOI: 10.4018/978-1-4666-4253-9.ch005

distributed algorithms (Lynch, 1996; Tel, 2000), which should in the future enable us to consider essential distributed features, such as fairness, safety, liveness and infinite evolutions. In our approach, algorithms are non-deterministic, not necessarily constrained to return exactly the same result.

Fully asynchronous P systems are characterized by the absence of any system clock, let alone a global one; however, an outside observer may very well use a clock to time the evolutions. Our approach, based on classical notions in distributed algorithms, as presented by Tel (2000), does *not* require any change in the *static* description of P systems, only their *evolutions* differ (i.e., the underlying runtime engine works differently): (1) for each cell, each step starts after a *random delay t* (after the preceding step); (2) for each cell, each step, once started, takes *zero* time (i.e., it occurs instantaneously); (3) for each message, its transmission *delay t* is *random* (from its origin until it arrives at its target).

A full version of this paper appears as a CDMTCS report (Nicolescu & Wu, 2011b).

2. PRELIMINARIES

We assume that the reader is familiar with the basic terminology and notations, such as alphabets, strings, multisets, relations, graphs, nodes (vertices), edges, directed graphs (digraphs), directed acyclic graphs (dags), arcs, depth-first search (DFS), breadth-first search (BFS), spanning tree, DFS and BFS spanning trees.

In this paper, we use a *simple P module*—an umbrella concept, which is general enough to cover several basic *synchronous* P system families, with *states*, *priorities*, *promoters* and *duplex* channels. In this basic model, the cells evolve *synchronously*. For the full definition of P modules and modular compositions, we refer readers to Dinneen, Kim, and Nicolescu (2010c). Essentially, a simple P module is a system, $\Pi = (O, \sigma 1, \sigma_2, \ldots, \sigma_n, \delta)$, where:

1. O is a finite non-empty alphabet of *elementary objects*;
2. $\sigma 1, \sigma_2, \ldots, \sigma_n$ are cells, of the form $\sigma_i = (Q_i, S_{i,0}, w_{i,0}, R_i)$, $1 \le i \le n$, where:
   a. Q_i is a finite set of *states*;
   b. $S_{i,0} \in Q_i$ is the *initial state*;
   c. $w_{i,0} \in O^*$ is the *initial multiset* of objects;
   d. R_i is a finite *ordered* set of rewriting/communication *rules* of the form: $S\ x \rightarrow_{\alpha} S'\ x'\ (y)_{\beta}\ |_{z}$, where: $S, S' \in Q_i$, $x, x', y, z \in O^*$, $\alpha \in \{\min, \max\}$, $\beta \in \{\uparrow, \downarrow, \updownarrow\}$.
3. δ is a set of *digraph* (*head, tail*) arcs on $\{1, 2, \ldots, n\}$, without reflexive arcs, representing *duplex* channels between cells.

The membrane structure is a digraph with duplex channels, so heads can send messages to tails *and* tails to heads. Rules are prioritized and are applied in *weak priority* order (Păun, 2006). The general form of a rule, which transforms state S to state S', is $S\ x \rightarrow_{\alpha} S'\ x'\ (y)_{\beta}\ |_{z}$. This rule consumes multiset x, and then (after all applicable rules have consumed their left-hand objects) produces multiset x', in the same cell (*here* mode). Also, it produces multiset y and sends it, by *replication* (*repl* mode), to all heads ("up"), to all tails ("down") or to all heads and tails ("up and down"), according to the target indicator $\beta \in \{\uparrow, \downarrow, \updownarrow\}$.

Additionally, we also use a targeted sending, $\beta = \uparrow_j, \downarrow_j, \updownarrow_j$, where j is either an arc label. Each arc has two labels—at its tail and at its head. Arc labels can be used for directing messages to a specific target cell. An arc, $\gamma = (\sigma_i, \sigma_j)$, which is not explicitly labelled, is implicitly labelled with the indices of the two cells, i.e., in this case, γ's labels are j, for its tail, and i, for its head.

Operator $\alpha \in \{\min, \max\}$ describes the rewriting mode. In the *minimal* mode, an applicable rule is applied once. In the *maximal* mode, an applicable rule is used as many times as possible and all rules with the same states S and S' can be applied in the maximally parallel manner. Finally, the optional z indicates a multiset of promoters, which enables the rule, but is not consumed (Ionescu & Sburlan, 2004).

Note: Our algorithms use duplex channels and work regardless of specific arc orientation. Therefore, to avoid superfluous details, the structure of our sample P systems will be given as undirected graphs, with the assumption that the results will be the same, regardless of actual arc orientation.

Extensions: We use an extended version of the basic P module framework, described above. Specifically, we assume that each cell σ_i contains a unique *cell ID symbol* ι_i, which is used as an *immutable promoter*. We also allow high-level rules, with a simple form of *complex symbols* and *free variable* matching.

To explain these additional features, consider rule 3.1 of algorithm 3: $S_3\ a\ n_j \rightarrow_{\min.\min} S_4\ a\ (c_i) \updownarrow_j |\iota_i$. This *generic* rule uses complex symbols n_j and c_i, where j and i are free variables, which could match anything, but, in the considered scenario, they will only match cell IDs. Briefly: (1) according to the *first* min, this rule is *instantiated once*, for one of the existing n_j symbols (if any), while promoter, ι_i, constrains i to the cell ID index of the current cell, σ_i; (2) according to the *second* min, the instantiated rule is *applicable once*, i.e., if applied, it consumes one a and one n_j, produces one a and sends one c_i to neighbor j (if this neighbor exists).

We thus extend the rewriting mode of generic rules, by considering all four possible combinations of the instantiation and rewriting modes: min.min, min.max, max.min, max.max. The interpretation of min.min, min.max and max.max modes is straightforward. While other interpretations could be considered, the mode max.min indicates that the generic rule is instantiated as *many* times as possible (without superfluous instances, which are not applicable) and each one of the instantiated rules is applied *once*, if possible. The instantiations are ephemeral, created when rules are tested for applicability and disappearing at the end of the step.

As an example, consider a system with N cells, $\sigma_1, \sigma_2, \ldots, \sigma_N$, where cell σ_1 has two structural neighbors, σ_2 and σ_3, is in state S_3 and contains multiset $a^2 n_2 n_3^2$. Consider also all possible instantiations of the following rule, ρ_α, where α is one of the four extended rewriting modes:

$$(\rho_\alpha)\ S_3\ a\ n_j \rightarrow_\alpha S_4\ a\ (c_i) \updownarrow_j |\iota_i.$$

The high-level rule $\rho_{\min.\min}$ generates one of the two low-level instances: either $S_3\ a\ n_2 \rightarrow_{\min} S_4\ a\ (c_1)\updownarrow_2$ or $S_3\ a\ n_3 \rightarrow_{\min} S_4\ a\ (c_1)\updownarrow_3$. $\rho_{\min.\max}$ generates one of the two low-level instances: either $S_3\ a\ n_2 \rightarrow_{\max} S_4\ a\ (c_1)\updownarrow_2$ or $S_3\ a\ n_3 \rightarrow_{\max} S_4\ a\ (c_1)\updownarrow_3$. $\rho_{\max.\min}$ generates the two low-level instances: $S_3\ a\ n_2 \rightarrow_{\min} S_4\ a\ (c_1)\updownarrow_2$ and $S_3\ a\ n_3 \rightarrow_{\min} S_4\ a\ (c_1)\updownarrow_3$. $\rho_{\max.\max}$ generates the two low-level instances: $S_3\ a\ n_2 \rightarrow_{\max} S_4\ a\ (c_1)\updownarrow_2$ and $S_3\ a\ n_3 \rightarrow_{\max} S_4\ a\ (c_1)\updownarrow_3$.

3. ASYNCHRONOUS P SYSTEMS

We define *asynchronous* P systems as follows. The rule format of asynchronous P systems is exactly the same as for synchronous P systems, i.e., $S\ x \rightarrow_\alpha S'\ x'\ (y)_\beta |_z$, including all mentioned extensions. However, we focus on typical distributed systems, where communications take substantially longer than actual local computations, and we consider that the message delay is totally unpredictable. As previously mentioned, in such systems, we assume: (1) for each cell, each step starts after a random delay t; (2) for each cell, each step takes zero time; (3) each message arrives after a random delay t.

Synchronous P systems can be considered as a special case of asynchronous P systems, where all step and transmission delays are one, i.e., $t = 1$. We typically assume that messages sent over the same arc arrive in FIFO order (queue)—but one could also consider that messages arrive in arbitrary order (multiset instead of queue).

For the purpose of *time complexity*, the time unit is chosen to be greater than any step or transmission delay, i.e., all such delays are real numbers in the closed unit interval, i.e., $t \in [0, 1]$. The *runtime complexity* of an asynchronous system is the *supremum* over all possible evolutions.

We illustrate these concepts with several known fundamental distributed algorithms (e.g., for DFS and BFS), mostly as presented by Tel (2000). For a more complete coverage, we refer readers to our report (Nicolescu & Wu, 2011b). First, we look at the same Echo algorithm, in two different distributed runtime scenarios: (1) synchronously and (2) asynchronously.

The Echo algorithm is a wave algorithm (Tel, 2000). It starts from a source cell, which broadcasts forward messages. These forward messages transitively reach all cells and, at the end, are reflected back to the initial source. The forward phase establishes a *virtual spanning tree* and the return phase is supposed to follow up its branches. The tree is virtual because it does not involve any structural change; instead, virtual child-parent links are established by pointer symbols. The algorithm terminates when the source cell receives the reflected messages from all its neighbors.

This algorithm requires that each cell "knows" all its neighbors (structural heads and tails). However, one could augment it with a preliminary phase which builds this knowledge; e.g., by Algorithm 2 (described in Section 3.1). For the moment, let us assume that each cell already knows all neighbors' IDs.

Scenario 1 in Figure 1 assumes that all messages arrive in one time unit, i.e., in *synchronous* mode. The forward and return phases take the same time, i.e., D time units each, where D is the diameter of the underlying graph, G. Scenario 2 in Figure 2 assumes that some messages travel much faster than others, which is possible in *asynchronous* mode: $t = \epsilon$, where $0 < \epsilon \ll 1$. In this case, the forward and return phases take very different times; D and N-1 time units, respectively, where N is the number of nodes of graph G.

Algorithm 1 (Echo Algorithm)

Input: All cells start in the same quiescent state, S_3, and with the same set of rules. Each cell, σ_i, contains an immutable cell ID symbol, ι_i. All cells know their neighbors, i.e., they have topological awareness, which are indicated by pointer symbols, n_j (e.g., as built by Algorithm 2). The source cell, σ_s, is additionally marked with one symbol, a, which triggers the process.

Output: All cells end in the same final state (S_4), and cell IDs are intact. Cell σ_s is still marked with one a and all other cells contain DFS spanning tree pointer symbols, indicating parents, p_j.

Figure 1. Echo algorithm in synchronous mode, or in a special case of the asynchronous mode, when all messages are propagated with the same delay, t = 1. Edges with arrows indicate child-parent arcs in the virtual spanning tree built by the algorithm. Thick arrows near edges indicate messages. Each of the (b), (c), (d) steps takes one time unit.

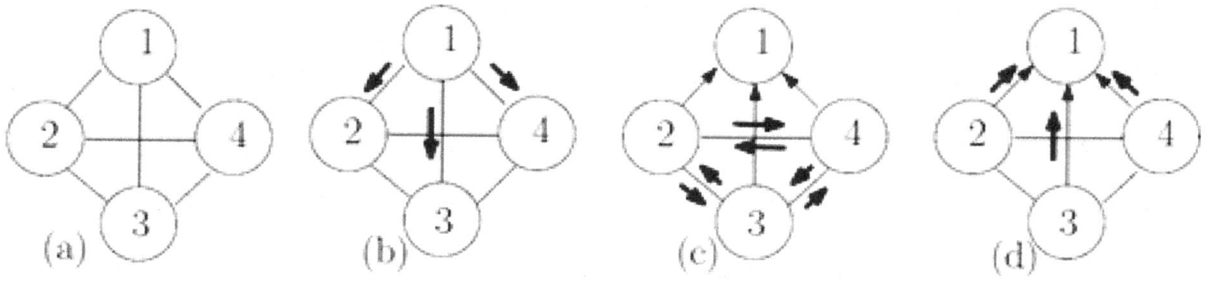

Figure 2. Echo algorithm in asynchronous mode, one possible evolution, with different forward and return times. Dotted thick arrows near edges indicate messages still in transit. Each of the (a), (b), (c), (d) steps takes ϵ time units; each of the (e), (f), (g), (h) steps take one time unit.

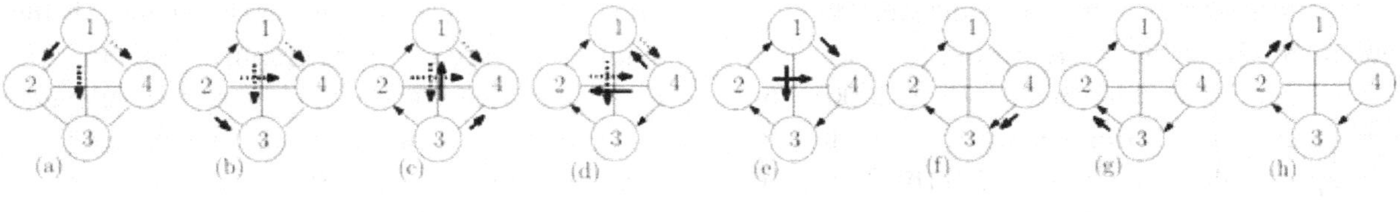

Rules

3. **Rules for state S_3:**
   1. $S_3 n_j \to_{\text{max.min}} S_4 w_j (c_i t) \updownarrow_j | a\iota_i$
   2. $S_3 c_j n_j \to_{\text{min.min}} S_4 p_j$
   3. $S_3 c_j n_j \to_{\text{min.min}} S_4 p_j (x_i) \updownarrow_j | \iota_i$
   4. $S_3 t \to_{\text{max}} S_4$
4. **Rules for state S_4:**
   1. $S_4 w_j c_j \to_{\text{max.min}} S_4$
   2. $S_4 w_j r_j \to_{\text{max.min}} S_4$
   3. $S_4 w_j p_k \to_{\text{max.min}} S_4 w_j p_k$
   4. $S_4 w_j a \to_{\text{max.min}} S_4 w_j a$
   5. $S_4 c_j \to_{\text{max.min}} S_4$
   6. $S_4 r_j \to_{\text{max.min}} S_4$
   7. $S_4 p_j \to_{\text{max.min}} S_4 p_j (r_i t) \updownarrow_j | t\iota_i$
   8. $S_4 t \to_{\text{max}} S_4$

Table 1 and Table 2 show the evolution of Algorithm 1 in the synchronous and asynchronous modes, respectively, and highlight the two spanning trees of Figure 1 and Figure 2.

Our Echo algorithm uses the following symbols: a marks the source cell; c_j is the echo signal sent by cell σ_j; r_j is the echo response sent by cell σ_j; w_j indicates that the cell waits for an echo response from cell σ_j, or an echo signal, which, in this case, is animated with an echo response; p_j indicates the virtual spanning tree parent; t is an auxiliary symbol accompanying the token, which enables further processing by a lower priority rule after the token has been consumed.

The source cell, σ_s, indicated by one symbol a, sends echo signals, c_s, to all its neighbors (rule 3.1). Upon receiving echo signals, cell σ_i selects one of the sending neighbors, say c_j, as its virtual tree parent, and creates a pointer to it, p_j (rule 3.2). Further, cell σ_i sends echo signals, c_i, to all its other (non-parent) neighbors (rule 3.3). When a cell, σ_i receives an echo signal, c_j or an echo response, r_j, from its neighbor, σ_j, it deletes the corresponding waiting indicator, w_j (rules 4.1–2). After σ_i has received echo signals from all its neighbors, it sends the echo response, r_i, to its parent, p_j (rule 4.7), or if $\sigma_i = \sigma_s$, the algorithm terminates. Otherwise, it has to wait (rule 4.3).

Table 1. Traces of Algorithm 1 for Figure 1 (synchronous mode)

Time	σ_1	σ_2	σ_3	σ_4
0	$S_3\iota_1 a n_2 n_3 n_4$	$S_3\iota_2 n_1 n_3 n_4$	$S_3\iota_3 n_1 n_2 n_4$	$S_3\iota_4 n_1 n_2 n_3$
1	$S_4\iota_1 a w_2 w_3 w_4$	$S_3\iota_2 n_1 n_3 n_4 c_1 t$	$S_3\iota_3 n_1 n_2 n_4 c_1 t$	$S_3\iota_4 n_1 n_2 n_3 c_1 t$
2	$S_4\iota_1 a w_2 w_3 w_4$	$S_4\iota_2 \mathbf{p_1} w_3 w_4 c_3 c_4\, t^2$	$S_4\iota_3 \mathbf{p_1} w_2 w_4 c_2 c_4\, t^2$	$S_4\iota_4 \mathbf{p_1} w_2 w_3 c_2 c_3\, t^2$
3	$S_4\iota_1 a w_2 w_3 w_4 r_2 r_3 r_4\, t^3$	$S_4\iota_2 \mathbf{p_1}$	$S_4\iota_3 \mathbf{p_1}$	$S_4\iota_4 \mathbf{p_1}$
4	$S_4\iota_1 a$	$S_4\iota_2 \mathbf{p_1}$	$S_4\iota_3 \mathbf{p_1}$	$S_4\iota_4 \mathbf{p_1}$

Table 2. Traces of Algorithm 1 for Figure 2 (one possible evolution in the asynchronous mode)

Time	σ_1	σ_2	σ_3	σ_4
0	$S_3\iota_1an_2n_3n_4$	$S_2\iota_2n_1n_3n_4$	$S_1\iota_3n_2n_4n_3$	$S_1\iota_4n_3n_5n_1$
1 ε	$S_4\iota_1aw_2w_3w_4$	$S_3\iota_2n_1n_3n_4c_1t$	$S_1\iota_3n_2n_4n_3$	$S_1\iota_4n_3n_5n_1$
2 ε	$S_4\iota_1aw_2w_3w_4$	$S_4\iota_2\mathbf{p_1}w_3w_4$	$S_3\iota_3n_2n_4n_3c_2t$	$S_1\iota_4n_3n_5n_1$
3 ε	$S_4\iota_1aw_2w_3w_4c_3t$	$S_4\iota_2\mathbf{p_1}w_3w_4$	$S_4\iota_3\mathbf{p_2}w_4w_3$	$S_3\iota_4n_3n_5n_1c_3t$
4 ε	$S_4\iota_1aw_2w_4c_4t$	$S_4\iota_2\mathbf{p_1}w_3w_4c_4t$	$S_4\iota_3\mathbf{p_2}w_4w_3$	$S_4\iota_4\mathbf{p_3}w_5w_1$
1	$S_4\iota_1aw_2$	$S_4\iota_2\mathbf{p_1}w_3$	$S_4\iota_3\mathbf{p_2}w_4w_3c_1t$	$S_4\iota_4\mathbf{p_3}w_5w_1c_1c_2\,t^2$
2	$S_4\iota_1aw_2$	$S_4\iota_2\mathbf{p_1}w_3$	$S_4\iota_3\mathbf{p_2}r_4tw_4$	$S_4\iota_4\mathbf{p_3}$
3	$S_4\iota_1aw_2$	$S_4\iota_2\mathbf{p_1}w_3r_3t$	$S_4\iota_3\mathbf{p_2}$	$S_4\iota_4\mathbf{p_3}$
4	$S_4\iota_1ar_2tw_2$	$S_4\iota_2\mathbf{p_1}$	$S_4\iota_3\mathbf{p_2}$	$S_4\iota_4\mathbf{p_3}$
5	$S_4\iota_1a$	$S_4\iota_2\mathbf{p_1}$	$S_4\iota_3\mathbf{p_2}$	$S_4\iota_4\mathbf{p_3}$

3.1. Discovering Neighbors

Echo and most of our distributed P algorithms mentioned in this paper require that cells are aware of their local topology, i.e., each cells knows its neighbors' IDs. This can be build by running a preliminary Phase I, in which cells discover their neighbors. In our previous papers (Nicolescu, Dinneen, & Kim, 2009; Dinneen, Kim, & Nicolescu, 2010b), we have developed broadcast-based P algorithms to discover local topology and local neighbors, in the synchronous setting. In this paper, we propose a crisper broadcast-based algorithm, Algorithm 2, which uses fewer symbols. This algorithm is also a wave algorithm (Tel, 2000).

In this algorithm, the source cell never learns that all cells have terminated. If this is required, the rules can be supplemented with a convergecast phase, which will inform the source cell of the overall termination. Usually, this is not required, if a subsequent Phase II starts three time units after this algorithm. This delay guarantees that each cell will have had enough time to compute its neighbor discovery.

Algorithm 2 (Discovering Cell Neighbors)

Input: All cells start in the same initial state, S_0, with the same set of rules. Each cell, σ_i, contains a cell ID symbol, ι_i, which is *immutable* and used as a *promoter*. Additionally, the source cell, σ_s, is marked with one symbol, a.

Output: All cells end in the same state, S_3. On completion, each cell contains its cell ID symbol, ι_i, and neighbor pointers, n_j. The source cell, σ_s, is still marked with symbol a.

Rules

0. **Rules for state S_0:**
   1. $S_0\ a \rightarrow_{\min} S_1\ ay\ (z) \updownarrow$
   2. $S_0\ z \rightarrow_{\min} S_1\ y\ (z) \updownarrow$
   3. $S_0\ z \rightarrow_{\max} S_1$
1. **Rules for state S_1:**
   1. $S_1\ y \rightarrow_{\min.\min} S_2\ (n_i) \updownarrow |\iota_i$
   2. $S_1\ z \rightarrow_{\max} S_2$
2. **Rules for state S_2:**
   1. $S_2 \rightarrow_{\min} S_3$
   2. $S_2\ z \rightarrow_{\max} S_3$

Traces of Table 3 highlight the neighborhoods of Figure 3, computed in three time units (in the synchronous mode), after receiving the first signal, z.

The source cell, σ_s, which is marked by one symbol, a, broadcasts signal z, to all cells, and enters state S_1. Each cell receiving z produces one symbol, y, and changes to state S_1. Superfluous z signals are discarded. Then, in S_1, each cell that has symbol y, sends its own ID, which appears as

Table 3. Traces of Algorithm 2 for Figure 3. Highlighted entries indicate steps when cells have effectively terminated this algorithm

Time	σ_1	σ_2	σ_3	σ_4	σ_5	σ_6
0	$S_0 \iota_1 a$	$S_0 \iota_2$	$S_0 \iota_3$	$S_0 \iota_4$	$S_0 \iota_5$	$S_0 \iota_6$
1	$S_1 \iota_1 ay$	$S_0 \iota_2 z$	$S_0 \iota_3$	$S_0 \iota_4 z$	$S_0 \iota_5$	$S_0 \iota_6$
2	$S_2 \iota_1 az_2$	$S_1 \iota_2 \mathbf{n}_1 yz$	$S_0 \iota_3 z_2$	$S_1 \iota_4 \mathbf{n}_1 yz$	$S_0 \iota_5 z$	$S_0 \iota_6$
3	$S_3 \iota_1 a\mathbf{n}_2\mathbf{n}_4$	$S_2 \iota_2 \mathbf{n}_1\mathbf{n}_4 z$	$S_1 \iota_3 \mathbf{n}_2\mathbf{n}_4 yz$	$S_2 \iota_4 \mathbf{n}_1\mathbf{n}_2 z^2$	$S_1 \iota_5 \mathbf{n}_4 yz$	$S_0 \iota_6 z^2$
4	$S_3 \iota_1 a\mathbf{n}_2\mathbf{n}_4$	$S_3 \iota_2 \mathbf{n}_1\mathbf{n}_3\mathbf{n}_4$	$S_2 \iota_3 \mathbf{n}_2\mathbf{n}_4\mathbf{n}_5 z$	$S_3 \iota_4 \mathbf{n}_1\mathbf{n}_2\mathbf{n}_3\mathbf{n}_5$	$S_2 \iota_5 \mathbf{n}_3\mathbf{n}_4 z$	$S_1 \iota_6 \mathbf{n}_3\mathbf{n}_5 y$
5	$S_3 \iota_1 a\mathbf{n}_2\mathbf{n}_4$	$S_3 \iota_2 \mathbf{n}_1\mathbf{n}_3\mathbf{n}_4$	$S_3 \iota_3 \mathbf{n}_2\mathbf{n}_4\mathbf{n}_5\mathbf{n}_6$	$S_3 \iota_4 \mathbf{n}_1\mathbf{n}_2\mathbf{n}_3\mathbf{n}_5$	$S_3 \iota_5 \mathbf{n}_3\mathbf{n}_4\mathbf{n}_6$	$S_2 \iota_6 \mathbf{n}_3\mathbf{n}_5$
6	$S_3 \iota_1 a\mathbf{n}_2\mathbf{n}_4$	$S_3 \iota_2 \mathbf{n}_1\mathbf{n}_3\mathbf{n}_4$	$S_3 \iota_3 \mathbf{n}_2\mathbf{n}_4\mathbf{n}_5\mathbf{n}_6$	$S_3 \iota_4 \mathbf{n}_1\mathbf{n}_2\mathbf{n}_3\mathbf{n}_5$	$S_3 \iota_5 \mathbf{n}_3\mathbf{n}_4\mathbf{n}_6$	$S_3 \iota_6 \mathbf{n}_3\mathbf{n}_5$

subscript in a complex symbol, n_i, to all its neighbors. In S_2, cells accumulate the received neighbor symbols, n_j, discard superfluous z symbols and enter S_3.

Remark: After receiving the broadcast signal, z, each cell needs three more time units to find its neighbors.

4. DISTRIBUTED DEPTH-FIRST SEARCH (DFS)

Depth-first search (DFS) and breadth-first search (BFS) are graph traversal algorithms, which construct a DFS spanning tree and a BFS spanning tree, respectively. Figure 3 shows the structure of a sample P system, Π, based on an "undirected" graph, G, and one possible *virtual* DFS spanning tree, T. We use quotation marks to indicate that G actually is a *directed* graph, but we do not care about arc orientation. The spanning tree is virtual, as it is described by "soft" pointer symbols, not by "hard" structural arcs.

DFS is a fundamental technique, inherently *sequential*, or so it appears. Several distributed DFS algorithms have been proposed, which attempt to make DFS run faster on distributed systems, such as the classical DFS (Tel, 2000), Awerbuch's DFS (Awerbuch, 1985), Cidon's DFS (Cidon, 1988), Sharma and Iyengar's DFS (Sharma & Iyengar, 1989), Makki and Havas's DFS (Makki & Havas, 1996), Sense of Direction (SoD) DFS (Tel, 2000). We refer the reader to a fundamental text, which covers all these algorithms (Tel, 2000).

Figure 3. P system Π, based on an "undirected" graph and one possible virtual DFS spanning tree. Thick arrows indicate virtual child-parent arcs in this tree, linked by pointer symbols.

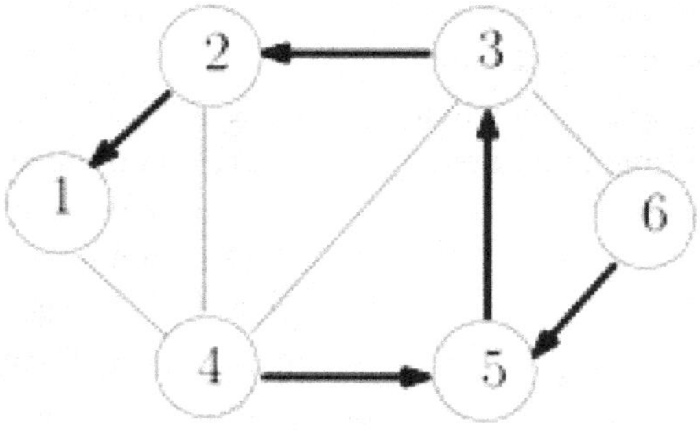

Several articles have proposed various synchronous P algorithms for DFS, as different implementations of the classical DFS discussed in Section 4.1. Gutiérrez-Naranjo et al. (2010) proposed a DFS algorithm using inhibitors to avoid visiting already-visited neighbor cells. Dinneen et al. (2010a) proposed a P algorithm to find disjoint paths in a digraph, using a distributed DFS strategy, which avoids visiting already-visited cells by changing the state of visited cells (Dinneen et al., 2010b). Bernardini et al. (2008) proposed a DFS algorithm in their P system synchronization solution. This approach uses an operator, $mark_+$, to select one not-yet-visited cell, indicated by a zero (0) polarity, and then mark the cell as visited, by changing the polarity to plus (+). The cell that performs a $mark_+$ operation implicitly records which child cell has been visited or not, without any message exchange.

Next, we present the asynchronous P system implementations of several well-known distributed DFS algorithms, which leverage the parallel and distributed characteristics of P systems. Due to the lack of space, we present only the classical and Awerbuch's DFS. For Cidon's, Sharma et al.'s, Makki et al.'s and Sense of Direction (SoD) DFS, we refer readers to our report (Nicolescu & Wu, 2011b).

4.1. Classical DFS

The classical DFS algorithm is based on Tarry's traversal algorithm, which traverses all arcs *sequentially*, in both directions, using a visiting *token* (Tel, 2000). Each cell records a list of *possibly-unvisited* neighbors, i.e., neighbor cells which are not known to have been visited. Because it traverses each arc twice, serially, the classical DFS algorithm is not the most efficient distributed DFS algorithm. The algorithm terminates when the source cell receives a backtrack token, and it has no more possibly-unvisited neighbors.

Figure 4 shows one snippet of the evolution of the classical DFS algorithm. We assume that the search started from cell σ_1 and has just backtracked to cell σ_5, after building path $\sigma_1.\sigma_2.\sigma_3.\sigma_5.\sigma_6$. In stage (a), cell σ_5 sends the token to the only one remaining possibly-unvisited cell, cell σ_4. Then in stage (b), because cell σ_4 was indeed unvisited, it sets cell σ_5 as its virtual tree parent and sends the token to one of its possibly-unvisited neighbors, cell σ_1. In stage (c), however, cell σ_1 has already been visited, so it returns the token to cell σ_4. Similarly, in stage (d), cell σ_4 tries cell σ_2, which sends back the token in stage (e); in stage (f), cell σ_4 tries cell σ_3, which sends back the token in stage (g). In stage (h), cell σ_4 has no

Figure 4. An example of classical DFS algorithm in the synchronous mode. Arcs with arrows indicate child-parent arcs in the virtual spanning tree built by the algorithm. Thick arrows near arcs indicate visiting tokens.

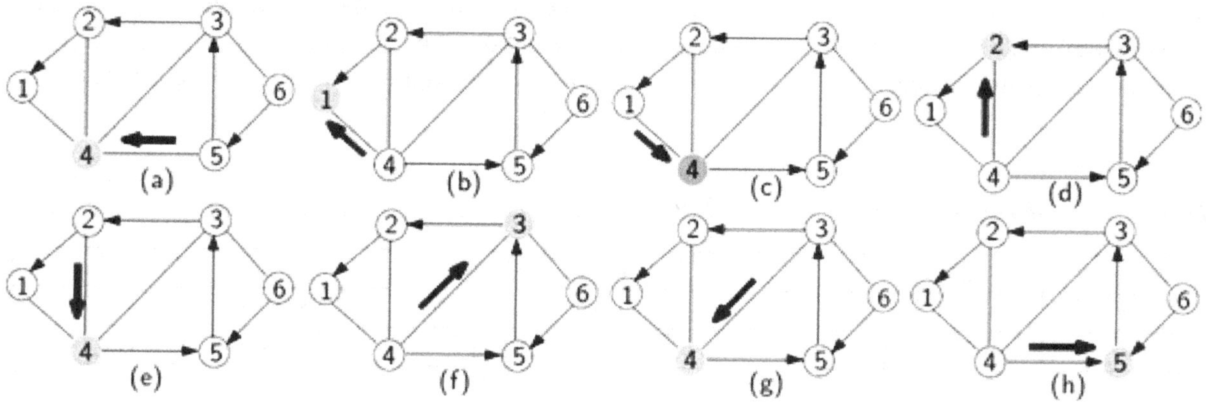

more possibly-unvisited neighbors, thus, it sends its backtrack token to its parent, cell σ_5. Note that, in this algorithm, cell σ_4 needlessly probes cells σ_1, σ_2 and σ_3, which have already been visited.

Algorithm 3 (Classical DFS)

Input: Same as in Algorithm 1.

Output: All cells end in the same final state (S_5), and cell IDs are intact. Cell σ_s is still marked with one a; all other cells contain DFS spanning tree pointer symbols, indicating parents, p_j.

Rules

3. **Rules for state S_3:**
    1. $S_3\, an_j \rightarrow_{\text{min.min}} S_4\, a\, (c_i) \updownarrow_j |\iota_i$
    2. $S_3\, c_j n_j n_k \rightarrow_{\text{min.min}} S_4\, p_j\, (c_i) \updownarrow_k |\iota_i$
    3. $S_3\, c_j n_j \rightarrow_{\text{min.min}} S_5\, p_j\, (x_i)\, l_j |\iota_i$
4. **Rules for state S_4:**
    1. $S_4\, c_j n_j \rightarrow_{\text{min.min}} S_4\, (x_i) \updownarrow_j |\iota_i$
    2. $S_4\, x_j n_k \rightarrow_{\text{min.min}} S_4\, (c_i) \updownarrow_k |\iota_i$
    3. $S_4\, x_j p_k \rightarrow_{\text{min.min}} S_5\, p_k\, (x_i) \updownarrow_k |\iota_i$
    4. $S_4\, x_j \rightarrow_{\text{min.min}} S_5$

Table 4 shows the initial and final configuration for P system Π of Figure 3 and highlights one possible DFS spanning tree.

In our algorithm for classical DFS, neighbor pointers, n_j, indicate *possibly-unvisited* neighbors and are erased as soon as that neighbor is known as visited. Additionally, we use the following symbols: a marks the source cell; c_j is the forward search token sent by cell σ_j; x_j is the backtrack token sent by cell σ_j; p_j points to the cell's *parent* in the virtual spanning tree.

The source cell, σ_s, indicated by a symbol, a, sends its token, c_s, to one of its possibly-unvisited neighbors, σ_j (rule 3.1). On receiving a c_j token, an unvisited cell, σ_i, selects one possibly-unvisited neighbor, and sends its token, c_i (rule 3.2). Otherwise, if σ_i has no more possibly-unvisited neighbors, it sends its backtrack token, x_i, to its parent, σ_j (rule 3.3). On receiving a c_j token, a visited cell, σ_i, sends back the token to the sending neighbor (rule 4.1).

Cell σ_i erases n_j, when it receives a c_j token from cell σ_j (rules 3.2, 3.3, 4.1, 4.2), or when it sends its c_i token to a neighbor (rules 3.2, 4.2).

When cell σ_i receives a backtrack token, it sends its c_i token to a possibly-unvisited neighbor, if any (rule 4.2). Otherwise, cell σ_i sends its backtrack token, x_i, to its parent, σ_k (rule 4.3). The algorithm terminates when the source cell, σ_s, receives a backtrack token, and it has no more possibly-unvisited neighbors (rule 4.4).

4.2. Awerbuch DFS

Awerbuch's algorithm (Awerbuch, 1985) and other more efficient algorithms improve time complexity by having the visiting token traversing tree arcs only, all other arcs are traversed in parallel, by auxiliary messages. In this algorithm, each cell knows exactly if a neighbor has been visited or not, i.e., there are no possible-unvisited cells that have actually been visited. When a cell is visited for the first time, it *notifies* all neighbors in *parallel* and *waits* until it receives all neighbors' *acknowledgments*. After this, the cell can visit any unvisited neighbor. Thus, this algorithm avoids probing the already visited neighbors. The algorithm termi-

Table 4. Partial Trace of Algorithm 3 for Figure 3

Time Unit	σ_1	σ_2	σ_3	σ_4	σ_5	σ_6
0	$S_3\iota_1 an_2n_4$	$S_3\iota_2n_1n_3n_4$	$S_3\iota_3n_2n_4n_5n_6$	$S_3\iota_4n_1n_2n_3n_5$	$S_3\iota_5n_3n_4n_6$	$S_3\iota_6n_3n_5$
19	$S_5\iota_1 a$	$S_5\iota_2\mathbf{p_1}$	$S_5\iota_3\mathbf{p_2}$	$S_5\iota_4\mathbf{p_5}$	$S_5\iota_5\mathbf{p_3}$	$S_5\iota_6\mathbf{p_5}$

nates when the source cell receives a backtrack token, and it has no more unvisited neighbors.

Figure 5 shows one snippet of the evolution of Awerbuch's DFS algorithm, in the synchronous mode. We assume that the search started from cell σ_1 and has just backtracked to cell σ_5, after building path $\sigma_1.\sigma_2.\sigma_3.\sigma_5.\sigma_6$. Also, cell σ_4 knows that cells σ_1, σ_2 and σ_3 have been visited. In stage (a), cell σ_5 forwards the visiting token to its only unvisited neighbor, cell σ_4. Then, in stage (b), cell σ_4 sets cell σ_5 as its parent, and notifies all its other neighbors, i.e., cells σ_1, σ_2 and σ_3, that it has too been visited. In stage (c), cell σ_4 receives acknowledgments from its neighbors, σ_1, σ_2 and σ_3. (In the asynchronous mode, cell σ_4 waits until it receives all the due acknowledgments.) In stage (d), cell σ_4 knows that cells σ_1, σ_2 and σ_3, have been visited, so it sends the backtrack token to its parent, cell σ_5, avoiding probing cells σ_1, σ_2 and σ_3 needlessly.

Algorithm 4 (Awerbuch DFS)

Input: Same as in Algorithm 1.

Output: Similar to Algorithm 3, but the final state is S_4. Also, cells may contain "garbage" symbols, which can be cleared, by using a few more steps.

Rules

3. **Rules for state S_3:**
   1. $S_3\, v_j n_j \rightarrow_{\text{max.min}} S_3\, m_j\, (b_i)\updownarrow_j | \iota_i$
   2. $S_3\, n_j \rightarrow_{\text{max.min}} S_4\, n_j w_j\, (v_i)\updownarrow_j \wedge | a\iota_i$
   3. $S_3\, c_j m_j \rightarrow_{\text{min.min}} S_4\, p_j | n_k$
   4. $S_3\, c_j m_j \rightarrow_{\text{min.min}} S_4\, p_j | m_k$
   5. $S_3\, c_j m_j \rightarrow_{\text{min.min}} S_5\, p_j$
   6. $S_3\, n_j \rightarrow_{\text{max.min}} S_4\, n_j w_j\, (v_i)\updownarrow_j | t\iota_i$
   7. $S_3\, m_j \rightarrow_{\text{max.min}} S_4\, m_j w_j\, (v_i)\updownarrow_j | t\iota_i$
   8. $S_3\, a \rightarrow_{\text{min}} S_4\, at$
4. **Rules for state S_4:**
   1. $S_4\, w_j \rightarrow_{\text{max.min}} S_4 | b_j$
   2. $S_4\, w_j p_k t \rightarrow_{\text{max.min}} S_4\, w_j p_k t$
   3. $S_4\, b_j \rightarrow_{\text{max.min}} S_4$
   4. $S_6\, n_k x_j\, t \rightarrow_{\text{min.min}} S_4\, m_k\, (c_i t)\updownarrow_k | \iota_i$
   5. $S_6\, p_k x_j\, t \rightarrow_{\text{min.min}} S_4\, p_k\, (x_i t)\updownarrow_k | \iota_i$
   6. $S_4\, an_j \rightarrow_{\text{min.min}} S_4\, am_j\, (c_i t)\updownarrow_j | t\iota_i$
   7. $S_4\, ax_j\, t \rightarrow_{\text{min.min}} S_4\, a$
   8. $S_4\, p_k n_j \rightarrow_{\text{min.min}} S_4\, p_k m_j\, (c_i t)\updownarrow_j | t\iota_i$
   9. $S_4\, p_j \rightarrow_{\text{min.min}} S_4\, p_j\, (x_i t)\updownarrow_j | t\iota_i$
   10. $S_4\, v_j \rightarrow_{\text{max.min}} S_4\, m_j\, (b_i)\updownarrow_j | \iota_i$
   11. $S_4\, t \rightarrow_{\text{min}} S_4$

Table 5 shows the initial and final configuration for P system Π of Figure 3 and highlights one possible DFS spanning tree.

Our version of Awerbuch's algorithm uses the following symbols: m_j points to a *non-parent* visited neighbor, σ_j; n_j points to an *unvisited* neighbor, σ_j; p_j points to the cell's *parent* in the

Figure 5. An example of Awerbuch's DFS algorithm in synchronous mode. Arcs with arrows indicate child-parent arcs in the virtual spanning tree built by the algorithm. Thick arrows near arcs indicate visiting tokens. Thin arrows near arcs indicate auxiliary messages. The elements in braces beside cell σ_i indicate the visited neighbors known by σ_i, with σ_i's parent in bold.

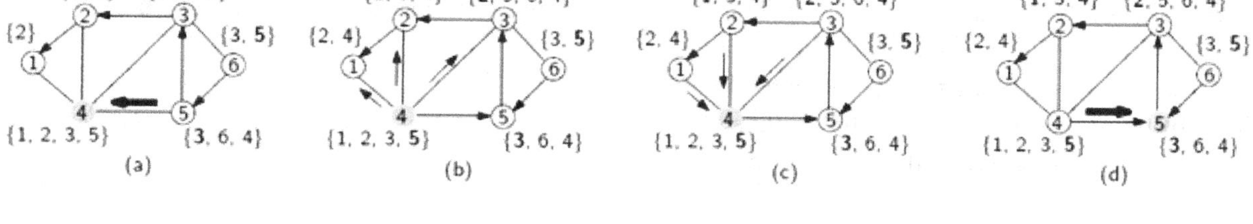

Table 5. Partial Trace of Algorithm 4 for Figure 3

Time Unit	σ_1	σ_2	σ_3	σ_4	σ_5	σ_6
0	$S_3 \iota_1 a n_2 n_4$	$S_3 \iota_2 n_1 n_3 n_4$	$S_3 \iota_3 n_2 n_4 n_5 n_6$	$S_3 \iota_4 n_1 n_2 n_3 n_5$	$S_3 \iota_5 n_3 n_4 n_6$	$S_3 \iota_6 n_3 n_5$
23	$S_5 \iota_1 a$...	$S_5 \iota_2 \mathbf{p}_{1...}$	$S_5 \iota_3 \mathbf{p}_{2...}$	$S_5 \iota_4 \mathbf{p}_{5...}$	$S_5 \iota_5 \mathbf{p}_{3...}$	$S_5 \iota_6 \mathbf{p}_{5...}$

virtual spanning tree; b_j is the acknowledgment from cell σ_j; c_j is the forward search token sent by cell σ_j; x_j is the backtrack token sent by cell σ_j; w_j indicates waiting for cell σ_j's acknowledgment; v_j is a visiting notification send by cell σ_j; t is an auxiliary symbol accompanying the token, which enables further processing by a lower priority rule after the token has been consumed. More detailed explanations and traces appear in our report (Nicolescu & Wu, 2011b).

4.3 Other Distributed DFS Algorithms

Cidon's algorithm (Cidon, 1988) improves Awerbuch's algorithm by not using acknowledgments, therefore removing a delay. The token holding cell does not wait for the neighbors' acknowledgments, but visits a neighbor at the same time when sending its visiting notification. However, it needs to record the most recently used cell, to solve cases when visiting notifications arrive after the visiting token.

Sharma et al.'s (1989) algorithm further improves time complexity, at the cost of increasing the message size, by including a *list* of visited cells when passing the visiting *token* (Tsin, 2002). Thus, it eliminates unnecessary message exchanges to inform neighbors of visited status.

Makki et al.'s algorithm improves Sharma et al.'s algorithm by using a *dynamic backtracking* technique. It keeps track of the most recent *split point*, i.e., the lowest ancestor node. When the search backtracks to a node, if the node has a non-tree edge to its split point, it backtracks to the split point directly via that edge, rather than following the longer tree path to its split point.

Another competitive algorithm is based on the existence of a Sense of Direction (SoD) arc labelling. We do not elaborate this here.

For P systems versions of all these algorithms, we refer the reader to our report (Nicolescu & Wu, 2011b).

5. DISTRIBUTED BREADTH-FIRST SEARCH (BFS)

BFS is a fundamental technique, inherently *parallel*, or so it appears. There are a number of distributed BFS algorithms, which speed up BFS in distributed systems, such as Synchronous BFS, Asynchronous BFS, an improved Asynchronous BFS with known graph diameter, Layered BFS, Hybrid BFS (Lynch, 1996).

Our previous research proposed a BFS-based P algorithm to find disjoint paths, and empirical results show that BFS can leverage the parallel and distributed characteristics of P systems (Nicolescu & Wu, 2011a). In this paper, we first present a P implementation of synchronous BFS algorithm (SyncBFS) (Lynch, 1996) and discuss how SyncBFS succeeds in the synchronous mode but *fails* in the asynchronous mode. Next, we propose a P implementation of an algorithm which works correctly in the asynchronous mode, the simple asynchronous BFS algorithm (AsyncBFS) (Lynch, 1996), and we show how it works in both synchronous and asynchronous scenarios.

5.1. Synchronous BFS

SyncBFS is a *wave* algorithm (Tel, 2000); it produces a BFS spanning tree in synchronous mode, but it often fails in asynchronous mode. Initially, the source cell broadcasts out a visiting token. On receiving the visiting token, an unmarked cell marks itself and chooses a parent from one of the cells from which the visiting token arrived. Then, in the first round after the cell gets marked, it sends a visiting token to all its non-parent neighbors. The algorithm terminates when no more cells are marked. However, the source cell never learns that all cells have terminated. If this is required, the rules can be supplemented with a convergecast phase, which will inform the source cell of the overall termination.

Figure 6(a) through 6(g) illustrates how SyncBFS works in the synchronous mode. Initially, in stage (a), cell σ_2 sends a visiting token to all its neighbors. In stage (b), on receiving the token, the unmarked cells, σ_1, σ_4 and σ_5, mark themselves and set cell σ_2 as its parent. Then in stage (c), the marked cells, σ_1, σ_4 and σ_5 send a visiting token to all their non-parent neighbors. The following stages are similar, and finally produce the BFS spanning tree in the stage (g). Figure 6(h) shows one possible evolution of SyncBFS in the asynchronous mode. The visiting token from σ_2 to σ_5 is delayed and arrives in σ_5 after σ_6 records its parent as σ_5. The resulting spanning tree is not a BFS spanning tree.

Algorithm 5 (Synchronous BFS)

Input: Same as in Algorithm 1.

Synchronous output: All cells end in the same final state, S_5. On completion, each cell, σ_i, still contains its cell ID symbol, ι_i. The source cell, σ_s, is still marked with one a. All other cells contain BFS spanning tree pointer symbols, indicating parents, p_j.

Figure 6. (a)–(g): An example of SyncBFS in synchronous mode. Arcs with arrows indicate child-parent arcs in the virtual spanning tree built by the algorithm. Thick arrows near arcs indicate visiting tokens. The result (g) is a BFS spanning tree. (h): A spanning tree which is not BFS, which can be built in the asynchronous mode. The dotted arrow indicates that the visiting token from σ_2 to σ_5 is delayed and arrives in σ_5 after σ_6 records its parent as σ_5.

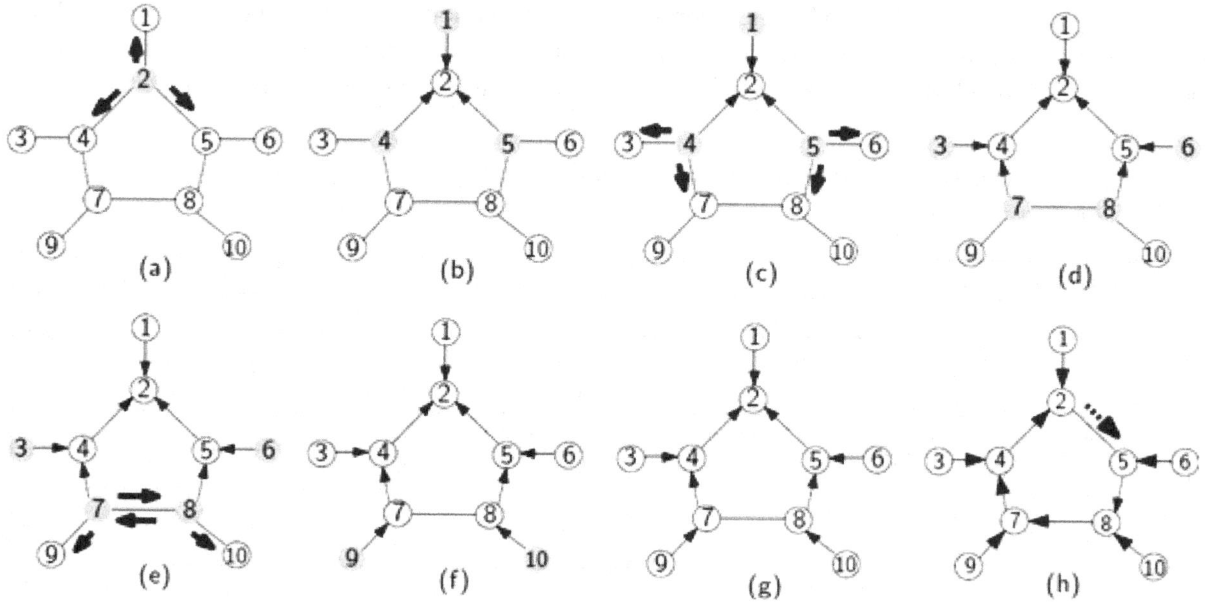

Rules

3. **Rules for state S_3:**
   1. $S_3\, a \rightarrow_{\min} S_4\, a$
   2. $S_3\, c_j n_j \rightarrow_{\min.\min} S_4\, p_j$
4. **Rules for state S_4:**
   1. $S_4\, n_j \rightarrow_{\max.\min} S_5\, (c_i) \updownarrow_j \iota_i$
   2. $S_4 \rightarrow_{\min} S_5$
5. **Rules for state S_5:**
   1. $S_5\, c_j \rightarrow_{\max.\max} S_5$

In Table 6(a) the "(Sync)" row indicates the BFS spanning tree built in the synchronous mode, as in Figure 6(g) (there is only one BFS tree in this case); and (b) the "(Async)" row indicates one spanning tree that can possibly result in the asynchronous mode, as in Figure 6(h). The resulting spanning tree is not a BFS spanning tree.

Our synchronous BFS implementation uses the following symbols: c_j is the visiting token sent by cell σ_j; n_j indicates a non-parent neighbor; p_j is the cell's parent in the virtual spanning tree. State S_3 indicates that the cell is unvisited; states S_4 and S_5 indicate that the cell is visited.

The source cell, σ_s, indicated by a, firstly marks itself by entering state S_4 (rule 3.1). In each round, if cell σ_i is marked, it sends its token to all its non-parent neighbors, σ_j (rule 4.1). A marked cell changes to state S_5 (rule 4.2), in which it ignores any further received token (rule 5.1). On receiving the token, c_j (from cell σ_j), an unmarked cell, σ_i, records its parent as p_j, marks itself by entering state S_4, and erases n_j (rule 3.2). The algorithm terminates when no more cells are marked, but the source cell does not know that all cells have terminated.

5.2. Asynchronous BFS

AsyncBFS supplements SyncBFS with rules that correct the parent destination and guarantees a BFS spanning tree (instead of an arbitrary spanning tree). The algorithm terminates when no more parent destinations need to be corrected, but in the basic version, the source cell does not know this. If termination detection is required, the rules can be supplemented with a complex convergecast phase, which will inform the source cell of the overall termination.

Figure 7 shows one snippet of an asynchronous evolution of AsyncBFS algorithm. We assume that the search started from cell σ_2 and has just arrived at cell σ_5, via path $\sigma_2.\sigma_4.\sigma_7.\sigma_8.\sigma_5$. Also, the visiting token directly sent from cell σ_2 has not arrived in cell σ_5. Each cell records its *distance* from the source cell, measured in *path lengths.* We initially set the source cell's distance to 0. In stage (a), cell σ_5, which is at distance 4 from σ_1, broadcasts its visiting token and the distance, 5, to all its non-parent neighbors, cells σ_2 and σ_6. In stage (b), because cell σ_2 has been marked as visited, it ignores cell σ_5's visiting token. Cell σ_6 is

Table 6. Partial Trace of Algorithm 5 for Figure 6 in the synchronous mode and one possible result in the asynchronous mode

Time	σ_1	σ_2	σ_3	σ_4	σ_5
0	$S_3\iota_1 n_2$	$S_3\iota_2 a n_1 n_4 n_5$	$S_3\iota_3 n_4$	$S_3\iota_4 n_2 n_3 n_7$	$S_3\iota_5 n_2 n_6 n_8$
(Sync)8	$S_5\iota_1\mathbf{p}_2$...	$S_5\iota_2 a$...	$S_5\iota_3\mathbf{p}_4$...	$S_5\iota_4\mathbf{p}_2$...	$S_5\iota_5\mathbf{p}_2$...
(Async)14	$S_5\iota_1\mathbf{p}_2$...	$S_5\iota_2 a$...	$S_5\iota_3\mathbf{p}_4$...	$S_5\iota_4\mathbf{p}_2$...	$S_5\iota_5\mathbf{p}_8$...
Time	σ_6	σ_7	σ_8	σ_9	σ_{10}
0	$S_3\iota_6 n_5$	$S_3\iota_7 n_4 n_8 n_9$	$S_3\iota_8 n_5 n_7 n_{10}$	$S_3\iota_9 n_7$	$S_3\iota_{10} n_8$
(Sync)8	$S_5\iota_6\mathbf{p}_5$...	$S_5\iota_7\mathbf{p}_4$...	$S_5\iota_8\mathbf{p}_5$...	$S_5\iota_9\mathbf{p}_7$...	$S_5\iota_{10}\mathbf{p}_8$...
(Async)14	$S_5\iota_6\mathbf{p}_5$...	$S_5\iota_7\mathbf{p}_4$...	$S_5\iota_8\mathbf{p}_7$...	$S_5\iota_9\mathbf{p}_7$...	$S_5\iota_{10}\mathbf{p}_8$...

unvisited, so it sets cell σ_5 as its parent, records its distance as 5, and marks itself as visited. In stage (c), we assume that the visiting token from cell σ_2 arrives. Cell σ_5 finds that the distance notified by cell σ_2, 1, is shorter than its recorded distance, 4, so it changes its distance to 1 and corrects its parent destination, by changing it from cell σ_8 to σ_2. Then, in stage (d), cell σ_5 notifies all its non-parent neighbors, cells σ_6 and σ_8, of the new distance. Cell σ_6 changes its distance to 2 (it still keeps its parent as cell σ_5), and cell σ_8 changes distance and changes its parent to cell σ_5. In stage (e), cell σ_8 notifies cell σ_7 and σ_{10} of the new distance. Cell σ_{10} changes its distance to 3, but cell σ_7 ignores σ_8's notification, because the notified distance, 3, is longer than its recorded distance, 2. Finally, the algorithm terminates when no more notifications are sent, but the source cell does not know that all cells have terminated.

Algorithm 6 (Asynchronous BFS)

Input: Same as in Algorithms 1 (and 5).

Output: Similar to Algorithm 5 (running in synchronous mode), but the final state is S_5. Also, cells may contain "garbage" symbols, which can be cleared, by using more steps.

Figure 7. An example of AsyncBFS algorithm in asynchronous mode. Arcs with arrows indicate child-parent arcs in the virtual spanning tree built by the algorithm. Thick arrows near arcs indicate visiting tokens. The dotted arrow indicates that the visiting token from σ_2 to σ_5 is delayed and arrives in σ_5 after σ_6 records its parent as σ_5. The number beside each cell indicates the cell's distance from the source cell, σ_2.

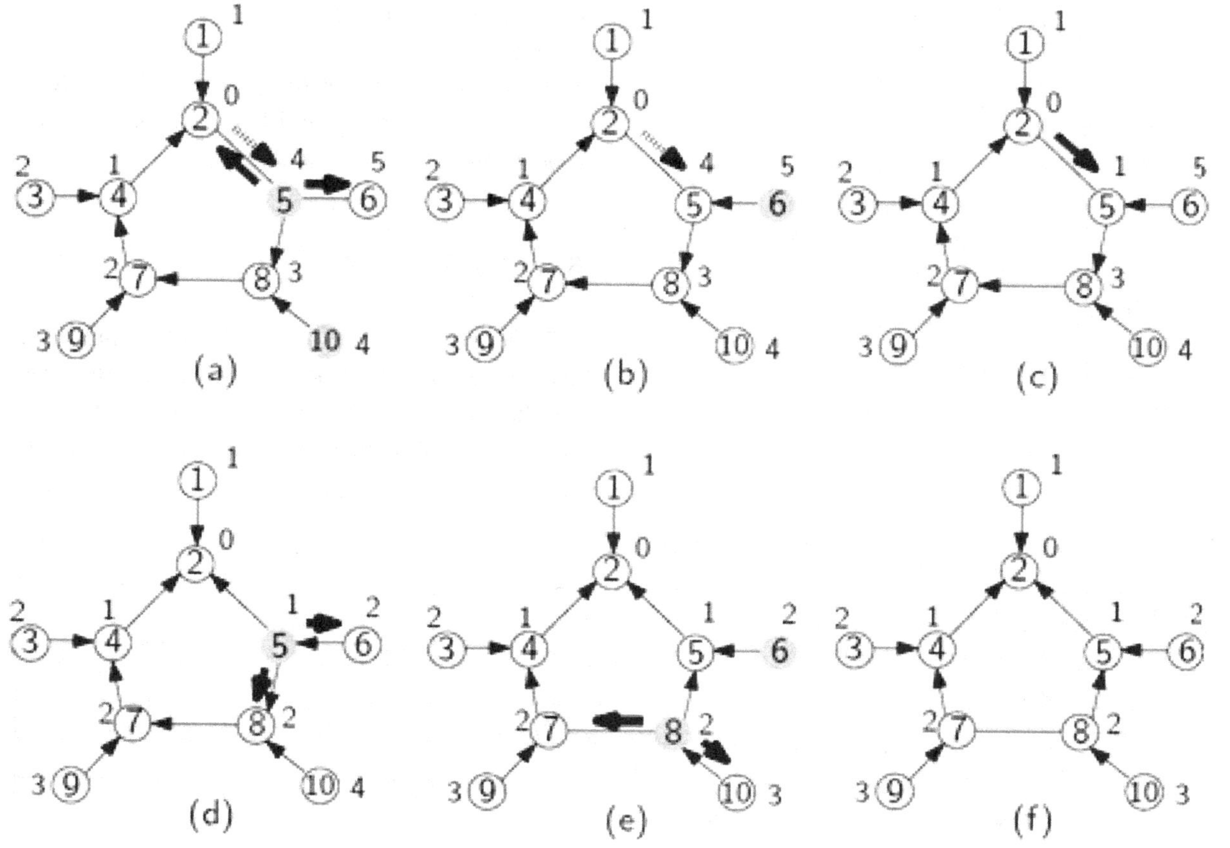

Rules

3. **Rules for state S_3:**
   1. $S_3 \rightarrow_{\min} S_4 h_j \mid a$
   2. $S_3 n_j \rightarrow_{\max.\min} S_4 m_j (c_i t g_i g_i) \updownarrow_j \mid a \iota_i$
   3. $S_3 c_j n_j \rightarrow_{\min.\min} S_4 p_j m_j \mid t$
4. **Rules for state S_4:**
   1. $S_4 \rightarrow_{\max.\min} S_5 (c_i t) \updownarrow_j \mid t n_j \iota_i$
   2. $S_4 g_j \rightarrow_{\min.\min} S_5 h (g_i g_i) \updownarrow \mid t p_j \iota_i$
   3. $S_4 g_j \rightarrow_{\min.\max} S_5 h (g_i) \updownarrow \mid t p_j \iota_i$
   4. $S_4 n_j \rightarrow_{\max.\min} S_5 m_j \mid t$
   5. $S_4 \rightarrow_{\min} S_5 \mid a$
   6. $S_4 t \rightarrow_{\min} S_5$
5. **Rules for state S_5:**
   1. $S_5 h \rightarrow_{\min.\max} S_6 e \mid c_j$
   2. $S_5 g_j \rightarrow_{\min.\max} S_6 g_j u_j x_j \mid c_j$
   3. $S_5 g_j \rightarrow_{\min.\max} S_6 g_j u_j \mid c_j$
   4. $S_5 g_j \rightarrow_{\max.\max} S_6 g_j \mid c_j$
   5. $S_5 g_j \rightarrow_{\max.\max} S_5$
6. **Rules for state S_6:**
   1. $S_6 g_j e \rightarrow_{\min.\max} S_6 \mid t x_j$
   2. $S_6 p k \rightarrow_{\max.\min} S_6 \mid e t$
   3. $S_6 c_j m_j \rightarrow_{\min.\min} S_6 p_j m_j \mid e t x_j$
   4. $S_6 c_j \rightarrow_{\max.\min} S_6 \mid t x_j$
   5. $S_6 u_j \rightarrow_{\min.\min} S_6 h (g_i g_i) \updownarrow \mid e t x_j \iota_i$
   6. $S_6 u_j \rightarrow_{\min.\max} S_6 h (g_i) \updownarrow \mid e t x_j \iota_i$
   7. $S_6 m_j \rightarrow_{\max.\min} S_6 m_j (c_i t) \updownarrow_j \mid e t \iota_i$
   8. $S_6 e \rightarrow_{\max} S_6 \mid t$
   9. $S_6 g_j u_j \rightarrow_{\min.\max} S_6 \mid x_j$
   10. $S_6 u_j \rightarrow_{\min.\max} S_6 h \mid x_j$
   11. $S_6 x_j \rightarrow_{\min.\min} S_5$
   12. $S_6 t \rightarrow_{\min} S_6$

Table 7 shows the initial and final configuration for P system Π of Figure 7 and highlights the BFS spanning tree (there is only one BFS tree in this case).

In this algorithm, we represent a non-negative integer, r, by $r + 1$ occurrences of a base symbol (hence, one occurrence for zero).

Our asynchronous BFS implementation uses the following symbols: h^{r+1} indicates that r is the length of the shortest path so-far from σ_s; g_j^{r+1} indicates that r is the length of a new path from σ_s, σ_s....σ_j.σ_i; e's and u_j's are temporary copies of h's and g_j's, respectively, used for path lengths' comparisons; x_j indicates that the ongoing path length comparison matches h's against g_j's; n_j points to an unvisited neighbor; m_j points to a visited neighbor (including the cell's parent); c_j is the visiting token sent by cell σ_j; p_j points to the cell's parent in the virtual spanning tree; t is an auxiliary symbol accompanying a token, which enables further processing by a lower priority rule, after the token has been consumed. States S_3 and S_4 indicate that the cell is unvisited; states S_5 and S_6 indicate that the cell is visited. More detailed explanations and traces appear in our report (Nicolescu & Wu, 2011b).

6. COMPLEXITY

All our distributed DFS and BFS implementations, except the SoD implementation, assume that each cell knows its neighbors' IDs (heads and tails). Our SoD implementation assumes that each cell

Table 7. Partial Trace of Algorithm 6 for Figure 7

Time	σ_1	σ_2	σ_3	σ_4	σ_5
0	$S_3 \iota_1 n_2$	$S_3 \iota_2 a n_1 n_4 n_5$	$S_3 \iota_3 n_4$	$S_3 \iota_4 n_2 n_3 n_7$	$S_3 \iota_5 n_2 n_6 n_8$
12	$S_5 \iota_1 \mathbf{p}_2$...	$S_5 \iota_2 a$...	$S_5 \iota_3 \mathbf{p}_4$...	$S_5 \iota_5 \mathbf{p}_2$...	$S_5 \iota_6 \mathbf{p}_2$...
Time	σ_6	σ_7	σ_8	σ_9	σ_{10}
0	$S_3 \iota_6 n_5$	$S_3 \iota_7 n_4 n_8 n_9$	$S_3 \iota_8 n_5 n_7 n_{10}$	$S_3 \iota_9 n_7$	$S_3 \iota_{10} n_8$
12	$S_4 \iota_6 \mathbf{p}_5$...	$S_4 \iota_7 \mathbf{p}_4$...	$S_4 \iota_8 \mathbf{p}_5$...	$S_4 \iota_9 \mathbf{p}_7$...	$S_4 \iota_{10} \mathbf{p}_8$...

Table 8. DFS (Figure 3) and BFS (Figure 6) algorithms comparisons, including empirical and theoretical complexity (time units)

	Algorithm	P Time	Time Compl.	Message Compl.	Needs
DFS	Classical	18	$2M$	$2M$	Local cell IDs
	Awerbuch	22	$4N$-2	$4M$	Local cell IDs
	Cidon	10	$2N$-2	$\leq 4M$	Local cell IDs
	Sharma	14	$2N$-2	$\leq 2N$-2	Global cell IDs
	SoD	10?	$2N$-2	$\leq 2N$-2	Sense of Direction (Z_n)
	Makki	13	$(1 + r)N$	$(1 + r)N$	Global cell IDs (or SoD)
BFS	Sync	8	$O(D)$	$O(M)$	Local IDs
	Simple Async	9	$O(DN)$	$O(NM)$	Local IDs
	Simple Async2	?	$O(D^2)$	$O(DM)$	D, Local IDs
	Layered Async	?	$O(D^2)$	$O(M + DN)$	Local IDs
	Hybrid Async	?	$O(Dk + D^2/k)$	$O(Mk + DN/k)$	Local IDs

knows the labels of its adjacent arcs (incoming and outgoing). In complexity analysis, we skip over a preliminary phase which could build such knowledge, see Algorithm 2. All our P system DFS implementations take one final time unit, to prompt the source cell to discard the token; we omit this time unit in the complexity analysis.

Table 8 shows the complexity of our P system DFS and BFS implementations, in terms of time units. The runtime complexity of our DFS P system implementations is similar to the standard distributed DFS algorithms; it is not exactly the same, because not all pseudocode tasks can be carried in one step by the rewriting rules of a P system. The complexity of our SoD algorithm must be considered with a grain of salt, for the reasons explained in SoD high-level pseudo-code. The runtime complexity of our SyncBFS and AsyncBFS implementations is also consistent with the runtime complexity of standard algorithms.

We also compare the number of lines in the algorithm pseudocodes and the number of rules in our P algorithms in Table 9. We can see that, except Sharma et al.'s algorithm, the number of rules in our P algorithms is smaller than the number of lines in the corresponding algorithm pseudocodes.

Table 9. Comparisons of the number of lines in the algorithm pseudocodes and the number of rules in our P algorithms

	Algorithm	Number of Lines in Pseudocode	Number of Rules in P Algorithm
DFS	Classical	22	7
	Awerbuch	30	19
	Cidon	38	25
	Sharma	15	19
	Makki	33	26
BFS	SoD	16	12?
	Sync	n/a	5
	Simple Async	27	26

7. CONCLUSION

We proposed a new approach to fully asynchronous P systems, and a matching complexity measure, both inspired from the field of distributed algorithms. We validated our approach by implementing several well-known distributed depth-first search (DFS) and breadth-first search (BFS) algorithms. We believe that these are the first P implementations of the standard distributed DFS and BFS algorithms. Empirical results show that, in terms of P steps, the runtime complexity of our distributed P algorithms is the same as the runtime complexity of standard distributed DFS and BFS.

Several interesting questions remain open. We intend to complete this quest by completing the implementation of the SoD algorithm and by implementing three other, more sophisticated, distributed BFS algorithms and compare their performance against the standard versions. We also intend to elaborate the foundations of fully asynchronous P systems and further validate this, by investigating a few famous critical problems, such as building minimal spanning trees. Finally, we intend to formulate fundamental distributed asynchronous concepts, such as fairness, safety and liveness, and investigate methods for their proofs.

REFERENCES

Awerbuch, B. (1985). A new distributed depth-first-search algorithm. *Information Processing Letters*, *20*(3), 147–150. doi:10.1016/0020-0190(85)90083-3.

Bernardini, F., Gheorghe, M., Margenstern, M., & Verlan, S. (2008). How to synchronize the activity of all components of a P system? *International Journal of Foundations of Computer Science*, *19*(5), 1183–1198. doi:10.1142/S0129054108006224.

Casiraghi, G., Ferretti, C., Gallini, A., & Mauri, G. (2005). A membrane computing system mapped on an asynchronous, distributed computational environment. In R. Freund, G. Păun, G. Rozenberg, & A. Salomaa (Eds.), *Proceedings of the 6th International Workshop on Membrane Computing* (LNCS 3850, pp. 159-164).

Cavaliere, M., Egecioglu, O., Ibarra, O., Ionescu, M., Păun, G., & Woodworth, S. (2008). Asynchronous spiking neural P systems: Decidability and undecidability. In M. Garzon & H. Yan (Eds.), *Proceedings of the 13th International Meeting on DNA Computing* (LNCS 4848, pp. 246-255).

Cavaliere, M., Ibarra, O. H., Păun, G., Egecioglu, O., Ionescu, M., & Woodworth, S. (2009). Asynchronous spiking neural P systems. *Theoretical Computer Science*, *410*, 2352–2364. doi:10.1016/j.tcs.2009.02.031.

Cavaliere, M., & Mura, I. (2008). Experiments on the reliability of stochastic spiking neural P systems. *Natural Computing*, *7*, 453–470. doi:10.1007/s11047-008-9086-8.

Cavaliere, M., & Sburlan, D. (2004). Time and synchronization in membrane systems. *Fundamenta Informaticae*, *64*, 65–77.

Cidon, I. (1988). Yet another distributed depth-first-search algorithm. *Information Processing Letters*, *26*, 301–305. doi:10.1016/0020-0190(88)90187-1.

Dinneen, M. J., Kim, Y.-B., & Nicolescu, R. (2010a). Edge- and node-disjoint paths in P systems. *Electronic Proceedings in Theoretical Computer Science*, *40*, 121–141. doi:10.4204/EPTCS.40.9.

Dinneen, M. J., Kim, Y.-B., & Nicolescu, R. (2010b). Edge- and vertex-disjoint paths in P modules. In *Proceedings of the Workshop on Membrane Computing and Biologically Inspired Process Calculi* (pp. 117-136).

Dinneen, M. J., Kim, Y.-B., & Nicolescu, R. (2010c). P systems and the Byzantine agreement. *Journal of Logic and Algebraic Programming*, *79*(6), 334–349. doi:10.1016/j.jlap.2010.03.004.

Freund, R. (2005). Asynchronous P systems and P systems working in the sequential mode. In G. Mauri, G. Paun, M. J. Pérez-Jiménez, G. Rozenberg, & A. Salomaa (Eds.), *Proceedings of the 5th International Workshop on Membrane Computing* (LNCS 3365, pp. 36-62).

Frisco, P. (2004). The conformon-P system: A molecular and cell biology-inspired computability model. *Theoretical Computer Science*, *312*, 295–319. doi:10.1016/j.tcs.2003.09.008.

Gutiérrez-Naranjo, M. A., & Pérez-Jiménez, M. J. (2010). Depth-first search with P systems. In *Proceedings of the 11th International Conference on Membrane Computing* (pp. 257-264).

Ionescu, M., & Sburlan, D. (2004). On P systems with promoters/inhibitors. *Journal of Universal Computer Science*, *10*(5), 581–599.

Kleijn, J., & Koutny, M. (2006). Synchrony and asynchrony in membrane systems. In H. J. Hoogeboom, G. Paun, G. Rozenberg, & A. Salomaa (Eds.), *Proceedings of the 7th International Workshop on Membrane Computing* (LNCS 4361, pp. 66-85).

Lynch, N. A. (1996). *Distributed algorithms*. San Francisco, CA: Morgan Kaufmann.

Makki, S. A. M., & Havas, G. (1996). Distributed algorithms for depth-first search. *Information Processing Letters*, *60*, 7–12. doi:10.1016/S0020-0190(96)00141-X.

Nicolescu, R., Dinneen, M. J., & Kim, Y.-B. (2009). Discovering the membrane topology of hyperdag P systems. In G. Păun, M. J. Pérez-Jiménez, A. Riscos-Núñez, G. Rozenberg, & A. Salomaa (Eds.), *Proceedings of the International Workshop on Membrane Computing* (LNCS 5957, pp. 410-435).

Nicolescu, R., & Wu, H. (2011a). *BFS solution for disjoint paths in P systems* (Tech. Rep. No. CDMTCS-399). Auckland New Zealand: University of Auckland.

Nicolescu, R., & Wu, H. (2011b). *Asynchronous P systems* (Tech. Rep. No. CDMTCS-406). Auckland, New Zealand: University of Auckland.

Pan, L., Zeng, X., & Zhang, X. (2011). Time-free spiking neural p systems. *Neural Computation*, *23*, 1320–1342. doi:10.1162/NECO_a_00115.

Păun, G. (1998). Computing with membranes. *Journal of Computer and System Sciences*, *61*, 108–143. doi:10.1006/jcss.1999.1693.

Păun, G. (2006). Introduction to membrane computing. In Ciobanu, G., Pérez-Jiménez, M. J., & Păun, G. (Eds.), *Applications of membrane computing* (pp. 1–42). New York, NY: Springer.

Păun, G., Rozenberg, G., & Salomaa, A. (2010). *The Oxford handbook of membrane computing*. New York, NY: Oxford University Press.

Sharma, M. B., & Iyengar, S. S. (1989). An efficient distributed depth-first-search algorithm. *Information Processing Letters*, *32*, 183–186. doi:10.1016/0020-0190(89)90041-0.

Tel, G. (2000). *Introduction to distributed algorithms*. Cambridge, UK: Cambridge University Press.

Tsin, Y. H. (2002). Some remarks on distributed depth-first search. *Information Processing Letters*, *82*, 173–178. doi:10.1016/S0020-0190(01)00273-3.

Yuan, Z., & Zhang, Z. (2007). Asynchronous spiking neural P system with promoters. In M. Xu, Y. Zhan, J. Cao, & Y. Liu (Eds.), *Proceedings of the 7th International Conference on Advanced Parallel Processing Technologies* (LNCS 4847, pp. 693-702).

This work was previously published in the International Journal of Natural Computing Research (IJNCR), Volume 2, Issue 2, edited by Leandro Nunes de Castro, pp. 1-18, copyright 2011 by IGI Publishing (an imprint of IGI Global).

Chapter 6
Simulating Spiking Neural P Systems Without Delays Using GPUs

F. Cabarle
University of the Philippines Diliman, Philippines

H. Adorna
University of the Philippines Diliman, Philippines

M. A. Martínez-del-Amor
University of Seville, Spain

ABSTRACT

In this paper, the authors discuss the simulation of a P system variant known as Spiking Neural P systems (SNP systems), using Graphics Processing Units (GPUs). GPUs are well suited for highly parallel computations because of their intentional and massively parallel architecture. General purpose GPU computing has seen the use of GPUs for computationally intensive applications, not just in graphics and video processing. P systems, including SNP systems, are maximally parallel computing models taking inspiration from the functioning and dynamics of a living cell. In particular, SNP systems take inspiration from a type of cell known as a neuron. The nature of SNP systems allowed for their representation as matrices, which is an elegant step toward their simulation on GPUs. In this paper, the simulation algorithms, design considerations, and implementation are presented. Finally, simulation results, observations, and analyses using a simple but non-trivial SNP system as an example are discussed, including recommendations for future work.

DOI: 10.4018/978-1-4666-4253-9.ch006

1. INTRODUCTION

The trend for massively parallel computation is moving from the more common multi-core CPUs towards GPUs for several significant reasons (Kirk, 2010; NVIDIA Corporation, 2010; Top 500, 2011). One important reason for such a trend includes the fraction of the power consumption of GPUs compared to the set-up and infrastructure in CPU clusters in order to obtain a comparable level of performance (NVIDIA CUDA Developers, 2011). Another important reason is that GPUs are architectured for *massively parallel computations* since unlike most general purpose multicore CPUs, a large part of the architecture of GPUs are devoted to parallel execution of arithmetic operations, and not on control and caching like in the CPUs (Kirk, 2010; NVIDIA Corporation, 2010; Garland et al., 2008). GPUs are currently the leading devices in high-throughput and supercomputing architectures (Garland & Kirk, 2010). Arithmetic operations are at the heart of many basic operations as well as scientific computations, and these are performed with larger speedups when done in parallel as compared to performing them sequentially. In order to perform these arithmetic operations on the GPU, there is a set of techniques called *GPGPU* (General Purpose computations on the GPU) which allow programmers to do computations on GPUs and not be limited to just graphics and video processing only (Harris, 2005).

P systems, under *Membrane computing*, are Turing complete (for several P system variants) computing models that perform computations non-deterministically, exhausting all possible computations at any given time (Chen et al., 2008). This type of unconventional model of computation was introduced by Gheorghe Păun in 1998 and takes inspiration and abstraction, similar to other members of *Natural computing* (e.g., DNA/molecular computing, neural networks, quantum computing), from nature (Păun, Ciobanu, & Pérez-Jiménez, 2006; P Systems, 2011; Păun, 2000). Specifically, P systems try to mimic the constitution and dynamics of the living cell in information processing: the multitude of elements inside it, and their interactions within themselves and their environment, or outside the cell's *skin* (the cell's outermost membrane). Before proceeding, we clarify what is meant by saying nature *computes*: computation in this case involves reading information from memory from past or present stimuli, then rewrite and retrieve this data as stimuli from the environment, process the gathered data and act accordingly due to this processing (Gross, 1998).

SNP systems differ from other types of P systems precisely because they are *mono-membranar* and the working alphabet contains only *one object type*. These characteristics, among others, are meant to capture the workings of a special type of cell known as the *neuron*. Neurons, such as those in the human brain, communicate or 'compute' by sending indistinct signals more commonly known as action potential or *spikes* (Ionescu, Păun, & Yokomori, 2006)

It has been shown that SNP systems, given their nature can be represented by matrices (Zeng, Adorna, Martínez-del-Amor, & Pan, 2010; Zeng, Adorna, Martínez-del-Amor, Pan, & Pérez-Jiménez, 2011). This representation allowed the design and implementation of an SNP system simulator using parallel devices such as GPUs.

Since the time P systems were presented, many simulators and software applications have been produced (Díaz, Graciani, Gutiérrez-Naranjo, Pérez-Hurtado, & Pérez-Jiménez, 2010). In terms of *High Performance Computing*, many P system simulators have also been designed for clusters of computers (Ciobanu & Wenyuan, 2004), for reconfigurable hardware as in Field-programmable Gate Arrays or FPGAs (Nguyen, Kearney, & Gioiosa, 2010b, 2010a), and even for GPUs (Cecilia et al., 2010b, 2010a). All of these efforts have shown that parallel architectures are well-suited in performance to simulate P systems.

However, these previous works on hardware are designed to simulate *cell-like* P system variants, which are among the first P system variants to have been introduced. Thus, the efficient simulation of *neural-like* variants (SNP systems) is a new challenge that requires novel attempts. Previous software related to SNP systems have been limited to verifications only, run in CPUs (Gutiérrez-Naranjo, Pérez-Jiménez, & Ramírez-Martínez, 2008).

A matrix representation of SNP systems is quite intuitive and natural due to their graph-like configurations and properties (shown in the succeeding sections). On the other hand, *linear algebra* operations have been efficiently implemented on parallel platforms and devices in the past years. For instance, there is a large number of algorithms implementing *matrix-vector* operations on GPUs. These algorithms offer huge performance since dense linear algebra readily maps to the data-parallel architecture of GPUs (Volkov & Demmel, 2008; Fatahalian, Sugerman, & Hanrahan, 2004).

It would thus seem then that a matrix represented SNP system simulator, implemented on highly parallel computing devices such as GPUs, be a natural confluence of the earlier points made. The matrix representation of SNP systems bridges the gap between the theoretical yet still computationally powerful SNP systems and the applicative and more tangible GPUs, via an SNP system simulator.

The design and implementation of the simulator, including the algorithms deviced, architectural considerations, are then implemented using the Compute Unified Device Architecture (CUDA). CUDA programming model, launched by NVIDIA in mid-2007, is a hardware and software architecture for issuing and managing computations on their most recent GPU families (G80 family onward), making the GPU operate as a highly parallel computing device (NVIDIA CUDA Developers, 2011). It extends the widely known ANSI C programming language, allowing programmers to easily design scalable and parallel software on the GPU, avoiding the use of low-level graphical primitives. CUDA also provides other benefits for the programmer such as abstracted and automated scaling of the parallel executed code.

This paper starts out by introducing and defining the type of SNP system that will be simulated. Afterwards the NVIDIA CUDA model and architecture are discussed, baring the scalability and parallelization CUDA offers. Followed by the design of the simulator, constraints and considerations, as well as the details of the algorithms used to realize the SNP system are discussed. The simulation results are eventually presented, as well as observations and analysis of these results. The paper ends by providing the conclusions and future work.

2. SPIKING NEURAL P SYSTEMS

The type of SNP systems focused on by this paper are those without delays i.e., those that spike or transmit signals the moment they are able to do so (Zeng et al., 2010, 2011). Variants which allow for delays before a neuron produces a spike, are also available (Ionescu et al., 2006). An SNP system without delay of degreee m is of the form:

$$\Pi = (O, \sigma_1, \ldots, \sigma_m, syn, in, out)$$

where:

1. $O = \{a\}$ is the alphabet made up of only one object, the system spike a.
2. $\sigma_1, \ldots, \sigma_m$ are neurons of the form $\sigma_i(n_i, R_i)$, $1 \leq i \leq m$, where:
   a. $n_i \geq 0$ gives the initial number of a's i.e., spikes contained in neuron σ_i.
   b. R_i is a finite set of rules with two forms:
      i. (b-1) $E/a^c \rightarrow a^p$, are known as *spiking rules*, where E is a regular expression over a, and $c \geq 1$, such that $p \geq 1$ number of spikes are

produced, one for each adjacent neuron with σ_i as the originating neuron and $a^c \in L(E)$.

ii. (b-2) $a^s \rightarrow \lambda$, are known as *forgetting rules*, for $s \geq 1$, such that for each rule $E/a^c \rightarrow a$ of type (b-1) from R_i, $a^s \notin L(E)$.

iii. (b-3) $a^c \rightarrow a$, a special case of (b-1) where $E = a^c$, and $p=1$.

3. $syn=\{(i,j) \mid 1 \leq i, j \leq m, i \neq j\}$
4. $in, out \in \{1,2,\ldots,m\}$ are the input and output neurons, respectively.

Rules of type (b-1) are applied if neuron σ_i contains a multiplicity of a (c copies) that is generated by the regular expression E. By $L(E)$ we mean the language generated by E. Using this type of rule, it consumes c spikes from the neuron, producing a spike to each of the neurons connected to it via a synapse. In this manner, for rules of type (b-2) if σ_i contains s spikes, then s spikes are forgotten or removed once the rule is applied.

The non-determinism of SNP systems comes with the fact that more than one rule can be applied at a given time, given enough spikes. The rule to be used is chosen non-deterministically in the neuron. However, at most one rule is applied per neuron at any given time (Ionescu et al., 2006; Zeng et al., 2010, 2011). The neurons in an SNP system operate in parallel and in unison, under a global clock (Ionescu et al., 2006). For Figure 1 no input neuron is present, but σ_3 (neuron 3) is the output neuron, hence the arrow pointing towards the environment and not to another neuron. One possible result of computation is the time difference between the first spike of the system and the succeeding spikes.

The SNP system in Figure 1 is Π, a 3 neuron system whose neurons are labeled (σ_1 to σ_3) and whose rules have a total system ordering from (1) to (5), taken from Zeng et al. (2011). σ_1 has an initial number of 2 spikes (hence the a^2 seen inside it). There is no *in* (input neuron), but σ_3 is the *out*. More formally,

$\Pi = (\{a\}, \sigma_1, \sigma_2, \sigma_3, syn, out)$ where $\sigma_1 = (2, R_1, R_2)$, $n_1 = 2$, $R_1 = \{a^2/a \rightarrow a\}$, $R_2 = \{a^2 \rightarrow a\}$ (σ_2 and σ_3 and their n_i s and R_i s can be similarly shown), $syn = \{(1,2), (1,3), (2,1), (2,3)\}$ are the synapses for Π.

A matrix representation of an SNP system makes use of the following vectors and matrix definitions (Zeng et al., 2010, 2011).

Configuration vector C_k is the vector containing all spikes in every neuron on the kth computation step, where C_0 is the initial vector containing all spikes in the system at the beginning of the computation. For Π (Figure 1) the initial configuration vector is $C_0 = <2,1,1>$.

Spiking vector S_k shows at a given configuration C_k if a rule is applicable (has value *1*) or not

Figure 1. SNP system Π

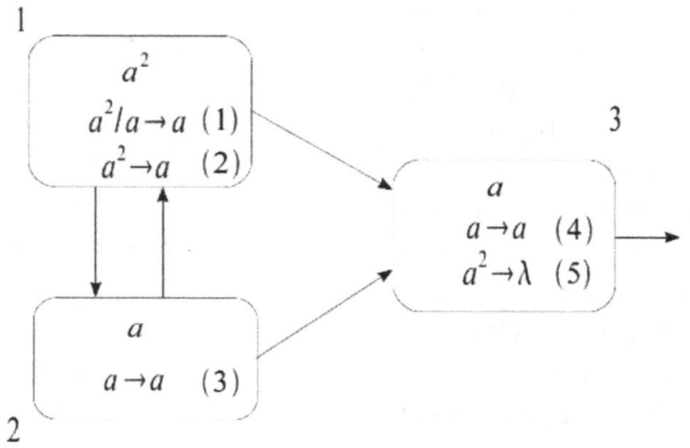

(has value 0 instead). For Π we have the spiking vector $S_0 = <1,0,1,1,0>$ given C_0. Note that a 2nd spiking vector, $S'_0 = <0,1,1,1,0>$, is possible if we use rule (2) over rule (1) instead (but not both at the same time, hence we cannot have a vector equal to $<1,1,1,1,0>$, so this S_k is invalid). *Validity* in this case means that only one among several applicable rules is used and thus represented in the S_k.

Spiking transition matrix M_Π is a matrix comprised of a_{ij} elements where a_{ij} is given as:

- $-c$, if rule r_i is in σ_j and is applied consuming c spikes;
- p, if rule r_i is in σ_s ($s \neq j$ and $(s,j) \in syn$) and is applied producing p spikes in total;
- 0, if rule r_i is in σ_s ($s \neq j$ and $(s,j) \notin syn$).

For Π, the M_Π is as follows:

$$M_\Pi = \begin{pmatrix} -1 & 1 & 1 \\ -2 & 1 & 1 \\ 1 & -1 & 1 \\ 0 & 0 & -1 \\ 0 & 0 & -2 \end{pmatrix}$$

In such a scheme, rows represent rules and columns represent neurons.

Finally, the following equation provides the configuration vector at the $(k+1)^{th}$ step, given the configuration vector and spiking vector at the kth step, and M_Π:

$$C_{k+1} = C_k + S_k * M_\Pi \qquad (1)$$

3. THE NVIDIA CUDA ARCHITECTURE

NVIDIA, a well known manufacturer of GPUs, released in 2007 the CUDA programming model and architecture (NVIDIA CUDA Developers, 2011). Using extensions of the widely known C language, a programmer can write parallel code which will then execute in multiple threads within multiple thread blocks, each contained within a grid of (thread) blocks. These grids belong to a single device i.e., a single GPU. Each device/GPU has multiple cores, each capable of running its own *block of threads.* The program run in the CUDA model scales up or down, depending on the number of cores the programmer currently has in a device. This scaling is done in a manner that is abstracted from the user, and is efficiently handled by the architecture as well. Parallelized code will run faster in CUDA with more cores than with fewer ones (NVIDIA Corporation, 2010).

Figure 2 shows another important feature of the CUDA model: the host and the device parts. The host (i.e., the CPU) controls the execution flow while the device (i.e., the GPU/s) is a highly-parallel *co-processor.* A function known as a *kernel function*, is a function called from the host but executed in the device.

CUDA C provides versions of the standard C language functions, e.g., the standard C function *malloc* has the CUDA C function counterpart

Figure 2. CUDA programming architecture (adapted from Cecilia et al., 2010a)

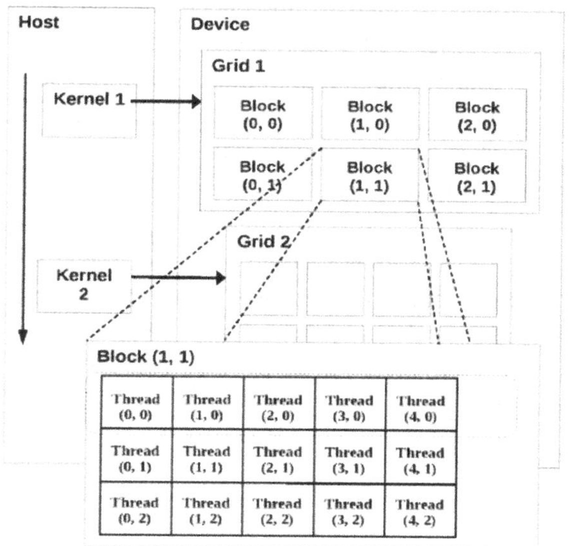

cudaMalloc, and the standard C function *free* has *cudaFree* as its CUDA C counterpart. CUDA C specific functions, e.g., *cudaMemcpy*, which, given an input of pointers and the size to copy (computed by the *sizeof* function), moves data from host to device (parameter *cudaMemcpyHostToDevice)* or device to host (*cudaMemcpyDeviceToHost*).

A kernel function call uses the triple < and > operator. For example, the kernel function *add<<<N,1>>>(dev_a, dev_b, dev_c)* adds the values per element (and each element is associated to one thread) of the device variables *dev_a* and *dev_b* sent to the device, collected in variable *dev_c* before being sent back to the host. The variable *N* in this case allows the programmer to specify a number of *N* threads which will execute the *add* kernel function in parallel, with '1' specifying only one block of thread for all *N* threads.

Since the kernel function is executed in parallel in the device, the function needs to have its inputs moved from the host to the device, and then back to the host after computation ends. This movement of data back and forth should be minimized in order to obtain more efficiency in execution time. Implementing an equation such as (1), which involves multiplication and addition between vectors and a matrix, can be done in parallel with the previous considerations in mind. In this case, C_k, S_k, and M_Π are loaded, manipulated, and pre-processed within the host code, before being sent to the kernel function. To represent C_k, S_k, and M_Π, text files are created to house each input, whereby each element of the vector or matrix is entered in the file in order, from left to right, with blank spaces as delimiters. M_Π however is entered in row-major order format (a linear array representation, whereby rows are placed one after another, left to right and top to bottom) i.e., for the matrix M_Π, the row-major order version is simply: *-1, 1, 1, -2, 1, 1, 1, -1, 1, 0, 0, -1, 0, 0, -2*. Row major ordering is a well-known ordering and representation of matrices for their linear as well as parallel manipulation in corresponding algorithms (Kirk, 2010). Once all computations are done for the $(k+1)^{th}$ configuration, the result of Equation 1 is then collected and moved from the device back to the host, where they can once again be operated on by the host. It is also important to note that these operations in the host provide logic and control on the inputs, while the device provides the arithmetic or computational 'muscle', the laborious task of working on multiple data at a given time in parallel. This division of labor illustrates the current dichotomy of the CUDA programming model (Cecilia et al., 2010b).

Once all 3 initial and necessary inputs are loaded (see Equation 1) the device is first instructed to perform multiplication between the S_k and M_Π. Vectors are treated and automatically formatted by the host code to appear as single row matrices, since vectors can be considered as such. Multiplication is done per element (one element is in one thread of the device), and then the products are collected and summed to produce a single element of the resulting vector.

Once multiplications of all the S_ks to M_Π are done, the results are added to the C_ks, once again element per element. Each element belongs to one thread, and all threads are executed in parallel. For this simulator, the host code consists largely of the programming language *Python*, a well-known high-level, object oriented programming (OOP) language. The reason for using a high-level language such as Python is because the initial inputs, as well as succeeding ones resulting from exhaustively applying the rules and Equation 1 require manipulation of the vector/matrix values as *strings*, and not just integral values. The host code/Python part thus implements the logic and control as mentioned earlier, while in it, the device/GPU code written in CUDA C executes the parallel parts. Python is also well known for being widely used in computational sciences (Langtangen, 2009).

4. SIMULATOR DESIGN AND IMPLEMENTATION

The current SNP simulator, based on the type of SNP systems without delays, is capable of implementing rules of the form (b-3). Rules are entered in the same manner as the earlier mentioned vectors and matrix, as blank space delimited values (from one rule to the other, belonging to the same neuron) and $ delimited (from one neuron to another). For Π in Figure 1, the file *r* containing the blank space and *$* delimited values is as follows: *2 2 $ 1 $ 1 2*. That is, rule (1) has the value 2 in the file *r*. Another implementation consideration was the use of *lists* in Python, since unlike dictionaries or tuples, lists in Python are *mutable*, which is a direct requirement of the vector/matrix value manipulations to be performed later on. Hence $C_k = <2, 1, 1>$ is represented as [2,1,1] in Python. That is, at the kth configuration of the system, the number of spikes of σ_1 are given by accessing the index (starting at zero) of the Python *list* variable *confVec*, in this case if *confVec*=[2,1,1], then *confVec*[0]=2 gives the number of spikes available at that time for σ_1, *confVec*[1]=1 for σ_2, and so on. The file *r*, which contains the ordered list of neurons and the rules that comprise each of them, is represented as a *list of sub-lists* in Python. For Π we have: *r*=[[2,2],[1],[1,2]].

Rules of σ_1 are given by accessing the sub-lists of *r* i.e., rule (1) is given by *r*[0][0]=2 and rule (4) is given by *r*[2][0]=1. We also have the input file *M*, which holds the Python *list* version of M_Π.

Algorithm 1. Overview of SNP system simulation algorithm

Input: C_k, M_Π, $r = [R_1 \ldots R_i]$

Output: *allGenCk* (list of all C_k) all their corresponding S_k

Require: *Ck, M, r* (file versions of C_k, M_Π, and *r, respectively)*

I. **(HOST)** Load input files. *M, r* are loaded once only. C_0 is also loaded once, then *Ck* afterwards.

II. **(HOST)** Determine if rule/s in *r* is/are applicable based on the number of spikes (n_i) present in each neuron in file *Ck*. Generate all valid and possible spiking vectors in a list of lists *Sk*, given the 3 inputs. (*Sks* are the file counterparts of S_k*s*).

III. **(DEVICE)** Run kernel function on *Sk* the current *Ck* and compute Equation 1 in parallel. Produce the next *Cks*.

IV. **(HOST+DEVICE)** Repeat steps I to IV, till at least one of the two *Stopping criteria* is encountered.

The general simulation algorithm is shown in Algorithm 1. Each part in Algorithm 1 indicates which part/s the simulator code runs in, either in the device (DEVICE) or in the host (HOST) part. Step *I* of Algorithm 1 loads the inputs needed to run the simulation. Step *II* generates all valid and possible S_ks given the inputs. Step *III* executes the kernel functions which implements Equation 1 in parallel. Step *IV* makes the algorithm stop with *2 stopping criteria*: (a) when a *zero vector* (a vector of zeros only) is encountered, or (b) when all distinct configuration have been produced in the computation. In particular, the computation of Π is finite for each natural number *n,* i.e., given a series of configurations $C_0 \rightarrow \ldots \rightarrow C_j \rightarrow \ldots \rightarrow C_k$, if $C_{k+1} = C_j$, then we check if C_j still has other possible C_i for *i* not in *{0, 1, …, k}*, and we do this for the series *{0, 1, …, k}*.

Figure 3 provides a graphical illustration of the simulation with respect to the host and device parts. Here we see that C_{k+1}s (in Figure 3 there are *n* of them) are all computed in parallel using the kernel functions called from the host. The host parts of the simulation however are run sequentially.

Another important point to notice is that either of the stopping criterion could allow for a deeply nested computation tree, one that can continue executing for a significantly lengthy amount of time even with a multi-core CPU and even the more parallelized GPU. The computation length (time) and depth (tree) will depend on the number of rules and neurons, their interconnections and the n_is. These 'larger' SNP systems would thus require equally larger, and faster GPU setups.

The more detailed algorithm for part *II* of Algorithm 1 is seen in Algorithm 2. Recall from the definition of an SNP system that we have *m* number of neurons. We related *m* to our implementation by noticing the cardinality of the Python list *r* i.e., $|r|=m$. This means the file *r* (a Python list of lists) has sub-lists equal to the number of neurons.

As an illustration of Algorithm 2, we consider Π as an input to our SNP system simulator. Recall

Figure 3. The simulation flow, with the host and device parts emphasized

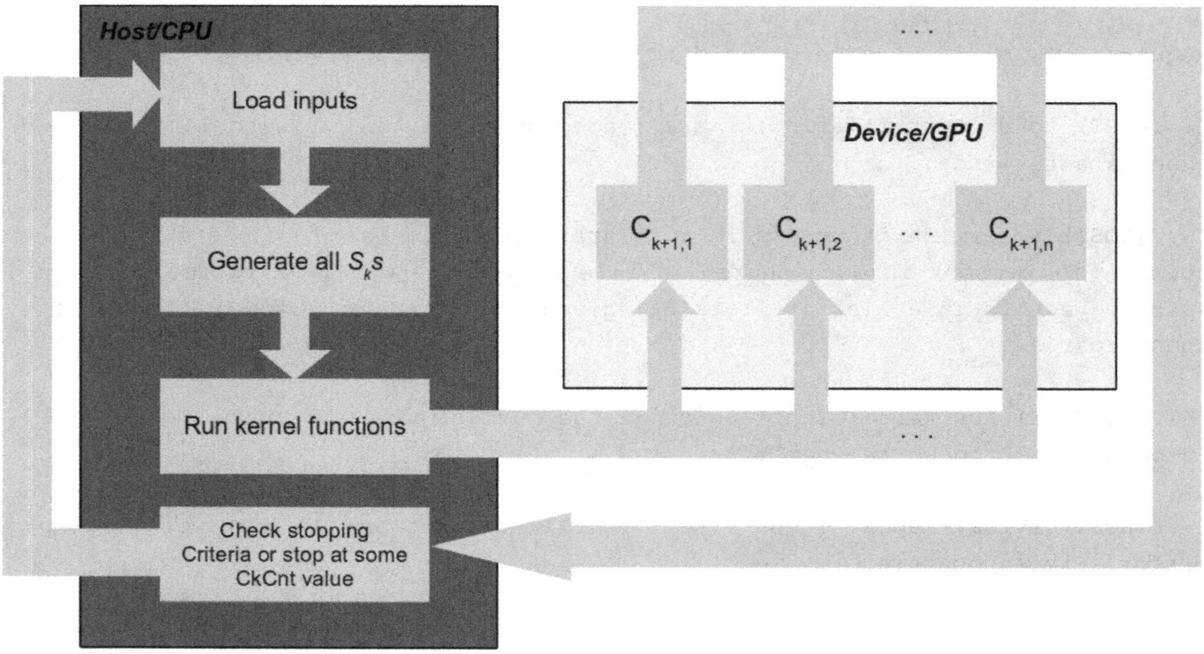

Algorithm 2. Further details of part II of Algorithm 1

```
II-1
Input: tmp, copy of r
Output: Modified tmp
  foreach neuron, idx in tmp do
            cnt = 1; // idx = index per tmp
            foreach rule, idx2 in neuron do
                        if spikMultip E then
                                  tmp[idx][idx2] = cnt;
                                  increment cnt by 1;
                        end
                        else
                                  tmp[idx][idx2] = 0;
                        end
            end
  end
II-2
Input: tmp
Output: tmp2, list of lists (the {1,0} strings per neuron).
  tmp2 = emptyCopy(tmp); //'empty' Python list copy of tmp
  foreach neuron, idx in tmp do
           tmpstrn = ''; /* empty string,
                       later of length |tmp[idx][idx2]| */
           foreach rule ∈ neuron,idx2, and rule ≠ 0 do
                       tmpstrn = '1' at idx2, '0' elsewhere;
                       Append tmpstrn into tmp2[idx][idx2];
           end
  end
II-3
Input: tmp2
Output: tmp3, list containing all possible and valid S_ks.
  foreach (i,j) pair in tmp2, i < j, 0 ≤ i < (m − 2), 1 ≤ j < m do
      Distribute and concatenate strings elements of tmp2[i] to tmp2[j];
      increment i,j by 1;
  end
```

that C_0 = <*2, 1, 1*> for Π, including its S_k, M_Π and the rule list R_i (Figure 1). We introduce variables of the form *idx* to mean the index of the current Python list element. Initially from II-1 of Algorithm 2, we have *tmp*=*r*=[[2,2],[1],[1,2]], where sub-lists in *tmp* are the number of spikes needed by *E* of each rule e.g., R_1 requires two spikes to fire, R_3 requires only one spike to fire. Applying II-1 of Algorithm 2 with *tmp* produces a modified *tmp*=[[1,2],[1],[1,0]] (output of II-2). We now have a *tmp* which we have marked with increasing integer values the rules which are applicable and which are not (has a zero value).

Continuing II-2, we generate all possible and valid S_ks from *tmp* by going through each neuron (each element of *tmp*) since we know which elements (rules) per neuron match *E*. We then produce a new list, *tmp*2, which is made up of a sub-list of strings from all possible and valid *{1,0}* strings i.e., S_k*s* per neuron. At the end of II-2 we have *tmp*2= [['10', '01'], ['1'], ['10']] . The reason for the values of *tmp*2 is obvious: *tmp*2[0][0] is the case where R_1 is applied and R_2 isn't (string '10'); *tmp*2[0][1] is the case where R_2 is applied and not R_1, and so on.

Illustrating II-3 of Algorithm 2, given *tmp*2 from II-2 we pair up the neurons in order, and then exhaustively distribute every element of the first neuron in the pair to the elements of the 2nd neuron in the pair. This pairing and distribution of strings will first be stored temporarily in *tmpstrn* and then be collected (concatenated) in a new list, *tmp*3. It is important to note that the distribution order is imperative as they relate to the meaning and value of the produced S_ks. The final output of the sub-algorithm for the generation of all valid and possible S_ks is a list, *tmp*3 = ['10110', '01110'] which we have mentioned earlier when we first introduced the concept of S_k in Section 2.

5. SIMULATION RESULTS, OBSERVATIONS, AND ANALYSES

The SNP system simulator (combination of Python and CUDA C) implements the algorithms in Section 4. The C_k tree for Π with C_0 = [2,1,1] went down as deep as *confVec*=109. At that point, all configuration vectors for all possible and valid spiking vectors have been produced. The Python list variable *allGenCk* collects all the C_ks produced. In Algorithm 2 all the values of *tmp*3 are added to *allGenCk*. Thus each time a new and unique C_k is produced, it is added to *allGenCk* to facilitate the 2nd stopping criteria, preventing an infinite loop in the simulation. The final value of *allGenCk* for the above simulation run is collected:

allGenCk = ['2-1-1', '2-1-2', '1-1-2', '2-1-3', '1-1-3', '2-0-2', '2-0-1', '2-1-4', '1-1-4', '2-0-3', '1-1-1', '0-1-2', '0-1-1', '2-1-5', '1-1-5', '2-0-4', '0-1-3', '1-0-2', '1-0-1', '2-1-6', '1-1-6', '2-0-5', '0-1-4', '1-0-3', '1-0-0', '2-1-7', '1-1-7', '2-0-6', '0-1-5', '1-0-4', '2-1-8', '1-1-8', '2-0-7', '0-1-6', '1-0-5', '2-1-9', '1-1-9', '2-0-8', '0-1-7', '1-0-6', '2-1-10', '1-1-10', '2-0-9', '0-1-8', '1-0-7', '0-1-9', '1-0-8', '1-0-9']

It is also noteworthy that the simulation for Π did not stop at the 1st stopping criteria (arriving at a zero vector i.e., C_k = [0,0,0]) since Π generates all natural counting numbers greater than 1, hence a loop (an infinite one) is to be expected. The simulation run shown above stopped with the 2nd stopping criteria from Section 4. Thus the simulation was able to exhaust all possible configuration vectors and their spiking vectors, stopping only since a repetition of an earlier generated *confVec*/C_k would introduce a loop (triggering the 2nd stopping criteria). Graphically (though not shown exhaustively) the computation tree for Π is shown in Figure 4.

The *confVecs* followed by (...) are the *confVecs* that went deeper, i.e., produced more C_ks than Figure 4 has shown.

6. CONCLUSION AND FUTURE WORK

Using a highly parallel computing device such as a GPU, and the NVIDIA CUDA programming model, an SNP system simulator was successfully designed and implemented as per the objective of this work. The simulator was shown to model the workings of an SNP system without delay using the system's matrix representation. The

Figure 4. The computation tree showing the output of the simulator with Π as input

```
211
├── 112
│   ├── 201
│   │   ├── 011
│   │   └── 111
│   │       └── 201
│   └── 202
│       ├── 011
│       ├── 012
│       │   ├── 101
│       │   │   └── 100
│       │   └── 102
│       │       ├── 100
│       │       └── 101
│       ├── 111
│       └── 112
└── 212
    ├── 112
    ├── 113
    │   ├── 202
    │   └── 203
    │       ├── 012
    │       ├── 013
    │       │   ├── 102
    │       │   └── 103
    │       │       ├── 101
    │       │       └── 102
    │       ├── 112
    │       └── 113
    ├── 212
    └── 213
        ├── 113
        ├── 114
        │   ├── 203
        │   └── 204 (...)
        ├── 213
        └── 214
            ├── 114
            ├── 115 (...)
            ├── 214
            └── 215 (...)
```

use of a high level programming language such as Python for host tasks, mainly for logic, string representation and manipulation of values (vector/matrix elements) has provided the necessary expressive power to implement the algorithms. The algorithms presented were able to produce and exhaust all possible and valid configuration and spiking vectors. For the device tasks, CUDA allowed the manipulation of the NVIDIA CUDA enabled GPU which took care of repetitive and highly parallel computations (vector-matrix addition and multiplication essentially).

Future versions of the SNP system simulator will focus on several improvements. These improvements include the use of an optimized algorithm for matrix computations on the GPU without requiring the input matrix to be transformed into a square matrix (this is currently handled by the simulator by padding zeros to an otherwise non-square matrix input). Finally, deeper understanding of the CUDA architecture, such as inter- thread/block communication, for very large systems with equally large matrices, is required. These improvements as well as the current version of the simulator should also be run in a machine or setup with higher versions of GPUs supporting NVIDIA CUDA.

ACKNOWLEDGMENT

Francis Cabarle is supported by the DOST-ERDT scholarship program. Henry Adorna is funded by the DOST-ERDT research grant and the Alexan professorial chair of the UP Diliman Department of Computer Science, University of the Philippines Diliman. They would also like to acknowledge the Algorithms and Complexity laboratory for the use of Apple iMacs with NVIDIA CUDA enabled GPUs for this work. Miguel A. Martínez–del–Amor is supported by "Proyecto de Excelencia con Investigador de Reconocida Valía" of the "Junta de Andalucìa" under grant P08-TIC04200, and the support of the project TIN2009–13192 of the "Ministerio de Educación y Ciencia" of Spain, both co-financed by FEDER funds. Finally, they would also like to thank the valuable insights of Mr. Neil Ibo.

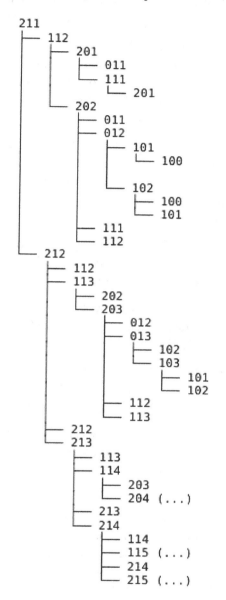

REFERENCES

Cecilia, J., García, J., Guerrero, G., Martínez-del-Amor, M., Pérez-Hurtado, I., & Pérez-Jiménez, M. (2010a). Simulating a p system based efficient solution to sat by using GPUs. *Journal of Logic and Algebraic Programming, 79*(6), 317–325. doi:10.1016/j.jlap.2010.03.008.

Cecilia, J., García, J., Guerrero, G., Martínez-del-Amor, M., Pérez-Hurtado, I., & Pérez-Jiménez, M. (2010b). Simulation of p systems with active membranes on cuda. *Briefings in Bioinformatics, 11*(3), 313–322. doi:10.1093/bib/bbp064.

Chen, H., Ionescu, M., Ishdorj, T. O., Păun, A., Păun, G., & Pérez-Jiménez, M. (2008). Spiking neural p systems with extended rules: Universality and languages. *Natural Computing: An International Journal, 7*(2), 147–166. doi:10.1007/s11047-006-9024-6.

Ciobanu, G., & Wenyuan, G. (2004). P systems running on a cluster of computers. In C. Martín-Vide, G. Mauri, G. Paun, G. Rozenberg, & A. Salomaa (Eds.), *Proceedings of the International Workshop on Membrane Computing* (LNCS 2933, pp. 289-328).

Díaz, D., Graciani, C., Gutiérrez-Naranjo, M., Pérez-Hurtado, I., & Pérez-Jiménez, M. (2010). In Păun, G., Rozenberg, G., & Salomaa, A. (Eds.), *The Oxford handbook of membrane computing* (p. 17). New York, NY: Oxford University Press.

Fatahalian, K., Sugerman, J., & Hanrahan, P. (2004). Understanding the efficiency of GPU algorithms for matrix-matrix multiplication. In *Proceedings of the ACM SIGGRAPH/EUROGRAPHICS Conference on Graphics Hardware* (pp. 133-137).

Garland, M., & Kirk, D. B. (2010). Understanding throughput-oriented architectures. *Communications of the ACM, 53*(11), 58–66. doi:10.1145/1839676.1839694.

Garland, M., Le Grand, S., Nickolls, J., Anderson, J., Hardwick, J., & Morton, S. (2008). Parallel computing experiences with cuda. *IEEE Micro, 28*, 13–27. doi:10.1109/MM.2008.57.

Gross, M. (1998). Molecular computation. In Gramss, T., Bornholdt, S., Gross, M., Mitchel, M., & Pellizzari, T. (Eds.), *Non-standard computation*. New York, NY: John Wiley & Sons.

Gutiérrez-Naranjo, M., Pérez-Jiménez, M., & Ramírez-Martínez, D. (2008). A software tool for verification of spiking neural p systems. *Natural Computing, 7*(4), 485–497. doi:10.1007/s11047-008-9083-y.

Harris, M. (2005). Mapping computational concepts to GPUs. In *Proceedings of the ACM SIGGRAPH Courses* (p. 50).

Ionescu, M., Păun, G., & Yokomori, T. (2006). Spiking neural p systems. *Fundamenta Informaticae, 71*(2-3), 279–308.

Kirk, D., & Hwu, W. (2010). *Programming massively parallel processors: A hands on approach*. San Francisco, CA: Morgan Kaufmann.

Langtangen, H. P. (2009). *Python scripting for computational science (Texts in computational science and engineering)* (3rd ed.). New York, NY: Springer.

Nguyen, V., Kearney, D., & Gioiosa, G. (2010a). An extensible, maintainable and elegant approach to hardware source code generation in reconfig-p. *Journal of Logic and Algebraic Programming, 79*(6), 383–396. doi:10.1016/j.jlap.2010.03.013.

Nguyen, V., Kearney, D., & Gioiosa, G. (2010b). A region-oriented hardware implementation for membrane computing applications and its integration into reconfig-p. In G. Paun, M. J. Pérez-Jiménez, A. Riscos-Núñez, G. Rozenberg, & A. Salomaa (Eds.), *Proceedings of the 10th International Workshop on Membrane Computing* (LNCS 5957, pp. 385-409).

NVIDIA Corporation. (2010). *Nvidia cuda c programming guide 3.0*. Retrieved from http://developer.download.nvidia.com/compute/cuda/3_0/toolkit/docs/NVIDIA_CUDA_Programming-Guide.pdf

NVIDIA CUDA Developers. (2011). *Resources page*. Retrieved from http://developer.nvidia.com/page/home.html

Păun, G. (2000). Computing with membranes. *Journal of Computer and System Sciences*, *61*, 108–143. doi:10.1006/jcss.1999.1693.

Păun, G., Ciobanu, G., & Pérez-Jiménez, M. (2006). *Applications of membrane computing*. New York, NY: Springer.

Systems, P. (2011). *Resource website*. Retrieved from http://ppage.psystems.eu/

Top 500. (2011). *Supercomputer sites*. Retrieved from http://www.top500.org

Volkov, V., & Demmel, J. (2008). Benchmarking GPUs to tune dense linear algebra. In *Proceedings of the ACM/IEEE Conference on Supercomputing* (p. 31).

Zeng, X., Adorna, H., Martínez-del-Amor, M., & Pan, L. (2010). When matrices meet brains. In *Proceedings of the Eighth Brainstorming Week on Membrane Computing* (pp. 255-266).

Zeng, X., Adorna, H., Martínez-del-Amor, M., Pan, L., & Pérez-Jiménez, M. (2011). Matrix representation of spiking neural p systems. In M. Gheorghe, T. Hinze, G. Paun, G. Rozenberg, & A. Salomaa (Eds.), *Proceedings of the 11th International Conference on Membrane Computing* (LNCS 6501, pp. 377-392).

This work was previously published in the International Journal of Natural Computing Research (IJNCR), Volume 2, Issue 2, edited by Leandro Nunes de Castro, pp. 19-31, copyright 2011 by IGI Publishing (an imprint of IGI Global).

Chapter 7
P Colonies of Capacity One and Modularity

Luděk Cienciala
Silesian University in Opava, Czech Republic

Lucie Ciencialová
Silesian University in Opava, Czech Republic

Miroslav Langer
Silesian University in Opava, Czech Republic

ABSTRACT

In this paper, the authors continue the investigation of P colonies introduced in Kelemen, Kelemenová, and Păun (2004). This paper examines a class of abstract computing devices composed of independent agents, acting and evolving in a shared environment. The first part is devoted to the P colonies of the capacity one. The authors present improved results concerning the computational power of the P colonies with capacity one and without using checking programs. The second part of the paper examines the modularity of the P colonies. The authors then divide the agents into modules.

1. INTRODUCTION

P colonies were introduced (Kelemen, Kelemenová, & Păun, 2004) as formal models of a computing device inspired by membrane systems and formal grammars called colonies. This model is inspired by structure and functioning of a community of living organisms in a shared environment.

The independent organisms living in a P colony are called agents or cells. Each agent is represented by a collection of objects embedded in a membrane. The number of objects inside each agent is the same and constant during computation. The environment contains several copies of the basic environmental object denoted by *e*. The object *e* appears in arbitrary large number of copies in the environment.

DOI: 10.4018/978-1-4666-4253-9.ch007

With each agent a set of programs is associated. The program, which determines the activity of the agent, is very simple and depends on content of the agent and on multiset of objects placed in the environment. Agent can change content of the environment by programs and through the environment it can affect the behavior of other agents.

This interaction between agents is a key factor in functioning of the P colony. In each moment each object inside the agent is affected by executing the program.

For more information about P colonies see Kelemen and Kelemenová (2005) and about P systems generaly see Păun, Rozenberg, and Salomaa (2009) or P Systems (2004).

2. DEFINITIONS

Throughout the paper we assume that the reader is familiar with the basics of the formal language theory.

We use *NRE* to denote the family of the recursively enumerable sets of natural numbers. Let Σ be the alphabet. Let Σ^* be the set of all words over Σ (including the empty word ε). We denote the length of the word $w \in \Sigma^*$ by $|w|$ and the number of occurrences of the symbol $a \in \Sigma$ in w by $|w|_a$.

A multiset of objects M is a pair $M = (V, f)$, where V is an arbitrary (not necessarily finite) set of objects and f is a mapping $f: V \to N$; f assigns to each object in V its multiplicity in M. The set of all multisets with the set of objects V is denoted by V^*. The set $U \subseteq V$ is called the support of M and is denoted by $supp(M)$ if for all

$x \in U$ $f(x) \neq 0$ holds. The cardinality of M, denoted by $|M|$, is defined by $|M| = \Sigma_a \in_V f(a)$. Each multiset of objects M with the set of objects $U = \{a_1, \ldots, a_n\}$ can be represented as a string w over alphabet U, where

$$| w |_{a_i} = f(a_i); 1 \leq i \leq n.$$

Obviously, all words obtained from w by permuting the letters represent the same multiset M. The ε represents the empty multiset.

2.1. P Colonies

We briefly recall the notion of P colonies. A P colony consists of agents and an environment. Both the agents and the environment contain objects. With each agent a set of programs is associated. The program is formed from rules. There are two types of rules in the programs. The first type of rules, called the evolution rules, are of the form $a \to b$. It means that the object a inside the agent is rewritten (evolved) to the object b. The second type of rules, called the communication rules, are of the form $c \leftrightarrow d$. When the communication rule is performed, the object c inside the agent and the object d outside the agent swap their places. Thus after execution of the rule, the object d appears inside the agent and the object c is placed outside the agent.

In Kelemen and Kelemenová (2005) the set of programs was extended by the checking rules. These rules give an opportunity to the agents to opt between two possibilities. The rules are in the form r_1/r_2. If the checking rule is performed, then the rule r_1 has higher priority to be executed over the rule r_2 It means that the agent checks whether the rule r_1 is applicable. If the rule can be executed, then the agent is compulsory to use it. If the rule r_1 cannot be applied, then the agent uses the rule r_2.

Definition: The P colony of the capacity k is a construct

$\Pi = (A, e, f, V_E, B_1, ..., B_n)$, where

- A is an alphabet of the colony, its elements are called objects,
- $e \in A$ is the basic object of the colony,
- $f \in A$ is the final object of the colony,
- V_E is a multiset over $A - \{e\}$,

- B_i, $1 \leq i \leq n$, are agents, each agent is a construct $B_i = (O_i, P_i)$, where
  - O_i is a multiset over A, it determines the initial state (content) of the agent, $|O_i| = k$,
  - $P_i = \{p_{i,1}, \ldots, p_{i,k_i}\}$ is a finite multiset of programs, where each program contains exactly k rules, which are in one of the following forms each:
    - $a \to b$, called the evolution rule,
    - $c \leftrightarrow d$, called the communication rule,
    - r_1/r_2, called the checking rule; r_1, r_2 are evolution rules or communication rules.

An initial configuration of the P colony is an $(n+1)$-tuple of strings of objects present in the P colony at the beginning of the computation. It is given by the multiset O_i for, $1 \leq i \leq n$ and by the set V_E. Formally, the configuration of the P colony Π is given by $(w_1, w_2, \ldots, w_n)$, where $|w_i| = k$, $1 \leq i \leq n$, w_i represents all the objects placed inside the i-th agent, and $w_E \in (A - \{e\})^*$ represents all the objects in the environment different from the object e.

In the paper parallel model of P colonies will be studied. It means that at each step of the parallel computation each agent tries to find one usable program. If the number of applicable programs are higher than one, then the agent chooses one of the programs nondeterministically. At one step of the computation the maximal possible number of agents are active.

Let the programs of each P_i be labeled in a one-to-one manner by labels in a set $lab(P_i)$ in such a way that $lab(P_i) \cap lab(P_j) = \emptyset$ for $i \neq j$, $1 \leq i, j \leq n$.

To express derivation step formally, we introduce following four functions for the agent using the rule r of program $p \in P$ with objects w in the environment:

For the rule r which is $a \to b$, $c \leftrightarrow d$, and for multiset $w \in V^*$ we define:

$left(a \to b, w) = a$	$left(c \leftrightarrow d, w) = \varepsilon$
$left(a \to b, w) = b$	$right(c \leftrightarrow d, w) = \varepsilon$
$\text{export}(a \to b, w) = \varepsilon$	$\text{export}(c \leftrightarrow d, w) = c$
$\text{import}(a \to b, w) = \varepsilon$	$\text{import}(c \leftrightarrow d, w) = d$

For checking rules the functions *left*, *right*, *export* and *import* are defined in a similar way.

For a program p and any $\alpha \in \{left, right, export, import\}$, let be $\alpha(p, w) = \cup_{r \in p} \alpha(r, w)$. A transition from a configuration to another is denoted as $(w_1, \ldots, w_n; w_E) \Rightarrow (w'_1, \ldots, w'n; w'_E)$ where the following conditions are satisfied:

- There is a set of program labels P with $|P| \leq n$ such that
- $p, p' \in P$, $p \neq p'$, $p \in lab(P_j)$ implies $p' \notin lab(P_j)$,
- for each $p \in P$, $p \in lab(P_j)$, $left(p, w_E) \cup export(p, w_E) = w_j$ and $\cup_{p \in P} import(p, w_E) \subseteq w_E$.
- Furthermore, the chosen set P is maximal, i.e., if any other program $r \in \cup_{1 \leq i \leq n} lab(P_i)$, $r \notin P$ is added to P, then the conditions listed are not satisfied.

Now, for each j, $1 \leq j \leq n$, for which there exists a $p \in P$ with $p \in lab(P_j)$, let be $w'_j = right(p, w_E) \cup import(p, w_E)$. If there is no $p \in P$ with $p \in lab(P_j)$ for some j, $1 \leq j \leq n$, then let be $w'_j = w_j$ and moreover, let be

$$w_E' = w_E - \bigcup_{p \in P} \text{import}(p, w_E) \cup \bigcup_{p \in P} \text{export}(p, w_E)$$

A configuration is halting if the set of program labels P satisfying the conditions above cannot vary from the empty set. A set of all possible halting configurations is denoted by H. A halting computation can be associated with the result of the computation. It is given by the number of copies of the special symbol f present in the environment. The set of numbers computed by a P colony Π is defined as

$$N(\Pi) = \{|v_E|_f \mid (w_1, ..., w_n; V_E) \Rightarrow^* (v_1, ..., v_n; v_E) \in H\},$$

where $(w_1, ..., w_n; V_E)$ is the initial configuration, $(v_1, ..., v_n; v_E)$ is a halting configuration, and $\Rightarrow^*$ denotes the reflexive and transitive closure of $\Rightarrow$.

Consider a P colony $\Pi = (A, e, f, V_E, B_1, ..., B_n)$. The maximal number of programs associated with the agents in the P colony Π are called the height of the P colony Π. The degree of the P colony Π is the number of agents in it. The third parameter characterizing the P colony is the capacity of the P colony Π describing the number of the objects inside each agent.

Let us use the following notations: $NPCOL_{par}(k, n, h)$ for the family of all sets of numbers computed by the P colonies working in a parallel, using no checking rules and with the capacity at most k, the degree at most n and the height at most h. If we allow the checking rules, then the family of all sets of numbers computed by the P colonies is denoted by $NPCOL_{par}K(k, n, h)$.

P colony is a kind of P systems. The original model of P systems is introduced, defined and its properties are described in e.g., Păun (2000, 2002). More about the P colonies is available in e.g., Cienciala, Ciencialová, and Langer (2011), Csuhaj-Varjú, Kelemen, Kelemenová, Păun, and Vaszil (2006), and Csuhaj-Varjú, Margenstern, and Vaszil (2006).

2.2. Register Machines

The aim of the paper is to characterize the size of the families $NPCOL_{par}(k, n, h)$ comparing them with the recursively enumerable sets of numbers. To meet the target, we use the notion of a register machine.

Definition: (Minsky, 1967) A register machine is the construct $M = (m, H, l_0, l_h, P)$ where:

- m is the number of registers,
- H is the set of instruction labels,
- l_0 is the start label, l_h is the final label,
- P is a finite set of instructions injectively labeled with the elements from the set H.

The instructions of the register machine are of the following forms:

l_1: $(ADD(r), l_2, l_3)$ - Add 1 to the content of the register r and proceed to the instruction (labeled with) l_2 or l_3.

l_1: $(SUB(r), l_2, l_3)$ -If the register r stores the value different from zero, then subtract 1 from its content and go to instruction l_2, otherwise proceed to instruction l_3.

l_h: *HALT* - Stop the machine. The final label l_h is only assigned to this instruction.

Without loss of generality, it can be assumed that in each *ADD*-instruction l_1: $(ADD(r), l_2, l_3)$ and in each conditional *SUB*-instruction l_1: $(SUB(r), l_2, l_3)$, the labels l_1, l_2, l_3 are mutually distinct.

The register machine M computes a set $N(M)$ of numbers in the following way: the computation starts with all registers empty (hence storing the number zero) and with the instruction labeled l_0. The computation proceeds by applying the instructions indicated by the labels (and the content of registers allows its application). If it reaches the halt instruction, then the number stored at that time in the register 1 is said to be computed by M and hence it is introduced in $N(M)$ (Because of the nondeterminism in choosing the continuation of the computation in the case of *ADD*-instructions, $N(M)$ can be an infinite set). It is known (Minsky, 1967) that in this way we can compute all sets of numbers which are Turing computable.

Moreover, we call a register machine partially blind (Greibach, 1978) if we interpret a subtract instruction in the following way: l_1: $(SUB(r), l_2, l_3)$ - if there is a value different from zero in the register r, then subtract one from its contents and go to instruction l_2 or to instruction l_3; if there is stored zero in the register r when attempting to decrement the register r, then the program ends without yielding a result.

When the partially blind register machine reaches the final state, the result obtained in the first register is only taken into account if the remaining registers store value zero. The family of sets of non-negative integers generated by partially blind register machines is denoted by NRM_{pb}. The partially blind register machine accepts a proper subset of NRE.

3. P COLONIES WITH ONE OBJECT INSIDE THE AGENT

In this section we analyze the behavior of P colonies with only one object inside each agent of P colonies. It means that each program is formed by only one rule, either the evolution rule or the communication rule. If all agents have their programs with the evolution rules, the agents "live only for themselves" and do not communicate with the environment.

Following results were proved:

- $NPCOL_{par}(1,*,7) = NRE$ in Cienciala and Ciencialová (2006)
- $NPCOL_{par}K(1,4,*) = NRE$ in Ciencialová, Cienciala, and Kelemenová (2007)
- $NPCOL_{par}(1,2,*) \supseteq NRM_{pb}$ in Ciencialová, Cienciala, and Kelemenová (2007)

Theorem 1: $NPCOL_{par}(1,4,*) = NRE$.

Proof: We construct a P colony simulating the computation of a register machine. Because there are only copies of e in the environment and inside the agents, we have to initialize a computation by generating the initial label l_0. After generating the symbol l_0, the agent stops. It can continue its activity only by using a program with the communication rule. Two agents will cooperate in order to simulate the ADD and SUB - instructions. Let us consider an m-register machine $M = (m, H, l_0, l_h, P)$ and present the content of the register i by the number of copies of a specific object a_i in the environment. We construct the P colony

$\Pi = (A, e, f, \emptyset, B_1, \ldots, B_4)$ with:

- $A = \{ l_i, L_i, l'_i, k_i, k'_i, L'_i, m_i, m_i', m_i'' M_i, M'_i, D_i, y_i, n_i \mid 0 \leq i \leq |H| \} \cup \cup\{a_i \mid 0 \leq i \leq m\} \cup \{A_r^{\,i} \mid \text{for every } l_1: (SUB(r), l_2, l_3) \in H\} \cup \{e, d, C\}$
- $f = a_1$,
- $B_i = (e, P_i)$, $1 \leq i \leq 4$.

1. To initialize simulation of computation of M we define the agent $B_1 = (e, P_1)$ with a set of programs (Tables 1-6 in the Appendix):

Agent B_1 generates label corresponding to the first instruction of the register machine M.

2. We need an additional agent to generate a special object d. This agent will be working during whole computation. In each pair of steps the agent B_2 places a copy of d to the environment. This agent stops working when it consumes the symbol which is generated by the simulation of the instruction l_h from the environment.

The P colony $\langle e \to l_0 \rangle$; starts its computation in the initial configuration $(e, e, e, e, \varepsilon)$. In the first subsequence of steps of computation of the P colony Π only agents B_1, B_2 can apply their programs.

3. To simulate the ADD-instruction $l_1: (ADD(r), l_2, l_3)$, we define two agents B_1 and B_3 in the P colony Π. These agents help each other to add a copy of the object a_r and the object l_2 or l_3 into the environment.

This pair of agents generates two objects. One object increments the value of the particular register and the second one defines the instruction from which simulation will continue. One agent is not able to generate both objects corresponding to the simulation of one instruction, because at the moment of placing all of its content into the environment via the communication rules, it does not know which instruction it simulates. It nondeterministically chooses one of the possible instructions (program 7). Now it is necessary to check whether the agent has chosen the right instruction. For this purpose the second agent slightly changes first generated object (programs 13, 14, 15). The first agent swaps this changed object for the new one generated only if it belongs to the same instruction (program 8). If this is not done successfully, the computation never stops because of absence of the halting object for the agent B_2.

4. For each *SUB*-instruction l_1: $(SUB(r), l_2, l_3)$, the following programs are introduced in the sets P_1, P_3 and in the set P_4:

Agents B_1, B_3 and B_4 collectively check the state of particular register and generate label of following instruction. The first part of simulation is similar to the first part of simulation of the *ADD*-instruction. Agents B_1 and B_3 generate two objects corresponding to this *SUB*-instruction (programs 19 – 22, 36 – 39). Then agent B_1 generates object $A_1{}^r$ (program 23) – it will try to execute subtraction (instruction l_1) from the register r. If it succeeds (program 24) it will generate object y_1 and it will be waiting until object l_2 appears in the environment (programs 27 – 33). If subtraction is not successful - there is no object a_r in the environment –then the agent will wait for object k_1‘. This object is generated by agent B_3 executing programs 40 and 41. Then agent B_1 generates object n_1 and waits for object l_2 (programs 28 – 32 and 34, 35). Part of the simulation is determined to purify the environment from redundant objects (programs in P_4 and programs 43 and 44).

5. The halting instruction l_h is simulated by the agent B_1 with a subset of programs:

The agent places the object l_h into the environment, from where it can be consumed by the agent B_2 and by this the agent B_2 stops its activity.

The P colony Π correctly simulates computation of the register machine M. The computation of Π starts with no object a_r placed in the environment in the same way as the computation of M starts with zeros in all registers. The computation of Π stops if the symbol l_h is placed inside the agent B_2 in the same way as M stops by executing the halting instruction labeled l_h. Consequently, $N(M) = N(\Pi)$ and because the number of agents equals four, the proof is complete.

Theorem 2: $NPCOL_{par}(1,*,8) = NRE$.

Proof: We construct a P colony simulating the computation of a register machine. Because there are only copies of e in the environment and inside the agents, we have to initialize a computation by generating the initial label l_0. After generating the symbol l_0 this agent stops and it can start its activity only by using a program with the communication rule. Two agents will cooperate in order to simulate the *ADD* and *SUB* instructions.

Let us consider an m-register machine $M = (m, H, l_0, l_h, P)$ and present the content of the register i by the number of copies of a specific object a_i in the environment. We construct the P colony

$\Pi = (A, e, f, \varnothing, B_1, ..., B_n)$, $n \leq 5|H|+2$, where:

- $A = \{l_i, l'_i, k_i, i, i', m_i, L_i, D_i \mid 0 \leq i \leq |H|\} \cup \{a_i \mid 0 \leq i \leq m\} \cup \{e, d\}$
- $f = a_1$,
- $B_i = (e, P_i)$, $1 \leq i \leq 5|H|+2$.

1. To initialize simulation of computation of M, we define the agent $B_1 = (e, P_1)$ with a set of programs (Tables 7-10 in the Appendix):

We need an additional agent to generate a special object d. This agent will be working during whole computation. In each pair of steps the agent B_2 places a copy of d to the environment.

The P colony Π starts its computation in the initial configuration (e, e, e,… e,ε). In the first subsequence of steps of the P colony Π, only the agents B_1 and B_2 can apply their programs.

2. To simulate the ADD-instruction l_1: (ADD(r), l_2, l_3), there are two agents $\langle e \rightarrow d \rangle$; and $\langle d \leftrightarrow e \rangle$; in the P colony Π. These agents help each other to add one copy of the object a_r and the object l_2 or l_3 to the environment.
3. For each SUB-instruction l_1: (SUB(r), l_2, l_3), the below mentioned programs are introduced in the sets $\langle d \leftrightarrow l_h \rangle$; and in the set Π
4. The halting instruction l_h is simulated by agent B_2 which consumes the object l_h and that stops the computation.

The P colony Π correctly simulates the computation of the register machine M. The computation of the $\langle l_1 \rightarrow D_1 \rangle$, starts with no object a_r, which indicates the content of the register r, placed in the environment, in the same way as the computation in the register machine M starts with zeros in all registers. Then the agents simulate the computation by simulating ADD- and SUB-instructions. The computation of the P colony Π stops if the symbol l_h is placed inside the corresponding agent as well as the register machine M stops by executing the halting instruction labeled l_h. Consequently, $N(M) = N(\Pi)$ and because the number of agents equals four, the proof is complete.

4. MODULARITY IN THE TERMS OF P COLONIES

During the evolution unicellular organisms have evolved into multicellular. Some cells specialized their activities for the particular function and have to cooperate with other specialized cells to be alive. In that way the organs have evolved and living organisms have become more complex. But the cooperating organs and more complex living organisms are more sophisticated, live longer and their life is improving.

From the previous section we can observe that some agents in the P colonies are providing the same function during the computation. This inspired us to introduce the modules in the P colonies. We have defined five modules, where each of them is providing one specific function.

Figure 1. Modular P colony

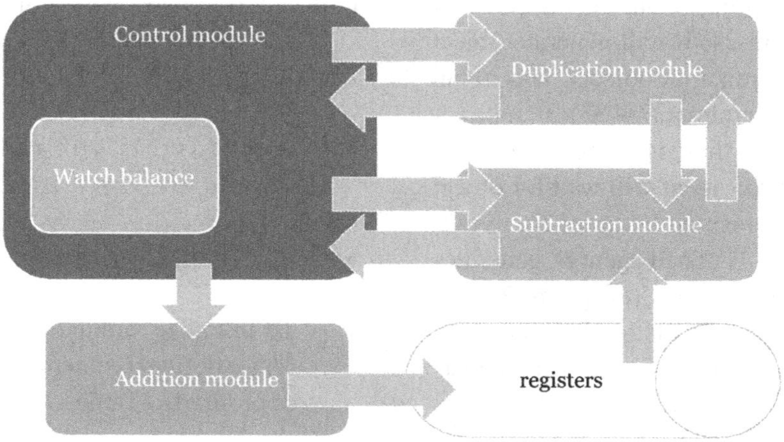

These modules are the module for the duplication, the module for the addition, the module for the subtraction, the balance-wheel module, the control module (Figure 1).

Modularity is not a new approach in the P systems therory. The modules are defined in Riscos-Núñez (2004) and Frisco (2004). Definition of each module's function is given in the proof of following theorem.

Theorem 3: $NPCOL_{par}(1,9,*) = NRE$.

Proof: Let us consider a register machine M with m registers. We construct the P colony $\Pi = (A, e, f, \varnothing, B_1, B_2, \ldots, B_9)$, simulating a computation of the register machine M with:

- $A = \{J, J', V, Q\} \cup \{l_i, l_i', l_i'', L_i, L_i', L_i'', E_i \mid l_i \in H\} \cup \{a_r \mid 1 \leq r \leq m\}$
- $f = a_1$
- $B_i = (O_i, P_i), O_i = \{e\}, 1 \leq i \leq 9$

We can group the agents of the P colony into five modules. Each module needs for its work an input and requires some objects. The result of its computation is an output:

1. The module for the duplication (uses 2 agents, Tables 11-15)):

The duplicating module is activated when the object D_i appears in the environment. This object carries a message "Duplicate object i.".

Duplicating module duplicates requested object.

2. The module for the addition (uses 1 agent):

The module for the addition adds one symbol a_r into the environment.

3. The module for the subtraction (uses 3 agents):

The module for the subtraction removes requested object from the environment.

4. The balance-wheel module (uses 1 agent):

The balance-wheel module "keeps the computation alive". It inserts the objects d into the environment until it consumes a special symbol f' from the environment. This action makes it stop working. The object f' gets into the environment from the duplicating module which is activated by the simulation of the halt instruction by the control module.

5. Control module (uses 2 agents):

   a. initialization: First agent in this module generates label of the first instruction of the register machine. (Table 16 in the Appendix)
   b. adding instruction l_1: $(ADD(r), l_2, l_3)$: (Table 17 in the Appendix)
   c. subtracting instruction l_1: $(SUB(r), l_2, l_3)$: (Table 18 in the Appendix)
   d. halting instruction l_h: (Table 19 in the Appendix)

The control module controls all the computation. It determines which instruction will be simulated and sends the commands (objects) to other modules to achieve execution of simulation of instruction. It starts with simulation of instruction labeled l_0 and halts when it generates object l_h.

The P colony Π correctly simulates any computation of the register machine M.

5. CONCLUSION

In this paper we have proved that the P colonies with capacity $k = 1$ and degree $n = 4$ and the P colonies with capacity $k = 1$ and height $h = 8$

without checking programs are computationally complete. In Section 4 we have shown that the P colonies with capacity $k = 1$ and degree $n = 9$ without checking programs are computationally complete. Although the this result is worse than the previous results, the main contribution of this section is grouping the agents into the modules, which can be suitable for programing or planning experiments in vitro.

ACKNOWLEDGMENT

This work has been supported by the Grant Agency of the Czech Republic grants No. 201/06/0567 and SGS/5/2010.

REFERENCES

Cienciala, L., & Ciencialová, L. (2006). Variations on the theme: P colonies. In *Proceedings of the 1st International WFM Workshop*, Ostrava, Czech Republic (pp. 27-34).

Cienciala, L., Ciencialová, L., & Langer, M. (2011). P colonies with capacity one and modularity. In *Proceedings of the Ninth Brainstorming Week on Membrane Computing* (pp. 71-90).

Ciencialová, L., Cienciala, L., & Kelemenová, A. (2007). On the number of agents in P colonies. In *Proceedings of the 8th Workshop on Membrane Computing*, Thessaloniki, Greece. (pp. 227-242).

Csuhaj-Varjú, E., Kelemen, J., Kelemenová, A., Păun, G., & Vaszil, G. (2006). Cells in environment: P colonies. *Multiple-valued Logic and Soft Computing*, *12*(3-4), 201–215.

Csuhaj-Varjú, E., Margenstern, M., & Vaszil, G. (2006). P colonies with a bounded number of cells. In *Proceedings of the 7th Workshop on Membrane Computing*, Leiden, The Netherlands (pp. 311-322).

Frisco, P. (2004). The conformon-P system: A molecular and cell biology inspired computability model. *Theoretical Computer Science*, *312*(2-3), 295–319. doi:10.1016/j.tcs.2003.09.008.

Greibach, S. A. (1978). Remarks on blind and partially blind one-way multicounter machines. *Theoretical Computer Science*, *1*(7), 311–324. doi:10.1016/0304-3975(78)90020-8.

Kelemen, J., & Kelemenová, A. (2005). On P colonies, a biochemically inspired model of computation. In *Proceedings of the 6th International Symposium of Hungarian Researchers on Computational Intelligence*, Budapest, Hungary (pp. 40-56).

Kelemen, J., Kelemenová, A., & Păun, G. (2004). Preview of P colonies: A biochemically inspired computing model. In *Proceedings of the Ninth International Conference on the Simulation and Synthesis of Living Systems*, Boston, MA (pp. 82-86).

Minsky, M. L. (1967). *Computation: Finite and infinite machines*. Upper Saddle River, NJ: Prentice Hall.

P systems. (2004). *Resources website*. Retrieved from http://ppage.psystems.eu/

Păun, G. (2000). Computing with membranes. *Journal of Computer and System Sciences*, *61*, 108–143. doi:10.1006/jcss.1999.1693.

Păun, G. (2002). *Membrane computing: An introduction*. Berlin, Germany: Springer-Verlag.

Păun, G., Rozenberg, G., & Salomaa, A. (2009). *The Oxford handbook of membrane computing*. New York, NY: Oxford University Press.

Riscos-Núñez, A. (2004). *Cellular programming: Efficient resolution of NP complete numerical problems*. Unpublished doctoral dissertation, Universidad de Sevilla, Sevilla, Spain.

APPENDIX

Table 1.

P_1	
1:	$\langle k_1 \to L_1' \rangle$,

Table 2.

P_2					
2:	$\langle e \leftrightarrow D_1 \rangle$,	3:	$\langle e \leftrightarrow l_1' \rangle$;	4:	$\langle D_1 \leftrightarrow d \rangle$,

Table 3.

P_1		P_1		P_3		P_3	
5:	$\langle L_1' \to L_1 \rangle$,	9:	$\langle D_1 \to k_1 \rangle$,	13:	$\langle l_1' \to a_r \rangle$;	16:	$\langle d \to l_1' \rangle$,
6:	$\langle L_1 \to l_2 \rangle$,	10:	$\langle k_1 \leftrightarrow e \rangle$,	14:	$\langle a_r \leftrightarrow e \rangle$;	17:	$\langle l_1' \leftrightarrow k_1 \rangle$,
7:	$\langle L_1 \to l_3 \rangle$,	11:	$\langle l_1 \to D_1 \rangle$,	15:	$\langle k_1' \to n_1 \rangle$,	18:	$\langle e \leftrightarrow D_1 \rangle$,
8:	$\langle e \leftrightarrow y_1 \rangle$;	12:	$\langle D_1 \leftrightarrow d \rangle$,				

Table 4.

P_1	P_1	P_3	P_3
19: $\langle n_1 \leftrightarrow m_1 \rangle$,	28: $\langle D_1 \to k_1 \rangle$,	36: $\langle y_1 \to l_2 \rangle$;	45: $\langle d \to l_1' \rangle$,
20: $\langle m_1 \to m_1' \rangle$,	29: $\langle k_1 \leftrightarrow e \rangle$,	37: $\langle l_2 \leftrightarrow e \rangle$;	46: $\langle l_1' \leftrightarrow k_1 \rangle$,
21: $\langle m_1' \to m_1'' \rangle$,	30: $\langle e \leftrightarrow l_1' \rangle$,	38: $\langle e \leftrightarrow n_1 \rangle$;	47: $\langle k_1 \to A_1^r \rangle$,
22: $\langle m_1'' \to M_1 \rangle$,	31: $\langle l_1' \to k_1' \rangle$,	39: $\langle n_1 \to l_3 \rangle$;	48: $\langle A_1^r \leftrightarrow a_r \rangle$,
23: $\langle M_1 \leftrightarrow l_2 \rangle$,	32: $\langle k_1' \leftrightarrow e \rangle$,	40: $\langle l_3 \leftrightarrow e \rangle$;	49: $\langle A_1^r \leftrightarrow k_1' \rangle$,
24: $\langle M_1 \leftrightarrow M_1' \rangle$,	33: $\langle e \leftrightarrow A_1^r \rangle$,	41: $\langle A_1^r \leftrightarrow k_1' \rangle$,	50: $\langle M_1' \leftrightarrow l_3 \rangle$,
25: $\langle A_1^r \to m_1 \rangle$,	34: $\langle y_1 \leftrightarrow m_1 \rangle$,	42: $\langle m_1 \leftrightarrow e \rangle$,	
26: $\langle e \leftrightarrow M_1 \rangle$,	35: $\langle d \leftrightarrow k_1' \rangle$,	43: $\langle e \leftrightarrow M_1' \rangle$,	
27: $\langle M_1 \to d \rangle$,		44: $\langle k_1' \to e \rangle$,	

Table 5.

P_4:		
51: $\langle M_1' \to e \rangle$,	53: $\langle l_h \leftrightarrow d \rangle$,	55: $\langle e \to l_0 \rangle$,
52: $\langle l_0 \leftrightarrow d \rangle$,	54: $\langle e \to d \rangle$,	56: $\langle d \leftrightarrow e \rangle$,

Table 6.

P_1
57: $\langle d \leftrightarrow l_h \rangle$,

Table 7.

P_1:	
1: $B_{l_1^1}$	2: $B_{l_1^2}$

Table 8.

P_2:		
3: $P_{l_1^1}$	4: $P_{l_1^1}$	5: $P_{l_1^2}$

Table 9.

$\langle e \leftrightarrow l_1 \rangle$, :	$\langle d \rightarrow l_3 \rangle$, :	$\langle e \leftrightarrow D_1 \rangle$, :
6: $\langle l_1 \rightarrow D_1 \rangle$,	10: $\langle l_2 \leftrightarrow e \rangle$,	13: $\langle D_1 \rightarrow a_r \rangle$,
7: $\langle D_1 \leftrightarrow d \rangle$,	11: $\langle l_3 \leftrightarrow e \rangle$,	14: $\langle a_r \leftrightarrow e \rangle$,
8: $\langle d \rightarrow l_2 \rangle$,	12: $P_{l_1^1}, P_{l_1^2}, P_{l_1^3}, P_{l_1^4}$,	15: $P_{l_1^5}$:
9: $P_{l_1^1}$		

Table 10.

$P_{l_1^1}$		$P_{l_1^2}$		$P_{l_1^4}$		$\langle e \leftrightarrow l_1 \rangle,$	
16:	$\langle d \rightarrow m_1 \rangle,$	19:	$\langle e \leftrightarrow D_1 \rangle,$	21:	$\langle e \leftrightarrow k_1 \rangle;$	32:	$\langle l_1 \rightarrow D_1 \rangle,$
17:	$\langle m_1 \leftrightarrow e \rangle,$	20:	$\langle D_1 \rightarrow k_1 \rangle,$	22:	$\langle k_1 \rightarrow 1' \rangle;$	33:	$\langle D_1 \leftrightarrow d \rangle,$
18:	$\langle k_1 \leftrightarrow e \rangle,$			23:	$\langle 1' \leftrightarrow e \rangle;$	34:	$P_{l_1^3}$
$P_{l_1^3}$		$P_{l_1^5}$		$P_{l_1^5}$		$\langle e \leftrightarrow m_1 \rangle,$	
24:	$\langle l_2 \leftrightarrow e \rangle,$	28:	$\langle e \leftrightarrow 1 \rangle,$	35:	$\langle 1' \rightarrow e \rangle;$	39:	$\langle m_1 \rightarrow 1 \rangle,$
25:	$\langle 1 \leftrightarrow 1' \rangle,$	29:	$\langle 1 \rightarrow d \rangle,$	36:	$\langle L_3 \rightarrow l_3 \rangle;$	40:	$\langle 1 \leftrightarrow a_r \rangle,$
26:	$\langle 1' \rightarrow L_3 \rangle,$	30:	$\langle d \leftrightarrow 1' \rangle,$	37:	$\langle l_3 \leftrightarrow e \rangle;$	41:	$\langle a_r \rightarrow l_2 \rangle,$
27:	$\langle L_3 \leftrightarrow e \rangle,$	31:	$\langle d \leftrightarrow L_3 \rangle,$	38:	Π		

Table 11.

P_1				P_2			
1:	$\langle e \leftrightarrow D_i \rangle,$	5:	$\langle J_i \leftrightarrow F_i \rangle,$	8:	$\langle e \leftrightarrow D'_i \rangle,$	12:	$\langle J_i \leftrightarrow i' \rangle,$
2:	$\langle D_i \leftrightarrow D'_i \rangle,$	6:	$\langle F_i \rightarrow i \rangle,$	9:	$\langle D'_1 \rightarrow F_i \rangle,$	13:	$\langle i' \leftrightarrow e \rangle,$
3:	$\langle D'_1 \leftrightarrow d \rangle,$	7:	$\langle i \leftrightarrow e \rangle,$	10:	$\langle F_i \leftrightarrow e \rangle,$		
4:	$\langle d \rightarrow J_i \rangle$			11:	$\langle e \leftrightarrow J_i \rangle$		

Table 12.

input:	one object D_i
output:	one object i after 10 steps and one object i' after 11 steps
requirements:	one object d

Table 13.

P_1	
1:	$\langle e \leftrightarrow A_r \rangle$,
2:	$\langle A_r \rightarrow a_r \rangle$,
3:	$\langle a_r \leftrightarrow e \rangle$
input:	one object A_r
output:	one object a_r after 4 steps
requirements:	$\varnothing$

Table 14.

P_1		P_1		P_2		P_3	
1:	$\langle e \leftrightarrow S_r \rangle$,	9:	$\langle d \leftrightarrow C_r' \rangle$,	11:	$\langle e \leftrightarrow B_r' \rangle$,	19:	$\langle e \leftrightarrow y' \rangle$;
2:	$\langle S_r \rightarrow D_{B_r} \rangle$,	10:	$\langle C_r' \rightarrow e \rangle$,	12:	$\langle B_r' \rightarrow C_r' \rangle$,	20:	$\langle y' \rightarrow y \rangle$;
3:	$\langle D_{B_r} \leftrightarrow d \rangle$,			13:	$\langle C_r' \leftrightarrow a_r \rangle$,	21:	$\langle y \leftrightarrow C_r \rangle$;
4:	$\langle d \leftrightarrow B_r \rangle$,			14:	$\langle C_r' \leftrightarrow C_r \rangle$,	22:	$\langle C_r \rightarrow e \rangle$;
5:	$\langle B_r \rightarrow E_r \rangle$,			15:	$\langle a_r \rightarrow y' \rangle$,		
6:	$\langle E_r \rightarrow E_r' \rangle$,			16:	$\langle C_r \rightarrow n \rangle$,		
7:	$\langle E_r' \rightarrow C_r \rangle$,			17:	$\langle y' \leftrightarrow e \rangle$,		
8:	$\langle C_r \leftrightarrow d \rangle$,			18:	$\langle n \leftrightarrow e \rangle$,		
input:	one object B_r						
output:	one object y after 23 steps or one object n after 22 steps						
requirements:	two objects d, object a_r (if there is at least one in the environment)						
uses:	duplication module						

Table 15.

P_1	
1:	$\langle e \to d \rangle,$
2:	$\langle d \leftrightarrow e \rangle,$
3:	$\langle d \leftrightarrow f' \rangle,$

Table 16.

P_1	
1:	$\langle e \to l_0 \rangle,$

Table 17.

P_1		*notes*
1:	$\langle l_1 \to D_1 \rangle,$	
2:	$\langle D_1 \leftrightarrow d \rangle,$	⇒ Duplication module
3:	$\langle d \leftrightarrow 1 \rangle,$	⇐ Duplication module
4:	$\langle 1 \to A_r \rangle,$	
5:	$\langle A_r \leftrightarrow 1' \rangle,$	⇐ Duplication module ⇒ Addition module
6:	$\langle 1' \to l_2 \rangle,$	
7:	$\langle 1' \to l_3 \rangle,$	

Table 18.

P_1	notes	P_2
1: $\langle l_1 \to D_1 \rangle$,		16: $\langle e \leftrightarrow L_1 \rangle$,
2: $\langle D_1 \leftrightarrow d \rangle$,	⇒ Duplication module	17: $\langle L_1 \to K_1 \rangle$,
3: $\langle d \leftrightarrow 1 \rangle$,	⇐ Duplication module	18: $\langle K_1 \leftrightarrow e \rangle$,
4: $\langle 1 \to S_r \rangle$,		19: $\langle e \leftrightarrow L_1' \rangle$,
5: $\langle S_r \leftrightarrow 1' \rangle$,	⇐ Duplication module ⇒ Subtraction module	20: $\langle e \leftrightarrow L_1'' \rangle$,
6: $\langle 1' \to L_1 \rangle$,		21: $\langle L_1' \to l_2 \rangle$,
7: $\langle L_1 \leftrightarrow y \rangle$,	⇐ Subtraction module	22: $\langle L_1'' \to l_3 \rangle$,
8: $\langle L_1 \leftrightarrow n \rangle$,	⇐ Subtraction module	23: $\langle l_2 \leftrightarrow e \rangle$,
9: $\langle y \to L_1' \rangle$,		24: $\langle l_3 \leftrightarrow e \rangle$,
10: $\langle n \to L_1'' \rangle$,		
11: $\langle L_1' \leftrightarrow K_1 \rangle$,		
12: $\langle L_1' \leftrightarrow K_1 \rangle$,		
13: $\langle K_1 \to d \rangle$,		
14: $\langle d \leftrightarrow l_2 \rangle$,		
15: $\langle D \leftrightarrow l_3 \rangle$,		

Table 19.

P_1		*notes*
1:	$\langle l_h \to D_f \rangle,$	
2:	$\langle D_f \leftrightarrow d \rangle,$	$\Rightarrow$ Duplication module
3:	$\langle d \leftrightarrow f \rangle,$	$\Leftarrow$ Duplication module

This work was previously published in the International Journal of Natural Computing Research (IJNCR), Volume 2, Issue 2, edited by Leandro Nunes de Castro, pp.32-46, copyright 2011 by IGI Publishing (an imprint of IGI Global).

Chapter 8
Local Search with P Systems: A Case Study

Miguel A. Gutiérrez-Naranjo
University of Sevilla, Spain

Mario J. Pérez-Jiménez
University of Sevilla, Spain

ABSTRACT

Local search is currently one of the most used methods for finding solutions in real-life problems. It is usually considered when the research is interested in the final solution of the problem instead of the how the solution is reached. In this paper, the authors present an implementation of local search with Membrane Computing techniques applied to the N-queens problem as a case study. A CLIPS program inspired in the Membrane Computing design has been implemented and several experiments have been performed. The obtained results show better average times than those obtained with other Membrane Computing implementations that solve the N-queens problem.

1. INTRODUCTION

Searching is the basis of many processes in Artificial Intelligence. The key point is that many real-life problems can be stated as a *space of states*: a *state* is the description of the world at a given instant (expressed in some language) and two states are linked by a *transition* if the second state can be reached from the previous one by applying one *elementary operation*. By using these concepts, a searching tree where the nodes are the states, the root is the starting state and the edges are the actions considered. Given an initial state, a sequence of transitions to one of the final states is searched.

By using this abstraction, searching methods have been deeply studied by themselves, forgetting the real-world problem which they fit. The studies consider aspects as the completeness (if the searching method is capable of finding a solution if it exists), complexity in time and space, and optimality (if the found solution is *optimal* in some sense). By considering the searching tree, classical search has focused on the order in which

DOI: 10.4018/978-1-4666-4253-9.ch008

the nodes should be explored. In this classical search two approaches are possible: the former is *blind search*, where the search is guided only by the topology of the tree and no information is available from the states; the latter is called *informed search* and some information about the features of the nodes is used to define a *heuristics* to decide the next node to explore.

Searching problems have been previously studied in the framework of Membrane Computing. In Gutiérrez-Naranjo and Pérez-Jiménez (2010), a first study on depth-first search in the framework of Membrane Computing was presented. In this paper we go further with the study of searching methods in Membrane Computing by exploring local search. We consider the N-queens problem as a case study and we present a family of P systems which solves it by implementing local search ideas.

The paper is organized as follows: First we recall some basic definitions related to local search. Then, we recall the problem used as a case study: the *N*-queens problem, previously studied in the framework of Membrane Computing in Gutiérrez-Naranjo, Martínez-del-Amor, Pérez-Hurtado, and Pérez-Jiménez (2009). Next, we provide some guidelines of the implementation of local search in our case study and show some experimental results. The paper finishes with some final remarks.

2. LOCAL SEARCH

Classical search algorithms explore the space of states systematically. This exploration is made by keeping one or more paths in memory and by recording the alternatives in each choice point. When a final state is found, the path, that is, the sequence of *transitions*, is considered as the solution of the problem. Nonetheless, in many problems, we are only interested in the found state, not properly in the path of transitions. For example, in job-shop scheduling, vehicle routing or telecommunications network optimization, we are only interested in the final state (a concrete disposition of the objects in the world), not in the way in which this state is achieved.

If the sequence of elementary transitions is not important, a good alternative to classical searching algorithms is *local search*. This type of search operates using a single state and its set of neighbors. It is not necessary to keep in memory how the current state has been obtained.

Since these algorithms do not systematically explore the states, they do not guarantee that a final state can be found, i.e., they are not complete. Nonetheless, they have two advantages that make them interesting in many situations:

- Only a little piece of information is stored, so very little memory (usually constant) is used.
- These algorithms can often find a reasonable solution in an extremely large space of states where classical algorithms are unsuitable.

The basic strategy in local search is considering a current state and, if it is not a final one, then it moves to one of its neighbors. This movement is not made randomly. In order to decide where to move, a *measure of goodness* is introduced in local search. In this way, the movement is performed towards the best neighbor or, at least, a neighbor who improves the current measure of goodness. It is usual to visualize the *goodness* of a state as its height in some geometrical space. In this way, we can consider a landscape of states and the target of the searching method is to arrive to the *global maximum*. This metaphor is useful to understand some of the drawbacks of this method: *flat regions*, where the neighbors are as good as the current state, or *local maximum* where the neighbors are worse than the current state, but it is not a *global maximum*. A deep study of local search is out of the scope of this paper. Further information can be found in Russell and Norvig (2002).

In this paper we will only consider the basic algorithm of local search: Given a *set of states*, *a movement operator* and *a measure to compare states*

3. THE N-QUEENS PROBLEM

Through this paper we will consider the *N*-queens problem as a case study. It is a generalization of a classic puzzle known as the 8-queens puzzle. The original one is attributed to the chess player Max Bezzel and it consists of putting eight queens on an 8×8 chessboard in such way that none of them is able to capture any other using the standard movement of the queens in chess, i.e., only one queen can be placed on each row, column and diagonal line (Hoffman, Loessi, & Moore, 1969; Bernhardsson, 1991).

In Gutiérrez-Naranjo et al. (2009), a first solution to the *N*-queens problem in the framework of Membrane Computing was shown. For that aim, a family of deterministic P systems with active membranes was presented. In this family, the *N*-th element of the family solves the *N*-queens problem and the last configuration encodes *all* the solutions of the problem.

In order to solve the problem, a truth assignment that satisfies a formula in conjunctive normal form (CNF) is searched. This problem is exactly SAT, so the solution presented in Gutiérrez-Naranjo et al. (2009) uses a modified solution for SAT from Pérez-Jiménez, Romero-Jiménez, and Sancho-Caparrini (2003). Some experiments were presented by running the P systems with an updated version of the P-lingua simulator (García-Quismondo, Gutiérrez-Escudero, Pérez-Hurtado, Pérez-Jiménez, & Riscos-Núñez, 2009). The experiments were performed on a system with an Intel Core2 Quad CPU (a single processor with 4 cores at 2,83Ghz), 8GB of RAM and using a C++ simulator under the operating system Ubuntu Server 8.04. According to the representation in Gutiérrez-Naranjo et al. (2009), the 3-queens problem is expressed by a formula in CNF with 9 variables and 31 clauses. The input multiset has 65 elements and the P system has 3185 rules. Along the computation, 2^9=512 elementary membranes need to be considered in parallel. Since the simulation was carried out on a uniprocessor system, these membranes were evaluated sequentially. The 117-th configuration was a halting one. It took 7 seconds to reach it and it has an object No in the environment. As expected, this means that three queens cannot be placed on a 3×3 chessboard satisfying the restrictions. In the 4-queens problem, four non-attacking queens are searched on a

Algorithm 1.

```
0. We start with a state randomly chosen.
1. We check if the current state is a final one.
1.1. If so, we finish. The system outputs the current state.
1.2. If not, we look for a movement which reaches a better state.
1.2.1. If it exists, we randomly choose one of the possible movements.
The reached state becomes the current state and we go back to 1.
1.2.2. If it does not exist, we go back to 0.
```

4×4 chessboard. According to the representation, the problem can be expressed by a formula in CNF with 16 variables and 80 clauses. Along the computation, 2^{16}=65536 elementary membranes were considered in the same configuration and the P system has 13622 rules. The simulation takes 20583 seconds (> 5 hours) to reach the halting configuration. It is the 256-th configuration and in this configuration one object Yes appears in the environment. This configuration has two elementary membranes encoding the two solutions of the problem (Gutiérrez-Naranjo et al., 2009).

In Gutiérrez-Naranjo and Pérez-Jiménez (2010), a study of depth-first search in the framework of Membrane Computing was presented. The case study was also the *N*-queens problem. An *ad hoc* CLIPS program was written based on a Membrane Computing design. Some experiments were performed on a system with an Intel Pentium Dual CPU E2200 at 2,20 GHz, 3GB of RAM and using CLIPS V6.241 under the operating system Windows Vista. Finding one solution took 0,062 seconds for a 4×4 board and 15,944 seconds for a 20×20 board.

4. A P SYSTEM FAMILY FOR LOCAL SEARCH

In this section we give a sketch of the design of a P system family which solves the N-queens problem by using local search, $\prod=\{\prod(N)\}_{N\in N}$. Each P system Π(N) solves the N-queens problem in a non-deterministic way, according to the searching method. The membrane structure does not change along the computation and we use electrical charges on the membranes as in the model of active membranes1.

One *state* is represented by an *N*×*N* chess board where *N* queens have been placed. In order to limit the number of possible states, we consider an important restriction: we consider that there is only one queen in each column and in each row. By using this restriction, we only need to check the diagonals in order to know whether a board is a solution to the problem or not.

These boards can be easily represented in Membrane Computing. For the P system Π(N), we consider a membrane structure which contains N elementary membranes labelled with 1,…,N and N objects y_i i∈{1,…,N} in the skin. By using rules of type $y_i[\ ]_j \to [y_i]_j$ the objects y_i are non-deterministically sent into the membranes and the object y_i inside a membrane with label j is interpreted as a queen placed on the row i of the column j. For example, the partial configuration $[[y_1]_1\ [y_5]_2\ [y_3]_3\ [y_4]_4\ [y_2]_5$ is a membrane representation of the board in Figure 1.

In order to know if one state is better than another, we need to consider a measure. The natural measure is to associate to any board the number of collisions (Sosic & Gu, 1994): The number of collisions on a diagonal line is one less than the number of queens on the line, if the line is not empty, and zero if the line is empty. The sum of collisions on all diagonal lines is the total number of collisions between queens. For ex-

Figure 1. Five queens on a board. We consider the origin of coordinates at bottom left

ample, if we denote by d_p the descendant diagonal for squares (i,j) where i+j=p and by u_q the ascendant diagonal for squares (i,j) where i−j=q, then the board shown in Figure 1 has 3 collisions: 2 in u_0 and 1 in d_7. This basic definition of collisions of a state can be refined in a Membrane Computing algorithm. As we will see below, in order to compare two boards, it is not important the exact amount of collisions when they are greater than 3.

Other key definitions in the algorithm are the concepts of neighbor and movement. In this paper, a movement is the interchange of columns of two queens by keeping the rows. In other words, if we have one queen at (i,j) and another at (k,s), after the movement these queens are placed at (i,s) and (k,j). It is trivial to check that, for each movement, if the original board does not have two queens on the same column and row, then the final one does not have it. The definition of neighbor depends on the definition of movement: the state s_2 is a neighbor of state s_1 if it can be reached from s_1 with one movement.

According to these definitions, the local search algorithm for the *N*-queens problem can be written as shown in Algorithm 2.

At this point, three basic questions arise from the design of Membrane Computing: (1) how the number of collisions of a board is computed? (2) how a *better* state is searched? and (3) how a movement is performed?

4.1. Computing Collisions

The representation of an N×N board is made by using N elementary membranes where the objects y1,...,yN are placed. These N elementary membranes, with labels 1,...,N, are not the unique elementary membranes in the membrane structure. There are 2N−1 ascendant and 2N−1 descendant diagonals in an N×N board. As pointed above, we denote the ascendant diagonals as u-N+1, ..., uN-1 where the index p in u_p denotes that the diagonal corresponds to the squares (i,j) with i−j=p. Analogously, the descendant diagonals are denoted by d2, ..., dN+N where the index q in d_q denotes that the diagonal corresponds to the squares (i,j) with i+j=q.

Besides the *N* elementary membranes with labels 1,...,*N* for encoding the board, we also place 4*N*−2 elementary membranes in the structure, with labels $u_{-N+1}, \ldots, u_{N-1}, d_2, \ldots, d_{N+N}$. These membranes will be used to compute the collisions.

Bearing in mind the current board, encoded by membranes with an object $[y_i]_j$, we can use rules of type $[y_i]_j \rightarrow d_{i+j}\, u_{i-j}$. These rules are triggered in parallel and they produce as many objects d_q (resp. u_p) as queens which are placed on the diagonal d_q (resp. u_p).

Objects d_q and u_p are sequentially sent into the elementary membranes labelled by d_q and u_p. In a first approach, one can consider a counter z_i which evolves to z_{i+1} inside each elementary

Algorithm 2.

```
0. We start with a randomly chosen state;
1.- We check if the number of collisions of the current state is zero;
1.1. If so, we finish. The halting configuration codifies the solution board.
1.2. If not, we look for movements which reach a state with a lower number of
collisions.
1.2.1. If they exist, we randomly choose one of the possible movements.
The reached state becomes the current state and we go back to 1.
1.2.2. If they do not exist, we go back to 0.
```

membrane when an object d_q or u_p is sent in. By using this strategy, the index i of z_i denotes how many objects have crossed the membrane, or in other words, how many queens are placed on the corresponding diagonal.

This strategy has an important drawback. In the worst case, if all the queens are placed on the same diagonal, at least N steps are necessary in order to count them. In our design, this is not necessary. As we will see, we only need to know if the number of queens in each diagonal is 0, 1, 2, or more than 2. Due to the parallelism of the P systems, this can be checked in a constant number of steps regardless of the number of queens.

Technically, after using a complex set of rules where the electrical charges are used to control the flow of objects, each membrane d_q sends to the skin a complex object of type dq(DAq,DBq,DCq,DDq) where DAq, DBq, DCq, DDq $\in \{0,1\}$ codify the number of queens on the diagonal (for u_p the development is analogous, with the notation up(UAp,UBp,UCp,UDp)). We consider four possibilities:

- **d_q(1,0,0,0):** The 1 in the first coordinate denotes that there is no queen placed on the diagonal and the diagonal is ready to receive one queen after a movement.
- **d_q(0,1,0,0):** The 1 in the second coordinate denotes that there is one queen placed on the diagonal. This diagonal does not contain collisions but it should not receive more queens.
- **d_q(0,0,1,0):** The 1 in the third coordinate denotes that there are two queens placed on the diagonal. This diagonal has one collision which can be solved by a unique appropriate movement.
- **d_q(0,0,0,1):** The 1 in the fourth diagonal denotes that there are more than two queens placed on the diagonal. This diagonal has several collisions and it will have at least one collision even if one movement is performed.

Bearing in mind that a diagonal is ready to receive queens (0 queens) or it needs to send queens to another diagonal (2 or more queens), we can prevent if a movement produces an improvement in the whole number of collisions before performing the movement. We do not need to perform the movement and then to count the number of collisions in order to know if the movement decreases the number of collisions. In order to do that, we distinguish if the pair of queens to be moved are placed on the same diagonal or not.

Firstly, let us consider two queens placed in the squares (i,j) and (k,s) of the same ascendant diagonal, i.e., $i-j=k-s$. We wonder if the movement of interchanging the columns of two queens by keeping the rows will improve the total number of collisions. In other words, we wonder if removing the queens from (i,j) and (k,s) putting them at (i,s) and (k,j) improves the board.

In order to answer this question we consider the following objects:

- **$u_{i-j}(0,0,UC_{i-j},UD_{i-j})$:** The ascendant diagonal u_{i-j} has at least 2 queens, so the first two coordinates are 0. The parameters UC_{i-j}, UD_{i-j} can be 0 or 1, but exactly one of them is 1.
- **$d_{i+j}(0,DB_{i+j},DC_{i+j},DD_{i+j})$ and $d_{k+s}(0,DB_{k+s},DC_{k+s},DD_{k+s})$:** The descendent diagonals and d_{k+s} have at least 1 queen, so the first coordinate is 0. The remaining ones can be 0 or 1, but exactly one of them is 1.

It is easy to check that the reduction in the whole amount of collisions produced by the removal of the queens from the squares (i,j) and (k,s) is

Analogously, in order to compute the change in the number of collisions produced by the placement of two queens in the squares (i,s), (k,j) we consider $d_{i+s}(DA_{i+s},DB_{i+s},DC_{i+s},DD_{i+s})$, $u_{i-s}(UA_{i-s}, UB_{i-s}, Uc_{i-s}, UD_{i-s})$ and $u_{k-j}(UA_{k-j}, UB_{k-j}, UC_{k-j}, UD_{k-j})$.

By using this notation, it is easy to check that the augmentation in the number of collisions is $4 - (DA_{i+s} + UA_{i-s} + UA_{k-j}$.

The movement represents an improvement in the general situation of the board if the reduction in the number of collisions is greater than the augmentation. This can be easily expressed with a simple formula depending on the parameters.

This is the key point in our Membrane Computing algorithm, since we do not need to perform the movement and then to check if we have an improvement, but we can evaluate it *a priori*, by exploring the objects placed in the skin. Obviously, if the squares share a descendant diagonal, the situation is symmetric.

If the queens do not share a diagonal, the study is analogous, but the obtained formula by considering that we get a *feasible movement* if the reduction is greater than the augmentation is slightly different.

From a technical point of view, we consider a finite set of rules with the following interpretation: *If the corresponding set of objects*

$u_{i-j}(UA_{i-j},UB_{i-j},UC_{i-j},UD_{i-j})$
$d_{i+j}(DA_{i+j},DB_{i+j},DC_{i+j},DD_{i+j})$

$u_{k-s}(UA_{k-s},UB_{k-s},UC_{k-s},UD_{k-s})$
$d_{k+s}(DA_{k+s},DB_{k+s},DC_{k+s},DD_{k+s})$

$u_{i-s}(UA_{i-s},UB_{i-s},UC_{i-s},UD_{i-s})$
$d_{i+s}(DA_{i+s},DB_{i+s},DC_{i+s},DD_{i+s})$

$u_{k-j}(UA_{k-j},UB_{k-j},UC_{k-j},UD_{k-j})$
$d_{k+j}(DA_{k+j},DB_{k+j},DC_{k+j},DD_{k+j})$

is placed in the skin, then the movement of queen from (i,j) and (k,s) to (i,s) and (k,j) improves the number of collisions.

In the general case, there will be many possible applications of rules of this type. The P system chooses one of them in a non-deterministic way. The application of the rule introduces an object $change_{iks}$ in the skin. After a complex set of rules, this object produces a new configuration and the cycle starts again.

The design of the P system depends on *N*, the number of queens, and it is rather complex from a technical point of view. It uses cooperation, inhibitors and electrical charges in order to control the flow of objects. In particular, a set of rules halts the P system if a board with zero collisions is reached and another set of rules re-starts the P system (i.e., it produces a configuration equivalent to the initial one) if no more improvements can be achieved from the current configuration.

Figure 2 shows a solution found with the corresponding P system for the 5-queens problem. We start with a board with all the queens in the main ascendant diagonal (upper left). The number of collisions in this diagonal (and in the whole board) is 4. By changing queens from the columns 2 and 5, we obtain the board shown in Figure 1 with 3 collisions (upper right in Figure 2). In the next step, the queens from columns 1 and 5 are

Figure 2. Starting from a configuration C_0 with 4 collisions (up-left) we can reach C_1 with 3 collisions (up-right); then C_2 with 2 collisions (bottom-left) and finally C_3 with 0 collisions (bottom-right), which is a solution to the 5-queens problem

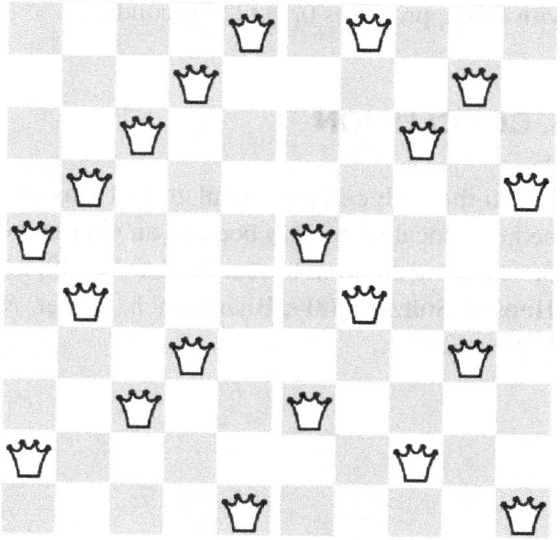

changed, and we get a board with 2 collisions, produced because the two main diagonals have two queens each (bottom left). Finally, by changing queens is the columns 1 and 3, we get a board with no collisions that represents a solution to the 5-queens problem (bottom right).

5. EXPERIMENTAL RESULTS

An *ad hoc* CLIPS[2] program was written *inspired* on this Membrane Computing design[3]. Some experiments were performed on a system with an Intel Pentium Dual CPU E2200 at 2,20 GHz, 3GB of RAM and using CLIPS V6.241 under the operating system Windows Vista.

Due to the random choosing of the initial configuration and the non-determinism of the P system for choosing the movement, 20 experiments have been performed for each number N of queens for $N \in \{10,20,\ldots,200\}$ in order to get an informative parameter. We have considered the average of these 20 experiments on the number of P system steps and the number of seconds. Table 1 shows the result of the experiments.

Notice, for example, that in the solution presented in Gutiérrez-Naranjo and Pérez-Jiménez (2010), the solution for 20 queens was obtained after 15,944 seconds. The average time obtained with this approach is 0.133275 seconds.

6. CONCLUSION

Due to the high computational cost of classical methods, local search has become an alternative for searching solution to real-life hard problems (Hoos & Stützle, 2004; Bijarbooneh, Flener, & Pearson, 2009).

In this paper we present a first approach to the problem of local search by using Membrane Computing and we have applied it to the N-queens problem as a case study. As a future work, several possibilities arise: One of them is to improve the design from a P system point of view, maybe considering new ingredients; a second one is to consider new case studies closer to real-life problems; a third one is to implement the design in parallel architectures and compare the results with the ones obtained with a one-processor computer.

Table 1. Experimental results

Number of Queens	Average Number of Steps	Average Number of Secs.
10	141.35	0.0171549
20	166.25	0.133275
30	270.9	0.717275
40	272.7	1.71325
50	382.4	4.75144
60	453.85	9.65071
70	495.45	16.9358
80	637.6	33.1815
90	625	47.3944
100	757.6	80.6878
110	745.75	113.635
120	841.75	157.937
130	891.25	216.141
140	983.7	311.71
150	979.75	381.414
160	1093	541.022
170	1145.5	683.763
180	1206.25	872.504
190	1272.256	1089.13
200	1365.25	1423.89

ACKNOWLEDGMENT

The authors acknowledge the support of the projects TIN-2009-13192 of the Ministerio de Ciencia e Innovación of Spain and the support of the Project of Excellence of the Junta de Andalucía, grant P08-TIC-04200.

REFERENCES

Bernhardsson, B. (1991). Explicit solutions to the N-queens problem for all. *ACM SIGART Bulletin*, *2*(2), 7. doi:10.1145/122319.122322.

Bijarbooneh, F. H., Flener, P., & Pearson, J. (2009). Dynamic demand-capacity balancing for air traffic management using constraint-based local search: First results. In *Proceedings of the 6th International Workshop on Local Search Techniques in Constraint Satisfaction* (Vol. 5, pp. 27-40).

García-Quismondo, M., Gutiérrez-Escudero, R., Pérez-Hurtado, I., Pérez-Jiménez, M. J., & Riscos-Núñez, A. (2009). An overview of P-lingua 2.0. In G. Păun, M. J. Pérez-Jiménez, A. Riscos-Núñez, G. Rozenberg, & A. Salomaa (Eds.), *Proceedings of the 10th International Workshop on Membrane Computing* (LNCS 5957, pp. 264-288).

Gutiérrez-Naranjo, M. A., Martínez-del-Amor, M. A., Pérez-Hurtado, I., & Pérez-Jiménez, M. J. (2009). Solving the N-queens puzzle with P systems. In *Proceedings of the Seventh Brainstorming Week on Membrane Computing*, Seville, Spain (Vol. 1, pp. 199-210).

Gutiérrez-Naranjo, M. A., & Pérez-Jiménez, M. J. (2010). Depth-first search with P systems. In M. Gheorghe, T. Hinze, G. Păun, G. Rozenberg, & A. Salomaa (Eds.), *Proceedings of the Eleventh International Conference on Membrane Computing* (LNCS 6501, pp. 257-264).

Hoffman, E., Loessi, J., & Moore, R. (1969). Constructions for the solution of the N queens problem. *National Mathematics Magazine*, *42*, 66–72.

Hoos, H. H., & Stützle, T. (2004). *Stochastic local search: Foundations & applications* (1st ed.). San Francisco, CA: Morgan Kaufmann.

Păun, G. (2002). *Membrane computing: An introduction*. Berlin, Germany: Springer-Verlag.

Păun, G., Rozenberg, G., & Salomaa, A. (Eds.). (2010). *The Oxford handbook of membrane computing*. Oxford, UK: Oxford University Press.

Pérez-Jiménez, M. J., Romero-Jiménez, Á., & Sancho-Caparrini, F. (2003). Complexity classes in models of cellular computing with membranes. *Natural Computing*, *2*(3), 265–285. doi:10.1023/A:1025449224520.

Russell, S. J., & Norvig, P. (2002). *Artificial intelligence: A modern approach* (2nd ed.). Upper Saddle River, NJ: Prentice Hall.

Sosic, R., & Gu, J. (1994). Efficient local search with conflict minimization: A case study of the N-queens problem. *IEEE Transactions on Knowledge and Data Engineering*, *6*(5), 661–668. doi:10.1109/69.317698.

ENDNOTES

1. We assume that the reader is familiar with the concepts of Membrane Computing. We refer to Păun (2002) for basic information in this area and to Păun, Rozenberg, and Salomaa (2010) for a comprehensive presentation and the web site http://ppage.psystems.eu for up-to-date information.
2. CLIPS is an expert system tool originally developed by the Software Technology Branch (STB), NASA/Lyndon B. Johnson Space Center, see http://clipsrules.sourceforge.net/.
3. Available from the authors.

This work was previously published in the International Journal of Natural Computing Research (IJNCR), Volume 2, Issue 2, edited by Leandro Nunes de Castro, pp. 47-55, copyright 2011 by IGI Publishing (an imprint of IGI Global).

Chapter 9
Forward and Backward Chaining with P Systems

Sergiu Ivanov
Academy of Sciences of Moldova, Moldova
& Technical University of Moldova, Moldova

Artiom Alhazov
Academy of Sciences of Moldova, Moldova
& Università degli Studi di Milano-Bicocca, Italy

Vladimir Rogojin
Helsinki University, Finland
& Academy of Sciences of Moldova, Moldova

Miguel A. Gutiérrez-Naranjo
Academy of Sciences of Moldova, Moldova
& University of Sevilla, Spain

ABSTRACT

One of the concepts that lie at the basis of membrane computing is the multiset rewriting rule. On the other hand, the paradigm of rules is profusely used in computer science for representing and dealing with knowledge. Therefore, establishing a "bridge" between these domains is important, for instance, by designing P systems reproducing the modus ponens-based forward and backward chaining that can be used as tools for reasoning in propositional logic. In this paper, the authors show how powerful and intuitive the formalism of membrane computing is and how it can be used to represent concepts and notions from unrelated areas.

1. INTRODUCTION

The use of rules is one of the most common paradigms in computer science for dealing with knowledge. Given two pieces of knowledge V and W, expressed in some language, the rule $V \to W$ is usually considered as a causal relation between V and W. This representation is universal in science. For example, in chemistry, V and W can be metabolites and $V \to W$ a chemical reaction. In this case, V represents the reactants which are consumed in the reaction and W is the obtained product. In propositional logic, $V \to W$, with $V = v_1 \vee v_2 \vee \ldots \vee v_n$ and $W = w_1 \vee w_2 \vee \ldots \vee w_n$, is a representation of the clause $\neg v_1 \vee \neg v_2 \vee \ldots \vee \neg v_n \vee w_1 \vee w_2 \vee \ldots \vee w_m$.

DOI: 10.4018/978-1-4666-4253-9.ch009

An important problem is deriving new knowledge: given a knowledge base $KB = (A, R)$, where A is a set of known atoms and R is a set of rules of type $V \rightarrow W$, the problem is to know if a new atom g can be obtained from the known atoms and rules. We will call this problem a *reasoning problem* and it will be denoted by $\langle A, R, g \rangle$.

In computer science, there are two basic methods for seeking a solution of a reasoning problem, both of them based on the inference rule known as Generalized Modus Ponens: the former is data-driven and it is known as *forward chaining*, the latter is query-driven and it is called *backward chaining* (Apt, 1990).

As one should observe, even though logic inference rules and multiset rewriting rules originate from totally different areas of mathematics and computer science and represent unrelated notions, their concepts have some similarities. In particular, no information about the ordering of elements in both left- and right-hand sides of the rules of both types is used. On the other hand, the inference rules could be thought of as set rewriting rules, while multiset rewriting rules operate at multisets. However, multiset rewriting rules could be interpreted as set rewriting rules if one ignores the multiplicity of elements of the multiset. Therefore we could represent sets of facts in P systems as multisets of objects and inference rules as multiset rewriting rules. When one considers the set of facts represented in a region of a P system, one only considers the underlying set of the region's multiset.

2. DEFINITIONS

2.1. Formal Logic Preliminaries

An *atomic formula* (also called an *atom*) is a formula with no deeper structure. An atomic formula is used to express some fact in the context of a given problem (Jago, 2007). The *universal set* of atoms is denoted with U. U is finite. For a set A, $|A|$ is the number of elements in this set (cardinality).

A *knowledge base* is a construct $KB = (A, R)$ where $A = \{a_1, a_2, \ldots, a_n\} \subseteq U$ is the set of known atoms and R is the set of rules of the form $V \rightarrow W$, with $V, W \subseteq U$.

In propositional logic, the *derivation* of a proposition is done via the inference rule known as Generalized Modus Ponens:

$$\frac{P_1, P_2, \ldots, P_n, \quad P_1 \wedge P_2 \wedge \ldots \wedge P_n \rightarrow Q}{Q}$$

The meaning of this is as follows: if $P_1 \wedge P_2 \wedge \ldots \wedge P_n \rightarrow Q$ is a known rule and $\{P_1, P_2, \ldots, P_n\} \subseteq A$ then, Q can be derived from this knowledge. Given a knowledge base $KB = (A, R)$ and an atomic formula $g \in U$, we say that g can be derived from KB, denoted by $KB \vdash g$, if there exists a finite sequence of atomic formulas $F_1, F_2, \ldots, F_k$ such that $F_k = g$ and for each $i \in \{1, 2, \ldots, k\}$ one of the following claims holds:

- $F_i \in A$;
- F_i can be derived via Generalized Modus Ponens from R and the set of atoms $\{F_1, F_2, \ldots, F_{i-1}\}$.

It is important to remark that for rules $V \rightarrow W$ we can require $|W| = 1$ without losing generality (Lloyd, 1987).

This definition of derivation provides two algorithms to answer the question of knowing if an atom g can be derived from a knowledge base KB. The first one is known as *forward chaining* and it is an example of data-driven reasoning, i.e., the starting point is the known data. The dual situation is the *backward chaining,* where the reasoning is query-driven (Bratko, 2001).

A deep study of both algorithms is out of the scope of this paper. We briefly recall their basic forms.

Forward Chaining

INPUT: A reasoning problem $\langle A, R, g \rangle$

INITIALIZE: *Deduced* = *A*, *Deduced'* = $\varnothing$

```
while Deduced ≠ Deduced' do
    Deduced' ← Deduced
    for all (P_1 ∧ P_2 ∧ ... P_n → Q) ∈ R,
{P_1, P_2, ..., P_n} ⊆ Deduced' do
        if Q = g then
            return true
        else
            Deduced ← Deduced ∪ {Q}
        end if
    end for
end while
if g ∉ Deduced then
    return false
end if
```

Backward Chaining

INPUT: A reasoning problem $\langle A, R, g \rangle$

The solution is obtained by a call *Reduce*(g,$\varnothing$).

Reduce (t, V)

INPUT: Target fact *t*, set of visited facts *V*

```
if t ∈ A then
  return true
else if t ∈ V then
  return false
else
   return ⋁_{(P_1 P_2 ... P_n → t) ∈ R} ( ⋀_{i=1}^{n} Reduce(P_i, V ∪ {t}) )
end if
```

In this paper we present several different transformations of a tuple $\langle A, R, g \rangle$ into P systems and prove that forward chaining and backward chaining can be represented and performed in the usual semantics of membrane computing. We will write multisets in string notation. We will use the symbol $(\cdot)$ to denote multiset union.

In this paper, $v_1 v_2 \ldots v_n$ may mean either a conjunction of atoms in an inference rule or a multiset of objects representing such a conjunction. Which of these is actually meant should be clear from the context.

2.2. Transitional P Systems

The reader is assumed familiar with the fundamental notions of membrane computing. A *transitional* membrane system is defined by a tuple (Păun, 2002):

$$\Pi = \left(O, \mu, w_1, w_2, \ldots, w_m, R_1, R_2, \ldots, R_m, i_0\right),$$

where

O is a finite set of objects,

μ is a hierarchical structure of m membranes, bijectively labeled by 1,…, m; the interior of each membrane defines a region; the environment is referred to as region 0,

w_i is the initial multiset in region i, $1 \le i \le m$

R_i is the set of rules of region i, $1 \le i \le m$

i_0 is the output region; in this paper i_0 is the skin.

The rules of a membrane system have the form $u \to v$, where $u \in O^+$ and $v \in O^*$. In the case of non-cooperative rules $u \in O$. We will not consider target indications because we will focus on single-membrane P systems in this paper.

The rules are applied in a maximally parallel way; no further rule should be applicable to the objects which do not evolve in the next step. The choice of rules is non-deterministic.

In transitional P systems with promoters/inhibitors we consider rules of the following forms:

- $u \to v|_a, a \in O$: This rule is only allowed to be applied when the membrane it is associated with contains at least an instance of a; a is called the *promoter* of this rule;

- $u \to v|_{\neg a}, a \in O$: This rule is only allowed to be applied when the membrane it is associated with contains no instances of a; a is called the *inhibitor* of this rule.

Articles containing further definitions can be found on (P Systems, 2011).

2.3. P Systems with Active Membranes

A P system with *active membranes* is defined by a tuple (Păun, Rozenberg, & Salomaa, 2010; Krishna, 1999):

$\Pi = \left(O, H, E, \mu, w_1, w_2, \ldots, w_m, R, i_0\right)$, where

O is a finite set of objects,
H is the alphabet of names of membranes,
E is the set of electrical charges; in this paper $E = \{-, +, 0\}$,
μ is a hierarchical structure of m membranes, bijectively labeled by 1,…, m,
w_i is the initial multiset in region i, $1 \le i \le m$
R is the set of rules,
i_0 is the output region; in this paper i_0 is the skin.

The rules in P systems with active membranes can be of the following five basic types (Păun, Rozenberg, & Salomaa, 2010):

a. $\left[a \to v\right]_h^e$, $h \in H$, $e \in \{+, -, 0\}$, $a \in O$, $v \in O^*$; in this paper we consider the extension $a \in O^+$;

b. $a\left[\ \right]_h^{e_1} \to \left[b\right]_h^{e_2}$, $h \in H$, $e_1, e_2 \in \{+, -, 0\}$, $a, b \in O$;

c. $\left[a\right]_h^{e_1} \to \left[\ \right]_h^{e_2} b$, $h \in H$, $e_1, e_2 \in \{+, -, 0\}$, $a, b \in O$;

d. $\left[a\right]_h^e \to b$, $h \in H \setminus \{s\}$, $e \in \{+, -, 0\}$, $a, b \in O$;

e. $\left[a\right]_h^{e_1} \to \left[b\right]_h^{e_2} \left[c\right]_h^{e_3}$, $h \in H \setminus \{s\}$, $e_1, e_2, e_3 \in \{+, -, 0\}$, $a, b, c \in O$.

The rules apply to elementary membranes, i.e., membranes which do not contain other membranes inside.

The rules are applied in the usual non-deterministic maximally parallel manner, with the following details: any object can be subject of only one rule of any type and any membrane can be subject of only one rule of types (b) – (e). Rules of type (a) are not counted as applied to membranes, but only to objects. This means that, when a rule of type (a) is applied, the membrane can also evolve by means of a rule of another type. If a rule of type (e) is applied to a membrane, and its inner objects evolve at the same step, it is assumed that first the inner objects evolve and then the division takes place, so that the result of applying rules inside the original membrane is replicated in the two new membranes.

3. FORWARD CHAINING

Let us consider the reasoning problem $\langle A, R, g\rangle$. Forward chaining basically consists in finding all facts that can be derived from A according to R and checking whether g is among these facts.

We will now try to design a transitional P system which will implement forward chaining. We will focus on constructing a non-uniform solution, because in this way we will be able to map inference rules directly to multiset rewriting rules in P systems.

In the first approach we will look at the propositional rule $V \to W$ from our knowledge base as at an evolution rule of a P system where all the objects in both sides of the rule have multiplicity one. Before we start, we need to introduce some considerations.

- First of all, in P systems the objects in the LHS (left-hand side) of the rule are consumed when the rule is applied. This limitation can be avoided by considering $V \to VW$ instead of $V \to W$.
- Copying the LHS into the RHS (right-hand side) introduces undesirable effects. One of them is that a rule can be applied indefinitely many times. This can be avoiding by considering a rule $\gamma_i V \to VW$ for every $r_i \equiv V \to W$.
- The answer YES can be easily produced by using a rule $g \to$ YES. As soon as g is generated, the object YES is produced. The answer NO should be produced if no new atoms can be deduced any more, but the goal g has not been obtained.

We construct a P system implementing chaining according to the remarks given above:

$\Pi_0 =$, where

$$U_0 = U \cup \{\text{YES}\} \cup \{\gamma_i \mid 1 \le i \le n\},$$

$$w_s^{(0)} = \gamma_1 \gamma_2 \cdots \gamma_n,$$

$$R_0 = \left\{ \begin{matrix} \gamma_i V \to VW \mid (r_i : V \to W) \\ \in R, 1 \le i \le n \end{matrix} \right\} \cup \{g \to \text{YES}\}$$

$n = |R|$.

Here U is the universal set of facts. The rules come from R and the objects of in the alphabet of the system come from A and R. Note that labeling the inference rules in R is done injectively.

We placed the initial set of facts A into the skin membrane and let some multiset rewriting rules easily obtained from R simulate the forward chaining inference process according to the set of inference rules R. The rule $g \to$ YES is waiting for the goal to appear in the region.

Π_0 always stops, and there is a YES in

$$R_0 \cup \{t_i \to t_{i+1} \mid 0 \le i \le n\} \cup \{t_{n+1} \to \text{NO}, \text{YES NO} \to \text{YES}\}$$

when g can be derived from the facts in A.

To place a NO in the skin at proper times requires a further observation that the upper bound on the number of steps Π_0 makes is $n + 1$. Indeed, all rules in R_0 may be applied only once and $|R_0| = |R| + 1 = n + 1$. If after $n + 1$ steps the symbol YES has not been produced, the system should produce a NO. In the following P system Π_1 we have implemented the timer:

$$\Pi_1 = \left(U_1, [\ ]_s, w_s^{(1)}, R_1, s\right), \text{ where}$$

$$U_1 = U_0 \cup \{t_i \mid 0 \le i \le n+1\} \cup \{\text{NO}\},$$

$$w_s^{(1)} = w_s^{(0)} \cdot t_0,$$

$$R_1 = \begin{matrix} R_0 \cup \{t_i \to t_{i+1} \mid 0 \le i \le n\} \\ \cup \{t_{n+1} \to \text{NO}, \text{YES NO} \to \text{YES}\} \end{matrix}.$$

Π_1 will stop in either $n + 1$ steps if a NO has been produced, or in $n + 2$ if a YES has been produced.

To assure that the system always stops when no rules are being applied, we can use rules with inhibitors. Consider the following P system:

$$\Pi_2 = \left(U_2, [\ ]_s, w_s^{(2)}, R_2, s\right), \text{ where}$$

$$U_2 = U_0 \cup \{t, p, \text{NO}\},$$

$$w_s^{(2)} = w_s^{(0)} \cdot tp,$$

$$R_2 = \left\{ \begin{matrix} \gamma_i V \to VWp \mid_{\neg\text{YES}} \mid (r_i : V \to W) \\ \in R, 1 \le i \le n \end{matrix} \right\}$$

$\cup\left\{p \rightarrow \lambda, t \rightarrow \mathrm{NO}\mid_{\neg p}, gt \rightarrow \mathrm{YES}\right\}.$

Any rule application produces an instance of *p*, which is immediately erased. While rules are still being applied, *p* is always present in the system and thus *t* cannot change into NO. When rules are not being applied any more, *p* is erased from the system and *t* evolves into NO. If a rule application adds the goal symbol *g* to the system, *g* consumes *t* and produces YES. Thus, when no more rules can be applied, the system always needs two more steps to produce a NO. When the goal fact is produced, the system always needs one more step to produce a YES.

The last problem to solve is cleaning up, so that the system only contains either YES or NO. This is pretty obvious:

$$\Pi_f^{(1)} = \Pi_3 = \left(U_2, [\ ]_s, w_s^{(2)}, R_3, s\right), \text{ where}$$

$$R_3 = R_2 \cup \left\{a \rightarrow \lambda \mid_{\neg p} \mid a \in U \cup \left\{\gamma_i \mid 1 \le i \le n\right\}\right\}.$$

When the system produces a YES, the application of rules derived from *R* stops and *p* is not produced any more. This allows the rules $a \rightarrow \lambda \mid_{\neg p}$ to clean everything in one extra step. When there are no more rules derived from *R* to apply, *p* is not produced either, which triggers the clean-up. Note that the clean-up procedure does not considerably alter the number of steps Π_3 needs to solve the problem.

4. A DIFFERENT APPROACH TO FORWARD CHAINING

We will now consider a P system $\Pi_f^{(2)}$ with a single membrane, and a set of rules of type $v \rightarrow w \mid_{\neg i;p}$ where *i*, *p*, *v*, *w* are objects of the alphabet.

We will translate a rule $r_i \equiv u_1 u_2 \ldots u_n \rightarrow v$ from *R* into *n* rules: $\rho_{ij} \equiv r_{ij} \rightarrow r_{ij+1} \mid_{\neg v;u_j}$ for $j \in \left\{1, 2, \ldots, n-1\right\}$ and $\rho_{in} \equiv r_{in} \rightarrow v \mid_{\neg v;u_j}$. Note that we require that the right-hand side of every rule in *R* should contain exactly one fact. We will also add the following rules to implement the timer:

$$\left\{t_k \rightarrow t_{k+1} \mid_{\neg g;t_k} \mid 1 \le k \le l-1\right\} \cup$$
$$\left\{t_k \rightarrow \mathrm{YES} \mid_{\neg \mathrm{NO};g} \mid 0 \le k \le l\right\}$$

$$\cup\left\{t_l \rightarrow \mathrm{NO} \mid_{\neg g;t_l}\right\}$$

The following rules will clean up the regions of the system:

$$\left\{a \rightarrow \lambda \mid_{\neg \mathrm{NO};\mathrm{YES}} \mid a \in \Gamma \setminus \left\{\mathrm{YES}\right\}\right\} \cup$$
$$\left\{b \rightarrow \lambda \mid_{\neg \mathrm{YES};\mathrm{NO}} \mid b \in \Gamma \setminus \left\{\mathrm{NO}\right\}\right\}$$

Here *g* is the goal fact and Γ is the alphabet of the P system.

The alphabet contains all the atoms from *U*, the symbols $\left\{\mathrm{YES}, \mathrm{NO}\right\}$, all t_k, $1 \le k \le l$, and all the r_{ij} where *i* is the index of the corresponding rule from *R* and *j* is the index of an atom in the LHS of the rule r_i.

In the initial configuration the skin membrane contains all objects from *A*, an object t_0, and all objects $r_{i1}, 1 \le i \le \mid R \mid$.

The rules ρ_{ij} are meant to check whether all left-hand-side symbols of the rule r_i are present in the system. If this condition is satisfied, the right-hand side of the rule r_i is added.

Example: Consider the tuple $\left\langle A, R, g\right\rangle$ with $A = \left\{a, b\right\}$ and $R = \left\{r_1 \equiv ab \rightarrow c, r_2 \equiv bc \rightarrow d\right\}$. From this deduction problem we can construct the P system $\Pi = \left(\Gamma, w, R_f\right)$ where

- The alphabet is $\Gamma = \begin{Bmatrix} a, b, c, d, r_{11}, r_{12}, r_{21}, r_{22}, \\ t_1, t_2, t_3, t_4, \text{YES}, \text{NO} \end{Bmatrix}$;
- The initial multiset in the unique membrane is $w = abr_{11}r_{21}t_0$;
- The rules ρ_{ij} are:

$$\rho_{11} \equiv r_{11} \to r_{12} \mid_{\neg c;a} \quad \rho_{21} \equiv r_{21} \to r_{22} \mid_{\neg d;b}$$
$$\rho_{12} \equiv r_{12} \to c \mid_{\neg c;b} \quad \rho_{22} \equiv r_{22} \to d \mid_{\neg d;c}$$

In the initial configuration $C_0 = \left[abr_{11}r_{21}t_0\right]$ rules ρ_{11} and ρ_{21} can be applied, which yields the configuration $C_1 = \left[abr_{12}r_{22}t_1\right]$. In C_1 the rule ρ_{12} can be applied and we obtain $C_2 = \left[abcr_{22}t_2\right]$. Now, by applying ρ_{22}, we obtain $C_3 = \left[abcdt_3\right]$. Since the goal fact has appeared in the system, t_3 will evolve into a YES: $C_4 = \left[abcd\text{YES}\right]$. In the next step all symbols but YES will be erased: $C_5 = \left[\text{YES}\right]$.

$\Pi_f^{(2)}$ works by transforming the symbols ρ_{i1} into the corresponding right-hand sides of rules $\left(r_{i1} \equiv V_i \to a\right) \in R,\ a_i \in U$ if all the symbols in the left-hand side of the rule r_i are present in the skin region. Thus the system never produces the right-hand side of a rule if not all of the symbols in the left-hand side of the rule are present in the skin region. This means that the set of facts the system derives is always a subset of the set of facts that can be derived from *A* by Generalized Modus Ponens.

On the other hand, independently of the order in which the symbols in the left-hand side of the rule appear in the system, if all of the symbols in the left-hand side of the rule r_i are present in the skin region, the promoters of the rules $\rho_{ij}, 1 \le j \le \mid V \mid$, guarantee that r_{i1} is transformed into a_i. This means that the system produces at least all facts that can be derived from *A* by Generalized Modus Ponens.

5. BACKWARD CHAINING

As usual, when implementing backward chaining in P systems, we would like to take as much advantage as possible of the parallelism offered by these devices. The obvious way to exploit parallelism is exploring the branches of the deduction tree in parallel.

Since we would like to explore a number of branches in parallel and since these branches are completely independent of one another, it would be natural to investigate each branch in a separate region.

This brings us to the conclusion that P systems with active membranes are a good candidate for implementing backward chaining. However, in P systems with active membranes one can only divide a membrane into two children membranes. A way to avoid this limitation is to demand the set $R_w = \left\{V \to w \mid \left(V \to w\right) \in R\right\}$ have no more than two elements. Any set of rules *R* can be transformed to satisfy this constraint by substituting every set of rules:

$$R_w = \left\{V_1 \to w, V_2 \to w, \ldots, V_n \to w\right\},\ n > 2$$

with

$$\left\{z_{i-1} \to z_i, V_{i+1} \to z_i \mid 2 \le i \le n-2\right\} \cup$$
$$\left\{z_{n-2} \to w, V_n \to w, V_1 \to z_1, V_2 \to z_1\right\}$$

The corresponding symbols $z_i, 1 \le i \le n-2$, should be added to the new set of facts U'.

We introduce two notations, $(')$ and $('')$ on a multiset:

$$W = w_1 w_2 \ldots w_n,\ W \in U^+:$$
$$W'' = w_1'' w_2'' \ldots w_n'' \text{ and}$$
$$W' = w_1' w_2' \ldots w_n'.$$

We also consider the corresponding specialization of these notations for sets.

Given that R satisfies the constraints specified above, consider the following P system with active membranes:

$$\Pi_b = \left(U_b, \{k, s\}, [[\ ]_k]_s, w_k, w_s, R_b, s\right), \text{ where}$$

$$U_b = U \cup U' \cup U'' \cup \{\rho_i \mid (r_i : V_i \rightarrow w_i) \in R\}$$

$$\cup \{f_0, f_1, c_0, c_1, c_2, c_3, l, p, q, \$_0, \$_1, \#\}$$

$$\cup \{t_i \mid 0 \leq i \leq 7\} \cup \{\text{YES}, \text{NO}\},$$

$$R_b = \left\{ \begin{array}{l|} [w'']_k^0 \rightarrow [\rho_i]_k^+ [\rho_j]_k^+ \\ \exists \{V_i \rightarrow w, V_j \rightarrow w\} \subseteq R, V_i \neq V_j \end{array} \right\}$$

$$\cup \left\{ \begin{array}{l|} [w'']_k^0 \rightarrow [\rho_i]_k^+ [\#]_k^+ \\ \exists (V_i \rightarrow w) \in R, \bar{\exists}(\alpha \rightarrow w) \in R, \alpha \neq V_i \end{array} \right\}$$

$$\cup \left\{ [t_{i-1} \rightarrow t_i]_s^0 \middle| 1 \leq i \leq 6 \right\}$$

$$\cup \left\{ [\rho_i \rightarrow q c_0 f_0 V_i]_k^+ \middle| \exists (V_i \rightarrow \alpha) \in R, \alpha \subseteq U \right\}$$

$$\cup \left\{ [f_0 \rightarrow f_1]_k^+, [l]_k^+ \rightarrow [\ ]_k^0 l, [l]_s^0 \rightarrow [\ ]_s^+ l, [l \rightarrow \lambda]_s^+ \right\}$$

$$\cup \left\{ [f_1 a \rightarrow a l]_k^+ \middle| a \in U \right\}$$

$$\cup \left\{ [c_{i-1} \rightarrow c_i]_k^+ \middle| 1 \leq i \leq 3 \right\}$$

$$\cup \left\{ [c_3 \rightarrow \lambda]_k^0, [c_3]_k^+ \rightarrow \$_0 \right\}$$

$$\cup \left\{ \begin{array}{l} [\$_0 \rightarrow \$_1 \text{YES}]_s^+, [\$_0 \rightarrow \text{YES}]_s^0, \\ [\text{YES NO} \rightarrow \text{YES}]_s^+, \end{array} \right.$$

$$\left. [\$_1]_s^0 \rightarrow [\ ]_s^+ \$_1 \right\}$$

$$\cup \left\{ [t_{i-1} \rightarrow t_i]_s^0 \middle| 1 \leq i \leq 6 \right\}$$

$$\cup \left\{ \begin{array}{l} [t_6 \rightarrow p t_7]_s^0, [t_7 \rightarrow t_2]_s^+, [t_7 \rightarrow \lambda]_s^0, \\ [p \rightarrow \text{NO}]_s^0, \end{array} \right.$$

$$\left. [p]_s^+ \rightarrow [\ ]_s^0 p \right\},$$

$$w_k = qgA', w_s = t_0.$$

This system decides, using backward chaining, whether g can be derived from A according to the rules in R. Handling cycles in inference rules $(\{a \rightarrow b, b \rightarrow a\})$ is a matter of further research.

Π_b starts with a single worker membrane with the label k, which contains the goal symbol g and A'. All primed symbols in the worker membrane are the symbols which have already been reduced once. The system will never reduce the same symbol twice in a worker membrane. The rule $[qa \rightarrow a'a'']_k^0$ marks g as reduced and creates a double primed copy of it. Double primed symbols are symbols which are meant to be reduced.

The system includes two types of operations for reducing symbols: $[w'']_k^0 \rightarrow [\rho_i]_k^+ [\rho_j]_k^+$ and $[w'']_k^0 \rightarrow [\rho_i]_k^+ [\#]_k^+$. The first operation is done in the cases when $|R_w| = 2$. It creates two new worker membranes with polarization + for each of the two left-hand sides of the rules used for reduction. The second operation is performed when $|R_w| = 1$. This operation creates two worker membranes, but one of them contains # which will not allow the membrane to evolve further. It is important to realize that, even if $|R_w| = 1$, the corresponding P system rule need employ a membrane to avoid attempts to apply rules multiple times.

In any of the newly created membranes, the rule $[\rho_i \to qc_0f_0V_i]_k^+$ introduces the actual left-hand side of the corresponding inference rule, as well as several service symbols. In the next step the rule $[aa' \to a']_k^+$ removes any of the new symbols which have already been reduced. At the same time f_0 evolves into f_1 and c_0 into c_1. In the next step f_1 verifies whether not primed symbols are still present in the membrane. If there indeed are such symbols, an l is produced, which eventually re-polarizes the worker membrane to 0, thus re-launching the process of application of inference rules. The role of the symbol q is to assure that only one not yet reduced symbol is reduced.

In parallel with the rule $[aa' \to a']_k^+$, the rule $[aa \to a]_k^+$ is applied. It removes the duplicates which appear in situations when the worker membrane contains a and b and reduces b by the rule $V \to b$, $a \in V$. Note that the rule removing the already reduced symbols and the reduction rule cannot be applicable to the same symbol in the same time, which removes concurrency effects.

If the worker membrane contains no more symbols which have not yet been reduced, Π_b concludes that we have discovered a resolution of g to the set of known atoms A. Since the rule $[f_1a \to al]_k^+$ does not produce the symbol l, the symbols c_i evolve until c_3 ejects a $\$_0$ into the skin region. This symbol will eventually produce YES.

The skin membrane contains symbols t_i which check whether there still is some activity in the system. Each application of an inference rule (or two inference rules, when $|R_w| = 2$) takes 6 steps. At the very beginning, the symbol t_0 evolves into t_6. If $\exists(V \to g) \in R$, when t_6 is produced in the skin region, the skin region will also contain an l. t_6 evolves into pt_7 and, at the same time, l polarizes the skin membrane to +. This makes t_7 evolve into t_2, thus restarting the t_i loop, while p resets the skin polarization to 0.

If, however, no worker membrane produces an l any more, when p is produced in the skin, the skin polarization stays at 0. This forces p to produce a NO and erase t_7, thus breaking the t_i loop.

The symbol $\$_0$ will always appear in the skin region at the same time as pt_7. Two situations are possible: if there has just been at least one l in the skin, the skin will have polarization +. In this case t_2 is produced and p is erased. At the same time, $\$_0$ produces a $\$_1$ and YES. $\$_1$ polarizes the skin to +, thus stopping the t_i loop. In the other situation no instances of l are produced and, when pt_7 is produced in the skin, the polarization of this membrane is 0. In this case p will produce a NO, while t_7 will be erased, thus breaking the t_i loop. At the same time $\$_0$ will produce a YES which will erase NO in the next step.

6. CONCLUSION

In this paper we continued exploring the possibilities of solving reasoning problems with P systems, a topic which was started in Gutiérrez et al. (2004). The computing devices of membrane computing, P systems, look appealing in this context due to two main reasons: the similarity of inference rules and multiset rewriting rules and the maximal parallelism. The similarity of the two types of rules allows a relatively natural transformation of reasoning problems into P systems and a rather efficient exploitation of the maximal parallelism.

We have only focused on zero-order logic in this paper, which resulted in quite simple P systems for forward chaining problems and more complicated devices for backward chaining. The difference in complexity appears because of the inherently recursive nature of backward chaining; and since one of our goals was to exploit the maximal parallelism, in the case of backward chaining we needed to branch off parallel explorations for each of the possibilities arousing at every reasoning step (after every SLD resolution).

This paper does not attempt to be exhaustive. One of the most evident questions is whether the P systems suggested in this paper can be optimized in the number of rules or control symbols. Another optimization criterion is the speed of the system. Although it is clear that all P systems have the time complexity $O(|R|)$, Π_b is about six times slower on average than $\Pi_f^{(1)}$.

ACKNOWLEDGMENT

AA gratefully acknowledges the project RetroNet by the Lombardy Region of Italy under the ASTIL Program (regional decree 6119, 20100618). MAGN acknowledges the support of the projects TIN-2009-13192 of the Ministerio de Ciencia e Innovación of Spain and the support of the Project of Excellence of the Junta de Andalucía, grant P08-TIC-04200.

REFERENCES

Apt, K. R. (1990). Logic programming. In van Leeuwen, J. (Ed.), *Handbook of theoretical computer science*. Amsterdam, The Netherlands: Elsevier.

Bratko, I. (2001). *PROLOG programming for artificial intelligence* (3rd ed.). Reading, MA: Addison-Wesley.

Gutiérrez-Naranjo, M. A., & Rogozhin, V. (2004). Deductive databases and P systems. *Computer Science Journal of Moldova*, *12*(1), 34.

Jago, M. (2007). *Formal logic. Penrith*. Cumbria, UK: Humanities-Ebooks LLP.

Krishna, S. N., & Rama, R. (1999). A variant of P systems with active membranes: Solving NP-complete problems. *Romanian Journal of Information Science and Technology*, *2*(4), 357–367.

Lloyd, J. W. (1987). *Foundations of logic programming* (2nd ed.). Berlin, Germany: Springer-Verlag.

Păun, G. (2002). *Membrane computing: An introduction*. Berlin, Germany: Springer-Verlag.

Păun, G., Rozenberg, G., & Salomaa, A. (Eds.). (2010). *The Oxford handbook of membrane computing*. Oxford, UK: Oxford University Press.

Systems, P. (2011). *Resources website*. Retrieved from http://ppage.psystems.eu/

This work was previously published in the International Journal of Natural Computing Research (IJNCR), Volume 2, Issue 2, edited by Leandro Nunes de Castro, pp. 56-66, copyright 2011 by IGI Publishing (an imprint of IGI Global).

Chapter 10
Towards Automated Verification of P Systems Using Spin

Raluca Lefticaru
University of Pitesti, Romania

Cristina Tudose
University of Pitesti, Romania

Florentin Ipate
University of Pitesti, Romania

ABSTRACT

This paper presents an approach to P systems verification using the Spin model checker. The authors have developed a tool which implements the proposed approach and can automatically transform P system specifications from P-Lingua into Promela, the language accepted by the well known model checker Spin. The properties expected for the P system are specified using some patterns, representing high level descriptions of frequently asked questions, formulated in natural language. These properties are automatically translated into LTL specifications for the Promela model and the Spin model checker is run against them. In case a counterexample is received, the Spin trace is decoded and expressed as a P system computation. The tool has been tested on a number of examples and the results obtained are presented in the paper.

1. INTRODUCTION

The relatively new field of Membrane Computing has known a fast development and many applications have been reported (Ciobanu, Păun, & Pérez-Jiménez, 2006), especially in biology and bio-medicine, but also in unexpected directions, such as economics, approximate optimization and computer graphics (Frisco, 2009; Păun, Rozenberg, & Salomaa, 2010). Also, a large number of software tools for simulating P systems have been developed, many of them with the purpose of dealing with real world problems, such as those arisen from biology (Cardona, Colomer, Margalida, Pérez-Hurtado, Pérez-Jiménez, & Sanuy, 2010). Similarly to other nature inspired computing mod-

DOI: 10.4018/978-1-4666-4253-9.ch010

els or evolutionary strategies, P systems have been employed to tackle computationally hard problems (Păun, 2001; Pérez-Jiménez & Riscos-Núñez, 2005). An overview of the state of the art in P system software can be found in Păun, Rozenberg, and Salomaa (2010), chapter 17. The P-Lingua framework, one of the most promising software projects in membrane computing, proposes a new programming language, aiming to become a standard for the representation and simulation of P systems (García-Quismondo, Gutiérrez-Escudero, Martínez-del-Amor, Orejuela-Pinedo, & Pérez-Hurtado, 2009; Martínez-del-Amor, Pérez-Hurtado, Pérez-Jiménez, & Riscos-Núñez, 2010).

After designing a P system that aims to solve a given problem, a validation is needed to ensure that the proposed model corresponds to what it is expected. Automated tools, such as model checkers, would be very useful to prove or disprove 'on-the-fly' that the P system meets the expected specification. *Model checking* is an automated technique for verifying if a model meets a given specification (Clarke, Grumberg, & Peled, 1999). It has been applied for verifying models of hardware and software designs, such as sequential circuits designs, communication protocols, concurrent systems, etc. A *model checker* is a tool that receives as input a property expressed as a temporal logic formula and a model of the system, given as an operational specification, and verifies, through the entire state space, whether the property holds or not. If a property violation is discovered then a counterexample is returned, that details why the model does not satisfy the property specified. Two widely used temporal specification languages in model checking are Linear Temporal Logic (LTL) and Computation Tree Logic (CTL) (Clarke, Grumberg, & Peled, 1999). Spin is probably the most well-known LTL model checker (Holzmann, 2003; Ben-Ari, 2005). It was written by Gerard Holzmann in the '80, developed over three decades at Bell Laboratories and it received in 2001 the prestigious ACM System Software Award. The transition systems accepted by SPIN (Simple Promela INterpreter) are described in the modelling language Promela (Process Meta Language) and the LTL formulas are checked using the algorithm advocated in Gerth, Peled, Vardi, and Wolper (1995).

In this paper we present an approach to automatic translation of P systems into executable specifications in Promela, the language accepted by the Spin model checker, and their formal verification using Spin. The paper intends to realize a bridge between P-Lingua, a very promising framework for defining and simulating P systems, and Spin, one of the most successful model checkers. The tool presented in the paper assists in designing and verifying P systems by automatically transforming the P-Lingua specifications into Promela. The properties expected for the P system are specified in a 'natural language', using a user-friendly interface, then are automatically translated into LTL specifications for the Promela model; furthermore, the Spin model checker is run against them. In case a counterexample is received, the Spin trace is decoded and expressed in terms of a P system derivation.

Model checking based verification of P systems is a topic which has attracted a significant amount of research in the last years; the main tools used so far are Maude (Andrei, Ciobanu, & Lucanu, 2005), Prism (Romero-Campero, Gheorghe, Bianco, Pescini, Pérez-Jiménez, & Ceterchi, 2006; Bernardini, Gheorghe, Romero-Campero, & Walkinshaw, 2007), NuSMV (Lefticaru, Ipate, & Gheorghe, 2010; Gheorghe, Ipate, Lefticaru, & Dragomir, 2011), Spin (Ipate, Lefticaru, & Tudose, 2011) and ProB (Ipate & Ţurcanu, 2011). Previous work (Ipate, Lefticaru, & Tudose, 2011) shows that Spin can cope better with the state explosion problem associated with modeling and verifying P systems. This paper makes further advances in this area. Firstly, each model checker uses a particular language for describing the models accepted. The activity of specifying a P system in a certain language, such as Promela for Spin, or SMV for NuSMV, can be tedious and error-prone. Many model checking tools cannot directly implement the transitions of a P system working in maximally parallel mode and, consequently, the models obtained are complex, because they are simulating the parallelism using many sequential operations. With this respect, the tool presented here automatically transforms a P system definition file into an executable specification for the Spin model checker. The input file is the P-Lingua specification of a P system, which is an easy way of expressing the P systems and can also be used for simulation with the P-Lingua framework.

Secondly, the executable specifications written for different model checkers are not functionally equivalent with the P systems, for example they can contain extra states and variables corresponding to intermediate steps, which have no correspondence in the P system configurations (Ipate, Lefticaru, & Tudose, 2011). For this reason, the P system properties that need to be verified should be reformulated as properties of the executable implementation. The tool described in this paper takes the properties expressed in a natural language and transforms them directly into LTL formulas for the Promela model. For more details rearding LTL formulas or the Spin model checker, see for example (Pnueli, 1977; Clarke, Grumberg, & Peled, 1999; Ben-Ari, 2005). The tool hides all the specialized information of the Spin model checker and provides the answer (true or false); in case a counterexample is found, this is decoded and expressed as a P system computation.

The paper is structured as follows. We start by describing the theoretical foundations of this approach in the next section; then the proposed framework is presented and some examples are given. Finally, the conclusions are drawn in the last section.

2. P SYSTEM SPECIFICATION IN PROMELA

In this section we will present the theoretical background for verifying P systems using the Spin model checker, as proposed in Ipate, Lefticaru, and Tudose (2011). Before we proceed, we formally introduce the concepts of P system and Kripke structure to be used in this paper.

The following definition refers to cell-like P systems, with transformation and communication rules (Păun, 2002).

Definition 1: *A P system is a tuple* $\Pi = (V, \mu, w_1, \ldots, w_n, R_1, \ldots, R_n)$, where V is a finite set, called alphabet; μ defines the membrane structure, which is a hierarchical arrangement of n compartments called regions delimited by membranes - these membranes and regions are identified by integers 1 to n; w_i, $1 \leq i \leq n$, represents the initial multiset occurring in region i; R_i, $1 \leq i \leq n$, denotes the set of processing rules applied in region i.

The membrane structure, μ, is denoted by a string of left and right brackets $\left([_i \text{ and }]_i\right.$, each with the label of the membrane *i*, it points to; μ also describes the position of each membrane in the hierarchy. The rules in each region have the form $u \rightarrow (a_1, t_1) \ldots (a_m, t_m)$, where *u* is a multiset of symbols from V, $a_i \in V, t_i \in \{ \textit{in, out, here} \}, 1 \leq i \leq m$. When such a rule is applied to a multiset *u* in the current region, *u* is replaced by the symbols a_i with t_i = *here;* symbols a_i with t_i = *out* are sent to the outer region or outside the system when the current region is the external compartment and symbols a_i with t_i = *in* are sent into one of the regions contained in the current one, arbitrarily chosen. In the following definitions and examples when the target indication is *here*, the pair $(a_i, here)$ will be replaced by a_i. The rules are applied in maximally parallel mode which means that they are used in all the regions at the same time and in each region all the objects to which a rule *can* be applied *must* be the subject of a rule application (Păun, 2000). Electrical charges, from the set $\{+; -; 0\}$, can also be associated with membranes, as described in (Păun, 2002). A *configuration* of the P system Π, is a tuple $c = (u_1, \ldots, u_n)$, where $u_i \in V^*$, is the multiset associated with region i, $1 \le i \le n$. A computation of a configuration c_2 from c_1 using the maximal parallelism mode is denoted by $c_1 \Rightarrow c_2$. In the set of all configurations we will distinguish halting configurations; $c = (u_1, \ldots, u_n)$ is a *halting configuration* if there is no region *i* such that u_i can be further developed.

Definition 2: *A Kripke structure over a set of atomic propositions AP is a four tuple* $M = (S, H, I, L)$, where S is a finite set of states; $I \subseteq S$ is a set of initial states; $H \subseteq S \times S$ is a transition relation that must be left-total, that is, for every state $s \in S$ there is a state $s' \in S$ such that $(s, s') \in H$; $L : S \to 2^{AP}$ is an interpretation function, that labels each state with the set of atomic propositions true in that state.

In Ipate, Gheorghe, and Lefticaru (2010) it is explained how an associated Kripke structure can be built for a given P system. For this, the object multiplicities in the P systems membranes have to be restricted to a finite domain and so additional state variables and predicates are defined, following the guidelines from Dang, Ibarra, Li, and Xie (2005, 2006). However, as explained in Ipate, Lefticaru, and Tudose (2011), the Spin model checker cannot directly implement this model and the Promela implementation is not functionally equivalent to the P system.

In the following, we will present the transformation of a simple P system into a Promela model. For more details, Ipate, Lefticaru, and Tudose (2011) can be consulted and some examples can be downloaded from the following web page http://fmi.upit.ro/evomt/psys/psys_spin.html. Consider the one-membrane P system $\Pi = (V, \mu, w, R)$, with the alphabet $V = \{a_1, \ldots, a_k\}$ and the set of rules $R = \{r_1, \ldots, r_m\}$ (each rule r_i has the form $u_i \to v_i$, $u_i, v_i \in V^*$). The Promela implementation of the P system will contain:

- *k* variables $a_i \in V$, $1 \le i \le k$, labelled exactly like the objects from *V*, each showing the number of occurrences of each object in the membrane;
- At most *k* auxiliary variables, labelled like the objects from the alphabet *V* plus a suffix *p*, each showing the number of occurrences of each object a_i produced in the current computation step;
- *m* variables n_i, $1 \le i \le m$, each showing the number of applications of each rule $r_i \in R$;
- One variable *state* showing the current state of the model, $state \in \{running, halt, crash\}$;
- One boolean variable *bStateInS* expressing if the current configuration in the Promela model represents a state in the P system; *bStateInS* is *false* when intermediary steps are executed and *true* when the computation is over (a step in the P system derivation is completed); a corresponding atomic proposition pInS will evaluate whether *bStateInS* holds;
- Two constants, *Max,* the upper bound for the number of occurrences of each object $a_i \in V$, $1 \le i \le k$, and *Sup*, the upper bound for the number of applications of each rule r_i, $1 \le i \le m$;
- A set of propositions, which will be used in the LTL formulas; they are introduced by *#define* and named suggestively. For example, *#define pn1* (n1>0) is used to check if the rule r_1 has been applied at least once, *#define pa1 (a==1)* checks if the number of objects of type *a* is exactly 1.

In order to describe in Promela one computation step of a P system, a set of operations, additional variables and intermediary states are needed. For example, consider $\Pi_1 = \left(V_1, \mu_1, w_1, R_1\right)$, a simple one-membrane P system having

$$V_1 = \left\{s, a, b, c\right\},\ \mu_1 = \left[\ _1\right]_1,\ w_1 = s,$$
$$R_1 = \left\{r_1 : s \to ab; r_2 : a \to c; r_3 : b \to bc; r_4 : b \to c\right\}.$$

The code excerpt in Box 1 corresponds to Π_1, when the current state is *running*:

The do-od loop realizes the non-deterministic application of the rules. It is followed by an if statement deciding the next state from the set {*halt,crash,running*}. The code is self-explanatory, for more details Ipate, Lefticaru, and Tudose (2011) can be consulted, so we will focus next on the properties to be checked.

The P system semantics is implemented for Spin as a sequence of transitions (or operations) and, consequently, additional intermediary states are introduced into the model. Naturally, we consider that the intermediary states cannot form infinite loops, and so every possible path in the Promela executable model will contain infinitely often states corresponding to the P system configurations. From these assumptions, it follows that every path in the P system has at least one corresponding path in the Promela model and vice versa. Furthermore, restrictions on the multiplicity of objects and rules applied are imposed, as explained earlier.

The next step needed for model checking P systems with Spin is reformulating the properties to be verified in equivalent formulas for the associated Promela model. For example, a property like 'always $b > 0$' (the number of occur-

Box 1.

```
bStateInS = false;
n1 = 0; n2 = 0; n3 = 0; n4 = 0;
ap = 0; bp = 0; cp = 0;
do
        :: s > 0 -> s = s - 1; n1 = n1 + 1; ap = ap + 1; bp = bp + 1
        :: a > 0 -> a = a - 1; n2 = n2 + 1; cp = cp + 1
        :: b > 0 -> b = b - 1; n3 = n3 + 1; bp = bp + 1; cp = cp + 1
        :: b > 0 -> b = b - 1; n4 = n4 + 1; cp = cp + 1
        :: else -> break
od;
a = a + ap; b = b + bp; c = c + cp;
if
        :: ( a > Max || b > Max || c > Max || s > Max ||
                n1 > Sup || n2 > Sup || n3 > Sup || n4 > Sup ) ->
                        state = crash; bStateInS = true
        :: else ->
                if
                        :: s == 0 && a == 0 && b == 0 ->
                                state = halt; bStateInS = true
                        :: else ->
                                state = running; bStateInS = true
                fi
fi
```

rences of b objects is always greater than 0) should become for the Promela model 'Globally $b > 0$ or not *pInS*' (we expect $b > 0$ only for configurations corresponding to the P system, but not for the intermediary steps). In Table 1 we summarize the transformations of all LTL formulas for the Promela specification, as they are formally proved in Ipate, Lefticaru, and Tudose (2011).

3. TOOL DESCRIPTION

The P system model-checking approach presented above has been implemented in a software tool, which can perform 'on-the-fly' verification of properties expressed in a natural language. The tool, as well as the specifications of the P systems used in our tests, can be downloaded from the web page http://fmi.upit.ro/evomt/psys/psys_spin.html. An advantage of this tool is that the users do not need to be experts in formal verification or to write complex, specialized LTL formulas, in order to apply the model checking verification technique. They only need to specify the P system, using P-Lingua, to choose the type of property to be checked and the conversion to Promela is performed automatically. If the property is false, the counterexample returned by Spin is parsed by the tool and represented as a P system computation.

In order to use the tool, the next steps are required:

- The user specifies the P-system in P-Lingua. He/she can also check, using the P-Lingua parsers, if the P system definition file is syntactically correct.
- The P-system is automatically transformed into a Promela specification.
- The user specifies some basic configuration properties over the system variables.
- The user selects a type of property to be verified, given in natural language, and the basic propositions involved in that property.
- The property is then automatically translated into an LTL formula suitable for the generated Promela model.
- The verification of the P system is performed automatically and if the answer returned by Spin is *false*, the tool will provide a counterexample expressed as a P system computation (with the configurations and set of rules applied at each step).

The main drawback of the application of previous model checking approaches to formal verification of P systems is the difficulty for non-expert users to formulate the appropriate properties in temporal logic. In our case, this could be further amplified by the fact that the LTL formulas would have to be transformed as described earlier. To alleviate this problem, we define some *patterns*, representing high level descriptions of frequently

Table 1. Reformulating the P system properties for the Promela implementation

<table>
<tr><th>Property</th><th>LTL Specification</th></tr>
<tr><td>$\mathbf{G}p$</td><td>[] (p || !pInS)</td></tr>
<tr><td>$\mathbf{F}p$</td><td><> (p && pInS)</td></tr>
<tr><td>pUq</td><td>(p || !pInS) U (q && pInS)</td></tr>
<tr><td>$\mathbf{X}p$</td><td>X (!pInS U (p && pInS))</td></tr>
<tr><td>pRq</td><td>(p && pInS) V (q || !pInS)</td></tr>
<tr><td>$\mathbf{G}\left(p \to q\right)$</td><td>[] (!p || q || !pInS)</td></tr>
<tr><td>$\mathbf{G}\left(p \to \mathrm{F}q\right)$</td><td>[] ((p → <> (q && pInS)) || !pInS)</td></tr>
</table>

asked questions, formulated in *natural language*. These patterns, which simplify the specification of properties to be verified, are employed in our tool.

Let *AP* be a set of atomic propositions. An example of such proposition could be: *the number of b objects from a membrane m is greater than 0*. Let $p \in AP$. A basic configuration property φ over *AP* is defined as:

$$\varphi ::= p \mid \varphi \vee \varphi \mid \varphi \wedge \varphi \mid$$

Each pattern is given as a natural language phrase that contains one or more basic configuration properties. The patterns considered so far are (in what follows φ and ψ are basic configuration properties, the statement must hold on every computation):

- **Invariance** $(\mathrm{G}\ \varphi)$**:** A configuration in which φ is true must persist indefinitely.
- **Occurrence** $(\mathrm{F}\ \varphi)$**:** A configuration where φ is true will eventually occur.
- **Next Occurrence** $(\mathrm{X}\ \varphi)$**:** A configuration where φ is true will occur after initial configuration.
- **Sequence** $(\varphi\ \mathrm{U}\ \psi)$**:** A configuration where φ is true is reachable and is necessarily preceded all the time by a configuration in which ψ is true.
- **Dual of Sequence** $(\varphi\ \mathrm{R}\ \psi)$**:** Along the computation up to and including the first configuration where φ is true, ψ holds. However, a configuration where φ is true is not required to hold eventually.
- **Consequence** $(\mathrm{G}(\varphi \rightarrow \mathrm{F}\ \psi)\ )$**:** If a configuration where φ is true occurs, then a configuration where ψ is true will eventually occur.
- **Instantly Consequence** $(\mathrm{G}(\varphi \rightarrow\ \psi)\ )$**:** If a configuration where φ is true occurs, then ψ holds also in that configuration.

These patterns can be used to formulate frequently asked questions, without worrying about their transformation into a temporal logic formula suited for our model. The transformation is performed automatically, employing the formulas from Table 1.

4. CASE STUDIES

In this section, we present some examples of P system properties we have verified using the framework introduced earlier. In order to simplify the presentation, we consider only one-membrane P systems. The first example is Π_1, the P system defined previously. This is a simple P system, that has been used in several papers. In order to facilitate the comparison with other representations, such as SMV (Ipate, Gheorghe, & Lefticaru, 2010) or Event-B (Ipate & Ţurcanu, 2011), Π_1 is presented among the examples on which we illustrate our approach. The other P systems have different properties, that can be verified (e.g., the number of *c* objects is always the square of *b* objects), or present polarizations.

4.1. Simple P Systems

Consider the following one-membrane P system:

$\Pi_1 = (V_1, \mu_1, w_1, R_1)$, having $V_1 = \{s, a, b, c\}$,
$\mu_1 = [\,_1]_1$, $w_1 = s$,
$R_1 = \{r_1 : s \rightarrow ab; r_2 : a \rightarrow c; r_3 : b \rightarrow bc; r_4 : b \rightarrow c\}$.

In order to realize the verification of the desired properties, the basic configuration propositions, which are part of the formulas must be specified first, as described in Table 2.

The first two columns are introduced by the user and they represent the basic configuration property and its name (or ID). The propositions from the third column are based on the previous two and they are inserted automatically in the Promela specification. Having the basic proposi-

Table 2. Set of basic configuration properties defined for Π_1

<table>
<tr><th>Prop. ID</th><th>Property</th><th>Promela Proposition</th></tr>
<tr><td>pab1</td><td>a==1 && b==1</td><td>#define pab1 (a==1 && b==1)</td></tr>
<tr><td>pab0</td><td>a==0 || b==0</td><td>#define pab0 (a==0 || b==0)</td></tr>
<tr><td>pc0</td><td>c==0</td><td>#define pc0 (c==0)</td></tr>
<tr><td>pa0c2</td><td>a==0 && c==2</td><td>#define pa0c2 (a==0 && c==2)</td></tr>
<tr><td>ps0</td><td>s==0</td><td>#define ps0 (s==0)</td></tr>
<tr><td>pa0</td><td>a==0</td><td>#define pa0 (a==0)</td></tr>
<tr><td>pa1</td><td>a==1</td><td>#define pa1 (a==1)</td></tr>
<tr><td>pc2</td><td>c==2</td><td>#define pc2 (c==2)</td></tr>
<tr><td>p1</td><td>s>0</td><td>#define p1 (s>0)</td></tr>
</table>

tion defined, more complex properties can be translated from a natural language into LTL formulas and verified using Spin. A set of properties checked for Π_1 is presented in Table 3.

A counter example is received for every false property, e.g., $s \Rightarrow ab$ corresponds to the second verified property from Table 3, which states that in the next configuration $a = 0 \wedge b = 0$. Similarly, the third property, expressing the invariance of *c* objects, *c* = *0*, is falsified by $s \Rightarrow ab \Rightarrow bc^2$.

Consider the following one-membrane P system:

$$\Pi_2 = \left(V_2, \mu_2, w_2, R_2\right),\ V_2 = \left\{s, a, b, c, x\right\},$$

$$\mu_2 = \left[{}_1\right]_1,\ w_2 = s,$$

$$R_2 = \left\{r_1 : s \to abcx; r_2 : a \to ab; r_3 : b \to bc^2; r_4 : x \to xc\right\}.$$

The computation of this P system is $s \Rightarrow abcx \Rightarrow ab^2c^4x \Rightarrow ab^3c^9x \Rightarrow ab^4c^{16}x \Rightarrow \ldots$ and it does not halt. It can be easily observed that in every configuration the number of occurrences of *c* objects is the square of the number of *b* objects. Some properties, which take into account the values of the variables in the previous

Table 3. Set of properties verified for Π_1

<table>
<tr><th>Properties</th><th>LTL Specifications for Spin</th><th>Truth</th></tr>
<tr><td>Next occurrence: pab1</td><td>X (!pInS U (pab1 && pInS))</td><td>true</td></tr>
<tr><td>Next occurrence: pab0</td><td>X (!pInS U (pab0 && pInS))</td><td>false</td></tr>
<tr><td>Invariance: pc0</td><td>[] (pc0 || !pInS)</td><td>false</td></tr>
<tr><td>Occurrence: pa0c2</td><td><> (pa0c2 && pInS)</td><td>true</td></tr>
<tr><td>Dual of sequence: ps0, pc0</td><td>(ps0 && pInS) V (pc0 || !pInS)</td><td>true</td></tr>
<tr><td>Sequence: pc0, pa0</td><td>((pc0) || !pInS) U ((pa0) && pInS)</td><td>true</td></tr>
<tr><td>Instantly consequence: pb0, pa0</td><td>[] (!pb0 || pa0 || !pInS)</td><td>true</td></tr>
<tr><td>Consequence: p1, p2</td><td>[] ((p1 → <> (p2 && pInS)) || !pInS)</td><td>true</td></tr>
</table>

Table 4. Set of basic configuration properties defined for Π_2

Prop. ID	Property	Promela Proposition
pbc	c==b*b	#define pbc (c==b*b)
p2	c-2*b_old-c_old-1==0	#define p2 (c-2*b_old-c_old-1==0)
pStep1	step>=1	#define pStep1 (step>=1)
pb	b==b_old+1	#define pb (b==b_old+1)
pc16	c==16	#define pc16 (c==16)
px0	x==0	#define px0 (x==0)
px1	x==1	#define px1 (x==1)

Table 5. Sample of properties verified for Π_2

Properties	LTL Specifications for Spin	Truth
Invariance: pbc	[] (pbc || !pInS)	true
Occurrence: pc16	<> (pc16 && pInS)	true
Instantly consequence: pStep1, pb	[] (!pStep1 || pb || !pInS)	true
Instantly consequence: pStep1, p2	[] (!pStep1 || p2 || !pInS)	true
Sequence: px0, px1	(px0 || !pInS) U (px1 && pInS)	true

Table 6. Set of basic configuration properties defined for Π_3

Prop. ID	Property	Promela Proposition
pa3	a%3==0	#define pa3 (a%3==0)
pagt0	a>0	#define pagt0 (a>0)
pba	b%a==0	#define pba (b%a==0)
pch0	ch==0	#define pch0 (ch==0)
pch1	ch==1	#define pch1 (ch==1)
pbcd	(b==c && c==d)	#define pbcd ((b==c && c==d))

Table 7. Sample of properties verified for Π_3

Properties	LTL Specifications for Spin	Truth
Invariance: pa3	[] ((pa3) || !pInS)	true
Instantly consequence: pagt0, pba	[] (!pagt0 || pba || !pInS)	true
Instantly consequence: ch0, pbcd	[] (!pch0 || pbcd || !pIns)	true
Instantly consequence: ch1, pbcd	[] (!pch1 || pbcd || !pInS)	false

configuration, *var_old*, and the current computation *step*, are defined in Table 4 and the results of their verification are shown in Table 5.

4.2. P Systems with Polarizations

Consider the following P system with charges:

$\Pi_3 = (V_3, \mu_3, w_3, R_3)$, having

$V_3 = \{a, b, c, d\}$, $\mu_3 = [_1]_1$, $w_3 = a^3$,

$$R_3 = \{ r_1 : [a]_1^- \rightarrow [a, d]_1^0 ; r_2 : [a]_1^0 \rightarrow [ab]_1^+ ; r_3 : [a]_1^+ \rightarrow [ac]_1^- \}.$$

The computation of this P system is

$$[a^3]_1^0 \Rightarrow [a^3b^3]_1^+ \Rightarrow [a^3b^3c^3]_1^- \Rightarrow [a^3b^3c^3d^3]_1^0 \Rightarrow [a^3b^6c^3d^3]_1^+ \Rightarrow [a^3b^6c^6d^3]_1^- \Rightarrow \ldots$$

and it does not halt. It can be easily observed that the number of each object is always a multiple of 3; also, if the charge is 0, then the number of occurrences of b, c, d is equal. Examples of properties which can be formulated and verified are given in Tables 6 and 7.

5. CONCLUSION AND FUTURE WORK

In this paper, we present a method to automatically verify P systems using the Spin model checker. The theoretical foundations of this approach have been presented in Ipate, Lefticaru, and Tudose (2011) and its advantages have been shown, in comparison to previous work, that use another main stream model checker, NuSMV (Lefticaru, Ipate, & Gheorghe, 2010).

The tool presented in this paper is intended to help designing and verifying P systems by automatically transforming the P-Lingua specifications into Promela, the language accepted by the Spin model checker. The P system properties are specified in a natural language, after which they are translated automatically into LTL specifications for the Promela model and then the Spin model checker is run against them. In case a counterexample is received, the Spin trace is decoded and expressed as a P system computation.

Future work consists in extending the tool to accept other classes of P systems, with division and dissolving rules. More experiments will be performed to determine the performance of the Spin model checker for more complex systems, such as those solving computationally hard problems, i.e., SAT problems.

ACKNOWLEDGMENT

This work was supported by CNCSIS - UEFISCSU, project number PNII - IDEI 643/2008.

REFERENCES

Andrei, O., Ciobanu, G., & Lucanu, D. (2005). Executable specifications of P systems. In G. Mauri, G. Păun, M. J. Pérez-Jiménez, G. Rozenberg, & A. Salomaa (Eds.), *Proceedings of the 5th International Workshop on Membrane Computing* (LNCS 3365, pp. 126-145).

Ben-Ari, M. (2005). *Principles of the Spin model checker*. London, UK: Springer.

Bernardini, F., Gheorghe, M., Romero-Campero, F. J., & Walkinshaw, N. (2007). A hybrid approach to modeling biological systems. In G. Eleftherakis, P. Kefalas, G. Paun, G. Rozenberg, & A. Salomaa (Eds.), *Proceedings of the 8th International Conference on Membrane Computing* (LNCS 4860, pp. 138-159).

Cardona, M., Colomer, M. A., Margalida, A., Pérez-Hurtado, I., Pérez-Jiménez, M. J., & Sanuy, D. (2010). A P system based model of an ecosystem of some scavenger birds. In G. Paun, M. J. Pérez-Jiménez, A. Riscos-Núñez, G. Rozenberg, & A. Salomaa (Eds.), *Proceedings of the 10th International Workshop on Membrane Computing* (LNCS 5957, pp. 182-195).

Ciobanu, G., Păun, G., & Pérez-Jiménez, M. J. (Eds.). (2006). *Applications of membrane computing*. Berlin, Germany: Springer-Verlag.

Clarke, E. M., Grumberg, O., & Peled, D. A. (1999). *Model checking*. Cambridge, MA: MIT Press.

Dang, Z., Ibarra, O. H., Li, C., & Xie, G. (2005). On model-checking of P systems. In C. S. Calude, M. J. Dinneen, G. Paun, M. J. Pérez-Jímenez, & G. Rozenberg (Eds.), *Proceedings of the 4th International Conference on Unconventional Computation* (LNCS 3699, pp. 82-93).

Dang, Z., Ibarra, O. H., Li, C., & Xie, G. (2006). On the decidability of model-checking for P systems. *Journal of Automata. Languages and Combinatorics*, *11*(3), 279–298.

Frisco, P. (2009). *Computing with cells: Advances in membrane computing*. Oxford, UK: Oxford University Press. doi:10.1093/acprof:oso/9780199542864.001.0001.

García-Quismondo, M., Gutiérrez-Escudero, R., Martínez-del-Amor, M. A., Orejuela-Pinedo, E., & Pérez-Hurtado, I. (2009). P-Lingua 2.0: A software framework for cell-like P systems. *International Journal of Computers, Communications & Control*, *4*(3), 234–243.

Gerth, R., Peled, D., Vardi, M. Y., & Wolper, P. (1995). Simple on-the-fly automatic verification of linear temporal logic. In *Proceedings of the International Symposium on Protocol Specification Testing and Verification* (pp. 3-18).

Gheorghe, M., Ipate, F., Lefticaru, R., & Dragomir, C. (2011). An integrated approach to P systems formal verification. In M. Gheorghe, T. Hinze, G. Paun, G. Rozenberg, & A. Salomaa (Eds.), *Proceedings of the 11th International Workshop on Membrane Computing* (LNCS 6501, pp. 226-239).

Holzmann, G. (2003). *The spin model checker: Primer and reference manual* (1st ed.). Reading, MA: Addison-Wesley.

Ipate, F., Gheorghe, M., & Lefticaru, R. (2010). Test generation from P systems using model checking. *Journal of Logic and Algebraic Programming*, *79*(6), 350–362. doi:10.1016/j.jlap.2010.03.007.

Ipate, F., Lefticaru, R., & Tudose, C. (2011). Formal verification of P systems using spin. *International Journal of Foundations of Computer Science*, *22*(1), 133–142. doi:10.1142/S0129054111007897.

Ipate, F., & Ţurcanu, A. (2011). Modelling, verification and testing of P systems using Rodin and ProB. In *Proceedings of the Ninth Brainstorming Week on Membrane Computing* (pp. 209-220).

Lefticaru, R., Ipate, F., & Gheorghe, M. (2010). Model checking based test generation from P systems using P-lingua. *Romanian Journal of Information Science and Technology*, *13*(2), 153–168.

Martínez-del-Amor, M. A., Pérez-Hurtado, I., Pérez-Jiménez, M. J., & Riscos-Núñez, A. (2010). A P-Lingua based simulator for tissue P systems. *Journal of Logic and Algebraic Programming*, *79*, 374–382. doi:10.1016/j.jlap.2010.03.009.

Păun, G. (2000). Computing with membranes. *Journal of Computer and System Sciences*, *61*(1), 108–143. doi:10.1006/jcss.1999.1693.

Păun, G. (2001). P systems with active membranes: Attacking NP-complete problems. *Journal of Automata. Languages and Combinatorics*, *6*(1), 75–90.

Păun, G. (2002). *Membrane computing: An introduction*. Berlin, Germany: Springer-Verlag.

Păun, G., Rozenberg, G., & Salomaa, A. (Eds.). (2010). *The Oxford handbook of membrane computing*. Oxford, UK: Oxford University Press.

Pérez-Jiménez, M. J., & Riscos-Núñez, A. (2005). Solving the subset-sum problem by P systems with active membranes. *New Generation Computing*, *23*(4), 339–356. doi:10.1007/BF03037637.

Pnueli, A. (1977). The temporal logic of programs. In *Proceedings of the 18th Annual Symposium on Foundations of Computer Science* (pp. 46-57).

Romero-Campero, F. J., Gheorghe, M., Bianco, L., Pescini, D., Pérez-Jiménez, M. J., & Ceterchi, R. (2006). Towards probabilistic model checking on P systems using PRISM. In H. J. Hoogeboom, G. Paun, G. Rozenberg, & A. Salomaa (Eds.), *Proceedings of the 7th International Workshop on Membrane Computing* (LNCS 4361, pp. 477-495).

This work was previously published in the International Journal of Natural Computing Research (IJNCR), Volume 2, Issue 3, edited by Leandro Nunes de Castro, pp. 1-12, copyright 2011 by IGI Publishing (an imprint of IGI Global).

Chapter 11
MP Modelling of Glucose–Insulin Interactions in the Intravenous Glucose Tolerance Test

Vincenzo Manca
University of Verona, Italy

Luca Marchetti
University of Verona, Italy

Roberto Pagliarini
University of Verona, Italy

ABSTRACT

The Intravenous Glucose Tolerance Test is an experimental procedure used to study the glucose-insulin endocrine regulatory system. An open problem is to construct a model representing simultaneously the entire regulative mechanism. In the past three decades, several models have appeared, but they have not escaped criticisms and drawbacks. In this paper, the authors apply the Metabolic P systems theory for developing new physiologically based models of the glucose-insulin system, which can be applied to the IVGTT. Ten data-sets obtained from literature were considered and an MP model was found for each, which fits the data and explains the regulations of the dynamics. Finally, each model is analysed to define a common pattern which explains, in general, the action of the glucose-insulin control system.

1. INTRODUCTION

Glucose is the primary source of energy for body cells. It is transported from the intestines or liver to body cells via the bloodstream, and is absorbed by the cells with the intervention of the hormone insulin produced by the pancreas. Blood glucose concentration is a function of the rate of glucose which enters the bloodstream, the glucose appearance, balanced by the rate of glucose which is removed from the circulation, the glucose disappearance. Normally, in mammals

DOI: 10.4018/978-1-4666-4253-9.ch011

this concentration is tightly regulated as a part of metabolic homeostasis. Indeed, although several exogenous factors, like food intake and physical exercise, affect the blood glucose concentration level, the pancreatic endocrine hormones insulin and glucagon[1] keep this level in the range 70 – 110 mg/dl. When the blood glucose concentration level is high, the pancreatic $\beta-$cells release insulin which lowers that concentration by inducing the uptake of the excess glucose by the liver and other cells and by inhibiting hepatic glucose production. On the contrary, when the glucose level is low, the pancreatic $\alpha-$cells release glucagon that results in increasing the blood glucose level by acting on liver cells and causing them to release glucose into the blood[2] (Figure 1).

If the plasma glucose concentration level is constantly out of the usual range, then we are in presence of blood glucose problems. In particular, when this level is constantly higher than the range upper bound (which is referred to as *hyperglycemia*), we are in presence of *Diabetes*: a dreadfully severe and pervasive illness which concerns a good number of structures in the body. Diabetes is classified into two main categories known as *type I* and *type II*, respectively. Type I, 5–10% of all categories of diabetes, results from autoimmune destruction of β-cells and the pancreas is no longer capable of making insulin. Therefore, daily insulin injections are necessary. Diabetes of type II refers to the remaining 90% and occurs when the pancreas produces insulin but cells fail to use it properly. In both the types of diabetes, the illness can lead to several complications like retinopathy, nephropathy, peripheral neuropathy and blindness. This motivates researches to study the glucose-insulin endocrine regulatory system. In particular, the glucose-insulin system has been the object of repeated mathematical modelling attempts. The majority of the proposed models were devoted to the study of the glucose-insulin dynamics by considering experimental data obtained by the *intravenous glucose tolerance test*, shortly *IVGTT*, and the *oral glucose tolerance test*, shortly *OGTT*. In these models, the insulin-glucose system is assumed to be com- posed of two linked subsystems modelling the insulin action and the glucose kinetics, respectively. Since the action of insulin is delayed with respect to plasma glucose, the subsystems of insulin action typically includes a delay.

Figure 1. The glucose homeostasis

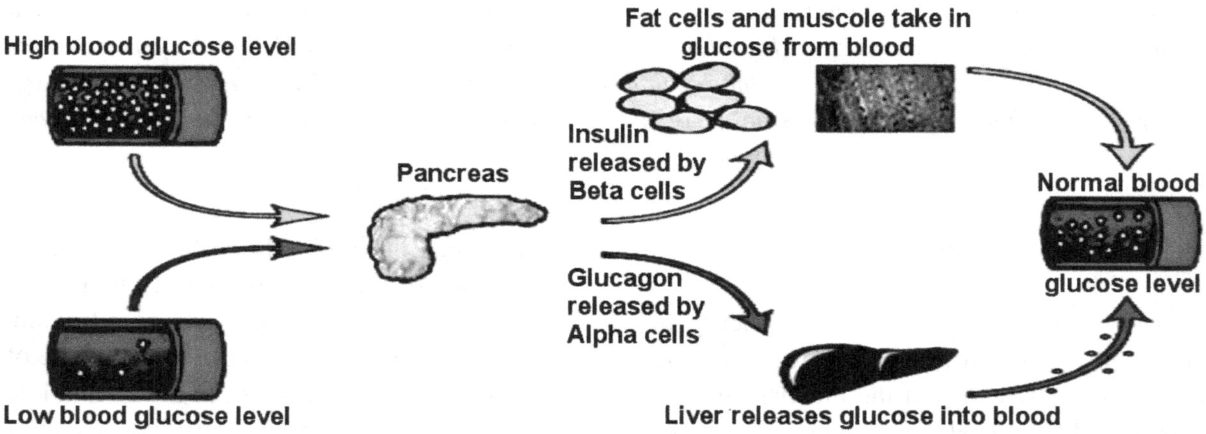

The intravenous glucose tolerance test focuses on the metabolism of glucose in a period of 3 hours starting from the infusion of a bolus of glucose at time t = 0. It is based on the assumption that, in a healthy person, the glucose concentration decreases exponentially with time following the loading dose (Figure 2). It has been recommended as a method to assess the use of insulin in order to identify subjects which may be diabetics (National Diabetes Data Group, 1979). However, considering the limits of the existing mathematical models, a need exists to have reliable mathematical models representing the glucose-insulin system. The mere fact that several models have been proposed (Boutayeb & Chetouani, 2006; Makroglou, Li, & Kuang, 2006; Mari, 2002) shows that mathematical and physiological considerations have to be carefully integrated when attempting to represent the glucose-insulin regulatory mechanism. In particular, in order to model the IVGTT, a reasonably simple model is required. It has to have a few parameters to be estimated and has to have dynamics consistent with physiology and experimental data. Further, the model formulation, while applicable to model the IVGTT, should be logically and easily extensible to model other envisaged experimental procedures.

2. MATHEMATICAL MODELS OF THE INTRAVENOUS GLUCOSE TOLERANCE TEST

A variety of mathematical models, statistical methods and algorithms have been proposed to understand different aspects of diabetes. In this section we briefly review the two mathematical models which had the most important impact in diabetology for modelling the intravenous glucose tolerance test. They have been useful to assess physiological parameters and to study the glucose-insulin interactions. However, they have not escaped from criticism and drawbacks.

Although several other models have been proposed (Bergman, Finegood, & Ader, 1985), the real start of modelling glucose-insulin dynamics is due to the *minimal model* developed in Bergman, Ider, Bowden, and Cobelli (1979) and Toffolo, Bergman, Finegood, Bowden, and Cobelli (1980). It has been characterized as the simplest model which is able to describe the glucose metabolism reasonably well by using the smallest set of identifiable and meaningful parameters (Bergman et al., 1979; Pacini & Bergman, 1986). Several versions based on the minimal model have been proposed, and the reader can find further information on them in Bergman et al. (1985) and Cobelli and Mari (1983). The minimal model has been formulated by using the following system of differential equations:

$$\frac{dG(t)}{dt} = -\left(p_1 + X(t)\right)G(t) + p_1 G_b$$

$$\frac{dX(t)}{dt} = -p_2 X(t) + p_3\left(I(t) - I_b\right) \quad (1)$$

$$\frac{dI(t)}{dt} = p_4\left(G(t) - p_5\right)t - p_6\left(I(t) - I_b\right)$$

where G(t) [mg/dl] and I (t) [μUI/ml] are plasma glucose and insulin con- centrations at time t [min], respectively, and (G(t) − p5) is assumed to be 0 when G(t) < p5. X (t) [min-1] is an auxiliary function which models the time delay of the insulin consumption on glucose. Gb and Ib are the subject baseline blood glucose and insulin concentrations, while pi, for i = 1, 2, . . ., 6, are the model parameters (we refer the reader to Bergman et al., 1979; Toffolo et al., 1980 for all the details connected to these parameters).

Although (1) is very useful in physiology research, it is based on some oversimplified mathematical representations. In fact, the artificial unobservable variable X (t) is introduced to model the delay in the action of insulin. Therefore the dynamical model has been proposed in Gaetano and Arino (2000):

$$\frac{dG(t)}{dt} = -b_1 G(t) - b_4 I(t) G(t) + b_7$$

$$G(t) \equiv G_b \quad \forall t \in [-b_5, 0) \qquad (2)$$

$$\frac{dI(t)}{dt} = -b_2 I(t) + \frac{b_6}{b_5} \int_{t-b_5}^{t} G(s) ds.$$

It is a delay integro-differential equation model which is a more realistic representation of the glucose-insulin dynamics which follows an IVGTT. Al- though it retains the physiological hypotheses underlying the first equation of (1), non-observable state variables are not introduced. Moreover, the physiological assumption underlying the third equation of (1), that pancreas is able to linearly increase its rate of insulin production with respect to the time, is not taken into account. The dynamical model assumes that the glucose concentration depends 1) on insulin-independent net glucose tissue uptake, 2) on spontaneous disappearance and 3) on constant liver glucose production. The insulin concentration, instead, is assumed to depend 1) on a spontaneous constant-rate decay, which is due to the insulin catabolism, and 2) on pancreatic secretion. In particular, the insulin secretion at time t is assumed to be proportional to the average value in the b_5 minutes which precede t, where b_5 is assumed to lie in a range from 5 to 30.

The integral term in (2) represents the *decaying memory kernel* (Cushing, 1977), which is introduced to model the time delay. The physiologic meaning of the delay kernel reflects the pancreas sensitivity to the blood glucose concentration. At a given time t, the pancreas will produce insulin at a rate proportional to the suitably weighted average of the plasma glucose concentrations in the past.

The dynamical model allows simultaneous estimation of both insulin secretion and glucose uptake parameters. However, it is conceivable that the dynamical model may not be considerable appropriate under all circumstances (Mukhopadhyay, Gaetano, & Arino, 2004). This is due to the fact that the IVGTT data related to several subjects could be best fitted by using different delay kernels. Therefore, an extension of (2) is proposed in Mukhopadhyay et al. (2004), where a generic weight function ω is introduced in the delay integral kernel modelling the pancreatic response to glucose level. In this way, the second equation of (2) becomes:

$$\frac{dI(t)}{dt} = -b_2 I(t) + b_6 \int_0^{\infty} \omega(s) G(t-s) ds \qquad (3)$$

where $\omega(s)$ is assumed to be a non-negative square integrable function on $\mathsf{R}^+ = [0, \infty)$, such that $\int_0^{\infty} \omega(s) ds = 1$ and $\int_0^{\infty} s \cdot \omega(s) ds$ is equal to the average time delay. The idea is that different patient populations show different shapes of the kernel function ω, and then suitable parametrization of such a function could offer the possibility to differentiate between patient populations by means of experimental parameter identification.

An alternative approach for dealing with time delay is analysed in Li, Kuang, and Li (2001), where the authors propose a model which includes (2) and (3) as special cases. In this model, the delay is modelled by using a Michaelis-Menten form, and the effective secretion of insulin at time t is assumed to be regulated by the concentrations of glucose in the b_5 minutes which precede time t instead of the average amount in that period.

3. MP MODELLING

An important problem of systems biology is the mathematical definition of a dynamical system which explains the observed behaviour of a phenomenon by increasing what is already known about it. An important line of re- search of biological modelling is aimed at defining new classes of discrete models avoiding some limitations of classical continuous models based on ordinary differential equations (ODEs). In fact, very often, the evaluation of the kinetic reaction rates is problematic because it may require measurements hardly accessible in living organisms. Moreover, these measurements dramatically alter the context of the investigated processes. In contrast to ODEs, *Metabolic P systems* (MP systems) (Manca, Bianco, & Fontana, 2005; Manca, 2010a, 2009, 2010b), based on Păun's P systems (Păun, 2002), were introduced for modelling *metabolic systems*.

In MP systems no single instantaneous kinetics are addressed, but rather the variation of the whole system under investigation is considered, at discrete time points, separated by a specified macroscopic interval τ. The dynamics is given along a sequence of steps and, at each step, it is governed by partitioning the matter among reactions which transform it. Metabolic P systems proved to be promising in many contexts and their applicability was tested in many situations where differential models are prohibitive due to the unavailability or the unreliability of the kinetic rates (Manca, 2010b; Manca & Marchetti, 2010a, 2010b, 2011; Manca, Pagliarini, & Zorzan, 2009; Castellini, Franco, & Pagliarini, 2011).

A Metabolic P system (Manca, 2010a) is essentially a multiset grammar where multiset transformations are regulated by functions. Namely, a rule like $a + b \rightarrow c$ means that a number u of molecules of kind a and u of kind b are replaced by u molecules of type c. The value of u is the flux of the rule application. Assume to consider a system at some time steps $i = 0, 1, 2, \ldots, t$, and consider a substance x that is produced by rules r_1, r_3 and is consumed by rule r_2. If $u_1[i]$, $u_2[i]$, $u_3[i]$ are the fluxes of the rules r_1, r_2, r_3 respectively, in the passage from step i to step i + 1, $i \in N$, the set of natural numbers, then the variation of substance x is given by:

$$x[i + 1] - x[i] = u_1[i] - u_2[i] + u_3[i].$$

In an MP system it is assumed that in any state the flux of each rule r_j is provided by a state function ϕ_j called *regulator* of the rule. Substances, reactions, and regulators (plus parameters which are variables different from substances occurring as arguments of regulators) specify the following discrete dynamics $(x[i] | i \in N)$ for any substance x, starting from the given value x[0], called EMA (Equational Metabolic Algorithm):

$$x[i + 1] = x[i] + \sum_{j=1}^{m} \alpha j \; uj \; [i] \qquad (4)$$

where m is the number of rules and α_j are the coefficients of fluxes acting on substance x. Moreover, a *temporal interval* τ, a conventional *mole size* ν, and substances masses are considered, which specify the time and population (discrete) granularities respectively. They are *scale factors* that do not enter directly in the definition of the dynamics of a system, but are essential for interpreting it at a specific physical level of mass and time granularity. In the following the MP dynamics we will present are computed in MATLAB by applying the EMA formula given in (4).

Here we apply an algorithm, called *Log-Gain Stoichiometric Stepwise Regression* (LGSS) (Manca & Marchetti, 2011), to define new MP models which describe the glucose-insulin dynamics in the IVGTT. LGSS represents the most recent solution, in terms of MP systems, of the inverse dynamics problem, that is, of the identification of (discrete) mathematical models exhibiting an observed dynamics and satisfying all the constraints required by the specific knowledge about the modelled phenomenon. The LGSS algorithm combines and extends the log-gain principles developed in the MP system theory (Manca, 2009, 2010b) with the classical method of Stepwise Regression (Hocking, 1976), which is a statistical regression technique based on Least Squares Approximation and a statistical F-test (Draper & Smith, 1981). The logic of this algorithm is quite complex because it combines several features for a systematic search procedure in suitable parameter spaces. We refer to the cited paper for details and motivations and to textbooks of statistics (Aczel & Sounderpandian, 2006) for the main statistical concepts (correlation and multiple coefficient of determination) on which our model evaluations are based.

The first MP grammar we give is the one of Table 1 which models the dynamics depicted in Figure 2. The model is given by 2 substances (G for the blood glucose level and I for the level of insulin) and 4 rules, the first two related to glucose and the others related to insulin: 1) r_1: constant release of glucose in the blood, 2) r_2: glucose disappearance due to a term which represents the normal decay of glucose (depending on G) and to a term which indicate the action of insulin (depending on both G and I), 3) r_3: release of insulin by the pancreas which depends on the blood glucose level, and iv) r_4: normal decay of insulin.

Table 1. The MP grammar which models the dynamics given in Figure 2 ($\tau = 2$ min)

$r_1 : \varnothing \rightarrow G$	$\phi_1 = 0.6$
$r_2 : G \rightarrow \varnothing$	$\phi_2 = 0.12G + 1.6 \cdot 10^{-6} G^2 I$
$r_3 : \varnothing \rightarrow I$	$\phi_3 = 49.9 + 0.1G^3$
$r_4 : I \rightarrow \varnothing$	$\phi_4 = 0.84I$

The MP grammar is defined for a value of τ of two minutes[3] (which gives the length of the time interval between two consecutive computed steps) and allows the calculation of the curves depicted in Figure 2. The dynamics is quite close to the data-set we started from. In fact, the multiple coefficients approximation for glucose and insulin (Aczel & Sounderpandian, 2006), are equal to 0.94 and 0.87 respectively[4]. The usage of the term G^3 in ϕ_3, against the possibility of choosing monomials of G with lower degree, expresses the high sensitivity of the pancreas β−cells for the blood glucose level when they release insulin.

The formula of each regulator has been calculated by means of LGSS which selects suitable linear combinations starting from a set of possible basic functions, called regressors, associated to each rule (constants, I, G, I^2, G^2, GI, I^3, G^3, G^2 I and GI^2) satisfying some natural constraints due to the biological meaning of the variables. However, the MP grammar given in Table 1 does not take into account the time delays which occur in the insulin release and this reduces the precision of the model. In fact, if we consider the dynamics of Figure 2, the simulation fails to describe the insulin peak which occurs between the 20th and the 40th minute. This missing peak is quite small and for this reason our approximation seems to be enough precise, but if we try to define new MP grammars for other data-sets related to the IVGTT, we reach very soon situations in which the missing peaks are very high causing a dramatic loss of precision.

In the differential models introduced in Section 2, the delay of the insulin release is approached by adding artificial substances or by considering a delay integral kernel. Here, instead, we solve the problem by assuming that ϕ_3 is given by linear combinations of monomials of G and of its "memories". This permits pointing out in a more natural and detailed way the different delays which act in the insulin production. If we indicate by $G^t = (G[i] | 0 \leq i \leq t)$ the vector containing the time-series of glucose in a given data-set, we define

Figure 2. The dynamics calculated by means of the MP grammar given in Table 1. The plots are related to a IVGTT data-set starting from the time of the glucose injection. The glucose dynamics is given on the left, while the insulin dynamics is given on the right.

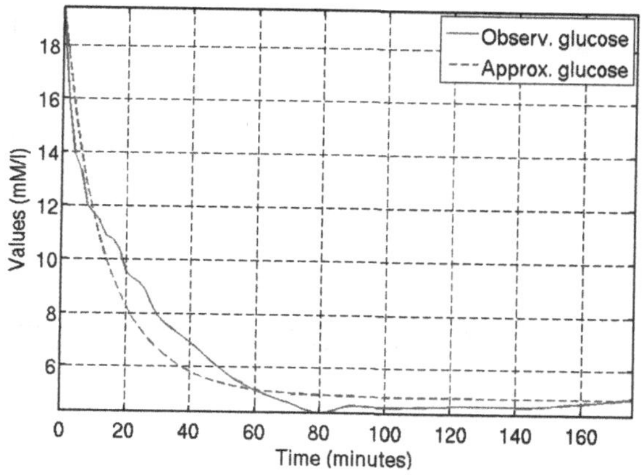

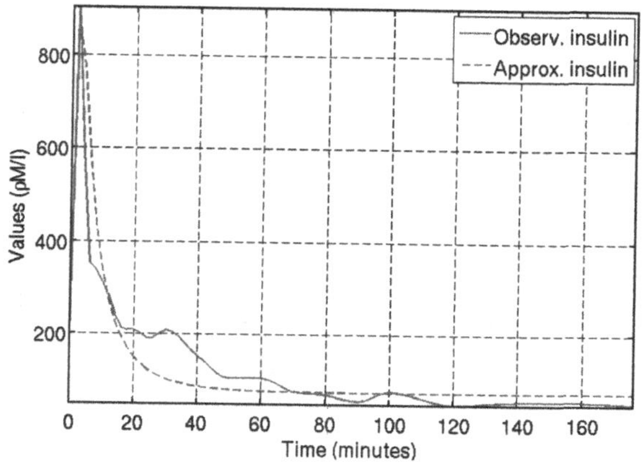

the time-series G^t_{-m} related to the memory of glucose shifted m steps after as the vector where G_b is the basal value of the blood glucose level[5]. Memories are very simple to be managed in MP systems and increase a lot the approximation power of the models as showed in Manca and Marchetti (2010b), where memories have been applied in the context of periodical function approximation.

$$G^t_{-m} = (\underbrace{G_b, G_b, \ldots, G_b}_{m\ times}, G[0], G[1], \ldots, G[t-m])$$

The extension of the MP grammar of Table 1 which considers glucose memories is given in Table 2, while the new calculated dynamics is depicted in Figure 3. The new model provides a better data fitting for the insulin curve. The multiple coefficient of determination for the insulin is increased from 0.87 to 0.95. Moreover ϕ_3 gives now an idea of the different phases which act in the blood release of insulin by pointing out their strength (given by the degree of the selected monomials) and their delay (given by the delay of the selected memories).

Table 2. The MP grammar which models the dynamics given in $\left(U_0, [\ ]_s, w_s^{(0)}, R_0, s\right)$ *Figure 3* ($\tau = 2$ *min) enriched with the usage of glucose memories (subscripts give the delay in minutes of each memory)*

$r_1 : \varnothing \rightarrow G$	$\phi_1 = 0.6$
$r_2 : G \rightarrow \varnothing$	$\phi_2 = 0.12G + 1.6 \cdot 10^{-6} G^2 I$
$r_3 : \varnothing \rightarrow I$	$\phi_3 = 1.5 \cdot 10^{-5} G^6 + 0.25 G^2_{-6} + 0.17 G^2_{-8} + 2.65 G_{-16} + 3.6 G_{-26}$
$r_4 : I \rightarrow \varnothing$	$\phi_4 = 0.65I$

Figure 3. The dynamics calculated by means of the MP grammar given in Table 2

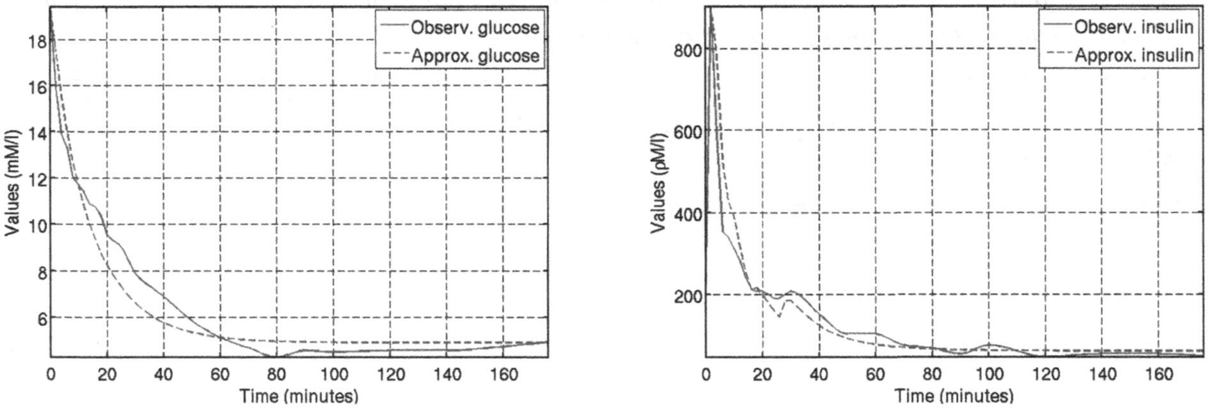

In our analysis we considered ten different data-sets published in literature and obtained by applying the intravenous glucose tolerance test to ten healthy patients. All subjects have negative family histories for diabetes and other endocrine diseases. During the test, the patients were on no medications and had no current illness. Each test has been performed during the morning after an overnight fast, and for the three days preceding the test each subject followed a diet composed of 55% carbohydrates, 30% fats, and 15% proteins. The curves of the considered data-sets are very different from each other, especially the curve related to the insulin dynamics which exhibits values and peaks of different height and at different delays. In all the cases, however, we found MP models which provide good data fitting (the average of the calculated multiple coefficients of determination for all the models is greater than 0.95 for both glucose and insulin). In Table 3 we provide the regulators related to four of the considered data-sets, and the plotting of the corresponding calculated dynamics for the insulin. The depicted dynamics exhibit examples of all the different scenarios we observed concerning the insulin release in our data-sets. We can have situations where the insulin curve exhibits many peaks which model the different release phases, or we can have dynamics without significant peaks but that are in any case modelled by a delayed insulin secretion (this is the case of data-set 1).

The total number of monomials used to define ϕ_3 can be changed by acting on the thresholds used by LGSS during the computing of its statistical tests. The models provided here have been defined trying to balance their simplicity with their power of approximation. Each model provides a sort of picture of the metabolism of the subject which have been analysed. This is reflected in the form of the regulators which is different in each model. The form of ϕ_3 changes according to the different pancreatic response to the increasing of the blood glucose level which we found to be different for each person. This confirms experimentally the idea introduced in the analysis of the dynamical model (Mukhopadhyay et al., 2004) regarding the different forms of the kernel function ω in (3). By analysing the correlations between the ϕ_3 regulators, we observed that some of them are uncorrelated while others exhibit common behaviours. This could be an experimental evidence that patients can be differentiated by considering the behaviour of ϕ_3, as suggested in Mukhopadhyay et al. (2004) where is indicated the possibility of differentiating between patient populations by considering the form and the parameters of the kernel function.

Table 3. MP regulation and the calculated insulin dynamics related to four of the considered data-sets ϕ_3, min)

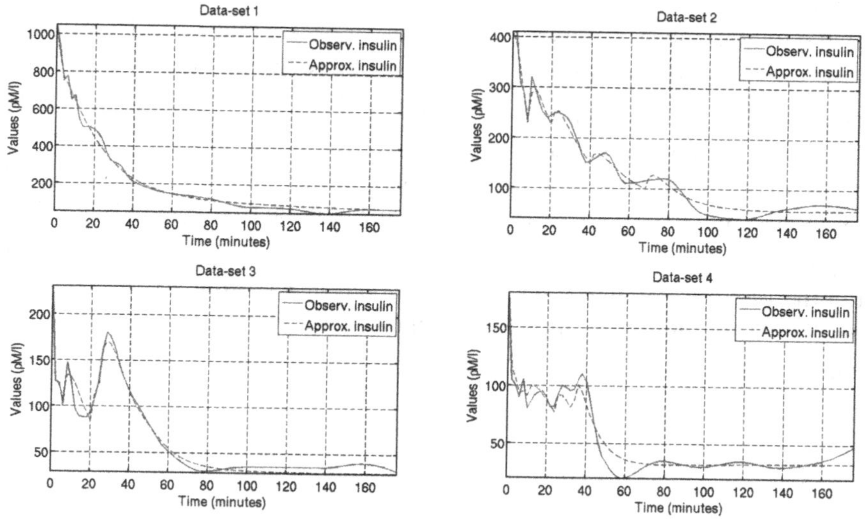

Data-set	Regulators
1	$\varphi_1 = 0.011$ $\varphi_2 = 6.6 \cdot 10^{-5} GI$ $\varphi_3 = 0.5 G_{-4}^2$ $\varphi_4 = 0.16 I$
2	$\varphi_1 = 0.056$ $\varphi_2 = 5.2 \cdot 10^{-4} I + 8.1 \cdot 10^{-5} GI$ $\varphi_3 = 3.76 \cdot 10^{-6} G^7 + 0.74 G_{-8}^2 + 0.02 G_{-20}^3 + 0.21 G_{-40}^2 + 10^{-4} G_{-68}^5$ $\varphi_4 = 0.49 I$
3	$\varphi_1 = 0.12$ $\varphi_2 = 0.02 G + 1.9 \cdot 10^{-4} GI$ $\varphi_3 = 0.04 G_{-2}^3 + 3.3 \cdot 10^{-5} G_{-6}^6 + 0.44 G_{-20}^2 + 0.04 G_{-24}^3$ $\varphi_4 = 0.5 I$
4	$\varphi_1 = 0.11$ $\varphi_2 = 6.2 \cdot 10^{-4} GI$ $\varphi_3 = 0.1 G_{-2}^2 + 0.9 G_{-6} + 1.07 G_{-10} + 2.4 \cdot 10^{-4} G_{-24}^4$ $+ 5.4 \cdot 10^{-7} G_{-32}^6 + 5.3 \cdot 10^{-8} G_{-34}^7$ $\varphi_4 = 0.4 I$

Even if we found differences in the regulation governing the release of insulin, it is possible to recognize a common pattern. The topmost chart of Figure 4 provides the total number of models which use, in ϕ_3 a memory with delay given in the x-axis. Here a common logic in the usage of memories becomes evident. Moreover we distinguish two peaks in the first ten minutes which agree with literature. In vivo, insulin secretion is biphasic with a first phase burst in insulin secretion occurring within the first ten minutes and a second phase that is long some hours (Gerich, 2002). The two peaks we observe perfectly fit with the first phase of insulin secretion and recall the first and the second pancreatic peaks introduced in the analysis of the minimal model (Bergman et al., 1979; Toffolo et al., 1980). The strength of the peaks is emphasized by the chart on the bottom of Figure 4 where the memory usage is weighted with respect to the degree of the corresponding monomials used in $(\tau = 2$. Here we can see that the first peak is twice the second one and that the release of insulin follows an oscillatory pattern according to experimental results, as reported in Gilon, Ravier, Jonas, and Henquin (2002).

Figure 4. Bar charts which give the total number of MP models that use a memory with delay given in the x-axis. In the chart on the bottom the number of models is weighted by considering the degree of the corresponding monomials used in the models.

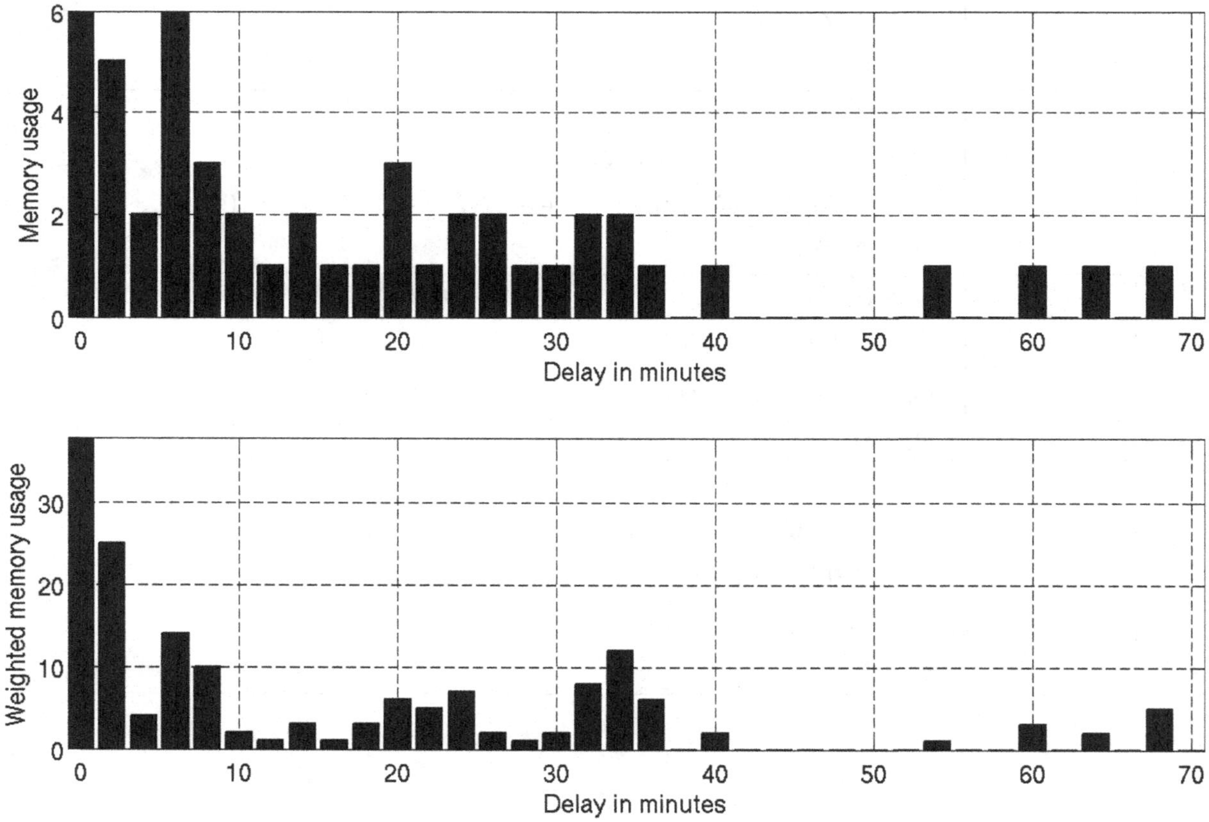

4. CONCLUSION AND ONGOING WORK

The main goal of this work was to study the possible application of MP systems as an alternative to model the intravenous glucose tolerance test. After having briefly described the test, in Section 2 we reviewed two mathematical models which had the most important impacts in diabetology and we analysed their limits and drawbacks. In Section 3 we proposed the use of Metabolic P systems to model the IVGTT data-sets by combining some principles of MP systems with statistical techniques to obtain MP models of IVGTT. Our preliminary results and analysis suggest that MP models seem to provide comprehensive tools for discovering personalized glucose-insulin dynamics. In fact, our regression approach allows us a quantitative analysis which could highlight results which have been only theorized during the development of the differential models. Further analysis should permit to characterize the differentiation between subjects by considering physiological parameters such as the height, the weight, the work, the sport activity, and so on. Despite these differences, we are working in order to point out common features in the regulation governing the release of insulin.

REFERENCES

Aczel, A., & Sounderpandian, J. (2006). *Complete business statistics*. New York, NY: McGraw-Hill.

Bergman, R., Finegood, D., & Ader, M. (1985). Assessment of insulin sensitivity in vivo. *Endocrine Reviews*, *6*(1), 45–86. doi:10.1210/edrv-6-1-45.

Bergman, R., Ider, Y., Bowden, C., & Cobelli, C. (1979). Quantitative estimation of insulin sensitivity. *American Journal of Physiology. Endocrinology and Metabolism*, *236*(6), 667–677.

Boutayeb, A., & Chetouani, A. (2006). A critical review of mathematical models and data used in diabetology. *Biomedical Engineering Online*, *5*(43).

Castellini, A., Franco, G., & Pagliarini, R. (2011). Data analysis pipeline from laboratory to MP models. *Natural Computing*, *10*(1), 55–76. doi:10.1007/s11047-010-9200-6.

Cobelli, C., & Mari, A. (1983). Validation of mathematical models of complex endocrine-metabolic systems: A case study on a model of glucose regulation. *Medical & Biological Engineering & Computing*, *21*(4), 390–399. doi:10.1007/BF02442625.

Cushing, J. (1977). *Integrodifferential equations and delay models in population dynamics*. Berlin, Germany: Springer-Verlag.

Draper, N., & Smith, H. (1981). *Applied regression analysis* (2nd ed.). New York, NY: John Wiley & Sons.

Gaetano, A. D., & Arino, O. (2000). Mathematical modelling of the intravenous glucose tolerance test. *Journal of Mathematical Biology*, *40*(2), 136–168. doi:10.1007/s002850050007.

Gerich, J. (2002). Redefining the clinical management of type 2 diabetes: Matching therapy to pathophysiology. *European Journal of Clinical Investigation*, *32*, 46–53. doi:10.1046/j.1365-2362.32.s3.6.x.

Gilon, P., Ravier, M., Jonas, J., & Henquin, J. (2002). Control mechanisms of the oscillations of insulin secretion in vitro and in vivo. *Diabetes*, *51*(1), 144–151. doi:10.2337/diabetes.51.2007.S144.

Hocking, R. (1976). The analysis and selection of variables in linear regression. *Biometrics*, 32.

Li, J., Kuang, Y., & Li, B. (2001). Analysis of IVGTT glucose-insulin interaction models with time delay. *Discrete and Continuous Dynamical Systems–Series B*, *1*(1), 103–124. doi:10.3934/dcdsb.2001.1.103.

Makroglou, A., Li, J., & Kuang, Y. (2006). Mathematical models and software tools for the glucose-insulin regulatory system and diabetes: An overview. *Applied Numerical Mathematics*, *56*(3), 559–573. doi:10.1016/j.apnum.2005.04.023.

Manca, V. (2009). Log-gain principles for metabolic P systems. In Condon, A., Harel, D., & Kok, J. (Eds.), *Algorithmic bioprocesses, natural computing series* (pp. 585–605). Berlin, Germany: Springer-Verlag. doi:10.1007/978-3-540-88869-7_28.

Manca, V. (2010a). Fundamentals of metabolic P systems. In P˘aun, G., & Rozenberg, G. (Eds.), *Oxford handbook of membrane computing*. Oxford, UK: Oxford University Press.

Manca, V. (2010b). Metabolic P systems. *Scholarpedia*, *5*(3), 9273. doi:10.4249/scholarpedia.9273.

Manca, V., Bianco, L., & Fontana, F. (2005). Evolutions and oscillations of P systems: Theoretical considerations and application to biological phenomena. In G. Mauri, G. Paun, M. J. Pérez-Jiménez, G. Rozenberg, & A. Salomaa (Eds.), *Proceedings of the 5th International Workshop on Membrane Computing* (LNCS 3365, pp. 63-84).

Manca, V., & Marchetti, L. (2010a). Goldbeter's mitotic oscillator entirely modeled by MP systems. In M. Gheorghe, T. Hinze, G. Păun, G. Rozenberg, & A. Salomaa (Eds.), *Proceedings of the 11th International Workshop on Membrane Computing* (LNCS 6501, pp. 273-284).

Manca, V., & Marchetti, L. (2010b). Metabolic approximation of real periodical functions. *Journal of Logic and Algebraic Programming*, *79*, 363–373. doi:10.1016/j.jlap.2010.03.005.

Manca, V., & Marchetti, L. (2011). Log-gain stoichiometic stepwise regression for MP systems. *International Journal of Foundations of Computer Science*, *22*(1), 97–106. doi:10.1142/S0129054111007861.

Manca, V., Pagliarini, R., & Zorzan, S. (2009). A photosynthetic process modelled by a metabolic P system. *Natural Computing*, *8*(4), 847–864. doi:10.1007/s11047-008-9104-x.

Mari, A. (2002). Mathematical modeling in glucose metabolism and insulin secretion. *Current Opinion in Clinical Nutrition and Metabolic Care*, *5*(5), 495–501. doi:10.1097/00075197-200209000-00007.

Martini, F. (2008). *Fundamentals of anatomy and physiology* (8th ed.). Upper Saddle River, NJ: Benjamin Cummings.

Mukhopadhyay, A., Gaetano, A. D., & Arino, O. (2004). Modelling the intravenous glucose tolerance test: A global study for single-distributed-delay model. *Discrete and Continuous Dynamical Systems - Series B*, *4*(2), 407–417. doi:10.3934/dcdsb.2004.4.407.

National Diabetes Data Group. (1979). Classification and diagnosis of diabetes mellitus and other categories of glucose intolerance. *Diabetes*, *28*(28), 1039–1057.

Pacini, G., & Bergman, R. (1986). Minmod: A computer program to calculate insulin sensitivity and pancreatic responsivity from the frequently sampled intravenous glucose tolerance test. *Computer Methods and Programs in Biomedicine*, *23*(2), 113–122. doi:10.1016/0169-2607(86)90106-9.

Păun, G. (2002). *Membrane computing: An introduction*. Berlin, Germany: Springer-Verlag.

Toffolo, G., Bergman, R., Finegood, D., Bowden, C., & Cobelli, C. (1980). Quantitative estimation of beta cell sensitivity to glucose in the intact organism: A minimal model of insulin kinetics in the dog. *Diabetes*, *29*(12), 979–990. doi:10.2337/diabetes.29.12.979.

ENDNOTES

1. Others gluco-regulatory hormones are: amylin, GLP-1, glucose-dependent insulinotropic peptide, epinephrine, cortisol, and growth hormone.
2. We refer the reader to Martini (2008) for a deeper description of the processes that underlies the glucose-insulin system.
3. In order to maintain the models as accurate as possible, we adopt here a time unit τ of two minutes because it is the minimal time granularity used in the data-sets we considered.
4. The coefficient value ranges from 1, when the regression model perfectly fits the data, to 0 according to the goodness of the model fit.
5. Since during the IVGTT the glucose level gradually returns to its basal level, here we assume G_b to be equal to the last value of the considered glucose time-series.

This work was previously published in the International Journal of Natural Computing Research (IJNCR), Volume 2, Issue 3, edited by Leandro Nunes de Castro, pp. 13-24, copyright 2011 by IGI Publishing (an imprint of IGI Global).

Chapter 12
Implementation on CUDA of the Smoothing Problem with Tissue-Like P Systems

Francisco Peña-Cantillana
University of Sevilla, Spain

Daniel Díaz-Pernil
University of Sevilla, Spain

Hepzibah A. Christinal
University of Sevilla, Spain & Karunya University, India

Miguel A. Gutiérrez-Naranjo
University of Sevilla, Spain

ABSTRACT

Smoothing is often used in Digital Imagery for improving the quality of an image by reducing its level of noise. This paper presents a parallel implementation of an algorithm for smoothing 2D images in the framework of Membrane Computing. The chosen formal framework has been tissue-like P systems. The algorithm has been implemented by using a novel device architecture called CUDA (Compute Unified Device Architecture) which allows the parallel NVIDIA Graphics Processors Units (GPUs) to solve many complex computational problems. Some examples are presented and compared; research lines for the future are also discussed.

1. INTRODUCTION

The study of digital images (Shapiro & Stockman, 2001) has seen a large progress over the last decades. The aim of dealing with an image in its digital form is improving its quality, in some sense, or simply achieving some artistic effect. The physical properties of camera technology are inherently linked to different sources of noise, so the application of a smoothing algorithm is necessary for reducing such noise within an image.

In this paper we use Membrane Computing techniques for smoothing 2D images with tissue-like P systems. We refer to Păun (2002) for basic information in this area and to Păun, Rozenberg, and Salomaa (2010) for a comprehensive presentation and the web site http://ppage.psystems.eu for the up-to-date information. The algorithm has been implemented by using a novel device architecture called CUDA (Compute Unified Device Architecture, http://www.nvidia.com/object/cudahomenew.html). CUDA is a general purpose

DOI: 10.4018/978-1-4666-4253-9.ch012

parallel computing architecture that allows the parallel NVIDIA Graphics Processors Units (GPUs) to solve many complex computational problems (for a good overview, the reader can refer to Owens et al., 2008) in a more efficient way than on a CPU. This architecture has been previously used in Membrane Computing (Cecilia et al., 2010a, 2010b) but, to the best of our knowledge, this is the first time that it is used for implementing a smoothing algorithm.

Dealing with Digital Images has several features which make it suitable for techniques inspired by nature. One of them is that it can be parallelized and locally solved. Regardless how large the picture is, the smoothing process can be performed in parallel in different local areas. Another interesting feature is that the basic necessary information can be easily encoded by bio-inspired representations. In the literature, one can find several attempts for bridging problems from Digital Imagery with Natural Computing as the works by Ceterchi et al. (2003) and Ceterchi, Mutyam, Păun, and Subramanian (2003) or the work by Chao and Nakayama where Natural Computing and Algebraic Topology are linked by using Neural Networks (Chao & Nakayama, 1996). Recently, new approaches have been presented in the framework of Membrane Computing (Christinal, Díaz-Pernil, Gutiérrez-Naranjo, & Pérez-Jiménez, 2010; Díaz-Pernil, Gutiérrez-Naranjo, Molina-Abril, & Real, 2010). Christinal, Díaz-Pernil, and Real (2009a, 2009b, 2010) started a new bio-inspired research line where the power and efficiency of tissue-like P systems were applied to topological processes for 2D and 3D digital images.

The paper is organised as follows: Firstly, we recall some basics of tissue-like P systems and the foundations of Digital Imagery. Next we present our P systems family and a simple example showing different results by using different thresholds. In Section 3 we present the implementation in CUDA of the algorithm and show an illustrative example, including a comparison of the times obtained in the different variants. The paper finishes with some final remarks and hints for future work.

2. PRELIMINARIES

In this section we provide some basics on the used P system model, tissue-like P systems, and on the foundation of Digital Imagery.

Tissue-like P systems (Martín-Vide, Păun, Pazos, & Rodríguez-Patón, 2003) have two biological inspirations: intercellular communication and cooperation between neurons. The common mathematical model of these two mechanisms is a network of processors dealing with symbols and communicating these symbols along channels specified in advance.

Formally, a *tissue-like P system* with input of degree $q \geq 1$ is a tuple

$$\Pi=(\Gamma, \Sigma, E, w_1,\ldots,w_q, R, i_\Pi, o_\Pi)$$

where

1. Γ is a finite *alphabet*, whose symbols will be called *objects*;
2. $\Sigma(\subset\Gamma)$ is the input alphabet;
3. $E\subseteq\Gamma$ is the alphabet of objects in the environment;
4. $w_1,\ldots,w_q$ are strings over Γ representing the multisets of objects associated with the cells at the initial configuration;
5. R is a finite set of communication rules of the form $(i,u/v,j)$ for $i,j \in\{0,1,2,\ldots,q\}$, $i\neq j$, $u,v \in \Gamma^*$;
6. $i_\Pi \in\{1,2,\ldots,q\}$ is the input cell;
7. $o_\Pi \in\{0,1,2,\ldots,q\}$ is the output cell.

A tissue-like P system of degree $q\geq1$ can be seen as a set of q cells (each one consisting of an elementary membrane) labelled by $1,2,\ldots,q$. We will use 0 to refer to the label of the environment, i_Π denotes the input cell and o_Π denotes the output cell (which can be the region inside a cell or the environment). The strings $w_1,\ldots,w_q$ describe the multisets of objects placed in the cells of the P system. We interpret that $E\subseteq\Gamma$ is the set of objects placed in the environment, each one of them available in an arbitrary large amount of copies.

The communication rule $(i,u/v,j)$ can be applied over two cells labelled by i and j such that u is contained in cell i and v is contained in cell j. The application of this rule means that the objects of the multisets represented by u and v are interchanged between the two cells. Note that if either $i=0$ or $j=0$ then the objects are interchanged between a cell and the environment.

Rules are used as usual in the framework of membrane computing, that is, in a maximally parallel way (a universal clock is considered). In one step, each object in a membrane can only be used for one rule (non-deterministically chosen when there are several possibilities), but any object which can participate in a rule of any form must do it, i.e., in each step we apply a maximal set of rules.

A *configuration* is an instantaneous description of the P system Π. Given a configuration, we can perform a computation step and obtain a new configuration by applying the rules in a parallel manner as it is shown above. A *computation* is a sequence of computation steps such that either it is infinite or it is finite and the last step yields a halting configuration (i.e., no rules can be applied to it). Then, a computation halts when the system reaches a halting configuration.

Next we recall some basics on Digital Imagery (we refer the interested reader to Ritter, Wilson, & Davidson, 1990 for a detailed introduction). A *point set* is simply a topological space consisting of a collection of objects called points and a topology which provides notions as *nearness* of two points, the *connectivity* of a subset of the point set, the *neighbourhood* of a point, *boundary points*, and *curves* and *arcs*.

For a point set $X \subseteq Z$, a *neighbourhood function* from X in Z, is a function . For each point $x \in X$, $N(x) \subseteq Z$. The set $N(x)$ is called a *neighbourhood* for x.

There are two neighbourhood function on subsets of which are of particular importance in image processing, the *von Neumann* neighbourhood and the *Moore* neighbourhood. The first one is defined by $N(x)=\{y: y=(x_1 \pm j, x_2)$ or $y=(x_1, x_2 \pm k)$, $j,k \in \{0,1\}\}$, where $x=(x_1, x_2) \in X \subset Z^2$. While the Moore neighbourhood is defined by $M(x)=\{ y=(x_1 \pm j, x_2 \pm k),\ j,k \in \{0,1\} \}$, where $x=(x_1, x_2) \in X \subset Z^2$. The von Neumann and Moore neighbourhood are also called the *four neighbourhood* (4-adjacency) and *eight neighbourhood* (8-adjacency), respectively.

An *Z-valued image* on X is any element of . Given an Z-valued image, i.e.,, then Z is called the set of possible range values of I and X the spatial domain of I. The graph of an image is also referred to as the *data structure representation* of the image. Given the data structure representation $I=\{(x,I(x)): x \in X\}$, then an element $(x,I(x))$ is called a *picture element* or *pixel*. The first coordinate x of a pixel is called the *pixel location* or *image point*, and the second coordinate $I(x)$ is called the *pixel value* of I at location x. Usually, we consider an ordered set $C \subseteq Z$ called the *set of colours*.

A *region* could be defined by a subset of the domain of I whose points are all mapped to the same (or similar) pixel value by I. So, we can consider the region as the set $\{x \in X: I(x)=i\}$ but we prefer to consider a region r as a maximal connected subset of a set like . We say two regions r_1, r_2 are adjacent when at less a pair of pixel and are adjacent. We say and are *border pixels*. If we say is an *edge pixel*. The set of connected edge pixels with the same pixel value is called a *boundary* between two regions.

The purpose of image enhancement is to improve the visual appearance of an image, or to transform an image into a form that is better suited for human interpretation or machine analysis. There exists a multitude of image enhancement techniques, as are averaging of multiple images, local averaging, Gaussian smoothing, max-min sharpening transform, etc.

One of the forms to enhancement an image could be eliminate non important regions of an image, i.e., remove regions which do not provide relevant information. This technique is known as smoothing.

2.1. A Family of Tissue-Like P Systems

Given an image with pixels ($n \in N$) and r a threshold ($r \in N$) which represents the upper bound of the distance between related colours, we define a tissue-like P system whose input is given by the pixels of the image encoded by the objects, where $1 \leq i,j \leq n$ and $a \in C$. Next, we shall give some outlines how to prove that our *smoothing problem* can be solved in a logarithmic number of steps using a family of tissue-like P systems Π.

We define a family of tissue-like P systems to do a smoothing of a 2D image. For each image of size with $n \in N$, we consider the tissue-like P system with input of degree 1:

$$\prod(r,n)=(\Gamma, \Sigma, E, w_1, R, i_{\Pi}, o_{\Pi})$$

where

- $\Gamma=\Sigma \cup E$,
- $\Sigma=\{a_{ij}: a \in C, 1\leq i,j\leq n\}$,
- $E=\{a_{ij}: a \in C, 1\leq i,j\leq n\}$,
- $w_1 = \varnothing$,
- R is the following set of communication rules:
    - $(1, a_{ij}\, b_{kl} \,/\, a_{ij}\, a_{kl}, 0)$,
        - for $1\leq i,j\leq n$,
        - $a,b \in C$, $a<b$ and $d(a,b) \leq r$,

These rules are used to simplify the image. If we have two colours whose distance in the set of colours of the image is lower than a given threshold r, then the colour with a higher value is replaced by a lower one. Of this manner, we change the regions structure.

- $i_{\Pi}=o_{\Pi}=1$.

Each P system works as follows: We take pairs of adjacent pixels and change the col or of the pixel with lower col or. We do it in a parallel way with all the possible pairs of pixels. In the next step, we will repeat the previous process, but the colours of the pixels may have been changed. So, in the worst case, a linear number of steps are necessary to do all the possible changes to obtain a smoothing of our image.

2.2. A Simple Example

In this section, we show the results obtained by the application of our method. Our input image (of size 30×30) can be seen in Figure 1. In this case, 0 represents the white colour and 30 represents the black colour.

Working with different thresholds provides different results as we can observe in Figure 2. If we take r=5, then we get the first image, and when the threshold is r=10 the second image is obtained. By using this method, it is clear that the structure of regions is (more or less) conserved with a threshold of r=5 and we need to a high number to obtain a more simplified image. Moreover, we can observe in both cases the col or of regions is similar to the regions of input image in this method. Therefore, we can use this technique for smoothing images, and clarify the structure of a region without eliminate important information.

Bearing in mind the size of the input data is, representing by h the number of the elements of the set C and considering r as the threshold used with both membrane solutions, the amount of necessary resources for defining the P systems of our family and the complexity of our problem is determined in Table 1.

3. PARALLEL IMPLEMENTATION

GPUs constitute nowadays a solid alternative for high performance computing, and the advent of CUDA allows programmers a friendly model to accelerate a broad range of applications. GPUs are especially well-suited to address problems that can

Figure 1. An example

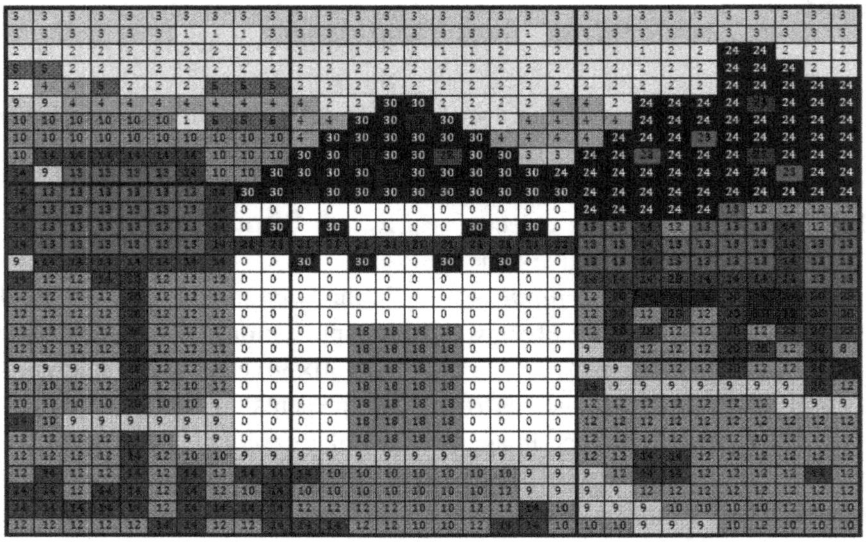

be expressed as data-parallel computations. GPUs can support several thousand of concurrent threads providing a massively parallel environment. This parallel technology is suitable for parallel computational paradigms by providing an efficient framework for real parallel implementations.

In this paper, we present a parallel software tool which implements our membrane approach for smoothing images. It has been developed by using Microsoft Visual Studio 2008 Professional Edition (C++) with the plugging Parallel Nsight (CUDA) under Microsoft Windows 7 Professional with 32 bits.

To implement the P systems, CUDA C, an extension of C for implementations of executable kernels in parallel with graphical cards NVIDIA has been used. It has been necessary the *nvcc compiler* of CUDA Toolkit. Moreover, we use libraries from openCV to the treatment of input and output images. Microsoft Visual Studio 2008 is responsible for calling to the compilers to build the objects, and to link them with the final program. This allows us to deal with images stored in .BMP, .JPG, .PNG, or .TIF formats among others.

The experiments have been performed on a computer with a CPU Intel Pentium 4 650, with support for HT technology which allows to work like two CPUs of 32 bits to 3412 MHz. It has 2 MB of L2 cache memory and 1 GB DDR SDRAM of main memory with 64 bits bus wide to 200 MHz. Moreover, it has a hard disc of 160 GB SATA2 with a transfer rate of 300 Mbps in

Figure 2. Theoretical smoothness of Figure 1

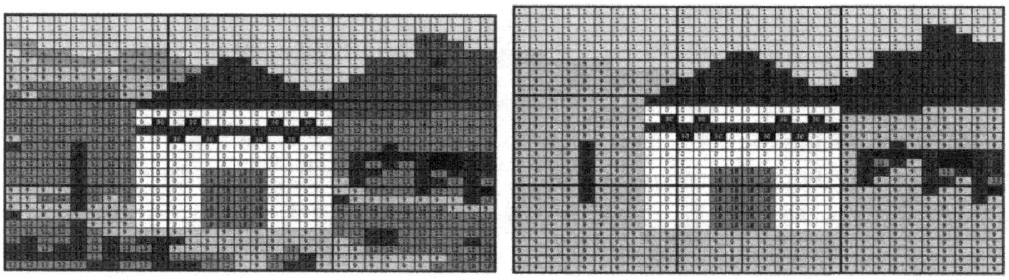

Table 1. Complexity and resources

Smoothing Problem	
Complexity	**Dynamical**
Number of steps of a computation	O(n)
Necessary Resources	
Size of the alphabet	
Initial number of cells	1
Initial number of objects	0
Number of rules	
Upper bound for the length of the rules	4

a 8 MB buffer. The graphical card (GPU) is an NVIDIA Geforce 8600 GT composed by 4 *Stream Processors* with a total of 32 cores to 1300 MHz and executes 512 threads per block as maximum. It has a 512 MB DDR2 main memory, but 499 MB could be used by processing in a 128 bits bus to 700 MHz. So, the transfer rate obtained is by 22.4 Gbps. For constant memory used 64 KB and for shared memory 16 KB. Its Compute Capability is 1.1 (from 1.0 to 2.1), then we can obtain a lot of improvements in the efficiency of the algorithms.

We have developed two applications of our P systems. In this case, we consider the natural order in the gray-scale set of colours $C = \{0,\ldots,255\}$. In the first one, we have considered a deterministic implementation, where the Moore neighbourhood is considered. The system checks if the rules can be applied for eight adjacent pixels. In the second one, we have considered a random selection of an adjacent pixel to work. In this case, the system checks only one possibility randomly chosen. This way, we simulate the characteristic non determinism of P systems using randomness. Moreover, we have decided to stop the system before the halting configuration, because more than an appropriate number of parallel steps of processing could make too much uniform the output image. In fact, in the deterministic version, the process could finish before the pre-fixed number of steps. So, the system needs some time to check this possibility. In the second one, it is not necessary to look at this question.

We consider the image of size 640×400 in Figure 3. When we take the deterministic application of our software, we can check that if we use an threshold r=50, our software smooths the original image (Figure 4) using 44 parallel steps. Nonetheless, when we work with a higher threshold, new important regions are changed, and the output image is different (Figure 5).

When we consider the random version of our software, we can check that if we use an threshold r=50 we need 300 steps, but the differences with

Figure 3. Original image

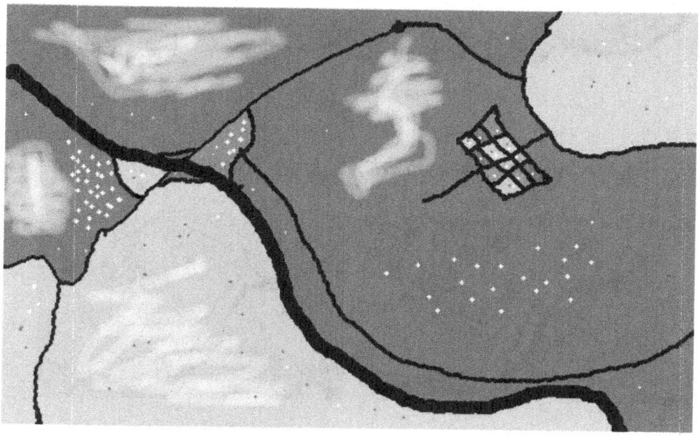

Figure 4. Deterministic version. Threshold 50: 0, 5, 10, 20, 32 and 44 steps, respectively.

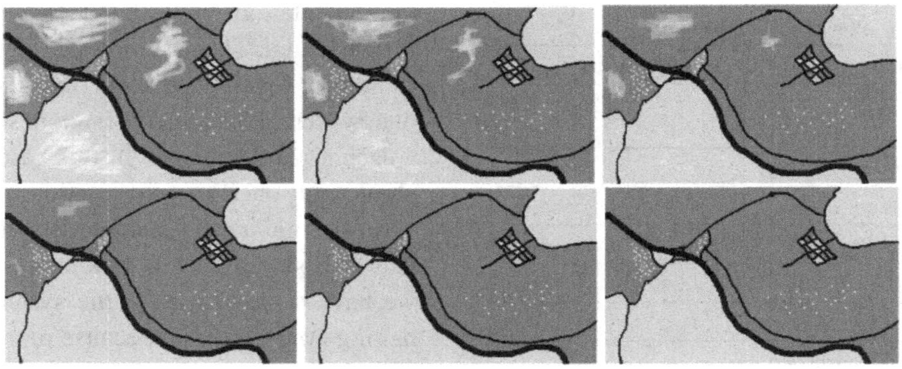

Figure 5. Deterministic version. Left image: Threshold 75, step 193. Right image: Threshold 125, step 193.

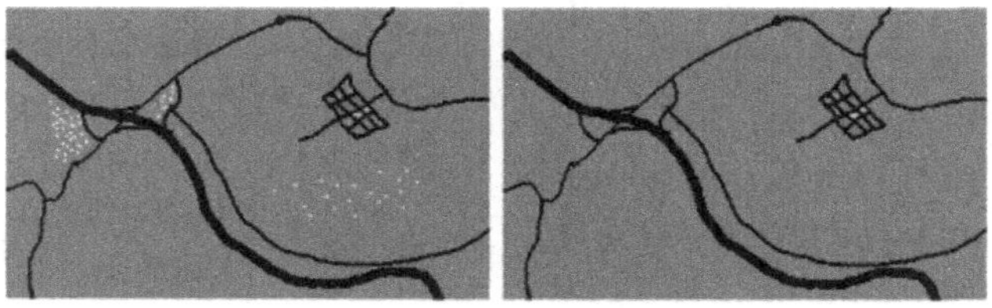

Figure 6. Random version. Threshold 50: 0, 50, 100, 150, 200 and 300 Steps, respectively

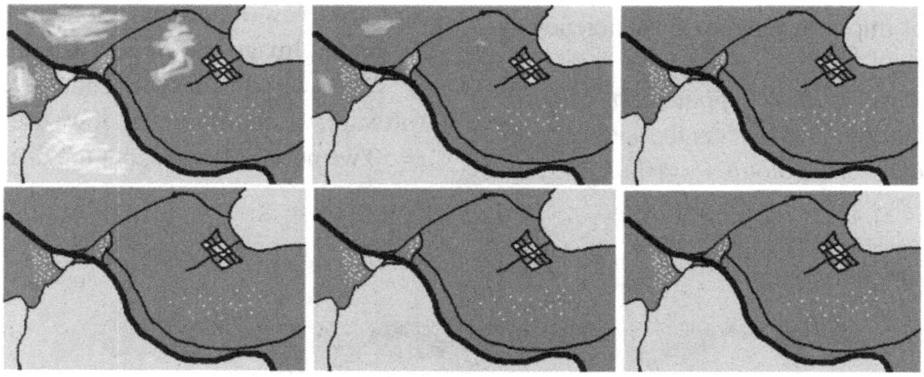

Figure 7. Random version. Left image: Threshold 75, step 1000. Right image: Threshold 125, step 800

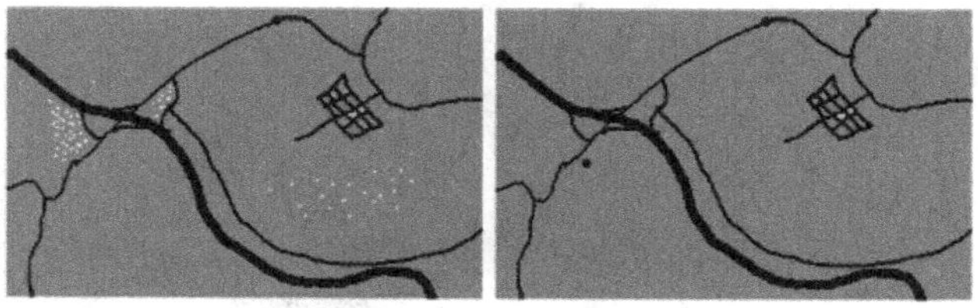

the resulting image with 150 or 200 steps are minimum, as we can see in Figure 6. When we take higher thresholds, as in the Figure 7, we can check that new regions have different colours.

Table 2 shows the running times of our software for both cases with different thresholds, shown in the examples. We can observe that the deterministic version of our software needs less time with respect to the random version. In the first one, it applies eight rules for each pixels while, in the second one, it applies only one rule for each pixel. Moreover, we need an additional running time to implement the random in each step for each pixel.

Finally, we have done some experiments with our software to know what happened if we work with images of different size. We have checked our software with images until size 512×512 in both versions. The deterministic version needs much time with bigger images, and the random version does not work with those images. This is a physical problem with our graphical card, because the shared memory is small.

4. CONCLUSION AND FUTURE WORK

In this paper, three emergent research fields are put together. Firstly, as pointed in Christinal et al. (2009a) and Christinal, Díaz-Pernil, and Real (2010), Membrane Computing has features as the encapsulation of the information, a simple representation of the knowledge and parallelism, which are appropriate with dealing with digital images. Nonetheless, the use of the intrinsic parallelism of Membrane Computing techniques cannot be implemented in current one-processor computers, so the potential advantages of the theoretical design are lost.

In this paper we show that the drawback of using one-processor computers for implementing Membrane Computing designs can be avoided by using the parallel architecture CUDA. This new technology provides the hardware needed for a real parallel implementation of Membrane Computing algorithms.

Considering this paper as a starting point, several research lines are open: From Digital Imagery, new parallel algorithms can be proposed or adapted to the new technology, from the Membrane Computing side, new design or different P system models can be explored. From the hardware point of view, the advances in the new technology CUDA open new possibilities for going on with the research.

ACKNOWLEDGMENT

DDP and MAGN acknowledge the support of the projects TIN2008-04487-E and TIN-2009-13192 of the Ministerio de Ciencia e Innovación of Spain and the support of the Project of Excellence with *Investigador de Reconocida Valía* of the Junta de Andalucía, grant P08-TIC-04200. HC acknowledges the support of the project MTM2009-12716 of the Ministerio de Educación y Ciencia of Spain and the project PO6-TIC-02268 of Excellence of Junta de Andalucìa, and the "CATAM" PAICYT research group FQM-296.

Table 2. Running times of the experiments

Version\ Thresholds	Computation Steps	Running Time
Determ. \ 50	44	536.522 ms
Determ. \ 75	193	1582.098 ms
Determ. \ 125	193	1563.660 ms
Random \ 50	300	6823.683 ms
Random \ 75	1000	21537.701 ms
Random \ 100	800	17332.891 ms

REFERENCES

Cecilia, J. M., García, J. M., Guerrero, G. D., Martínez-del-Amor, M. A., Pérez-Hurtado, I., & Pérez-Jiménez, M. J. (2010a). Simulating a P system based efficient solution to SAT by using GPUs. *Journal of Logic and Algebraic Programming*, *79*(6), 317–325. doi:10.1016/j.jlap.2010.03.008.

Cecilia, J. M., García, J. M., Guerrero, G. D., Martìnez-del-Amor, M. A., Pérez-Hurtado, I., & Pérez-Jiménez, M. J. (2010b). Simulation of P systems with active membranes on CUDA. *Briefings in Bioinformatics*, *11*(3), 313–322. doi:10.1093/bib/bbp064.

Ceterchi, R., Gramatovici, R., Jonoska, N., & Subramanian, K. G. (2003). Tissue-like P systems with active membranes for picture generation. *Fundamenta Informaticae*, *56*(4), 311–328.

Ceterchi, R., Mutyam, M., Păun, G., & Subramanian, K. G. (2003). Array-rewriting P systems. *Natural Computing*, *2*(3), 229–249. doi:10.1023/A:1025497107681.

Chao, J., & Nakayama, J. (1996). Cubical singular simplex model for 3D objects and fast computation of homology groups. In *Proceedings of the 13th International Conference on Pattern Recognition* (Vol. 4, pp. 190-194).

Christinal, H. A., Díaz-Pernil, D., Gutiérrez-Naranjo, M. A., & Pérez-Jiménez, M. J. (2010). Thresholding of 2D images with cell-like P systems. *Romanian Journal of Information Science and Technology*, *13*(2), 131–140.

Christinal, H. A., Díaz-Pernil, D., & Real, P. (2009a, November 15-18). Segmentation in 2D and 3D image using tissue-like P system. In E. Bayro-Corrochano & J. O. Eklundh (Eds.), *Proceedings of the 14th Ibero-American Conference on Progress in Pattern Recognition, Image Analysis, Computer Vision, and Applications*, Guadalajara, Jalisco, Mexico (LNCS 5856, pp. 169-176).

Christinal, H. A., Díaz-Pernil, D., & Real, P. (2009b, November 24-27). Using membrane computing for obtaining homology groups of binary 2D digital images. In P. Wiederhold & R. P. Barneva (Eds.), *Proceedings of the 13th International Workshop on Combinatorial Image Analysis*, Playa del Carmen, Mexico (LNCS 5852, pp. 383-396).

Christinal, H. A., Díaz-Pernil, D., & Real, P. (2010). P systems and computational algebraic topology. *Journal of Mathematical and Computer Modelling*, *52*(11-12), 1982–1996. doi:10.1016/j.mcm.2010.06.001.

Díaz-Pernil, D., Gutiérrez-Naranjo, M. A., Molina-Abril, H., & Real, P. (2010). A bio-inspired software for segmenting digital images. In A. K. Nagar, R. Thamburaj, K. Li, Z. Tang, & R. Li (Eds.), *Proceedings of the IEEE Fifth International Conference on Bio-inspired Computing: Theories and Applications*, Beijing, China (Vol. 2, p. 1377-1381).

Martín-Vide, C., Păun, G., Pazos, J., & Rodríguez-Patón, A. (2003). Tissue P systems. *Theoretical Computer Science*, *296*(2), 295–326. doi:10.1016/S0304-3975(02)00659-X.

Owens, J. D., Houston, M., Luebke, D., Green, S., Stone, J. E., & Phillips, J. C. (2008). GPU computing. *Proceedings of the IEEE*, *96*(5), 879–899. doi:10.1109/JPROC.2008.917757.

Păun, G. (2002). *Membrane computing: An introduction*. Berlin, Germany: Springer-Verlag.

Păun, G., Rozenberg, G., & Salomaa, A. (Eds.). (2010). *The Oxford handbook of membrane computing*. Oxford, UK: Oxford University Press.

Ritter, G. X., Wilson, J. N., & Davidson, J. L. (1990). Image algebra: An overview. *Computer Vision Graphics and Image Processing*, *49*(3), 297–331. doi:10.1016/0734-189X(90)90106-6.

Shapiro, L. G., & Stockman, G. C. (2001). *Computer vision*. Upper Saddle River, NJ: Prentice Hall.

This work was previously published in the International Journal of Natural Computing Research (IJNCR), Volume 2, Issue 3, edited by Leandro Nunes de Castro, pp. 25-34, copyright 2011 by IGI Publishing (an imprint of IGI Global).

Chapter 13
Elementary Active Membranes Have the Power of Counting

Antonio E. Porreca
Università degli Studi di Milano–Bicocca, Italy

Alberto Leporati
Università degli Studi di Milano–Bicocca, Italy

Giancarlo Mauri
Università degli Studi di Milano–Bicocca, Italy

Claudio Zandron
Università degli Studi di Milano–Bicocca, Italy

ABSTRACT

P systems with active membranes have the ability of solving computationally hard problems. In this paper, the authors prove that uniform families of P systems with active membranes operating in polynomial time can solve the whole class of PP decision problems, without using nonelementary membrane division or dissolution rules. This result also holds for families having a stricter uniformity condition than the usual one.

1. INTRODUCTION

P systems with active membranes (Păun, 2001) are known to solve computationally hard problems in polynomial time by trading space for time: an exponential number of membranes are created in polynomial time by using division rules, and then massive parallelism is exploited, e.g., to explore the whole solution space of an NP-complete problem in parallel.

When we allow nonelementary division rules, i.e., rules that can be applied to membranes containing further membranes, even PSPACE-complete problems become solvable in polynomial time (Sosík, 2003; Alhazov, Martín-Vide, & Pan, 2003). The general idea is that nonelementary division allows us to construct a binary tree-shaped membrane structure, isomorphic to the parse tree of the formula resulting from the expansion of universal and existential quantifiers into conjunctions and disjunctions, according to the equivalences

$$\forall x \varphi(x) \Leftrightarrow \varphi(0) \wedge \varphi(1)$$
$$\exists x \varphi(x) \Leftrightarrow \varphi(0) \vee \varphi(1)$$

DOI: 10.4018/978-1-4666-4253-9.ch013

We also know that no problem outside PSPACE can be solved in polynomial time, as this is also an upper bound (Sosík & Rodríguez-Patón, 2007): in symbols, we have $\mathrm{PMC}_{\mathrm{AM}} = \mathrm{PSPACE}$.

On the other hand, when no division at all is allowed the resulting P systems can be shown to be no more powerful than polynomial-time Turing machines (Zandron, Ferretti, & Mauri, 2001).

The "intermediate" case, when the only membranes that can divide are elementary (i.e., leaves of the tree corresponding to the membrane structure), is possibly the most interesting one. The exponential number of membranes that may be created cannot be structured into a binary tree: hence, the algorithm above can only be applied to formulae having just one kind of quantifier. This is enough to solve the SAT problem (Zandron et al., 2001) and its complement (which are respectively NP- and coNP-complete), where only existentially (resp., universally) quantified variables are allowed.[1] However, the corresponding complexity class $\mathrm{PMC}_{\mathrm{AM}(-n)}$ still lacks a characterisation in terms of Turing machines. Alhazov et al. (2009) have shown how PP- and #P-complete problems can be solved without nonelementary division, but their result is not directly related to the class $\mathrm{PMC}_{\mathrm{AM}(-n)}$, as it requires some form of post-processing or the use of non-standard rules. In this paper, we improve the previous NP $\cup$ coNP lower bound to PP within the standard framework of active membranes. This is an improved version of the paper "P systems with active membranes: Beyond NP and coNP" presented by the authors at the Eleventh International Conference on Membrane Computing (Porreca, Leporati, Mauri, & Zandron, 2010).

2. PRELIMINARIES

We use P systems with restricted elementary active membranes, which are defined as follows.

Definition 1: A *P system with restricted elementary active membranes* of initial degree $d \geq 1$ is a tuple $\Pi = (\Gamma, \Lambda, \mu, w_1, \ldots, w_d, R)$, where:

- Γ is a finite alphabet of symbols (the objects);
- Λ is a finite set of labels for the membranes;
- μ is a membrane structure (i.e., a rooted *unordered* tree) consisting of d membranes enumerated by $1,\ldots,d$; furthermore, each membrane is labeled by an element of Λ, not necessarily in a one-to-one way;
- $w_1,\ldots,w_d$ are strings over Γ, describing the initial multisets of objects placed in the d regions of μ;
- R is a finite set of rules.

Each membrane possesses, besides its label and position in μ, another attribute called *electrical charge* (or polarization), which can be either neutral (0), positive (+) or negative (–) and is always neutral before the beginning of the computation.

The rules are of the following kinds:

Object evolution rules, of the form $\left[a \rightarrow w\right]_h^\alpha$

They can be applied inside a membrane labeled by h, having charge α and containing an occurrence of the object a; the object a is rewritten into the multiset w (i.e., a is removed from the multiset in h and replaced by every object in w).

Send-in communication rules, of the form $a\left[\;\right]_h^\alpha \rightarrow \left[b\right]_h^\beta$

They can be applied to a membrane labeled by h, having charge α and such that the external region contains an occurrence of the object a; the object a is sent into h becoming b and, simultaneously, the charge of h is changed to β.

Send-out communication rules, of the form $\left[a\right]_h^\alpha \rightarrow \left[\;\right]_h^\beta b$

They can be applied to a membrane labeled by h, having charge α and containing an occurrence of the object a; the object a is sent out from h to the outside region becoming b and, simultaneously, the charge of h is changed to β.

Elementary division rules, of the form $[a]_h^{\alpha} \rightarrow [b]_h^{\beta} [c]_h^{\gamma}$

They can be applied to a membrane labeled by h, having charge α, containing an occurrence of the object a but having no other membrane inside (an *elementary membrane*); the membrane is divided into two membranes having label h and charge β and γ; the object a is replaced, respectively, by b and c while the other objects in the initial multiset are copied to both membranes.

Each instantaneous configuration of a P system with active membranes is described by the current membrane structure, including the electrical charges, together with the multisets located in the corresponding regions. A computation step changes the current configuration according to the following set of principles:

- Each object and membrane can be subject to at most one rule per step, except for object evolution rules (inside each membrane any number of evolution rules can be applied simultaneously).
- The application of rules is *maximally parallel*: each object appearing on the left-hand side of evolution, communication, dissolution or elementary division must be subject to exactly one of them (unless the current charge of the membrane prohibits it). The same reasoning applies to each membrane that can be involved to communication, dissolution, elementary or non-elementary division rules. In other words, the only objects and membranes that do not evolve are those associated with no rule, or only to rules that are not applicable due to the electrical charges.
- When several conflicting rules can be applied at the same time, a nondeterministic choice is performed; this implies that, in general, multiple possible configurations can be reached after a computation step.
- While all the chosen rules are considered to be applied simultaneously during each computation step, they are logically applied in a bottom-up fashion: first, all evolution rules are applied to the elementary membranes, then all communication, dissolution and division rules; then the application of rules proceeds towards the root of the membrane structure. In other words, each membrane evolves only after its internal configuration has been updated.
- The outermost membrane cannot be divided or dissolved, and any object sent out from it cannot re-enter the system again.

A *halting computation* of Π is a finite sequence of configurations $\vec{C} = (C_0, \ldots, C_k)$, where C_0 is the initial configuration, every C_{i+1} is reachable by C_i via a single computation step, and no rules can be applied anymore in C_k. A *non-halting* computation $\vec{C} = (C_i : i \in \mathbb{N})$ consists of infinitely many configurations, again starting from the initial one and generated by successive computation steps, where the applicable rules are never exhausted.

P systems can be used as *recognisers* by employing two distinguished objects YES and NO; exactly one of these must be sent out from the outermost membrane during each computation, in order to signal acceptance or rejection respectively; we also assume that all computations are halting. If all computations starting from the same initial configuration are accepting, or all are rejecting, the P system is said to be *confluent*. If this is not necessarily the case, then we have a *non-confluent* P system, and the overall result is established as for nondeterministic Turing machines: it is acceptance iff an accepting computation exists.

In order to solve decision problems (i.e., decide languages), we use *families* of recogniser P systems $\Pi = \{\Pi_x : x \in \Sigma^*\}$. Each input x is associated with a P system Π_x that decides the membership of x in the language $L \subseteq £^*$ by accepting or rejecting. The mapping $x \mapsto \Pi_x$ is restricted, in order to be computable is restricted, in order to be computable efficientlyand uniformly for each input length.

Definition 2: A family of P systems $\Pi = \{\Pi_x : x \in \Sigma^*\}$ is said to be *(polynomial-time) uniform* if the mapping $x \mapsto \Pi_x$ can be computed by two deterministic polynomial-time Turing machines F (for "family") and E (for "encoding") as follows:

- The machine F, taking as input *the length n of x* in unary notation, constructs a P system Π_n with a distinguished input membrane (the P systems structure Π_n is common for all inputs of length n).
- The machine E, on input x, outputs a multiset w_x (an encoding of the specific input x).
- Finally, Π_x is simply Π_n with w_x added to the multiset placed inside its input membrane.

Notice that this definition of uniformity is possibly weaker than the other one commonly used in membrane computing (Peréz-Jiménez, Jiménez, & Sancho-Caparrini, 2003), where the Turing machine F maps each input x to a P system $\Pi_{s(x)}$, where $s : £^* \to \mathbb{N}$ is a measure of the size of the input (in our case, $s(x)$ is always $|x|$). In particular, complexity classes defined using this restricted uniformity condition are not always formally known to be closed under polynomial-time reductions[2]. See Murphy and Woods (2011) for further details on uniformity conditions, including constructions using weaker devices than polynomial-time Turing machines.

Any explicit encoding of Π_x is allowed as output, as long as the number of membranes and objects represented by it does not exceed the length of the whole description, and the rules are listed one by one. This restriction is enforced in order to mimic a (hypothetical) realistic process of construction of the P systems, where membranes and objects are presumably placed in a constant amount during each construction step, and require actual physical space in proportion to their number. For instance, the membrane structure can be represented by brackets, and the multisets as strings (i.e., in unary notation); this is a *permissible encoding* in the sense of Murphy and Woods (2011).

Finally, we describe how time complexity for families of recogniser P systems is measured.

Definition 3: A uniform family of P systems $\Pi = \{\Pi_x : x \in \Sigma^*\}$ is said to decide the language $L \subseteq £^*$ (in symbols $L(\Pi) = L$) in time $f : \mathbb{N} \to \mathbb{N}$ iff, for each $x \in £^*$ $x \in L$ $x \notin L$;

The system Π_x accepts if and rejects if ;

- Each computation of Π_x halts within $f(|x|)$ computation steps.

We denote by $\mathrm{PMC}_{\mathrm{AM}(-n,-d)}$ the class of languages (equivalently, decision problems) which can be decided in polynomial time by uniform families of P systems with restricted elementary active membranes.

In this paper we use uniform families of P systems to solve a variant of the SAT problem. Hence, we set the relevant notation and describe how Boolean formulae can be encoded in order to simplify a uniform solution.

Given a set of $m \geq 3$ variables $X_m = \{x_1, \ldots, x_m\}$, the number of clauses of 3 variables (without repeated variables, and ignoring permutations of literals) is given by $8\binom{m}{3}$, the number of 3-element subsets times the 2^3 ways to negate them. Hence, a 3CNF formula φ can be encoded as an $8\binom{m}{3}$-bit string, where the i-th bit is 1 iff the i-th clause (under some fixed ordering) appears in φ.

Notice that $8\binom{m}{3} = \frac{4}{3}m^3 - 4m^2 + \frac{8}{3}m$ is a polynomial.

In this paper, we will order the clauses according to the enumeration printed by the recursive algorithm of Figure 1.

Example 1 (Encoding): The clauses over 4 variables $X_4 = \{x_1,\ldots,x_4\}$, in the order given by the algorithm of Figure 1, are the following ones:

$x_1 \vee x_2 \vee x_3$ $\quad x_1 \vee x_2 \vee \bar{x}_3$

$x_1 \vee \bar{x}_2 \vee x_3$ $\quad x_1 \vee \bar{x}_2 \vee \bar{x}_3$

$\bar{x}_1 \vee x_2 \vee x_3$ $\quad \bar{x}_1 \vee x_2 \vee \bar{x}_3$

$\bar{x}_1 \vee \bar{x}_2 \vee x_3$ $\quad \bar{x}_1 \vee \bar{x}_2 \vee \bar{x}_3$

$x_1 \vee x_2 \vee x_4$ $\quad x_1 \vee x_2 \vee \bar{x}_4$

$x_1 \vee \bar{x}_2 \vee x_4$ $\quad x_1 \vee \bar{x}_2 \vee \bar{x}_4$

$\bar{x}_1 \vee x_2 \vee x_4$ $\quad \bar{x}_1 \vee x_2 \vee \bar{x}_4$

$\bar{x}_1 \vee \bar{x}_2 \vee x_4$ $\quad \bar{x}_1 \vee \bar{x}_2 \vee \bar{x}_4$

$x_1 \vee x_3 \vee x_4$ $\quad x_1 \vee x_3 \vee \bar{x}_4$

$x_1 \vee \bar{x}_3 \vee x_4$ $\quad x_1 \vee \bar{x}_3 \vee \bar{x}_4$

$\bar{x}_1 \vee x_3 \vee x_4$ $\quad \bar{x}_1 \vee x_3 \vee \bar{x}_4$

$\bar{x}_1 \vee \bar{x}_3 \vee x_4$ $\quad \bar{x}_1 \vee \bar{x}_3 \vee \bar{x}_4$

$x_2 \vee x_3 \vee x_4$ $\quad x_2 \vee x_3 \vee \bar{x}_4$

$x_2 \vee \bar{x}_3 \vee x_4$ $\quad x_2 \vee \bar{x}_3 \vee \bar{x}_4$

$\bar{x}_2 \vee x_3 \vee x_4$ $\quad \bar{x}_2 \vee x_3 \vee \bar{x}_4$

$\bar{x}_2 \vee \bar{x}_3 \vee x_4$ $\quad \bar{x}_2 \vee \bar{x}_3 \vee \bar{x}_4$

Figure 1. A recursive, polynomial-time algorithm that enumerates all clauses of 3 out of m variables

```
PRINT-CLAUSES(m)
    IF m > 3 THEN
        PRINT-CLAUSES(m − 1)
    END
    FOR i ← 1 to m − 2 DO
        FOR j ← i + 1 to m − 1 DO
            PRINT "xi ∨ xj ∨ xm"
            PRINT "xi ∨ xj ∨ x̄m"
            PRINT "xi ∨ x̄j ∨ xm"
            PRINT "xi ∨ x̄j ∨ x̄m"
            PRINT "x̄i ∨ xj ∨ xm"
            PRINT "x̄i ∨ xj ∨ x̄m"
            PRINT "x̄i ∨ x̄j ∨ xm"
            PRINT "x̄i ∨ x̄j ∨ x̄m"
        END
    END
END
```

Then, the formula

$$\varphi = (x_1 \vee x_2 \vee \bar{x}_3) \wedge (\bar{x}_1 \vee \bar{x}_2 \vee \bar{x}_3) \wedge (x_1 \vee \bar{x}_3 \vee \bar{x}_4) \wedge (\bar{x}_2 \vee \bar{x}_3 \vee x_4)$$

is encoded as the following sequence of $8\binom{4}{3} = 32$ bits

$\varphi =$

0100 0001 0000 0000 0001 0000 0000 0010

because the clauses actually appearing are the 2nd, 8th, 20th, and 31st ones.

Besides being computable in polynomial time with respect to m, this ordering has the following important property: the sequence of clauses over m variables is a prefix of the sequence of clauses over m' variables whenever $m' \geq m$. As a consequence, each formula over m variables can also be considered as a formula over m' variables by padding its encoding to the correct length. For instance, the formula φ of Example 1 can be interpreted as a formula over *five* variables $x_1,\ldots,x_5$ if its encoding is padded to length $8\binom{5}{3} = 80$ by a string of 48 zeroes, i.e., as $\varphi 0^{48}$.

We now consider the following decision problem.

Problem 1 (Threshold-3SAT): Given a Boolean formula φ over m variables and a non-negative integer $k < 2^m$, do more than k assignments (out of 2^m) satisfy it?

Notice that we can force all valid instances (φ,k) of Problem 1 to have a description of length exactly $8\binom{m}{3} + m$ for some m, as every number in the range $[0,2^m)$ can be represented using m bits. This will be useful in the next section.

The problem Threshold-3SAT subsumes a whole class of languages related to the counting version of problems in NP.

Definition 4: The complexity class PP consists of all problems solvable in polynomial time by nondeterministic Turing machines having the following acceptance criterion: the machine accepts its input iff more than half the computations are accepting.

Proposition 1: Threshold-3SAT *is* PP*-hard.*

Proof: We reduce the following standard PP-complete problem (Papadimitriou, 1994, p. 256) to Threshold-3SAT.

Problem 2 (Majority-SAT): Given a Boolean formula φ in CNF, having c clauses over m variables and such that each variable occurs at most once per clause, do more than half the assignments (i.e., more than 2^{m-1} assignments) satisfy it?

The reduction is similar to that from SAT to 3SAT described in Garey and Johnson (1979, p. 48). We first transform φ into a formula having *at most* three literals per clause. Observe that φ is satisfied iff the formula obtained by replacing a clause of $p > 3$ literals $\bigvee_{i=1}^{p} \ell_i$ with

$$(y \Leftrightarrow \ell_1 \vee \ell_2) \wedge \left(y \vee \bigvee_{i=1}^{p} \ell_i \right)$$

is also satisfied, assuming y is a new variable. In CNF, that is equivalent to

$$\left(\overline{\ell_1} \vee y\right) \wedge \left(\overline{\ell_2} \vee y\right) \wedge \left(\ell_1 \vee \ell_2 \vee \overline{y}\right) \wedge \left(y \vee \bigvee_{i=3}^{p} \ell_i\right).$$

This substitution doubles the number of total assignments of the formula, due to the addition of a new variable, but the number of *satisfying* ones is left unchanged, as the value of y is forced to be equal to $\ell_1 \vee \ell_2$. The substitution decreases by one the number of literals of the initial clause; by repeating the process $p - 3$ times, and then again to any other clause having more than three literals, we obtain a formula φ' having at most three literals per clause, and the same number of satisfying assignments as φ. The number of variables of φ' is bounded by $m + cm$, as the number of new variables per clause introduced (denoted by $p - 3$ above) is less than m, and there are c original clauses.

Next, we transform every clause of one or two literals into a clause of exactly three. A clause of a single literal ℓ is replaced by

$$\left(\ell \vee z_1 \vee z_2\right) \wedge \left(\ell \vee \overline{z}_1 \vee z_2\right) \wedge \left(\ell \vee z_1 \vee \overline{z}_2\right) \wedge \left(\ell \vee \overline{z}_1 \vee \overline{z}_2\right),$$

where z_1 and z_2 are new variables, which is clearly satisfied iff ℓ is. Each replacement like this one multiplies by $2^2 = 4$ the number of satisfying assignments of the whole formula, as the values of z_1 and z_2 are actually irrelevant.

A clause of two literals $\ell_1 \vee \ell_2$ is replaced by

$$\left(\ell_1 \vee \ell_2 \vee z\right) \wedge \left(\ell_1 \vee \ell_2 \vee \overline{z}\right),$$

where z is a new variable, which is also equivalent to the original clause but doubles the number of satisfying assignments of the formula.

Call φ'' the formula obtained from φ' by replacing single and 2-literal clauses by conjunctions of 3-literal clauses as described above, and let q be the number of variables added in the process (notice that q is $O(cm)$). Then it should be clear that φ has more than 2^{m-1} satisfying assignments iff φ' does, and the latter is equivalent to φ'' having more than 2^{m+q-1} satisfying assignments.

Since the mapping $R(\varphi) = (\varphi'', 2^{m+q-1})$ is computable in polynomial time with respect to c and m, it is a reduction from MAJORITY-SAT to THRESHOLD-3SAT.

3. SOLVING THRESHOLD-3SAT

In order to solve THRESHOLD-3SAT we design a polynomial time, deterministic Turing machine F (for "family") such that, for each n of the form $8\binom{m}{3} + m$, the output of $F(1^n)$ is a P system Π_n that solves the problem for all inputs of length n.

The input provided to Π_n is computed by another polynomial time Turing machine E (for "encoding") that, given an m-variable 3CNF formula as described in the previous section and an integer k, outputs the following set of objects:

$$E(\varphi,k) = \left\{C_i : the\, i-th\, clause\, does\, not\, appear\, in\, \varphi, for\, 1 \le i \le 8\binom{m}{3}\right\} \cup \{\mathrm{k}_i : the\, i-th\, bit\, of\, k\, (counting\, from\, 0)\, is\, 1, for\, 1 \le i \le m-1\}$$

Example 2: The formula φ given in Example 1, together with the integer $k = 12$, are encoded as the following set of objects: $E(\varphi,k) = \{C_i : 1 \le i \le 32\, and\, i \notin \{2, 8, 20, 31\}\} \cup \{\mathrm{k}_2, \mathrm{k}_3\}$.

The initial configuration of Π_n, input multiset excluded, is the following one:

$$E(\varphi,k) = \left\{C_i : \text{the } i\text{-th clause does not appear in } \varphi, for\, 1 \le i \le 8\binom{m}{3}\right\} \cup \{\mathrm{k}_i : \text{the } i\text{-th bit of } k \text{ (counting from0) is 1, for } 1 \le i \le m-1\}$$

$$C_0 = \left[\left[\mathrm{i}_{n-m}\right]_{\mathrm{E}}^0 \left[\,\right]_{\mathrm{K}_0}^0 \cdots \left[\,\right]_{\mathrm{K}_{m-1}}^0 \mathrm{o}_{t-1} \mathrm{no}_{t+3}\right]_{\mathrm{in}}^0$$

where $t = 4n - 3m + 4$ is the number of computation steps the objects O and NO have to wait before taking an active role during the computation (see Phase 5). The multiset encoding $E(\varphi,k)$ is placed inside the input membrane IN, and then the computation proceeds according to the following five phases:

1. Initialise the contents of the membranes by moving the input objects to their target membrane.
2. Generate all possible assignments for φ by using elementary division rules; each division sets the truth value of a variable to true on one side, and false on the other.
3. Check if each assignment satisfies the input formula φ by generating objects corresponding to each satisfied clause, and then verifying if all of them appear; if so, an object is sent out to the outermost membrane.
4. Count the number of satisfying assignments, testing whether it is larger than k, by "deleting" k of the objects produced during the previous phase.
5. Output the correct answer.

The fourth phase, first suggested by Alhazov et al. (2009), differentiates our solution from the standard algorithm schema, common in membrane computing, for solving NP-complete problems[3].

Phase 1 (Initialise): In the first computation steps, the objects C_i, corresponding to the clauses that do not appear in the input formula φ, are moved to membrane E using the communication rules

$$[\mathrm{NO}_1 \rightarrow \mathrm{NO}_0]^{+}_{\mathrm{IN}} \; (R_1)$$

This takes a number of steps at most equal to $n-m$ (i.e., to the maximum number of clauses in φ). In the mean time, the object I_{n-m} has its subscript decreased by one for $n-m-1$ computation steps, and is finally replaced during the $(n-m)$-th step, using the rules

$$[\mathrm{i}_i \rightarrow \mathrm{i}_{i-1}]^{0}_{\mathrm{E}} \qquad \mathit{for}\ 1 \leq i \leq n-m\ (R_2)$$

$$[\mathrm{i}_0 \rightarrow \mathrm{x}_1 \cdots \mathrm{x}_m \mathrm{w}_m]^{0}_{\mathrm{E}} \; (R_3)$$

Hence, after $n-m$ computation steps, membrane E contains C_i for each missing clause, and the variable-objects $\mathrm{x}_1,\ldots,\mathrm{x}_m$.

At the same time, the objects K_i are first moved to their respective membranes in the first time step, making them positively charged

$$\mathrm{k}_i\ [\ ]^{0}_{\mathrm{k}_i} \rightarrow [\mathrm{k}_i]^{+}_{\mathrm{k}_i} \qquad \mathit{for}\ 0 \leq i \leq m-1 \,(R_4)$$

then each K_i divides its membrane i times:

$$[\mathrm{k}_j]^{+}_{\mathrm{k}_i} \rightarrow [\mathrm{k}_{j-1}]^{+}_{\mathrm{k}_i} [\mathrm{k}_{j-1}]^{+}_{\mathrm{k}_i} \quad (R_5)$$
$$\mathit{for}\ 0 \leq i \leq m-1 \ \ \mathit{and}\ 1 \leq j \leq i.$$

After at most m steps (the largest possible subscript is $m-1$), there are exactly k positively charged membranes among those having label $\mathrm{K}_0,\ldots,\mathrm{K}_{m-1}$.

The total duration of Phase 1 is $n-m$ steps.

Phase 2 (Generate): The variable-objects $\mathrm{x}_1,\ldots,\mathrm{x}_m$ are used to generate all the truth assignments inside multiple copies of membrane E. This is accomplished by using the division rules

$$[\mathrm{x}_i]^{0}_{\mathrm{e}} \rightarrow [\mathrm{t}_i]^{0}_{\mathrm{e}}\ [\mathrm{f}_i]^{0}_{\mathrm{e}} \qquad \mathit{for}\ 1 \leq i \leq m. \,(R_6)$$

After m steps, 2^m copies of membrane E exist, each one containing a different truth assignment to the variables $x_1,\ldots,x_m$ of φ: the occurrence of T_i (resp., F_i) indicates that x_i is set to true (resp., false) in that particular assignment.

Simultaneously, the subscript of object w_m (standing for "wait m steps") is decreased by one each step:

$$[\mathrm{w}_i \rightarrow \mathrm{w}_{i-1}]_{\mathrm{e}}^{0} \qquad for\ 1 \le i \le m. (R_7)$$

When the counter reaches 0, the objects w_0 are sent out from each copy of membrane E while changing its charge according to the following rule:

$$[\mathrm{w}_0]_{\mathrm{e}}^{0} \rightarrow [\ ]_{\mathrm{e}}^{+}\ \mathrm{w}_0. (R_8)$$

When membrane E is positively charged, the objects T_i and F_i are replaced by the set of clause-objects corresponding to all the clauses satisfied by that particular value of variable x_i (whether they are actually part of formula φ or not):

$$[\mathrm{t}_i \rightarrow C_{i_1} \cdots C_{i_\ell}]_{\mathrm{e}}^{+}$$
$$for\ 1 \le i \le m, where\, clause\ i_j\, contains\, literal\ x_i \qquad (R_9)$$

$$[\mathrm{f}_i \rightarrow C_{i_1} \cdots C_{i_\ell}]_{\mathrm{e}}^{+}$$
$$for\ 1 \le i \le m, where\, clause\ i_j\, contains\, literal\ \overline{x_i}. \qquad (R_{10})$$

Notice that $\ell = 4\begin{pmatrix} m-1 \\ 2 \end{pmatrix} = 2m^2 - 6m + 4$, as this is the number of clauses over m variables where a particular literal occurs.

At the same time, each copy of w_0 is brought back as s_0 to a copy of membrane E by using the following rule in a maximally parallel way:

$$\mathrm{w}_0\ [\ ]_{\mathrm{e}}^{+} \rightarrow [\mathrm{s}_0]_{\mathrm{e}}^{+}. (R_{11})$$

The total duration of Phase 2 is $m + 2$ steps.

Phase 3 (Check): The occurrence of s_i inside a copy of membrane E denotes the fact that the first i clauses (according to the enumeration described above) have been found to be satisfied by the assignment corresponding to that membrane. We assume that the clauses which do not appear in φ are satisfied by default; indeed, this is precisely the reason why the corresponding C_i objects were placed inside membrane E in Phase 1.

When membrane E is positively charged, the object C_1 is sent out from E (as the "junk" object #), changing the charge to negative:

$$[C_1]_{\mathrm{e}}^{+} \rightarrow [\ ]_{\mathrm{e}}^{-}\ \#. (R_{12})$$

When E is negative, object s_i is sent out; at the same time, the objects C_i, for $i \ge 2$, are temporarily "primed", and all remaining copies of C_1 are discarded:

$$[\mathrm{s}_i]_{\mathrm{e}}^{-} \rightarrow [\ ]_{\mathrm{e}}^{-}\ \mathrm{s}_i \qquad for\ 0 \le i \le n - m - 1 (R_{13})$$

$$[C_i \rightarrow C'_i]_{\mathrm{e}}^{-} \qquad for\ 2 \le i \le n - m (R_{14})$$

$$[C_1 \rightarrow \#]_{\mathrm{e}}^{-}. (R_{15})$$

In the next step, the objects C'_i become C_{i-1}; this way, during this phase the system only needs to check for the presence of object C_1 for $n - m$ times.

$$[C'_i \rightarrow C_{i-1}]_{\mathrm{e}}^{-} \qquad for\ 2 \le i \le n - m. (R_{16})$$

At the same time, the object s_i is brought back in (if $i < n - m$), its subscript incremented by one, while changing the charge of E to positive in order to resume the checking of clauses:

$$\mathrm{s}_i\ [\ ]_{\mathrm{e}}^{-} \rightarrow [\mathrm{s}_{i+1}]_{\mathrm{e}}^{+} \qquad for\, 0 \le i \le n - m - 1. \qquad (R_{17})$$

If s_{n-m} is finally found inside E, it is sent out to signal that the formula is fully satisfied under that particular assignment:

$$[\mathrm{s}_{n-m}]_{\mathrm{e}}^{+} \rightarrow [\ ]_{\mathrm{e}}^{0}\ \mathrm{s}_{n-m}. (R_{18})$$

Hence, after the $3n - 3m + 1$ steps of Phase 3, the outermost membrane IN contains a copy of s_{n-m} for each assignment that satisfies φ.

Phase 4 (Count): In the next step, k copies of s_{n-m} (or all of them, if less than k exist) are "deleted" from membrane IN by sending them into any of the membranes having label $K_0, \ldots, K_{m-1}$; these membranes are set to negative in the process, so that no membrane gets more than one copy of s_{n-m}:

$$s_{n-m} \; [\;]_{k_i}^{+} \rightarrow [\#]_{k_i}^{-} \qquad \textit{for } 0 \le i \le m-1. \qquad (R_{19})$$

Recall that the number of positively charged membrane K_i is exactly k. Hence, after this single step there are one or more copies of s_{n-m} left inside membrane IN if and only if the number of satisfying assignments of φ was greater than k.

Phase 5 (Output): The objects o_t and NO_{t+2}, initially located inside membrane IN, work as counters during Phases 1–4 (whose total duration is precisely $t = 4n - 3m + 4$ steps) according to the following rules:

$$[o_i \rightarrow o_{i-1}]_{\text{in}}^{0} \qquad \textit{for } 1 \le i \le t+1 \; (R_{20})$$

$$[no_i \rightarrow no_{i-1}]_{\text{in}}^{0} \qquad \textit{for } 2 \le i \le t+3. \qquad (R_{21})$$

When the subscript of o_i reaches 0, Phase 5 begins and o_0 is sent out, thus "opening" membrane IN for output by setting its charge to positive:

$$[o_0]_{\text{in}}^{0} \rightarrow [\;]_{\text{in}}^{+} \; \#. \; (R_{22})$$

If any object s_{n-m} is found inside IN, it is sent out as YES in the next step, changing the charge to negative:

$$[s_{n-m}]_{\text{in}}^{+} \rightarrow [\;]_{\text{in}}^{-} \; yes. \; (R_{23})$$

Otherwise, membrane IN remains positive, and the object NO_0, produced by the rule

$$[no_1 \rightarrow no_0]_{\text{in}}^{+} \; (R_{24})$$

is sent out as NO in the following step:

$$[no_0]_{\text{in}}^{+} \rightarrow [\;]_{\text{in}}^{-} \; no. \; (R_{25})$$

The duration of Phase 5 is either 2 or 3 steps, depending on whether the number of assignments satisfying φ is greater than k or not.

This algorithm allows us to solve the THRESHOLD-3SAT problem in linear time $O(n+m) = O(n)$.

Theorem 1: THRESHOLD-3SAT $\in \text{PMC}_{\text{AM}(-n,-d)}$.

Proof: Let Π be the family of P systems described above. We show that Π can be constructed in polynomial time by two Turing machines F and E.

The machine F, on input 1^n (where $n = |(\varphi,k)|$) first computes the unique positive root of the polynomial

$$p(m) = 8\binom{m}{3} + m - n$$

thus establishing the number of variables. This can be done in polynomial time with respect to n simply by trying all integers up to n.

Then F outputs the initial configuration C_0 of Π_n, which can be easily computed in polynomial time from n and m. Finally, the set of rules $R_1 \bigcup \cdots \bigcup R_{25}$ is output. Each of the sets R_i can be computed in polynomial time; the most complicated ones are R_9 and R_{10}, which require enumerating the clauses using the algorithm of Figure 1.

The P system Π_n itself, on input $E(\varphi,k)$, only requires $O(n)$ time (and $O(n2^m)$ space) to output YES or NO, without using any nonelementary division or dissolution rules; this establishes that the problem is in $\mathrm{PMC}_{\mathrm{AM}(-n,-d)}$.

If the machines F and E receive a malformed input, i.e., any input having length $n \neq 8\binom{m}{3} + m$ for all $m \leq n$, then F produces a fixed P system that sends out the NO object immediately (while E produces an empty multiset).

4. SOLVING THE OTHER PP PROBLEMS

Solving one PP-complete problem by a uniform family of P systems with restricted elementary membranes implies $\mathrm{PP} \subseteq \mathrm{PMC}_{\mathrm{AM}(-n,-d)}$ if the uniformity condition is defined as in Peréz-Jiménez et al. (2003), as closure under polynomial-time reductions is immediate. However, our uniformity condition is possibly weaker, as the P system associated with each input only depends on its size and not on the specific input itself, and the class $\mathrm{PMC}_{\mathrm{AM}(-n,-d)}$ defined in this way is currently not known to be closed under polynomial-time reductions. Hence, to prove the PP inclusion we operate as follows.

Theorem 2: $\mathrm{PP} \subseteq \mathrm{PMC}_{\mathrm{AM}(-n,-d)}$.

Proof: Let $L \in \mathrm{PP}$, and let R be a Turing machine reducing L to the problem THRESHOLD-3SAT in polynomial time $p(n)$, where n is the length of the instance of L. We describe two polynomial-time Turing machines F' and E' constructing a family of P systems Π', also running in polynomial time, such that $L(\Pi') = L$.

The machine F', on input 1^n (where $n = |x|$), constructs a P system able to solve the largest THRESHOLD-3SAT formula that might be produced as the output of R; if the actual output of R is smaller than that, we can pad it to the correct length by adding enough zeroes. Let f be defined as follows:

$$f(n) = \min \left\{ n' : n' \geq n \text{ and } n' = 8\binom{m'}{3} + m' \text{ for some } m' \right\}$$

that is, $f(n)$ is the smallest integer of the form $8\binom{m'}{3} + m'$ greater than or equal to n. Then, F' behaves as follows:

$$F'(1^n) = F\left(1^{f(p(n))}\right) = \Pi_{f(p(n))}.$$

Since R runs in time $p(n)$, the P system $\Pi_{f(p(n))}$ is large enough to receive as input any formula φ obtained via the reduction R, as $|R(x)| = |(\varphi,k)| \leq p(|x|)$, as long as it is padded to length $f(p(n))$ as described above.

Notice that the value $f(n)$ can be obtained in polynomial time with respect to n by simply computing $8\binom{m'}{3} + m'$ for all integers m' until n is reached or exceeded; furthermore, $f(n)$ itself is at most polynomial in n (e.g., a trivial upper bound is $8\binom{n}{3} + n$).

The encoding machine E', on input x, produces an output formula encoding φ', obtained from $(\varphi,k) = R(x)$ as follows:

$$\varphi' = \varphi 0^{\ell} \text{ where } \ell = f(p(n)) - |\varphi|.$$

Recall from Section 2 that $\varphi 0^{\ell}$ is indeed a valid encoding of a formula, having exactly the same clauses of φ *but over m' variables instead of the original m* (where m' *satisfies* $f(p(n)) = 8\binom{m'}{3} + m'$). The number of required assignments k has to be adjusted accordingly: every assignment of the original formula φ corresponds to $2^{m'-m}$ assignments of φ' (obtained by extending it with arbitrary values to the new variables) that satisfy it iff the original assignment satisfies φ, since the new $m' - m$ variables do not actually appear in φ'. Hence, we define $k' = 2^{m'-m}.k$.

Summarising, the machine E' behaves as follows:

$$E'\left(x\right) = E(\varphi 0^{\ell}, 2^{m'-m} k)$$

where $(\varphi,k) = R(x)$.

Since $(\varphi',k') \in$ THRESHOLD-3SAT iff $(\varphi,k) \in$ THRESHOLD-3SAT by construction, and the latter is equivalent to $x \in L$ by reduction, we obtain $L \in \mathrm{PMC}_{\mathrm{AM}(-n,-d)}$. But L was an arbitrary PP language: hence the inclusion $\mathrm{PP} \subseteq \mathrm{PMC}_{\mathrm{AM}(-n,-d)}$ holds as required.

5. CONCLUSION

Uniform families of P systems with active membranes without nonelementary division and dissolution rules have been proved to be able to solve all PP problems in polynomial time; this property holds even when the uniformity condition is the same as that used for traditional families of circuits (Vollmer, 1999). The current bounds on the computing power of these P systems, in terms of complexity classes for Turing machines, are thus

$$\mathrm{PP} \subseteq \mathrm{PMC}_{\mathrm{AM}(-n,-d)} \subseteq \mathrm{PSPACE} = \mathrm{PMC}_{\mathrm{AM}},$$

where neither inclusion is known to be proper. Further improvements on the PP lower bound are expected, as it is plausible that P systems like those of the family Π solving THRESHOLD-3SAT described in this paper can be used as "modules" in larger P systems, thus providing a way to simulate an oracle for a PP-complete problem. Furthermore, it is still possible that $\mathrm{PMC}_{\mathrm{AM}(-n,-d)}$ actually coincides with PSPACE, thus showing that nonelementary membrane division (and possibly dissolution) do not increase the efficiency of P systems with active membranes.

REFERENCES

Alhazov, A., Burtseva, L., Cojocaru, S., & Rogozhin, Y. (2009). Solving PP-complete and #P-complete problems by P systems with active membranes. In D. Corne, P. Frisco, G. Păun, G. Rozenberg, & A. Salomaa (Eds.), *Proceedings of the International Conference on Membrane Computing* (LNCS 5391, pp. 108-117).

Alhazov, A., Martín-Vide, C., & Pan, L. (2003). Solving a PSPACE-complete problem by recognizing P systems with restricted active membranes. *Fundamenta Informaticae*, *58*, 67–77.

Garey, M. R., & Johnson, D. S. (1979). *Computers and intractability: A guide to the theory of NP-completeness*. New York, NY: W. H. Freeman & Co..

Murphy, N., & Porreca, A. E. (2010). First steps towards linking membrane depth and the polynomial hierarchy. In *Proceedings of the Eighth Brainstorming Week on Membrane Computing* (pp. 255-266).

Murphy, N., & Woods, D. (2011). The computational power of membrane systems under tight uniformity conditions. *Natural Computing*, *10*, 613–632. doi:10.1007/s11047-010-9244-7.

Papadimitriou, C. M. (1994). *Computational complexity*. Reading, MA: Addison-Wesley.

Păun, G. (2001). P systems with active membranes: Attacking NP-complete problems. *Journal of Automata. Languages and Combinatorics*, *6*, 75–90.

Peréz-Jiménez, M., Jiménez, A. R., & Sancho-Caparrini, F. (2003). Complexity classes in models of cellular computing with membranes. *Natural Computing*, *2*, 265–285. doi:10.1023/A:1025449224520.

Porreca, A. E., Leporati, A., Mauri, G., & Zandron, C. (2010). P systems with elementary active membranes: Beyond NP and coNP. In M. Gheorghe, T. Hinze, G. Paun, G. Rozenberg, & A. Salomaa (Eds.), *Proceedings of the 11th International Conference on Membrane Computing* (LNCS 6501, pp. 338-347).

Sosík, P. (2003). The computational power of cell division in P systems: Beating down parallel computers? *Natural Computing*, *2*, 287–298. doi:10.1023/A:1025401325428.

Sosík, P., & Rodríguez-Patón, A. (2007). Membrane computing and complexity theory: A characterization of PSPACE. *Journal of Computer and System Sciences*, *73*, 137–152. doi:10.1016/j.jcss.2006.10.001.

Vollmer, H. (1999). *Introduction to circuit complexity: A uniform approach*. New York, NY: Springer.

Zandron, C., Ferretti, C., & Mauri, G. (2001). Solving NP-complete problems using P systems with active membranes. In *Proceedings of the Second International Conference on Unconventional Models of Computation* (pp. 289-301).

ENDNOTES

1. Some further partial results relating quantifier alternations and nonelementary division depth, albeit in the slightly different framework of P systems with active membranes without charges, have been obtained (Murphy & Porreca, 2010).
2. This might complicate proofs of inclusions among complexity classes, although one can usually find a proof not relying on closure under polynomial-time reductions, as in the present paper.
3. Indeed, by eliminating the fourth phase (or, equivalently, by choosing $k = 0$) we obtain essentially a uniform version of the original solution to SAT described by Zandron et al. (2001).

This work was previously published in the International Journal of Natural Computing Research (IJNCR), Volume 2, Issue 3, edited by Leandro Nunes de Castro, pp. 35-48, copyright 2011 by IGI Publishing (an imprint of IGI Global).

Chapter 14
Linear Time Solution to Prime Factorization by Tissue P Systems with Cell Division

Xingyi Zhang
Anhui University, China

Yunyun Niu
Huazhong University of Science and Technology, China

Linqiang Pan
Huazhong University of Science and Technology, China

Mario J. Pérez-Jiménez
University of Sevilla, Spain

ABSTRACT

Prime factorization is useful and crucial for public-key cryptography, and its application in public-key cryptography is possible only because prime factorization has been presumed to be difficult. A polynomial-time algorithm for prime factorization on a quantum computer was given by P. W. Shor in 1997. In this work, it is considered as a function problem, and in the framework of tissue P systems with cell division, a linear-time solution to prime factorization problem is given on biochemical computational devices – tissue P systems with cell division, instead of computational devices based on the laws of quantum physical.

1. INTRODUCTION

In math, *prime factorization* is the breaking down of a composite number into smaller primes, which when multiplied together equal the original integer. Currently, though the prime factorization problem is not known to be NP-hard, no efficient algorithm is publicly known. It is generally considered intractable. The presumed computational hardness of this problem is at the heart of several algorithms in cryptography such as RSA (Rivest, Shamir, & Adleman, 1978).

DOI: 10.4018/978-1-4666-4253-9.ch014

Many areas of mathematics and computer science have been brought to bear on the prime factorization problem, including elliptic curves, algebraic number theory, and quantum computing. A polynomial-time algorithm for prime factorization on a quantum computer was given by Shor in 1997. This will have significant implications for cryptography if a large quantum computer is ever built. However, before a practical quantum computer appears, it is still of interest to find any reasonable computational devices for solving the prime factorization problem. In this work, we shall give a linear-time solution to prime factorization on a class of biochemical computational devices – *tissue P systems with cell division*, instead of computational devices based on the laws of quantum physical.

Tissue P systems with cell division is a class of computational devices in *membrane computing*. Membrane computing is an emergent branch of natural computing, which is inspired by the structure and the functioning of living cells, as well as the organization of cells in tissues, organs, and other higher order structures. The devices in membrane computing, called *P systems*, provide distributed parallel and non-deterministic computing models. Since Păun (2000) introduced the first P system, this area is heavily investigated. Please refer to the monographs of membrane computing (Păun, Rozenberg, & Salomaa, 2010; Frisco, 2009) for general information in this area, and to the membrane computing web site (P systems web page) for the up-to-date information.

Informally, a P system consists of a membrane structure, in the compartments of which one places multisets of objects which evolve according to given rules in a synchronous, non-deterministic, maximally parallel manner. *Tissue P systems* are a class of P systems, where membranes are placed in the nodes of a graph. It is a net of processors dealing with objects and communicating these objects along channels specified in advance. The communication among cells is based on symport/antiport rules, which was introduced to P systems in Păun and Păun (2002). Symport rules move objects across a membrane together in one direction, whereas antiport rules move objects across a membrane in opposite directions. This model has two biological inspirations (Martín-Vide, Pazos, Păun, & Rodríguez-Patón, 2003): intercellular communication and cooperation between neurons. In Păun, Pérez-Jiménez, and Riscos-Núñez (2008), tissue P systems are endowed with the ability of producing new cells based on the mitosis or cellular division, thus obtaining the ability of generating an exponential amount of workspace in polynomial time. Such variant of tissue P systems is called *tissue P systems with cell division*.

Tissue P systems with cell division were widely investigated for solving NP-complete problems. Some of them deal with non-numerical NP-complete decision problems, such as the SAT problem (Păun et al., 2008), 3-coloring problem (Díaz-Pernil, Gutiérrez-Naranjo, Pérez-Jiménez, & Riscos-Núñez, 2008), vertex cover (Díaz-Pernil, Gutiérrez-Naranjo, Pérez-Jiménez, & Riscos-Núñez, 2008). Others deal with numerical NP-complete decision problems, that is, decision problems whose instances consist of sets or sequences of integer numbers, such as subset sum (Díaz-Pernil, Gutiérrez-Naranjo, Pérez-Jiménez, & Riscos-Núñez, 2007) and partition problem (Díaz-Pernil, Gutiérrez-Naranjo, Pérez-Jiménez, & Riscos-Núñez, 2010). Although prime factorization we shall consider is a numerical problem, it is neither a decision problem nor an optimization problem. In this work, we shall construct a family of tissue P systems with cell division, which can decompose integer numbers in a linear time with respect to the length of binary representation of the integer to be factored. As a result of computation, a prime number is sent to a given output membrane, instead of yes or no. Note that in this work the linear-time solution to the prime factorization problem is achieved by time-space trade-off, so an exponential space will be used during the computation.

Up to now, besides there are two polynomial-time solutions to prime factorization by P systems with active membranes (Leporati, Zandron, & Mauri, 2007; Obtulowicz, 2001), one well known polynomial algorithm that solves the factorization problem is based on quantum computer (Shor, 1997). As in the case of quantum computers, the solution given in this work indicates the powerful computing power of tissue P systems with cell division; although at this moment nobody knows how to build a biochemical computer.

2. PRELIMINARIES

An *alphabet* Σ is a finite non-empty set, whose elements are called *objects*. An ordered sequence of objects is a *string*. The number of objects in a string u is the *length* of the string, and it is denoted by u. As usual, the empty string (with length 0) will be denoted by λ. The set of strings of length n built with objects from the alphabet Σ is denoted by Σ^n and $\Sigma^* = \cup_{n\geq 0} \Sigma^n$. A *language* over Σ is a subset from Σ^*.

A *multiset* m over a set A is a pair (A, f), where $f : A \to \mathbb{N}$ is a mapping. If $m = (A, f)$ is a multiset, then its *support* is defined as $\sup p(m) = \{x \in A \,|\, f(x) > 0\}$ and its *size* is defined as $\sum_{x\in A} f(x)$. A multiset is empty (resp. finite) if its support is the empty set (resp. finite).

If $m = (A, f)$ is a finite multiset ove A, and $\sup p(m) = \{a_1, ..., a_k\}$, then it will be denoted as $m = \{\{a_1^{f(a_1)}, ..., a_k^{f(a_k)}\}\}$. That is, superscripts indicate the multiplicity of each element. If $f(x) = 0$ for any $x \in A$, then this element is omitted.

3. TISSUE P SYSTEMS WITH CELL DIVISION

In Martín-Vide, Pazos, Păun, and Rodríguez-Patón, (2002) and Martín-Vide et al. (2003), the first definition of the model of tissue P systems was proposed, where the membrane structure did not change along the computation. We now shall recall a model of *tissue P systems with cell division* based on the cell-like model of P systems with membranes division (Păun et al., 2008). The biological inspiration of this model is clear: live tissues are not *static* network of cells, since new cells are generated by membrane fission in a natural way.

The main features of this model, from the computational point of view, are that cells are not polarized (the contrary holds in the cell-like model of P systems with active membranes, see Păun (2002); the cells obtained by division have the same labels as the original cell and if a cell is divided, its interaction with other cells or with the environment is blocked during the division process. In some sense this means that while a cell is dividing it closes its communication channels with other cells and with the environment.

In what follows, we will define a function computed by a family of P systems with cell division using binary encoding.

Formally, a *(function) computing tissue P system with cell division with input* of degree $q \geq 1$ is a tuple of the form

$\Pi = (\Gamma, \Sigma, w_1, ..., w_q, \varepsilon, \Re, i_{in}, i_{out})$ where:

1. Γ is the alphabet of objects;
2. Σ is an input alphabet strictly contained in Γ;
3. $w_1, ..., w_q$ are strings over Γ, describing the initial multisets of objects placed in the cells of the system at the beginning of the computation;

4. $\varepsilon \subseteq \Gamma$ is the set of objects in the environment in unbounded number of copies;
5. $\Re$ is a finite set of rules of the following forms:
   a. $(i, u / v, j)$, for $i, j \in \{0, 1, 2, ..., q\}, i \neq j,\ u, v \in \Gamma^*$; *Communication rules*; $1, 2, ..., q$ identify the cells of the system, 0 is the environment; when applying a rule $(i, u / v, j)$, the objects of the multiset represented by u are sent from region i to region j and simultaneously the objects of the multiset v are sent from region j to region $i(|u| + |v|$ is called the length of the communication rule $(i, u / v, j))$;
   b. $[a]_i \rightarrow [b]_i[c]_i$, where $i \in \{1, 2, ..., q\},\ a, b, c \in \Gamma$, and $i \neq i_{out}$; *Division rules*; in reaction with an object a, the cell is divided into two cells with the same label; all the objects in the original cells are replicated and copies of them are placed in each of the new cells, with the exception of the object a, which is replaced by the object b in the first new cell and by c in the second one; the output cell cannot be divided;
6. $i_{in} \in \{1, 2, ..., q\}$ is the input cell;
7. $i_{out} \in \{0, 1, 2, ..., q\}$ is the output cell; specifically, if $i_{out} = 0$, then the output cell is the environment.

The rules of a system as above are used in the non-deterministic maximally parallel manner. In each step, all cells which can evolve must evolve in a maximally parallel way (in each step the system applies a multiset of rules which is maximal, no further rule can be added). This way of applying rules has only one restriction when a cell is divided; the division rule is the only one which is applied for that cell in that step; the objects inside that cell do not evolve by means of communication rules. The labels of cells precisely identify the rules which can be applied to them. This is also the case for the new generated cells.

A configuration of a tissue P system with cell division is described by all multisets of objects over Γ associated with all the cells present in the system and the multiset of objects over $\Gamma - \varepsilon$ associated with environment. The initial configuration of the system Π with input $w \in \Sigma^*$ is the tuple $(w_1, w_2, ..., w_{i_{in}} w, ..., w_q; \varnothing)$; that is, the corresponding configuration after adding the multiset w to the content of the input cell i_{in}. The computation starts from the initial configuration and proceeds as defined above. When there is no rule can be applied, the computation stops. Only halting computations give a result. If $C = \{C^i\}_{i<r}$ is a halting computation, where C^i represents the configuration of the system at step i, then the result of computation $Output(C) = (C_{b_1}^{r-1}(i_{out}), C_{b_2}^{r-1}(i_{out}), ..., C_{b_n}^{r-1}(i_{out}))$, where $C_{b_n}^{r-1}(i_{out})$, $1 \leq j \leq n$, is the multiplicity of object b_j in the region i_{out} in the halting configuration C^{r-1}.

For prime factorization problem, the factors are smaller-equal than the integer to be factored. This fact enables us to find a reasonable encoding for prime factorization problem. Specifically, we shall use the method from Leporati, Zandron, and Gutiérrez-Naranjo (2006) to encode binary numbers by multisets of objects. Let $x_{k-1}, ..., x_1, x_0$ (with $k \geq 1$) be the binary representation of integer $x \geq 0$, that is, $x = \sum_{i=0}^{k-1} x_i 2^i$. We use the objects from the following alphabet A_k, for $k \geq 1$:

$$A_k = \{\langle b, j \rangle | b \in \{0, 1\}, j \in \{0, 1, ..., k\}\}$$

Objects $\langle b, j \rangle$ is used to represent bit b in position j in the binary encoding of an integer number. Hence, to represent the above number x we will use the following multiset (actually, a set) of objects:

$$\langle x_{k-1}, k-1\rangle, ..., \langle x_1, 1\rangle, \langle x_0, 0\rangle$$

Let us remark that the alphabet A_k depends on the length of the binary representation of the number x. Moreover, it is clear that with A_k we can represent all integer numbers in the range $0, 1, ..., 2^k - 1$. In order to distinguish between the objects that represent the bits of different integers A and B, a leading label A, B are used to mark each element in the multiset. To this aim, the alphabet A_k is modified as follows:

$$A_k^{'} = \{\langle l, b, j\rangle \,|\, l \in \{A, B\}, b \in \{0,1\}, j \in \{0, 1, ..., k\}\}$$

In this way, the i-th bit of A (that is, a_i) and the j-th bit of B (that is, b_j) are represented by the objects $\langle A, a_i, i\rangle$ and $\langle B, b_j, j\rangle$, respectively.

In general, we give the following definition of function computed by a family of P systems with cell division using binary encoding.

Definition 1: We say that a partial function $f : \mathbb{N} \to \mathbb{N}$ is computed in polynomial time by a family $\Pi = \{\Pi(t) \,|\, t \in \mathbb{N}\}$ of tissue P systems with cell division using binary encoding if the following holds:

- The family Π is polynomially uniform by Turing machines, that is, there exists a deterministic Turing machine working in polynomial time which constructs the system $\Pi(t)$ from $t \in \mathbb{N}$.
- There exists a pair (cod, s) of polynomial-time computable functions over the domain $D(f)$ of function f such that:
  - for each $u \in D(f)$, $s(u)$ is a natural number and $cod(u)$ is an input multiset of the system $\Pi(s(u))$;
  - the family Π is polynomially bounded with regard to (f, cod, s), that is, there exists a polynomial function p, such that for each $u \in D(f)$ every computation of $\Pi(s(u))$ with input $cod(u)$ is halting and, moreover, it performs at most $p(|u|)$ steps;
  - the family Π is sound with regard to (f, cod, s), that is, for each $u \in D(f)$, if there exists a computation C of $\Pi(s(u))$ with input $cod(u)$ and the objects in region i_{out} in the last configuration of C encode $(\beta_1, ..., \beta_q) \in \mathbb{N}^q$, then $f(u) = (\beta_1, ..., \beta_q)$;
  - the family Π is complete *with regard to* (f, cod, s), that is, for each $u \in D(f)$, if $f(u) = (\beta_1, ..., \beta_q) \in \mathbb{N}^q$, then in every computation of $\Pi(s(u))$ with input $cod(u)$, the objects in region i_{out} in the last configuration encode $(\beta_1, ..., \beta_q)$.

4. A LINEAR TIME SOLUTION TO THE FACTORIZATION PROBLEM

Let us first recall the definition of the prime factorization problem, which can be stated as follows: given an integer N, find an integer d with $1 < d < N$ that divides N. It is trivially in the class FNP, but we do not known whether it lies in class FP or not (FNP and FP are the function problem extensions of the decision problem classes NP and P). The prime factorization problem is generally considered intractable, which means that no polynomial-time (with respect to the instance size) algorithm is known that solves it on every instance; and it is the version solved by most practical implementations. Note that deciding whether N is a composite number is much easier than the problem of finding the factors of N. Specifically, it can be solved in polynomial time (with respect to the number of digits of N) with the AKS primality test (Agrawal, Kayal, & Saxena, 2004). In this work, we shall consider a restricted version of prime factorization problem, based on the following two facts. (1) Given an algorithm for integer factorization, one can factor any integer down to its constituent prime factors by repeated application of this algorithm. (2) Not all numbers of a given length are equally hard to factor. Semiprimes (the product of two prime numbers) are believed as the hardest instances of integer factorization for currently known techniques.

Problem 1: NAME: factorization.

- **INSTANCE:** $N = A \cdot B$ (the dot here means multiplication), where A and B are prime numbers with $A < B$.
- **OUTPUT:** B.

Next, we shall construct a family $\{\Pi(k)\}_{k\in\mathbb{N}}$ of tissue P systems with cell division to factor the integer number which is the product of two prime numbers, where each system $\Pi(k)$ can decompose all such numbers of length *k* in binary form, provided that an appropriate input multiset is given. Note that if the input is not a product of two primes, then two cases arise: (1) the input is a prime; (2) the input is a product of more than two primes. In the first case, the system will output no result. As for the second case, the system will output each prime. The technique of time-space trade-off is used to factor the product of two prime numbers in linear time, so an exponential space will be generated during the computation. The construction is a brute force algorithm, which consists of the following stages:

- **Generation Stage:** By division, all the possible pairs of integer numbers of length k in binary form are produced (one pair for each membrane with label 2).
- **Pre-Checking Stage:** In this stage, the product of each pair of integer numbers of length k is calculated.
- **Checking Stage:** The system checks whether or not there exists a pair of integer numbers such that their product equals to the number N to be composed.
- **Output Stage:** The system sends to the output region a prime number.

For each $k \in \mathbb{N}$,

$$\Pi(k) = (\Gamma(k), \Sigma(k), w_1, w_2, w_3, \Re(k), \varepsilon(k), i_{in}, i_{out})$$

with the following components:

$$\Gamma(k) = \Sigma(k) \cup \{a_i, b_i, \langle X,0,i\rangle, f_i, g_i \mid 0 \le i \le k-1\} \cup$$

$$\begin{aligned}
&\{\langle A,j,i\rangle, \langle B,j,i\rangle, \langle A',j,i\rangle, \mid 0 \le i \le k-1, 0 \le j \le 1\} \cup \\
&\{\langle B',j,i\rangle, \langle A'',j,i\rangle, \langle B'',j,i\rangle \mid 0 \le i \le k-1, 0 \le j \le 1\} \cup \\
&\{\langle A_l,j,i\rangle \mid 0 \le i \le k-1, 0 \le j \le 1, 0 \le l \le \lceil \lg k \rceil + 1\} \cup \\
&\{\langle B_l,j,i\rangle \mid 0 \le i \le k-1, 0 \le j \le 1, 0 \le l \le \lceil \lg k \rceil + 1\} \cup \\
&\{c_i \mid 0 \le i \le 4k + \lceil \lg 2k \rceil + \lceil \lg k \rceil + 4\} \cup \{z, h\} \cup \\
&\{c'_i \mid 1 \le i \le \lceil \lg k \rceil + 2k + 2\} \cup \{\langle C,1,i\rangle \mid 0 \le i \le 2k-1\} \cup \\
&\{\langle C,0,i\rangle \mid 0 \le i \le 2k-2\} \cup \{d_i \mid -1 \le i \le k-2\} \cup \\
&\{e_i \mid -1 \le i \le k-1\} \cup \{\langle i,j\rangle \mid 0 \le i,j \le k-1\}
\end{aligned}$$

$$\Sigma(k) = \{\langle N,0,i\rangle, \langle N,1,i\rangle \mid 0 \le i \le k-1\}.$$

$$w_1 = \{\{c_0\}\}.$$

$$\begin{aligned}
w_2 = &\{\{a_0, a_1, \ldots, a_{k-1}, b_0, b_1, \ldots, b_{k-1}, z\}\} \cup \\
&\{\{\langle i,j\rangle \mid 0 \le i,j \le k-1\}\}
\end{aligned}$$

$$w_3 = \lambda.$$

$\Re(k)$ is the set of rules:

Division Rules:

$$r_{1,i} \equiv [a_i]_2 \to [\langle A,0,i\rangle]_2[\langle A,1,i\rangle]_2 \text{ for } 0 \le i \le k-1$$

$r_{2,i} \equiv [b_i]_2 \to [\langle B,0,i\rangle]_2[\langle B,1,i\rangle]_2$ for $0 \le i \le k-1$

Communication Rules:

$r_{3,i} \equiv (1, c_i / c_{i+1}^2, 0)$ for $0 \le i \le 2k-1$

$r_4 \equiv (1, c_{2k} / z, 2)$;

$r_{5,i} \equiv (2, c_{2k+i} / c_{2k+i+1}^2, 0)$ for $0 \le i \le \lceil \lg 2k \rceil - 1$

$r_{6,i,j} \equiv (2, c_{2k\lceil \lg 2k \rceil} \lceil A, j, i \rceil / c_{2k+\lceil \lg 2k \rceil+1} \langle A_0, j, i \rangle, 0)$,

for $0 \le i \le k-1, 0 \le j \le 1$;

$r_{7,i,j} \equiv (2, c_{2k+\lceil \lg 2k \rceil} \lceil B, j, i \rceil / c_{2k+\lceil \lg 2k \rceil+1} \langle B_0, j, i \rangle, 0)$

for $0 \le i \le k-1, 0 \le j \le 1$;

$r_8 \equiv (2, c_{2k+\lceil \lg 2k \rceil+1} / c_1' c_{2k+\lceil \lg 2k \rceil+2}, 0)$;

$r_{9,i} \equiv (2, c_{2k+\lceil \lg 2k \rceil+i} / c_{2k+\lceil \lg 2k \rceil+i+1}, 0)$,

for $2 \le i \le \lceil \lg k \rceil + 2k + 3$;

$r_{10,i} \equiv (2, c_i' / c_{i+1}', 0)$,

for $1 \le i \le \lceil \lg k \rceil + 2k + 1$;

$r_{11,i,j,l} \equiv (2, \langle A_l, j, i \rangle / \langle A_{l+1}, j, i \rangle^2, 0)$,

for $0 \le i \le k-1$, $0 \le j \le 1, 0 \le l \le \lceil \lg k \rceil$;

$r_{12,i,j,l} \equiv (2, \langle B_l, j, i \rangle / \langle B_{l+1}, j, i \rangle^2, 0)$,

for $0 \le i \le k-1$, $0 \le j \le 1$, $0 \le l \le \lceil \lg k \rceil$;

$r_{13,i,j} \equiv (2, \langle A_{\lceil \lg k \rceil+1}, 0, i \rangle \langle B_{\lceil \lg k \rceil+1}, 0, j \rangle \langle i, j \rangle / \langle C, 0, i+j \rangle, 0)$

for $0 \le i, j \le k-1$;

$r_{14,i,j} \equiv (2, \langle A_{\lceil \lg k \rceil+1}, 0, i \rangle \langle B_{\lceil \lg k \rceil+1}, 1, j \rangle \langle i, j \rangle / \langle C, 0, i+j \rangle, 0)$

for $0 \le i, j \le k-1$;

$r_{15,i,j} \equiv (2, \langle A_{\lceil \lg k \rceil+1}, 1, i \rangle \langle B_{\lceil \lg k \rceil+1}, 0, j \rangle \langle i, j \rangle / \langle C, 0, i+j \rangle, 0)$

for $0 \le i, j \le k-1$;

$r_{16,i,j} \equiv (2, \langle A_{\lceil \lg k \rceil+1}, 1, i \rangle \langle B_{\lceil \lg k \rceil+1}, 1, j \rangle \langle i, j \rangle / \langle C, 1, i+j \rangle, 0)$

for $0 \le i, j \le k-1$;

$r_{17,i} \equiv (2, \langle C, 0, i \rangle \langle C, o, i \rangle / \langle C, 0, i \rangle, 0)$

for $0 \le i \le 2k-2$;

$r_{18,i} \equiv (2, \langle C, 0, i \rangle \langle C, 1, i \rangle / \langle C, 1, i \rangle, 0)$,

for $0 \le i \le 2k-2$;

$r_{19,i} \equiv (2, \langle C, 1, i \rangle \langle C, 1, i \rangle / \langle C, 0, i \rangle \langle C, 1, i+1 \rangle, 0)$

for $0 \le i \le 2k-2$;

$r_{20,i,j} \equiv (2, c'_{\lceil \lg k \rceil + 2k+2} \langle C,1,i \rangle \langle N,j,k-1 \rangle / \lambda, 0)$,

for $k \le i \le 2k-1$, $0 \le j \le 1$;

$r_{21,i,j} \equiv (2, c_{2k+\lceil \lg 2k \rceil + \lceil \lg k \rceil + 4} \langle C,j,i \rangle \langle N,j,i \rangle / \langle X,0,i \rangle, 0,$

for $0 \le i \le k-1$, $0 \le j \le 1$;

$r_{22} \equiv (2, \langle X,0,k-1 \rangle / d_{k-2}, 0)$;

$r_{23,i} \equiv (2, d_i \langle X,0,i \rangle / d_{i-1}, 0)$,

for $0 \le i \le k-2$;

$r_{24} \equiv (2, d_{-1} / e_{k-1}, 0)$;

$r_{25,i,j} \equiv (2, \langle A_{\lceil \lg k \rceil+1}, j, i \rangle \langle B_{\lceil \lg k \rceil+1}, j, i \rangle e_i / \langle A_{\lceil \lg k \rceil+1}, j, i \rangle$

$\langle B_{\lceil \lg k \rceil+1}, j, i \rangle e_{i-1}, 0)$,

for $0 \le i \le k-1$, $0 \le j \le 1$;

$r_{26} \equiv (2, e_{-1} / f_0, 0)$;

$r_{27,i} \equiv (2, \langle A_{\lceil \lg k \rceil+1}, 1, i \rangle \langle B_{\lceil \lg k \rceil+1}, 0, i \rangle e_i / \langle A_{\lceil \lg k \rceil+1}, 1, i \rangle$

$\langle B_{\lceil \lg k \rceil+1}, 0, i \rangle f_0, 0)$,

for $0 \le i \le k-1$;

$r_{28,i,j} \equiv (2, f_i \langle B_{\lceil \lg k \rceil+1}, j, i \rangle / f_{i+1} \langle B', j, i \rangle, 0)$,

for $0 \le i \le k-2$, $0 \le j \le 1$;

$r_{29,j} \equiv (2, f_{k-1} \langle B_{\lceil \lg k \rceil+1}, j, k-1 \rangle / \langle B', j, k-1 \rangle, 0)$,

for $0 \le j \le 1$;

$r_{30,i} \equiv (2, \langle B', 1, i \rangle / \langle B'', 1, i \rangle h, 0)$,

for $1 \le i \le k-1$,

$r_{31,i} \equiv (2, \langle B', 0, i \rangle h / \langle B'', 0, i \rangle h, 0)$,

for $0 \le i \le k-1$;

$r_{32,i,j} \equiv (2, \langle B'', j, i \rangle / \lambda, 3)$,

for $0 \le i \le k-1, 0 \le j \le 1$;

$r_{33,i} \equiv (2, \langle A_{\lceil \lg k \rceil+1}, 0, i \rangle \langle B_{\lceil \lg k \rceil+1}, 1, i \rangle e_i / \langle A_{\lceil \lg k \rceil+1}, 0, i \rangle$

$\langle B_{\lceil \lg k \rceil+1}, 1, i \rangle g_0, 0)$,

for $0 \le i \le k-1$;

$r_{34,i,j} \equiv (2, g_i \langle A_{\lceil \lg k \rceil+1}, j, i \rangle / g_{i+1} \langle A', j, i \rangle, 0)$,

for $0 \le i \le k-2$, $0 \le j \le 1$;

$r_{35,j} \equiv (2, g_{k-1} \langle A_{\lceil \lg k \rceil + 1}, j, k-1 \rangle / \langle A', j, k-1 \rangle, 0),$

for $0 \le j \le 1$;

$r_{36,i} \equiv (2, \langle A', 1, i \rangle / \langle A'', 1, i \rangle h, 0),$

for $1 \le i \le k-1$;

$r_{37,i} \equiv (2, \langle A', 0, i \rangle h / \langle A'', 0, i \rangle h, 0),$

for $0 \le i \le k-1$;

$r_{38,i,j} \equiv (2, \langle A'', j, i \rangle / \lambda, 3),$

for $0 \le i \le k-1$, $0 \le j \le 1$.

- $\varepsilon(k) = \Gamma(k)$.
- $i_{in} = 2$ is the *input cell.*
- $i_{out} = 3$ is the *output cell.*

4.1. An Overview of the Computation

A family of tissue P systems with cell division is constructed as above. Let u be an instance of the prime factorization problem, where N is the integer number to be decomposed and k is the number of bits needed to represent N. Then we consider a size mapping on the set of instances defined as $s(u) = k$. The coding of the instance is the multiset

$cod(u) = \{\{\langle N, i_{k-1}, k-1 \rangle, \langle N, i_{k-2}, k-2 \rangle, \ldots, \langle N, i_0, 0 \rangle\}\},$

where $i_j = 0$ or 1 $(0 \le j \le k-1)$ is the bit at position *j* in the binary encoding of N. In what follows, we will informally describe how the tissue P system with cell division $\Pi(s(u))$ with input $cod(u)$ works.

Let us start with the generation stage. This stage has two parallel processes, which are described in two items.

- On one hand, in the cell with label 1 by using the rule $r_{3,i}$ the object c_i is doubled until step $2k$; starting from c_0 object c_i grows its subscript by one in each step. Therefore, 4^k copies of c_{2k} are obtained in the cell with label 1 at step $2k$.
- On the other hand, in the cell with label 2 the division rules $r_{1,i}$ and $r_{2,i}$ are applied. For each object a_i (which is used to generate the two possible bits at position *i* in the binary encoding of integer number *A*), two cells labeled by 2 are produced, one of them containing a new object $\langle A, 0, i \rangle$ and the other one containing another new object $\langle A, 1, i \rangle$. Object $\langle A, 0, i \rangle$ (resp. $\langle A, 1, i \rangle$) represents the fact that the bit at position *i* in the binary encoding of *A* is 0 (resp. 1). Similarly, for each object b_i (which is used to generate the two possible bits at position *i* in the binary encoding of integer number *B*), two cells labeled by 2 are also produced, one of them containing a new object $\langle B, 0, i \rangle$ and the other one containing another new object $\langle B, 1, i \rangle$. The objects a_i, b_i are non-deterministically chosen, after 2*k* steps of division we obtain exactly 4^k cells with label 2, each of them containing an encoding of one possible pair of integer numbers *A* and *B* whose val-

ues range from 0 to $2^k - 1$. The object z is duplicated, hence a copy of z appears in each cell with label 2. Note that after step 2^k the cells with label 2 cannot divide anymore, because the objects a_i and b_i are exhausted.

The pre-checking stage starts from step $2k+1$. In this stage, the product of each pair of integer numbers in cell with label 2 is calculated. At the step $2k+1$, there are 4^k copies of c_{2k} in the cell with label 1, and there are 4^k cells with label 2, each of them containing a copy of z, so the rule r_4 is enabled and applied. Due to the fact that at that step there will exist exactly 2^{2k} copies of z, in different cells labeled 2, each cell with label 2 gets precisely one copy of c_{2k}. In the next $\lceil \lg 2k \rceil$ steps, by the rule $r_{5,i}$, the object c_{2k+i} is duplicated and its subscript increases by one in each step; so at step $2k + \lceil \lg 2k \rceil + 1$, there are at least $2k$ copies of $c_{2k+\lceil \lg 2k \rceil}$ in each cell with label 2. Once object $c_{2k+\lceil \lg 2k \rceil}$ is generated, by the rules $r_{6,i,j} - r_{7,i,j}$, each copy of objects $\langle A, j, i \rangle$ and $\langle B, j, i \rangle$, $0 \le i \le k-1$, $0 \le j \le 1$ together with a copy of object $c_{2k+\lceil \lg 2k \rceil}$, is traded for one copy of objects $\langle A_0, j, i \rangle$, $\langle B_0, j, i \rangle$, and one copy of object $c_{2k+\lceil \lg 2k \rceil+1}$ at step $2k + \lceil \lg 2k \rceil + 2$.

From step $2k + \lceil \lg 2k \rceil + 3$ to step $2k + \lceil \lg 2k \rceil + \lceil \lg k \rceil + 3$, by the rules $r_{11,i,j,l}$ and $r_{12,i,j,l}$, the objects $\langle A_l, j, i \rangle$ and $\langle B_l, j, i \rangle$ duplicate themselves until getting at least $k+1$ copies of objects $\langle A_{\lceil \lg k \rceil+1}, j, i \rangle$ and $B_{\lceil \lg 2k \rceil+1}, j, i$. In the following computation, k copies of these objects are used to obtain the product of integer numbers A and B, while the other copy of these objects is used to output the computed result.

For any two k-bits integer numbers $A = \sum_{i=0}^{k-1} x_i 2^i$ ($x_i = 0$ or 1) and $B = \sum_{i=0}^{k-1} y_i 2^i$ ($y_i = 0$ or 1), the product of A and B can be written as $A \cdot B = \sum_{i=0}^{k-1} \sum_{j=0}^{k-1} x_i y_j 2^{i+j}$. In order to get the product, we will first compute the contribution of each pair of bits x_i and y_j, and then sum all the contributions. Specifically, the rules $r_{13,i,j} - r_{16,i,j}$ are used to get the contribution of each pair of bits; the rules $r_{17,i} - r_{19,i}$ are used to get the sum of all contributions. Since each cell with label 2 contains at least $k+1$ copies of objects $\langle A_{\lceil \lg k \rceil+1}, j, i \rangle$ and $\langle B_{\lceil \lg k \rceil+1}, j, i \rangle$, $j = 1$ or 0, the process of computing the product of each pair of bits a_i and b_j only needs one step, which produces some bits of the result C as well as the carry bits. It takes at most $2k$ steps to sum all the bits by the rules $r_{17,i} - r_{19,i}$. In this way, after step $4k + \lceil \lg 2k \rceil + \lceil \lg k \rceil + 4$ the product of two integer numbers in each cell with label 2 is computed and the pre-checking stage is finished. At this moment, the subscript of object c_i reaches $4k + \lceil \lg 2k \rceil + \lceil \lg k \rceil + 3$ by the rules r_8 and $r_{9,i}$, while the subscript of object c'_i reaches $\lceil \lg k \rceil + 2k + 2$ by the rule $r_{10,i}$.

The checking stage starts from step $4k + \lceil \lg 2k \rceil + \lceil \lg k \rceil + 5$ with the application of the rules $r_{20,i,j}$, $r_{21,i,j}$, r_{22} and $r_{23,i}$. The rules $r_{20,i,j}$ are used to check whether the "efficient" length of bits of the product is greater than $k-1$, i.e., whether there exists at least one position i, $k \le i \le 2k-1$, in the product having bit 1. Checking that the bits higher than $k-1$ are all zero could be done in the same way as checking that lower bits match those of N. If there exists such position in the binary encoding of the product, then the product must be greater than N. In this case, at least one of objects $\langle C, 1, i \rangle$,

$k \leq i \leq 2k-1$, must appear in this cell. By the rule $r_{20,i,j}$, object $\langle N, j, k-1\rangle$, $j=0$ or 1, is removed. The rules $r_{21,i,k-1}$ and r_{22} cannot be used without object $\langle N, j, k-1\rangle$, thus this cell with label 2 will not send objects to the output cell. If the bit on each position i such that $k \leq i \leq 2k-1$ equals to 0, then at that step only the rule $r_{9,\lceil \lg k\rceil+2k+3}$ can be used by which object $c_{4k+\lceil \lg 2k\rceil+\lceil \lg k\rceil+3}$ is traded for $c_{4k+\lceil \lg 2k\rceil+\lceil \lg k\rceil+4}$. The rues $r_{21,i,j}$, r_{22} and $r_{23.i}$ are used to check whether the product equals to n.

- If the product equals to N in a cell with label 2, then all objects $\langle X, 0, i\rangle$, $0 \leq i \leq k-1$, should be produced in this cell by the rule $r_{21,i,j}$. The rules r_{22} and $r_{23,i}$ are used to check whether all objects $\langle X, 0, i\rangle$, $0 \leq i \leq k-1$ are produced. It is performed one bit by one bit, starting from the most significant bit. The object $\langle X, 0, k-1\rangle$ is traded for d_{k-2}, then d_{k-2} and $\langle X, 0, k-2\rangle$ are traded for d_{k-3}, and the process continues until the position 0 is checked and the object d_{-1} is produced. Since the length of the integer number N is k, this process takes k steps. The computation passes to the output stage from step $5k+\lceil \lg 2k\rceil+\lceil \lg k\rceil+7$.
- If the product does not equal to N in a cell with label 2, then at least one object $\langle X, 0, i\rangle$, $0 \leq i \leq k-1$, will not be produced in this cell. Without loss of generality, we assume that the first object not appearing in this cell is $\langle X, 0, s\rangle$, starting from the most significant bit, where $0 \leq s \leq k-1$. By the rules r_{22} and $r_{22,i}$, it is not difficult to find that object d_{s-1} will not be produced and the application of rules in that cell finishes. That means that this cell will not send any objects to the output cell.

The output stage starts from step $5k+\lceil \lg 2k\rceil+\lceil \lg k\rceil+7$. In this stage, if the product of two integer numbers equals to N and the two numbers are also equal, then one of them will be outputted to the output cell; if the product of two integer numbers equals to N and the two numbers are not equal, then the smaller one will be outputted to the output cell. According to the checking stage, if the product of two integer numbers equals to N in a cell with label 2, then the object d_{-1} appears in this cell. The object d_{-1} is traded for e_{k-1}. The rules $r_{25,i,j}$, $r_{27,i}$ and $r_{33,i}$ are used to check which integer number is smaller or whether they are equal. If object e_{-1} appears, then the two integer numbers are equal, and the integer number corresponding to objects $\langle B_{\lceil \lg k\rceil+1}, j, i\rangle$ is outputted to the output cell labeled by 3 by the rules r_{26}, $r_{28,i,j} - r_{32,i,j}$. If two integer numbers are not equal, then object f_0 or g_0 should appear and object e_{-1} does not appear. If object f_0 appears in the cell with label 2, it means that the integer number corresponding to objects $\langle A_{\lceil \lg k\rceil+1}, j, i\rangle$ is greater than the integer number corresponding to objects $\langle B_{\lceil \lg k\rceil+1}, j, i\rangle$, and the integer number corresponding to objects $\langle B_{\lceil \lg k\rceil+1}, j, i\rangle$ is outputted to the output cell with label 3 by the rules $r_{28,i,j} - r_{32,i,j}$ in the case that this integer number does not equal integer number 1. Note that the rules $r_{30,i} - r_{31,i}$ are used to check whether the smaller integer number that corresponds to objects $\left\langle B_{\lceil \lg k \rceil+1}, j, i \right\rangle$ equals integer number 1 and in the negative case this integer number is outputted to the output cell with label 3 in the form of $\left\langle B'', j, i \right\rangle$. If object g_0 appears in the cell with label 2, it means the fact that the integer number corresponding to objects $\left\langle A_{\lceil \lg k \rceil+1}, j, i \right\rangle$ is less than the number corresponding to objects $\left\langle B_{\lceil \lg k \rceil+1}, j, i \right\rangle$, and the integer number corresponding to objects $\left\langle A_{\lceil \lg k \rceil+1}, j, i \right\rangle$ is outputted to the output cell with label 3 in the form of $\left\langle A'', j, i \right\rangle$, by the rules $r_{34,i,j} - r_{38,i,j}$ when this integer number does not equal integer number 1. This stage takes no more than 3*k*+3 steps, and in the case that two integer numbers are equal, the output stage takes exactly 3*k*+3 steps. So the computation of the system stops after step $8k + \lceil \lg 2k \rceil + \lceil \lg k \rceil + 9$, and the computation result can read out from the objects in the output cell with label 3.

4.2. Necessary Resources

From the overview of the computation, it can be found that the family $\{\Pi(k)\}_{k \in \mathbb{N}}$ constructed above can solve the factorization problem in a linear time with respect to the size of the integer to be factored. In what follows, we point out that this family of tissue P systems with cell division can be constructed in polynomial time by deterministic Turing machine.

It is easy to check that the rules of a system $\Pi(k)$ of the family are defined recursively from the value *k*. The necessary resources to build an element of the family are of a polynomial order, as shown below:

- **Size of the Alphabet:** $k^2 + 39k + (4k+2) + \lceil \lg k \rceil + \lceil \lg 2k \rceil.$ $+9 \in O(k^2)$
- **Initial Number of Cells:** $3 \in O(1)$.
- **Initial Number of Objects:** $k^2 + 2k + 2 \in O(k^2)$.
- **Number of Rules:**

$$4k^2 + 43k + \lceil \lg 2k \rceil + (4k+2)\lceil \lg k \rceil + 2 \in O(k^2).$$

- **Maximal Length of a Rule:** $6 \in O(1)$.

Therefore, a deterministic Turing machine can build the tissue P system $\Pi(k)$ in a polynomial time with respect to *k*.

5. CONCLUSION AND COMMENTS

Prime factorization problem is not in itself a widely useful problem. It has become useful only because it has been found to be crucial for public-key cryptography, and this application is in turn possible only because they have been presumed to be difficult. Currently, no deterministic polynomial-time algorithm executed on Turing machines is known to solve the problem for every possible instance. It is thus of interest to explore any possible and reasonable way to solve prime factorization problem because of its importance in public-key cryptography.

Prime factorization problem is neither decision problem nor optimization problem. In this work, it is considered as a function problem, and in the framework of tissue P systems with cell division, a linear-time solution to prime factorization problem is given. The initial structure of the systems is very simple, which consists of three cells. The system is initialized with inputting into the input cell the multiset that expresses the integer number *n* to be factored. After a linear time with respect to the size of *N* (i.e., $8k + \lceil \lg 2k \rceil + \lceil \lg k \rceil + 9$ steps), we can read out one factor of *N* in the output cell.

P systems are a highly distributed parallel model of computation. Currently, nobody knows how to build a biochemical computer/an artificial tissue-like computer. P systems may be implemented using molecules, cells or a large computer network such as the Internet. Although it goes beyond the scope of this work to discuss the implementation of P systems, clearly, it is of particular interest and it is a big challenging topic.

ACKNOWLEDGMENT

The work was supported by National Natural Science Foundation of China (61033003, 61003038, 61003131 and 30870826), Ph.D. Programs Foundation of Ministry of Education of China (20100142110072), Fundamental Research Funds for the Central Universities (2010ZD001), and the Opening Foundation of Key Laboratory of University of Science and Technology of China for High-Performance Computing and Applications (NHPCC-KF-1102), and Scientific Research Foundation for Doctor of Anhui University (02203104). Mario J. Pérez-Jiménez also acknowledges the support of the project TIN2009-13192 of the Ministerio de Ciencia e Innovación of Spain, cofinanced by FEDER funds, and the "Proyecto de Excelencia con Investigador de Reconocida Valía" of the Junta de Andalucía under grant P08-TIC04200.

REFERENCES

Agrawal, M., Kayal, N., & Saxena, N. (2004). PRIMES is in P. *The Annals of Mathematics*, *160*(2), 781–793. doi:10.4007/annals.2004.160.781.

Díaz-Pernil, D., Gutiérrez-Naranjo, M. A., Pérez-Jiménez, M. A., & Riscos-Núñez, A. (2007). Solving subset sum in linear time by using tissue P systems with cell division. In J. Mira & J. R. Alvarez (Eds.), *Proceedings of the Second International Work-Conference on Bio-inspired Modeling of Cognitive Tasks* (LNCS 4527, pp. 170-179).

Díaz-Pernil, D., Gutiérrez-Naranjo, M. A., Pérez-Jiménez, M. A., & Riscos-Núñez, A. (2008). A uniform family of tissue P systems with cell division solving 3-COL in a linear time. *Theoretical Computer Science*, *404*, 76–87. doi:10.1016/j.tcs.2008.04.005.

Díaz-Pernil, D., Gutiérrez-Naranjo, M. A., Pérez-Jiménez, M. A., & Riscos-Núñez, A. (2008). Computational efficiency of cellular division in tissue-like membrane systems. *Romanian Journal of Information Science and Technology*, *11*(3), 229–241.

Díaz-Pernil, D., Gutiérrez-Naranjo, M. A., Pérez-Jiménez, M. A., & Riscos-Núñez, A. (2010). A linear time solution to the partition problem in a cellular tissue-like model. *Journal of Computational and Theoretical Nanoscience*, *7*(5), 884–889. doi:10.1166/jctn.2010.1435.

Frisco, P. (2009). *Computing with cells: Advances in membrane computing*. New York, NY: Oxford University Press. doi:10.1093/acprof:oso/9780199542864.001.0001.

Leporati, A., Zandron, C., & Gutiérrez-Naranjo, M. A. (2006). P systems with input in binary form. *International Journal of Foundations of Computer Science*, *17*(1), 127–146. doi:10.1142/S0129054106003735.

Leporati, A., Zandron, C., & Mauri, G. (2007). Solving the factorization problem with P systems. *Progress in Natural Science*, *17*(4), 471–478. doi:10.1080/10020070708541025.

Martín-Vide, C., Pazos, J., Păun, G., & Rodríguez-Patón, A. (2002). A new class of symbolic abstract neural nets: Tissue P systems. In O. H. Ibarra & L. Zhang (Eds.), *Proceedings of the 8th Annual International Conference on Computing and Combinations* (LNCS 2387, pp. 290-299).

Martín-Vide, C., Pazos, J., Păun, G., & Rodríguez-Patón, A. (2003). Tissue P systems. *Theoretical Computer Science, 296*, 295–326. doi:10.1016/S0304-3975(02)00659-X.

Obtulowicz, A. (2001). On P systems with active membranes solving the integer factorization problem in a polynomial time. In C. S. Calude, G. Paun, G. Rozenberg, & A. Salomaa (Eds.), *Proceedings of the Mathematical, Computer Science, and Molecular Computing Points of View: Multiset Processing* (LNCS 2235, pp. 267-285).

Păun, A., & Păun, G. (2002). The power of communication: P systems with symport/antiport. *New Generation Computing, 20*(3), 295–305. doi:10.1007/BF03037362.

Păun, G. (2000). Computing with membranes. *Journal of Computer and System Sciences, 61*(1), 108–143. doi:10.1006/jcss.1999.1693.

Păun, G., Pérez-Jiménez, M. J., & Riscos-Núñez, A. (2008). Tissue P systems with cell division. *International Journal of Computers, Communications & Control, 3*(3), 295–302.

Păun, G., Rozenberg, G., & Salomaa, A. (2010). *Handbook of membrane computing*. New York, NY: Oxford University Press.

Rivest, R. L., Shamir, A., & Adleman, L. M. (1978). A method for obtaining digital signatures and public-key cryptosystems. *Communications of the ACM, 21*(2), 120–126. doi:10.1145/359340.359342.

Shor, P. W. (1997). Polynomial-time algorithms for prime factorization and discrete logarithms on a quantum computer. *SIAM Journal on Computing, 26*(5), 1484–1509. doi:10.1137/S0097539795293172.

Systems, P. (2011). *Resources website*. Retrieved from http://ppage.psystems.eu/

This work was previously published in the International Journal of Natural Computing Research (IJNCR), Volume 2, Issue 3, edited by Leandro Nunes de Castro, pp. 49-60, copyright 2011 by IGI Publishing (an imprint of IGI Global).

Chapter 15
Unorganized Machines:
From Turing's Ideas to Modern Connectionist Approaches

Levy Boccato
University of Campinas (UNICAMP), Brazil

Everton S. Soares
University of Campinas (UNICAMP), Brazil

Marcos M. L. P. Fernandes
Faculdade de Engenharia de Sorocaba (FACENS), Brazil

Diogo C. Soriano
Federal University of ABC (UFABC), Brazil

Romis Attux
University of Campinas (UNICAMP), Brazil

ABSTRACT

This work presents a discussion about the relationship between the contributions of Alan Turing – the centenary of whose birth is celebrated in 2012 – to the field of artificial neural networks and modern unorganized machines: reservoir computing (RC) approaches and extreme learning machines (ELMs). Firstly, the authors review Turing's connectionist proposals and also expose the fundamentals of the main RC paradigms – echo state networks and liquid state machines, - as well as of the design and training of ELMs. Throughout this exposition, the main points of contact between Turing's ideas and these modern perspectives are outlined, being, then, duly summarized in the second and final part of the work. This paper is useful in offering a distinct appreciation of Turing's pioneering contributions to the field of neural networks and also in indicating some perspectives for the future development of the field that may arise from the synergy between these views.

1. INTRODUCTION

Alan Mathison Turing (1912-1954) is widely regarded as one of the foremost mathematicians of the 20th century (Hawking, 2007), especially due to his proof of the impossibility of existence of a general solution to the *Entscheidungs problem* posed by David Hilbert (Turing, 1936). Albeit Alonzo Church, in a completely independent fashion, has reached the same conclusion using the formalism known as λ-calculus (Epstein & Carnielli, 2008) – which would play a role of its own in theoretical computer science (Russell & Norvig, 2009), - Turing's proof was striking in

DOI: 10.4018/978-1-4666-4253-9.ch015

the sense that it embodied, in an abstract (though almost tangible) way, the essence of the computing machines that were to occupy a preponderant role in the technological history of mankind from the 1940s up to present day. A result of this nature has the weight of a lifetime achievement, but, for Turing, it was only a sort of "first peak" in an intellectual trajectory that would also leave marks in other chapters of the history of the last century.

In September 1938, the same year in which he concluded his PhD under Church's supervision, Turing reported to Government Code and Cypher School (GCCS) at Bletchley Park (Hodges, 1992). Hence began a work on the decryption of the naval Enigma cipher that had a remarkable impact on the British war effort, which suffered immensely from the action of the German submarines. The concurrent problem of speech coding allowed Turing to have contact with the Bell Labs team, which apropos included Claude Shannon, who shared many of Turing's views regarding what can be broadly termed "information science." In a *tour the force* involving cryptography, early signal processing theory and electronics, Turing conceived a voice-encoding device called *Delilah* ("the biblical deceiver of men," as explained in Hodges (1992)), the prototype of which was built in 1944. The system, however, never had the chance of playing the practical role for which it was intended.

In parallel with these developments, Turing cultivated an interest that was central enough to leave a definite mark in his post-war research *corpus*: the idea of building a *thinking machine* (Leavitt, 2006). This idea is organically related to many of his earlier intellectual pursuits,[1] and also to certain philosophical convictions forged in the course of his personal history.

One particular effort was very influential in the development of the field of artificial intelligence (AI) (Russell & Norvig, 2009): the attempt to formalize the notion of machine intelligence using an imitation game that is now termed *Turing test*. The test is discussed in a work (Turing, 1950) that is an immense pleasure to read, not only for its unique style, but also for its cornucopia of brilliant insights into many aspects and key questions associated with the later development of AI.

Interestingly, Turing also made other important contributions to the field that, in spite of their relevance, are even presently, relatively little known. Among these contributions, we highlight, in this paper, Turing's ideas on the design of neural networks – which, thanks to works like Teuscher (2001), Copeland (2004), and Copeland and Proudfoot (1999), are starting to receive a more fit appreciation. These ideas can be, from a historical standpoint, considered as a development of the logical approach to neural modeling introduced by Warren McCulloch and Walter Pitts (1943). However, as we will discuss later on, Turing's connectionist perspective is also very rich in its early use of recurrence and, particularly, of unorganized architectures. These features establish a number of interesting parallels with some recent neural approaches – like reservoir computing (Lukosevicius & Jaeger, 2009) and extreme learning machines (Huang, Zhu, & Siew, 2006) - and also with a number of investigations concerning the connectivity pattern of the nervous system. These connections have not, to the best of our knowledge, hitherto been explored. It is our belief that they can be useful not only in historiographical terms, but also as indicative of promising research subjects.

This work is organized as follows: in Section 2, we review Turing's seminal ideas introduced in the report *Intelligent Machinery*, focusing on his contributions to the field of neural networks through the proposal of the so-called unorganized machines; then, in Sections 3 and 4, we describe in detail two modern connectionist paradigms – reservoir computing and extreme learning machines – that revive the idea of "disorganization"; the conceptual links between these approaches and Turing's ideas are duly established in Section 5, in which we also discuss interesting perspectives for future research that may benefit from this synergy. Finally, Section 6 concludes the paper.

2. TURING'S NEURAL NETWORKS

In 1948, Turing delivered to Sir Charles Darwin, head of the National Physical Laboratory (NPL), in London, the report entitled *Intelligent Machinery*, describing the main results of his research concerning the possibility that computational machines exhibit intelligent behavior analogous to that engendered by the human brain. In his own words: *"I propose to investigate the question as to whether it is possible for machinery to show intelligent behaviour"* (Turing, 1968). Unfortunately, *Intelligent Machinery* did not receive the deserved appreciation at the time, having remained unpublished until 1968; fourteen years after Turing's death. Recently, due to the efforts of Teuscher (2001), Copeland (2004) and others, this landmark work has been progressively disseminated and its valuable contributions are finally being properly acknowledged.

In this remarkably original report, Turing anticipated several key concepts that would later be central to the field of artificial/computational intelligence. For instance, the use of search mechanisms inspired in evolution theory, such as genetic algorithms (Holland, 1975) and evolution strategies (Schwefel, 1981), can be found *in nuce* in what he called "evolutionary or genetic search" (Turing, 1968). Nonetheless, *Intelligent Machinery* is mainly devoted to a discussion about machine learning, in which Turing anticipates the approach modernly known as connectionism (Turing, 1968).

It is important to stress that the idea of using a network composed of interconnected simple processing units had already been addressed in the work of McCulloch and Pitts (1943), which, curiously, was not cited by Turing. However, the differences between the proposed network models aside, Turing took one step further by developing the notion that random arrangements of neurons can be suitably trained via external interference in order to compute a specific function, in an early proposal of a supervised learning paradigm (Turing, 1968; Teuscher, 2001).

With the purpose of investigating the emergence of intelligent behavior in machines, the possibility of which he was absolutely convinced of, Turing proposed the study of structures built from certain kind of standard components that are largely random in their construction, which are termed *unorganized machines (networks)*. In particular, Turing conceived two types of unorganized machines, referred to as A-type and B-type, and also a modified version of the B-type architecture, which received from Teuscher (2001) the name of BI-type. A peculiar feature of this last structure is the fact that, due to the presence of interference signals, an external agent (teacher) is capable of modifying the operation mode of each connection within the network aiming to adapt it to perform a desired function.

After this preamble, we describe, in the following, the neural network models proposed by Turing.

2.1. A-Type Networks

The first – and also the most simple – unorganized machine introduced by Turing is made up from a sufficiently high number of interconnected processing units (neurons). Each neuron: (*i*) can assume one of two possible states (0 or 1) at each time instant; (*ii*) is connected to a central synchronizing unit from which synchronizing pulses are emitted at equal intervals of time (*T*); (*iii*) has exactly two input terminals, $x_1(t)$ and $x_2(t)$, and produces a single output $y(t)$ according to the following expression:

$$y(t+1) = 1 - x_1(t)x_2(t) \tag{1}$$

Hence, each neuron computes the logical function NAND between its input signals, as shown in Table 1.

Turing's option for the use of a NAND function as the basic unit within unorganized machines was probably motivated by the fact that any logical function can be implemented exclusively using NAND elements (Ercegovac, Lang, & Moreno, 1998; Teuscher, 2001). Consequently, it is possible to affirm that universal Turing machines with a truncated tape can be simulated with the aid of A-type machines (Teuscher, 2001).

However, in order that an A-type network present a specific behavior, it is necessary to carefully design its topology and to choose the number of neurons, as well as their initial states, which can be an arduous task. Additionally, it is important to mention that A-type machines do not allow external parameter update during their operation. Figure 1 depicts a generic A-type unorganized machine containing five neurons.

2.2. B-Type Networks

The distinctive characteristic of B-type networks is the fact that each neural connection has an interference node that presents different operation modes. This offers the possibility of reinforcing useful connections and of eliminating the useless ones. Each interference node consists of a small A-type network containing three neurons that, depending on the initial states, may: (*i*) invert the input signal; (*ii*) interrupt the transmission of any information, forcing the output to "1" or (*iii*) alternately behave as described in (*i*) and (*ii*). In Figure 2, we display the representation adopted by Turing for a B-type connection, as well as the A-type network that constitutes the interference node, whereas Figure 3 exemplifies a B-type network.

Table 1. Update of the neuron state as a function of the inputs

$x_1(t)$	$x_2(t)$	$y(t+1)$
0	0	1
0	1	1
1	0	1
1	1	0

Figure 1. A-type network

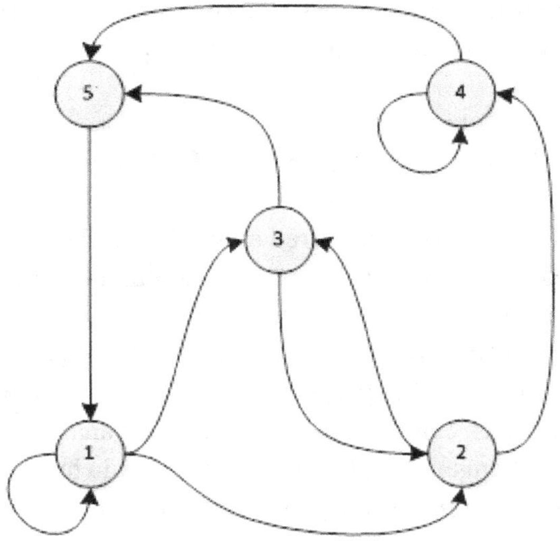

Apparently, B-type networks do not present significant modifications with respect to A-type machines. In fact, since the B-type link is, in essence, an A-type network, it is correct to state that all B-type networks are also A-type networks. However, Turing's motivation was to proceed towards more flexible structures that allowed some kind of training/adaptation to perform specific tasks.

In this context, B-type networks can be seen as an intermediate step: on the one hand, the organization of the connections still needs to be performed at the moment the network is conceived; on the other hand, it is possible to modify the network behavior by acting directly on the connections among the existing neurons.

Figure 2. B-type connection

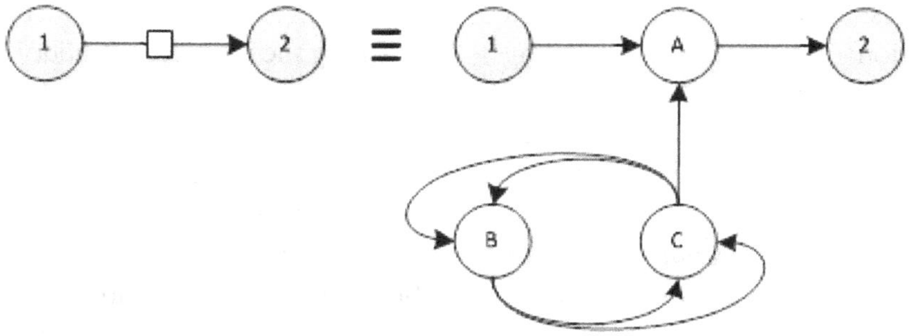

2.3. BI-Type Networks

Finally, Turing proposed a modification in the B-type connection structure through the insertion of two interference inputs i_1 and i_2, as shown in Figure 4.

This new class of unorganized machines, called BI-type networks by Teuscher (2001) ("I" stands for interference), offers the interesting perspective of adjusting the operation mode of each interference node by choosing the values of external input signals. Thus, the intention underlying the proposal of B-type networks becomes clearer: Turing's purpose was to construct a kind of switch formed by the same basic processing element - i.e., NAND neurons, - allowing for an external agent (teacher) to adapt its operation mode in order that the whole network achieve a desired behavior.

According to Turing, "*the cortex of an infant is an unorganised machine, which can be organised by suitable interfering training*" (Turing, 1968). In this sense, BI-type networks engender the process of education (training) that, according to Turing, was the responsible for organizing the human brain structure and enabling the learning of desired tasks, since these structures bring interference inputs that can be accessed and modified by an external agent.

Figure 3. B-type network

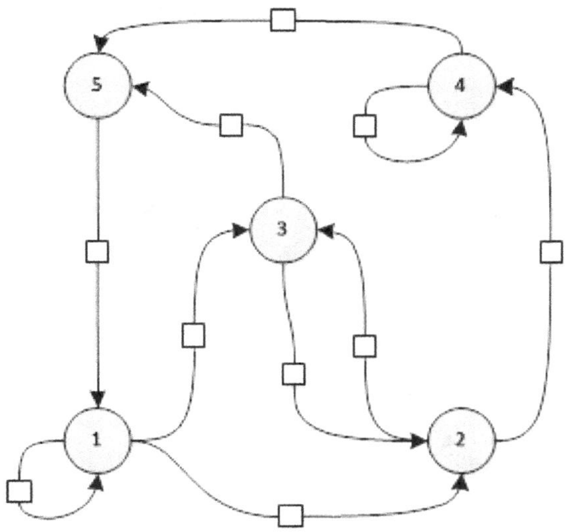

2.4. Discussion

In spite of their simplicity in terms of architecture and formulation, the unorganized machines proposed by Turing are capable of producing very

Figure 4. BI-type connection

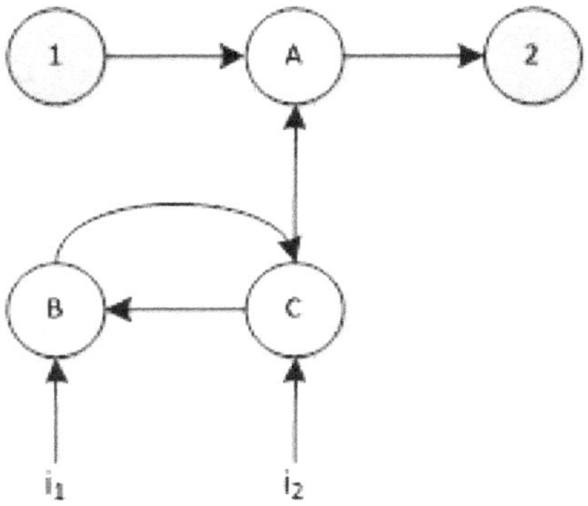

complex behaviors. Indeed, as remarked in Section 2.1, A-type networks can be used to implement any logical function (Teuscher, 2001). Turing also believed that, as occurs with A-type, B-type and BI-type networks could reproduce any logical function, thus being capable of implementing a universal machine with a truncated tape: "*In particular with a B-type unorganised machine with sufficient units one can find initial conditions which will make it into a universal machine with a given storage capacity*" (Turing, 1968).

Notwithstanding, as evinced in Copeland and Proudfoot (1996), Teuscher and Sanchez (2001), and Teuscher (2001), this claim is not correct. In fact, there are simple logical operations that cannot be implemented via B-type networks, such as the exclusive disjunction (XOR) of a pair of inputs.

Fortunately, with simple modifications in the B-type link, it is possible to solve this problem. As discussed in Copeland and Proudfoot (1996), Turing's claim concerning the computational power of B-type networks becomes true if the available operation modes of the interference node are interrupt and pass, instead of the original invert (also called interchange) mode. Then, the authors suggested the addition of another interference node in each connection, so that the new link can pass through the input signal or interrupt the transmission. Figure 5 illustrates the corresponding connection model.

A similar solution has been introduced by Teuscher (2001): to invert the input signal before reaching the interference node. This was accomplished by inserting another A-type neuron in the neural connection, as shown in Figure 6, which is functionally equivalent to the previous proposal, but simpler.

Last, but not least, *Intelligent Machinery* brought another innovative contribution: aiming to exemplify the organization process of an unorganized machine, Turing defined the so-called P-type machines, which can be seen as universal machines without a tape, and whose description is initially incomplete and random. These structures were then subject to pain and pleasure stimuli according to the decisions made and their description was progressively adapted based on the reward. In Turing's simple experiments, it is possible to notice an interesting conceptual link with the idea of reinforcement learning (Sutton & Barto, 1998).

Undoubtedly, *Intelligent Machinery* represents a breakthrough in the study of machine learning, discussing and developing important concepts in the field of artificial intelligence, neuroscience and philosophy of mind that were well ahead of its time. We will illustrate this assertion following a course different from that of the crucial efforts of Copeland, Proudfoot, Teuscher, and others, in that our emphasis will be on the points of contact between Turing's ideas and modern unorganized

Figure 5. Copeland's and Proudfoot's proposal

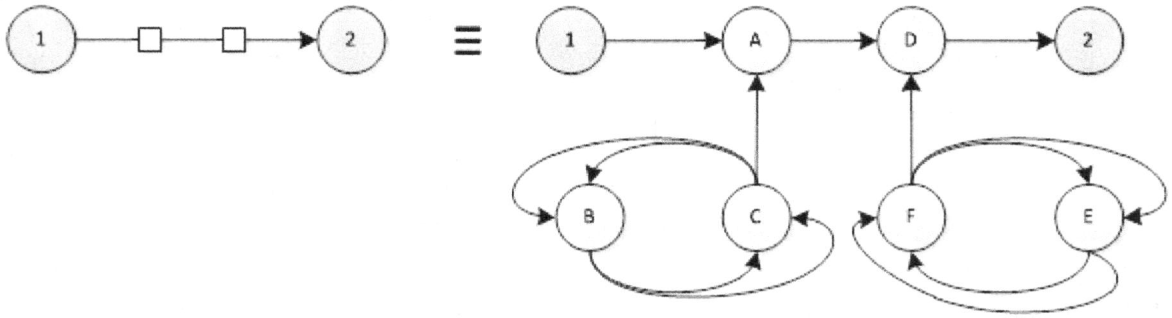

Figure 6. (a) TB-Type Connection and (b) TBI-Type Connection

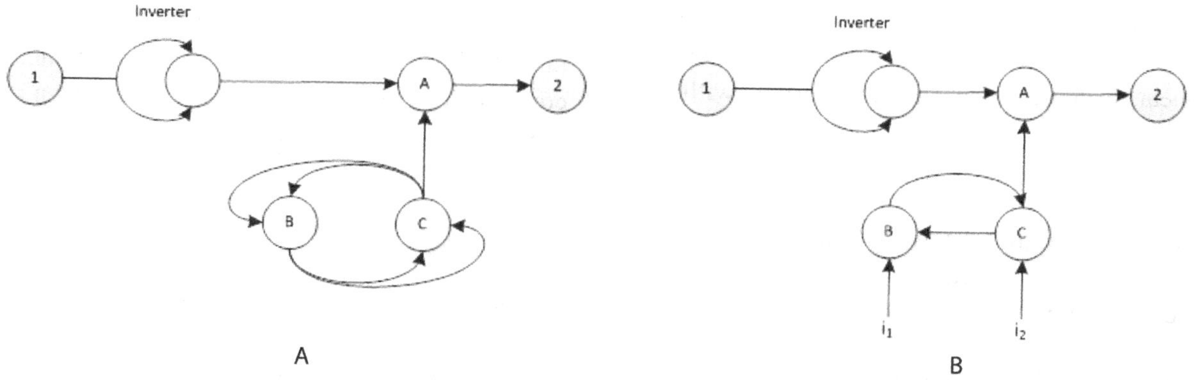

connectionist approaches – particularly reservoir computing (RC) and extreme learning machines (ELMs). The fundamentals of these two approaches will be discussed in the following.

3. RESERVOIR COMPUTING

Recurrent neural networks (RNNs) can be regarded as powerful computational tools for solving complex and dynamic problems by virtue of: (1) the presence of feedback connections, which enables the development of an internal memory that captures the time history of the input signals; and (2) the nonlinear character of the processing elements, which offers flexibility of creating a vast range of nonlinear mappings. In fact, these structures present the universal approximation property, as shown in Funahashi and Nakamura (1993), and reveal important conceptual associations with the idea of universal Turing machines (Kilian & Siegelmann, 1996).

The effective use of RNNs nonetheless requires the adaptation of all connection weights, including those associated with the recurrent links, which, within a supervised learning framework, brings certain well-known difficulties. For instance, calculating the gradient of the error function becomes a computationally expensive task due to the feedback loops. Other common obstacles involve slow convergence rates and instability of both the training process and the network operation.

In this context, echo state networks (ESNs), proposed by Jaeger (2001), and liquid state machines (LSMs), proposed by Maass, Natschläger, and Markram (2002), offer a creative solution to this dilemma and establish a new recurrent neural network training paradigm known as reservoir computing (RC) (Verstraeten, Schrauwen, D'Haene, & Stroodbandt, 2007; Lukosevicius & Jaeger, 2009).

The standard RC architecture consists of: (*i*) a highly interconnected and recurrent network of nonlinear processing elements, called dynamical reservoir (or "liquid," in the usual LSM nomenclature), which is capable of preserving information about the history of the input signals; (*ii*) an adaptive linear readout, which is responsible for combining the reservoir signals in order to approximate the desired outputs.

The attractive feature of the RC approaches lies in the possibility of preserving, to a certain extent, the processing capability inherent to a recurrent structure without incurring in the aforementioned drawbacks associated with the RNN training process. These objectives are elegantly achieved by defining the reservoir connection weights without resorting to any information concerning the desired task, fixing their values according to some predefined criterion. Hence, the overall training process consists in adapting the coefficients of the linear readout, which can be performed with the aid of linear regression methods (Lukosevicius & Jaeger, 2009).

Figure 7 exhibits the basic RC architecture, as well as highlights the fact that the adaptation process employing an error signal is confined to the free parameters of the output layer.

3.1. Echo State Networks

Consider a discrete-time RNN structure, as displayed in Figure 7, with K inputs, N internal units and L outputs. The reservoir input stimuli are grouped in vector $\mathbf{u}(n) = [u_1(n) \ \ldots \ u_K(n)]^T$, whereas the reservoir state is represented by $\mathbf{x}(n) = [x_1(n) \ \ldots \ x_N(n)]^T$ and is updated according to the following expression:

$$\mathbf{x}(n+1) = \mathbf{f}(\mathbf{W}^{in}\mathbf{u}(n+1) + \mathbf{W}\mathbf{x}(n) + \mathbf{W}^{back}\mathbf{y}(n)), \quad (2)$$

where $\mathbf{W}^{in}$, $\mathbf{W}$ and $\mathbf{W}^{back}$ denote the input, the internal recurrent and the output feedback connection weights, respectively, and $\mathbf{f}(\cdot) = (f_1(\cdot) \ \ldots \ f_N(\cdot))$ specifies the activation functions of the internal units. The vector $\mathbf{y}(n) = [y_1(n) \ \ldots \ y_L(n)]^T$ contains the network outputs, which are determined by means of linear combinations of the reservoir states, as shown in the following expression:

$$\mathbf{y}(n+1) = \mathbf{W}^{out}\mathbf{x}(n+1), (3)$$

where $\mathbf{W}^{out}$ is the output weight matrix.

In his seminal work, Jaeger conceived an important conceptual element – the echo state property – which establishes that the reservoir states tend to reflect the recent history of the input signals as long as the reservoir weight matrix W satisfies specific spectral conditions (Jaeger, 2001). This useful property allows the process of designing the ESN reservoir to be performed independently and previously to the network training, since the emergence of an effective memory of the input history is ensured, so that the weights of the recurrent connections can be arbitrarily assigned and remain fixed. Consequently, only the readout parameters are effectively trained with the aid of an error signal, and, due to its linear character, this task essentially involves a least-squares solution.

However, in order that the network performs satisfactorily, the reservoir should offer a sufficiently rich and diverse repertoire of dynamical

Figure 7. RC architecture and training process

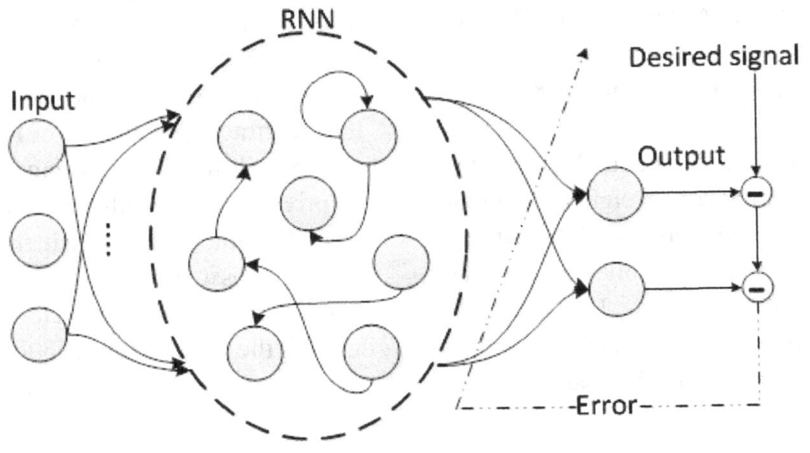

behaviors to the adaptive readout. Having these aspects in mind, Jaeger proposed a simple strategy: to create a random and sparse weight matrix W (Jaeger, 2001). The sparse nature of such matrix aims to decouple groups of neurons, contributing to the emergence of individual dynamical behaviors.

Since their proposal, echo state networks have been applied in a myriad of important problems, such as system identification (Jaeger, 2003), time series prediction (Jaeger & Hass, 2004; Sacchi, Ozturk, Principe, Cameiro, & da Silva, 2007; Verplancke et al., 2010), and channel equalization (Boccato, Lopes, Attux, & Von Zuben, 2011), and the obtained results were very promising. Nonetheless, the research field is still in its infancy, and different possibilities to improve the original paradigms are being constantly investigated. In particular, several works were devoted to the study and development of different schemes for the reservoir design which, in a certain sense, seek to increase the diversity and the quality of the dynamical behaviors originated in the recurrent layer, like (Ozturk, Xu, & Principe, 2007; Schrauwen, Wardermann, Verstraeten, Steil, & Stroodbandt, 2008; Boedecker, Obst, Mayer, & Asada, 2009). In addition to this perspective, other works (Butcher, Verstraeten, Schrauwen, Day, & Haycock, 2010; Boccato, Lopes, Attux, & Von Zuben, 2011; Boccato, Lopes, Attux, & Von Zuben, 2012), have focused on proposing new readout structures with the purpose of achieving a more effective use of the signals coming from the reservoir. These, along with practical applications, are essentially the mainstream research lines involving echo state networks.

3.2. Liquid State Machines

Independently of and simultaneously to the development of ESNs, a similar reservoir computing paradigm called liquid state machine (LSM) has emerged within a conceptual framework closer to neuroscience, aiming to study some computational abilities of the brain. This architecture, as originally proposed by Maass, Natschläger, and Markram (2002), relies on a computational model that maps input time functions (given by streams of numbers or bits) in output streams (Maass, 2007) - which is done by a special filter with fading memory - and a readout stage as previously shown in Figure 7.

The filter is related to dynamical systems that define the reservoir and the term "liquid" is justified by the dynamical patterns associated with the reservoir response to an external input. In contrast with ESNs, a LSM has its reservoir based on more realistic models of neurons, which provides a promising basis for generating a multidimensional higher-order state space for suitably performing generic computational tasks. Naturally, the computational power of a LSM will depend on how the liquid properties match the computational problem to be solved, something that is proved in rigorous mathematical terms in Maass, Natschläger, and Markram (2002), giving rise to what Maass (2007) calls separation and approximation properties for LSMs. In consonance with the rationale of reservoir computing, the "liquid" also exhibits a sparse connection between neurons (Maass, Natschläger, & Markram, 2004) that evokes Turing's connectionist formulations as described in Section 2. Moreover, the LSM paradigm establishes an important connection between unorganized network theory and some structural aspects of biological networks, as those identified by Yamazaki and Tanaka (2007) in the context of cerebellum organization and computational properties.

4. EXTREME LEARNING MACHINES

Feedforward neural networks (FNNs) have been extensively used in the context of information processing, especially because of their attractive capability of universal approximation of nonlinear input-output mappings (Haykin, 1998). As occurs with RNNs, it is necessary to adapt all connection weights in order that the network presents an adequate behavior, which has been typically carried out with the aid of learning algorithms based on classical nonlinear optimization techniques (Luenberger, 2003).

Although the absence of feedback connections simplifies the computation of the derivatives of the error function, there still remain certain difficulties, especially for practical real-time applications, due to slow convergence and costly hardware implementation of the usual training algorithms. In this context, extreme learning machines (ELMs) (Huang, Zhu, & Siew, 2004, 2006) represent an interesting alternative to circumvent these limitations. The proposed solution to accelerate the training process of single-hidden layer feedforward neural networks consists in randomly assigning the parameters – connection weights and bias – of the hidden neurons, which means that only the coefficients of the linear output layer are effectively adapted according to an error signal.

By relinquishing the adaptation of the hidden layer parameters, the network training process is converted into finding the optimum coefficients of the output linear combiner, which can be easily solved with the aid of linear regression methods. Hence, ELMs avoid the backpropagation of an error signal and the use of iterative methods (Haykin, 1998), as well as the possibility of convergence to local minima, which represents an improvement in terms of training simplicity and efficiency at the expense of a loss of structural generality.

This creative approach receives important theoretical support from a rigorous proof which demonstrates that, for FNNs with a single hidden layer, under certain conditions, it is not imperative to adapt the intermediate neuron parameters if the activation functions of the hidden nodes are infinitely differentiable (Huang, Zhu, & Siew, 2006). Moreover, there are interesting evidences that associate the use of the Moore-Penrose generalized inverse to compute the least-squares solution of the output weights with a potential improvement in the network generalization capability (Bartlett, 1998; Huang, Zhu, & Siew, 2006).

It is possible to notice the strong resemblance between the key ideas underlying ELMs and RC approaches: in both cases, the internal neural structures – the dynamical reservoir and the hidden layer - are not subject to adaptation, being the training process strictly focused on the linear combiner at the output. Indeed, we may even consider ELMs as a feedforward counterpart to echo state networks. As a consequence, the mathematical description of ELMs is quite similar to that of ESNs, and Equations 2 and 3 remain valid, with the caveat that W and $\mathbf{W}^{back}$ must be set to zero as ELMs do not possess recurrent connections. Figure 8 displays the basic ELM architecture.

The impressive results obtained with ELMs in applications involving time series prediction and pattern classification have encouraged further investigations of this new approach, and recent efforts led to the development of extended versions of ELMs, such as online sequential ELMs (Liang, Huang, Saratchandran, & Sundararajan, 2006; Huang, Wang, & Lan, 2011), fully complex ELMs (Li, Huang, Saratchandran, & Sundararajan, 2005; Huang, Li, Chen, & Siew, 2008; Huang, Wang, & Lan, 2011), incremental ELMs (Huang, Chen, & Siew, 2006; Huang & Chen, 2007; Huang & Chen, 2008; Huang, Wang, & Lan, 2011) and kernel-based ELMs (Frénay & Verleysen, 2011; Huang, Zhou, Ding, & Zhang, 2012). For more details on state-of-art ELMs, we refer the reader to the survey of G.-B. Huang et al., (2011).

5. REFLECTIONS ON THE POINTS OF CONTACT BETWEEN TURING'S NETWORKS AND MODERN UNORGANIZED MACHINES

The exposition provided in Sections 3 and 4 revealed the conceptual and motivational similarities between reservoir computing approaches and extreme learning machines. Both proposals

Figure 8. ELM architecture and training process

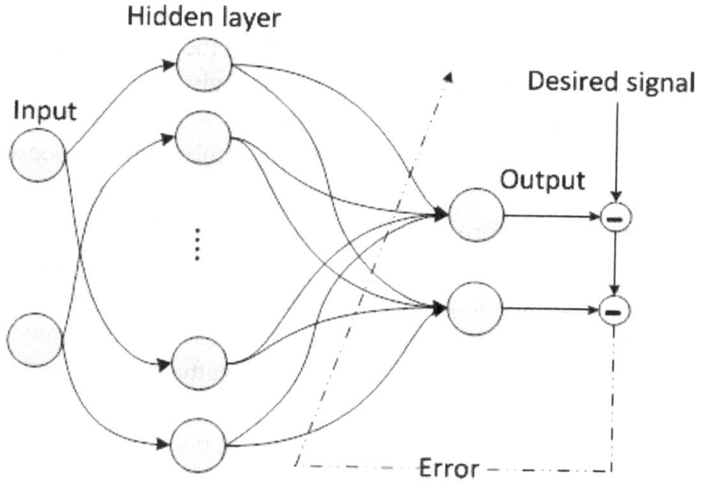

are characterized by the use of untrained layers of neurons whose activations are combined by a linear readout, which leads to significant advantages in terms of tractability and simplicity of the adaptation process.

Interestingly, these approaches also converge in the sense that they evoke the idea of "disorganization", a biological aspect that was taken into account in early works about neural networks, like (Rosenblatt, 1958) and, as will be discussed in more detail, in (Turing, 1968), under the guise of structures like random reservoir/hidden layer. In fact, since the reservoir (liquid or hidden layer), is not subject to training, there will always be a part of the RC and ELM structures that remains essentially unorganized.

We are now in an adequate position to present in a systematic way that which we consider to be the main contribution of this paper: an analysis of the points of contact between Turing's pioneering views on connectionism and the *modus operandi* of modern unorganized machines. We use the expression "in a systematic way" because we believe that the main aspects of this analysis have been outlined in previous sections, which faces us essentially with the task of producing a synthesis.

The most important aspect to be highlighted is the noticeable similarity between the structure of Turing's Boolean networks and reservoir computing methods. This similarity is of a twofold nature, referring to the existence of a recurrent layer with neurons whose connection pattern is not defined in a supervised fashion that can be complemented by specific elements devised to incorporate the information brought by a reference signal/response.

It should be kept in mind that, in spite of this similarity, the motivation underlying the two sets of proposals is fundamentally different. Turing, as discussed in Section 2, reached an unorganized architecture by reflecting on the process of development of the human nervous system from embryogenesis to children education. On the other hand, the RC and ELM paradigms are derived from considerations of a more practical nature, which arise from viewing neural networks as function/dynamical system approximators and seeking a good compromise insofar as the training process is concerned. It is important to mention, by the way, that the latter standpoint has been dominant in the field of neural networks as a consequence of the renaissance of the field in the 1980s, which naturally led to a certain emphasis on optimization, model selection and statistics. Turing's work, in this context, becomes crucial, as it provides the neural network research program with an opportunity to "come full circle" and "harmonize" itself with the natural computing standpoint from which it arose.

As for the need for converting the information processed by the unorganized network of neurons, it took different shapes in Turing's work and in modern machines. This is due to the nature of the involved signals: Turing dealt with Boolean sequences, whereas RC and ELMs can rely on classical least squares methods that suit quite well real (and also complex) numbers. It should also be kept in mind that we live in a world in which computational resources are vastly available, which offers possibilities of developing, with the aid of simulations, stochastic training approaches that Turing never had the chance of testing. This makes his contribution more impressive, as the fundamental duality between disorganization and supervision was completely fathomed by him, and, moreover, his solutions to deal with it were quite ingenious.

A point for potential cross-fertilization seems to be the perspective of modifying Turing's network to generate a Boolean version of an echo state network, and, perhaps, to find a potential equivalent to the echo state property (Jaeger, 2001). This could be of immense value to the simplification of system modeling under finite alphabets, which typically gives rise to combinatorial optimization problems. It would also be a relevant contribution to signal processing in the context of finite fields (Gutch, Gruber, Yeredor, & Theis, 2012), a research field that may bring important contributions to applications ranging from channel coding to genomic data analysis.

In addition to what has been discussed so far, it is important to remark that certain recent achievements of complex system theory and neuroscience also present interesting similarities with the essential aspects of Turing's connectionist proposal. For instance, the recent transposition of graph theory to the anatomic study of cerebral connectivity (Scannell, Burns, Hilgetag, O'Neil, & Young, 1999) has highlighted features like: (1) segregated information processing regions working in parallel; (2) a dense connective structure between neurons in each segregated processing region; and (3) a relative low number of sparse connections between different dedicated processing regions in order to build a distributed processing apparatus. These features might indicate the possibility that groups of neurons connected according to complex patterns be, in a certain sense, responsible for delivering "pre-processed" information to a more controlled layer responsible for higher level data fusion/processing, evoking the basic structures discussed in Sections 2 through 4.

It is our genuine belief that the fact that Turing's views, built in the early infancy of neural networks, show such intimate connections with the fundamental aspects of modern unorganized machines is a tribute to his ability to detect the essential factors underlying information processing, as well as a clear invitation to neural network researches to revisit with a fresh spirit the legacy of "founding fathers" like him.

6. CONCLUSION

In this work, we presented a review of Turing's ideas on connectionist computing devices, and also discussed the basic elements of modern unorganized machines, like reservoir computing methodologies and extreme learning machines. During this exposition and in an specific section, we attempted to highlight the many conceptual points of contact between these two research programs, having in view two aims: (*i*) to make a contribution, in the centenary of his birth, to a more precise evaluation of Alan Turing's profound views on computational intelligence; (*ii*) to indicate concrete possibilities of original developments brought by these views, which exhale, more than sixty years later, the unmistakable *fraîcheur* of a brilliant mind that deserves to be ranked among the most original mankind has ever produced.

Perhaps it is suitable – if not inevitable – to conclude this work with a paraphrase of the words attributed to the Marquis de Laplace: "Lisez Turing, lisez Turing, c'est notre maître à tous."[2]

ACKNOWLEDGMENT

The authors would like to thank FAPESP and CNPq for the financial support.

REFERENCES

Bartlett, P. L. (1998). The sample complexity of pattern classification with neural networks: The size of the weights is more important than the size of the network. *IEEE Transactions on Information Theory*, *44*(2), 525–536. doi:10.1109/18.661502.

Boccato, L., Lopes, A., Attux, R., & Von Zuben, F. J. (2011). An echo state network architecture based on Volterra filtering and PCA with application to the channel equalization problem. In *Proceedings of the International Joint Conference on Neural Networks* (pp. 580-587).

Boccato, L., Lopes, A., Attux, R., & Von Zuben, F. J. (2012). An extended echo state network using volterra filtering and principal component analysis. *Neural Networks*, *32*, 292–302. doi:10.1016/j.neunet.2012.02.028.

Boedecker, J., Obst, O., Mayer, N. M., & Asada, M. (2009). Initialization and self-organized optimization of recurrent neural network connectivity. *HFSP Journal*, *3*(5), 340–349. doi:10.2976/1.3240502.

Butcher, J., Verstraeten, D., Schrauwen, B., Day, C., & Haycock, P. (2010). Extending reservoir computing with random static projections: A hybrid between extreme learning and RC. In *Proceedings of the 18th European Symposium on Artificial Neural Networks* (pp. 303-308).

Copeland, B. J. (2004). *The essential Turing*. Oxford, UK: Oxford University Press.

Copeland, B. J., & Proudfoot, D. (1996). On Alan Turing's anticipation of connectionism. *Synthese*, *108*, 361–377. doi:10.1007/BF00413694.

Copeland, B. J., & Proudfoot, D. (1999). Alan Turing's forgotten ideas in computer science. *Scientific American*, *280*(4), 77–81. doi:10.1038/scientificamerican0499-98.

Epstein, R., & Carnielli, W. A. (2008). *Computability: Computable functions, logic and the foundations of mathematics* (3rd ed.). Socorro, NM: Advanced Reasoning Forum.

Ercegovac, M. D., Lang, T., & Moreno, J. H. (1998). *Introduction to digital systems*. New York, NY: John Wiley & Sons.

Frénay, B., & Verleysen, M. (2011). Parameter-insensitive Kernel in extreme learning for non-linear support vector regression. *Neurocomputing*, *74*(16), 2526–2531. doi:10.1016/j.neucom.2010.11.037.

Funahashi, K.-I., & Nakamura, Y. (1993). Approximation of dynamical systems by continuous time recurrent neural networks. *Neural Networks*, *6*(6), 801–806. doi:10.1016/S0893-6080(05)80125-X.

Gutch, H. W., Gruber, P., Yeredor, A., & Theis, F. J. (2012). ICA over finite fields - Separability and algorithms. *Signal Processing*, *92*(8), 1796–1808. doi:10.1016/j.sigpro.2011.10.003.

Hawking, S. (2007). *God created the integers*. New York, NY: Running Press.

Haykin, S. (1998). *Neural networks: A comprehensive foundation*. Upper Saddle River, NJ: Prentice Hall.

Hodges, A. (1992). *Alan Turing: The enigma*. New York, NY: Vintage.

Holland, J. (1975). *Adaptation in natural and artificial systems*. Ann Arbor, MI: University of Michigan Press.

Huang, G.-B., & Chen, L. (2007). Convex incremental extreme learning machine. *Neurocomputing*, *70*(16-18), 3056–3062. doi:10.1016/j.neucom.2007.02.009.

Huang, G.-B., & Chen, L. (2008). Enhanced random search based incremental extreme learning machine. *Neurocomputing*, *71*(16-18), 3460–3468. doi:10.1016/j.neucom.2007.10.008.

Huang, G.-B., Chen, L., & Siew, C.-K. (2006). Universal approximation using incremental constructive feedforward networks with random hidden nodes. *IEEE Transactions on Neural Networks*, *17*(4), 879–892. doi:10.1109/TNN.2006.875977.

Huang, G.-B., Li, M.-B., Chen, L., & Siew, C.-K. (2008). Incremental extreme learning machine with fully complex hidden nodes. *Neurocomputing*, *71*(4-6), 576–583. doi:10.1016/j.neucom.2007.07.025.

Huang, G.-B., Wang, D. H., & Lan, Y. (2011). Extreme learning machines: A survey. *International Journal of Machine Learning and Cybernetics*, *2*(2), 107–122. doi:10.1007/s13042-011-0019-y.

Huang, G.-B., Zhou, H., Ding, X., & Zhang, R. (2012). Extreme learning machine for regression and multiclass classification. *IEEE Transactions on Systems, Man, and Cybernetics. Part B, Cybernetics*, *42*(2), 513–529. doi:10.1109/TSMCB.2011.2168604.

Huang, G.-B., Zhu, Q.-Y., & Siew, C.-K. (2004). Extreme learning machine: A new learning scheme of feedforward neural networks. In *Proceedings of the International Joint Conference on Neural Networks* (pp. 985-990).

Huang, G.-B., Zhu, Q.-Y., & Siew, C.-K. (2006). Extreme learning machine: Theory and applications. *Neurocomputing*, *70*(1-3), 489–501. doi:10.1016/j.neucom.2005.12.126.

Jaeger, H. (2001). *The echo state approach to analyzing and training recurrent neural networks* (GMD Report No. 148). St. Augustin, Germany: German National Research Center for Information Technology.

Jaeger, H. (2003). Adaptive nonlinear system identification with echo state networks. In *Proceedings of the Conference on Advances in Neural Information Processing Systems* (pp. 593-600).

Jaeger, H., & Hass, H. (2004). Harnessing nonlinearity: Predicting chaotic systems and saving energy in wireless communication. *Science*, *304*(5667), 78–80. doi:10.1126/science.1091277.

Kilian, J., & Siegelmann, H. (1996). The dynamic universality of sigmoidal neural networks. *Information and Computation*, *128*(1), 48–56. doi:10.1006/inco.1996.0062.

Leavitt, D. (2006). *The man who knew too much: Alan Turing and the invention of the computer*. New York, NY: W. W. Norton.

Li, M.-B., Huang, G.-B., Saratchandran, P., & Sundararajan, N. (2005). Fully complex extreme learning machine. *Neurocomputing*, *68*, 306–314. doi:10.1016/j.neucom.2005.03.002.

Liang, N.-Y., Huang, G.-B., Saratchandran, P., & Sundararajan, N. (2006). A fast and accurate on-line sequential learning algorithm for feedforward networks. *IEEE Transactions on Neural Networks*, *17*(6), 1411–1423. doi:10.1109/TNN.2006.880583.

Luenberger, D. G. (2003). *Linear and nonlinear programming* (2nd ed.). New York, NY: Springer.

Lukosevicius, M., & Jaeger, H. (2009). Reservoir computing approaches to recurrent neural network training. *Computer Science Review, 3*(3), 127–149. doi:10.1016/j.cosrev.2009.03.005.

Maass, W. (2007). Liquid computing. In S. B. Cooper, B. Löwe, & A. Sorbi (Eds.), *Proceedings of the Third International Conference on Computation and Logic in the Real World* (LNCS 4497, pp. 507-516).

Maass, W., Natschläger, T., & Markram, H. (2002). Real-time computing without stable states: A new framework for neural computation based on perturbations. *Neural Computation, 14*(11), 2531–2560. doi:10.1162/089976602760407955.

Maass, W., Natschläger, T., & Markram, H. (2004). Fading memory and kernel properties of generic cortical microcircuit models. *Journal of Physiology, Paris, 98*(4-6), 315–330. doi:10.1016/j.jphysparis.2005.09.020.

McCulloch, W., & Pitts, W. (1943). A logical calculus of the ideas immanent in nervous activity. *The Bulletin of Mathematical Biophysics, 5*(4), 115–133. doi:10.1007/BF02478259.

Ozturk, M. C., Xu, D., & Principe, J. C. (2007). Analysis and design of echo state networks. *Neural Computation, 19*(1), 111–138. doi:10.1162/neco.2007.19.1.111.

Rosenblatt, F. (1958). The perceptron: A probabilistic model for information storage and organization in the brain. *Psychological Review, 65*(6), 386–408. doi:10.1037/h0042519.

Russell, S., & Norvig, P. (2009). *Artificial intelligence: A modern approach*. Upper Saddle River, NJ: Prentice Hall.

Sacchi, R., Ozturk, M. C., Principe, J. C., Carneiro, A. A., & da Silva, I. N. (2007). Water inflow forecasting using echo state network: A Brazilian case study. In *Proceedings of the International Joint Conference on Neural Networks* (pp. 2403-2408).

Scannell, J. W., Burns, G. A., Hilgetag, C. C., O'Neil, M. A., & Young, M. P. (1999). The connectional organization of the cortico-thamalic system of the cat. *Cerebral Cortex, 9*(3), 277–299. doi:10.1093/cercor/9.3.277.

Schrauwen, B., Wardermann, M., Verstraeten, D., Steil, J. J., & Stroodbandt, D. (2008). Improving reservoirs using intrinsic plasticity. *Neurocomputing, 71*(7-9), 1159–1171. doi:10.1016/j.neucom.2007.12.020.

Schwefel, H.-P. (1981). *Numerical optimization of computer models*. New York, NY: John Wiley & Sons.

Sutton, R., & Barto, A. (1998). *Reinforcement learning*. Cambridge, MA: MIT Press.

Teuscher, C. (2001). *Turing's connectionism: An investigation of neural networks architectures*. New York, NY: Springer.

Teuscher, C., & Sanchez, E. (2001). A revival of Turing's forgotten connectionist ideas: Exploring unorganized machines. In *Proceedings of the Sixth Neural Computation and Psychology Workshop on Connectionist Models of Learning, Development and Evolution* (pp. 153-162).

Turing, A. M. (1936). On computable numbers, with an application to the entscheidungsproblem. *Proceedings of the London Mathematical Society, 42*, 230–265. doi:10.1112/plms/s2-42.1.230.

Turing, A. M. (1950). Computing machinery and intelligence. *Mind, 59*(236), 433–460. doi:10.1093/mind/LIX.236.433.

Turing, A. M. (1968). Intelligent machinery. In Evans, C. R., & Robertson, A. D. (Eds.), *Cybernetics: Key papers*. Baltimore, MD: University Park Press.

Verplancke, T., Van Looy, S., Steurbaut, K., Benoit, D., De Turck, F., De Moor, G., & Decruyenaere, J. (2010). A novel time series analysis approach for prediction of dialysis in critically ill patients using echo-state networks. *BMC Medical Informatics and Decision Making*, *10*(4).

Verstraeten, D., Schrauwen, B., D'Haene, M., & Stroodbandt, D. (2007). An experimental unification of reservoir computing methods. *Neural Networks*, *20*(3), 391–403. doi:10.1016/j.neunet.2007.04.003.

Yamazaki, T., & Tanaka, S. (2007). The cerebellum as a liquid state machine. *Neural Networks*, *20*(3), 290–297. doi:10.1016/j.neunet.2007.04.004.

ENDNOTES

1. Two examples that illustrate this assertion are the formal/mechanical embodiment of human calculation that is the *raison d'être* of a Turing machine (Turing, 1936) and Turing's interest in automated chess playing (Hodges, 1992).
2. The original reads "Lisez Euler, lisez Euler...," i.e., "Read Euler, read Euler..."

This work was previously published in the International Journal of Natural Computing Research (IJNCR), Volume 2, Issue 4, edited by Leandro Nunes de Castro, pp. 1-16, copyright 2011 by IGI Publishing (an imprint of IGI Global).

Chapter 16
The Grand Challenges in Natural Computing Research:
The Quest for a New Science

Leandro Nunes de Castro
Natural Computing Laboratory (LCoN), Mackenzie University, Brazil

Renato Dourado Maia
State University of Montes Claros, Brazil

Rafael Silveira Xavier
Natural Computing Laboratory (LCoN), Mackenzie University, Brazil

Alexandre Szabo
Natural Computing Laboratory (LCoN), Mackenzie University, Brazil

Rodrigo Pasti
Laboratory of Bioinformatics and Bio-Inspired Computing (LBiC), State University of Campinas (UNICAMP), Brazil

Daniel Gomes Ferrari
Natural Computing Laboratory (LCoN), Mackenzie University, Brazil

ABSTRACT

An important premise of Natural Computing is that some form of computation goes on in Nature, and that computing capability has to be understood, modeled, abstracted, and used for different objectives and in different contexts. Therefore, it is necessary to propose a new language capable of describing and allowing the comprehension of natural systems as a union of computing phenomena, bringing an information processing perspective to Nature. To develop this new language and convert Natural Computing into a new science it is imperative to overcome three specific Grand Challenges in Natural Computing Research: Transforming Natural Computing into a Transdisciplinary Discipline, Unveiling and Harnessing Information Processing in Natural Systems, Engineering Natural Computing Systems.

DOI: 10.4018/978-1-4666-4253-9.ch016

1. COMPUTING: YESTERDAY, TODAY, AND TOMORROW

The history of *computing* is much longer than the history of the *Computer Science* discipline. Whilst computing is related with the representation of numbers and can be traced back to even earlier than mathematical concepts, Computer Science, as we understand it today, is more related with the computer hardware, software and technology. Since Computer Science appeared formally in the 1940s it has been alternating its focus of attention (Denning, 2008):

- **1940s:** Study of automatic computing;
- **1950s:** Study of information processing;
- **1960s:** Study of phenomena surrounding computers;
- **1970s:** Study of what can be automated;
- **1980s:** Study of computation;
- **2000s:** Study of information processes, both natural and artificial.

From the early days of computer science, by the 1940s, researchers have been interested in tracing parallels and designing computational models and abstractions of natural phenomena. A pioneer example in this direction was the work performed by McCulloch and Pitts (1943), in which they proposed a logical model of how neurons process information. With the advent of computers, this type of research became even broader and deeper. New, interdisciplinary areas of investigation emerged based on efforts combining a natural science, e.g., Biology, Physics and Chemistry, with Computing. Examples include the Artificial Neural Networks, Evolutionary Algorithms, Artificial Immune Systems, and many others.

Not so long ago these research fields existed by themselves in a disconnected fashion, but by the early to mid 2000, the first volume of the pioneer Natural Computing journal was released (Rozenberg, 2002) and the first textbook of the field was published (de Castro, 2006). With these initiatives, the field became more consistent and gained the status of discipline (de Castro, 2007; Kari & Rozenberg, 2008; Johnson, 2009; Rozenberg et al., 2012).

Computing promoted a revolution in all sciences and in our way of life. Its capability of automatically and quickly processing information gave birth to various solutions and discoveries, from genome sequencing to weather forecasting. Computing is now ubiquitous and the way we interact with computers is changing rapidly as well. People relate, check-in to places, talk, share data, etc., all via networked computers. Even the interface is changing, computers no longer need to have a physical keyboard and a mouse, they can be used to synthesize natural phenomena, to design algorithms for solving complex problems, and many other functions. It is now time to raise an important question:

1.1. What is the Future of Computing?

An exploration of such question in any science, beyond computing, gives rise to what can be called the Grand Challenges. The advancement of all areas, including computing, requires a deep thinking about its current status and what are the main challenges to be transposed, so that major breakthroughs can be achieved. Over the World, Grand Challenges have been discussed in areas such as Global Health (e.g., The Grand Challenges in Global Health – http://www.grandchallenges.org), but have received a lot of attention in Computer Science (e.g., the USA CRA Conference on Grand Research Challenges in Computer Science and Engineering – http://www.cra.org; the UK Grand Challenges in Computing Research – http://www.ukcrc.org.uk; and the Brazilian Grand Challenges in Computer Science – http://www.sbc.org.br).

The Grand Challenges aim at defining research questions that tend to be important for science and technology in the long term, identifying and characterizing potential grand research problems. These may allow the formulation of R&D projects capable of producing major scientific advancements, with practical applications for society and technology. For a theme to be considered a Grand Challenge it has to satisfy some premises, such as an emphasis in advancing science, a vision beyond specific projects, a clear and objective success evaluation, and it has to be ambitious and visionary. Examples of Grand Challenges in Computing include the management of information in massive volumes of distributed, multimedia data, the computational modeling of complex systems, an investigation into the impact of the transition from silicon to other technologies, a more participatory and universal access to knowledge and information, and a high quality technology development (http://www.sbc.org.br).

The discussion addressed in this paper is more related to the *Grand Challenges in Natural Computing Research* than to specific topics within the field. This is primarily motivated by two perceptions. Over the past years, an uncountable number of natural computing approaches, for instance, algorithms based on immune systems, evolutionary biology, insect swarms many others, have been proposed (de Castro, 2007; Kari & Rozenberg, 2008; Johnson, 2009; Masulli & Mitra, 2009; Parpinelli & Lopes, 2011; Rozenberg et al., 2012). Computer Science by itself is changing rapidly, also influenced by the Natural Computing contributions. Therefore, and bearing in mind the focus on Natural Computing of this work, the previous question can be narrowed down to:

1.2. What is the Future of Natural Computing?

Before trying to answer this particular question, there is a more fundamental one to be discussed: What is computing? There have been tentative answers to this question in various contexts and, thus, computing is leaving the Computer Science domain to broader perspectives. During the 1930s, Gödel (1934), Church (1936), Post (1936), and Turing (1937) independently provided the first definitions of computing. Despite these and several other efforts, including some very recent ones, to define computing and computation (e.g., computation as symbol manipulation (Conery, 2010), computation as a process (Frailey, 2010), and computation as a physical process (Deutsch, 2012)) the question of what is computation, such as questions like "what is life?" and "what is intelligence?" is one that may never have a satisfactory, globally accepted, answer, because new discoveries and maturing understandings always result in novel insights and perspectives (Denning, 2010). For now, we are going to assume these more contemporary views that some form of computation goes on in Nature (Ballard, 1997; Brent & Buck, 2006; de Castro, 2006; Denning, 2007; Cohen, 2009; Schwenk et al., 2009; Crnkovic, 2010, 2011a; Gelende, 2011; Mitchel, 2011; Penrose, 2012; Zenil, 2012a, 2012b), and this will influence in a higher or lower level the discipline that came to be known as Natural Computing.

A straightforward, though, important conclusion is that computing is not a human invention; it already exists in the Universe and is responsible for its very origin (Zenil, 2012). Thus, there is natural and artificial computing. And artificial computing makes use of Nature itself to work, but in a way that is manipulated by humans. The hypothesis, thus, becomes "Is Computer Science a Natural Science?" (Denning, 2007; Mitchel, 2011). This hypothesis raises another question "Why studying natural systems and what are the advantages and benefits of this study?" At least one biased answer to this question becomes clearer with the maturation of Natural Computing over the past decades. Transposing natural phenomena to computing and engineering makes it possible to solve challenging problems found in these and virtually any other area. In the opposite direction, computing may be of much use for the exploration of Nature.

This context paves the ground to present Natural Computing within a New Computing Paradigm. It is now time to move forward and start thinking about a New Science based on Natural Computing. To do so, it is necessary to have some further advancements in the field and, more importantly, to break some paradigms. These will be called here The Grand Challenges in Natural Computing Research.

This paper is organized as follows. Section 2 briefly reviews and extends the Natural Computing scope, and Section 3 introduces the Grand Challenges in Natural Computing Research. The work is concluded in Section 4 with a discussion of what has been proposed.

2. NATURAL COMPUTING REVISITED

Computing can be found in three different contexts within Natural Computing: complex problem solving, synthesis of natural phenomena, and computing with novel natural materials (de Castro, 2007). In all cases, a proper understanding of natural phenomena is the basis for new ideas and for the understanding of how computing is realized. Such understanding is often obtained through the use of computer modeling, for instance, planet dynamics (Cohen, 2000), immunology (Hart et al., 2007), chemical reaction networks (Bersini et al., 2006), bacteria (Xavier et al., 2011), species diversity (Gavrilets & Vose, 2005), among many others (e.g., Gotelli & Kelley, 1993; de Jong, 2002; Chen et al., 2003; Cohen & Harel, 2007; Bersini & Lenaerts, 2009; Cohen, 2009; de Aguiar et al., 2009). These models have become so important in the understanding of nature that a new natural computing branch is proposed here to incorporate the computer modeling of natural phenomena. Thus, natural computing can now be defined as (Figure 1):

Figure 1. Natural computing and its four branches

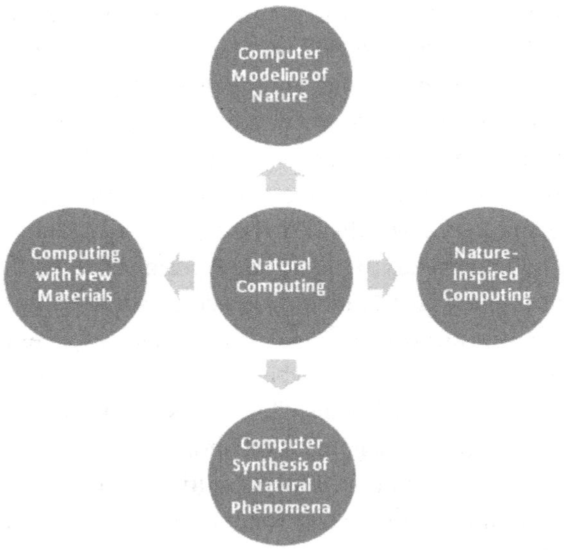

1. **Computer Modeling of Natural Phenomena:** This branch investigates natural phenomena by means of computer modeling;
2. **Computing Inspired by Nature:** It makes use of nature as inspiration for the development of problem solving techniques. The main idea of this branch is to develop computational tools (algorithms) by taking inspiration from nature for the solution of complex problems;
3. **Computational Synthesis of Natural Phenomena:** It is basically a synthetic process aimed at creating life-like patterns, forms, behaviors, and organisms. Its products can be used to mimic various natural phenomena, thus increasing our understanding of nature and insights about "life-as-we-know-it" and "life-as-it-could-be"; and
4. **Computing with Novel Natural Materials:** This branch focuses on the use of natural materials, different from silicon, to perform computation, thus constituting a true novel computing paradigm that comes to complement or supplement the current silicon-based computers.

An important premise of Natural Computing is that there is some form of computation or information processing going on in nature, and that computing capability can be understood, modeled, abstracted and used for different objectives and in different contexts. Therefore, it is necessary to propose a new language capable of describing and allowing the comprehension of natural systems as a union of computing phenomena, bringing an information processing perspective to nature. Key efforts in this direction include the works of Brent and Bruck (2006), Lloyd (2006), de Castro (2007), Denning (2007), Gelende (2011), Mitchel (2011), Deutsch (2012), Zenil (2012a, 2012b), and Crnkovic (2010, 2011a, 2011b). This introduces the following definition for Natural Computing:

Natural Computing is a Science Concerned with the Investigation and Design of Information Processing in Natural and Computational Systems: Based on Biology, Physics, Chemistry, Engineering and Computer Science, it emerges as a new science with transdisciplinary concepts aimed at understanding computing in nature and applying it in several different contexts, from a better comprehension of nature to the design of novel complex problem solving tools. This aim and scope gives rise to the *Grand Challenges in Natural Computing Research*.

3. THE GRAND CHALLENGES IN NATURAL COMPUTING RESEARCH

If one is to pursue the maturity of the field and a position that reflects its broadness of scope and applications, Natural Computing would necessarily become a New Science. To reach that maturity level, three specific Grand Challenges in Natural Computing Research will be detached: Transforming Natural Computing into a Transdisciplinary Discipline, Unveiling and Harnessing Information Processing in Natural Systems, Engineering Natural Computing Systems.

3.1. Transforming Natural Computing into a Transdisciplinary Discipline

As with all major research areas, Natural Computing is maturing. Its maturation can be seen in the disciplinary approaches (Jantsch, 1972): multi- and interdisciplinary, throughout time, from the past to the present and until the stage Natural Computing should be: *transdisciplinarity*. However, before delving into the need to transform Natural Computing into a transdisciplinary science, it is important to understand its multi- and interdisciplinary natures.

Multidisciplinarity, which refers to knowledge associated with more than one discipline, has been the basis for the proposal and existence of Natural Computing. The literature is permeated with Natural Computing works based on Biology, Physics, Chemistry and Computer Science. Algorithms inspired by how the immune system responds to pathogens, how evolution occurs in nature, how brains process information and how insects solve foraging and other problems form part of the core of the field. In all cases, knowledge specific from one field, for instance entomology, has to be acquired and used in conjunction with knowledge from another field (e.g., computer science) so that new algorithms are designed.

Interdisciplinarity, that is, new knowledge extensions between or beyond disciplines, or the combination of disciplines into a new single one, has also been part of the origins for Natural Computing. Artificial Neural Networks, Evolutionary Algorithms, Artificial Immune Systems, Swarm Intelligence, Artificial Life, Fractal Geometry, Molecular Computing and Quantum Computing are all interdisciplinary approaches by themselves that are part of Natural Computing. As a single discipline, it was formalized in 2006 (de Castro, 2006) with the publication of the first textbook of the field, though there were already some initiatives around the world concerning courses and journals dedicated to the subject. Thus, this new discipline borrowed concepts from the natural and computer sciences to introduce computing related to nature, incorporating several interdisciplinary proposals already available.

The next step in Natural Computing Research corresponds to the Grand Challenge proposed here: to reach the unicity of knowledge in a single language and, thus, formalize natural computing as a science that has as main goal to understand computing in natural phenomena and use it for diverse applications. As such, the fundamental sciences would come side by side with Natural Computing instead of simply be used as a basis to study it. The meaning and complexity of this challenge reside in the following question:

How to Transpose Natural Computing into a Transdisciplinary Context? To illustrate the role of natural computing and this Grand Challenge, Figure 2, Figure 3, and Figure 4 depicts how the inter-, multi- and transdisciplinarity maturation of Natural Computing has occurred.

Figure 2. Relationships among the various fundamental disciplines and natural computing. Natural computing uses ideas from biology, physics, chemistry and computer science in a multidisciplinary approach.

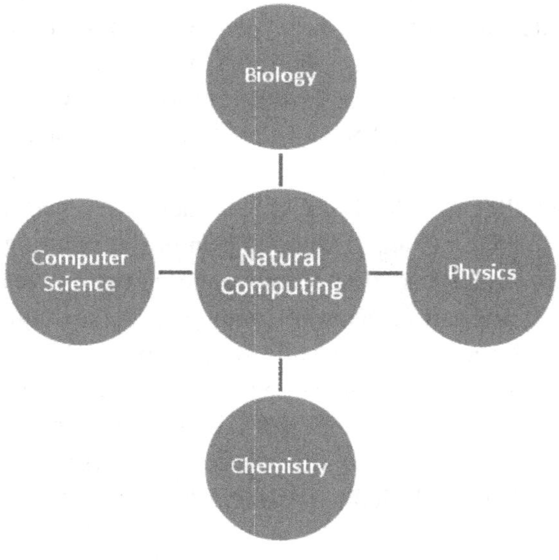

Figure 3. Relationships among the various fundamental disciplines and natural computing. Knowledge is exchanged among disciplines so as to promote natural computing.

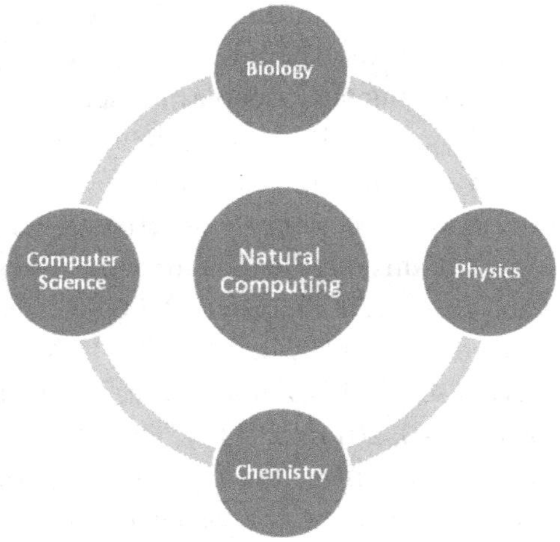

A *transdisciplinary* research requires the use of knowledge from two or more disciplines with a common goal: to create a more holistic, boundary-free, approach. Transdisciplinarity means that, instead of a collaboration of disciplines, it is a unicity of organized thinking that lies within a context beyond the individual disciplines themselves. The term, originally introduced by Jean Piaget in 1970 (Nicolescu, 2008), defines well the idea of what we are looking for, and can be assumed a core element in the Natural Computing concept as a new science, aggregating the proposition of a new language to the understanding of computing in natural phenomena.

Its fundamentals reside in the knowledge available from nature in Physics, Chemistry, Biology, Engineering and Computer Science. Under the transdisciplinary Natural Computing umbrella, Natural Computing is itself a Natural Science. The knowledge within Computer Science does not directly explain natural phenomena, but gives birth to the first steps towards the understanding of computing in nature (Brent & Bruck, 2006; Lloyd, 2006; de Castro, 2007; Denning, 2007; Gelende, 2011; Mitchel, 2011; Deutsch, 2012; Zenil, 2012a, 2012b; Crnkovic, 2010, 2011a, 2011b).

Figure 4. Relationships among the various fundamental disciplines and natural computing. A new science emerges uniting knowledge from various disciplines, resulting in a more holistic approach with no specific boundaries among disciplines.

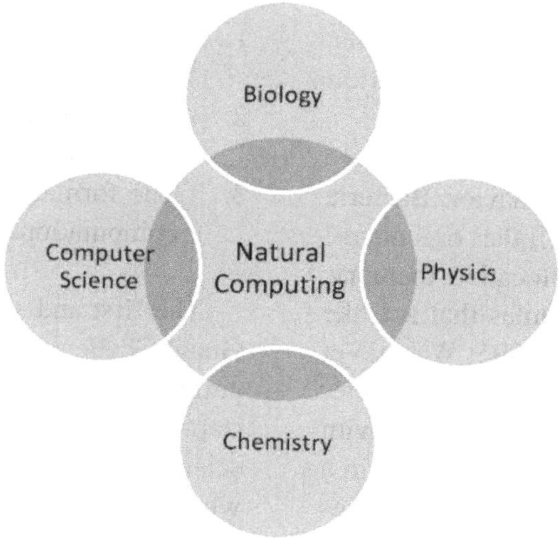

3.2. Unveiling and Harnessing Information Processing in Natural Systems

In 1983, Richard Feynman told his Caltech students: "Computer science differs from physics in that it is not actually a science. It does not study natural objects. Neither is it mathematics. It's like engineering – about getting to do something, rather than dealing with abstractions" (Feynman, 1996). This concept of Computer Science was consistent with how researchers from other fields understood computers and computing. However, some researchers saw computing as a natural science, for information processing had been observed in the realm of various phenomena, in different fields of investigation.

Nobel Laureate and Caltech President David Baltimore commented: "Biology is today an information science" (Denning, 2001). The classic definition of computing is becoming obsolete: computer science is increasing its scope to the study of natural and artificial information processes (Denning, 2007; Zenil, 2012a, 2012b). However, if computing is concerned with information processing, either natural or artificial, it is necessary to first answer the following question: What is information?

The word information comes from the Latin word *informare*, which means to give shape, mold, organize, but this is still an imprecise and conflicting definition. According to Floridi (2010), information is a powerful and elusive concept that can be associated with several explanations, depending on the goal. Lloyd (2006), by contrast, places a more pragmatic view of information as a measure of order, a universal measure applicable to any structure or system. Thus, information quantifies the instructions necessary for the production of an organization. This concept of information naturally leads to the perspective of Nature as an information processor: from a set of information one obtains, by means of processing, a different set of information.

Natural sciences research has, for long, described Nature based on informational events that occur in the Universe. Thus, one can suggest that these sciences are, in essence, particular languages continuously built to describe and understand information processing (Computing) that guides Natural Systems. Natural Sciences are, therefore, endowed with many languages to describe the same fundamental principles, to elucidate the same fundamental phenomenon: information processing – computing.

An example of computing going on in nature is related to bacteria colony behavior. Bacteria colonies behave like multicellular organisms, with cell differentiation, task allocation, memory, and, in some cases, even modules that act like reproduction organs (Shapiro, 1995; Wakano et al., 2003; Xavier et al., 2011). Thus, each bacterium must be able to sense and communicate with other units in the colony to perform its task in a coordinated manner. The cooperative activities carried out by members of the colony generate a social intelligence, which allows the colony to learn from their environment. In other words, bacterial intelligence depends on the interpretation of chemical messages and distinction between internal and external information. Thus, a colony can be viewed as a system that analyzes contextual information from its environment, generates new information and retrieves information from the past through a process in two levels:

1. The processing performed by a molecular network of individual bacteria, and
2. The processing of information carried out by the network of molecular communication that forms the colony and its interaction with the environment.

From a classical perspective of a computer system, based on Von Neumann's architecture, a colony of bacteria represents a computer system with memory and a control/processing unit with input-output processes. The main conceptual difference between the classical view and a bacteria colony is that in the latter processing occurs in distinct levels of abstractions, in a hierarchical and distributed manner.

This example, which presented in a basic form the information processing in a colony of bacteria, was built based on the following sequence of steps:

1. A proper understanding of the natural phenomenon;
2. The identification of the information processes of the natural phenomenon; and
3. The formalism of the natural system as a computational one.

The first and second steps are related to the Grand Challenge of consolidating Natural Computing as a transdisciplinary science: the first step requires a strong involvement with the basic science of the natural system under investigation, whilst the second step requires the observation of the natural system behavior under a computational perspective. The third step involves defining the computational architecture of the natural system. Altogether, these three steps represent one of the Grand Challenges in Natural Computing Research: to unveil and harness information processing in natural systems.

An important question has to be raised here: *What is the Natural Computing role in this Informational Natural Sciences Era?* Overcoming this challenge will bring two important benefits to Computing and Nature:

1. **A Rethinking (and probably Redesign) of Computing:** Since the early days of computing, most computational devices are based on Turing Machines (TM) and the Von Neumann (VN) architecture. More recently, computing with molecules, photons, and other types of natural materials has been considered. In some cases, data representation, storage and processing are performed in completely different forms from those currently known to most of us. The question is: Why do we still compute using the same, old-fashioned, TM/VN paradigms? As far as we properly understand how informa-

tion is processed in Nature and learn how to use it for computing, a completely new perspective on computing may arise. Some researchers have already started pursuing this line of thought (Feynman, 1996; de Silva & Uchiyama, 2007; Denning, 2007; Conery, 2010; Frailey, 2010; Crnkovic, 2010, 2011a, 2011b; Gelende, 2011; Mitchel, 2011; Deutsch, 2012; Penrose, 2012; Zenil, 2012a, 2012b).

2. **A New Form of Interacting With and Using Nature:** The way humans interact with Nature has gone from the extraction and cultivation of animal and food to the observation of phenomena for the design of novel complex problem solving algorithms. The former has been the basis of our very existence so far, and the latter has been broadly used by Natural Computing researchers to innovate and solve problems in various knowledge domains. Unveiling and harnessing the information processing of Nature will inevitably force us to go one level up in the evolutionary scale; we will be able to interact with Nature more organically, symbiotically, not only for providing us shelter and food in a sustainable manner, but for helping us to harness its power for computing.

3.3. Engineering Natural Computing Systems

Natural systems are open systems that communicate with the environment presenting a complex and emergent behavior. That is, the global behavior of a natural system is a result of local interactions of lower level components. Complex biological systems must be modeled as self-referential, self-organizing, and auto-generative component systems whose computational behavior goes far beyond the TM/VN paradigm (Kampis, 1991). A component system is a computer that, when running its instructions (software), builds a new hardware. Then, there is a computer that restructures itself in a hardware-software non-dissociable interaction: the hardware defines the software, and the software defines the hardware.

As such, computing in natural systems does not occur in isolation, and the architecture of the natural system is fluid and interactive. Computing in one level is the implementation of the laws that govern the interaction of parts that compose that level and communicate with other ones (Crnkovic, 2011a). This gives an idea of the difficulty in designing and implementing nature-inspired computational systems, for it requires decentralization (no central control), locality (a sense of neighborhood), and, most often, multilevel computing (e.g., micro and macro level) (Xavier et al., 2011; Fernandez-Marquez et al., 2012).

Although natural computing researchers have been using mechanisms inspired by natural phenomena to design computational tools for solving complex problems, research on the engineering side of natural computing has been most often performed in an ad hoc fashion, without any standards. Despite that, the idea of creating a methodology to design nature-inspired systems is not new, though normally restricted to specific areas, such as the recent proposals in artificial immune systems (de Castro, 2001), self-organizing systems (Brueckener et al., 2005), and amorphous computing (Nagpal & Mamei, 2004).

One could think of engineering Natural Computing following the standards of software engineering: requisites, analysis, design, implementation, verification, and testing (Puviani et al., 2012). However, the nature-inspired methodology requires a subdivision in the design phase that involves the initial identification of bioinspired mechanisms followed by a modeling phase, a refining and a simulation or prototyping of these mechanisms. Within this design phase, Fernandez-Marquez et al. (2012) proposed the use of specific design patterns based on a series of mechanisms available in the nature-inspired literature. The initial phase defines which patterns must be used, the refining phase defines the patterns and entities dynamics, and the simulation phase is responsible for the implementation of the design patterns. The classification of the patterns is performed in three layers: *basic patterns* (that define the basic mechanisms to be used individually or in conjunction to form more complex patterns), *composed patterns* (also known as intermediary patterns, formed by combining lower level mechanisms), and *high level patterns* (formed by mechanisms well-known from the literature, such as flocking, foraging and quorum sensing).

These methodologies altogether are first steps towards a modularization and standardization of natural system behaviors that may be used for the engineering of nature-inspired systems. However, there is still much to explore that has not yet been described by natural sciences or never used for the design of natural computing approaches. None of these methodologies is definitive and, thus, the engineering of natural computing systems is still a Grand Challenge for the field. And this design requires deep thinking about questions such as (Mitchel, 2011): How is information represented in a natural system? How information is read and written in such system? How is information processed? What are the design standards to engineer Natural Computing approaches? Despite that, an important question that remains to be answered is:

- To What Degree Defining Standards for the Engineering of Natural Computing Systems is a Limiting Factor for the Creative Development of the Field?

4. DISCUSSION

From a global perspective, Natural Computing represents an environment of intellectual synergy that instigates the scientific community to reflect and rethink ideas and proposals in a transdisciplinary way. To build this environment, the following questions must be constantly revisited and updated:

- What is information?
- What is computing?
- How computing can limit our knowledge?
- How computing in natural systems can expand our knowledge?

The exploration of these questions can be the departure point for the development of Natural Computing as a robust science that serves the purpose of representing a common language for scientists to discuss the computational processes of natural systems. It is necessary to establish this two-way road between natural and artificial systems, having Natural Computing as a transdisciplinary bridge for new discoveries and interactions.

The present paper raised the question "what is the future of Natural Computing research." This question is relevant, because what it has been seen over the past years a number of publications in the field which, in some cases, boil down to the same approach designed with a different metaphor. Also, the field has matured, grown, and though some more holistic perspectives have been already proposed (de Castro, 2007; Kari & Rozenberg, 2008; Johnson, 2009; Rozenberg et al., 2012), it still lacks a more coherent analysis and more consistent guidelines of where to go and how to grow and mature. Based on these, this paper proposed three Grand Challenges in Natural Computing Research: Transforming Natural Computing into a Transdisciplinary Discipline, Unveiling and Harnessing Information Processing in Natural Systems, and Engineering Natural Computing Systems. The final goal is a single one: *To transform Natural Computing into a New Science.*

ACKNOWLEDGMENT

The authors thank CNPq, Fapesp, Capes and MackPesquisa for the financial support.

REFERENCES

Astrom, K. J., Borisson, U., Ljung, L., & Wittenmark, B. (1977). Theory and applications of self-tuning regulators. *Automatica*, *13*(5), 457–476. doi:10.1016/0005-1098(77)90067-X.

Back, T., & Schwefel, H. (1993). An overview of evolutionary algorithms for parameter optimization. *Evolutionary Computation*, *1*(1), 1–23. doi:10.1162/evco.1993.1.1.1.

Ballard, D. (1997). *An introduction to natural computation*. Cambridge, MA: MIT Press.

Bersini, H., Lenaerts, T., & Santos, F. (2006). Growing biological networks: Beyond the gene duplication model. *Journal of Theoretical Biology*, *241*(3), 488–505. doi:10.1016/j.jtbi.2005.12.012 PMID:16442124.

Brent, R., & Bruck, J. (2006). Can computers help to explain biology? *Nature*, *440*(23), 416–417. doi:10.1038/440416a PMID:16554784.

Britton, N. F. (1986). *Reaction-diffusion equations and their applications to biology*. New York, NY: Academic Press.

Brueckner, S. A., Serugendo, G. D. M., Karageorgos, A., & Nagpal, R. (Eds.). (2005). *Proceedings of the Third International Workshop on Engineering Self-Organizing Systems* (LNCS 3464). Berlin, Germany: Springer-Verlag.

Camazine, S., Deneubourg, J.-L., Franks, N. R., Sneyd, J., Theraulaz, G., & Bonabeau, E. (2001). *Self-organization in biological systems*. Princeton, NJ: Princeton University Press.

Chen, T., He, H. L., & Church, G. M. (1999). Modeling gene expression with differential equations. In *Proceedings of the Pacific Symposium on Biocomputing* (pp. 29-40).

Chen, V. C. P., Tsui, K.-L., & Barton, R. R. (2006). A review on design, modeling and applications of computer experiments. *IIE Transactions*, *38*(4), 273–291. doi:10.1080/07408170500232495.

Church, A. (1936). A note on the entscheidungsproblem. *American Journal of Mathematics*, *58*, 345–363. doi:10.2307/2371045.

Cohen, I. R. (2000). *Tending Adam's garden: Evolving the cognitive immune self*. New York, NY: Academic Press.

Cohen, I. R. (2009). Real and artificial immune systems: Computing the state of the body. *Nature Reviews. Immunology*, *7*, 569–574. doi:10.1038/nri2102 PMID:17558422.

Cohen, I. R., & Harel, D. (2007). Explaining a complex living system: dynamics Multi-scaling and emergence. *Journal of the Royal Society, Interface*, *4*, 175–182. doi:10.1098/rsif.2006.0173 PMID:17251153.

Conery, J. S. (2010, November). Computation is symbol manipulation. In *Proceedings of the Ubiquity Symposium on What is Computation?* (article 4).

Crnkovic, G. D. (2010). Biological information and natural computation. In Vallverdú, J. (Ed.), *Thinking machines and the philosophy of computer science: Concepts and principles* (pp. 36–52). Hershey, PA: IGI Global. doi:10.4018/978-1-61692-014-2.ch003.

Crnkovic, G. D. (2011a). Dynamics of information as natural computation. *Information*, *2*(3), 460–477. doi:10.3390/info2030460.

Crnkovic, G. D. (2011b). Significance of models of computation, from Turing model to natural computation. *Minds and Machines*, *21*(2), 301–322. doi:10.1007/s11023-011-9235-1.

de Aguiar, M. A. M., Barange, M., Baptestini, E. M., Kaufman, L., & Bar-Yam, Y. (2009). Global patterns of speciation and diversity. *Nature*, *460*(16), 384–387. doi:10.1038/nature08168 PMID:19606148.

de Castro, L. N. (2001). *Immune engineering: Development and application of computational tools inspired by artificial immune systems* (Unpublished doctoral dissertation). Computer and Electrical Engineering School, Unicamp, Brazil.

de Castro, L. N. (2006). *Fundamentals of natural computing: Basic concepts, algorithms, and applications*. Boca Raton, FL: CRC Press.

de Castro, L. N. (2007). Fundamentals of natural computing: An overview. *Physics of Life Reviews*, *4*(1), 1–36. doi:10.1016/j.plrev.2006.10.002.

de Jong, H. (2002). Modeling and simulation of genetic regulatory systems: A literature review. *Journal of Computational Biology*, *9*(1), 67–103. doi:10.1089/10665270252833208 PMID:11911796.

de Silva, A. P. (2005). Molecular logic gets loaded. *Nature*, *4*, 15–16. doi:10.1038/nmat1301.

de Silva, A. P., & Uchiyama, S. (2007). Molecular logic and computing. *Nature Nanotechnology*, *2*, 399–410. doi:10.1038/nnano.2007.188 PMID:18654323.

Denning, P. J. (Ed.). (2001). *The invisible future: The seamless integration of technology in everyday life*. New York, NY: McGraw-Hill.

Denning, P. J. (2007). Computing is a natural science. *Communications of the ACM*, *50*(7), 13–18. doi:10.1145/1272516.1272529.

Denning, P. J. (2008). Computing field: Structure. In Wah, B. (Ed.), *Wiley encyclopedia of computer science and engineering*. New York, NY: Wiley Interscience.

Denning, P. J. (2010, November). Opening statement. In *Proceedings of the Ubiquity Symposium on What is Computation?* (article 1).

Deutsch, D. (2012). What is computation? (How) does nature compute? In Zenil, H. (Ed.), *A computable universe: Understanding computation & exploring nature as computation*. Singapore: World Scientific.

Fernandez-Marquez, J. L., Serugendo, G. D. M., Montagna, S., Viroli, M., & Arcos, J. L. (2012). Description and composition of bio-inspired design patterns: A complete overview. *Natural Computing*. doi:10.1007/s11047-012-9324-y PMID:22962549.

Feynman, R. P. (1996). *The Feynman lectures on computation*. Reading, MA: Addison-Wesley.

Floridi, L. (2010). *The philosophy of information*. Oxford, UK: Oxford University Press.

Frailey, D. J. (2010, November). Computation is process. In *Proceedings of the Ubiquity Symposium on What is Computation?* (article 5).

Gatenby, R. A., & Gawlinski, E. T. (1996). A reaction-diffusion model of cancer invasion. *Cancer Research*, *56*, 5745–5753. PMID:8971186.

Gavrilets, S., & Vose, A. (2005). Dynamic patterns of adaptive radiation. *Proceedings of the National Academy of Sciences of the United States of America*, *12*(50), 18040–18045. doi:10.1073/pnas.0506330102 PMID:16330783.

Gelende, E. (2011, February). Natural computation. In *Proceedings of the Ubiquity Symposium on What is Computation?* (article 1).

Gödel, K. (1934). *On undecidable propositions of formal mathematics*. Princeton, NJ: Institute for Advanced Study.

Gotelli, N. J., & Kelley, W. G. (1993). A general model of metapopulation dynamics. *Oikos*, *68*(1), 36–44. doi:10.2307/3545306.

Goutsias, J., & Lee, N. H. (2007). Computational and experimental approaches for modeling gene regulatory networks. *Current Pharmaceutical Design*, *13*(14), 1415–1436. doi:10.2174/138161207780765945 PMID:17504165.

Hart, E., Bersini, H., & Santos, F. (2007). How affinity influences tolerance in an idiotypic network. *Journal of Theoretical Biology*, *249*(3), 422–436. doi:10.1016/j.jtbi.2007.07.019 PMID:17904580.

Johnson, C. (2009). Teaching natural computation. *IEEE Computational Intelligence Magazine*, *4*(1), 24–30. doi:10.1109/MCI.2008.930984.

Kampis, G. (1991). *Self-modifying systems in biology and cognitive science: A new framework for dynamics, information, and complexity* (1st ed.). Oxford, UK: Pergamon.

Kari, L., & Rozenberg, G. (2008). The many facets of natural computing. *Communications of the ACM*, *51*, 72–83. doi:10.1145/1400181.1400200.

Kauffman, S. (1995). *At home in the universe: The search for the laws of self-organization and complexity*. Oxford, UK: Oxford University Press.

Lavesson, N., & Davidsson, P. (1999). Quantifying the impact of learning algorithm parameter Tuning. In *Proceedings of the 21st National Conference on Artificial Intelligence* (pp. 1165-1173).

Ledoux, S. F. (2002). Defining natural sciences. *Behaviorology Today*, *5*(1), 34–36.

Lehn, J.-M. (2002). Toward self-organization and complex matter. *Science*, *295*(5564), 2400–2403. doi:10.1126/science.1071063 PMID:11923524.

Lenaerts, T., & Bersini, H. (2009). A synthon approach to artificial chemistry. *Artificial Life*, *15*(189-103.

Lloyd, S. (2006). *Programming the universe: A quantum computer scientist takes on the cosmos*. New York, NY: Knopf.

Masulli, F., & Mitra, S. (2009). Natural computing methods in bioinformatics: A survey. *Information Fusion*, *10*(3), 211–216. doi:10.1016/j.inffus.2008.12.002.

McCulloch, W., & Pitts, W. H. (1943). A logical calculus of the ideas immanent in nervous activity. *The Bulletin of Mathematical Biophysics*, *5*, 115–133. doi:10.1007/BF02478259.

Mitchel, M. (2011, February). Biological computation. In *Proceedings of the Ubiquity Symposium on What is Computation?* (article 3).

Nagpal, R., & Mamei, M. (2004). Engineering amorphous computing systems. *Multiagent Systems, Artificial Societies, and Simulated Organizations*, *11*, 303–320. doi:10.1007/1-4020-8058-1_19.

Nicolescu, B. (Ed.). (2008). *Transdisciplinarity: Theory and practice*. New York, NY: Hampton Press.

Parpinelli, R. S., & Lopes, H. S. (2011). New inspirations in swarm intelligence: A survey. *International Journal of Bio-Inspired Computation*, *3*(1), 1–16. doi:10.1504/IJBIC.2011.038700.

Penrose, R. (2012). Foreword. In Zenil, H. (Ed.), *A computable universe: Understanding computation & exploring nature as computation*. Singapore: World Scientific.

Post, E. (1936). Finite combinatory processes - Formulation 1. *Journal of Symbolic Logic*, *1*, 103–105. doi:10.2307/2269031.

Puviani, M., Serugendo, G. D. M., Frei, R., & Cabri, G. (2012). A method fragments approach to methodologies for engineering self-organizing systems. *ACM Transactions on Autonomous and Adaptive Systems*, *7*(3), 1–33. doi:10.1145/2348832.2348836.

Regev, A., & Shapiro, E. (2002). Cellular abstractions: Cells as computation. *Nature*, *419*, 343. doi:10.1038/419343a PMID:12353013.

Rozenberg, G. (Ed.). (2002). *Natural Computing: An International Journal*. New York, NY: Springer.

Rozenberg, G., Bäck, T., & Kok, J. N. (Eds.). (2012). *Handbook of natural computing*. New York, NY: Springer. doi:10.1007/978-3-540-92910-9.

Schwenk, K., Padilla, D. K., Bakkenand, G. S., & Full, R. J. (2009). Grand challenges in organismal biology. *Integrative and Comparative Biology*, *49*(1), 7–14. doi:10.1093/icb/icp034 PMID:21669841.

Shapiro, J. A. (1995). The significances of bacterial colony patterns. *BioEssays*, *17*(7), 597–607. doi:10.1002/bies.950170706 PMID:7646482.

Turing, A. (1937). On computable numbers, with an application to the entschei-dungsproblem. *Proceedings of the London Mathematical Society*, *42*, 230–265. doi:10.1112/plms/s2-42.1.230.

Wakano, J. Y., Maenosono, S., Komoto, A., Eiha, N., & Yamaguchi, Y. (2003). Self-organized pattern formation of a bacteria colony modeled by a reaction diffusion system and nucleation theory. *Physical Review Letters*, *90*(25), 258102. doi:10.1103/PhysRevLett.90.258102 PMID:12857171.

Xavier, R. S., Omar, N., & de Castro, L. N. (2011). Bacterial colony: Information processing and computational behavior. In *Proceedings of the Third World Congress on Nature and Biologically Inspired Computing* (pp. 446-450).

Zenil, H. (Ed.). (2012a). *A computable universe: Understanding computation & exploring nature as computation*. Singapore: World Scientific.

Zenil, H. (2012b). Introducing the computable universe. In Zenil, H. (Ed.), *A computable universe: Understanding computation & exploring nature as computation*. Singapore: World Scientific.

This work was previously published in the International Journal of Natural Computing Research (IJNCR), Volume 2, Issue 4, edited by Leandro Nunes de Castro, pp. 17-30, copyright 2011 by IGI Publishing (an imprint of IGI Global).

Chapter 17
Trans-Canada Slimeways:
Slime Mould Imitates the Canadian Transport Network

Andrew Adamatzky
University of the West of England, UK

Selim G. Akl
Queen's University, Canada

ABSTRACT

Slime mould Physarum polycephalum builds up sophisticated networks to transport nutrients between distant parts of its extended body. The slime mould's protoplasmic network is optimised for maximum coverage of nutrients yet minimum energy spent on transportation of the intra-cellular material. In laboratory experiments with P. polycephalum we represent Canadian major urban areas with rolled oats and inoculated slime mould in the Toronto area. The plasmodium spans the urban areas with its network of protoplasmic tubes. The authors uncover similarities and differences between the protoplasmic network and the Canadian national highway network, analyse the networks in terms of proximity graphs and evaluate slime mould's network response to contamination.

1. INTRODUCTION

The increase of long-distance travel and subsequent reconfiguration of vehicular and social networks (Larsen, Urry, & Axhausen, 2006) requires novel and unconventional approaches towards analysis of dynamical processes in complex transport networks (Barrat, Barthelemy, & Vespignani, 2008) routing and localisation of vehicular networks (Olariu & Weigle, 2009) optimisation of interactions between different parts of a transport network during scheduling road expansion and maintenance (Taplin, Qiu, & Han, 2005) and shaping of transport network structure (Beuthe, Himanen, Reggiani, & Zamparini, 2004). The main goals of the paper are to uncover viable analogies between biological and human-made transport networks and to project behavioural traits of biological networks onto existing vehicular transport networks.

DOI: 10.4018/978-1-4666-4253-9.ch017

While choosing a biological object we want it to be experimental laboratory friendly, easy to cultivate and handle, and convenient to analyse its behaviour. Ants would indeed be the first candidate, and a great deal of impressive results has been published on ant-colony inspired computing (Dorigo & Statzle, 2004; Solnon, 2010), however ant colonies require substantial laboratory resources, experience and time in handling them. Actually very few, if any, papers were published on experimental laboratory implementation of ant-based optimisation, the prevalent majority of publications being theoretical. There is however an object which is extremely easy to cultivate and handle, and which exhibits remarkably good foraging behaviour and development of transport networks. This is the plasmodium of *Physarum polycephalum*.

Plasmodium is a vegetative stage of acellular slime mould *P. polycephalum*, a syncytium, that is, a single cell with many nuclei, which feeds on microscopic particles (Stephenson & Stempen, 2000).When foraging for its food the plasmodium propagates towards sources of food particles, surrounds them, secretes enzymes and digests the food. Typically, the plasmodium forms a congregation of protoplasm covering the food source. When several sources of nutrients are scattered in the plasmodium's range, the plasmodium forms a network of protoplasmic tubes connecting the masses of protoplasm at the food sources.

A life cycle of *P. polycephalum* is as following. When plasmodium is deprived of water or nutrients it switches to 'hibernation' mode and forms a hardened mass called sclerotium. Sclerotium can survive without food or water for years. When moistened, the sclerotium returns to the state of plasmodium. When exposed to bright light and starved, the plasmodium switches to fructification phase. It grows sporangia. When a spore gets into a favourable environment, it releases a single-cell myxamoeba. Myxamoebas can live as they are for a long time. In the presence of water a myxamoeba is transformed into a swarm cell with two flagellas. Swarm cells can swim. Myxamoebas and swarm cells can reproduce asexually, by simple division. During changes of environment from good to bad, myxamoebas and swarm cells can form spheroidal micro-cysts with cellulose walls. When enough myxamoebas or swarm cells are present in the volume, they begin sexual reproduction and form a zygote. The zygote divides mitotically and forms a multi-nuclear single cell — the plasmodium.

The plasmodium is a unique user-friendly biological substrate from which experimental prototypes of massive-parallel amorphous biological computers are designed (Adamatzky, 2010). During its foraging behaviour the plasmodium spans scattered sources of nutrients with a network of protoplasmic tubes. The protoplasmic network is optimised to cover all sources of food and to provide a robust and speedy transportation of nutrients and metabolites in the plasmodium body. The plasmodium's foraging behaviour can be interpreted as computation. Data are represented by spatial configurations of attractants and repellents, and results of computation by structures of a protoplasmic network formed by the plasmodium on the data sets (Nakagaki, Yamada, & Ueda, 2000). (Nakagaki, Yamada, & Toth, 2001; Adamatzky, 2010). The problems solved by plasmodium of *P. polycephalum* include shortest path (Nakagaki, Yamada, & Ueda, 2000; Nakagaki, Yamada, & Toth, 2001) implementation of storage modification machines (Adamatzky, 2007b). Voronoi diagram (Shirakawa, Adamatzky, Gunji, & Miyake, 2009), Delaunay triangulation (Adamatzky, 2010), logical computing (Tsuda, Aono, & Gunji, 2004), and process algebra (Schumann & Adamatzky, 2009); see overview in Adamatzky (2010).

Previously (Adamatzky, 2007a) we have evaluated a road-modeling potential of *P. polycephalum*, however no conclusive results were presented back in 2007. A step forward, namely, biological-approximation, or evaluation, of human-made road networks was done in our previous papers on approximation of motorways/highways in the United Kingdom (Adamatzky & Jones, 2010),

Mexico (Adamatzky, Martinez, Chapa-Vergara, Asomoza-Palacio, & Stephens, 2010), and the Netherlands (Adamatzky & Sloot, 2010) by plasmodium of *P. polycephalum*. For all three countries we found that, in principle, the network of protoplasmic tubes developed by plasmodium matches, at least partly, the network of human-made transport arteries. The shape of a country and the exact spatial distribution of urban areas (represented by source of nutrients) may play a key role in determining the exact structure of the plasmodium network. Also we suspect that a degree of matching between Physarum networks and motorway networks is determined by original government designs of motorways in any particular country. This is why it is so important to collect data on development of plasmodium networks in all major countries, and then undertake a comparative analysis.

The work described in this paper contributes to a general research effort currently underway in computer science, that is motivated by at least three goals:

- To provide additional evidence that "Nature computes." More precisely, we endeavour to show that the computational paradigm is capable of modelling Nature's work with great precision. Thus, when viewed as computations, the processes of Nature may be better explained and better understood.
- To exhibit examples of natural algorithms whose features are sufficiently attractive, so as to inspire effective algorithms for conventional computers. Nature's algorithms may be more efficient than conventional ones and may lead to better solutions for a variety of optimisation problems.
- To identify problems where natural processes themselves are the only viable approach towards a solution. Such problems may occur in environments where conventional computers are inept, in particular when living organisms, including the human body itself, are the subject of the computation.

What are unique properties of the Canadian transport system? The Canadian Highway System gives us a good example of a logically designed transportation system whose key goal is to connect all the provinces together by highways. The highway network was built as a federal-provincial territorial cooperative project with great effort taken in coordinating work on different parts. Another attractive property of the highway system is that it was designed to provide an access to remote areas where no regions of high population density exist.

The paper is structured as follows. We present experimental techniques used in Section 2. Properties of protoplasmic networks built by *P. polycephalum* are discussed in Section 3. We compare slime mould networks with the Canadian highway network in Section 4 and slime mould and human-made networks with proximity graphs in Section 5. In Section 6 we show how the slime mould transport network restructures in response to a spreading contamination.

2. METHODS

The plasmodium of *P. polycephalum* is cultivated in plastic containers, on paper kitchen towels sprinkled with still drinking water and fed with oat flakes (Asda's Smart Price Porridge Oats). For experiments we use 12 × 12 cm polyestyrene square Petri dishes. Agar plates, 2% agar gel (Select agar, Sigma Aldrich), are cut in a shape of Canada. We consider the eleven most populated urban areas U of Canada (Figure 1a) and five transport nodes:

1. Toronto area (including Hamilton, London, St. CatharinesNiagara, Windsor, Oshawa, Barrie, Guelph, and Kingston);

Figure 1. Experimental setup. (a) Urban areas and transport nodes to be represented by oat flakes, from Canada's National Highway System (2008), (b) Snapshot of protoplasmic transport network developed by P. polycephum; the snapshot is made on a highway map.

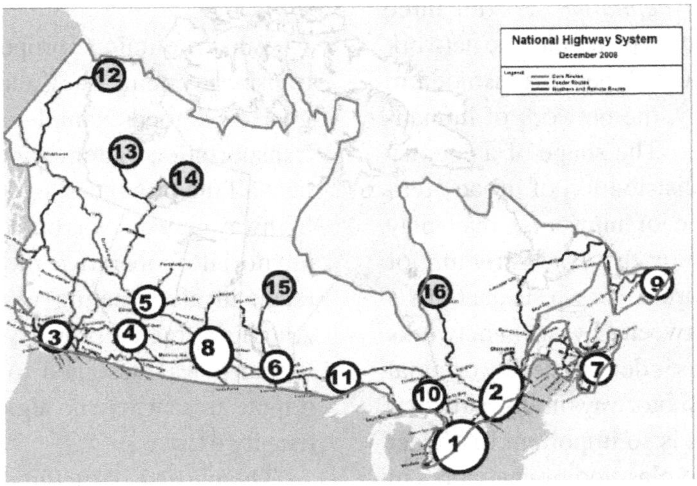

(a)

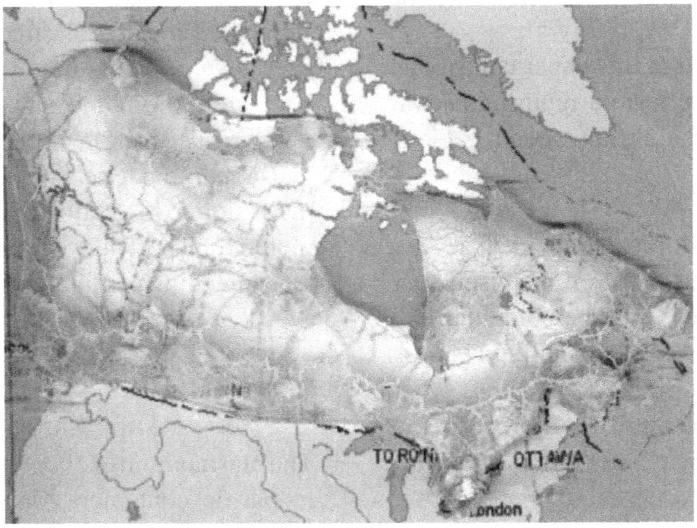

(b)

2. Montreal area (including OttawaGatineau, Quebec City, Sherbrooke, Trois-Rivieres);
3. Vancouver area (including Victoria, Abbotsford, Kelowna);
4. Calgary;
5. Edmonton;
6. Winnipeg;
7. Halifax-Moncton;
8. Saskatoon-Regina;
9. St. John's;
10. Sudbury;
11. Thunder Bay;
12. Inuvik;
13. Wrigley;

14. Yellowknife;
15. Thompson;
16. Radisson.

The last five entries from Inuvik to Radisson, are not highly populated urban areas. They are transport nodes added for completeness, i.e., to present slime mould with the same number of principal transport nodes as the human-made highways system (Figure 1a). Some transport nodes as Fort McMurray, La Ronge, Flin Flon, and so on, are not included in the list due to their proximity to already chosen major urban areas.

To project regions of U onto agar gel we place oat flakes in the positions of these regions of U (Figure 1). In each experiments we tried to match the size and shape of areas in (Figure 1) by selecting rolled oat of corresponding size and shape. At the beginning of each experiment a piece of plasmodium, usually already attached to an oat flake in the cultivation box, is placed in the Toronto area (region 1 in Figure 1a). The Petri dishes with plasmodium are kept in darkness, at temperature 22-25 C°, except for observation and image recording. Periodically (usually in 12 h or 24 h intervals) the dishes are scanned in Epson Perfection 4490. We undertook 23 experiments.

3. FORAGING ON URBAN AREAS

It usually takes the plasmodium of *P. polycephalum* 2-5 days to span all urban areas. How fast the plasmodium colonises the space depends on many unknown factors, including seasonal variations, plasmodium's age, etc. 'Younger' plasmodia, which were just recently 'woken up' from the sclerotium phase do usually colonise the experimental arena quicker than old plasmodia, which were replanted several times in culture boxes. Images of protoplasmic networks presented in the paper are taken when all oat flakes, representing U, were colonised by plasmodium. Examples of the protoplasmic networks are shown in Figure 2.

As every living creature does, the plasmodium of *P. polycephalum* rarely repeats its foraging pattern, and almost never builds *exactly* the same protoplasmic network twice. To generalise our experimental results we constructed a Physarum graph with weighted-edges. A Physarum graph is a tuple $P = (U, E, w)$, where U is a set of urban areas, E is a set edges, and $w: E \rightarrow [0, 1]$ associates each edge of E with a probability (or weights). For every two regions a and b from U there is an edge connecting a and b if a plasmodium's protoplasmic link is recorded at least in one of k experiments, and the edge (a, b) has a probability calculated as a ratio of experiments where protoplasmic link (a, b) occurred in the total number of experiments $k = 23$. For example, if we observed a protoplasmic tube connecting areas a and b in 5 experiments, the weight of edge (a, b) will be $w(a, b) = 5/23$. We do not take into account the exact configuration of the protoplasmic tubes but merely their existence. Further we will be dealing with threshold Physarum graphs $P(\theta) = \langle U, T(E), w, \theta \rangle$. The threshold Physarum graph is obtained from Physarum graph by the transformation: $T(E) = \{e \in E: w(e) > \theta\}$. That is all edges with weights less than or equal to θ are removed. Examples of threshold Physarum graphs for various values of θ are shown in Figure 3.

A 'raw' Physarum graph P(0) is a non-planar graph due to the presence of protoplasmic tube connecting Saskatoon-Regina (8) with Yellowknife (14) (Figure 3a). It also exhibits two cross-Canada transport links Inuvik (12) to Radisson (16) and Yellowknife (14) to Radisson (16). Nevertheless, these are links that might be considered as senseless from a geographical point of view because they are crossing massive mountains and forests.

Figure 2. Examples of protoplasmic networks developed by P. polycephalum on major urban areas and transport nodes U. Greyscale images.

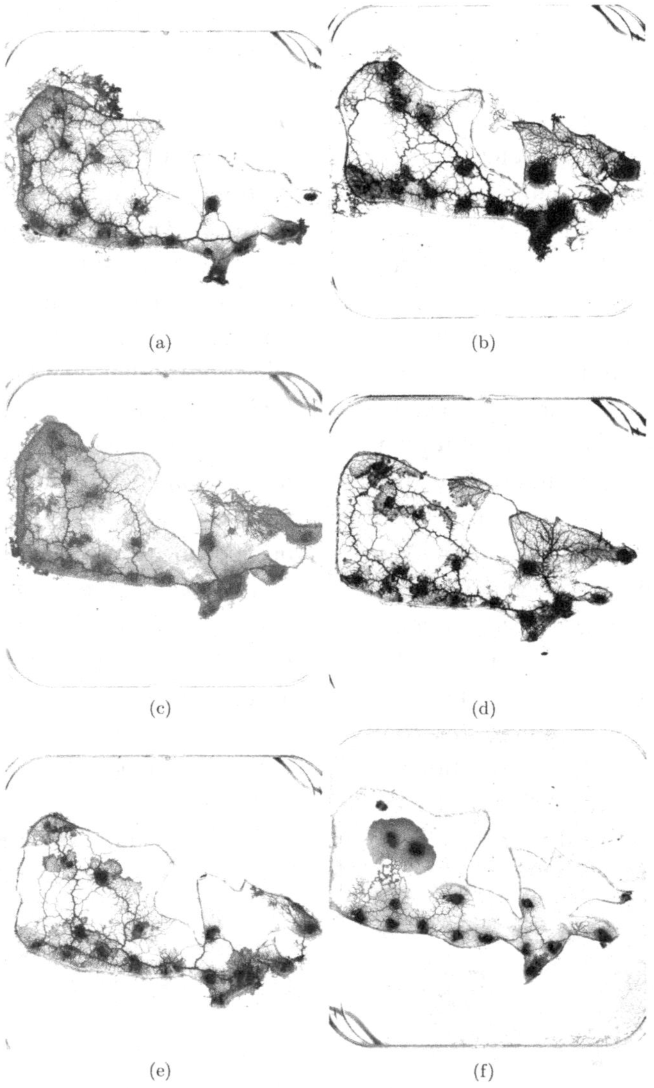

All three links disappear when we increase θ to 8 (Figure 3b). Four more links become trimmed off when $\theta = 8$: Sudbury (10) — Thompson (15), Montreal area (2) — Sudbury (10), Sudbury (10) — Radisson (16), Montreal area (2) — St. John's (9).

P(8/23) is the last connected graph in a series of threshold Physarum graphs, P(θ), $0 \leq \theta \leq 23$. Urban areas St. John's (9) and Radisson (16) become isolated in P(9/23) due to the disappearance of transport links from the Montreal area (2) to Radisson (16) and from Radisson (16) to St. John's (9) (Figure 3c).

The Physarum graph splits into a tree and two isolated nodes for $\theta = 17/23$ (Figure 3d). Five long distance routes from urban areas to transport nodes are removed: Vancouver area (3) — Inuvik (12), Vancouver area (3) — Wrigley (13), Edmonton (5) — Wrigley (13), Saskatoon-Regina (8) — Thompson (15), Winnipeg (6) — Thompson (15);

Figure 3. Configurations Physarum-graph P(θ) for various cutoff values of θ. Thickness of each edge is proportional to the edge's weight.

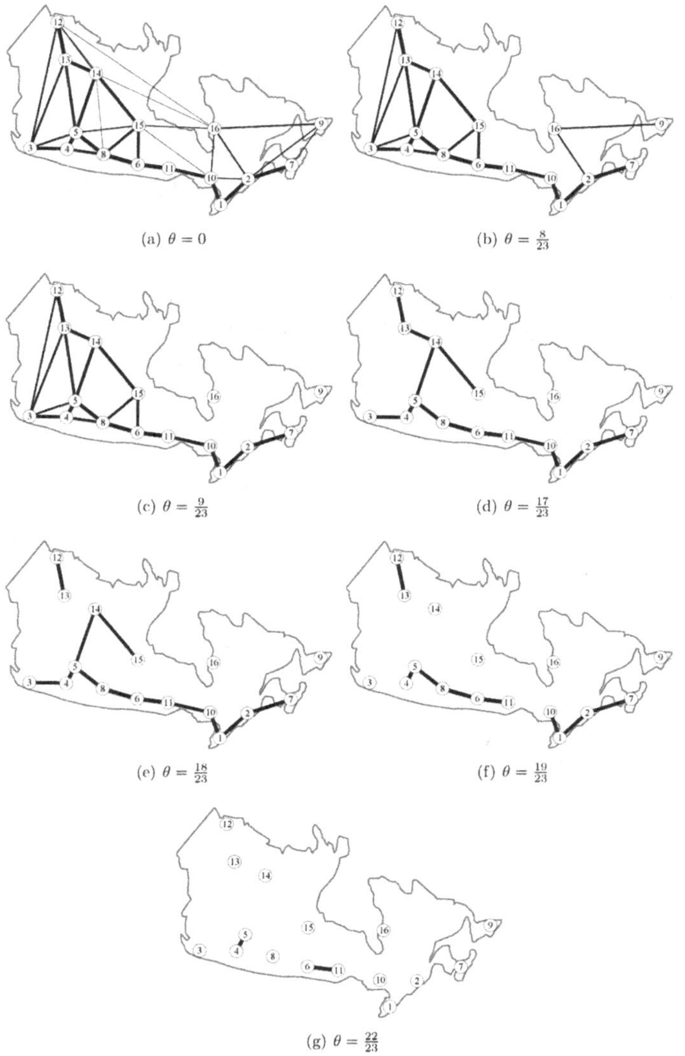

(a) $\theta = 0$ (b) $\theta = \frac{8}{23}$ (c) $\theta = \frac{9}{23}$ (d) $\theta = \frac{17}{23}$ (e) $\theta = \frac{18}{23}$ (f) $\theta = \frac{19}{23}$ (g) $\theta = \frac{22}{23}$

and, two short-distance routes between major urban areas: Vancouver area (3) — Edmonton (5) and Calgary (4) — Saskatoon-Regina (8).

The graph P(18/23) consists of several disconnected components: two isolated nodes, St. Johns (9) and Radisson (16), a two-node segment Inuvik (12) — Wrigley (13), and a tree spanning the rest of the urban areas (Figure 3e). A further increase of θ to 19/23 (Figure 3f) leads to the formation of

- **Five Isolated Nodes:** Vancouver area (3), St. Johns (9), Yellowknife (14), Thompson (15), Radisson (16);
- **A Segment:** Inuvik (12) — Wrigley (13);
- **A Chain:** Calgary (4) — Edmonton (5) — Saskatoon-Regina (8) — Winnipeg (6) — Thunder Bay (11);
- **A Chain:** Sudbury (10) — Toronto area (1) — Montreal area (2) — Halifax-Moncton (7).

Only segment-routes Calgary (4) to Edmonton (5) and Winnipeg (6) to Thunder Bay (11) are represented by protoplasmic tubes in almost all experiments (Figure 3g).

4. PHYSARUM NETWORK VS. HIGHWAY NETWORK

We construct the highway graph H as follows. Let U be a set of urban regions, for any two regions *a* and *b* from U, the nodes *a* and *b* are connected by an edge (*a*, *b*) if there is a motorway starting in *a* and passing in the vicinity of *b* and not passing in the vicinity of any other urban area $c \in U$. Highway graph H shown in Figure 4b is extracted from a scheme of the Canadian transport network (Figure 4a).

Finding 1: Physarum almost approximates the Canadian highway network.

'Raw' Physarum graph P(0) approximates 21 of 22 edges of highway graph H. Only one edge, Vancouver area (3) to Yellowknife (14), of the highway graph H is not represented by

Figure 4. Physarum vs highway network. (a) Highway network in Canada (Canada's National Highway System, 2008), (b) Highway graph H. (c-d-e) Intersection of threshold Physarum graph with highway graph for θ = 0, 8/23, 17/23.

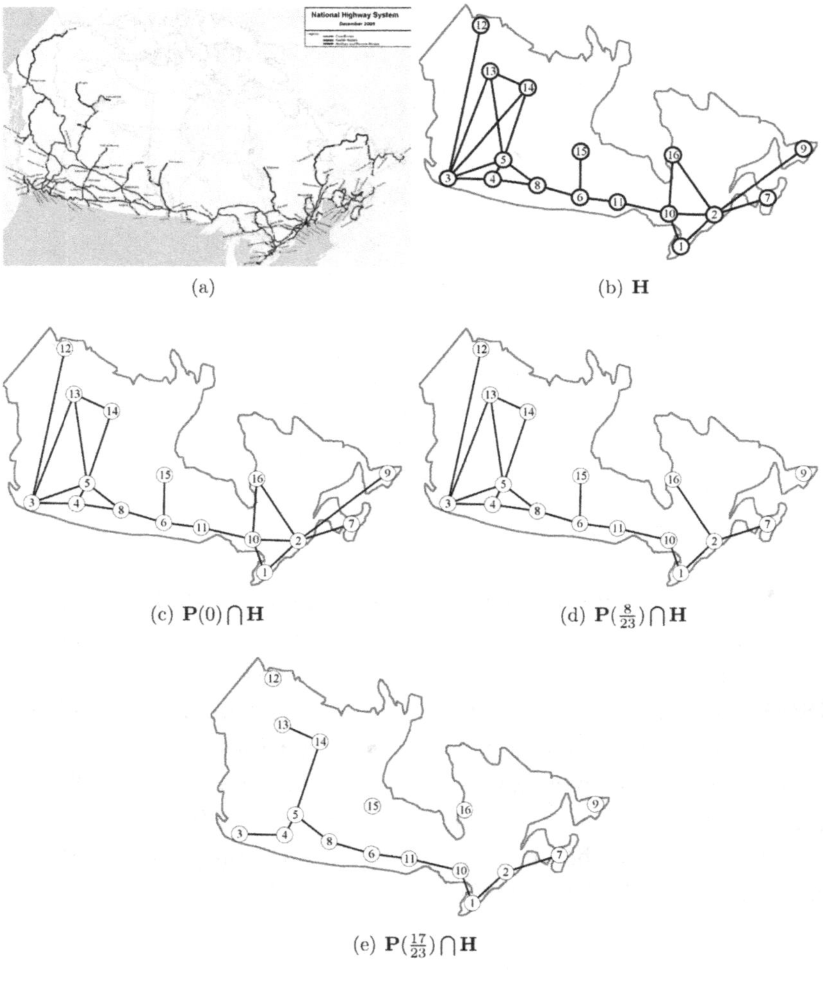

protoplasmic tubes in any of the 23 experiments undertaken (Figure 4c). The 'raw' physarum graph gives us a rather relaxed approximation because it includes even links which occurred just once in a set of experiments. Let us look at P(8/23) which represents links which occurred in over 35% of experiments. Physarum graph P(8/23) approximates 18 of 22 edges of H (Figure 4d). The only edges of H not represented in P(8/23) are Vancouver area to Yellowknife, Sudbury to Radisson, Sudbury to Montreal area, and St. John's to Montreal area.

Finding 2: A core component of the Physarum transport network and the Canadian highway network consists of a chain passing along the south border from Halifax-Monctron area to Edmonton, and a fork attached to Edmonton; the south branch of the fork is Edmonton — Calgary — Vancouver area and the north branch is Edmonton – Yellowknife – Wrigley.

The component above is the only connected component in the intersection of P(17/23) with H (Figure 4e).

5. PROXIMITY GRAPHS

A planar graph consists of nodes which are points of the Euclidean plane and edges which are straight segments connecting the points. A planar proximity graph is a planar graph where two points are connected by an edge if they are close in some sense. A pair of points is assigned a certain neighbourhood, and points of the pair are connected by an edge if their neighbourhood is empty. Here we consider the most common proximity graph as follows.

- **GG:** Points a and b are connected by an edge in the Gabriel Graph GG if disc with diameter $dist(a, b)$ centered in middle of the segment ab is empty (Gabriel & Sokal, 1969; Matula & Sokal, 1984) (Figure 5a).
- **RNG:** Points a and b are connected by an edge in the Relative Neighbourhood Graph RNG if no other point c is closer to a and b than $dist(a, b)$ (Toussaint, 1980) (Figure 5b).
- **MST:** The Euclidean minimum spanning tree (MST) (Nesetril, Milkova, & Nesetrilova, 2001) is a connected acyclic graph which has minimum possible sum of edges' lengths (Figure 5b).

In general, the graphs relate as MST $\subseteq$ RNG $\subseteq$ GG (Toussaint, 1980; Matula & Sokal, 1984; Jaromczyk & Toussaint, 1992).

Finding 3: For a given configuration of nodes of U RNG = MST.

The finding implies that the configuration of urban areas of U is 'spanning friendly.'

Finding 4: Let T_i be a minimum spanning tree rooted in node $i \in U$ then $T_i = T_j$ for any $i, j \in U$.

We demonstrated this by direct computation of all possible spanning trees on U.

Finding 5: St. John's and Inuvik urban areas are isolated in GG$\cap$H and RNG$\cap$H.
Finding 6: MST/{(Inuvik — Wrigley), (Halifax-Moncton — St. John's)} $\subset$ H.

This means that the Canadian highway network is almost optimal (Figure 5de). Intersections of Physarum graphs for principal values of threshold θ with the Gabriel graph and the minimum spanning tree are shown in Figure 6.

Finding 7: MST $\subset$ P(0).

Figure 5. Proximity graphs and their intersection with highway graph H. (a) Gabriel graph. (b) Relative neighbourhood graph and minimum spanning tree. (c) Intersection of Gabriel graph with highway graph. (d) Intersection of relative neighbourhood graph with highway graph.

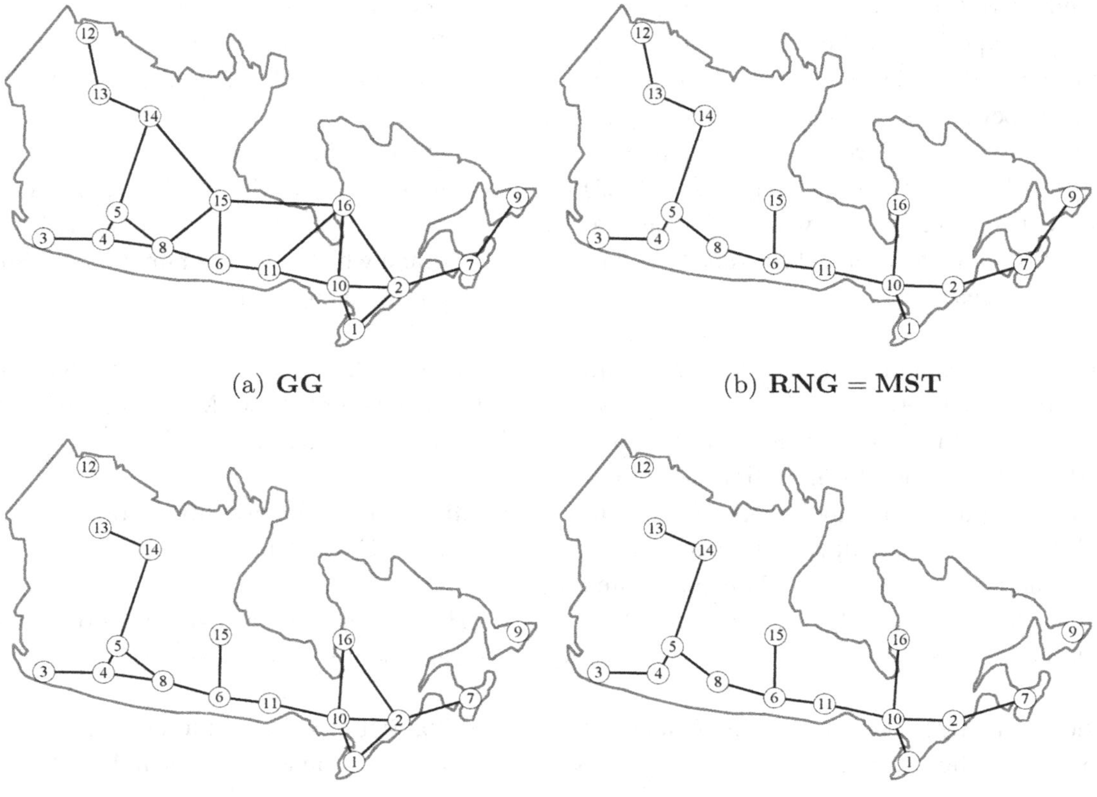

(a) **GG** (b) **RNG = MST** (c) **GG⋂H** (d) **RNG⋂H**

'Raw' Physarum includes an 'ideal' acyclic spanning network MST. This some- how characterises a good quality of a slime mould approximation of a transport network. The minimum spanning tree is not included in the high-threshold Physarum graph P(17/23). However, there is a 'strong' component of MST which is included in the high-threshold Physarum graph (Figure 6). The strong component is a tree rooted in the Toronto area. The tree's stem is Toronto — Sudbury — Thunder Bay — Winnipeg — Saskatoon-Regina — Edmonton. It has two end branches Edmonton — Calgary — Vancouver area and Edmonton — Yellowknife — Wrigley — Inuvik.

6. RESPONSE TO CONTAMINATION

To imitate propagating contamination we place a crystal of sea salt (SAXA Coarse Sea Salt, a crystal weight around 20 mg), in the place of the Bruce Nuclear Power station (eastern shore of Lake Huron, near Tiverton, Ontario). Inorganic salts are chemo-repellents for *P. polycephalum* therefore sodium chloride diffusing in agar gel causes plasmodium to retreat from a contaminated zone. We studied plasmodium's response circa 24 h after initiation of contamination. During 24 h a contamination zone expands as far as Winnipeg and Thompson in the west and St. John's in the east. In some cases contamination spreads

Figure 6. Intersection of (a-c-e) Gabriel graph GG and (b-d-f) minimum spanning tree MST with Physarum graphs P(θ) for (a-b) θ = 0, (cd) θ = 8/23, (ef) θ = 17/23

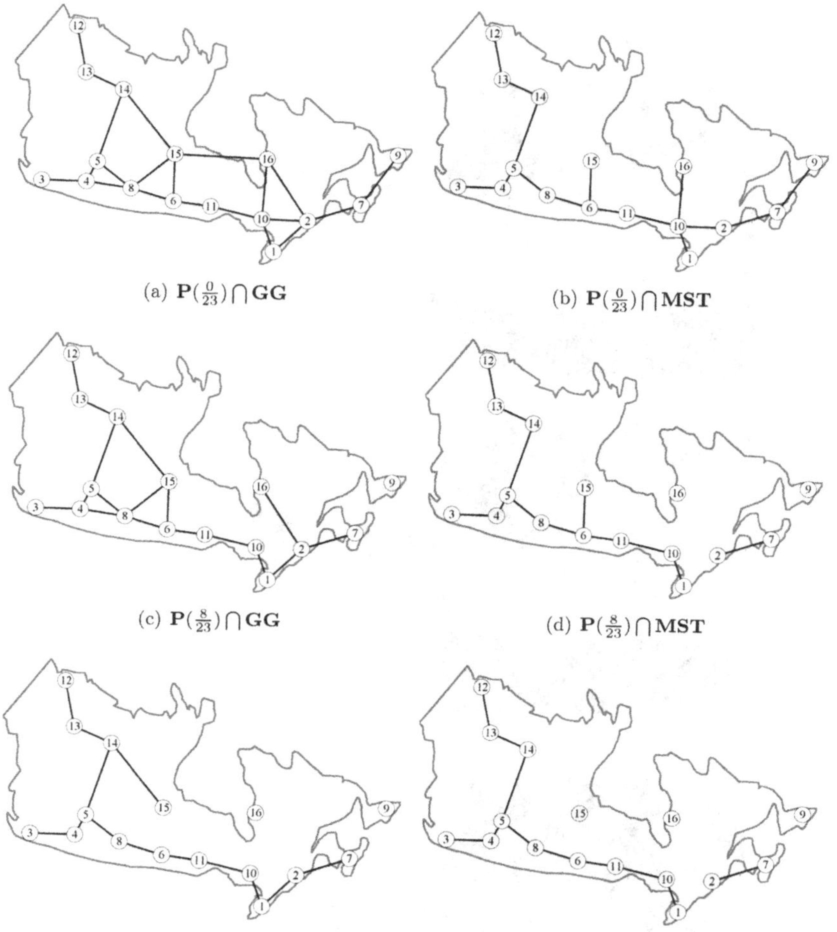

(a) $\mathbf{P}(\frac{0}{23})\bigcap\mathbf{GG}$

(b) $\mathbf{P}(\frac{0}{23})\bigcap\mathbf{MST}$

(c) $\mathbf{P}(\frac{8}{23})\bigcap\mathbf{GG}$

(d) $\mathbf{P}(\frac{8}{23})\bigcap\mathbf{MST}$

(e) $\mathbf{P}(\frac{17}{23})\bigcap\mathbf{GG}$

(f) $\mathbf{P}(\frac{17}{23})\bigcap\mathbf{MST}$

to cover the area Saskatoon-Moncton. In a few experiments the plasmodium colony occupying St. Jonn's remains unaffected.

Finding 8: In response to contamination propagating from the Bruce Nuclear Power station, the plasmodium of P. polycephalum takes one or more of the following actions: migrates outside Canada, enhances the transport network outside the contaminated zone, sprouts indiscriminately from urban areas and transport links.

The plasmodium's reactions are illustrated in Figure 7 and Figure 8. Four types of responses are observed in laboratory experiments.

- Plasmodium migrates outside Canada (Figure 7a and Figure 7b). Typical waves of migration are from Nunavut towards Baffin Bay and Greenland and from British Columbia towards Washington and Oregon in USA. Due to the growth substrate being an agar plate cut in the shape of Canada, the plasmodium ends up on the bare plastic bottom of a Petri dish, therefore it does not migrate far away from Canada.

Figure 7. Physarum response to contamination. (a-b) Migration outside Canada. (c–f) Compensating activation of transport net- work unaffected by contamination. (a-c-e) Original images. (b-d-f) Bi- narized images: only pixels from (a-c-e) which red and green compo- nents exceed 100 and blue component is less than 100 are drawn as black pixels in (bdf), otherwise white.

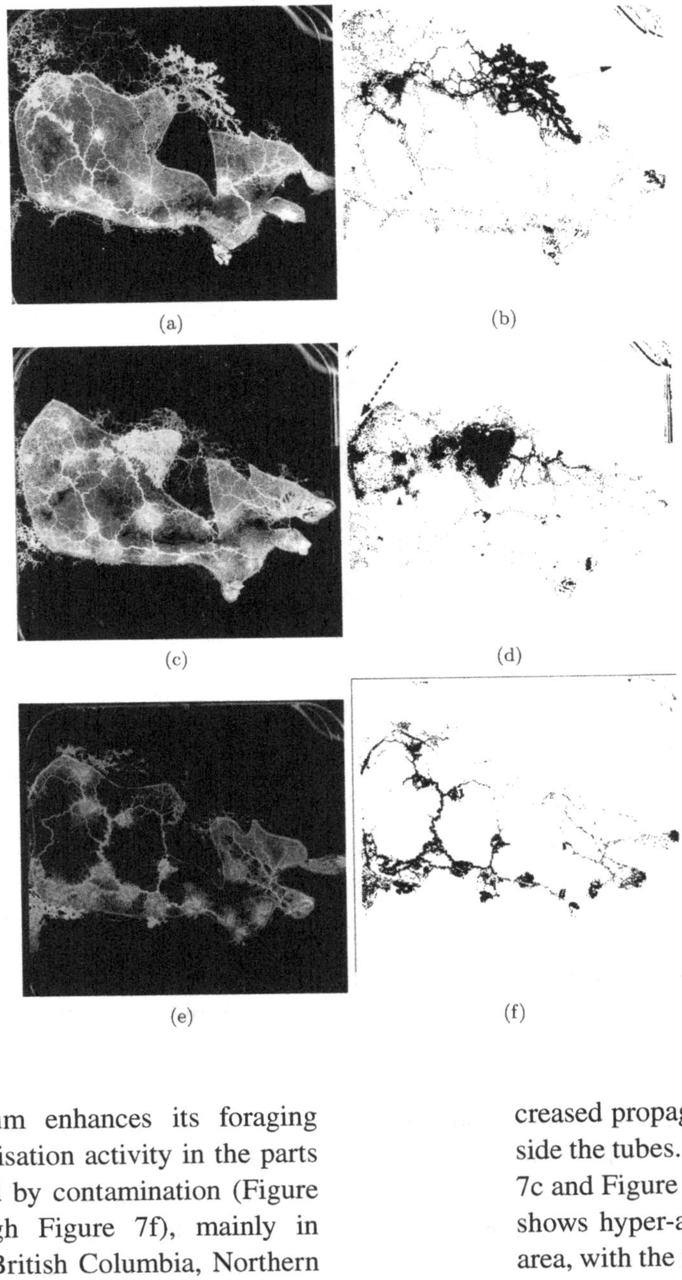

- Plasmodium enhances its foraging and colonisation activity in the parts unaffected by contamination (Figure 7c through Figure 7f), mainly in Alberta, British Columbia, Northern Territories, Yukon and Nunavut. Protoplasmic tubes themselves are often increased in size and intensity of their colours, which reflects increased propagation of cytoplasm inside the tubes. For example, in Figure 7c and Figure 7d plasmodium clearly shows hyper-activity in the Nunavut area, with the whole territory covered by spreading plasmodium. Figure 7c and Figure 7d illustrates hyper-activation of transport routes, particularly links Inuvik — Wrigley, Yelloknife

Figure 8. Physarum sprouting in response to contamination. (a-b) Sprouting from edges. (c-d) Sprouting from nodes. (a-c) Original colour images. (b-d) Binarized images.

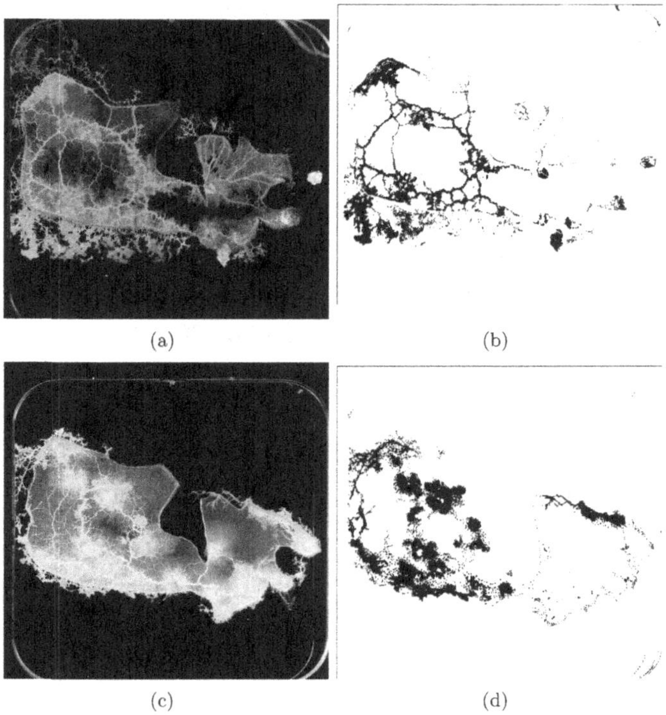

— Wrigley, Edmonton — Wrigley, Edmonton — Vancouver area, Saskatoon-Regina — Edmonton, and Winnipeg — Saskatoon.

- Plasmodium expands outside oat flakes and also produces processes protruding from the protoplasmic tubes (Figure 8a through Figure 7d). This a common reaction of plasmodium in response to mechanical damage, e.g., cutting of protoplasmic tubes (Adamatzky, 2010).

7. DISCUSSION

To imitate transport networks in Canada we represented major urban areas and transport nodes with oat flakes, inoculated plasmodium of *Physarum poly- cephalum*, allowed the plasmodium to span all oat flakes with its network of proto- plasmic tubes and analysed the structure of the protoplasmic network. We found that in over 75% of experiments *P. polycephalum* an acyclic transport network consisting of a chain spanning urban areas along the south boundary of Canada, from Halifax-Moncton to Vancouver area, with branches Edmonton to Yellowknife to Wrigley to Inuvik and Yellowknife to Thompson. In all experiments slime mould approximates all but Vancouver to Calgary links of Canadian highways networks. Both slime mould and Canadian highway networks have a strong spanning tree component and thus can be thought of as optimal transport networks. In laboratory experiments with slime mould we also detailed possible scenarios of transport network restructuring in a response to a spreading contamination. We believe our results make a substantial contribution towards nature-inspired analyses and design of human-made transport networks. Further experiments are necessary to determine how natural and geographical conditions, especially terrain, affect the exact topology of developing transport networks.

REFERENCES

Adamatzky, A. (2007a, March). *From reaction-diffusion to Physarum computing*. Paper presented at the Workshop on Unconventional Computing: Quo Vadis? Santa Fe, NM.

Adamatzky, A. (2007b). Physarum machine: Implementation of a Kolmogorov-Uspensky machine on a biological substrate. *Parallel Processing Letters*, *17*, 455–467. doi:10.1142/S0129626407003150.

Adamatzky, A. (2010). *Physarum machines*. Singapore: World Scientific.

Adamatzky, A., & Jones, J. (2010). Road planning with slime mould: If Physarum built motorways it would route M6/M74 through Newcastle. *International Journal of Bifurcation and Chaos in Applied Sciences and Engineering*. doi:10.1142/S0218127410027568.

Adamatzky, A., Martinez, G. J., Chapa-Vergara, S. V., Asomoza-Palacio, R., & Stephens, C. R. (2010). Approximating Mexican highways with slime mould. *Natural Computing: An International Journal*, *10*(3), 1195–1214. doi:10.1007/s11047-011-9255-z.

Adamatzky, A., & Sloot, P. (2010). *Bio-development of motorway networks in the Netherlands: Slime mould approach*. Retrieved from http://arxiv.org/abs/1209.2974

Barrat, A., Barthelemy, M., & Vespignani, A. (2008). *Dynamical processes in complex networks*. Cambridge, UK: Cambridge University Press. doi:10.1017/CBO9780511791383.

Beuthe, M., Himanen, V., Reggiani, A., & Zamparini, L. (Eds.). (2004). *Transport developments and innovations in an evolving*. Singapore: World Scientific.

Canada's National Highway System. (2008). *Condition report. St. John's, NL*. Canada: Council of Ministers Responsible for Transportation and Highway Safety.

Dorigo, M., & Statzle, T. (2004). *Ant colony optimization*. Cambridge, MA: Bradford Books. doi:10.1007/b99492.

Gabriel, K. R., & Sokal, R. R. (1969). A new statistical approach to geographic variation analysis. *Systematic Zoology*, *18*, 259–278. doi:10.2307/2412323.

Jaromczyk, J. W., & Toussaint, G. T. (1992). Relative neighborhood graphs and their relatives. *Proceedings of the IEEE*, *80*, 1502–1517. doi:10.1109/5.163414.

Kirkpatrick, D. G., & Radke, J. D. (1985). A framework for computational morphology. In Toussaint, G. (Ed.), *Computational geometry* (pp. 217–248). Amsterdam, The Netherlands: North-Holland.

Larsen, J., Urry, J., & Axhausen, K. (2006). *Mobilities, networks, geographies*. Aldershot, UK: Ashgate.

Matula, D. W., & Sokal, R. R. (1984). Properties of Gabriel graphs relevant to geographical variation research and the clustering of points in the same plane. *Geographical Analysis*, *12*, 205–222. doi:10.1111/j.1538-4632.1980.tb00031.x.

Nakagaki, T. (2001). Smart behavior of true slime mold in a labyrinth. *Research in Microbiology*, *152*, 767–770. doi:10.1016/S0923-2508(01)01259-1.

Nakagaki, T., Iima, M., Ueda, T., Nishiura, Y., Saigusa, T., & Tero, A. et al. (2007). Minimum-risk path finding by an adaptive amoeba network. *Physical Review Letters*, *99*, 068104. doi:10.1103/PhysRevLett.99.068104.

Nakagaki, T., Yamada, H., & Toth, A. (2001). Path finding by tube morphogenesis in an amoeboid organism. *Biophysical Chemistry*, *92*, 47–52. doi:10.1016/S0301-4622(01)00179-X.

Nakagaki, T., Yamada, H., & Ueda, T. (2000). Interaction between cell shape and contraction pattern in the *Physarum plasmodium. Biophysical Chemistry*, *84*, 195–204. doi:10.1016/S0301-4622(00)00108-3.

Nesetril, J., Milkova, E., & Nesetrilova, H. (2001). Otakar Boruvka on minimum spanning tree problem. *Discrete Mathematics*, *233*, 3–36. doi:10.1016/S0012-365X(00)00224-7.

Olariu, S., & Weigle, M. C. (2009). *Vehicular networks: From theory to practice*. Boca Raton, FL: Chapman and Hall/CRC. doi:10.1201/9781420085891.

Schumann, A., & Adamatzky, A. (2009, September 26-29). Physarum spatial logic. In *Proceedings of the 1st International Symposium on Symbolic and Numeric Algorithms for Scientific Computing*, Timisoara, Romania.

Shirakawa, T., Adamatzky, A., Gunji, Y.-P., & Miyake, Y. (2009). On simultaneous construction of Voronoi diagram and Delaunay triangulation by Physarum polycephalum. *International Journal of Bifurcation and Chaos in Applied Sciences and Engineering*, *19*(9). doi:10.1142/S0218127409024682.

Solnon, C. (2010). *Ant colony optimization and constraint programming*. New York, NY: Wiley-Interscience.

Stephenson, S. L., & Stempen, H. (2000). *Myxomycetes: A handbook of slime molds*. Portland, OR: Timber Press.

Taplin, J. H. E., Qiu, M., & Han, R. (2005). *Cost-benefit analysis and evolutionary computing: Optimal scheduling of interactive road projects*. Cheltenham, UK: Edward Elgar.

Tero, A., Kobayashi, R., & Nakagaki, T. (2006). *Physarum* solver: A biologically inspired method of road-network navigation. *Physica A*, *363*, 115–119. doi:10.1016/j.physa.2006.01.053.

Toussaint, G. T. (1980). The relative neighborhood graph of a finite planar set. *Pattern Recognition*, *12*, 261–268. doi:10.1016/0031-3203(80)90066-7.

Tsuda, S., Aono, M., & Gunji, Y.-P. (2004). Robust and emergent Physarum logical-computing. *Bio Systems*, *73*, 45–55. doi:10.1016/j.biosystems.2003.08.001.

This work was previously published in the International Journal of Natural Computing Research (IJNCR), Volume 2, Issue 4, edited by Leandro Nunes de Castro, pp. 31-46, copyright 2011 by IGI Publishing (an imprint of IGI Global).

Chapter 18
Ecosystems Computing:
Introduction to Biogeographic Computation

Rodrigo Pasti
Laboratory of Bioinformatics and Bio-Inspired Computing (LBiC), University of Campinas (UNICAMP), Brazil

Fernando José Von Zuben
Laboratory of Bioinformatics and Bio-Inspired Computing (LBiC), University of Campinas (UNICAMP), Brazil

Leandro Nunes de Castro
Natural Computing Laboratory (LCoN), Mackenzie University, Brazil

ABSTRACT

The main issue to be presented in this paper is based on the premise that Nature computes, that is, processes information. This is the fundamental of Natural Computing. Biogeographic Computation will be presented as a Natural Computing approach aimed at investigating ecosystems computing. The first step towards formalizing Biogeographic Computation will be given by defining a metamodel, a framework capable of generating models that compute through the elements of an ecosystem. It will also be discussed how this computing can be realized in current computers.

1. INTRODUCTION: THE NATURAL COMPUTING OF BIOGEOGRAPHY

By the 1940s, Computer Science was engaged in the study of automatic computing. One decade later came the study of information processing, followed by the study of phenomena surrounding computers, what can be automated, and then formal computation. In the new millennium, Computer Science has given attention to the investigation of information processing, both in Nature and the artificial (Denning, 2008).

Some researchers understand computing as a natural science, for information processes have been perceived in the essence of various phenomena in several fields of science. In the

DOI: 10.4018/978-1-4666-4253-9.ch018

book *The Invisible Future* (Denning, 2001), David Baltimore says "Biology is nowadays an information science." However, if computing is concerned with the study of information processing, what would be the computing of nature? That is, in what sense nature processes information? A consistent definition is given by Lloyd (2002): "all physical system registers information and, by evolving in time, operating in its context, changes information, transforms information or, if you prefer, processes information." Information here is a measure of order, organization, a universal measure applicable to any structure, any system (Lloyd, 2006). Understanding nature as an information processor gives us a new concept to the terminology computing, and that is exactly the fundamental basics of Natural Computing (de Castro, 2006, 2007). Several researchers, in many sciences, have already studied nature in such context:

- Immune systems (Cohen, 2009; Hart et al., 2007; de Castro & Timmis, 2002);
- Ecosystems (Gavrilets & Losos, 2009; de Aguiar et al., 2009; Gavrilets & Vose, 2005);
- Bees (Maia & de Castro, 2012; Lihoreau et al., 2010);
- Ants (Vittori et al., 2006; Pratt et al., 2002; Dorigo et al., 1996);
- Genes (Kauffman, 1993; Holland, 1992);
- Bacteria (Xavier et al., 2011, Mehta et al., 2009);
- Basic laws of nature (Dowek, 2012);
- All *universe* (Lloyd, 2006);
- Among many others (Schwenk et al., 2009; de Castro, 2007, 2006; Denning, 2007; Brent & Buck, 2006).

Just as with biogeography, the object of study here are ecosystems: individuals, species and environment. Starting with the premise that nature processes information, the main goal of this paper is to introduce a new research field aimed at investigating ecosystem computing, based on the knowledge of Biogeography and Natural Computing as sciences.

Ecosystems are highly complex and dynamic environments composed of a high number of interdependent variables defined in space and time (Provata et al., 2008; Harel, 2003; Milne, 1998; Kauffman, 1993; Jorgensen et al., 1992). They are usually studied by understanding their component parts, as the studies involving the dynamics of solar systems (Cohen, 2000), in which forces, such as gravity, are used to explain the emergence of its behaviors.

The composition of ecosystems obeys physical and chemical laws, but there is no set of fundamental laws that explain how they work (Cohen & Harel, 2007). The application of reductionist methods for the understanding of how living systems work is widely used, but shows clear limitations when the goal is to extract universal laws to explain these systems (Cohen, 2007; Fleck, 1979). It is possible to identify a scale of emergence going from simple molecules to a complex organism. Biogeography emphasizes the emergence of societies of living organisms (individuals and species), representing the highest level of Figure 1.

By analyzing this scenario from an information processing perspective and taking into account the fundamentals of Natural Computing, it is possible to note that the basic elements of an ecosystem compute and, thus, conclude that a formal definition for Biogeographic Computation, as a Natural Computing field of research, can be proposed as follows:

Biogeographic Computation (BC) is a research field in the realm of Natural Computing aimed at understanding ecosystems computing.

Biogeographic Computation is based on Biogeography and the transposition of knowledge from this field to a computing universe promoted by the fundamentals of Natural Computing, that

Figure 1. Emergence of behaviors and objects in different scales (based on the paper "Explaining a complex living system: dynamics, multi-scaling and emergence," by Cohen, 2007)

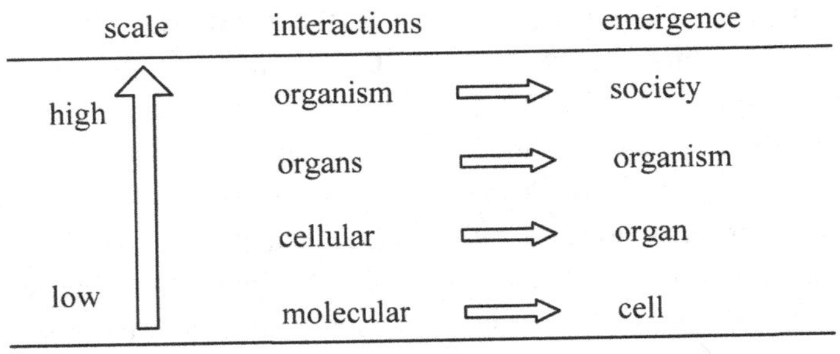

is, the observation of ecosystems from a computational perspective. As a first step towards understanding ecosystems computing, it will be introduced a framework, named *metamodel*, that will allow the realization of ecosystems computing in current computers, that is, based on Von Neumann's architecture (Stallings, 2003). Through the mathematical formalisms of the metamodel it will be possible to build *dynamic models* that represent the space-time evolution of ecosystems in discrete states, in which biogeographic processes are equivalent to state changes. Through time, it is possible to identify representative states that describe the reality of continuous transformations for a discrete and computable universe.

This paper is organized as follows. Section 2 reviews some elementary concepts for the proposal of Biogeographic Computation and it's metamodel, and Section 3 motivates the investigation and application of Biogeographic Computation. In Section 4 the metamodel is formalized. In Section 5 an application of metamodel is exemplified by means of a model that exhibits unique biogeographic patterns, analogous to those encountered in nature. Concluding remarks are presented in Section 6 together with future perspectives of Biogeographic Computation.

2. FUNDAMENTALS OF BIOGEOGRAPHY

Living beings are highly multiform. The diversity of organisms present on Earth is overwhelming. It is estimated that there are 50 million species on Earth, including animals, plants and microorganisms (Brown & Lomolino, 2005). In almost all regions of the planet, from the freezing deserts of the Arctic, the abyssal of oceans to the hot and humid forests, it is possible to find a large variety of living systems. In all of them, they are adapted to the conditions imposed by the habitats. Heredity is an important aspect related to the diversity of living organisms. Species often share extinct ancestors. A classical example cited by Brown and Lomolino (2005) is that all existing plant species share a common ancestor: a green algae that lived approximately 500 million years ago. Therefore, it is possible to define a Biogeography Science, for instance, according to Brown and Lomolino (2005):

Biogeography is a science concerned with documenting and understanding special models of biodiversity. It is the study of the distribution of organisms, in the past and in the present, and of the variation patterns that occurred on Earth, related to the number and types of living beings.

The occurrence of patterns in nature implies the existence of some processes. Thus, there is a variation in space and time promoted by them. The abstractions of Biogeographic Computation reside in these patterns and processes.

2.1. Ecosystems

An ecosystem is a set of living beings, the environment that they inhabit and all interactions of these organisms with the environment and one another. A forest, a river, a lake, a garden and the biosphere are all examples of an ecosystem. The ecosystems present three basic components: the communities of individuals and species (*biota* or *ecological community*); the physical or chemical elements of the environment, and the geographical space (*habitat*). Elements that compose all ecosystems are the *ecological niches* that describe the relational position of a species or population in its ecosystem, defining the way of life of any organism (Brown & Lomolino, 2005). The niches provide answers to the interactions of organisms and theirs with the environment, as in cases of competition by resources or predator-prey competitions (Schoener, 1991). In summary, there are some important concepts to be introduced:

- **Adaptation:** It is intimately related to natural selection, because it complements the notion of graded improvement. The adaptation level to the environment is what determines the path to be followed by natural selection: a response to the selection always occurs when a heritable feature is related with reproductive success; the outcome is an improvement in performance through generations of reproduction and differentiation.
- **Biological Isolation:** Determines the reproductive capability between two individuals. If there is an isolation, then two individuals cannot reproduce.
- Ecological Barrier: It includes any means that prevent a given species from occupying a new habitat. Notic also that when a species leaves its habitat, its adaptable features may not be sufficient for the survival in the new environment.
- **Geographical Isolation:** It occurs among two or more individuals and species when there are ecological barriers that severely restrict their contact.

There is no consensus on the definition of species (Brown & Lomolino, 2006). In the present paper, species will be treated in a specific manner, related to the concept of a *biological species*, which defines a species as a population of organisms that present biological isolation in relation to other populations, thus representing a separate evolutionary lineage (Brown & Lomolino, 2005; Coyne & Orr, 1999). The crossing between species that generated individuals with biological isolation may lead to the emergence of hybrid species.

2.2. Processes in Biogeography

The biogeographical processes explain geographical, ecological and evolutionary patterns, with the goal of describing and understanding how species occupy habitats, migrate, emerge, disappear, procreate, differentiate and adapt, from the simplest to the most complex ecosystem. All processes are well described and consolidated in the literature (Brown & Lomolino, 2005; Ridley, 2004; Coyne & Orr, 1999; Rosenzweig, 1995; Myers & Giller, 1991; Hegenveld, 1990; Simmons, 1982). The processes can be classified based on their type:

- **Geographical Processes:** Related to the Earth surface and spatial distribution of significant phenomena for ecosystems. This includes climate, tectonic and all other phenomena related to environmental changes.

- **Ecological Processes:** Directly related to individuals and species, such as dispersion and interactions.
- **Evolutionary Processes:** Related to the evolution of individuals and species. They can be divided into *macro* and *microevolutionary*.

Basically, the goal is to explain a wide range spatio-temperal events in an ecosystem. A single species can explore a whole ecosystem, transposing ecological barriers, evolving and giving origin to various descending species that can become completely different genetically from the ancestor species. When expanding its coverage, a species may or may not adapt itself to new environments. If adaptation is necessary, there are several evolutionary processes that lead to improvement in adaptation. If adaptation is not sufficient, or does not occur at all, a species, much likely, will become extinct. Biogeographical processes are the ones responsible for the theory that explains the diversity of species through space-time and not only related to the diversity among species, but also intraspecific diversity. Thus, it is important not only to understand how the diversity of species emerge, but also how individual diversity can lead to species diversity (Coyne & Orr, 1999; Magurran, 1999). Essentially, it is possible to emphasize the following biogeographical processes.

2.2.1. Geographical Process

- **Environmental Changes:** Includes all processes related to the transformation in geographic spaces and habitats. It can give rise to a series of natural patterns responsible for a great variety of habitats over time. In this context, it is possible to emphasize *vicariance,* responsible for habitat fragmentation and the appearance of ecological barriers. For instance, the emergence of an island can be viewed as a piece of land separated from a continent (Brown & Lomolino, 2005).

2.2.2. Ecological Process

- **Dispersion:** Deals with the movements of individuals and species through the geographical space. Dispersion can be the source of various emergent patterns. The *diffusion* involves the gradual spread of individuals and species outside their habitats through dispersion. It is a three-stage process: (1) repeated dispersion events that promote the occupation of novel habitats; (2) the establishment, through adaptation, in new environments; and (3) the composition of new populations that can give origin to new species. This process can be viewed as the start of dispersion. The definitions of dispersion and diffusion give rise to the definition of *dispersion routes* (Brown & Lomolino, 2005), which correspond to types of habitats in which species can disperse based on their adaptation. There are three dispersion routes: (1) *corridors*: allow individuals and species to migrate from an origin habitat to another without imposing limiting factors; populations remain with a balanced number of individuals; (2) *filters*: these are dispersion routes more restrictive than corridors; they selectively block the passage of individuals based on their adaptations, as a result, colonizers tend to represent a single subset of their initial population; and (3) *sweeptake routes*: these are rare dispersions, constituting a specific case of filters; a classic example is the colonization of isolated ocean islands. Additionally, when a migratory population fixes on a distant habitat, sufficient to maintain isolation from the other individuals of their species, the result is the *founder effect*.

2.2.3. Microevolutionary Processes

- **Natural Selection:** The selection of individuals and features favorable to the species. Favorable features that are inherited become more common in successive generations of a population of organisms that reproduce. The natural selection process is responsible for many patterns of evolution that can be found in nature. In a broad sense, it can be considered the force that models the evolutionary dynamics of the biotic components in ecosystems. Obviously, natural selection is a process that depends on many variables, all related to each element and interaction between them. It is possible to highlight the selective pressure effect, which dictates the survival of a phenotype or genotype in a population. When the selective pressure is intense to a point where few individuals survive through generations, that is, the number of individuals in a species is considerable less than in the previous generation, the result is the well-known bottleneck effect.
- **Mutation:** It is defined as any modification in the genetic material of an organism, including the altering or deletion of a single or many DNA nucleotides, and even a complete rearrangement *of a chromosome*.
- **Reproduction:** Two individuals, that are not biologically isolated, can reproduce sexually to generate new individuals through their parents' DNA. The individuals that migrate for a new area carry their genes with them and, if they reproduce, they introduce their genes in the local population, promoting the *gene or phenotype flow*. Reproduction can also occur asexually; that is, without an intercourse and, thus, without the exchange of genetic material from the parents.

2.2.4. Macroevolutionary Processes

- **Peripatric Speciation:**. It is the simplest and most common speciation process. It occurs when the populations are geographically isolated, such that the gene flow between them is almost completely interrupted. The causes of this type of speciation include the founder effect, through which a population, started by only a few colonizer individuals, contains just a small random sample of the alleles present in the ancestor population.
- **Sympatric Speciation:** It occurs due to chromosomal and mutation changes. During fertilization or the developmental process of the embryo, there is a chance that a rearrangement of the genetic material occurs. Individuals that suffered sympatric speciation are mutants in relation to their parents. These new individuals may generate a new species or still belong to an existing hybrid species.
- **Competitive (or Parapatric) Speciation:** It is the expansion of a species from a single to multiple habitats. When the original species is separated in subgroups, one explores the original habitat and the others the new habitats. When two or more habitats are occupied, the subgroups tend to diverge after some time, such that its individuals may develop biological isolation with the ancestor species.

- **Species Extinction:** The differential survival and the proliferation of species in geological time are determined by analogy with the differential survival and reproduction of individuals. Species or groups of species may disappear.

3. ARTIFICIAL ECOSYSTEMS: WHY TO STUDY?

The objects of study of Biogeographic Computation are the ecosystems. To move from the natural to the computational perspective, it is necessary to employ some type of representation that expresses computationally the existence of such ecosystems and the computation involved. Biogeographic Computation models have the following proposal: to represent ecosystems' elements and explain how they are processing information. The models can be seen as part of the essence of the Biogeographic Computation theory, because they move from the description of the real world to the computational world. Therefore, the objects of study of Biogeographic Computation are virtual or artificial ecosystems.

Artificial ecosystems are abstract universes consisting of basic elements represented by mathematical definitions. What elements are contained in these ecosystems depends on what types of computing one wants to reproduce. Formally, defining an artificial ecosystem is not an easy task, but one thing is clear: it is possible to describe and manipulate it arbitrarily. The crucial and most important aspect of the proposed Biogeographic Computation is the freedom to manipulate an artificial ecosystem. The starting point for this is the definition of the *metamodel* that represents an abstract definition of the ecosystem and its biogeographical processes. The metamodel allows the design of highly complex scenarios, like those found in natural ecosystems, with the following characteristics:

1. Information processing between elements with a high number of connections among themselves;
2. Endless possibilities of representing elements of ecosystems;
3. Individuals and species composing an adaptive system conditioned to interactions with one another and the environment;
4. Adaptation to different conditions lead to the emergence of different adaptive units through speciation processes;
5. Different types of speciation processes leading to a vast range of representations subject to the environment and the interactions of elements;
6. Systems with high levels of diversity represented by individuals, species and habitats;
7. Maximizing the exploration of the representation space due to the high diversity of individuals, species and habitats;
8. Self-organization and emergence.

Understanding the high complexity of ecosystems by using models generated by the metamodel aid the understanding of biogeography and the design of computational tools that take full advantage of the scenario presented. Complex problems of everyday life often have the same characteristics inherent to ecosystems - adaptive systems, diverse solutions, high connectivity, among many others, and this motivates the study of artificial ecosystems in order to solve such problems.

Several models and algorithms in the literature are included in the scope of Biogeography and Biogeographic Computation and make use of some of the features listed above. The creative freedom promoted by artificial ecosystems is found in these models, but there is no consensus representation for models in the literature. Taking as examples the following works of de Aguiar et al. (2009), Simon (2008), Vittori et al. (2006), de Castro (2006), Gavrilets and Vose (2005), and Vittori and Araujo (2001); they all represent models of Biogeographic Computation and each has its own formalism. To circumvent the situation described above the metamodel proposes a unified formalism, to be presented in Section 4.

Given the scenario provided by artificial ecosystems and biogeographical processes, the purpose of Biogeographic Computation becomes to design tools to extract features inherent and unique to ecosystems and biogeographical processes.

3.1. Research Areas of Biogeographic Computation

The tools used in the study of ecosystems computing are the computer models generated from the metamodel. There are two avenues of investigation: theoretical and practical. As a first proposal and starting point, the theory is grounded in the understanding of ecosystems through a computer language provided by the metamodel itself. The practice is the application of this theory to design models that solve complex problems.

In Natural Computing, empirical work will always be part of the process of understanding the computation of natural phenomena. The observation of ecosystems is an integral part of Biogeographic Computation: observe to understand computing. Empirical methods have featured in Biogeographic Computation, where observational studies of ecosystems may include regions from small to large continental areas, as reported by Nicholson et al. (2007), Brown and Lomolino (2005), Melville et al. (2005), Wiens and Donoghue (2004), Newton (2003), and Mayr and Diamond (2001). The knowledge contained in empirical work is then processed through the basics of Natural Computing, where natural elements are seen as information processors. The vast majority of computer models in the literature was proposed by observations performed and documented by other researchers. Obviously this does not prevent a Natural Computing researcher to perform field observations. Examples include the works of Vittori (Vittori et al., 2006; Vittori & Araujo, 2001), who observed an ecosystem of real ants, understood the computation performed by them and turned it into a tool to solve a telecommunication problem.

3.1.1. Biogeographic Computation Theory

Biogeographic Computation theory seeks to understand ecosystems through Natural Computing. The elements of ecosystems are information processors and, based on this premise, it is possible to make inferences about certain phenomena and behaviors through computer modeling. In several studies, it is possible to find attempts at understanding ecosystems following the premise of Biogeographic Computation. Several information processors in ecosystems are formalized in different contexts, for example:

- Bees from the species *Bombus terrestris* (Lihoreau et al., 2010);
- Adaptive radiation (Gavrilets & Losos, 2009; Gavrilets & Vose, 2005);
- Ants (Vittori et al., 2006; Pratt et al., 2002);
- Sympatric speciation (de Aguiar et al., 2009);
- Speciation and diversification in metapopulations (Gavrilets et al., 2000);
- Individual-based modeling (Grimm & Railsback, 2005).

Whatever the case, the objects of study are always ecosystems doing some kind of computation. By knowing how certain elements process information, the time and space limits lie in computing power, bringing down a major obstacle for the understanding of biogeography: the enormous time scale. Some processes take hundreds and even millions of years to occur, leaving only fossil records (Gavrilets & Losos, 2009; Brown & Lomolino, 2005). The manipulation of an abstract ecosystem may bring information about geological scales (millions of years) to computational scales (less than a second).

3.1.2. From Theory to Application

Complex problems can be found in various sciences and fields of research, such as Engineering (Pardalos et al., 2002), Economics (Dixit, 1990), Bioinformatics (Galperin & Koonin, 2003) and Marketing (Ricci et al., 2010). In all cases, there is something in common: the high complexity of these problems is an obstacle for obtaining satisfactory results. Problems of this nature are included in the scope of continuous (Bazaraa et al., 2006) and combinatorial optimization (Papadimitriou & Steiglitz, 1998), data clustering (Han et al., 2005), machine learning (Bishop, 2006), among others. Solving these problems is the goal of Biogeographic Computation: to use ecosystems' computing to solve complex problems.

In some situations it is possible to see that ecosystems' elements solve problems. As an example, consider the evolutionary processes, which provide progressive adaptation of species to certain habitats. Adaptation here can easily be translated into optimization, that is, adaptation is a continuous improvement process. A word of caution must be said here: species adaptation does not have a purpose or well defined objective. However, not only related to optimization, various types of problems have proven treatable by the theory of evolution, a fact confirmed by the entire line of research called Evolutionary Computation (Back et al., 2000), as well as other information processors in ecosystems:

- Artificial ants solving combinatorial problems (de Castro, 2006; Dorigo et al., 1996);
- Artificial bees solving optimization problems (Maia & de Castro, 2012);
- Dispersion (migration) of individuals in artificial habitats for solving continuous function optimization problems (Simon, 2008);
- Ant-inspired robotics (de Castro, 2006; Kube et al., 2004).

4. BIOGEOGRAPHIC COMPUTATION METAMODEL

In order to understand ecosystems' computing, it will be proposed here a framework called metamodel: a structured formalism that translates Biogeography into a set of mathematical definitions that represent elements and computations of ecosystems. The starting point is a 2-tuple, which represents the fundamental structure of the metamodel, serving as a template for the design of Biogeographic Computation models. The basic elements are the definition of an ecosystem and the definition of computing (or model dynamics).

Definition 1. Metamodel of Biogeographic Computation: It is defined as a 2-tuple $\mathcal{M}$ composed of two elements E and C that represent the definitions of ecosystem and computing, respectively:

$$\mathcal{M}=\langle E,C\rangle \quad (1)$$

A model generated by a metamodel exists if and only if there is an ecosystem and a computation to manage its dynamics through space and time.

4.1. Definitions that Characterize an Artificial Ecosystem

In the metamodel, there are three main components that represent an ecosystem: (1) the space of representation of the biota elements; (2) the geographic space; (3) and the set of relations. The biota and the geographical space have elements defined in spaces of representations, whilst relations define how elements of these spaces relate to one another.

Despite the broadness of these spaces, in practical implementations of Biogeographic Computation only a finite set of elements of the representation spaces will be part of the model. However, for every element considered, it should be possible to define all the relevant relationships that it establishes with other elements of the model.

Definition 2. Ecosystem: Defined as a 3-tuple $E = \langle I, H, R \rangle$, where I is the *Biota*, that is, representation space of individuals; H the geographical space; and R the set of relations.

Definition 3. Biota: Representation space I that allows characterizing the individuals who compose a biota. Consider p as the number of attributes that characterize each individual, a value dependent on each application.

Definition 4. Individual: Every individual $\mathbf{i}_j \in I$, j=1,..., o, is described by a vector of p attributes $\mathbf{i}_j = [\mathbf{i}_{j1}, \ldots, \mathbf{i}_{jp}]$.

Definition 5. Geographical Space: Representation space H that allows characterizing the habitats that compose the geographical space; that is, an environment in which the biota inhabit. Consider r as the number of attributes that characterize each habitat, a value dependent on each application.

Definition 6. Habitat: Each habitat $\mathbf{h}_t \in H$, t= 1,...,q, is described by a vector of r attributes $\mathbf{h}_t = [h_{t1}, \ldots, h_{tr}]$.

Definition 7. Set of Relations: Contains all the n relations that belong to a model; defined by $R = \{\rho_1, \ldots, \rho_n\}$. Each relation exclusively defines an interaction biota-biota, biota-habitat, or habitat-habitat; that is, a unique interaction of elements of I, or elements of I and H, or elements of H. Relations are directed, e.g., for two individuals $\mathbf{i}_j \overset{\rho}{\rightarrow} \mathbf{i}_g$, or undirected denoted by $\mathbf{i}_j \overset{\rho}{\rightarrow} \mathbf{i}_g$. They can be binary or take gradual values, e.g., over the interval [0,1]. Here are some simple examples, given an arbitrary relation ρ between individuals:

- $\mathbf{i}_j \overset{\rho}{\rightarrow} \mathbf{i}_g$: There is a relation ρ from $\mathbf{i}_j$ to $\mathbf{i}_g$.
- $\mathbf{i}_j \overset{\rho}{\rightarrow} \mathbf{i}_g$: There is a relation ρ from $\mathbf{i}_j$ to $\mathbf{i}_g$ and from $\mathbf{i}_g$ to $\mathbf{i}_j$ (between $\mathbf{i}_j$ and $\mathbf{i}_g$).
- $\mathbf{i}_j \overset{\bar{\rho}}{\rightarrow} \mathbf{i}_g$: There is no relation ρ from $\mathbf{i}_j$.to $\mathbf{i}_g$.
- $\mathbf{i}_j \overset{\bar{\rho}}{\rightarrow} \mathbf{i}_g$: There is no relation ρ from $\mathbf{i}_j$ to $\mathbf{i}_g$ and from $\mathbf{i}_g$ to $\mathbf{i}_j$ (between $\mathbf{i}_j$ and $\mathbf{i}_g$).

If the relations do not assume binary values, they are defined as follows: $\mathbf{i}_j \overset{\rho = x}{\rightarrow} \mathbf{i}_g$. To synthesize the representation, it is possible to represent relations of multiple elements in a single expression. Here is an example considering an arbitrary relation ρ among 3 individuals: $\{\mathbf{i}_j, \mathbf{i}_g\} \overset{\rho}{\rightarrow} \mathbf{i}_t$.

Every relation can be represented by a graph, which can be undirected or directed, weighted or not, according to their relation.

Definition 8. Relation Graph between Elements of an Ecosystem: The relations obtained for individuals $\mathbf{i}_j \in I$ and habitats $\mathbf{h}_t \in H$ lead to the production of relation graphs that represent networks of relations, where the vertices are the elements and the edges represent the presence or absence of the relation. In other words, it means that a graph P is a result of a relation $\rho \in R$.

The information about these relations depends on specific criteria relevant to the models. It is possible to use the relations as qualitative and/or quantitative measures of interactions. Relations are not processes, because they only describe associations between elements of the ecosystem. They can give different answers to different scenarios, provided by the ecosystems' computing. If there is no dynamics, relations provide invariant information in time and space. Eight relations are fundamental to the understanding of the metamodel, as follows:

Relation 1. Habitat Occupancy: Defined as ρ_{HO}, given an individual $\mathbf{i}_j$ and a habitat $\mathbf{h}_t$, ρ_{HO} provides the relation of occupancy of $\mathbf{i}_j$ in $\mathbf{h}_t : \mathbf{i}_j \xrightarrow{\rho_{HO}} \mathbf{h}_t$.

Relation 2. Adaptation: Defined as ρ_A, given an individual $\mathbf{i}_j$ and a habitat $\mathbf{h}_t$, ρ_A provides the adaptation relation of $\mathbf{i}_j$ in $\mathbf{h}_t$, allowing to infer the degree of adaptation x of an individual $\mathbf{i}_j$ in the habitat $\mathbf{h}_t : \mathbf{i}_j \xrightarrow{\rho_A = x} \mathbf{h}_t$.

Relation 3. Biological Isolation: Defined as ρ_{BI}, given two individuals $\{\mathbf{i}_j, \mathbf{i}_g\} \in I$, the relation ρ_{BI} provides the reproduction capability between $\mathbf{i}_j$ and $\mathbf{i}_g$. Two individuals are able to reproduce if and only if $\mathbf{i}_j \overset{\overline{\rho_{BI}}}{\leftrightarrow} \mathbf{i}_g$.

Relation 4. Habitat Neighborhood: Defined as ρ_{HN}, given two habitats $\{\mathbf{h}_t, \mathbf{h}_u\} \in H$, $_{HN}$ provides the relation of neighborhood between two habitats. If $\mathbf{h}_t \overset{HN}{\leftrightarrow} \mathbf{h}_u$ then $\mathbf{h}_t$ and $\mathbf{h}_u$ are neighbors, i.e., they are continuous habitats.

Relation 5. Ecological Barrier: Defined as ρ_{EB}, given an individual $\mathbf{i}_j \in I$, three habitats $\{\mathbf{h}_t, \mathbf{h}_u, \mathbf{h}_v\} \in \mathbf{h}$, where $\mathbf{h}_t \overset{\rho_{HN}}{\leftrightarrow} \mathbf{h}_u$, $\mathbf{h}_v \overset{\rho_{HN}}{\leftrightarrow} \mathbf{h}_u$ and $\mathbf{h}_v \overset{\overline{\rho_{HN}}}{\leftrightarrow} \mathbf{h}_t$, so $\mathbf{h}_u$ is a habitat that separates $\mathbf{h}_t$ from $\mathbf{h}_v$, the relations $\mathbf{i}_j \xrightarrow{\rho_{HO}} \mathbf{h}_t$ and $\mathbf{i}_j \xrightarrow{\overline{\rho_A}} \mathbf{h}_u$ imply an ecological barrier of $\mathbf{i}_j$ in $\mathbf{h}_v$, leading to $\mathbf{i}_j \xrightarrow{EB} \mathbf{h}_v$.

Relation 6. Geographical Isolation: Defined as ρ_{GI}, given two individuals $\{\mathbf{i}_j, \mathbf{i}_g\} \in I$ and three habitats $\{\mathbf{h}_t, \mathbf{h}_u, \mathbf{h}_v\} \in H$, where $\mathbf{h}_t \overset{\rho_{HN}}{\leftrightarrow} \mathbf{h}_u$, $\mathbf{h}_v \overset{\rho_{HN}}{\leftrightarrow} \mathbf{h}_u$ e $\mathbf{h}_v \overset{\overline{\rho_{HN}}}{\leftrightarrow} \mathbf{h}_t$, $\mathbf{h}_u$ is a habitat that separates $\mathbf{h}_t$ from $\mathbf{h}_v$, the relations $\mathbf{i}_j \xrightarrow{\rho_{HO}} \mathbf{h}_t$, $\mathbf{i}_g \xrightarrow{\rho_{HO}} \mathbf{h}_v$, $\mathbf{i}_j \xrightarrow{\rho_{EB}} \mathbf{h}_v$ e $\mathbf{i}_g \xrightarrow{\rho_{EB}} \mathbf{h}_t$ imply the existence of a geographic isolation between $\mathbf{i}_j$ and $\mathbf{i}_g : \mathbf{i}_j \overset{\rho_{GI}}{\leftrightarrow} \mathbf{i}_g$.

Relation 7. Trophic Relation. Defined as ρ_{TR}, given two individuals $\{\mathbf{i}_j, \mathbf{i}_g\} \in I$, where $\mathbf{i}_j \overset{\overline{\rho_{BI}}}{\leftrightarrow} \mathbf{i}_g$, the relation ρ_{TR} provides the trophic relation between $\mathbf{i}_j$ and $\mathbf{i}_g$. If $\mathbf{i}_j \xrightarrow{\rho_{TR}} \mathbf{i}_g$, then $\mathbf{i}_g$ feeds from $\mathbf{i}_j$.

Relation 8. Ancestry Relation: Defined as ρ_{AR} it describes the ancestry relation between individuals. Given two individuals $\{\mathbf{i}_j, \mathbf{i}_g\} \in I$, $\mathbf{i}_j$ is an ancestor of $\mathbf{i}_g$ if $\mathbf{i}_j \xrightarrow{\rho_{AR}} \mathbf{i}_g$. The relation is also defined to subsets that belong to i: $\{\mathbf{i}_1, \ldots, \mathbf{i}_y\} \xrightarrow{\rho_{AR}} \mathbf{i}_g$, or $\{\mathbf{i}_1, \ldots, \mathbf{i}_y\} \xrightarrow{\rho_{AR}} \{\mathbf{i}_1, \ldots, \mathbf{i}_w\}$.

4.1.1. Contextualizing Species

Speciation explains the appearance of new species along time. To understand this process, it is necessary to have an understanding of what is a species. This is also relevant to Biogeographic

Computation, where the following question can be made: what are species in artificial ecosystems? The answer lies in the relations of individuals, which can determine computationally the existence of species.

Definition 9. Biological Species of Sexual Individuals: A species S is a set of individuals, where for every pair $\{\mathbf{i}_j,\mathbf{i}_g\} \in I$, $j \neq g$, it is true that $\mathbf{i}_j \overset{\overline{\rho_{BI}}}{\leftrightarrow} \mathbf{i}_g$.

The definition of species obtained through the relation ρ_{BI} gives rise to a set of species $S_{BI} = \{S_1,\ldots,S_m\}$, where $S_l \subseteq I$, $l = 1, ..., m$. It is possible to conclude that $S_1\ S_2 \ldots S_m = \{\mathbf{i}_1,\ldots,\mathbf{i}_o\}$. Note that Definition 9 allows an individual $\mathbf{i}_j \in I$ to belong to two sets of species, leading to the definition of hybrid individuals.

Definition 10. Hybrid Individuals: Given two species $\{S_f,S_e\}\ S_{BI}$, a hybrid individual between S_f and S_e is an individual that belongs to the set $S_f \cap S_e$. If $S_f \cap S_e = \varnothing$, then there is no hybrid individual between S_f and S_e. This definition can account for three or more species.

It should be emphasized that other conformations of species sets can be obtained through different definitions of relations between individuals.

4.2. Definitions that Characterize Ecosystems Computing

The goal of the metamodel is to transpose the computation of biogeographical processes for a discrete computation, variant in time and space. Thus, the change of state of an artificial ecosystem is provided by the occurrence of processes that are responsible for the dynamic models, inserting discrete-time temporal variation in individuals and habitats.

Definition 11. Processes: Defined according to the taxonomy of biogeographical processes: ecological (ξ), geographical (φ), microevolutionary (μ) and macroevolutionary (M). Processes ξ, μ, M act upon individuals $\mathbf{i}_j \in I$, $j=1,..., o$ and processes φ act upon habitats $\mathbf{h}_t \in \mathbf{h}$, $t = 1,..., q$.

Definition 12. Set of Processes: Defined as a set $C = \{\xi_1,\xi_2,\ldots,\xi_x,\varphi_{x+1},\ldots,\varphi_y,\mu_{y+1},\ldots,\mu_d,M_{d+1},\ldots,M_c\}$ of c processes ξ, φ, μ or M. The values of x, y, and d represent the number o each process type, according to the biogeographic taxonomy. Set C defines the computation of all models. The processes can be applied following a specific order, but there may also be simultaneous execution of processes. The dynamics provided by the computation C has the following characteristics:

1. Discrete or continuous in time;
2. Acts on a state space that contains both discrete and continuous variables;
3. Stochastic or deterministic;
4. Linear or nonlinear.

The transformations in elements $\mathbf{i}_j \in I$ and $\mathbf{h}_t \in H$ can be represented through time by the systematic application of processes contained in the set C. Taking individuals $\mathbf{i}_j$ and habitats $\mathbf{h}_t$ at the time instant $k \in Z^+$, results in the extended notation $\mathbf{i}_j^{(k)}$ and $\mathbf{h}_t^{(k)}$. The application of processes implies updates of these sets in discrete instants of time. Any change in $\mathbf{i}_j^{(k)}$ and $\mathbf{h}_t^{(k)}$ can lead to changes in their relations. At time instants k, relations provide different responses to elements of the ecosystem, then a graph is the result of a relation $\rho \in R$ at time *k*. Consequently, a species $S_f \in S_{BI}$, may also have its conformation variant in time: $S_f^{(k)}$.

In the following, the metamodel processes will be presented. Additional definitions, representing cause and effect relations, are also provided.

Process 1. Dispersion: Defined as ξ_D. Given an individual $\mathbf{i}_j \in I$, it is considered that a subset of the attribute set represents its spatial location. The process ξ_D applies transformations in this subset of attributes.

During dispersion different individuals may occupy different habitats and cross ecological barriers, leading to the definition of dispersion routes, diffusion and the founder effect. All these events imply updating and redefining the relations of the elements of *I*, of the elements of *I* and *H*, and of the elements of *H*.

4.2.1. Dispersion Process Effects

- **Dispersion Routes:** Consider an individual $\mathbf{i}_j \in I$ and three habitats $\{\mathbf{h}_t, \overline{\mathbf{h}_u}, \mathbf{h}_v\} \in H$, where $\mathbf{h}_t \overset{\rho_{HN}}{\leftrightarrow} \mathbf{h}_u$ $\mathbf{h}_v \overset{\rho_{HN}}{\leftrightarrow} \mathbf{h}_u$ $\mathbf{h}_v \overset{\rho_{HN}}{\leftrightarrow} \mathbf{h}_t$, and . Then, $\mathbf{h}_u$ is a habitat that separates from $\mathbf{h}_t$. The existence of different types of dispersion routes can be deduced from the following relations: $\mathbf{i}_j \overset{\rho_{HO}}{\rightarrow} \mathbf{h}_t$ and $\mathbf{i}_j \overset{\rho_{EB}}{\rightarrow} \mathbf{h}_v$. Depending on ρ_{EB}, it is possible to define the existence of a corridor, a filter or a sweeptake route if the individual $\mathbf{i}_j$ occupies habitat $\mathbf{h}_v$: $\mathbf{i}_j \overset{\rho_{HO}}{\rightarrow} \mathbf{h}_v$ when dispersing.
- **Diffusion:** Occurs gradually by successive dispersions through dispersal routes. Consider a subset of individuals $\mathbf{i}_j \in I$, $j=1,..,y$, and a subset of habitats $\mathbf{h}_u \in H$, $u=1, ..., w$. Initially, in an instant, it is true that $\mathbf{i}_j \overset{\rho_{HO}}{\rightarrow} \mathbf{h}_u$. There are three stages that define the diffusion: (1) successive processes ξ_D; (2) occupation of different habitats in future instants: $\mathbf{i}_j \overset{\rho_{HO}}{\rightarrow} \mathbf{h}_t$, where $\mathbf{h}_t \not\subset \{\mathbf{h}_1, \ldots, \mathbf{h}_w\}$; and (3) finally it must be true that $\mathbf{i}_j \overset{\rho_A}{\rightarrow} \mathbf{h}_t$ for every $\mathbf{i}_j \overset{\rho_{HO}}{\rightarrow} \mathbf{h}_t$.
- **Founder effect**. Occurs gradually by successive dispersions. Assume a species $S_f \in S_{BI}$, three habitats $\{\mathbf{h}_t, \overline{\mathbf{h}_u}, \mathbf{h}_v\} \in H$, where $\mathbf{h}_t \overset{\rho_{HN}}{\leftrightarrow} \mathbf{h}_u$, $\mathbf{h}_v \overset{\rho_{HN}}{\leftrightarrow} \mathbf{h}_u$ and $\mathbf{h}_v \overset{\rho_{HN}}{\leftrightarrow} \mathbf{h}_t$. $\mathbf{h}_u$ is a habitat that separates $\mathbf{h}_t$ from $\mathbf{h}_v$. Given, in an instant $k \in Z^+$, a subset $\{\mathbf{i}_1, \ldots, \mathbf{i}_y\} \in S_f$, assume that $\{\mathbf{i}_1, \ldots, \mathbf{i}_y\} \overset{\rho_{HO}}{\rightarrow} \mathbf{h}_t$. Through successive dispersions, in a future instant of time, the founder effect occurs when $\{\mathbf{i}_1, \ldots, \mathbf{i}_y\} \overset{\rho_{HO}}{\rightarrow} \mathbf{h}_v$ and $\{\mathbf{i}_1, \ldots, \mathbf{i}_y\} \overset{\rho_A}{\rightarrow} \mathbf{h}_v$. The subset $\{\mathbf{i}_1, \ldots, \mathbf{i}_y\}$ is a founder population.

Process 2. Environmental Changes: Defined as φ_{EC}. Given a habitat $\mathbf{h}_t \in H$, the process φ_{EC} applies transformations in its attributes. It is possible to proceed in changes of abiotic factors and in the topology of $\mathbf{h}_t$. In the second case, there can be a habitat fragmentation of $\mathbf{h}_t$ in habitats $\mathbf{h}_1, \ldots, \mathbf{h}_y$.

4.2.2. Environmental Changes Effect

- **Vicariance:** Occurs gradually through successive environmental changes, resulting in habitat fragmentation of $\mathbf{h}_t \in H$ in $\mathbf{h}_1, \ldots, \mathbf{h}_y$. At time instant $k \in Z^+$, it is true that $\mathbf{i}_j \overset{\rho_{HO}}{\rightarrow} \mathbf{h}_t$ for a subset $\mathbf{i}_j \in S_f$,

$j=1,\ldots,m$, $S_f \in S_{BI}$. In a future instant of time, the fragmentation of h_t produces the vicariance condition when for any individuals $\{\mathbf{i}_j,\mathbf{i}_g\} \in S_f$ it is true that $\mathbf{i}_j \overset{\rho_{GI}}{\leftrightarrow} \mathbf{i}_g$.

Process 3. Sexual Reproduction: Defined as μ_R. Given two individuals $\{\mathbf{i}_j,\mathbf{i}_g\} \in I$, consider $\mathbf{h}_t \in H$, where $\{\mathbf{i}_j,\mathbf{i}_g\} \overset{\rho_{HO}}{\rightarrow} \mathbf{h}_t$ and $\mathbf{i}_j \overset{\overline{\rho_{BI}}}{\leftrightarrow} \mathbf{i}_g$. The process μ_R combines attributes $\mathbf{i}_j$ and $\mathbf{i}_g$ to generate a new individual $\mathbf{i}_*$.

4.2.3. Dispersion and Reproduction Effect

- **Genotypic or Phenotypic Flow**. Initially, at time instant $k \in Z^+$, consider two individuals $\{\mathbf{i}_j,\mathbf{i}_g\} \in I$ wher$\{\mathbf{i}_j,\mathbf{i}_g\} \overset{\rho_{HO}}{\rightarrow} \mathbf{h}_t$e the following conditions are true: $\mathbf{i}_j \overset{GI}{\leftrightarrow} \mathbf{i}_g$ e $\mathbf{i}_j \overset{\overline{\rho_{BI}}}{\leftrightarrow} \mathbf{i}_g$. In a future time instant, it can be true that $\{\mathbf{i}_j,\mathbf{i}_g\} \overset{\rho_{HO}}{\rightarrow} \mathbf{h}_t$. The occurrence of μ_R between $\mathbf{i}_j$ and $\mathbf{i}_g$ in this scenario represents a particular case of reproduction: genotypic or phenotypic flow.

Process 4. Mutation: Defined as μ_M. Given an individual $\mathbf{i}_j \in \mathbf{i}$, it is considered that a subset of its attributes represents its phenotype or genotype. The process μ_M applies transformations in this subset of attributes.

Process 5. Natural Selection: Defined as μ_{NS}. Given an individual $\mathbf{i}_j \in \mathbf{i}$, the process μ_{NS} determines the survival of $\mathbf{i}_j$. Consider $\mathbf{i}_j$ at time instant k, at time $k + 1$, $\mathbf{i}_j$ ceases to exist. Several factors are crucial in this process, including:

1. **Low Adaptation:** Given a habitat $\mathbf{h}_t \in \mathbf{h}$ where $\mathbf{i}_j \overset{\rho_{HO}}{\rightarrow} \mathbf{h}_t$ and $\mathbf{i}_j \overset{\overline{\rho_A}}{\rightarrow} \mathbf{h}_t$.
2. **Intraspecific Competition for Resources:** Given two individuals $\{\mathbf{i}_j,\mathbf{i}_g\} \in S_f$, where $S_f \in S_{BI}$, if $\{\mathbf{i}_j,\mathbf{i}_g\} \overset{\rho_{HO}}{\rightarrow} \mathbf{h}_t$, then there may exist an intraspecific competition.
3. **Interspecific Competition:** Given two individuals $\mathbf{i}_j \in S_f$ and $\mathbf{i}_g \in S_e$, where $\{S_f,S_e\} \in S_{BI}$ and $\{\mathbf{i}_j,\mathbf{i}_g\} \overset{\rho_{HO}}{\rightarrow} \mathbf{h}_t$, this scenario can lead to the existence of competition, determined by specific relations, for example: predator-prey, defined by $\mathbf{i}_j \overset{\rho_{TR}}{\rightarrow} \mathbf{i}_g$.
4. **Selective Pressure:** Represents the pressure that an entire ecosystem can exert on individuals and species. Thus, there are several factors that should be considered in a selective pressure, all related to the habitat characteristics and relations between individuals and species. In this case, the definition of a selective pressure relation may comprise several factors in a single relation, that will determine the survival of an individual $\mathbf{i}_j \in S_f$.

4.2.4. Natural Selection Effect

- **Bottleneck Effect:** Occurs gradually through natural selection. Initially, at time instant $k \in Z^+$, consider a species $S_f = \{\mathbf{i}_1,\ldots,\mathbf{i}_y\}$, $S_f \in S_{BI}$. At a future time instant, where $S_f = \{\mathbf{i}_1,\ldots,\mathbf{i}_w\}$, if $w \ll y$, then the bottleneck effect occurred.

Process 6. Extinction: Defined as M_E. Alters the conformation of the set when a species $S_f \in S_{BI}$ has cardinality $z=0$, i.e., $S_f = \varnothing$, then S_f ceases to exist.

Process 7. Sympatric Speciation: Defined as M_{SS}. Alters the conformation of the set S_{BI}, adding a new species S_*. Composed of individuals generated from the following situation: given $\{\mathbf{i}_j,\mathbf{i}_g\} \in S_f$, the process μ_R generates $\mathbf{i}_*$ such that $\mathbf{i}_* \overset{\rho_{BI}}{\leftrightarrow} \mathbf{i}_l$ for every $\mathbf{i}_l \in S_f$. By obtaining a set of individuals $\{\mathbf{i}_{*1},\ldots,\mathbf{i}_{*y}\}$ generated from this situation, if it is true that for every $\mathbf{i}_{*j}$ and $\mathbf{i}_{*g}$: $\mathbf{i}_{*j} \overset{\rho_{BI}}{\leftrightarrow} \mathbf{i}_{*g}$, then $\{\mathbf{i}_{*1},\ldots,\mathbf{i}_{*y}\}$ constitutes a new $S_f=\{\mathbf{i}_1,\ldots,\mathbf{i}_b\}$ species $S_* = \{\mathbf{i}_{*1},\ldots,\mathbf{i}_{*y}\}$.

Process 8. Alopatric Speciation: Defined as M_{AS}. Alters the conformation of the set S_{BI}, adding one or more new species S_*. Through the vicariance process, it is possible to obtain two (or more) subsets $\{\mathbf{i}_1,\ldots,\mathbf{i}_y\} \in S_f$ and $\{\mathbf{i}_1,\ldots,\mathbf{i}_w\} \in S_f$, where, $\{\mathbf{i}_1,\ldots,\mathbf{i}_w\} \overset{\rho_{HO}}{\rightarrow} \mathbf{h}_u$, $\{\mathbf{i}_1,\ldots,\mathbf{i}_y\} \overset{\rho_{GI}}{\leftrightarrow} \{\mathbf{i}_1,\ldots,\mathbf{i}_w\}$ at time instant $k \in Z^+$. After this isolation, by successive processes μ_R and μ_M, in a future time instant, subsets $\{\mathbf{i}_1,\ldots,\mathbf{i}_a\}$ and $\{\mathbf{i}_1,\ldots,\mathbf{i}_b\}$, where $\{\mathbf{i}_1,\ldots,\mathbf{i}_a\} \overset{\rho_{AR}}{\rightarrow} \{\mathbf{i}_1,\ldots,\mathbf{i}_y\}$ and, individuals may present the following condition: . Additionally, the following condition $\{\mathbf{i}_1,\ldots,\mathbf{i}_a\} \overset{\rho_{BI}}{\leftrightarrow} \{\mathbf{i}_1,\ldots,\mathbf{i}_y\}$ and $\{\mathbf{i}_1,\ldots,\mathbf{i}_b\} \overset{\rho_{BI}}{\leftrightarrow} \{\mathbf{i}_1,\ldots,\mathbf{i}_w\}$ indicates that it can be considered two new species: $S_{*f}=\{i_1,\ldots,i_a\}$ and $S_{*e}=\{\mathbf{i}_1,\ldots,\mathbf{i}_b\}$. Otherwise, only a new species S_* can be considered where $S_f=\{\mathbf{i}_1,\ldots,\mathbf{i}_a\}$ and or and $S_*=\{\mathbf{i}_1,\ldots,\mathbf{i}_a\}$.

Process 9. Peripatric Speciation: Defined as M_{PS}. Alters the conformation of the S_{BI} set, adding a new species S_*. Through dispersion, at a time instant consider two subsets: $\{\mathbf{i}_1,\ldots,\mathbf{i}_y\} \in S_f$ and $\{\mathbf{i}_1,\ldots,\mathbf{i}_w\} \in S_f$, where $\{\mathbf{i}_1,\ldots,\mathbf{i}_y\} \overset{\rho_{HO}}{\rightarrow} \mathbf{h}_t$, $\{\mathbf{i}_1,\ldots,\mathbf{i}_w\} \overset{\rho_{HO}}{\rightarrow} \mathbf{h}_u$, $\{\mathbf{i}_1,\ldots,\mathbf{i}_y\} \overset{\rho_{GI}}{\leftrightarrow} \{\mathbf{i}_1,\ldots,\mathbf{i}_w\}$, and $w \leftrightarrow y$. After this isolation, through successive processes μ_R and μ_M, in a future time instant, subsets $\{\mathbf{i}_1,\ldots,\mathbf{i}_a\}$ and $\{\mathbf{i}_1,\ldots,\mathbf{i}_b\}$, where $\{\mathbf{i}_1,\ldots,\mathbf{i}_a\} \overset{\rho_{AR}}{\rightarrow} \{\mathbf{i}_1,\ldots,\mathbf{i}_y\}$ and $\{\mathbf{i}_1,\ldots,\mathbf{i}_b\} \overset{\rho_{AR}}{\rightarrow} \{\mathbf{i}_1,\ldots,\mathbf{i}_w\}$, may present the following condition: $\{\mathbf{i}_1,\ldots,\mathbf{i}_a\} \overset{\rho_{BI}}{\leftrightarrow} \{\mathbf{i}_1,\ldots,\mathbf{i}_b\}$. The individuals $\{\mathbf{i}_1,\ldots,\mathbf{i}_b\}$ constitutes a new species S_*.

Process 10. Competitive Speciation: Defined as M_{CS}. Alters the conformation of the S_{BI} set, adding a new species S_*. Presents similarities with the process M_{PS}, where through *dispersion*, at a time instant $k \in Z^+$ consider two subsets: $\{\mathbf{i}_1,\ldots,\mathbf{i}_y\} \in S_f$ and $\{\mathbf{i}_1,\ldots,\mathbf{i}_w\} \in S_f$, where $\{\mathbf{i}_1,\ldots,\mathbf{i}_y\} \overset{\rho_{HO}}{\rightarrow} \mathbf{h}_t$, $\{\mathbf{i}_1,\ldots,\mathbf{i}_w\} \overset{\rho_{HO}}{\rightarrow} \mathbf{h}_u$, and $w \ll y$. The difference lies in the relation between populations, where it is true that $\{\mathbf{i}_1,\ldots,\mathbf{i}_y\} \overset{\overline{\rho_{GI}}}{\leftrightarrow} \{\mathbf{i}_1,\ldots,\mathbf{i}_w\}$. It may also be true that $\mathbf{h}_t \overset{\rho_{HN}}{\leftrightarrow} \mathbf{h}_u$. Through successive processes μ_R and μ_M, in a future time instant, subsets $\{\mathbf{i}_1,\ldots,\mathbf{i}_a\}$ and $\{\mathbf{i}_1,\ldots,\mathbf{i}_b\}$, where $\{\mathbf{i}_1,\ldots,\mathbf{i}_a\} \overset{\rho_{AR}}{\rightarrow} \{\mathbf{i}_1,\ldots,\mathbf{i}_y\}$ and

$\{\mathbf{i}_1,\ldots,\mathbf{i}_b\} \overset{\rho_{AR}}{\rightarrow} \{\mathbf{i}_1,\ldots,\mathbf{i}_w\}$, may present the following condition: $\{\mathbf{i}_1,\ldots,\mathbf{i}_a\} \overset{\rho_{BI}}{\leftrightarrow} \{\mathbf{i}_1,\ldots,\mathbf{i}_b\}$. The individuals $\{\mathbf{i}_1,\ldots,\mathbf{i}_b\}$ constitute a new species S_*.

5. BIOGEOGRAPHIC PATTERNS: CARRYING CAPACITY AND POPULATION EQUILIBRIUM ON ADAPTIVE SURFACES

Part of the main potentialities and unique properties of Biogeographic Computation and its metamodel will be explored in this section. Relations and biogeographic processes are used to explain the emergence of highly complex patterns in natural and artificial ecosystems. Emphasis here will be placed on adaptive radiation, which deals with the emergence and extinction of species over time (Brown & Lomolino, 2005; Myers & Giller, 1991), and will be simulated in a conceptual experiment designed to incorporate some relevant processes of Biogeography, according to the formalism presented in the previous section.

To achieve this, a biogeographic model was conceived. The details of the computational flow of the model will not be described here. Instead, all the processes that are involved will be listed and some results concerning the main emergent properties presented. Basically, speciation and spatio-temporal patterns will emerge as a consequence of adaptive radiation in a multimodal adaptive phenotypical landscape. Additionally, the number of exemplars (individuals) of each species will obey the relative quality of each ecological opportunity, directly associated with each local maximum of the adaptive surface. The existence of multiple ecological opportunities is directly connected with the multimodality of the adaptive surface. The attraction basin of each local optimum is considered an ecological opportunity (Rosenzweig, 1995, Wright, 1932): if individuals cross different attraction basins, then a speciation process is in course (Rosenzweig, 1995). As the model here describes individuals by using phenotypes, the biota is defined in a multidimensional real-valued space. Thus, it is possible to define the relations and processes using the metamodel:

- $R=\{\rho_A,\rho_{SP}\}$.
- $C=\{\mu_R,\mu_{NS},M_{SS}\}$.

More specifically, the relations are implemented as follows:

- ρ_A **(Adaptation):** Describes the interaction of individuals and habitats through adaptive surfaces;
- ρ_{SP} **(Selective Pressure):** Describes the selective pressure imposed by the environment over the individuals. Higher levels of adaptability imply lower selective pressures.

And the processes are implemented as:

- μ_R **(Reproduction):** Generation of new individuals with phenotypic variation;
- μ_{NS} **(Natural Selection):** Determination of the survival of phenotypes in a population based on their level of adaptability. Higher selective pressures indicate lower survival probabilities;
- M_{SS} **(Sympatric Speciation):** If a generated individual moves to another ecological opportunity, which can be properly detected, for instance, using results from Pasti *et al.* (2011), it gives rise to a new species.

In a problem solving context, an important analogy to be explored here is population-based optimization in a continuous space (Gallagher &

Frean, 2005). In this context, adaptive radiation can be interpreted as an effective process of looking for promising regions on multimodal optimization surfaces, so that the point that corresponds to the maximum (or minimum) of the optimization surface should be located. To illustrate the behavior of the conceptually described biogeographic model, the role of the multimodal adaptive surface will be artificially performed by the well-known Griewank benchmark function (Griewank, 1981) in 3D, for visualization purposes, and by the function number nine of the 2005 CEC Competition (Suganthan et al., 2005), also in 3D. The goal is to minimize both functions.

The Griewank function is composed of multiple global optima of the same quality, corresponding to the peaks of the surface, interspersed by valleys, as illustrated in the contours of Figure 2. Based on a single user-defined parameter that provides a threshold for the maximum total capacity of the population, the model starts with two individuals of the same species, randomly located in the phenotypical space, and the adaptive radiation promotes the differentiation of species and self-organization of the available resources so that the number of individuals in each ecological opportunity complies with its relative quality, which will be denoted here as the carrying capacity (Hui, 2006). Additionally, the population equilibrium is defined as the mean of the population size along generations, given that generally there is a tendency of producing an oscillatory behavior around the mean (Hui, 2006). Given that each ecological opportunity in the Griewank function has a similar relative quality, i.e., similar carrying capacity, a uniform distribution of the population size emerges. Note that the resulting number of species and exemplars per species are defined on-demand, according to the peculiarities of the adaptive surface. The most fundamental emergent property associated with adaptive radiation is the continued improvement in the average fitness of the individuals in the population, so that they tend to converge to the local maximum associated with each ecological opportunity, as shown in Figure 2.

On the other hand, in the case of function number nine of the 2005 CEC Competition, given that the carrying capacities of the ecological opportunities are now distinct, the size of the population for each species converges to a value proportional to the corresponding relative quality, as depicted in Figure 3.

The occurrence of speciation, the detection and exploitation of multiple ecological opportunities by means of adaptive radiation, and the self-organization of the number of individuals associated with each species, according to the relative carrying capacity of each ecological opportunity, are emergent properties in Biogeographic Computation. These emergent properties have been applied here in the conceptual context of adaptive phenotypical surfaces, opening the possibility of developing studies on dynamics of adaptive radiation, as well as optimization algorithms for a broad class of application scenarios, including optimization in uncertain environments (Jin & Branke, 2005).

6. DISCUSSION

This paper follows the premise that elements of ecosystems can be viewed as information processors. There are unique features inherent to ecosystems, such as diversity of species and habitats, which motivate the study and application of Biogeographic Computation in several contexts.

Being a conceptual paper founded on a well-established theory, the relevance of the proposed metamodel can be supported by two main reasons: (i) The absence of such a general and complete Biogeographic Computation formalism in the

Figure 2. Carrying capacity and population equilibrium achieved after convergence of a spatio-temporal simulation in an arbitrary multimodal adaptive phenotypical surface (3D Griewank function). Notation: population equilibrium/carrying capacity, after 100 generations.

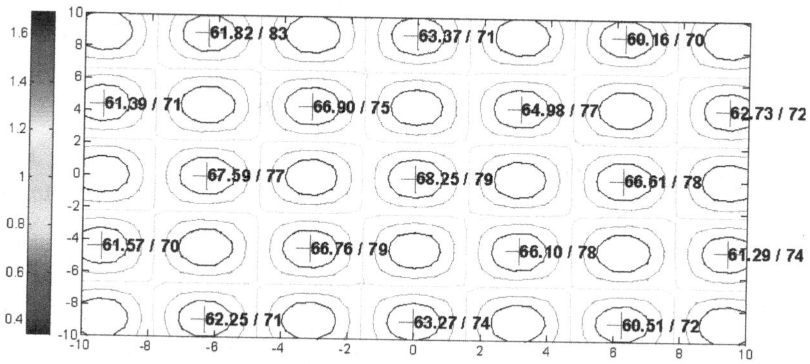

Figure 3. Carrying capacity and population equilibrium achieved after convergence of a spatio-temporal simulation in an arbitrary multimodal adaptive adaptive surface (function number 9 of 2005 CEC Competition). Notation: population equilibrium/carrying capacity, after 100 generations.

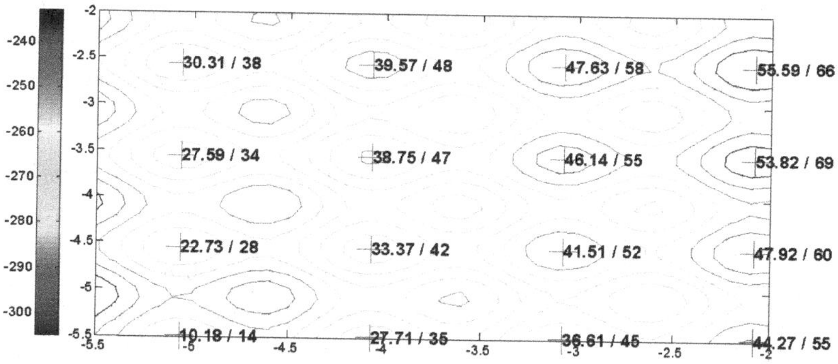

current literature; (ii) The maturity of the Biogeography research field, with convincing explanations for a wide range of spatio-temporal phenomena in ecosystems. The metamodel proposed in this paper may thus represent a proper framework to favor two avenues of research:

1. The theoretical investigation into novel models aimed at understanding ecosystems under the viewpoint of information processing, helping the validation of theories and propositions within Biogeography;
2. The development of innovative computational tools based on artificial ecosystems for solving complex problems.

Both avenues are yet to be explored and there are distinct aspects in the conceptual framework of Biogeographic Computation that may guide to spatio-temporal emergent phenomena not properly addressed in alternative natural computing frameworks. This was preliminarily explored in Section 5 of this paper by means of a simple but clear example of an artificial ecosystem derived from properly formalized processes and relations of Biogeography.

REFERENCES

Bäck, T., Fogel, D. B., & Michalewicz, Z. (2000a). *Evolutionary computation 1: Basic algorithms and operators*. Bristol, UK: Institute of Physics. doi:10.1887/0750306653.

Bazaraa, M., Sherali, H. D., & Shetty, C. M. (2006). *Nonlinear programming – Theory and algorithms* (3rd ed.). New York, NY: John Wiley & Sons. doi:10.1002/0471787779.

Bishop, C. M. (2006). *Pattern recognition and machine learning*. New York, NY: Springer.

Brent, R., & Bruck, J. (2006). Can computers help to explain biology? *Nature*, *440*(23), 416–417. doi:10.1038/440416a PMID:16554784.

Brown, J. H., & Lomolino, M. V. (2005). *Biogeography* (3rd ed.). Sunderland, MA: Sinauer.

Cohen, I. R. (2000). *Tending Adam's garden: Evolving the cognitive immune self.* London, UK: Academic Press.

Cohen, I. R. (2009). Real and artificial immune systems: Computing the state of the body. *Nature Reviews. Immunology*, *7*, 569–574. doi:10.1038/nri2102 PMID:17558422.

Cohen, I. R., & Harel, D. (2007). Explaining a complex living system: Dynamics, multi-scaling and emergence. *Journal of the Royal Society, Interface*, *4*(13), 175–182. doi:10.1098/rsif.2006.0173 PMID:17251153.

Coyne, J. A., & Orr, H. A. (1999). The evolutionary genetics of speciation. In Magurran, A. E., & May, R. M. (Eds.), *Evolution of biological diversity*. Oxford, UK: Oxford University Press.

de Aguiar, M. A. M., Barange, M., Baptestini, E. M., Kaufman, L., & Bar-Yam, Y. (2009). Global patterns of speciation and diversity. *Nature*, *460*(16), 384–387. doi:10.1038/nature08168 PMID:19606148.

de Castro, L. N. (2006). *Fundamentals of natural computing: Basic concepts, algorithms, and applications*. Boca Raton, FL: CRC Press.

de Castro, L. N. (2007). Fundamentals of natural computing: An overview. *Physics of Life Reviews*, *4*(1), 1–36. doi:10.1016/j.plrev.2006.10.002.

de Castro, L. N., & Timmis, J. (2002). *Artificial immune systems: A new computational intelligence approach*. Berlin, Germany: Springer-Verlag.

Denning, P. J. (2001). *The invisible future: The seamless integration of technology in everyday life*. New York, NY: McGraw-Hill.

Denning, P. J. (2007). Computing is a natural science. *Communications of the ACM*, *50*(7), 13–18. doi:10.1145/1272516.1272529.

Denning, P. J. (2008). The computing field: Structure. In Wah, B. (Ed.), *Wiley encyclopedia of computer science and engineering* (pp. 615–623). New York, NY: Wiley Interscience.

Dixit, A. G. (1990). *Optimization in economic theory*. Oxford, UK: Oxford University Press.

Dorigo, M., Maniezzo, V., & Colorni, A. (1996). The ant system: Optimization by a colony of cooperating agents. *IEEE Transactions on Systems, Man, and Cybernetics –Part B*, *26*(1), 29–41. doi:10.1109/3477.484436 PMID:18263004.

Dowek, G. (2012). The physical Church Thesis as an explanation of the Galileo Thesis. *Natural Computing, 11*(2), 247-251.

Gallagher, M., & Frean, M. (2005). Population-based continuous optimization, probabilistic modelling and mean shift. *Evolutionary Computation*, *13*(1), 29–42. doi:10.1162/1063656053583478 PMID:15901425.

Galperin, M. Y., & Koonin, E. V. (2003). *Frontiers in computational genomics*. Norfolk, UK: Caister Academic Press.

Gavrilets, S., & Aaron Vose, A. (2005). Dynamic patterns of adaptive radiation. *Proceedings of the National Academy of Sciences of the United States of America*, *12*(50), 18040–18045. doi:10.1073/pnas.0506330102 PMID:16330783.

Gavrilets, S., Acton, R., & Gravner, J. (2000). Dynamics of speciation and diversification in metapopulation dynamics. *Evolution; International Journal of Organic Evolution*, *54*(5), 1493–1501. PMID:11108578.

Gavrilets, S., & Losos, J. B. (2009). Adaptive radiation: Contrasting theory with data. *Science*, *323*(5915), 732–737. doi:10.1126/science.1157966 PMID:19197052.

Griewank, A. O. (1981). Generalized decent for global optimization. *Journal of Optimization Theory and Applications*, *34*, 11–39. doi:10.1007/BF00933356.

Grimm, V. R., & Railsback, S. F. (2005). *Individual-based modeling and ecology*. Princeton, NJ: Princeton University Press.

Han, J., Kamber, M., & Pei, J. (2005). *Data mining: Concepts and techniques* (2nd ed.). San Francisco, CA: Morgan Kaufmann.

Harel, D. (2003). A grand challenge for computing: Full reactive modeling of a multi-cellular animal. *Bulletin of the European Association for Theoretical Computer Science*, *81*, 226–235.

Hart, E., Bersini, H., & Santos, F. (2007). How affinity influences tolerance in an idiotypic network. *Journal of Theoretical Biology*, *249*(3), 422–436. doi:10.1016/j.jtbi.2007.07.019 PMID:17904580.

Hengeveld, R. (1990). *Dynamic biogeography*. Cambridge, UK: Cambridge University Press.

Holland, J. H. (1992). *Adaptation in natural and artificial systems: An introductory analysis with applications to biology, control, and artificial intelligence*. Cambridge, MA: Bradford Books.

Hui, C. (2006). Carrying capacity, population equilibrium, and environment's maximal load. *Ecological Modelling*, *192*, 317–320. doi:10.1016/j.ecolmodel.2005.07.001.

Jin, Y., & Branke, J. (2005). Evolutionary optimization in uncertain environments – A survey. *IEEE Transactions on Evolutionary Computation*, *9*(3), 303–317. doi:10.1109/TEVC.2005.846356.

Jorgensen, S. E., Patten, B. C., & Stragkraba, M. (1992). Ecosystems emerging: Toward an ecology of complex systems in a complex future. *Ecological Modelling*, *62*(1-3), 1–27. doi:10.1016/0304-3800(92)90080-X.

Kauffman, S. A. (1993). *The origins of order: Self-organization and selection in evolution*. Oxford, UK: Oxford University Press.

Kube, C. R., Parker, C. A. C., Wang, T., & Zhang, H. (2004). Biologically inspired collective robotics. In De Castro, L. N., & Von Zuben, F. J. (Eds.), *Recent developments in biologically inspired computing* (pp. 367–397). Hershey, PA: Idea Group. doi:10.4018/978-1-59140-312-8.ch015.

Lihoreau, M., Chittka, L., & Raine, N. E. (2010). Travel optimization by foraging bumblebees through readjustments of traplines after discovery of new feeding locations. *American Naturalist*, *176*(6), 744–757. doi:10.1086/657042 PMID:20973670.

Lloyd, S. (2002). *The computational universe*. Retrieved from http://edge.org/conversation/the-computational-universe

Lloyd, S. (2006). *Programming the universe: A quantum computer scientist takes on the cosmos*. New York, NY: Knopf.

Magurran, A. (1999). Population differentiation without speciation. In Magurran, A. E., & May, R. M. (Eds.), *Evolution of biological diversity*. Oxford, UK: Oxford University Press.

Maia, R. D., & de Castro, L. N. (2012). Bee colonies as model for multimodal continuous optimization: The OptBees algorithm. In *Proceedings of the IEEE Congress on Evolutionary Computation* (pp. 1-8).

Mayr, E., & Diamond, J. (2001). *The birds of Northern Melanesia: Speciation, ecology and biogeography*. Oxford, UK: Oxford University Press.

Mehta, P., Goyal, S., Long, T., Bassler, B. L., & Wingreen, N. (2009). Information processing and signal integration in bacterial quorum sensing. *Molecular Systems Biology*, *5*, 325. doi:10.1038/msb.2009.79 PMID:19920810.

Melville, J., Nicholson, G. E., Harmon, L. J., & Losos, J. B. (2005). Intercontinental community convergence of ecology and morphology in desert lizards. *Proceedings of the Royal Society of London*, *273*(1586), 557–563. doi:10.1098/rspb.2005.3328 PMID:16537126.

Milne, B. T. (1998). Motivation and benefits of complex systems approaches in ecology. *Ecosystems (New York, N.Y.)*, *1*, 449–456. doi:10.1007/s100219900040.

Myers, A. A., & Giller, P. S. (1991). *Analytical biogeography*. Boca Raton, FL: Chapman & Hall.

Newton, I. (2003). *Speciation and biogeography of birds*. New York, NY: Academic Press.

Nicholson, G. E., Harmon, L. J., & Losos, J. B. (2007). Evolution of Anolis Lizard Dewlap Diversity. *PLoS ONE*, *2*(3), e274. doi:10.1371/journal.pone.0000274 PMID:17342208.

Pardalos, P. M., & Resende, M. G. C. (Eds.). (2002). *Handbook of applied optimization*. Oxford, UK: Oxford University Press.

Pasti, R., Von Zuben, F. J., Maia, R. D., & Castro, L. N. (2011). Heuristics to avoid redundant solutions on population-based multimodal continuous optimization. In *Proceedings of the IEEE Congress on Evolutionary Computation* (pp. 2321-2328).

Pratt, S. C., Mallon, E. B., Sumpter, D. J. T., & Franks, N. R. (2002). Quorum sensing, recruitment, and collective decision-making during colony emigration by the ant Leptothorax albipennis. *Behavioral Ecology and Sociobiology*, *52*(2), 117–127. doi:10.1007/s00265-002-0487-x.

Provata, A., Sokolov, I. M., & Spagnolo, B. (2008). Ecological complex systems. *The European Physical Journal B - Condensed Matter and Complex Systems*, *65*(3), 307-314.

Ricci, F., Rokach, L., Shapira, B., & Kantor, P. B. (Eds.). (2010). *Recommender systems handbook*. New York, NY: Springer.

Ridley, M. (2004). *Evolution* (3rd ed.). Oxford, UK: Wiley-Blackwell.

Rosenzweig, M. L. (1995). *Species diversity in space and time*. Cambridge, UK: Cambridge University Press. doi:10.1017/CBO9780511623387.

Schoener, T. W. (1991). Ecological interactions. In Myers, A. A., & Giller, P. S. (Eds.), *Analytical biogeography*. Boca Raton, FL: Chapman & Hall.

Schwenk, G., Padilla, D. G., Bakkenand, G. S., & Full, R. J. (2009). Grand challenges in organismal biology. *Integrative and Comparative Biology*, *49*(1), 7–14. doi:10.1093/icb/icp034 PMID:21669841.

Simmons, I. (1982). *Biogeographical processes*. St. Leonards, NSW, Australia: Allen & Unwin.

Simon, D. (2008). Biogeography-based optimization. *IEEE Transactions on Evolutionary Computation*, *12*(6), 702–713. doi:10.1109/TEVC.2008.919004.

Suganthan, P. N., Hansen, N., Liang, J. J., Deb, K., Chen, Y. P., Auger, A., & Tiwari, S. (2005). *Problem definitions and evaluation criteria for the CEC 2005 special session on real-parameter optimization (Tech. Rep.)*. Singapore: Nanyang Technological University.

Vittori, G., & Araujo, A. F. R. (2001). Agent-oriented routing in telecommunications networks. *IEICE Transactions on Communications. E (Norwalk, Conn.)*, *84-B*(11), 3006–3013.

Vittori, G., Talbot, G., Gautrais, J., Fourcassié, V., Araujo, A. F. R., & Theraulaz, G. (2006). Path efficiency of ant foraging trails in an artificial network. *Journal of Theoretical Biology*, *239*(4), 507–515. doi:10.1016/j.jtbi.2005.08.017 PMID:16199059.

Wiens, J. J., & Donoghue, M. J. (2004). Historical biogeography, ecology and species richness. *Trends in Ecology & Evolution*, *19*(12), 639–644. doi:10.1016/j.tree.2004.09.011 PMID:16701326.

Wright, S. (1932). The roles of mutation, inbreeding, crossbreeding, and selection in evolution. In *Proceedings of the 6th International Congress of Genetics* (pp. 356-366).

Xavier, R. S., Omar, N., & de Castro, L. N. (2011). Bacterial colony: Information processing and computational behavior. In *Proceedings of the Third World Congress on Nature and Biologically Inspired Computing* (pp. 439-443).

This work was previously published in the International Journal of Natural Computing Research (IJNCR), Volume 2, Issue 4, edited by Leandro Nunes de Castro, pp. 47-67, copyright 2011 by IGI Publishing (an imprint of IGI Global).

Compilation of References

Aczel, A., & Sounderpandian, J. (2006). *Complete business statistics*. New York, NY: McGraw-Hill.

Adamatzky, A. (2007a, March). *From reaction-diffusion to Physarum computing*. Paper presented at the Workshop on Unconventional Computing: Quo Vadis? Santa Fe, NM.

Adamatzky, A., & Sloot, P. (2010). *Bio-development of motorway networks in the Netherlands: Slime mould approach*. Retrieved from http://arxiv.org/abs/1209.2974

Adamatzky, A. (2007b). Physarum machine: Implementation of a Kolmogorov-Uspensky machine on a biological substrate. *Parallel Processing Letters*, *17*, 455–467. doi:10.1142/S0129626407003150.

Adamatzky, A. (2010). *Physarum machines*. Singapore: World Scientific.

Adamatzky, A., & Jones, J. (2010). Road planning with slime mould: If Physarum built motorways it would route M6/M74 through Newcastle. *International Journal of Bifurcation and Chaos in Applied Sciences and Engineering*. doi:10.1142/S0218127410027568.

Adamatzky, A., Martinez, G. J., Chapa-Vergara, S. V., Asomoza-Palacio, R., & Stephens, C. R. (2010). Approximating Mexican highways with slime mould. *Natural Computing: An International Journal*, *10*(3), 1195–1214. doi:10.1007/s11047-011-9255-z.

Aghagolzadeh, M., Soltanian-Zadeh, H., Araabi, B., & Aghagolzadeh, A. (2007). A hierarchical clustering based on mutual information maximization. In *Proceedings of the IEEE International Conference on Image Processing* (Vol. 1).

Agrawal, M., Kayal, N., & Saxena, N. (2004). PRIMES is in P. *The Annals of Mathematics*, *160*(2), 781–793. doi:10.4007/annals.2004.160.781.

Agrawal, R. B., & Deb, K. (1994). Simulated binary crossover for continuous search space. *Complex Systems*, *9*, 115–148.

Alhazov, A., Burtseva, L., Cojocaru, S., & Rogozhin, Y. (2009). Solving PP-complete and #P-complete problems by P systems with active membranes. In D. Corne, P. Frisco, G. Păun, G. Rozenberg, & A. Salomaa (Eds.), *Proceedings of the International Conference on Membrane Computing* (LNCS 5391, pp. 108-117).

Alhazov, A., Martín-Vide, C., & Pan, L. (2003). Solving a PSPACE-complete problem by recognizing P systems with restricted active membranes. *Fundamenta Informaticae*, *58*, 67–77.

Andrei, O., Ciobanu, G., & Lucanu, D. (2005). Executable specifications of P systems. In G. Mauri, G. Păun, M. J. Pérez-Jiménez, G. Rozenberg, & A. Salomaa (Eds.), *Proceedings of the 5th International Workshop on Membrane Computing* (LNCS 3365, pp. 126-145).

Angeline, P. (1998). Using selection to improve particle swarm optimization. In *Proceedings of the IEEE Congress on Evolutionary Computation* (pp. 84-89). Washington, DC: IEEE Computer Society.

Antunes, C. H., Barrico, C., Gomes, A., Pires, D. F., & Martins, A. G. (2009). An evolutionary algorithm for reactive power compensation in radial distribution networks. *Applied Energy*, *86*, 977–984. doi:10.1016/j.apenergy.2008.09.008.

Apt, K. R. (1990). Logic programming. In van Leeuwen, J. (Ed.), *Handbook of theoretical computer science*. Amsterdam, The Netherlands: Elsevier.

Astrom, K. J., Borisson, U., Ljung, L., & Wittenmark, B. (1977). Theory and applications of self-tuning regulators. *Automatica*, *13*(5), 457–476. doi:10.1016/0005-1098(77)90067-X.

Asuni, G., Teti, G., Laschi, C., Guglielmelli, E., & Dario, P. (2005). A robotic head neuro-controller based on biologically-inspired neural models. In *Proceedings of the IEEE International Conference on Robotics and Automation* (pp. 2362-2367).

Awerbuch, B. (1985). A new distributed depth-first-search algorithm. *Information Processing Letters*, *20*(3), 147–150. doi:10.1016/0020-0190(85)90083-3.

Bäck, T., Fogel, D. B., & Michalewicz, Z. (2000a). *Evolutionary computation 1: Basic algorithms and operators*. Bristol, UK: Institute of Physics. doi:10.1887/0750306653.

Back, T., & Schwefel, H. (1993). An overview of evolutionary algorithms for parameter optimization. *Evolutionary Computation*, *1*(1), 1–23. doi:10.1162/evco.1993.1.1.1.

Ballard, D. (1997). *An introduction to natural computation*. Cambridge, MA: MIT Press.

Banks, A., Vincent, J., & Anyakoha, C. (2007). A review of particle swarm optimization. Part I: Background and development. *Natural Computing*, *6*, 467–484. doi:10.1007/s11047-007-9049-5.

Banks, A., Vincent, J., & Anyakoha, C. (2008). A review of particle swarm optimization. Part II: Hybridisation, combinatorial, multicriteria and constrained optimization, and indicative applications. *Natural Computing*, *7*, 109–124. doi:10.1007/s11047-007-9050-z.

Barrat, A., Barthelemy, M., & Vespignani, A. (2008). *Dynamical processes in complex networks*. Cambridge, UK: Cambridge University Press. doi:10.1017/CBO9780511791383.

Bartlett, P. L. (1998). The sample complexity of pattern classification with neural networks: The size of the weights is more important than the size of the network. *IEEE Transactions on Information Theory*, *44*(2), 525–536. doi:10.1109/18.661502.

Bazaraa, M., Sherali, H. D., & Shetty, C. M. (2006). *Nonlinear programming – Theory and algorithms* (3rd ed.). New York, NY: John Wiley & Sons. doi:10.1002/0471787779.

Ben-Ari, M. (2005). *Principles of the Spin model checker*. London, UK: Springer.

Bergman, R., Finegood, D., & Ader, M. (1985). Assessment of insulin sensitivity in vivo. *Endocrine Reviews*, *6*(1), 45–86. doi:10.1210/edrv-6-1-45.

Bergman, R., Ider, Y., Bowden, C., & Cobelli, C. (1979). Quantitative estimation of insulin sensitivity. *American Journal of Physiology. Endocrinology and Metabolism*, *236*(6), 667–677.

Bernardini, F., Gheorghe, M., Romero-Campero, F. J., & Walkinshaw, N. (2007). A hybrid approach to modeling biological systems. In G. Eleftherakis, P. Kefalas, G. Paun, G. Rozenberg, & A. Salomaa (Eds.), *Proceedings of the 8th International Conference on Membrane Computing* (LNCS 4860, pp. 138-159).

Bernardini, F., Gheorghe, M., Margenstern, M., & Verlan, S. (2008). How to synchronize the activity of all components of a P system? *International Journal of Foundations of Computer Science*, *19*(5), 1183–1198. doi:10.1142/S0129054108006224.

Bernhardsson, B. (1991). Explicit solutions to the N-queens problem for all. *ACM SIGART Bulletin*, *2*(2), 7. doi:10.1145/122319.122322.

Bersini, H., Lenaerts, T., & Santos, F. (2006). Growing biological networks: Beyond the gene duplication model. *Journal of Theoretical Biology*, *241*(3), 488–505. doi:10.1016/j.jtbi.2005.12.012 PMID:16442124.

Beuthe, M., Himanen, V., Reggiani, A., & Zamparini, L. (Eds.). (2004). *Transport developments and innovations in an evolving*. Singapore: World Scientific.

Bijarbooneh, F. H., Flener, P., & Pearson, J. (2009). Dynamic demand-capacity balancing for air traffic management using constraint-based local search: First results. In *Proceedings of the 6th International Workshop on Local Search Techniques in Constraint Satisfaction* (Vol. 5, pp. 27-40).

Birbil, C. I., & Fang, S.-C. (2003). An electromagnetism-like mechanism for global optimization. *Journal of Global Optimization*, *25*, 263–282. doi:10.1023/A:1022452626305.

Birbil, C. I., Fang, S.-C., & Sheu, R.-L. (2004). On the convergence of a population-based global optimization algorithm. *Journal of Global Optimization*, *30*, 301–318. doi:10.1007/s10898-004-8270-3.

Bishop, C. M. (2006). *Pattern recognition and machine learning*. New York, NY: Springer.

Bizzi, E., dAvella, A., Saltiel, P., & Trensch, M. (2002). Modular organization of spinal motor systems. *The Neuroscientist*, 8.

Boccato, L., Lopes, A., Attux, R., & Von Zuben, F. J. (2011). An echo state network architecture based on Volterra filtering and PCA with application to the channel equalization problem. In *Proceedings of the International Joint Conference on Neural Networks* (pp. 580-587).

Boccato, L., Lopes, A., Attux, R., & Von Zuben, F. J. (2012). An extended echo state network using volterra filtering and principal component analysis. *Neural Networks*, *32*, 292–302. doi:10.1016/j.neunet.2012.02.028.

Boedecker, J., Obst, O., Mayer, N. M., & Asada, M. (2009). Initialization and self-organized optimization of recurrent neural network connectivity. *HFSP Journal*, *3*(5), 340–349. doi:10.2976/1.3240502.

Boutayeb, A., & Chetouani, A. (2006). A critical review of mathematical models and data used in diabetology. *Biomedical Engineering Online*, *5*(43).

Braier, P., Berry, R., & Wales, D. (1990). How the range of pair interactions govern features of multidimensional potentials. *The Journal of Chemical Physics*, *93*(12), 8745–8756. doi:10.1063/1.459263.

Branke, J. (2008). Consideration of a partial user preferences in evolutionary multi-objective optimization. In J. Branke, K. Deb, K. Miettinen, & R. Slowinski (Eds.), *Proceedings of the Conference on Multiobjective Optimization - Interactive and Evolutionary Approaches* (LNCS 5252, pp. 157-178).

Branke, J., & Deb, K. (2004). Integrating user preferences into evolutionary multi-objective optimization. In Jin, Y. (Ed.), *Knowledge incorporation in evolutionary computation* (pp. 461–477). New York, NY: Springer.

Branke, J., Greco, S., Slowinski, R., & Zielniewicz, P. (2010). Interactive evolutionary multiobjective optimization driven by robust ordinal regression. *Bulletin of the Polish Academy of Sciences. Technical Sciences*, *58*(3), 347–358.

Branke, J., Kaußlera, T., & Schmeck, H. (2001). Guidance in evolutionary multi-objective optimization. *Advances in Engineering Software*, *32*, 499–507. doi:10.1016/S0965-9978(00)00110-1.

Brans, J.-P., & Mareschal, B. (1986). How to select and how to rank projects: The PROMETHEE method for MCDM. *European Journal on Operation Research*, *24*, 228–238. doi:10.1016/0377-2217(86)90044-5.

Bratko, I. (2001). *PROLOG programming for artificial intelligence* (3rd ed.). Reading, MA: Addison-Wesley.

Brent, R., & Bruck, J. (2006). Can computers help to explain biology? *Nature*, *440*(23), 416–417. doi:10.1038/440416a PMID:16554784.

Britton, N. F. (1986). *Reaction-diffusion equations and their applications to biology*. New York, NY: Academic Press.

Brown, J. H., & Lomolino, M. V. (2005). *Biogeography* (3rd ed.). Sunderland, MA: Sinauer.

Brueckner, S. A., Serugendo, G. D. M., Karageorgos, A., & Nagpal, R. (Eds.). (2005). *Proceedings of the Third International Workshop on Engineering Self-Organizing Systems* (LNCS 3464). Berlin, Germany: Springer-Verlag.

Buhler, M., Koditschek, D. E., & Kindlmann, P. J. (1994). Planning and control of a juggling robot. *The International Journal of Robotics Research*, *3*, 101–118. doi:10.1177/027836499401300201.

Butcher, J., Verstraeten, D., Schrauwen, B., Day, C., & Haycock, P. (2010). Extending reservoir computing with random static projections: A hybrid between extreme learning and RC. In *Proceedings of the 18th European Symposium on Artificial Neural Networks* (pp. 303-308).

Call, S., Zubarev, D., & Boldyrev, A. (2007). Global minimum structure searches via particle swarm optimization. *Journal of Computational Chemistry*, *28*(7), 1177–1186. doi:10.1002/jcc.20621.

Camazine, S., Deneubourg, J.-L., Franks, N. R., Sneyd, J., Theraulaz, G., & Bonabeau, E. (2001). *Self-organization in biological systems*. Princeton, NJ: Princeton University Press.

Canada's National Highway System. (2008). *Condition report. St. John's, NL*. Canada: Council of Ministers Responsible for Transportation and Highway Safety.

Cardona, M., Colomer, M. A., Margalida, A., Pérez-Hurtado, I., Pérez-Jiménez, M. J., & Sanuy, D. (2010). A P system based model of an ecosystem of some scavenger birds. In G. Paun, M. J. Pérez-Jiménez, A. Riscos-Núñez, G. Rozenberg, & A. Salomaa (Eds.), *Proceedings of the 10th International Workshop on Membrane Computing* (LNCS 5957, pp. 182-195).

Casiraghi, G., Ferretti, C., Gallini, A., & Mauri, G. (2005). A membrane computing system mapped on an asynchronous, distributed computational environment. In R. Freund, G. Păun, G. Rozenberg, & A. Salomaa (Eds.), *Proceedings of the 6th International Workshop on Membrane Computing* (LNCS 3850, pp. 159-164).

Castellini, A., Franco, G., & Pagliarini, R. (2011). Data analysis pipeline from laboratory to MP models. *Natural Computing*, *10*(1), 55–76. doi:10.1007/s11047-010-9200-6.

Cavaliere, M., Egecioglu, O., Ibarra, O., Ionescu, M., Păun, G., & Woodworth, S. (2008). Asynchronous spiking neural P systems: Decidability and undecidability. In M. Garzon & H. Yan (Eds.), *Proceedings of the 13th International Meeting on DNA Computing* (LNCS 4848, pp. 246-255).

Cavaliere, M., Ibarra, O. H., Păun, G., Egecioglu, O., Ionescu, M., & Woodworth, S. (2009). Asynchronous spiking neural P systems. *Theoretical Computer Science*, *410*, 2352–2364. doi:10.1016/j.tcs.2009.02.031.

Cavaliere, M., & Mura, I. (2008). Experiments on the reliability of stochastic spiking neural P systems. *Natural Computing*, *7*, 453–470. doi:10.1007/s11047-008-9086-8.

Cavaliere, M., & Sburlan, D. (2004). Time and synchronization in membrane systems. *Fundamenta Informaticae*, *64*, 65–77.

Cecilia, J. M., García, J. M., Guerrero, G. D., Martínez-del-Amor, M. A., Pérez-Hurtado, I., & Pérez-Jiménez, M. J. (2010a). Simulating a P system based efficient solution to SAT by using GPUs. *Journal of Logic and Algebraic Programming*, *79*(6), 317–325. doi:10.1016/j.jlap.2010.03.008.

Cecilia, J. M., García, J. M., Guerrero, G. D., Martìnez-del-Amor, M. A., Pérez-Hurtado, I., & Pérez-Jiménez, M. J. (2010b). Simulation of P systems with active membranes on CUDA. *Briefings in Bioinformatics*, *11*(3), 313–322. doi:10.1093/bib/bbp064.

Cecilia, J., García, J., Guerrero, G., Martínez-del-Amor, M., Pérez-Hurtado, I., & Pérez-Jiménez, M. (2010a). Simulating a p system based efficient solution to sat by using GPUs. *Journal of Logic and Algebraic Programming*, *79*(6), 317–325. doi:10.1016/j.jlap.2010.03.008.

Cecilia, J., García, J., Guerrero, G., Martínez-del-Amor, M., Pérez-Hurtado, I., & Pérez-Jiménez, M. (2010b). Simulation of p systems with active membranes on cuda. *Briefings in Bioinformatics*, *11*(3), 313–322. doi:10.1093/bib/bbp064.

Ceterchi, R., Gramatovici, R., Jonoska, N., & Subramanian, K. G. (2003). Tissue-like P systems with active membranes for picture generation. *Fundamenta Informaticae*, *56*(4), 311–328.

Ceterchi, R., Mutyam, M., Păun, G., & Subramanian, K. G. (2003). Array-rewriting P systems. *Natural Computing*, *2*(3), 229–249. doi:10.1023/A:1025497107681.

Chakraborty, U. K. (2008). *Advances in differential evolution*. New York, NY: Springer. doi:10.1007/978-3-540-68830-3.

Chao, J., & Nakayama, J. (1996). Cubical singular simplex model for 3D objects and fast computation of homology groups. In *Proceedings of the 13th International Conference on Pattern Recognition* (Vol. 4, pp. 190-194).

Chaudhuri, S., & Deb, K. (2010). An interactive multi-objective optimization and decision-making using evolutionary methods. *Applied Soft Computing*, *10*, 496–511. doi:10.1016/j.asoc.2009.08.019.

Chen, T., He, H. L., & Church, G. M. (1999). Modeling gene expression with differential equations. In *Proceedings of the Pacific Symposium on Biocomputing* (pp. 29-40).

Cheng, L., & Yang, J. (2007). Global minimum structures of morse clusters as a function of the range of the potential: 81 ≤ n ≤160. *The Journal of Physical Chemistry A, 111*, 5287–5293. doi:10.1021/jp072238g.

Chen, H., Ionescu, M., Ishdorj, T. O., Păun, A., Păun, G., & Pérez-Jiménez, M. (2008). Spiking neural p systems with extended rules: Universality and languages. *Natural Computing: An International Journal, 7*(2), 147–166. doi:10.1007/s11047-006-9024-6.

Chen, V. C. P., Tsui, K.-L., & Barton, R. R. (2006). A review on design, modeling and applications of computer experiments. *IIE Transactions, 38*(4), 273–291. doi:10.1080/07408170500232495.

Cherubini, A., Oriolo, G., Macrì, F., Aloise, F., Cincotti, F., & Mattia, D. (2007). A vision-based path planner/follower for an assistive robotics project. In *Proceedings of the Workshop on Robot Vision* (pp. 77-86).

Christinal, H. A., Díaz-Pernil, D., & Real, P. (2009a, November 15-18). Segmentation in 2D and 3D image using tissue-like P system. In E. Bayro-Corrochano & J. O. Eklundh (Eds.), *Proceedings of the 14th Ibero-American Conference on Progress in Pattern Recognition, Image Analysis, Computer Vision, and Applications*, Guadalajara, Jalisco, Mexico (LNCS 5856, pp. 169-176).

Christinal, H. A., Díaz-Pernil, D., & Real, P. (2009b, November 24-27). Using membrane computing for obtaining homology groups of binary 2D digital images. In P. Wiederhold & R. P. Barneva (Eds.), *Proceedings of the 13th International Workshop on Combinatorial Image Analysis*, Playa del Carmen, Mexico (LNCS 5852, pp. 383-396).

Christinal, H. A., Díaz-Pernil, D., Gutiérrez-Naranjo, M. A., & Pérez-Jiménez, M. J. (2010). Thresholding of 2D images with cell-like P systems. *Romanian Journal of Information Science and Technology, 13*(2), 131–140.

Christinal, H. A., Díaz-Pernil, D., & Real, P. (2010). P systems and computational algebraic topology. *Journal of Mathematical and Computer Modelling, 52*(11-12), 1982–1996. doi:10.1016/j.mcm.2010.06.001.

Church, A. (1936). A note on the entscheidungsproblem. *American Journal of Mathematics, 58*, 345–363. doi:10.2307/2371045.

Cidon, I. (1988). Yet another distributed depth-first-search algorithm. *Information Processing Letters, 26*, 301–305. doi:10.1016/0020-0190(88)90187-1.

Cienciala, L., & Ciencialová, L. (2006). Variations on the theme: P colonies. In *Proceedings of the 1st International WFM Workshop*, Ostrava, Czech Republic (pp. 27-34).

Cienciala, L., Ciencialová, L., & Langer, M. (2011). P colonies with capacity one and modularity. In *Proceedings of the Ninth Brainstorming Week on Membrane Computing* (pp. 71-90).

Ciencialová, L., Cienciala, L., & Kelemenová, A. (2007). On the number of agents in P colonies. In *Proceedings of the 8th Workshop on Membrane Computing*, Thessaloniki, Greece. (pp. 227-242).

Ciobanu, G., & Wenyuan, G. (2004). P systems running on a cluster of computers. In C. Martín-Vide, G. Mauri, G. Paun, G. Rozenberg, & A. Salomaa (Eds.), *Proceedings of the International Workshop on Membrane Computing* (LNCS 2933, pp. 289-328).

Ciobanu, G., Păun, G., & Pérez-Jiménez, M. J. (Eds.). (2006). *Applications of membrane computing*. Berlin, Germany: Springer-Verlag.

Clarke, E. M., Grumberg, O., & Peled, D. A. (1999). *Model checking*. Cambridge, MA: MIT Press.

Clerc, M., & Kennedy, J. (2002). The particle swarm explosion, stability, and convergence in a multidimensional complex space. *IEEE Transactions on Evolutionary Computation, 6*(1), 58–73. doi:10.1109/4235.985692.

Cobelli, C., & Mari, A. (1983). Validation of mathematical models of complex endocrine-metabolic systems: A case study on a model of glucose regulation. *Medical & Biological Engineering & Computing, 21*(4), 390–399. doi:10.1007/BF02442625.

Coelho, R. F., Bersini, H., & Bouillard, Ph. (2003). Parametrical mechanical design with constraints and preferences: Application to a purge valve. *Computer Methods in Applied Mechanics and Engineering, 192*, 4355–4378. doi:10.1016/S0045-7825(03)00418-3.

Coello, C. A. C. (2004). Handling preferences in evolutionary multi-objective optimization: A survey. In *Proceedings of the Congress on Evolutionary Computation* (pp. 30-37).

Coello, C. A. C., Veldhuizen, D. V., & Lamont, G. B. (2002). *Evolutionary algorithms for solving multiobjective problems*. Boston, MA: Kluwer Academic.

Cohen, I. R. (2000). *Tending Adam's garden: Evolving the cognitive immune self*. London, UK: Academic Press.

Cohen, I. R. (2000). *Tending Adam's garden: Evolving the cognitive immune self*. New York, NY: Academic Press.

Cohen, I. R. (2009). Real and artificial immune systems: Computing the state of the body. *Nature Reviews. Immunology*, *7*, 569–574. doi:10.1038/nri2102 PMID:17558422.

Cohen, I. R., & Harel, D. (2007). Explaining a complex living system: Dynamics, multi-scaling and emergence. *Journal of the Royal Society, Interface*, *4*(13), 175–182. doi:10.1098/rsif.2006.0173 PMID:17251153.

Combes, D., Le Ray, D., Lambert, F., Simmers, J., & Straka, H. (2008). An intrinsic feed-forward mechanism for vertebrate gaze stabilization. *Current Biology*, *18*(5), 241–243. doi:10.1016/j.cub.2008.02.018.

Conery, J. S. (2010, November). Computation is symbol manipulation. In *Proceedings of the Ubiquity Symposium on What is Computation?* (article 4).

Copeland, B. J. (2004). *The essential Turing*. Oxford, UK: Oxford University Press.

Copeland, B. J., & Proudfoot, D. (1996). On Alan Turing's anticipation of connectionism. *Synthese*, *108*, 361–377. doi:10.1007/BF00413694.

Copeland, B. J., & Proudfoot, D. (1999). Alan Turing's forgotten ideas in computer science. *Scientific American*, *280*(4), 77–81. doi:10.1038/scientificamerican0499-98.

Coyne, J. A., & Orr, H. A. (1999). The evolutionary genetics of speciation. In Magurran, A. E., & May, R. M. (Eds.), *Evolution of biological diversity*. Oxford, UK: Oxford University Press.

Crnkovic, G. D. (2010). Biological information and natural computation. In Vallverdú, J. (Ed.), *Thinking machines and the philosophy of computer science: Concepts and principles* (pp. 36–52). Hershey, PA: IGI Global. doi:10.4018/978-1-61692-014-2.ch003.

Crnkovic, G. D. (2011a). Dynamics of information as natural computation. *Information*, *2*(3), 460–477. doi:10.3390/info2030460.

Crnkovic, G. D. (2011b). Significance of models of computation, from Turing model to natural computation. *Minds and Machines*, *21*(2), 301–322. doi:10.1007/s11023-011-9235-1.

Csuhaj-Varjú, E., Margenstern, M., & Vaszil, G. (2006). P colonies with a bounded number of cells. In *Proceedings of the 7th Workshop on Membrane Computing*, Leiden, The Netherlands (pp. 311-322).

Csuhaj-Varjú, E., Kelemen, J., Kelemenová, A., Păun, G., & Vaszil, G. (2006). Cells in environment: P colonies. *Multiple-valued Logic and Soft Computing*, *12*(3-4), 201–215.

Cushing, J. (1977). *Integrodifferential equations and delay models in population dynamics*. Berlin, Germany: Springer-Verlag.

Cvetkovic, D., & Parmee, I. C. (2002). Preferences and their application in evolutionary multiobjective optimization. *IEEE Transactions on Evolutionary Computation*, *6*(1), 42–57. doi:10.1109/4235.985691.

Dang, Z., Ibarra, O. H., Li, C., & Xie, G. (2005). On model-checking of P systems. In C. S. Calude, M. J. Dinneen, G. Paun, M. J. Pérez-Jímenez, & G. Rozenberg (Eds.), *Proceedings of the 4th International Conference on Unconventional Computation* (LNCS 3699, pp. 82-93).

Dang, Z., Ibarra, O. H., Li, C., & Xie, G. (2006). On the decidability of model-checking for P systems. *Journal of Automata. Languages and Combinatorics*, *11*(3), 279–298.

Darwin, C. (2003). *The origin of species*. New York, NY: Signet Classic.

de Aguiar, M. A. M., Barange, M., Baptestini, E. M., Kaufman, L., & Bar-Yam, Y. (2009). Global patterns of speciation and diversity. *Nature*, *460*(16), 384–387. doi:10.1038/nature08168 PMID:19606148.

de Castro, L. N. (2001). *Immune engineering: Development and application of computational tools inspired by artificial immune systems* (Unpublished doctoral dissertation). Computer and Electrical Engineering School, Unicamp, Brazil.

de Castro, L. N. (2006). *Fundamentals of natural computing: Basic concepts, algorithms, and applications*. Boca Raton, FL: CRC Press.

de Castro, L. N. (2007). Fundamentals of natural computing: An overview. *Physics of Life Reviews*, *4*(1), 1–36. doi:10.1016/j.plrev.2006.10.002.

de Castro, L. N., & Timmis, J. (2002). *Artificial immune systems: A new computational intelligence approach*. Berlin, Germany: Springer-Verlag.

de Jong, H. (2002). Modeling and simulation of genetic regulatory systems: A literature review. *Journal of Computational Biology*, *9*(1), 67–103. doi:10.1089/10665270252833208 PMID:11911796.

de Melo, V. V., Vargas, D. V., & Delbem, A. C. B. (2010). *Uso de otimização contínua na resolução de problemas binários: um estudo com evolução diferencial e algoritmo filo-genético em problemas deceptivos aditivos*. Paper presented at the 2ª Escola Luso-Brasileira De Computação Evolutiva (elbce), Guimarães, Portugal.

de Silva, A. P. (2005). Molecular logic gets loaded. *Nature*, *4*, 15–16. doi:10.1038/nmat1301.

de Silva, A. P., & Uchiyama, S. (2007). Molecular logic and computing. *Nature Nanotechnology*, *2*, 399–410. doi:10.1038/nnano.2007.188 PMID:18654323.

Deaven, D., & Ho, K. (1995). Molecular geometry optimization with a genetic algorithm. *Physical Review Letters*, *75*, 288–291. doi:10.1103/PhysRevLett.75.288.

Deb, K. (1999). Solving goal programming problems using multi-objective genetic algorithms. In *Proceedings of the IEEE Congress on Evolutionary Computation* (pp. 77-84).

Deb, K., & Padhye, N. (2010). Development of efficient particle swarm optimizers by using concepts from evolutionary algorithms. In *Proceedings of the Genetic and Evolutionary Computation Conference* (pp. 55-62). New York, NY: ACM Press.

Deb, K. (1998). An efficient constraint handling method for genetic algorithms. *Computer Methods in Applied Mechanics and Engineering*, *186*, 311–338. doi:10.1016/S0045-7825(99)00389-8.

Deb, K. (2001). *Multi-objective optimization using evolutionary algorithms*. Chichester, UK: John Wiley & Sons.

Deb, K., Pratap, A., Agrawal, S., & Meyarivan, T. (2002). A fast and elitist multi-objective genetic algorithm: NSGA-II. *IEEE Transactions on Evolutionary Computation*, *6*(2), 182–197. doi:10.1109/4235.996017.

Deb, K., Sinha, A., Korhonen, P. J., & Wallenius, J. (2010). An interactive evolutionary multiobjective optimization method based on progressively approximated value functions. *IEEE Transactions on Evolutionary Computation*, *14*(5), 723–739. doi:10.1109/TEVC.2010.2064323.

Degallier, S., Santos, C., Righetti, L., & Ijspeert, A. (2006). Movement generation using dynamical systems: A humanoid robot performing a drumming task. In *Proceedings of the IEEE-RAS International Conference on Humanoid Robots* (pp. 512-517).

del Solar, J. R., & Vallejos, P. A. (2005). Motion detection and tracking for an aibo robot using camera motion compensation and kalman filtering. In D. Nardi, M. Riedmiller, C. Sammut, & J. Santos-Victor (Eds.), *Proceedings of the 8th Robot Soccer World Cup* (LNCS 3276 pp. 619-627).

Denning, P. J. (2010, November). Opening statement. In *Proceedings of the Ubiquity Symposium on What is Computation?* (article 1).

Denning, P. J. (2001). *The invisible future: The seamless integration of technology in everyday life*. New York, NY: McGraw-Hill.

Denning, P. J. (2007). Computing is a natural science. *Communications of the ACM*, *50*(7), 13–18. doi:10.1145/1272516.1272529.

Denning, P. J. (2008). The computing field: Structure. In Wah, B. (Ed.), *Wiley encyclopedia of computer science and engineering* (pp. 615–623). New York, NY: Wiley Interscience.

Denning, P. J. (Ed.). (2001). *The invisible future: The seamless integration of technology in everyday life*. New York, NY: McGraw-Hill.

Deutsch, D. (2012). What is computation? (How) does nature compute? In Zenil, H. (Ed.), *A computable universe: Understanding computation & exploring nature as computation*. Singapore: World Scientific.

di Pierro, F., Khu, S.-T., & Savic, D. A. (2007). An investigation on preference order ranking scheme for multiobjective evolutionary optimization. *IEEE Transactions on Evolutionary Computation, 11*(1), 17–45. doi:10.1109/TEVC.2006.876362.

Díaz, D., Graciani, C., Gutiérrez-Naranjo, M., Pérez-Hurtado, I., & Pérez-Jiménez, M. (2010). In Păun, G., Rozenberg, G., & Salomaa, A. (Eds.), *The Oxford handbook of membrane computing* (p. 17). New York, NY: Oxford University Press.

Díaz-Pernil, D., Gutiérrez-Naranjo, M. A., Molina-Abril, H., & Real, P. (2010). A bio-inspired software for segmenting digital images. In A. K. Nagar, R. Thamburaj, K. Li, Z. Tang, & R. Li (Eds.), *Proceedings of the IEEE Fifth International Conference on Bio-inspired Computing: Theories and Applications*, Beijing, China (Vol. 2, p. 1377-1381).

Díaz-Pernil, D., Gutiérrez-Naranjo, M. A., Pérez-Jiménez, M. A., & Riscos-Núñez, A. (2007). Solving subset sum in linear time by using tissue P systems with cell division. In J. Mira & J. R. Alvarez (Eds.), *Proceedings of the Second International Work-Conference on Bio-inspired Modeling of Cognitive Tasks* (LNCS 4527, pp. 170-179).

Díaz-Pernil, D., Gutiérrez-Naranjo, M. A., Pérez-Jiménez, M. A., & Riscos-Núñez, A. (2008). A uniform family of tissue P systems with cell division solving 3-COL in a linear time. *Theoretical Computer Science, 404*, 76–87. doi:10.1016/j.tcs.2008.04.005.

Díaz-Pernil, D., Gutiérrez-Naranjo, M. A., Pérez-Jiménez, M. A., & Riscos-Núñez, A. (2008). Computational efficiency of cellular division in tissue-like membrane systems. *Romanian Journal of Information Science and Technology, 11*(3), 229–241.

Díaz-Pernil, D., Gutiérrez-Naranjo, M. A., Pérez-Jiménez, M. A., & Riscos-Núñez, A. (2010). A linear time solution to the partition problem in a cellular tissue-like model. *Journal of Computational and Theoretical Nanoscience, 7*(5), 884–889. doi:10.1166/jctn.2010.1435.

Dinneen, M. J., Kim, Y.-B., & Nicolescu, R. (2010b). Edge- and vertex-disjoint paths in P modules. In *Proceedings of the Workshop on Membrane Computing and Biologically Inspired Process Calculi* (pp. 117-136).

Dinneen, M. J., Kim, Y.-B., & Nicolescu, R. (2010a). Edge- and node-disjoint paths in P systems. *Electronic Proceedings in Theoretical Computer Science, 40*, 121–141. doi:10.4204/EPTCS.40.9.

Dinneen, M. J., Kim, Y.-B., & Nicolescu, R. (2010c). P systems and the Byzantine agreement. *Journal of Logic and Algebraic Programming, 79*(6), 334–349. doi:10.1016/j.jlap.2010.03.004.

Dixit, A. G. (1990). *Optimization in economic theory*. Oxford, UK: Oxford University Press.

Dorigo, M., Maniezzo, V., & Colorni, A. (1996). The ant system: Optimization by a colony of cooperating agents. *IEEE Transactions on Systems, Man, and Cybernetics –Part B, 26*(1), 29–41. doi:10.1109/3477.484436 PMID:18263004.

Dorigo, M., & Statzle, T. (2004). *Ant colony optimization*. Cambridge, MA: Bradford Books. doi:10.1007/b99492.

Dowek, G. (2012). The physical Church Thesis as an explanation of the Galileo Thesis. *Natural Computing, 11*(2), 247-251.

Doye, J. P. K. (2006). Physical perspectives on the global optimization of atomic clusters. *Nonconvex Optimization and its Applications, 85*, 103-139.

Doye, J. P. K., Leary, R., Locatelli, M., & Schoen, F. (2004). Global optimization of morse clusters by potential energy transformations. *INFORMS Journal on Computing, 16*, 371–379. doi:10.1287/ijoc.1040.0084.

Doye, J. P. K., & Wales, D. (1997). Structural consequences of the range of the interatomic potential. A menagerie of clusters. *Journal of the Chemical Society, Faraday Transactions, 93*, 4233–4243. doi:10.1039/a706221d.

Draper, N., & Smith, H. (1981). *Applied regression analysis* (2nd ed.). New York, NY: John Wiley & Sons.

Eberhart, R. C., & Kennedy, J. (1995). A new optimizer using particle swarm theory. In *Proceedings of the Sixth International Symposium on Micro Machine and Human Science* (pp. 39-43). Washington, DC: IEEE Computer Society.

Epstein, R., & Carnielli, W. A. (2008). *Computability: Computable functions, logic and the foundations of mathematics* (3rd ed.). Socorro, NM: Advanced Reasoning Forum.

Ercegovac, M. D., Lang, T., & Moreno, J. H. (1998). *Introduction to digital systems*. New York, NY: John Wiley & Sons.

Fatahalian, K., Sugerman, J., & Hanrahan, P. (2004). Understanding the efficiency of GPU algorithms for matrix-matrix multiplication. In *Proceedings of the ACM SIGGRAPH/EUROGRAPHICS Conference on Graphics Hardware* (pp. 133-137).

Felsenstein, J. (2003). *Inferring phylogenies*. Sunderland, MA: Sinauer Associates.

Fernández, E., López, E., Bernal, S., Coello, C. A. C., & Navarro, J. (2010). Evolutionary multiobjective optimization using an outranking-based dominance generalization. *Computers & Operations Research*, *37*(2), 390–395. doi:10.1016/j.cor.2009.06.004.

Fernandez-Marquez, J. L., Serugendo, G. D. M., Montagna, S., Viroli, M., & Arcos, J. L. (2012). Description and composition of bio-inspired design patterns: A complete overview. *Natural Computing*. doi:10.1007/s11047-012-9324-y PMID:22962549.

Feynman, R. P. (1996). *The Feynman lectures on computation*. Reading, MA: Addison-Wesley.

Floridi, L. (2010). *The philosophy of information*. Oxford, UK: Oxford University Press.

Fonseca, C. M., & Fleming, P. J. (1993). Genetic algorithms for multiobjective optimization: Formulation, discussion and generalization. In *Proceedings of the Fifth International Conference on Genetic Algorithms*, San Mateo, CA (pp. 416-423).

Fonteix, C., Massebeuf, S., Pla, F., & Kiss, L. N. (2004). Multicriteria optimization of an emulsion polymerization process. *European Journal of Operational Research*, *153*, 350–359. doi:10.1016/S0377-2217(03)00157-7.

Frailey, D. J. (2010, November). Computation is process. In *Proceedings of the Ubiquity Symposium on What is Computation?* (article 5).

Frénay, B., & Verleysen, M. (2011). Parameter-insensitive Kernel in extreme learning for non-linear support vector regression. *Neurocomputing*, *74*(16), 2526–2531. doi:10.1016/j.neucom.2010.11.037.

Freund, R. (2005). Asynchronous P systems and P systems working in the sequential mode. In G. Mauri, G. Paun, M. J. Pérez-Jiménez, G. Rozenberg, & A. Salomaa (Eds.), *Proceedings of the 5th International Workshop on Membrane Computing* (LNCS 3365, pp. 36-62).

Frisco, P. (2004). The conformon-P system: A molecular and cell biology inspired computability model. *Theoretical Computer Science*, *312*(2-3), 295–319. doi:10.1016/j.tcs.2003.09.008.

Frisco, P. (2009). *Computing with cells: Advances in membrane computing*. New York, NY: Oxford University Press. doi:10.1093/acprof:oso/9780199542864.001.0001.

Frisco, P. (2009). *Computing with cells: Advances in membrane computing*. Oxford, UK: Oxford University Press. doi:10.1093/acprof:oso/9780199542864.001.0001.

Froltsov, V., & Reuter, K. (2009). Robustness of 'cut and splice' genetic algorithms in the structural optimization of atomic clsuters. *Chemical Physics Letters*, *473*, 363–366. doi:10.1016/j.cplett.2009.04.015.

Funahashi, K.-I., & Nakamura, Y. (1993). Approximation of dynamical systems by continuous time recurrent neural networks. *Neural Networks*, *6*(6), 801–806. doi:10.1016/S0893-6080(05)80125-X.

Gabriel, K. R., & Sokal, R. R. (1969). A new statistical approach to geographic variation analysis. *Systematic Zoology*, *18*, 259–278. doi:10.2307/2412323.

Gaetano, A. D., & Arino, O. (2000). Mathematical modelling of the intravenous glucose tolerance test. *Journal of Mathematical Biology*, *40*(2), 136–168. doi:10.1007/s002850050007.

Gallagher, M., & Frean, M. (2005). Population-based continuous optimization, probabilistic modelling and mean shift. *Evolutionary Computation*, *13*(1), 29–42. doi:10.1162/1063656053583478 PMID:15901425.

Galperin, M. Y., & Koonin, E. V. (2003). *Frontiers in computational genomics*. Norfolk, UK: Caister Academic Press.

García-Quismondo, M., Gutiérrez-Escudero, R., Pérez-Hurtado, I., Pérez-Jiménez, M. J., & Riscos-Núñez, A. (2009). An overview of P-lingua 2.0. In G. Păun, M. J. Pérez-Jiménez, A. Riscos-Núñez, G. Rozenberg, & A. Salomaa (Eds.), *Proceedings of the 10th International Workshop on Membrane Computing* (LNCS 5957, pp. 264-288).

García-Quismondo, M., Gutiérrez-Escudero, R., Martínez-del-Amor, M. A., Orejuela-Pinedo, E., & Pérez-Hurtado, I. (2009). P-Lingua 2.0: A software framework for cell-like P systems. *International Journal of Computers, Communications & Control*, *4*(3), 234–243.

García, S., Molina, D., Lozano, M., & Herrera, F. (2009). A study on the use of non-parametric tests for analyzing the evolutionary algorithms' behavior: A case study on the CEC'2005 special session on real parameter optimization. *Journal of Heuristics*, *15*, 617–644. doi:10.1007/s10732-008-9080-4.

Garey, M. R., & Johnson, D. S. (1979). *Computers and intractability: A guide to the theory of NP-completeness*. New York, NY: W. H. Freeman & Co..

Garland, M., & Kirk, D. B. (2010). Understanding throughput-oriented architectures. *Communications of the ACM*, *53*(11), 58–66. doi:10.1145/1839676.1839694.

Garland, M., Le Grand, S., Nickolls, J., Anderson, J., Hardwick, J., & Morton, S. (2008). Parallel computing experiences with cuda. *IEEE Micro*, *28*, 13–27. doi:10.1109/MM.2008.57.

Garza-Fabre, M., Pulido, G. T., & Coello, C. A. C. (2009). Ranking methods for many-objective optimization. In *Proceedings of the 8th Mexican International Conference on Artificial Intelligence* (pp. 633-645).

Gascuel, O., & Steel, M. (2006). Neighbor-joining revealed. *Molecular Biology and Evolution*, *23*(11), 1997. doi:10.1093/molbev/msl072.

Gatenby, R. A., & Gawlinski, E. T. (1996). A reaction-diffusion model of cancer invasion. *Cancer Research*, *56*, 5745–5753. PMID:8971186.

Gavrilets, S., & Aaron Vose, A. (2005). Dynamic patterns of adaptive radiation. *Proceedings of the National Academy of Sciences of the United States of America*, *12*(50), 18040–18045. doi:10.1073/pnas.0506330102 PMID:16330783.

Gavrilets, S., Acton, R., & Gravner, J. (2000). Dynamics of speciation and diversification in metapopulation dynamics. *Evolution; International Journal of Organic Evolution*, *54*(5), 1493–1501. PMID:11108578.

Gavrilets, S., & Losos, J. B. (2009). Adaptive radiation: Contrasting theory with data. *Science*, *323*(5915), 732–737. doi:10.1126/science.1157966 PMID:19197052.

Gavrilets, S., & Vose, A. (2005). Dynamic patterns of adaptive radiation. *Proceedings of the National Academy of Sciences of the United States of America*, *12*(50), 18040–18045. doi:10.1073/pnas.0506330102 PMID:16330783.

Gelende, E. (2011, February). Natural computation. In *Proceedings of the Ubiquity Symposium on What is Computation?* (article 1).

Gerich, J. (2002). Redefining the clinical management of type 2 diabetes: Matching therapy to pathophysiology. *European Journal of Clinical Investigation*, *32*, 46–53. doi:10.1046/j.1365-2362.32.s3.6.x.

Gerth, R., Peled, D., Vardi, M. Y., & Wolper, P. (1995). Simple on-the-fly automatic verification of linear temporal logic. In *Proceedings of the International Symposium on Protocol Specification Testing and Verification* (pp. 3-18).

Gheorghe, M., Ipate, F., Lefticaru, R., & Dragomir, C. (2011). An integrated approach to P systems formal verification. In M. Gheorghe, T. Hinze, G. Paun, G. Rozenberg, & A. Salomaa (Eds.), *Proceedings of the 11th International Workshop on Membrane Computing* (LNCS 6501, pp. 226-239).

Gilon, P., Ravier, M., Jonas, J., & Henquin, J. (2002). Control mechanisms of the oscillations of insulin secretion in vitro and in vivo. *Diabetes*, *51*(1), 144–151. doi:10.2337/diabetes.51.2007.S144.

Gödel, K. (1934). *On undecidable propositions of formal mathematics*. Princeton, NJ: Institute for Advanced Study.

Goldberg, D. E. (1989). *Genetic algorithms in search, optimization and machine learning* (1st ed.). Reading, MA: Addison-Wesley.

Goldberg, D. E. (2002). *The design of innovation: Lessons from and for competent genetic algorithms*. Boston, MA: Kluwer Academic.

Gotelli, N. J., & Kelley, W. G. (1993). A general model of metapopulation dynamics. *Oikos*, *68*(1), 36–44. doi:10.2307/3545306.

Goutsias, J., & Lee, N. H. (2007). Computational and experimental approaches for modeling gene regulatory networks. *Current Pharmaceutical Design*, *13*(14), 1415–1436. doi:10.2174/138161207780765945 PMID:17504165.

Greibach, S. A. (1978). Remarks on blind and partially blind one-way multicounter machines. *Theoretical Computer Science*, *1*(7), 311–324. doi:10.1016/0304-3975(78)90020-8.

Griewank, A. O. (1981). Generalized decent for global optimization. *Journal of Optimization Theory and Applications*, *34*, 11–39. doi:10.1007/BF00933356.

Grillner, S. (1985). Neurobiological bases of rhythmic motor acts in vertebrates. *Science*, *228*, 143–149. doi:10.1126/science.3975635.

Grimm, V. R., & Railsback, S. F. (2005). *Individual-based modeling and ecology*. Princeton, NJ: Princeton University Press.

Gross, M. (1998). Molecular computation. In Gramss, T., Bornholdt, S., Gross, M., Mitchel, M., & Pellizzari, T. (Eds.), *Non-standard computation*. New York, NY: John Wiley & Sons.

Grosso, A., Locatelli, M., & Schoen, F. (2007). A population-based approach for hard global optimization problems based on dissimilarity measures. *Mathematical Programming Services A*, *110*, 373–404. doi:10.1007/s10107-006-0006-3.

Gu, L., & Kanade, T. (2006). 3d alignment of face in a single image. In. *Proceedings of the IEEE Conference on Computer Vision and Pattern Recognition*, *1*, 1305–1312.

Gutch, H. W., Gruber, P., Yeredor, A., & Theis, F. J. (2012). ICA over finite fields - Separability and algorithms. *Signal Processing*, *92*(8), 1796–1808. doi:10.1016/j.sigpro.2011.10.003.

Gutiérrez-Naranjo, M. A., & Pérez-Jiménez, M. J. (2010). Depth-first search with P systems. In M. Gheorghe, T. Hinze, G. Păun, G. Rozenberg, & A. Salomaa (Eds.), *Proceedings of the Eleventh International Conference on Membrane Computing* (LNCS 6501, pp. 257-264).

Gutiérrez-Naranjo, M. A., & Pérez-Jiménez, M. J. (2010). Depth-first search with P systems. In *Proceedings of the 11th International Conference on Membrane Computing* (pp. 257-264).

Gutiérrez-Naranjo, M. A., Martínez-del-Amor, M. A., Pérez-Hurtado, I., & Pérez-Jiménez, M. J. (2009). Solving the N-queens puzzle with P systems. In *Proceedings of the Seventh Brainstorming Week on Membrane Computing*, Seville, Spain (Vol. 1, pp. 199-210).

Gutiérrez-Naranjo, M. A., & Rogozhin, V. (2004). Deductive databases and P systems. *Computer Science Journal of Moldova*, *12*(1), 34.

Gutiérrez-Naranjo, M., Pérez-Jiménez, M., & Ramírez-Martínez, D. (2008). A software tool for verification of spiking neural p systems. *Natural Computing*, *7*(4), 485–497. doi:10.1007/s11047-008-9083-y.

Han, J., Kamber, M., & Pei, J. (2005). *Data mining: Concepts and techniques* (2nd ed.). San Francisco, CA: Morgan Kaufmann.

Harel, D. (2003). A grand challenge for computing: Full reactive modeling of a multi-cellular animal. *Bulletin of the European Association for Theoretical Computer Science*, *81*, 226–235.

Harik, G. R. (1999). *Linkage learning via probabilistic modeling in the ecga* (Tech. Rep. No. 99010). Urbana, IL: University of Illinois at Urbana-Champaign.

Harik, G. R., Lobo, F. G., & Sastry, K. (2006). Linkage learning via probabilistic modeling in the extended compact genetic algorithm (ecga). In M. Pelikan, K. Sastry, & E. CantúPaz (Eds.), Scalable optimization via probabilistic modeling (p. 39-61). Berlin, Germany: Springer-Verlag.

Harik, G. R., Lobo, F. G., & Goldberg, D. E. (1999). The compact genetic algorithm. *IEEE Transactions on Evolutionary Computation*, *3*(4), 287–297. doi:10.1109/4235.797971.

Harris, M. (2005). Mapping computational concepts to GPUs. In *Proceedings of the ACM SIGGRAPH Courses* (p. 50).

Hart, E., Bersini, H., & Santos, F. (2007). How affinity influences tolerance in an idiotypic network. *Journal of Theoretical Biology*, *249*(3), 422–436. doi:10.1016/j.jtbi.2007.07.019 PMID:17904580.

Hartke, B. (1993). Global geometry optimization of clusters using genetic algorithms. *Journal of Physical Chemistry*, *97*, 9973–9976. doi:10.1021/j100141a013.

Hartke, B. (2004). Application of evolutionary algorithms to global cluster geometry optimization. In Johnston, R. L. (Ed.), *Applications of evolutionary computation in chemistry: Structure and bonding* (pp. 33–53). Berlin, Germany: Springer-Verlag.

Hawking, S. (2007). *God created the integers*. New York, NY: Running Press.

Haykin, S. (1998). *Neural networks: A comprehensive foundation*. Upper Saddle River, NJ: Prentice Hall.

Held, R., & Hein, A. (1963). Movement-produced stimulation in the development of visually guided behavior. *Journal of Comparative and Physiological Psychology*, *56*(5), 872–876. doi:10.1037/h0040546.

Hengeveld, R. (1990). *Dynamic biogeography*. Cambridge, UK: Cambridge University Press.

Higashi, N., & Iba, H. (2003). Particle swarm optimization with gaussian mutation. In *Proceedings of the IEEE Swarm Intelligence Symposium* (pp. 72-79). Washington, DC: IEEE Computer Society.

Hocking, R. (1976). The analysis and selection of variables in linear regression. *Biometrics*, 32.

Hodges, A. (1992). *Alan Turing: The enigma*. New York, NY: Vintage.

Hodgson, R. (2002). Particle swarm optimization applied to the atomic cluster optimization problem. In *Proceedings of the Genetic and Evolutionary Computation Conference* (pp. 68-73). New York, NY: ACM Press.

Hoffman, E., Loessi, J., & Moore, R. (1969). Constructions for the solution of the N queens problem. *National Mathematics Magazine*, *42*, 66–72.

Holden, N., & Freitas, A. (2005). A hybrid particle swarm/ant colony algorithm for the classification of hierarchical biological data. In *Proceedings of the IEEE Swarm Intelligence Symposium* (pp. 100-107). Washington, DC: IEEE Computer Society.

Holland, J. H. (1975). *Adaptation in natural artificial systems*. Ann Arbor, MI: University of Michigan Press.

Holland, J. H. (1992). *Adaptation in natural and artificial systems: An introductory analysis with applications to biology, control, and artificial intelligence*. Cambridge, MA: Bradford Books.

Holzmann, G. (2003). *The spin model checker: Primer and reference manual* (1st ed.). Reading, MA: Addison-Wesley.

Hoos, H. H., & Stützle, T. (2004). *Stochastic local search: Foundations & applications* (1st ed.). San Francisco, CA: Morgan Kaufmann.

Horn, J. (1997). Multicriterion decision making. In Bäck, T., Fogel, D., & Michalewicz, Z. (Eds.), *Handbook of evolutionary computation* (*Vol. 1*, pp. 1–15). New York, NY: Oxford University Press. doi:10.1887/0750308958/b386c85.

Hosoda, K., Sakamoto, K., & Asada, M. (1995). Trajectory generation for obstacle avoidance of uncalibrated stereo visual servoing without 3d reconstruction. In *Proceedings of the IEEE/RSJ International Conference on Intelligent Robots and Systems* (Vol. 1, p. 29).

Huang, G.-B., Zhu, Q.-Y., & Siew, C.-K. (2004). Extreme learning machine: A new learning scheme of feedforward neural networks. In *Proceedings of the International Joint Conference on Neural Networks* (pp. 985-990).

Huang, G.-B., & Chen, L. (2007). Convex incremental extreme learning machine. *Neurocomputing*, *70*(16-18), 3056–3062. doi:10.1016/j.neucom.2007.02.009.

Huang, G.-B., & Chen, L. (2008). Enhanced random search based incremental extreme learning machine. *Neurocomputing*, *71*(16-18), 3460–3468. doi:10.1016/j.neucom.2007.10.008.

Huang, G.-B., Chen, L., & Siew, C.-K. (2006). Universal approximation using incremental constructive feedforward networks with random hidden nodes. *IEEE Transactions on Neural Networks*, *17*(4), 879–892. doi:10.1109/TNN.2006.875977.

Huang, G.-B., Li, M.-B., Chen, L., & Siew, C.-K. (2008). Incremental extreme learning machine with fully complex hidden nodes. *Neurocomputing*, *71*(4-6), 576–583. doi:10.1016/j.neucom.2007.07.025.

Huang, G.-B., Wang, D. H., & Lan, Y. (2011). Extreme learning machines: A survey. *International Journal of Machine Learning and Cybernetics*, *2*(2), 107–122. doi:10.1007/s13042-011-0019-y.

Huang, G.-B., Zhou, H., Ding, X., & Zhang, R. (2012). Extreme learning machine for regression and multiclass classification. *IEEE Transactions on Systems, Man, and Cybernetics. Part B, Cybernetics*, *42*(2), 513–529. doi:10.1109/TSMCB.2011.2168604.

Huang, G.-B., Zhu, Q.-Y., & Siew, C.-K. (2006). Extreme learning machine: Theory and applications. *Neurocomputing*, *70*(1-3), 489–501. doi:10.1016/j.neucom.2005.12.126.

Hui, C. (2006). Carrying capacity, population equilibrium, and environment's maximal load. *Ecological Modelling*, *192*, 317–320. doi:10.1016/j.ecolmodel.2005.07.001.

Hutchinson, S., Hager, G., & Corke, P. (1996). A tutorial on visual servo control. *IEEE Transactions on Robotics and Automation*, *12*(5), 651–670. doi:10.1109/70.538972.

Imai, T. (2008). Interaction of the body, head, and eyes during walking and turning. *Experimental Brain Research*, *136*(1), 1–18. doi:10.1007/s002210000533.

Ionescu, M., Păun, G., & Yokomori, T. (2006). Spiking neural p systems. *Fundamenta Informaticae*, *71*(2-3), 279–308.

Ionescu, M., & Sburlan, D. (2004). On P systems with promoters/inhibitors. *Journal of Universal Computer Science*, *10*(5), 581–599.

Ipate, F., & Ţurcanu, A. (2011). Modelling, verification and testing of P systems using Rodin and ProB. In *Proceedings of the Ninth Brainstorming Week on Membrane Computing* (pp. 209-220).

Ipate, F., Gheorghe, M., & Lefticaru, R. (2010). Test generation from P systems using model checking. *Journal of Logic and Algebraic Programming*, *79*(6), 350–362. doi:10.1016/j.jlap.2010.03.007.

Ipate, F., Lefticaru, R., & Tudose, C. (2011). Formal verification of P systems using spin. *International Journal of Foundations of Computer Science*, *22*(1), 133–142. doi:10.1142/S0129054111007897.

Jaeger, H. (2001). *The echo state approach to analyzing and training recurrent neural networks* (GMD Report No. 148). St. Augustin, Germany: German National Research Center for Information Technology.

Jaeger, H. (2003). Adaptive nonlinear system identification with echo state networks. In *Proceedings of the Conference on Advances in Neural Information Processing Systems* (pp. 593-600).

Jaeger, H., & Hass, H. (2004). Harnessing nonlinearity: Predicting chaotic systems and saving energy in wireless communication. *Science*, *304*(5667), 78–80. doi:10.1126/science.1091277.

Jago, M. (2007). *Formal logic. Penrith.* Cumbria, UK: Humanities-Ebooks LLP.

Jain, A., Murty, M., & Flynn, P. (1999). Data clustering: A review. *ACM Computing Surveys*, *31*(3), 264–323. doi:10.1145/331499.331504.

Jaromczyk, J. W., & Toussaint, G. T. (1992). Relative neighborhood graphs and their relatives. *Proceedings of the IEEE*, *80*, 1502–1517. doi:10.1109/5.163414.

Jin, Y., & Sendhoff, B. (2002). Incorporation of fuzzy preferences into evolutionary multiobjective optimization. In *Proceedings of the 4th Asia Pacific Conference on Simulated Evolution and Learning* (Vol. 1, pp. 26-30).

Jin, Y., & Branke, J. (2005). Evolutionary optimization in uncertain environments – A survey. *IEEE Transactions on Evolutionary Computation*, *9*(3), 303–317. doi:10.1109/TEVC.2005.846356.

Johnson, C. (2009). Teaching natural computation. *IEEE Computational Intelligence Magazine*, *4*(1), 24–30. doi:10.1109/MCI.2008.930984.

Johnston, R. (2003). Evolving better nanoparticles: Genetic algorithms for optimising cluster geometries. *Dalton Transactions (Cambridge, England)*, *22*, 4193–4207. doi:10.1039/b305686d.

Jorgensen, S. E., Patten, B. C., & Stragkraba, M. (1992). Ecosystems emerging: Toward an ecology of complex systems in a complex future. *Ecological Modelling*, *62*(1-3), 1–27. doi:10.1016/0304-3800(92)90080-X.

Kampis, G. (1991). *Self-modifying systems in biology and cognitive science: A new framework for dynamics, information, and complexity* (1st ed.). Oxford, UK: Pergamon.

Kapur, A., Virji-Babul, N., Tzanetakis, G., & Driessen, P. F. (2005). Gesture-based affective computing on motion capture data. In *Proceedings of the First International Conference on Affective Computing and Intelligent Interaction* (Vol. 1, pp. 1-7).

Kari, L., & Rozenberg, G. (2008). The many facets of natural computing. *Communications of the ACM*, *51*, 72–83. doi:10.1145/1400181.1400200.

Kauffman, S. (1995). *At home in the universe: The search for the laws of self-organization and complexity*. Oxford, UK: Oxford University Press.

Kauffman, S. A. (1993). *The origins of order: Self-organization and selection in evolution*. Oxford, UK: Oxford University Press.

Kaushik, R., Marcinkiewicz, M., Xiao, J., Parsons, S., & Raphan, T. (2007). Implementation of bio-inspired vestibulo-ocular reflex in a quadrupedal robot. In *Proceedings of the IEEE International Conference on Robotics and Automation* (pp. 4861-4866).

Kelemen, J., & Kelemenová, A. (2005). On P colonies, a biochemically inspired model of computation. In *Proceedings of the 6th International Symposium of Hungarian Researchers on Computational Intelligence*, Budapest, Hungary (pp. 40-56).

Kelemen, J., Kelemenová, A., & Păun, G. (2004). Preview of P colonies: A biochemically inspired computing model. In *Proceedings of the Ninth International Conference on the Simulation and Synthesis of Living Systems*, Boston, MA (pp. 82-86).

Kennedy, J. (2003). Bare bones particle swarms. In *Proceedings of the IEEE Swarm Intelligence Symposium* (pp. 80-87). Washington, DC: IEEE Computer Society.

Kennedy, J., & Mendes, R. (2002). Population structure and particle swarm performance. In *Proceedings of the IEEE Congress on Evolutionary Computation* (pp. 1671-1676). Washington, DC: IEEE Computer Society.

Kennedy, J., & Eberhart, R. C. (1995). Particle swarm optimization. In[Washington, DC: IEEE Computer Society.]. *Proceedings of the IEEE International Conference on Neural Networks*, *IV*, 1942–1948. doi:10.1109/ICNN.1995.488968.

Kilian, J., & Siegelmann, H. (1996). The dynamic universality of sigmoidal neural networks. *Information and Computation*, *128*(1), 48–56. doi:10.1006/inco.1996.0062.

Kimura, H., Fukuoka, Y., & Cohen, A. H. (2007). Adaptive dynamic walking of a quadruped robot on natural ground based on biological concepts. *The International Journal of Robotics Research*, *26*(5), 475–490. doi:10.1177/0278364907078089.

Kirk, D., & Hwu, W. (2010). *Programming massively parallel processors: A hands on approach*. San Francisco, CA: Morgan Kaufmann.

Kirkpatrick, D. G., & Radke, J. D. (1985). A framework for computational morphology. In Toussaint, G. (Ed.), *Computational geometry* (pp. 217–248). Amsterdam, The Netherlands: North-Holland.

Kleijn, J., & Koutny, M. (2006). Synchrony and asynchrony in membrane systems. In H. J. Hoogeboom, G. Paun, G. Rozenberg, & A. Salomaa (Eds.), *Proceedings of the 7th International Workshop on Membrane Computing* (LNCS 4361, pp. 66-85).

Knowles, J., & Corne, D. (1999). The Pareto archived evolution strategy: A new baseline algorithm for multi-objective optimization. In *Proceedings of the Congress on Evolutionary Computation* (pp. 98-105).

Kraskov, A. (2008). *Synchronization and interdependence measures and their application to the electroencephalogram of epilepsy patients and clustering of data*. Retrieved from http://eprints.ucl.ac.uk/69978/

Kraskov, A., Andrzejak, R., & Grassberger, P. (2005). Hierarchical clustering based on mutual information. *Europhysics Letters*, *70*(2), 278. doi:10.1209/epl/i2004-10483-y.

Krink, T., & Loøvbjerg, M. (2002). The lifecycle model: Combining particle swarm optimization, genetic algorithms and hillclimbers. In J. JuliánMerelo Guervós, P. Adamidis, H.-G. Beyer, H.-P. Schwefel, & J.-L. Fernández-Villacañas (Eds.), *Proceedings of the 7th International Conference on Parallel Problem Solving from Nature* (LNCS 2439, pp. 621-630).

Krink, T., Vesterstroøm, J. S., & Riget, J. (2002). Particle swarm optimization with spatial particle extension. In *Proceedings of the IEEE Congress on Evolutionary Computation* (pp. 1474-1479). Washington, DC: IEEE Computer Society.

Krishna, S. N., & Rama, R. (1999). A variant of P systems with active membranes: Solving NP-complete problems. *Romanian Journal of Information Science and Technology*, *2*(4), 357–367.

Kube, C. R., Parker, C. A. C., Wang, T., & Zhang, H. (2004). Biologically inspired collective robotics. In De Castro, L. N., & Von Zuben, F. J. (Eds.), *Recent developments in biologically inspired computing* (pp. 367–397). Hershey, PA: Idea Group. doi:10.4018/978-1-59140-312-8.ch015.

Kurazume, R., & Hirose, S. (2000). Development of image stabilization system for remote operation of walking robots. In. *Proceedings of the IEEE International Conference on Robotics and Automation*, *2*, 1856–1861.

Langtangen, H. P. (2009). *Python scripting for computational science (Texts in computational science and engineering)* (3rd ed.). New York, NY: Springer.

Larrañaga, P., & Lozano, J. A. (2001). *Estimation of distribution algorithms: A new tool for evolutionary computation (genetic algorithms and evolutionary computation)*. New York, NY: Springer.

Larsen, J., Urry, J., & Axhausen, K. (2006). *Mobilities, networks, geographies*. Aldershot, UK: Ashgate.

Lavesson, N., & Davidsson, P. (1999). Quantifying the impact of learning algorithm parameter Tuning. In *Proceedings of the 21st National Conference on Artificial Intelligence* (pp. 1165-1173).

Leavitt, D. (2006). *The man who knew too much: Alan Turing and the invention of the computer*. New York, NY: W. W. Norton.

Ledoux, S. F. (2002). Defining natural sciences. *Behaviorology Today*, *5*(1), 34–36.

Lefticaru, R., Ipate, F., & Gheorghe, M. (2010). Model checking based test generation from P systems using P-lingua. *Romanian Journal of Information Science and Technology*, *13*(2), 153–168.

Lehn, J.-M. (2002). Toward self-organization and complex matter. *Science*, *295*(5564), 2400–2403. doi:10.1126/science.1071063 PMID:11923524.

Lemmon, A. R., & Milinkovitch, M. C. (2002). The metapopulation genetic algorithm: An efficient solution for the problem of large phylogeny estimation. *Proceedings of the National Academy of Sciences*, 10516-10521.

Lenaerts, T., & Bersini, H. (2009). A synthon approach to artificial chemistry. *Artificial Life*, *15*(189-103.

Lennard-Jones, J. E. (1931). Cohesion. *Proceedings of the Physical Society*, *43*, 461–482. doi:10.1088/0959-5309/43/5/301.

Leporati, A., Zandron, C., & Gutiérrez-Naranjo, M. A. (2006). P systems with input in binary form. *International Journal of Foundations of Computer Science*, *17*(1), 127–146. doi:10.1142/S0129054106003735.

Leporati, A., Zandron, C., & Mauri, G. (2007). Solving the factorization problem with P systems. *Progress in Natural Science*, *17*(4), 471–478. doi:10.1080/10020070708541025.

Lewis, P. O. (1998). A genetic algorithm for maximum-likelihood phylogeny inference using nucleotide sequence data. *Molecular Biology and Evolution*, *15*(3), 277–283.

Liang, N.-Y., Huang, G.-B., Saratchandran, P., & Sundararajan, N. (2006). A fast and accurate on-line sequential learning algorithm for feedforward networks. *IEEE Transactions on Neural Networks*, *17*(6), 1411–1423. doi:10.1109/TNN.2006.880583.

Lihoreau, M., Chittka, L., & Raine, N. E. (2010). Travel optimization by foraging bumblebees through readjustments of traplines after discovery of new feeding locations. *American Naturalist, 176*(6), 744–757. doi:10.1086/657042 PMID:20973670.

Li, J., Kuang, Y., & Li, B. (2001). Analysis of IVGTT glucose-insulin interaction models with time delay. *Discrete and Continuous Dynamical Systems–Series B, 1*(1), 103–124. doi:10.3934/dcdsb.2001.1.103.

Li, M.-B., Huang, G.-B., Saratchandran, P., & Sundararajan, N. (2005). Fully complex extreme learning machine. *Neurocomputing, 68*, 306–314. doi:10.1016/j.neucom.2005.03.002.

Liu, D., & Nocedal, J. (1989). On the limited memory method for large scale optimization. *Mathematical Programming B, 45*, 503–528. doi:10.1007/BF01589116.

Lloyd, S. (2002). *The computational universe*. Retrieved from http://edge.org/conversation/the-computational-universe

Lloyd, J. W. (1987). *Foundations of logic programming* (2nd ed.). Berlin, Germany: Springer-Verlag.

Lloyd, S. (2006). *Programming the universe: A quantum computer scientist takes on the cosmos*. New York, NY: Knopf.

Locatelli, M., & Schoen, F. (2002). Fast global optimization of difficult Lennard-Jones clusters. *Computational Optimization and Applications, 21*, 55–70. doi:10.1023/A:1013596313166.

Loøvbjerg, M., Rasmussen, T. K., & Krink, T. (2001). Hybrid particle swarm optimiser with breeding and subpopulations. In *Proceedings of the Third Genetic and Evolutionary Computation Conference* (pp. 469-476).

Luenberger, D. G. (2003). *Linear and nonlinear programming* (2nd ed.). New York, NY: Springer.

Lukosevicius, M., & Jaeger, H. (2009). Reservoir computing approaches to recurrent neural network training. *Computer Science Review, 3*(3), 127–149. doi:10.1016/j.cosrev.2009.03.005.

Lynch, N. A. (1996). *Distributed algorithms*. San Francisco, CA: Morgan Kaufmann.

Maass, W. (2007). Liquid computing. In S. B. Cooper, B. Löwe, & A. Sorbi (Eds.), *Proceedings of the Third International Conference on Computation and Logic in the Real World* (LNCS 4497, pp. 507-516).

Maass, W., Natschläger, T., & Markram, H. (2002). Real-time computing without stable states: A new framework for neural computation based on perturbations. *Neural Computation, 14*(11), 2531–2560. doi:10.1162/089976602760407955.

Maass, W., Natschläger, T., & Markram, H. (2004). Fading memory and kernel properties of generic cortical microcircuit models. *Journal of Physiology, Paris, 98*(4-6), 315–330. doi:10.1016/j.jphysparis.2005.09.020.

Magurran, A. (1999). Population differentiation without speciation. In Magurran, A. E., & May, R. M. (Eds.), *Evolution of biological diversity*. Oxford, UK: Oxford University Press.

Maia, R. D., & de Castro, L. N. (2012). Bee colonies as model for multimodal continuous optimization: The OptBees algorithm. In *Proceedings of the IEEE Congress on Evolutionary Computation* (pp. 1-8).

Makki, S. A. M., & Havas, G. (1996). Distributed algorithms for depth-first search. *Information Processing Letters, 60*, 7–12. doi:10.1016/S0020-0190(96)00141-X.

Makroglou, A., Li, J., & Kuang, Y. (2006). Mathematical models and software tools for the glucose-insulin regulatory system and diabetes: An overview. *Applied Numerical Mathematics, 56*(3), 559–573. doi:10.1016/j.apnum.2005.04.023.

Malis, E. (2004). Visual servoing invariant to changes in camera-intrinsic parameters. *IEEE Transactions on Robotics and Automation, 20*(1), 72–81. doi:10.1109/TRA.2003.820847.

Manca, V., & Marchetti, L. (2010a). Goldbeter's mitotic oscillator entirely modeled by MP systems. In M. Gheorghe, T. Hinze, G. Păun, G. Rozenberg, & A. Salomaa (Eds.), *Proceedings of the 11th International Workshop on Membrane Computing* (LNCS 6501, pp. 273-284).

Manca, V., Bianco, L., & Fontana, F. (2005). Evolutions and oscillations of P systems: Theoretical considerations and application to biological phenomena. In G. Mauri, G. Paun, M. J. Pérez-Jiménez, G. Rozenberg, & A. Salomaa (Eds.), *Proceedings of the 5th International Workshop on Membrane Computing* (LNCS 3365, pp. 63-84).

Manca, V. (2009). Log-gain principles for metabolic P systems. In Condon, A., Harel, D., & Kok, J. (Eds.), *Algorithmic bioprocesses, natural computing series* (pp. 585–605). Berlin, Germany: Springer-Verlag. doi:10.1007/978-3-540-88869-7_28.

Manca, V. (2010a). Fundamentals of metabolic P systems. In P˘aun, G., & Rozenberg, G. (Eds.), *Oxford handbook of membrane computing*. Oxford, UK: Oxford University Press.

Manca, V. (2010b). Metabolic P systems. *Scholarpedia*, *5*(3), 9273. doi:10.4249/scholarpedia.9273.

Manca, V., & Marchetti, L. (2010b). Metabolic approximation of real periodical functions. *Journal of Logic and Algebraic Programming*, *79*, 363–373. doi:10.1016/j.jlap.2010.03.005.

Manca, V., & Marchetti, L. (2011). Log-gain stoichiometic stepwise regression for MP systems. *International Journal of Foundations of Computer Science*, *22*(1), 97–106. doi:10.1142/S0129054111007861.

Manca, V., Pagliarini, R., & Zorzan, S. (2009). A photosynthetic process modelled by a metabolic P system. *Natural Computing*, *8*(4), 847–864. doi:10.1007/s11047-008-9104-x.

Mari, A. (2002). Mathematical modeling in glucose metabolism and insulin secretion. *Current Opinion in Clinical Nutrition and Metabolic Care*, *5*(5), 495–501. doi:10.1097/00075197-200209000-00007.

Marques, J. M. C., Llanio-Trujillo, J. L., Abreu, P. E., & Pereira, F. B. (2010). How different are two chemical structures? *Journal of Chemical Information and Modeling*, *50*(12), 2129–2140. doi:10.1021/ci100219f.

Martínez-del-Amor, M. A., Pérez-Hurtado, I., Pérez-Jiménez, M. J., & Riscos-Núñez, A. (2010). A P-Lingua based simulator for tissue P systems. *Journal of Logic and Algebraic Programming*, *79*, 374–382. doi:10.1016/j.jlap.2010.03.009.

Martini, F. (2008). *Fundamentals of anatomy and physiology* (8th ed.). Upper Saddle River, NJ: Benjamin Cummings.

Martins, J. P., Soares, A. H. M., Vargas, D. V., & Delbem, A. C. B. (2011). Multi-objective phylogenetic algorithm: Solving multi-objective decomposable deceptive problems. In R. H. C. Takahashi, K. Deb, E. F. Wanner, & S. Greco (Eds.), *Proceedings of the Sixth International Conference on Evolutionary Multi-criterion Optimization* (LNCS 6575, pp. 285-297).

Martín-Vide, C., Pazos, J., Păun, G., & Rodríguez-Patón, A. (2002). A new class of symbolic abstract neural nets: Tissue P systems. In O. H. Ibarra & L. Zhang (Eds.), *Proceedings of the 8th Annual International Conference on Computing and Combinations* (LNCS 2387, pp. 290-299).

Martín-Vide, C., Păun, G., Pazos, J., & Rodríguez-Patón, A. (2003). Tissue P systems. *Theoretical Computer Science*, *296*(2), 295–326. doi:10.1016/S0304-3975(02)00659-X.

Martín-Vide, C., Pazos, J., Păun, G., & Rodríguez-Patón, A. (2003). Tissue P systems. *Theoretical Computer Science*, *296*, 295–326. doi:10.1016/S0304-3975(02)00659-X.

Masulli, F., & Mitra, S. (2009). Natural computing methods in bioinformatics: A survey. *Information Fusion*, *10*(3), 211–216. doi:10.1016/j.inffus.2008.12.002.

Matos, V., & Santos, C. (2010). Omnidirectional locomotion in a quadruped robot: A CPG-based approach. In *Proceedings of the IEEE/RSJ International Conference on Intelligent Robots and Systems*, Taipei, Taiwan (pp. 3392-3397).

Matula, D. W., & Sokal, R. R. (1984). Properties of Gabriel graphs relevant to geographical variation research and the clustering of points in the same plane. *Geographical Analysis*, *12*, 205–222. doi:10.1111/j.1538-4632.1980.tb00031.x.

Mayr, E., & Diamond, J. (2001). *The birds of Northern Melanesia: Speciation, ecology and biogeography*. Oxford, UK: Oxford University Press.

McCulloch, W., & Pitts, W. (1943). A logical calculus of the ideas immanent in nervous activity. *The Bulletin of Mathematical Biophysics*, *5*(4), 115–133. doi:10.1007/BF02478259.

McCulloch, W., & Pitts, W. H. (1943). A logical calculus of the ideas immanent in nervous activity. *The Bulletin of Mathematical Biophysics*, *5*, 115–133. doi:10.1007/BF02478259.

Mehta, P., Goyal, S., Long, T., Bassler, B. L., & Wingreen, N. (2009). Information processing and signal integration in bacterial quorum sensing. *Molecular Systems Biology*, *5*, 325. doi:10.1038/msb.2009.79 PMID:19920810.

Melville, J., Nicholson, G. E., Harmon, L. J., & Losos, J. B. (2005). Intercontinental community convergence of ecology and morphology in desert lizards. *Proceedings of the Royal Society of London*, *273*(1586), 557–563. doi:10.1098/rspb.2005.3328 PMID:16537126.

Mendes, R. (2004). *Population topologies and their influence in particle swarm performance*. Unpublished doctoral dissertation, Universidade do Minho, Braga, Portugal.

Michel, O. (2004). Webots: Professional mobile robot simulation. *Journal of Advanced Robotics Systems*, *1*(1), 39–42.

Milne, B. T. (1998). Motivation and benefits of complex systems approaches in ecology. *Ecosystems (New York, N.Y.)*, *1*, 449–456. doi:10.1007/s100219900040.

Minsky, M. L. (1967). *Computation: Finite and infinite machines*. Upper Saddle River, NJ: Prentice Hall.

Mitchel, M. (2011, February). Biological computation. In *Proceedings of the Ubiquity Symposium on What is Computation?* (article 3).

Morse, P. (1929). Diatomic molecules according to the wave mechanics: Vibrational levels. *Physical Review*, *34*, 57–64. doi:10.1103/PhysRev.34.57.

Morzy, T., Wojciechowski, M., & Zakrzewicz, M. (2009). Pattern-oriented hierarchical clustering. In *Proceedings of the Third East European Conference on Advances in Databases and Information Systems* (pp. 179-190).

Mousseau, V., Slowinski, R., & Zielniewicz, P. (2000). A user-oriented implementation of the ELECTRE-TRI method integrating preference elicitation support. *Computers & Operations Research*, *27*, 757–777. doi:10.1016/S0305-0548(99)00117-3.

Mühlenbein, H., & Mahnig, T. (1999). Fda - a scalable evolutionary algorithm for the optimization of additively decomposed functions. *Evolutionary Computation*, *7*(4), 353–376. doi:10.1162/evco.1999.7.4.353.

Mukhopadhyay, A., Gaetano, A. D., & Arino, O. (2004). Modelling the intravenous glucose tolerance test: A global study for single-distributed-delay model. *Discrete and Continuous Dynamical Systems - Series B*, *4*(2), 407–417. doi:10.3934/dcdsb.2004.4.407.

Mullen, K., Ardia, D., Gil, D., Windover, D., & Cline, J. (2011). DEoptim: An R package for global optimization by differential evolution. *Journal of Statistical Software*, *40*(6), 1–26.

Murphy, N., & Porreca, A. E. (2010). First steps towards linking membrane depth and the polynomial hierarchy. In *Proceedings of the Eighth Brainstorming Week on Membrane Computing* (pp. 255-266).

Murphy, N., & Woods, D. (2011). The computational power of membrane systems under tight uniformity conditions. *Natural Computing*, *10*, 613–632. doi:10.1007/s11047-010-9244-7.

Myers, A. A., & Giller, P. S. (1991). *Analytical biogeography*. Boca Raton, FL: Chapman & Hall.

Nadeau, S., Amblard, B., Mesure, S., & Bourbonnais, D. (2003). Head and trunk stabilization strategies during forward and backward walking in healthy adults. *Gait & Posture*, *18*(3), 134–142. doi:10.1016/S0966-6362(02)00070-X.

Nagpal, R., & Mamei, M. (2004). Engineering amorphous computing systems. *Multiagent Systems, Artificial Societies, and Simulated Organizations*, *11*, 303–320. doi:10.1007/1-4020-8058-1_19.

Nakagaki, T. (2001). Smart behavior of true slime mold in a labyrinth. *Research in Microbiology*, *152*, 767–770. doi:10.1016/S0923-2508(01)01259-1.

Nakagaki, T., Iima, M., Ueda, T., Nishiura, Y., Saigusa, T., & Tero, A. et al. (2007). Minimum-risk path finding by an adaptive amoeba network. *Physical Review Letters*, *99*, 068104. doi:10.1103/PhysRevLett.99.068104.

Nakagaki, T., Yamada, H., & Toth, A. (2001). Path finding by tube morphogenesis in an amoeboid organism. *Biophysical Chemistry, 92*, 47–52. doi:10.1016/S0301-4622(01)00179-X.

Nakagaki, T., Yamada, H., & Ueda, T. (2000). Interaction between cell shape and contraction pattern in the *Physarum plasmodium. Biophysical Chemistry, 84*, 195–204. doi:10.1016/S0301-4622(00)00108-3.

National Diabetes Data Group. (1979). Classification and diagnosis of diabetes mellitus and other categories of glucose intolerance. *Diabetes, 28*(28), 1039–1057.

Nesetril, J., Milkova, E., & Nesetrilova, H. (2001). Otakar Boruvka on minimum spanning tree problem. *Discrete Mathematics, 233*, 3–36. doi:10.1016/S0012-365X(00)00224-7.

Newton, I. (2003). *Speciation and biogeography of birds*. New York, NY: Academic Press.

Nguyen, V., Kearney, D., & Gioiosa, G. (2010b). A region-oriented hardware implementation for membrane computing applications and its integration into reconfig-p. In G. Paun, M. J. Pérez-Jiménez, A. Riscos-Núñez, G. Rozenberg, & A. Salomaa (Eds.), *Proceedings of the 10th International Workshop on Membrane Computing* (LNCS 5957, pp. 385-409).

Nguyen, V., Kearney, D., & Gioiosa, G. (2010a). An extensible, maintainable and elegant approach to hardware source code generation in reconfig-p. *Journal of Logic and Algebraic Programming, 79*(6), 383–396. doi:10.1016/j.jlap.2010.03.013.

Nicholson, G. E., Harmon, L. J., & Losos, J. B. (2007). Evolution of Anolis Lizard Dewlap Diversity. *PLoS ONE, 2*(3), e274. doi:10.1371/journal.pone.0000274 PMID:17342208.

Nicolescu, R., & Wu, H. (2011a). *BFS solution for disjoint paths in P systems* (Tech. Rep. No. CDMTCS-399). Auckland New Zealand: University of Auckland.

Nicolescu, R., & Wu, H. (2011b). *Asynchronous P systems* (Tech. Rep. No. CDMTCS-406). Auckland, New Zealand: University of Auckland.

Nicolescu, R., Dinneen, M. J., & Kim, Y.-B. (2009). Discovering the membrane topology of hyperdag P systems. In G. Păun, M. J. Pérez-Jiménez, A. Riscos-Núñez, G. Rozenberg, & A. Salomaa (Eds.), *Proceedings of the International Workshop on Membrane Computing* (LNCS 5957, pp. 410-435).

Nicolescu, B. (Ed.). (2008). *Transdisciplinarity: Theory and practice*. New York, NY: Hampton Press.

NVIDIA Corporation. (2010). *Nvidia cuda c programming guide 3.0*. Retrieved from http://developer.download.nvidia.com/compute/cuda/3_0/toolkit/docs/NVIDIA_CUDA_ProgrammingGuide.pdf

NVIDIA CUDA Developers. (2011). *Resources page*. Retrieved from http://developer.nvidia.com/page/home.html

Obtulowicz, A. (2001). On P systems with active membranes solving the integer factorization problem in a polynomial time. In C. S. Calude, G. Paun, G. Rozenberg, & A. Salomaa (Eds.), *Proceedings of the Mathematical, Computer Science, and Molecular Computing Points of View: Multiset Processing* (LNCS 2235, pp. 267-285).

Olariu, S., & Weigle, M. C. (2009). *Vehicular networks: From theory to practice*. Boca Raton, FL: Chapman and Hall/CRC. doi:10.1201/9781420085891.

Oliveira, E., & Antunes, C. H. (2010a). An evolutionary algorithm based on an outranking relation for sorting problems. In *Proceedings of the IEEE International Conference on Systems Man and Cybernetics*, Istanbul, Turkey (pp. 2732-2739).

Oliveira, E., & Antunes, C. H. (2010b). An evolutionary algorithm guided by preferences elicited according to the ELECTRE TRI method principles. In P. Cowling & P. Merz (Eds.), *Proceedings of the 10th European Conference on Evolutionary Computation in Combinatorial Optimization* (LNCS 6022, pp. 214-225).

Owens, J. D., Houston, M., Luebke, D., Green, S., Stone, J. E., & Phillips, J. C. (2008). GPU computing. *Proceedings of the IEEE, 96*(5), 879–899. doi:10.1109/JPROC.2008.917757.

Ozturk, M. C., Xu, D., & Principe, J. C. (2007). Analysis and design of echo state networks. *Neural Computation, 19*(1), 111–138. doi:10.1162/neco.2007.19.1.111.

P systems. (2004). *Resources website.* Retrieved from http://ppage.psystems.eu/

Pacini, G., & Bergman, R. (1986). Minmod: A computer program to calculate insulin sensitivity and pancreatic responsivity from the frequently sampled intravenous glucose tolerance test. *Computer Methods and Programs in Biomedicine, 23*(2), 113–122. doi:10.1016/0169-2607(86)90106-9.

Panerai, F., Metta, G., & Sandini, G. (2000). Visuo-inertial stabilization in space-variant binocular systems. *Robot and Autonomous Systems*, 195-214.

Panerai, F., Metta, G., & Sandini, G. (2002). Learning visual stabilization reflexes in robots with moving eyes. *Neurocomputing, 48*(1-4), 323–337. doi:10.1016/S0925-2312(01)00645-2.

Pan, L., Zeng, X., & Zhang, X. (2011). Time-free spiking neural p systems. *Neural Computation, 23*, 1320–1342. doi:10.1162/NECO_a_00115.

Papadimitriou, C. M. (1994). *Computational complexity.* Reading, MA: Addison-Wesley.

Pardalos, P. M., & Resende, M. G. C. (Eds.). (2002). *Handbook of applied optimization.* Oxford, UK: Oxford University Press.

Parpinelli, R. S., & Lopes, H. S. (2011). New inspirations in swarm intelligence: A survey. *International Journal of Bio-Inspired Computation, 3*(1), 1–16. doi:10.1504/IJBIC.2011.038700.

Parreiras, R. O., Maciel, J. H. R. D., & Vasconcelos, J. A. (2006). The a posteriori decision in multiobjective optimization problems with smarts, Promethee II and a fuzzy algorithm. *IEEE Transactions on Magnetics, 42*(4), 1139–1142. doi:10.1109/TMAG.2006.871986.

Parreiras, R. O., & Vasconcelos, J. A. (2007). A multiplicative version of Promethee II applied to multiobjective optimization problems. *European Journal of Operational Research, 183*(2), 729–740. doi:10.1016/j.ejor.2006.10.002.

Pasti, R., Von Zuben, F. J., Maia, R. D., & Castro, L. N. (2011). Heuristics to avoid redundant solutions on population-based multimodal continuous optimization. In *Proceedings of the IEEE Congress on Evolutionary Computation* (pp. 2321-2328).

Patane, F., Laschi, C., Miwa, H., Guglielmelli, E., Dario, P., & Takanishi, A. (2004). Design and development of a biologically-inspired artificial vestibular system for robot heads. In *Proceedings of the IEEE/RSJ International Conference on Intelligent Robots and Systems* (pp. 1317-1322).

Păun, A., & Păun, G. (2002). The power of communication: P systems with symport/antiport. *New Generation Computing, 20*(3), 295–305. doi:10.1007/BF03037362.

Păun, G. (1998). Computing with membranes. *Journal of Computer and System Sciences, 61*, 108–143. doi:10.1006/jcss.1999.1693.

Păun, G. (2000). Computing with membranes. *Journal of Computer and System Sciences, 61*(1), 108–143. doi:10.1006/jcss.1999.1693.

Păun, G. (2001). P systems with active membranes: Attacking NP-complete problems. *Journal of Automata. Languages and Combinatorics, 6*(1), 75–90.

Păun, G. (2002). *Membrane computing: An introduction.* Berlin, Germany: Springer-Verlag.

Păun, G. (2006). Introduction to membrane computing. In Ciobanu, G., Pérez-Jiménez, M. J., & Păun, G. (Eds.), *Applications of membrane computing* (pp. 1–42). New York, NY: Springer.

Păun, G., Ciobanu, G., & Pérez-Jiménez, M. (2006). *Applications of membrane computing*. New York, NY: Springer.

Păun, G., Pérez-Jiménez, M. J., & Riscos-Núñez, A. (2008). Tissue P systems with cell division. *International Journal of Computers, Communications & Control, 3*(3), 295–302.

Păun, G., Rozenberg, G., & Salomaa, A. (2009). *The Oxford handbook of membrane computing*. New York, NY: Oxford University Press.

Păun, G., Rozenberg, G., & Salomaa, A. (2010). *Handbook of membrane computing*. New York, NY: Oxford University Press.

Păun, G., Rozenberg, G., & Salomaa, A. (2010). *The Oxford handbook of membrane computing*. New York, NY: Oxford University Press.

Păun, G., Rozenberg, G., & Salomaa, A. (Eds.). (2010). *The Oxford handbook of membrane computing*. Oxford, UK: Oxford University Press.

Pelikan, M., & Mühlenbein, H. (1999). Marginal distributions in evolutionary algorithms. In *Proceedings of the International Conference on Genetic Algorithms* (pp. 90-95).

Pelikan, M., Goldberg, D. E., & Cantú-Paz, E. (1999). BOA: The Bayesian optimization algorithm. In *Proceedings of the Genetic and Evolutionary Computation Conference*, Orlando, FL (Vol. 1, pp. 525-532).

Pelikan, M., Goldberg, D. E., & Lobo, F. G. (2002). A survey of optimization by building and using probabilistic models. *Computational Optimization and Applications*, *21*(1), 5–20. doi:10.1023/A:1013500812258.

Penrose, R. (2012). Foreword. In Zenil, H. (Ed.), *A computable universe: Understanding computation & exploring nature as computation*. Singapore: World Scientific.

Pereira, F. B., & Marques, J. M. C. (2008). A self-adaptive evolutionary algorithm for cluster geometry optimization. In *Proceedings of the Eight International Conference on Hybrid Intelligent Systems* (pp. 678-683). Washington, DC: IEEE Computer Society.

Pereira, F. B., & Marques, J. M. C. (2009). A study on diversity for cluster geometry optimization. *Evolutionary Intelligence*, *2*, 121–140. doi:10.1007/s12065-009-0020-5.

Pérez-Jiménez, M. J., & Riscos-Núñez, A. (2005). Solving the subset-sum problem by P systems with active membranes. *New Generation Computing*, *23*(4), 339–356. doi:10.1007/BF03037637.

Pérez-Jiménez, M. J., Romero-Jiménez, Á., & Sancho-Caparrini, F. (2003). Complexity classes in models of cellular computing with membranes. *Natural Computing*, *2*(3), 265–285. doi:10.1023/A:1025449224520.

Peréz-Jiménez, M., Jiménez, A. R., & Sancho-Caparrini, F. (2003). Complexity classes in models of cellular computing with membranes. *Natural Computing*, *2*, 265–285. doi:10.1023/A:1025449224520.

Pnueli, A. (1977). The temporal logic of programs. In *Proceedings of the 18th Annual Symposium on Foundations of Computer Science* (pp. 46-57).

Poli, R. (2008). Analysis of the publications on the applications of particle swarm optimization. *Journal of Artificial Evolution and Applications*.

Poli, R., Kennedy, J., & Blackwell, T. (2007). Particle swarm optimization: An overview. *Swarm Intelligence*, *1*, 33–57. doi:10.1007/s11721-007-0002-0.

Porreca, A. E., Leporati, A., Mauri, G., & Zandron, C. (2010). P systems with elementary active membranes: Beyond NP and coNP. In M. Gheorghe, T. Hinze, G. Paun, G. Rozenberg, & A. Salomaa (Eds.), *Proceedings of the 11th International Conference on Membrane Computing* (LNCS 6501, pp. 338-347).

Post, E. (1936). Finite combinatory processes - Formulation 1. *Journal of Symbolic Logic*, *1*, 103–105. doi:10.2307/2269031.

Pozzo, T., Berthoz, A., & Lefort, L. (1990). Head stabilization during various locomotor tasks in humans. *Experimental Brain Research*, *82*, 97–106. doi:10.1007/BF00230842.

Prado, R. S., Silva, R. C., Guimarães, F. G., & Neto, O. M. (2010). A new differential evolution based metaheuristic for discrete optimization. *International Journal of Natural Computing Research*, *1*(2), 15–32. doi:10.4018/jncr.2010040102.

Pratt, S. C., Mallon, E. B., Sumpter, D. J. T., & Franks, N. R. (2002). Quorum sensing, recruitment, and collective decision-making during colony emigration by the ant Leptothorax albipennis. *Behavioral Ecology and Sociobiology*, *52*(2), 117–127. doi:10.1007/s00265-002-0487-x.

Provata, A., Sokolov, I. M., & Spagnolo, B. (2008). Ecological complex systems. *The European Physical Journal B - Condensed Matter and Complex Systems*, *65*(3), 307-314.

Puviani, M., Serugendo, G. D. M., Frei, R., & Cabri, G. (2012). A method fragments approach to methodologies for engineering self-organizing systems. *ACM Transactions on Autonomous and Adaptive Systems*, *7*(3), 1–33. doi:10.1145/2348832.2348836.

Rachmawati, L., & Srinivasan, D. (2006, July). Preference incorporation in multi-objective evolutionary algorithms: A survey. *IEEE Congress on Evolutionary Computation*, Vancouver, BC, Canada (pp. 3385-3391).

Regev, A., & Shapiro, E. (2002). Cellular abstractions: Cells as computation. *Nature*, *419*, 343. doi:10.1038/419343a PMID:12353013.

Rekiek, B., De Lit, P., Pellichero, F., L'Eglise, T., Falkenauer, E., & Delchambre, A. (2000). Dealing with user's preferences in hybrid assembly lines design. In *Proceedings of the Management and Control of Production and Logistics Conference*.

Ricci, F., Rokach, L., Shapira, B., & Kantor, P. B. (Eds.). (2010). *Recommender systems handbook*. New York, NY: Springer.

Richer, T., & Blackwell, T. M. (2006). The Lévy particle swarm. In *Proceedings of the IEEE Congress on Evolutionary Computation* (pp. 3150-3157). Washington, DC: IEEE Computer Society.

Ridley, M. (2004). *Evolution* (3rd ed.). Oxford, UK: Wiley-Blackwell.

Righetti, L., & Ijspeert, A. J. (2008). Pattern generators with sensory feedback for the control of quadruped locomotion. In *Proceedings of the IEEE International Conference on Robotics and Automation* (pp. 819-824).

Riscos-Núñez, A. (2004). *Cellular programming: Efficient resolution of NP complete numerical problems*. Unpublished doctoral dissertation, Universidad de Sevilla, Sevilla, Spain.

Ritter, G. X., Wilson, J. N., & Davidson, J. L. (1990). Image algebra: An overview. *Computer Vision Graphics and Image Processing*, *49*(3), 297–331. doi:10.1016/0734-189X(90)90106-6.

Rivest, R. L., Shamir, A., & Adleman, L. M. (1978). A method for obtaining digital signatures and public-key cryptosystems. *Communications of the ACM*, *21*(2), 120–126. doi:10.1145/359340.359342.

Roberts, C., Johnston, R., & Wilson, N. (2000). A genetic algorithm for the structural optimization of morse clusters. *Theoretical Chemistry Accounts*, *104*, 123–130. doi:10.1007/s002140000117.

Romero-Campero, F. J., Gheorghe, M., Bianco, L., Pescini, D., Pérez-Jiménez, M. J., & Ceterchi, R. (2006). Towards probabilistic model checking on P systems using PRISM. In H. J. Hoogeboom, G. Paun, G. Rozenberg, & A. Salomaa (Eds.), *Proceedings of the 7th International Workshop on Membrane Computing* (LNCS 4361, pp. 477-495).

Rosenblatt, F. (1958). The perceptron: A probabilistic model for information storage and organization in the brain. *Psychological Review*, *65*(6), 386–408. doi:10.1037/h0042519.

Rosenzweig, M. L. (1995). *Species diversity in space and time*. Cambridge, UK: Cambridge University Press. doi:10.1017/CBO9780511623387.

Roy, B. (1996). *Multicriteria methodology for decision aiding*. Dordrecht, The Netherlands: Springer-Verlag.

Rozenberg, G. (Ed.). (2002). *Natural Computing: An International Journal*. New York, NY: Springer.

Rozenberg, G., Bäck, T., & Kok, J. N. (Eds.). (2012). *Handbook of natural computing*. New York, NY: Springer. doi:10.1007/978-3-540-92910-9.

Ruela, A. S., Cabral, R. D., Aquino, A. L., & Guimarães, F. G. (2010). Memetic and evolutionary design of wireless sensor networks based on complex network characteristics. *International Journal of Natural Computing Research*, *1*(2), 33–53. doi:10.4018/jncr.2010040103.

Russell, S. J., & Norvig, P. (2002). *Artificial intelligence: A modern approach* (2nd ed.). Upper Saddle River, NJ: Prentice Hall.

Russell, S., & Norvig, P. (2009). *Artificial intelligence: A modern approach*. Upper Saddle River, NJ: Prentice Hall.

Sacchi, R., Ozturk, M. C., Principe, J. C., Carneiro, A. A., & da Silva, I. N. (2007). Water inflow forecasting using echo state network: A Brazilian case study. In *Proceedings of the International Joint Conference on Neural Networks* (pp. 2403-2408).

Said, L. B., Bechikh, S., & Ghedira, K. (2010). The r-dominance: A new dominance relation for interactive evolutionary multicriteria decision making. *IEEE Transactions on Evolutionary Computation*, *14*(5), 801–818. doi:10.1109/TEVC.2010.2041060.

Saitou, N., & Nei, M. (1987). The neighbor-joining method: A new method for reconstructing phylogenetic trees. *Molecular Biology and Evolution*, *4*(4), 406–425.

Sanderson, A., & Weiss, L. (1980). Image-based visual servo control using relational graph error signals. *Proc. IEEE*, pp. 1074-1077.

Sandini, G., Metta, G., & Vernon, D. (2004). Robotcub: An open framework for research in embodied cognition. In *Proceedings of the 4th IEEE/RAS International Conference on Humanoid Robots* (Vol. 1, pp. 13-32).

Sastry, K. (2001). *Evaluation-relaxation schemes for genetic and evolutionary algorithms.* Unpublished master's thesis, University of Illinois at Urbana-Champaign, Urbana, IL.

Sastry, K., Pelikan, M., & Goldberg, D. (2004). Efficiency enhancement of genetic algorithms via building-block-wise fitness estimation. In *Proceedings of the IEEE Congress on Evolutionary Computing* (pp. 720-727).

Scannell, J. W., Burns, G. A., Hilgetag, C. C., O'Neil, M. A., & Young, M. P. (1999). The connectional organization of the cortico-thamalic system of the cat. *Cerebral Cortex*, *9*(3), 277–299. doi:10.1093/cercor/9.3.277.

Schoener, T. W. (1991). Ecological interactions. In Myers, A. A., & Giller, P. S. (Eds.), *Analytical biogeography*. Boca Raton, FL: Chapman & Hall.

Schrauwen, B., Wardermann, M., Verstraeten, D., Steil, J. J., & Stroodbandt, D. (2008). Improving reservoirs using intrinsic plasticity. *Neurocomputing*, *71*(7-9), 1159–1171. doi:10.1016/j.neucom.2007.12.020.

Schumann, A., & Adamatzky, A. (2009, September 26-29). Physarum spatial logic. In *Proceedings of the 1st International Symposium on Symbolic and Numeric Algorithms for Scientific Computing*, Timisoara, Romania.

Schwefel, H.-P. (1981). *Numerical optimization of computer models*. New York, NY: John Wiley & Sons.

Schwefel, H.-P. P. (1995). *Evolution and optimum seeking*. New York, NY: John Wiley & Sons.

Schwenk, G., Padilla, D. G., Bakkenand, G. S., & Full, R. J. (2009). Grand challenges in organismal biology. *Integrative and Comparative Biology*, *49*(1), 7–14. doi:10.1093/icb/icp034 PMID:21669841.

Shapiro, J. A. (1995). The significances of bacterial colony patterns. *BioEssays*, *17*(7), 597–607. doi:10.1002/bies.950170706 PMID:7646482.

Shapiro, L. G., & Stockman, G. C. (2001). *Computer vision*. Upper Saddle River, NJ: Prentice Hall.

Sharma, M. B., & Iyengar, S. S. (1989). An efficient distributed depth-first-search algorithm. *Information Processing Letters*, *32*, 183–186. doi:10.1016/0020-0190(89)90041-0.

Shi, Y., & Eberhart, R. C. (1998). A modified particle swarm optimizer. In *Proceedings of the IEEE International Conference on Evolutionary Computation* (pp. 69-73). Washington, DC: IEEE Computer Society.

Shibata, T., & Schaal, S. (2001). Biomimetic gaze stabilization based on feedback-error-learning with nonparametric regression networks. *Neural Networks*, *14*, 201–216. doi:10.1016/S0893-6080(00)00084-8.

Shirakawa, T., Adamatzky, A., Gunji, Y.-P., & Miyake, Y. (2009). On simultaneous construction of Voronoi diagram and Delaunay triangulation by Physarum polycephalum. *International Journal of Bifurcation and Chaos in Applied Sciences and Engineering*, *19*(9). doi:10.1142/S0218127409024682.

Shor, P. W. (1997). Polynomial-time algorithms for prime factorization and discrete logarithms on a quantum computer. *SIAM Journal on Computing*, *26*(5), 1484–1509. doi:10.1137/S0097539795293172.

Silva, A., Neves, A., & Costa, E. (2002). An empirical comparison of particle swarm and predator prey optimization. In M. O'Neill, R. F. E. Sutcliffe, C. Ryan, M. Eaton, & N. J. L. Griffith (Eds.), *Proceedings of 13th Irish International Conference on Artificial Intelligence and Cognitive Science* (LNCS 2464, pp. 103-110).

Simmons, I. (1982). *Biogeographical processes*. St. Leonards, NSW, Australia: Allen & Unwin.

Simon, D. (2008). Biogeography-based optimization. *IEEE Transactions on Evolutionary Computation*, *12*(6), 702–713. doi:10.1109/TEVC.2008.919004.

Smirnov, B., Strizhev, Y., & Berry, R. (1999). Structures of large morse clusters. *The Journal of Chemical Physics*, *110*(15), 7412–7420. doi:10.1063/1.478643.

Solnon, C. (2010). *Ant colony optimization and constraint programming*. New York, NY: Wiley-Interscience.

Soria, C. M., Carelli, R., Kelly, R., & Zannatha, J. M. I. (2006). Coordinated control of mobile robots based on artificial vision. *International Journal of Computers, Communications & Control*, *1*(2), 85–94.

Sosic, R., & Gu, J. (1994). Efficient local search with conflict minimization: A case study of the N-queens problem. *IEEE Transactions on Knowledge and Data Engineering*, *6*(5), 661–668. doi:10.1109/69.317698.

Sosík, P. (2003). The computational power of cell division in P systems: Beating down parallel computers? *Natural Computing*, *2*, 287–298. doi:10.1023/A:1025401325428.

Sosík, P., & Rodríguez-Patón, A. (2007). Membrane computing and complexity theory: A characterization of PSPACE. *Journal of Computer and System Sciences*, *73*, 137–152. doi:10.1016/j.jcss.2006.10.001.

Sousa, J., Matos, V., & Santos, C. (2010). A bio-inspired postural control for a quadruped robot: An attractor-based dynamics. In *Proceedings of the IEEE/RSJ International Conference on Intelligent Robots and Systems*, Taipei, Taiwan (pp. 5329-5334).

Sproewitz, A., Moeckel, R., Maye, J., Asadpour, M., & Ijspeert, A. J. (2007). Adaptive locomotion control in modular robotics. In *Proceedings of the Workshop on Self-Reconfigurable Robots/Systems and Applications* (pp. 81-84).

Stacey, A., Jancic, M., & Grundy, I. (2003). Particle swarm optimization with mutation. In *Proceedings of the IEEE Congress on Evolutionary Computation* (pp. 1425-1430). Washington, DC: IEEE Computer Society.

Stephenson, S. L., & Stempen, H. (2000). *Myxomycetes: A handbook of slime molds*. Portland, OR: Timber Press.

Stillinger, F. (1999). Exponential multiplicity of inherent structures. *Physical Review E: Statistical Physics, Plasmas, Fluids, and Related Interdisciplinary Topics*, *59*, 48–51. doi:10.1103/PhysRevE.59.48.

Storn, R., & Price, K. (1997). Differential evolution - a simple and efficient heuristic for global optimization over continuous spaces. *Journal of Global Optimization*, *11*(4), 341–359. doi:10.1023/A:1008202821328.

Studier, J., & Keppler, K. (1988). A note on the neighbor-joining algorithm of Saitou and Nei. *Molecular Biology and Evolution*, *5*(6), 729.

Suganthan, P. N., Hansen, N., Liang, J. J., Deb, K., Chen, Y. P., Auger, A., & Tiwari, S. (2005). *Problem definitions and evaluation criteria for the CEC 2005 special session on real-parameter optimization (Tech. Rep.)*. Singapore: Nanyang Technological University.

Sutton, R., & Barto, A. (1998). *Reinforcement learning*. Cambridge, MA: MIT Press.

Systems, P. (2011). *Resource website*. Retrieved from http://ppage.psystems.eu/

Taga, G. (1994). Emergence of bipedal locomotion through entrainment among the neuro-musculoskeletal system and the environment. In *Proceedings of the NATO Advanced Research Workshop and EGS Topical Workshop on Chaotic Advection, Tracer Dynamics and Turbulent Dispersion* (pp. 190-208).

Taplin, J. H. E., Qiu, M., & Han, R. (2005). *Cost-benefit analysis and evolutionary computing: Optimal scheduling of interactive road projects*. Cheltenham, UK: Edward Elgar.

Taroco, C. G., Carrano, E. G., & Neto, O. M. (2010). Robust design of power distribution systems using an enhanced multi-objective genetic algorithm. *International Journal of Natural Computing Research*, *1*(2), 92–112. doi:10.4018/jncr.2010040106.

Tel, G. (2000). *Introduction to distributed algorithms*. Cambridge, UK: Cambridge University Press.

Tero, A., Kobayashi, R., & Nakagaki, T. (2006). *Physarum* solver: A biologically inspired method of road-network navigation. *Physica A*, *363*, 115–119. doi:10.1016/j.physa.2006.01.053.

Teuscher, C., & Sanchez, E. (2001). A revival of Turing's forgotten connectionist ideas: Exploring unorganized machines. In *Proceedings of the Sixth Neural Computation and Psychology Workshop on Connectionist Models of Learning, Development and Evolution* (pp. 153-162).

Teuscher, C. (2001). *Turing's connectionism: An investigation of neural networks architectures*. New York, NY: Springer.

Thiele, L., Miettinen, K., Korhonen, P. J., & Molina, J. (2009). A preference-based interactive evolutionary algorithm for multiobjective optimization. *Evolutionary Computation Journal*, *17*(3), 411–436. doi:10.1162/evco.2009.17.3.411.

Toffolo, G., Bergman, R., Finegood, D., Bowden, C., & Cobelli, C. (1980). Quantitative estimation of beta cell sensitivity to glucose in the intact organism: A minimal model of insulin kinetics in the dog. *Diabetes*, *29*(12), 979–990. doi:10.2337/diabetes.29.12.979.

Top 500. (2011). *Supercomputer sites*. Retrieved from http://www.top500.org

Toussaint, G. T. (1980). The relative neighborhood graph of a finite planar set. *Pattern Recognition*, *12*, 261–268. doi:10.1016/0031-3203(80)90066-7.

Tsin, Y. H. (2002). Some remarks on distributed depth-first search. *Information Processing Letters*, *82*, 173–178. doi:10.1016/S0020-0190(01)00273-3.

Tsou, C.-S., & Kao, C.-H. (2006). An electromagnetism-like meta-heuristic for multi-objective optimization. In *Proceedings of the IEEE Congress on Evolutionary Computation* (pp. 1172-1178).

Tsuda, S., Aono, M., & Gunji, Y.-P. (2004). Robust and emergent Physarum logical-computing. *Bio Systems*, *73*, 45–55. doi:10.1016/j.biosystems.2003.08.001.

Turing, A. (1937). On computable numbers, with an application to the entschei-dungsproblem. *Proceedings of the London Mathematical Society*, *42*, 230–265. doi:10.1112/plms/s2-42.1.230.

Turing, A. M. (1936). On computable numbers, with an application to the entscheidungsproblem. *Proceedings of the London Mathematical Society*, *42*, 230–265. doi:10.1112/plms/s2-42.1.230.

Turing, A. M. (1950). Computing machinery and intelligence. *Mind*, *59*(236), 433–460. doi:10.1093/mind/LIX.236.433.

Turing, A. M. (1968). Intelligent machinery. In Evans, C. R., & Robertson, A. D. (Eds.), *Cybernetics: Key papers*. Baltimore, MD: University Park Press.

Vargas, D. V., & Delbem, A. C. B. (2010). *Algoritmo filo-genético* (Tech. Rep. No. 350). San Paulo, Brazil: Universidade de Sao Paulo.

Vargas, D. V., Delbem, A. C. B., & de Melo, V. V. (2010). *Algoritmo filo-genético*. Paper presented at the 2ª Escola Luso-Brasileira De Computação Evolutiva (elbce), Guimarães, Portugal.

Verplancke, T., Van Looy, S., Steurbaut, K., Benoit, D., De Turck, F., De Moor, G., & Decruyenaere, J. (2010). A novel time series analysis approach for prediction of dialysis in critically ill patients using echo-state networks. *BMC Medical Informatics and Decision Making*, *10*(4).

Verstraeten, D., Schrauwen, B., D'Haene, M., & Stroobandt, D. (2007). An experimental unification of reservoir computing methods. *Neural Networks*, *20*(3), 391–403. doi:10.1016/j.neunet.2007.04.003.

Vesterstrom, J., & Thomsen, R. (2004, June). A comparative study of differential evolution, particle swarm optimization, and evolutionary algorithms on numerical benchmark problems. In *Proceedings of the IEEE Congress on Evolutionary Computation*, Portland. *OR*, *3*, 1980–1987.

Vittori, G., & Araujo, A. F. R. (2001). Agent-oriented routing in telecommunications networks. *IEICE Transactions on Communications. E (Norwalk, Conn.)*, *84-B*(11), 3006–3013.

Vittori, G., Talbot, G., Gautrais, J., Fourcassié, V., Araujo, A. F. R., & Theraulaz, G. (2006). Path efficiency of ant foraging trails in an artificial network. *Journal of Theoretical Biology*, *239*(4), 507–515. doi:10.1016/j.jtbi.2005.08.017 PMID:16199059.

Volkov, V., & Demmel, J. (2008). Benchmarking GPUs to tune dense linear algebra. In *Proceedings of the ACM/IEEE Conference on Supercomputing* (p. 31).

Vollmer, H. (1999). *Introduction to circuit complexity: A uniform approach*. New York, NY: Springer.

Wakano, J. Y., Maenosono, S., Komoto, A., Eiha, N., & Yamaguchi, Y. (2003). Self-organized pattern formation of a bacteria colony modeled by a reaction diffusion system and nucleation theory. *Physical Review Letters*, *90*(25), 258102. doi:10.1103/PhysRevLett.90.258102 PMID:12857171.

Wiens, J. J., & Donoghue, M. J. (2004). Historical biogeography, ecology and species richness. *Trends in Ecology & Evolution*, *19*(12), 639–644. doi:10.1016/j.tree.2004.09.011 PMID:16701326.

Wille, L., & Vennik, J. (1985). Computational complexity of the ground-state determination of atomic clusters. *Journal of Physics. A, Mathematical and General*, *18*(8), 419–422. doi:10.1088/0305-4470/18/8/003.

Wörz, S., & Rohr, K. (2007). Spline-based elastic image registration with matrix-valued basis functions using landmark and intensity information. In F. A. Hamprecht, C. Schnörr, & B. Jähne (Eds.), *Proceedings of the 29th DAGM Conference on Pattern Recognition* (LNCS 4713, pp. 537-546).

Wright, S. (1932). The roles of mutation, inbreeding, crossbreeding, and selection in evolution. In *Proceedings of the 6th International Congress of Genetics* (pp. 356-366).

Wu, P., Yang, K.-J., & Fang, H.-C. (2006). A revised em-like algorithm + k-opt method for solving the traveling salesman problem. In *Proceedings of the First International Conference on Innovative Computing. Information and Control*, *1*, 546–549.

Xavier, R. S., Omar, N., & de Castro, L. N. (2011). Bacterial colony: Information processing and computational behavior. In *Proceedings of the Third World Congress on Nature and Biologically Inspired Computing* (pp. 439-443).

Xie, X., Zhang, W., & Yang, Z. (2002). Dissipative particle swarm optimization. In *Proceedings of the IEEE Congress on Evolutionary Computation* (pp. 1456-1461). Washington, DC: IEEE Computer Society.

Yamada, H., Mori, M., & Hirose, S. (2007). Stabilization of the head of an undulating snake-like robot. In *Proceedings of the IEEE/RSJ International Conference on Intelligent Robots and Systems* (pp. 3566-3571).

Yamazaki, T., & Tanaka, S. (2007). The cerebellum as a liquid state machine. *Neural Networks*, *20*(3), 290–297. doi:10.1016/j.neunet.2007.04.004.

Yuan, Z., & Zhang, Z. (2007). Asynchronous spiking neural P system with promoters. In M. Xu, Y. Zhan, J. Cao, & Y. Liu (Eds.), *Proceedings of the 7th International Conference on Advanced Parallel Processing Technologies* (LNCS 4847, pp. 693-702).

Yurtkuran, A., & Emel, E. (2010). A new hybrid electromagnetism-like algorithm for capacitated vehicle routing problems. *Expert Systems with Applications*, *37*, 3427–3433. doi:10.1016/j.eswa.2009.10.005.

Zandron, C., Ferretti, C., & Mauri, G. (2001). Solving NP-complete problems using P systems with active membranes. In *Proceedings of the Second International Conference on Unconventional Models of Computation* (pp. 289-301).

Zeiri, Y. (1995). Prediction of the lowest energy structure of clusters using a genetic algorithm. *Physical Review*, *51*, 2769–2772.

Zeng, X., Adorna, H., Martínez-del-Amor, M., & Pan, L. (2010). When matrices meet brains. In *Proceedings of the Eighth Brainstorming Week on Membrane Computing* (pp. 255-266).

Zeng, X., Adorna, H., Martínez-del-Amor, M., Pan, L., & Pérez-Jiménez, M. (2011). Matrix representation of spiking neural p systems. In M. Gheorghe, T. Hinze, G. Paun, G. Rozenberg, & A. Salomaa (Eds.), *Proceedings of the 11th International Conference on Membrane Computing* (LNCS 6501, pp. 377-392).

Zenil, H. (2012b). Introducing the computable universe. In Zenil, H. (Ed.), *A computable universe: Understanding computation & exploring nature as computation.* Singapore: World Scientific.

Zenil, H. (Ed.). (2012a). *A computable universe: Understanding computation & exploring nature as computation.* Singapore: World Scientific.

Zhang, W.-J., & Xie, X.-F. (2003). DEPSO: Hybrid particle swarm with differential evolution operator. In *Proceedings of the IEEE International Conference on Systems, Man and Cybernetics* (pp. 3816-3821). Washington, DC: IEEE Computer Society.

Zitzler, E., Laumanns, M., & Thiele, L. (2002). SPEA2: Improving the strength pareto evolutionary algorithm for multiobjective optimization. In *Proceedings of the Evolutionary Methods for Design, Optimisation and Control with Application to Industrial Problems* (pp. 95-100).

Zwickl, D. J. (2006). *Genetic algorithm approaches for the phylogenetic analysis of large biological sequence datasets under the maximum likelihood criterion.* Unpublished doctoral dissertation, University of Texas at Austin, Austin, TX.

About the Contributors

Leandro Nunes de Castro received a BSc degree in electrical engineering from the Federal University of Goias (Brazil, 1996) and MSc and PhD degrees in computer engineering from the State University of Campinas (Unicamp) (São Paulo, Brazil) in 1998 and 2001, respectively. He received a MBA (2007) in strategic business management from the Catholic University of Santos. He was a research associate with the Computing Laboratory at UKC (Canterbury, UK) from 2001 to 2002, a visiting lecturer at Unicamp from 2002 to 2003, a senior research fellow at the Wernher von Braun Center for Advanced Research from May to December 2004, and a visiting lecturer at the Universiti Technologi Malaysia (Johor, MY) in September 2005. In May 2003, he joined the Catholic University of Santos (UniSantos) as an assistant professor in computer science and established collaborations with the Federal University of Bahia (UFBA) and the Federal University of Minas Gerais (UFMG). Leandro is currently an associate professor at Mackenzie University. He has broad interest in all natural computing approaches with a particular emphasis on biologically inspired computing including artificial immune systems, artificial neural networks, evolutionary algorithms, swarm intelligence, fractal geometry, and artificial life. He is the main author of *Artificial Immune Systems: A New Computational Intelligence Approach* published by Springer-Verlag (UK, 2002), one of the editors of *Recent Developments in Biologically Inspired Computing* published by Idea Group Inc. (USA, 2004), and the author of *Fundamentals of Natural Computing: Basic Concepts, Algorithms, and Applications* published by CRC Press LLC (June 2006). He has published over seventy-five conference papers, twenty journal papers and six book chapters mostly covering natural computing approaches. He has been a member of the IEEE Computational Intelligence Society since 1999, ICARIS (International Conference on Artificial Immune Systems) Steering Committee since 2003, the Brazilian Society for Automation (SBA) since 1998, and the Brazilian Computing Society (SBC) since 2006. In February 2007 he started a company on natural computing, named "NatComp – from Nature to Business", which he is the Director of Research, Development, and Innovation (RDI).

* * *

Andrew Adamatzky is Professor of Unconventional Computing at the UWE, Bristol, UK. His research interests include non-standard and nature inspired computation, theoretical computer science, artificial intelligence and crowd dynamics, mathematical biology and psychology, non-linear sciences. His recent work has included development of logical and arithmetical circuits in excitable chemical media, slime mould, and liquid crystal figures; and also, development of intelligent massively parallel actuator arrays, formal languages and complexity of cellular automat models, and memristive devices. He authored several books on non-linear media based computers and artificial intelligence.

Henry Adorna obtained his BS (Mathematics) from FEATI University Manila in 1987 and his MS and PhD (Mathematics) both from the University of the Philippines Diliman (UPD) in 1996 and 2002, respectively. He is an Associate Professor of Theoretical Computer Science at the UPD. He is the current recipient of the Alexan Professorial Chair of the College of Engineering of the UPD. He wrote his dissertation on communication complexity under Juraj Hromkovic as a DAAD Sandwich Program Scholar at RWTH-Aachen from 2000 to 2002. He worked with Gheorge Paun and Mario Perez-Jimenez on communication complexity concept in membrane computing in 2009 during his post doctoral studies at Universidad de Sevilla under an ERDT Post-Doctoral grant from DOST-ERDT Program. His publications include discrete mathematics, formal languages, membrane computing, bioinformatics, and data visualization. His current research interests are membrane computing, and discrete mathematics.

Selim G. Akl holds a PhD degree from McGill University. He is a Professor of Computing at Queen's University, Kingston, Ontario, Canada, where he currently serves as Director of the Queen's School of Computing. Dr. Akl's research interests are in parallel and unconventional computation (including quantum and biomolecular computers and non-standard computational problems). He is author of Parallel Sorting Algorithms (Academic Press, 1985), The Design and Analysis of Parallel Algorithms (Prentice Hall, 1989), and Parallel Computation: Models and Methods (Prentice Hall, 1997), and a co-author of Parallel Computational Geometry (Prentice Hall, 1992) and Adaptive Cryptographic Access Control (Springer, 2010). Dr. Akl is editor in chief of Parallel Processing Letters and presently serves on the editorial boards of Computational Geometry, the International Journal of Parallel, Emergent, and Distributed Systems, the International Journal of Unconventional Computing, and the International Journal of High Performance Computing and Networking.

Artiom Alhazov, Ph. D., a researcher at the Institute of Mathematics and Computer Science of Moldova, graduated from the State University of Moldova, Chi inău, and defended his Ph. D. thesis "excellent unanimously" at the Research Group on Mathematical Linguistics, Tarragona, Spain. He completed two post-doctorate course at the Åbo Akademi University, Turku, Finland and the Hiroshima University, Higashi-Hiroshima, Japan. He is doing research in the domains of biological computing (including membrane computing), computer linguistics, complexity theory. He has published over 120 articles in this area, including 28 journal articles and 3 book chapters. He has extensive experience in both theoretical computer science and practical application development.

Tudor Bălănescu is professor in the Department of Computer Science, University of Piteşti, Romania. He received a PhD in mathematics from the University of Bucharest, Romania, where he worked before joining his current university. His research interests include automata and formal languages, parsing and compiling, formal semantics, mathematical linguistics, software engineering, and membrane computing.

Levy Boccato was born in Piracicaba, São Paulo, Brazil, in 1986. He received the BS degree in Computer Engineering in 2008, and the MS degree in Electrical Engineering, with emphasis on Computer Engineering, in 2010, all from the University of Campinas, São Paulo, Brazil. Currently, he is a PhD student at the same university. His main research interests include computational intelligence, artificial neural networks and reservoir computing, along with applications to signal processing tasks.

Francis George Cabarle obtained his bachelor's degree in Computer Engineering from the Electrical and Electronics Engineering Institute of the University of the Philippines Diliman (UPD) in 2009. He worked as an administrator of the High Performance Computing cluster facility of the UPD College of Science afterward. He is currently a graduate student in Computer Science in the Department of Computer Science's Algorithms and Complexity laboratory (AC lab). At the AC lab he works with Henry Adorna and other graduate students on Membrane computing, particularly implementing P systems on graphics processing units (GPUs). He is also currently a scholar under the DOST-ERDT program of the College of Engineering. His current publications include simulating SNP systems in GPUs, and is also interested in using GPUs for computational biology, as well as in parallel and distributed computations to solve hard problems.

A. Hepzibah Christinal is doing her Ph.D., in Mathematics in the Applied Mathematics Department at the University of Seville, Spain. She is currently working as Assistant Professor(SG) in Karunya University, Coimbatore, Tamilnadu, India. She is also a member of the Research Group on Computational Algebraic Topology and Applied Mathematics of the University of Seville. Her research interest includes Algebraic Topology, Digital image, Natural Computing and Optimization Techniques.

Luděk Cienciala works as a researcher in Institute of Computer Science of Silesian University in Opava from 1999. He finished Master degree at Faculty of Science in University of Ostrava in 1996. He received Ph.D. degree in Applied Mathematics from Faculty of Science in University of Ostrava in 2006. He teaches logic, graph theory, computer graphics and mathematics. His main areas of research are theoretical computer science, natural computing and computer graphics.

Lucie Ciencialová joint Institute of Computer Science of Silesian University in Opava in 2006 where she works as a researcher. She teaches theoretical computer science, mathematics, logic and information systems. She received Master degree in Computer Science from Silesian University in 2005. She finished Ph.D. studies at Silesian University in 2008 with Ph.D. thesis named "P colonies". Her interests include natural computing and web design.

Daniel Diaz Pernil obtained his Ph.D. in Mathematics in 2008. Currently, he is a professor in the Applied Mathematic I Department at the University of Seville, Spain. He is also a member of the Research Group on Computational Algebraic Topology and Applied Mathematics of the University of Seville. His research interest includes topics related to Algebraic Topologya, Digital Image and Natural Computing.

Miguel A. Gutiérrez-Naranjo obtained his Ph.D. in Mathematics in 2002. Currently, he is a professor in the Computer Science and Artificial Intelligence Department at the University of Seville, Spain. He is also a member of the Research Group on Natural Computing of the University of Seville. His research interest includes topics related to Artificial Intelligence and Natural Computing. He has coauthored more than 30 scientific papers in these areas.

Florentin Ipate received his PhD and MSc degrees from the University of Sheffield in 1995 and 1992, respectively, and his BSc from Politehnica University of Bucharest in 1991, all in Computer Science. He is now a professor of Computer Science with the University of Pitesti. He has been awarded the In Hoc Signo Vinces Prize for research and publications by the National Research Council for Higher Education in 2002 and the COPYRO Publishing Prize for Computer Science in 2000. FI's research interests are in specification and model based testing, formal specification languages for software systems, agile modelling and testing, modelling, verification and testing of biology-inspired computing systems. He has been involved, as principal investigator or co-investigator, in several EU or nationally funded RTD projects, involving teams from high-profile universities and world-leading industrial companies. His main research results have been published in a research monograph with Springer and in high profile journals.

Sergiu Ivanov graduated the Technical University of Moldova, Computer Science Department. He does not possess any scientific degrees as yet, but he is fully committed to continuing the research work he is currently doing. His domains of interest are natural computing, including but not limited to biologically inspired computational models (membrane computing), parallel and concurrent programming, functional programming. Ivanov possesses extensive experience in development of small applications and is currently collaborating with researchers in theoretical computer science to extend his theoretical research skills.

Miroslav Langer finished his master degree in 2004 at Institute of Computer Science, Faculty of Philosophy and Science of Silesian University in Opava. He is finishing his Ph. D. studies at the same institute nowadays. His scientific interests are formal languages and automata, grammar systems, algorithms and programming.

Raluca Lefticaru received her MSc degree in Computer Science and BSc from the University of Pitesti in 2006 and 2004, respectively. Currently, she is a finishing PhD student and teaching assistant at the University of Pitesti. Her research interests are formal specification methodologies and software testing, especially state-machine and Event-B based testing using evolutionary approaches, P systems testing and verification. She has written about 20 research papers, many of them published in important international conferences and journals. She has been involved, as co-investigator, in several nationally funded RTD projects and in one EU funded project. Vincenzo Manca is a Full Professor in Computer at the University of Verona. He obtained his degrees from the University of Pisa, under the guide of Alfonso Caracciolo di Forino and Ennio De Giorgi. He taught at the Universities of Udine and Pisa. His research interests cover a wide class of topics from mathematical logic, discrete mathematics, and theoretical computer science to the informational analysis of biological systems. At present, his investigation is focused on DNA Computing, Membrane Computing, and Synthetic Computational Biology. He published three books and over 130 scientific papers in international journals and scientific series, and was member in many international PC. He advised 7 Ph.D students, and tutored more than 40 M.Sc. students. He founded the bachelor in Bioinformatics at the University of Verona, and is member of the scientific committee of the "Computational BioMedical Center" (CBMC), at the same university.

Alberto Leporati is assistant professor in Computer Science at Università degli Studi di Milano-Bicocca, Italy. He has obtained a master degree and then a Ph.D. in the same field at Università degli Studi di Milano in 1998 and 2003, respectively. His research activity concerns various aspects of theoretical computer science, focusing in particular on the theory of computational complexity. In the past he has studied the computational power and efficiency of classical and quantum circuits. Since 2005 he studies the computational properties of membrane systems; in particular, the computational power of the variants obtained by selectively adding or removing one or more computational features. On these subjects, he has co-authored more than 50 scientific papers in international journals, contributed volumes and conference proceedings. He contributed to many research projects, financed by national funds, by the European Community and by the industry. He is member of the European Association for Theoretical Computer Science (EATCS). He is also member of the Program Committee of the International Conference on Membrane Computing.

Luca Marchetti, graduated in Computer Science, is now PhD student in Computer Science under the guide of Vincenzo Manca and works as research associate at the "Computational BioMedical Center" (CBMC) of the University of Verona. His research interests are mainly focused on Systems Biology, Natural Computing and, more specifically, on the developing of new techniques for modelling in silico natural phenomena by means of Metabolic P systems (MP systems). In the last year he defined, in collaboration with his mentor Vincenzo Manca, the Log-Gain Stoichiometric Stepwise regression algorithm (LGSS) which represents the most recent solution, in terms of MP systems, of the inverse dynamics problem, that is, the problem of identifying (discrete) mathematical models exhibiting an observed dynamics and satisfying all the constraints required by the specific knowledge about the modelled phenomenon. He is co-author of scientific papers published in journals, volumes, and conference proceedings.

Miguel Ángel Martínez del Amor received his degree in Computer Engineering from the Faculty of Computer Science of the University of Murcia (Spain) in June 2008. Currently, he is a Ph.D. student at the Department of Computer Science and Artificial Intelligence of the University of Seville (Spain). He is also a member of the Research Group on Natural Computing of the same university, and since 2009, he is a research fellow under grant from "Proyecto de Excelencia con Investigador de Reconocida Valía" P08-TIC04200 of the "Junta de Andalucía" (Spain). His main research interest is to joint Membrane Computing and High Performance Computing by using efficient computer simulations based on GPUs. He is also interested in using GPU computing for bioinformatics, computational Systems Biology, ecosystem modeling, physics and many other complex systems.

Giancarlo Mauri is full professor of Computer Science at the University of Milano-Bicocca. His research interests include: natural computing and unconventional computing models, in particular membrane systems and splicing systems; bioinformatics; computational systems biology, in particular stochastic modeling and simulation of biological systems and processes, biomedical data analysis. On these subjects, he published more than 200 scientific papers in international journals, contributed volumes and conference proceedings. He is currently member of the steering committees of the International Conference on Membrane Computing, of the International Conference on Unconventional Computing and Natural Computing and of the International Workshop on DNA Computer.

Radu Nicolescu is senior lecturer in the Department of Computer Science, University of Auckland, New Zealand. Prior to joining his current university, he worked in the University of Bucharest, Romania, and then in the industry, in Salzburg and Vienna. His scientific interests include automata and formal languages, parsing and compiling, combinatorial optimizations, information theory, distributed computing, software development, and models for parallel and distributed computing. He holds a PhD in mathematics from the University of Bucharest. He is a member of ACM and IEEE Computer Society.

Yunyun Niu was born in China on November 17, 1983. She received her master degree at Zhengzhou University of Light Industry in 2007. Currently, she is a PhD candidate in the Department of Control Science and Engineering, Huazhong University of Science and Technology. Her main research field is unconventional models of computation, especially, membrane computing.

Roberto Pagliarini graduated in Computer Science and earned his PhD in Computer Science at the University of Verona, where he is currently a post-doc research associate. He visited for eight mounts the Bioinformatic Group at the Cranfield University (UK). His research interests focus on Systems Biology, Natural Computing, and modelling of natural phenomena by means of Membrane Computing. In particular he investigates the possibility of obtaining efficient and systematic methods for defining membrane models from experimental data of given processes. Along this direction, he collaborated with the biochemistry and vegetal physiology group at Biotechnological Department of Verona University, in order to investigate computational models for crucial events related to photosynthetic organisms. Moreover, he is studying the possibility of inferring causality networks among species by developing and integrating specific statistical indexes. He is co-author of scientific papers published in journals, volumes, and conference proceedings.

Rodrigo Pasti has a degree in Computer Engineering from the Sao Francisco University (2004) and an MSc in Computer Science from the Catholic University of Santos (2007). He is currently a PhD student in the Faculty of Electrical and Computer Engineering (FEEC) at the State University of Campinas (Unicamp) and a researcher at the Laboratory of Bioinformatics and Bioinspired Computation (LBiC). He is a member and research associate at the Natural Computing Labora-tory (LCoN) of the Graduate Program in Electrical Engineering of Mackenzie University. He is also a lecturer of Artificial Intelligence in the Faculty of Computer Engineering of the Pontifical University of Campinas (PUCC). His main areas of research are Computational Intelligence, Natural Computing, Ecosystem Computing and Biogeographic Computation.

Francisco Antonio Peña-Cantillana studies Computer Engineering at the University of Seville, Spain. He is also a member of the Research Group on Natural Computing of the University of Seville. Currently, he is making his Final Project on the fields of Natural Computing, Digital Image and GPGPU using CUDA.

Mario J. Pérez-Jiménez received his degree in mathematics from the Barcelona University and the doctor degree in mathematics from the Sevilla University. In the past, he was associated professor at the University of Barcelona. Currently, he is full professor of Computer Science and Artificial Intelligence at the University of Sevilla, where is the head of the Research Group on Natural Computing. His main research fields are computational complexity theory, natural computing, membrane computing, bioinformatics, and computational modeling for systems biology and population biology. He has published twelve books in computer science and mathematics, and over 200 scientific papers in international journals (collaborating with many researchers worldwide). He is the main researcher in various European, Spanish and Andalusia research grants. He has been an independent expert to the evaluation of NEST (New and Emergent Science and Technology) proposals under the Sixth Framework Programme of the European Community, and from May 2006 he is an European Science Foundation peer reviewer.

Antonio E. Porreca was born in 1982. He is currently a Ph.D. student in computer science at Università degli Studi di Milano-Bicocca, Italy, where he also got his B.Sc. and M.Sc. in the same field in 2005 and 2008 respectively. His research interests include complexity theory, computability, and the theoretical aspects of natural computing. In particular, up to now his work has mainly focused on the complexity theory of membrane systems (P systems), and the formalisation and analysis of the space/time trade-off they are subject to when attempting to solve computationally hard problems.

Vladimir Rogohin, Ph. D., graduated the State University of Moldova and then obtained his Master Degree in Computer Science at the Åbo Akademy, Finland. He has then defended his Ph. D. thesis in computer science at the Turku Centre for Computer Science, Åbo Akademy. He has experience in programming both Web-based applications and stand-alone applications. Vladimir's current focus is at analysing complex networks which come from a number of biological and biomedical sources by applying discrete mathematics theory methods as well as at building and implementing mathematical models, methods and algorithms to explain the biomedical data related in particular to cancer research. The list of domains of Vladimir's expertise includes systems biology, biomodelling, bioinformatics, discrete mathematics, automata and formal languages, cellular computing, DNA computing.

Cristina Tudose is a finishing PhD student and teaching assistant at the University of Pitesti, Romania. She has graduated in 2004 and has received her MSc degree in Computer Science from the University of Pitesti in 2006. Her research areas are formal specification methodologies, testing and verification, domains in which she has already published the results of her research in important international conferences and journals. Her expertise includes temporal logics, algebraic specifications, and model checking. She has been involved, as co-investigator, in several nationally funded RTD projects and in two EU funded project. She has a good theoretical background and practical skills in software analysis, design and implementation.

Fernando José Von Zuben received his Dr.E.E. degree from the University of Campinas (Unicamp), Campinas, SP, Brazil, in 1996. He is currently the header of the Laboratory of Bioinformatics and Bio-inspired Computing (LBiC), and an Associate Professor at the Department of Computer Engineering and Industrial Automation, School of Electrical and Computer Engineering, Uni-versity of Campinas (Unicamp). The main topics of his research are computational intelligence, bioinspired computing, multivariate data analysis, and machine learning. He coordinates open ended research projects in these topics, tackling real-world problems in the areas of information technology, decision-making, pattern recognition, and discrete and continuous optimization.

Huiling Wu is a current PhD student in Department of Computer Science, University of Auckland, New Zealand. She was born in Guangzhou, China. She got her BSc degree (first class) in Department of Computer Science, Zhongshan (Sun Yat-sen) University in 2003 and a MSc degree (first class) in the Department of Computer Science, University of Auckland in 2007. After that, she worked as a software engineer in Nortel R&D, China. She continued her research and became a PhD candidate in Department of Computer Science, University of Auckland in 2009. Her research interests focus on P systems, parallel and distributed computing, and autonomic computing.

Claudio Zandron is associate professor of computer science at the University of Milan – Bicocca. His research interests concern the areas of formal languages, molecular computing models, DNA and membrane computing and computational complexity. Since 1996 he studies formal models based on the action of restriction enzymes over DNA molecules. Recently, he investigates Membrane Systems, a computational model inspired by the structure and functioning of the cell. He studied the computational power of some variants of this model, as well as time and space computational complexity aspects. He also considered their application in the framework of systems biology. He co-authored about 60 research paper, presented at international conferences or published in international scientific journals.

Xingyi Zhang was born in China on June 6, 1982. He received his doctor degree at Huazhong University of Science and Technology in 2009. Currently, he works in School of Computer Science and Technology, Anhui University. His main research field is unconventional models of computation, especially, membrane computing.

Index

T

U

V

Z